# RACING COLLECTIBLES

## IDENTIFICATION & VALUE GUIDE

from the editors of
**RACING COLLECTOR'S
PRICE GUIDE**

## COLLECTOR BOOKS
*A Division of Schroeder Publishing Co., Inc.*

The current values in this book should be used only as a guide. They are not intended to set prices, which vary from one section of the country to another. Auction prices as well as dealer prices vary greatly and are affected by condition and demand. Neither the editors nor the publisher assumes responsibility for any losses which might be incurred as a result of consulting this guide.

Cover design: Beth Summers
Book design: Joyce Cherry

**Searching For A Publisher?**

We are always looking for people knowledgeable within their fields. If you feel that there is a real need for a book on your collectible subject and have a large comprehensive collection, contact Collector Books.

Collector Books
P.O. Box 3009
Paducah, KY 42002-3009

www.collectorbooks.com

# Contents

## Dedication

To the late B. D. McClure who published our first price guide — *Collector's World, 1991.*

## Acknowledgments

**Our thanks to:**

James "Whit" King for his constant and continual enthusiasm working long hours to produce the first annual *Racing Collectibles Identification and Value Guide*

Our many friends in racing who have so willingly shared their information and photos

A few of many: Ron Byrd, Eddie Timberman, Kenny Brackett, Greenway Pauley, Doris Roberts, and Wanda Lund Early

We are very grateful to our associates whose help has made this guide possible:

Larry Hardin, L. H. Collectibles (336) 632-1753, www.lh-dist.com
Wayne and Debbie Keith, Just For Fun (336) 249-3907, www.just4fun.com.

A special thanks to Van Cox for his editorial contributions and to our staff members Chad McClure and Dianne McClure.

# Introduction

Are you a diehard NASCAR fan? If so, you are also probably a collector of racing memorabilia — whether you realize it or not. You may have display cases brimming with die-cast cars, or albums filled with trading cards, or an entire room dedicated to a particular driver like some of our hardcore collectors. Then again, you may have only a dozen or so old racing postcards stuffed in a shoebox somewhere or a few lapel pins stuck in the back corner of a desk drawer. In either case, you are a collector to some degree.

*Racing Collectibles* will identify, describe, and provide an estimated fair market value for more than two dozen different categories of racing's most coveted collectibles. This publication was written and compiled by the editors of *Racing Collector's Price Guide*, whose staff has provided the longest continuous coverage of the racing collectibles industry — dating back more than a decade.

The collecting of motorsports memorabilia has been around since the beginning of, well, racing. In the early days, there were very few manufactured souvenirs. Racing enthusiasts, hungry for some memento of their trip to the track, were happy to settle for what we'll call incidental collectibles. These items weren't necessarily made to be collectible, but ended up being so regardless. Count postcards, programs, ticket stubs, sheet metal,

and racer-worn apparel in this category. Also, in recent years, marketing gurus have used the burgeoning collectibility of NASCAR memorabilia to promote everything from soda pop to breakfast cereal.

A few NASCAR-themed trading cards and die-cast pieces began to appear during the '70s and early '80s. They were limited-edition novelties, however, released sporadically by manufacturers who were still a bit unsure of the market. In fact, it wasn't until 1988, that former Charlotte, North Carolina, sportscaster Jim McCulloch truly ushered in the era of collectibility with the introduction of the inaugural Maxx Race Cards set. The first mass-produced NASCAR card set was quicky devoured by the racing public. A year later, Racing Champions put the racing die-cast industry into high gear by releasing its now-famous "flat bottom" series. While this publication will not address die-cast or trading cards, it should be noted that those two categories have both complemented and enhanced the collectibility of the items described herein.

In the decade since, the collectibles industry has mushroomed into a multi-billion dollar per year bonanza. As NASCAR racing has become America's biggest spectator sport, the popularity of racing collectibles — both manufactured and incidental — has grown exponentially.

A number of variables come into play when determining the value of a particular collectible. Of course, the law of supply and demand figures most heavily in the equation. In racing, the more prominant names — drivers like Dale Earnhardt, Jeff Gordon, and Tony Stewart — are more collectible than most of their peers. Hence, their items merit higher values.

Geography is also a factor. Racing memorabilia is more plentiful in stock car racing's hotbed — the southeast — than in other areas. So an item may bring a substantially higher price in Oregon than in North Carolina. Autographed memorabilia is at a premium. However, race car drivers are much more accessible than other athletes. Consequently, some types of signed racing memorabilia may not appraise for quite as much as comparable "stick-and-ball" memorabilia — but the gap is closing rapidly. An autographed item is usually valued at or near the appraised price of the collectible plus the estimated value of the autograph.

Last but not least, the condition of the item is of utmost importance. Values reflected in *Racing Collectibles* are for collectibles in mint condition. Obviously, the most notable exception is race-used memorabilia: helmets, firesuits, crew uniforms, sheet metal. In that case, "used ain't abused."

So where is the best place to find NASCAR memorabilia? Well, there are a number of options. It's always a good idea for the collector to align himself with a reputable dealer who can help locate those hard-to-find items. Memorabilia shows and charity auctions are also great sources, as is the classified advertising section of any major racing magazine or newspaper. However, in today's electronic age, the Internet is by far the most valuable tool the collector will ever know. Whether it's an online auction or a dealer's homepage, the web is a winner. But remember, the chase is half the fun. So sit back, strap yourself in, and let's go collecting!

# AUTOGRAPHS

Driver autographs have become increasingly popular over the past few years. Since NASCAR drivers are much more accessible than athletes from other sports, their signatures are more plentiful and therefore don't carry quite the monetary value as those from the stick-and-ball venues. However, as NASCAR continues to grow, the drivers are becoming less accessible and, consequently those appraisals are on the rise.

Of course, counterfeiting of celebrity autographs has long been a problem for collectors. In racing, bogus signatures are most prevalent in the case of deceased drivers. So, before you shell out big bucks for a signature, take whatever steps are necessary to authenticate it.

Bobby Allison, signed photo . . . . . . . . . .15.00

Davey Allison, signed photo . . . . . . . . . .80.00
John Andretti, signed photo . . . . . . . . . . .8.00
Buddy Baker, signed photo . . . . . . . . . . .15.00
Johnny Benson, signed photo . . . . . . . . . .8.00
Brett Bodine, signed photo . . . . . . . . . . .8.00
Geoff Bodine, signed photo . . . . . . . . . . .8.00
Neil Bonnett, signed photo . . . . . . . . . . .60.00
Jeff Burton, signed photo . . . . . . . . . . .15.00
Ward Burton, signed photo . . . . . . . . . . .15.00
Dave Blaney, signed photo . . . . . . . . . . .8.00
Derrike Cope, signed photo . . . . . . . . . . .6.00
Dale Earnhardt, signed photo . . . . . . . .100.00
Dale Earnhardt, Jr., signed photo . . . . . .30.00
Bill Elliott, signed photo . . . . . . . . . . .20.00
Tim Flock, signed photo . . . . . . . . . . . .18.00
A. J. Foyt, signed photo . . . . . . . . . . . .25.00
Harry Gant, signed photo . . . . . . . . . . .12.00
Jeff Gordon, signed photo . . . . . . . . . . .30.00
Ernie Irvan, signed photo . . . . . . . . . . .15.00
Kenny Irwin, signed photo . . . . . . . . . . .15.00
Dale Jarrett, signed photo . . . . . . . . . . .18.00

Ned Jarrett, signed photo . . . . . . . . . . .15.00
Junior Johnson, signed photo . . . . . . . . .20.00
Matt Kenseth, signed photo . . . . . . . . . .15.00
Alan Kulwicki, signed photo . . . . . . . . . .75.00
Bobby Labonte, signed photo . . . . . . . . .18.00
Terry Labonte, signed photo . . . . . . . . . .18.00
Elmo Langley, signed photo . . . . . . . . . .15.00
Chad Little, signed photo . . . . . . . . . . . .8.00

Fred Lorenzen, signed photo . . . . . . . . . .20.00
Tiny Lund, signed photo, very hard to find in good shape . . . . . . . . . . . . . . . . . . .150.00
Dave Marcis, signed photo . . . . . . . . . . .8.00
Sterling Marlin, signed photo . . . . . . . . . .8.00
Mark Martin, signed photo . . . . . . . . . . .20.00
Jeremy Mayfield, signed photo . . . . . . . .12.00
Rob Moroso, signed photo . . . . . . . . . . .25.00
Ted Musgrave, signed photo . . . . . . . . . .6.00
Joe Nemechek, signed photo . . . . . . . . . .8.00
Steve Park, signed photo . . . . . . . . . . .15.00
Benny Parsons, signed photo . . . . . . . . .12.00
Adam Petty, signed photo . . . . . . . . . . .35.00

Kyle Petty, signed photo . . . . . . . . . . . .12.00
Richard Petty, signed photo . . . . . . . . . .15.00
"Tiger" Tom Pistone, signed photo . . . . . .10.00
Tim Richmond, signed photo . . . . . . . . . .50.00

Richard Petty, signed photo . . . . . . . . . . .15.00

Fireball Roberts, signed photo, very hard to find in
　good shape . . . . . . . . . . . . . . . . . .200.00
Ricky Rudd, signed photo . . . . . . . . . . . .12.00
Ken Schrader, signed photo . . . . . . . . . . .8.00
Wendell Scott, signed photo . . . . . . . . . .50.00
Mike Skinner, signed photo . . . . . . . . . . .8.00
Jimmy Spencer, signed photo . . . . . . . . .10.00
Tony Stewart, signed photo . . . . . . . . . .30.00
Dick Trickle, signed photo . . . . . . . . . . . .8.00
Curtis Turner, signed photo, very hard to find in
　good shape . . . . . . . . . . . . . . . .200.00

Lee Roy Yarborough, signed photo, very hard to
　find in good shape . . . . . . . . . . . . .125.00

Kenny Wallace, signed photo . . . . . . . . . .8.00
Rusty Wallace, signed photo . . . . . . . . . .22.00
Darrell Waltrip, signed photo . . . . . . . . .15.00
Michael Waltrip, signed photo . . . . . . . . .8.00
Cale Yarborough, signed photo . . . . . . . .15.00
Lee Roy Yarborough, signed photo, very hard to
　find in good shape . . . . . . . . . . . . .125.00

## BEAN BAG RACERS

　Beanie bag toys were the worldwide collectibles phenomenon of the past decade. Their immense popularity spread into the racing world with the introduction of bean bag race car replicas and driver-specific stuffed bears. The Redliners series, produced by long-time collectibles manufacturer Mary Meyer, joins Beanie Racers and RCCA Baby Racers as the most popular brands of bean bag race cars.

　The most sought-after NASCAR-themed bears are Driver Bears by Racing Champions, Speed Bean Bears, and Coca-Cola Bears — which are coveted by both NASCAR and Coca-Cola collectors. Most bean bag cars and stuffed bears have been produced within the past three years and have appreciated only slightly since their initial release. However, a few of the issues featuring the bigger name drivers have shown a better-than-average increase in value.

### BABY RACERS BY RCCA

2 Rusty Wallace, Ford Motorsports . . . . . .10.00
3 Dale Earnhardt, Goodwrench Plus . . . . .20.00

3 Dale Earnhardt, Jr., AC Delco . . . . . . . .10.00
24 Jeff Gordon, Dupont . . . . . . . . . . . . .10.00
88 Dale Jarrett, Quality Care . . . . . . . . . .10.00

### BEANIE RACERS

1 Steve Park, Pennzoil . . . . . . . . . . . . . .10.00
2 Rusty Wallace . . . . . . . . . . . . . . . . . .10.00

3 Dale Earnhardt, Goodwrench Plus . . . . .25.00
3 Dale Earnhardt, Jr., AC Delco . . . . . . .20.00
4 Bobby Hamilton, Kodak . . . . . . . . . . .10.00
6 Mark Martin, Valvoline . . . . . . . . . . .15.00
6 Mark Martin, Eagle One . . . . . . . . . .15.00
8 Hut Stricklin, Circuit City . . . . . . . . . .10.00
10 Ricky Rudd, Tide . . . . . . . . . . . . . .10.00
13 Jerry Nadeau, First Plus . . . . . . . . . .10.00
16 Ted Musgrave, Primestar . . . . . . . . .10.00
18 Bobby Labonte, Interstate . . . . . . . . .10.00
22 Ward Burton, MBNA . . . . . . . . . . . .10.00
26 Johnny Benson, Cheerios . . . . . . . . .10.00
30 Derrike Cope, Gumout . . . . . . . . . . .10.00
33 Ken Schrader . . . . . . . . . . . . . . . .10.00
41 Steve Grissom . . . . . . . . . . . . . . .10.00
42 Joe Nemechek, BellSouth . . . . . . . . .10.00
46 Jeff Green, First Union . . . . . . . . . . .10.00
94 Bill Elliott, McDonald's . . . . . . . . . . .15.00
94 Bill Elliott, McDonald's-Gold . . . . . . . .15.00
94 Bill Elliott, McDonald's-Mac Tonight . . . .15.00
96 David Green, Caterpillar . . . . . . . . . .10.00
97 Chad Little, John Deere . . . . . . . . . .10.00
99 Jeff Burton, Exide . . . . . . . . . . . . .10.00

### COCA-COLA BEARS

18 Bobby Labonte, Interstate . . . . . . . . .10.00
20 Tony Stewart, Home Depot . . . . . . . .15.00
28 Kenny Irwin, Texaco . . . . . . . . . . . .15.00
44 Kyle Petty, Hot Wheels . . . . . . . . . .10.00
45 Adam Petty, Sprint . . . . . . . . . . . . .21.00
88 Dale Jarrett, Quality Care . . . . . . . . .10.00
94 Bill Elliott, McDonald's . . . . . . . . . . .10.00
99 Jeff Burton, Exide . . . . . . . . . . . . .10.00

### DRIVER BEARS BY RACING CHAMPIONS

5 Terry Labonte . . . . . . . . . . . . . . . . .9.00
5 Terry Labonte, tie dye . . . . . . . . . . . .9.00
6 Mark Martin . . . . . . . . . . . . . . . . . .9.00
12 Jeremy Mayfield . . . . . . . . . . . . . . .9.00
60 Mark Martin . . . . . . . . . . . . . . . . .9.00
94 Bill Elliott . . . . . . . . . . . . . . . . . . .9.00
94 Bill Elliott, Most Popular Driver . . . . . . .9.00

97 Chad Little . . . . . . . . . . . . . . . . . .9.00
99 Jeff Burton . . . . . . . . . . . . . . . . . .9.00

### REDLINERS BY MARY MEYER

2 Rusty Wallace . . . . . . . . . . . . . . . .20.00
3 Dale Earnhardt, Goodwrench Plus . . . . .30.00
3 Dale Earnhardt, Pro Bass . . . . . . . . . .35.00
6 Mark Martin, Valvoline . . . . . . . . . . .20.00
24 Jeff Gordon, Dupont . . . . . . . . . . . .20.00
28 Kenny Irwin, Havoline . . . . . . . . . . .20.00
88 Dale Jarrett, Ford Credit . . . . . . . . . .20.00
99 Jeff Burton, Exide . . . . . . . . . . . . .20.00

### SPEED BEAN BEARS

Brickyard 400 Set: Dale Earnhardt, Ricky Rudd, Dale
  Jarrett, Jeff Gordon, Brickyard 400 Bear .50.00
2 Rusty Wallace . . . . . . . . . . . . . . . .10.00
3 Dale Earnhardt . . . . . . . . . . . . . . .25.00
3 Dale Earnhardt, Jr. . . . . . . . . . . . . .10.00
5 Terry Labonte . . . . . . . . . . . . . . . .10.00
6 Mark Martin . . . . . . . . . . . . . . . . .10.00
18 Bobby Labonte . . . . . . . . . . . . . . .10.00
20 Tony Stewart . . . . . . . . . . . . . . . .15.00
24 Jeff Gordon . . . . . . . . . . . . . . . . .10.00
88 Dale Jarrett . . . . . . . . . . . . . . . . .10.00
94 Bill Elliott . . . . . . . . . . . . . . . . . .10.00
99 Jeff Burton . . . . . . . . . . . . . . . . .10.00

### SPEEDIE BEANIES

3 Dale Earnhardt, Goodwrench Plus . . . . .15.00
5 Terry Labonte, Kellogg's . . . . . . . . . . .5.00
6 Mark Martin, Valvoline . . . . . . . . . . . .5.00
24 Jeff Gordon, Dupont . . . . . . . . . . . . .8.00
88 Dale Jarrett, Ford Credit . . . . . . . . . . .5.00

## CARDS

The trading card explosion of the early 1990s spawned a number of special interest card sets — some of which are still being produced today, albeit sporadically. Unlike the larger "annual" editions, these sets usually focus on a specific driver, team, or theme. Many were produced as promotional tools for corporate sponsors, race tracks, or the card companies themselves. Still other sets were offered by smaller card manufacturers whose niche was driver-specific sets.

The values of these card ensembles vary greatly from set to set, depending on the subject and availability. Some sets were released regionally, adding to the value in areas where they were not offered.

# METAL CARDS

Metal collector cards featuring NASCAR drivers made their debut about 10 years ago. Since then, production has been sporadic. Some metal cards were offered as promotional devices for the corporate world, while others were released by companies like Highland Mint as stand-alone collectibles.

In terms of monetary worth, metal cards have consistently held their own in the secondary market. However, the only cards showing any appreciable gain in value are those produced on NASCAR's top three or four superstars, as well as those who are now deceased.

### ALLIANCE RACING

Robert Pressley, 3 cards, 999 . . . . . . . . .75.00
Robert Pressley, car & card, 2,759 . . . . .35.00

### CARD DYNAMICS

Davey Allison, 5 card set, 4,000 . . . . . . .75.00
Davey Allison, 1992 Gant Oil Set, 5,000 . .65.00
Joe Amato, NHRA Drag Set, 10,000 . . . . .9.00
Kenny Bernstein, NHRA Drag Set, 10,000 . .9.00
Geoff Bodine, Double Eagle postcard, 500 .55.00
Geoff Bodine, 1993 Gant Oil Set, 6,000 . . .8.00
Geoff Bodine, Quik Chek Set, 5,000 . . . . .8.00
Dale Earnhardt, Blacktop Busch Series, 5,000 . . . . . . . . . . . . . . . . . . . . . . .25.00
Dale Earnhardt, rookie card, Earnhardt Set . . . . . . . . . . . . . . . . . . . . . . . .25.00
Dale Earnhardt, 1980 WC Champ, Earnhardt Set . . . . . . . . . . . . . . . . . . . . . . . .25.00
Dale Earnhardt, 1986 WC Champ, Earnhardt Set . . . . . . . . . . . . . . . . . . . . . . . .25.00
Dale Earnhardt, 1987 WC Champ, Earnhardt Set . . . . . . . . . . . . . . . . . . . . . . . .25.00
Dale Earnhardt, 1990 WC Champ, Earnhardt Set . . . . . . . . . . . . . . . . . . . . . . . .25.00
Dale Earnhardt, 1991 WC Champ, Earnhardt Set . . . . . . . . . . . . . . . . . . . . . . . .25.00
Dale Earnhardt, Double Eagle postcard, 500 . . . . . . . . . . . . . . . . . . . . . . .175.00
Dale Earnhardt, 1993 Gant Oil Set, 6,000 . . . . . . . . . . . . . . . . . . . . . . . .25.00
Dale Earnhardt, North State Chevrolet, 650 . . . . . . . . . . . . . . . . . . . . . . .175.00
Dale Earnhardt, Quik Chek Set, 7,000 . . . .14.00
Bill Elliott, 1992 Gant Oil Set, 5,000 . . . .25.00
Bill Elliott, 1993 Gant Oil Set, 6,000 . . . .10.00
Bill Elliott, Quik Chek Set, 5,000 . . . . . . . .8.00
Harry Gant, Blacktop Busch Series, 5,000 . .5.00
Harry Gant, 5 card set, 4,000 . . . . . . . . .25.00

Dale Earnhardt, North State Chevrolet, 650 . . . . . . . . . . . . . . . . . . . . . .175.00

Harry Gant, Double Eagle postcard, 500 . .55.00
Harry Gant, 1992 Gant Oil Set, 4,000 . . .25.00
Harry Gant, 1993 Gant Oil Set, 6,000 . . .10.00
Harry Gant, 1994 Gant Oil Set, 6,000 . . . .8.00
Harry Gant, North State Chevrolet, 2,000 .40.00
Harry Gant, Quik Chek Set, 5,000 . . . . . . .8.00
Jerry Glanville, 5 card set, 5,000 . . . . . .20.00
Jeff Gordon, Blacktop Busch Series, 5,000 . . . . . . . . . . . . . . . . . . . . . . .15.00
Jeff Gordon, Baby Ruth-Double Eagle postcard, 500 . . . . . . . . . . . . . . . . . . . . . . .110.00
Jeff Gordon, Dupont-Double Eagle postcard, 500 . . . . . . . . . . . . . . . . . . . . . . .100.00
Jeff Gordon, 1993 Gant Oil Set, 6,000 . . .20.00
Jeff Gordon, 1994 Gant Oil Set, 6,000 . . .12.00
Jeff Gordon, Quik Chek Set, 7,000 . . . . . .14.00
Steve Grissom, by Allsports, 500 . . . . . . .40.00
Steve Grissom, Blacktop Busch Series, 5,000 . . . . . . . . . . . . . . . . . . . . . . . .5.00
Eddie Hill, NHRA Drag Set, 10,000 . . . . . . .9.00
Ernie Irvan, 5 card set, 2,000 . . . . . . . . .35.00
Ernie Irvan, Blacktop Busch Series, 5,000 . .7.00
Ernie Irvan, Double Eagle postcard, 500 . .60.00
Ernie Irvan, 1992 Gant Oil Set, 4,000 . . . .30.00
Ernie Irvan, 1994 Gant Oil Set, 6,000 . . . .10.00
Ernie Irvan, Montgomery Motors Set, 1,000 . . . . . . . . . . . . . . . . . . . . . . .30.00
Ernie Irvan, North State Chevrolet, 2,000 .65.00
Dale Jarrett, 1993 Gant Oil Set, 6,000 . . .10.00
Alan Kulwicki, Blacktop Busch Series, 5,000 . . . . . . . . . . . . . . . . . . . . . . .15.00
Alan Kulwicki, 5 card set, 4,000 . . . . . . .75.00
Alan Kulwicki, 1992 Gant Oil Set . . . . . . .40.00

Alan Kulwicki, 1993 Gant Oil Set, 6,000 . .10.00
Alan Kulwicki, Quik Chek Set, 7,000 . . . . .12.00
Alan Kulwicki, Double Eagle postcard, 500 .85.00
Bobby Labonte, Blacktop Busch Series, 5,000 .7.00
Terry Labonte, Blacktop Busch Series, 5,000 .7.00
Sterling Marlin, 1992 Gant Oil Set, 4,000 .30.00

Mark Martin, Blacktop Busch Series, 5,000 .7.00
Mark Martin, Double Eagle postcard, 500 .70.00
Mark Martin, 1992 Gant Oil Set, 4,000 . .40.00
Mark Martin, 1994 Gant Oil Set, 6,000 . .10.00
Mark Martin, Montgomery Motors Set, 1,000 . . . . . . . . . . . . . . . . . . . . . . . .30.00
Mark Martin, Quik Chek Set, 5,000 . . . . .10.00
Kyle Petty, 5 card set, 4,000 . . . . . . . . .25.00
Kyle Petty, 1992 Gant Oil Set, 4,000 . . . .25.00
Kyle Petty, 1993 Gant Oil Set, 6,000 . . . .10.00

Kyle Petty, Quik Chek Set, 5,000 . . . . . . .8.00
Richard Petty, 1993 Gant Oil Set, 6,000 . .10.00
Richard Petty, Quik Chek Set, 5,000 . . . . .8.00
Robert Pressley, Blacktop Busch Series, 5,000 . . . . . . . . . . . . . . . . . . . . . . . .5.00
Don Prudhomme, NHRA Drag Set, 10,000 12.00
Shawna Robinson, by Allsports, 500 . . . .40.00
Ricky Rudd, 5 card set, 4,000 . . . . . . . .25.00
Morgan Shepherd, 1994 Gant Oil Set, 6,000 .8.00
Hut Stricklin, 1994 Gant Oil Set, 6,000 . . . .8.00
Rusty Wallace, 5 card set, 2,000 . . . . . .45.00
Rusty Wallace, Double Eagle postcard, 500 . . . . . . . . . . . . . . . . . . . . . . .70.00
Rusty Wallace, 1992 Gant Oil Set, 4,000 .40.00
Rusty Wallace, 1993 Gant Oil Set, 6,000 .10.00
Rusty Wallace, 1994 Gant Oil Set, 6,000 .10.00
Rusty Wallace, Montgomery Motors Set, 1,000 . . . . . . . . . . . . . . . . . . . . . . .30.00
Rusty Wallace, Quik Chek Set, 5,000 . . . .10.00
Darrell Waltrip, 5 card set, 4,000 . . . . . .25.00
Darrell Waltrip, 1992 Gant Oil Set, 4,000 .25.00
Darrell Waltrip, 1994 Gant Oil Set, 6,000 . .8.00
Michael Waltrip, 5 card set, 2,000 . . . . . .29.00

### JEFF GORDON FAN CLUB

Jeff Gordon, 3 card set, 1,200 . . . . . . . .75.00

### HIGHLAND MINT

Dale Earnhardt, bronze, 5,000 . . . . . . . .100.00
Dale Earnhardt, gold card, 500 . . . . . . .500.00
Dale Earnhardt, silver, 1,000 . . . . . . . . .200.00
Bill Elliott, bronze, 5,000 . . . . . . . . . . . .55.00

Dale Earnhardt, bronze, 5,000 . . . . . . .100.00

Bill Elliott, silver, 1,000 . . . . . . . . . . . . .240.00
Jeff Gordon, bronze, 5,000 . . . . . . . . . .90.00
Jeff Gordon, silver, 1,000 . . . . . . . . . . .360.00
Ernie Irvan, bronze, 5,000 . . . . . . . . . . .55.00
Ernie Irvan, silver, 1,000 . . . . . . . . . . .240.00
Mark Martin, bronze, 5,000 . . . . . . . . . . .60.00
Mark Martin, silver, 1,000 . . . . . . . . . . .245.00
Rusty Wallace, bronze, 5,000 . . . . . . . . .60.00
Rusty Wallace, silver, 1,000 . . . . . . . . .245.00

### METALLIC IMPRESSIONS

Bill Elliott, 1993 5 card set . . . . . . . . . .45.00

Bill Elliott, 1993 4" x 6" card . . . . . . . . .20.00

### TEXAS PETE

Joe Nemechek, card & die-cast car . . . . . .15.00

### SUPERIOR METALS

Derrike Cope, in binder, numbered . . . . . .5.00
Bill Elliott, in binder, numbered . . . . . . . .18.00
Harry Gant, in binder, numbered . . . . . . .15.00
Bobby Hamilton, in binder, numbered . . . . .9.00
Ernie Irvan, in binder, numbered . . . . . . .10.00
Sterling Marlin, in binder, numbered . . . . .12.00
Mark Martin, in binder, numbered . . . . . .18.00
Phil Parsons, in binder, numbered . . . . . . .9.00
Kyle Petty, in binder, numbered . . . . . . . .15.00
Richard Petty, in binder, numbered . . . . . .18.00
Ken Schrader, in binder, numbered . . . . . .15.00
Darrell Waltrip, in binder, numbered . . . . .15.00

## PROMO CARDS

Promo cards are basically what the name implies: promotional cards released by trading card manufacturers to provide advance publicity for upcoming sets. Action Packed released the first promo card in 1989. MAXX, Traks, Pro Set, Redline, and Gold Card followed suit two years later. At that point, it became common practice for manufacturers to release a promo card (or cards) in advance of each set.

Some promo cards are actually variations of a card that will appear in the set, while others are a totally unique, often elaborately decorated card. The early Action Packed and MAXX promo cards are generally considered to be the most valuable, with a few other special editions earning a pretty healthy appraisal.

### ACTION PACKED

Bobby Allison, 1993 #BA1 . . . . . . . . . . .20.00
Allison, Earnhardt, Gordon, Jarrett & Kulwicki,
 1993, 5 card set . . . . . . . . . . . . . .180.00
Mario Andretti, 1989 Indy . . . . . . . . . .130.00
Pancho Carter, 1989 Indy . . . . . . . . . .100.00

Dale Earnhardt, 1993 #DE1 . . . . . . . . . .55.00
Dale Earnhardt, 1994 #2R941 . . . . . . . .25.00
Dale Earnhardt, 1995 #DE2 . . . . . . . . . .20.00
Emerson Fittipaldi, 1989 Indy . . . . . . . . .100.00
Jeff Gordon, 1993 #JG1 . . . . . . . . . . . .55.00

Jeff Gordon, 1994 #2R942 . . . . . . . . . . .15.00

Jeff Gordon, 1994 #2R942G, 24k gold . .175.00
Jeff Gordon, 1994 #3R94S . . . . . . . . . .15.00
Jeff Gordon, 1995 #102 . . . . . . . . . . .15.00
Jeff Gordon, 1995 Country Set . . . . . . . .10.00
Jeff Gordon, 1996 Credentials Set . . . . .12.00
Jeff Gordon, 1996 Fan Photo, Club . . . . .4.00
Jeff Gordon, 1997 Action Packed Set . . . . .4.00
Eddie Hill, 1994 #DR1, Drag Racing . . . . .7.50
Dale Jarrett, 1993 #DJ1 . . . . . . . . . . .25.00
Dale Jarrett, 1994 #2R944 . . . . . . . . .5.00
Bobby Labonte, 1995 Country Set #46 . . .10.00
Alan Kulwicki, 1993 #AK1 . . . . . . . . . . .50.00

Alan Kulwicki & Davey Allison, 1993 #AK/DA . . . . . . . . . . . . . . . . . . .20.00
Alan Kulwicki & Davey Allison, 1993 #AKDA 24k Gold . . . . . . . . . . . . . . . . .100.00
Mark Martin, 1996 Credentials Set . . . . .2.00
Rick Mears, 1989 Indy . . . . . . . . . . . .100.00
Kyle Petty, #101, Mello Yello . . . . . . . . .9.00
Kyle Petty, #102 . . . . . . . . . . . . . . . .12.00
Kyle Petty, #103, Mello Yello . . . . . . . . .9.00
Kyle Petty, 1994 #KP1 . . . . . . . . . . . .5.00
Kyle Petty, 1994 #KP2 . . . . . . . . . . . .5.00
Kyle Petty, 1994 #2R943 . . . . . . . . . .10.00
Kyle Petty, 1994 #2R943G, 24k gold . . . .85.00
Richard Petty, 1993 #RP1 . . . . . . . . . . . .9.00
Richard Petty, 1993 #RP2 . . . . . . . . . . . .9.00
Richard Petty, 1993 #RP3 . . . . . . . . . . . .9.00
Richard Petty, 1993 #RP4 . . . . . . . . . . . .9.00
Richard Petty, 1993 #RP5 . . . . . . . . . . . .9.00
Richard Petty, 1993 #RP6 . . . . . . . . . . . .9.00
Ricky Rudd, 1994 #3R941 . . . . . . . . . . .5.00
Kenny Wallace, 1996 Credentials Set . . . . .1.00
Rusty Wallace, 1994 #2R945 . . . . . . . . .5.00
1995 150 SuperTruck . . . . . . . . . . . . . .5.00

## DYNAMICS

Kyle Petty, 1992 . . . . . . . . . . . . . . . .15.00

## CLASSIC-SCOREBOARD

Dale Earnhardt, 1995 $1,000 Phone Card .35.00
Dale Earnhardt, 1996 #HP96 . . . . . . . . .12.00
Dale Earnhardt, 1996 #RP96 . . . . . . . . .12.00
Dale Earnhardt, 1996 Assets Set . . . . . . .12.00
Dale Earnhardt, 1996 Images Set, #3 car .15.00

Jeff Gordon, 1995 Images Set . . . . . . . .18.00
Terry Labonte, 1997 "Texas Terry" Comes Home . . . . . . . . . . . . . . . . . . . . .15.00
1996 Speed Street . . . . . . . . . . . . . . . .10.00

## FINISH LINE

Davey Allison, 1993 . . . . . . . . . . . . . . .10.00
Assorted, 1993 Promo Sheet, 8½ x 11 . . .5.00
Assorted, 1994 4 card sheet, 8½ X 11 . . .2.00
Assorted, 1996 sheet . . . . . . . . . . . . . . .2.00
Harry Gant, 1994 . . . . . . . . . . . . . . . . .3.00
Scott Geoffrion, 1993 . . . . . . . . . . . . . .2.00
Jeff Gordon, 1993 . . . . . . . . . . . . . . .15.00
Jeff Gordon, 1994 Jeff Gordon, gold . . . . .8.00
Jeff Gordon, 1996 Phone Paks II Set . . . . .9.00
Terry & Bobby Labonte, 1993 . . . . . . . . .8.00
Terry Labonte, 1994 gold . . . . . . . . . . .5.00
Mark Martin, 1994 . . . . . . . . . . . . . . . .4.00
Mark Martin, 1996 Phone Paks Set, $2 Phone Card . . . . . . . . . . . . . . . . . . . . .5.00

Davey Allison, 1993 . . . . . . . . . . . . . . .10.00

Cory McClenathan, 1993 . . . . . . . . . . .2.00
Cruz Pedregon, 1993 . . . . . . . . . . . . .2.00
Rusty Wallace, 1994 . . . . . . . . . . . . .4.00
1993 NHRA cover card . . . . . . . . . . . . .50
1993 cover card . . . . . . . . . . . . . . .50
1994 cover card . . . . . . . . . . . . . . .50
1996 National Racing Convention . . . . . . .4.00

## FLEER

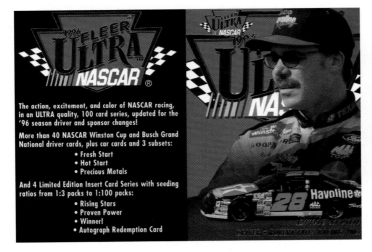

Ernie Irvan, 1996 Update Set . . . . . . . . .5.00
Jeff Gordon, 1996 Fleer Set, silver foil . . . .2.00
Jeff Gordon, 1996 Fleer Set, blue foil . . . . .4.00
Jeff Gordon, 1996 Flair Set . . . . . . . . . .10.00

Jeff Gordon, 1996 Fleer Set, blue foil . . . . .4.00

Mark Martin, 1997 Ultra Set . . . . . . . . . .5.00

## GOLD CARD

Terry Labonte, 1992 #A . . . . . . . . . . . .5.00
Terry Labonte, 1992 #B . . . . . . . . . . . .5.00
Terry Labonte, 1992 #C . . . . . . . . . . . .5.00

Rob Moroso, 1991 3 cardsheet . . . . . . . . .5.00
Kyle Petty, 1992, plastic . . . . . . . . . . .10.00
Richard Petty, 1992, white type . . . . . . . .15.00
Richard Petty, 1992, black type . . . . . . . .10.00
Michael Waltrip, 1992 #A . . . . . . . . . . .3.00
Michael Waltrip, 1992 #B . . . . . . . . . . .3.00
Michael Waltrip, 1992 #C . . . . . . . . . . .3.00

Kyle Petty, 1992, plastic . . . . . . . . . . . .10.00

### HI-TECH

1995 Lowes Racing Set, 3 cards . . . . . . .8.00

Davey Allison, 1993 Indy Tire Test Set . . . . .3.00
Dale Earnhardt, 1995 Brickyard 400 Set #P3 . . . . . . . . . . . . . . . . . .15.00
Ernie Irvan, 1995 Brickyard 400 Set #P2 . .6.00
Jeff Gordon, 1994 #2 . . . . . . . . . . . . . .10.00

Dale Earnhardt, 1995 Brickyard 400 Set #P3 . . . . . . . . . . . . . . . . . . . . .15.00

Mark Martin, 1995 Brickyard 400 Set #P1 .6.00
Kyle Petty, 1994 #3 . . . . . . . . . . . . . . .4.00
Richard Petty, 1994 #1 . . . . . . . . . . . . .5.00
Rusty Wallace, 1993 Indy Tire Test Set . . . .3.00

### MAXX

1992 The Winston . . . . . . . . . . . . . . . .5.00
Jeff Burton, 1995 Premier Series Set . . . . .2.00
Jeff Burton, 1995 Premier Series Set, Maxx Club . . . . . . . . . . . . . . . . . . . . . .2.00
Ricky Craven, 1996 Premier Series Set . . . .2.00

Bill Elliott, 1991 Set . . . . . . . . . . . . . . .75.00

Bill Elliott, 1992 black set . . . . . . . . . . .25.00
Bill Elliott, 1992 red set . . . . . . . . . . . . .25.00
Bill Elliott, 1993 green border . . . . . . . . .4.00
Bill Elliott, 1993 Premier Set . . . . . . . . .10.00
Bill Elliott, 1993 Premier Plus Set . . . . . .10.00
Bill Elliott, 1994 sample . . . . . . . . . . . . . .6.00
Bill Elliott, 1994 Club Maxx . . . . . . . . . . .10.00
Bill Elliott, 1994 Chromium . . . . . . . . . . .7.00
Bill Elliott, 1994 Premier Gold . . . . . . . . . .5.00
Bill Elliott, 1994 Premier without gold . . . . .5.00

Jeff Gordon, 1994 sample . . . . . . . . . . . .10.00
Jeff Gordon, 1995 Set, Every Second Counts .4.00
Jeff Gordon, 1995 Maxx Club . . . . . . . . . .7.00

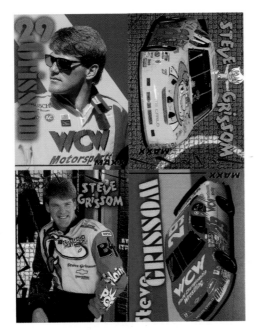

Steve Grissom, 1996 NSCC Convention
Sheet . . . . . . . . . . . . . . . . . . . . . .8.00

Dale Jarrett, 1996 NSCC Convention Sheet .10.00
Bobby Labonte, 1996 Odyssey Set . . . . . . .2.00
Terry Labonte, 1996, sealed . . . . . . . . . . .2.00
Sterling Marlin, 1996 Series 1 Set . . . . . . .2.00

Mark Martin & Steve Hmiel, 1995 St. Louis Con-
vention Sheet . . . . . . . . . . . . . . . . . .6.00
Ted Musgrave, 1994 Series II Set . . . . . . . .2.00
Ted Musgrave, 1995 Medallion Set, #16 Ford .3.00
Ricky Rudd, 1995 Series II Set . . . . . . . . . .2.00

Darrell Waltrip, 1995 Premier Plus Set . . . .2.00

## PINNACLE

Bobby Allison, 1996 Zenith Set . . . . . . . . .5.00
Loy Allen, 1995 #128 . . . . . . . . . . . . . . .3.00

Bobby Allison, 1996 Zenith Set, Club . . . . . .9.00
Geoff Bodine, 1995 #136 . . . . . . . . . . . .3.00
Dale Earnhardt, 1996 Racers Choice Set . .12.00

Dale Earnhardt, 1995 Zenith Set #132 . . .15.00
Bill Elliott, 1996 Club, #BE1, 3,000 . . . . .10.00
Bill Elliott, 1997 Precision Steel . . . . . . . .7.00
Jeff Gordon, 1995 Select Set #12 . . . . . .10.00
Jeff Gordon, 1996 Racers Choice . . . . . . .7.00
Jeff Gordon, 1995 #DM 8 . . . . . . . . . . .20.00
Dale Jarrett, 1996 Speedflix Set . . . . . . . .4.00
Dale Jarrett, 1997, 2 cards with coin . . . . .5.00
Terry Labonte, 1997 Racers Choice Set . . .3.00
Sterling Marlin, 1996 Racers Choice Set . . .2.00
Sterling Marlin, 1996 Team Pinnacle . . . . . .2.00

Jeff Gordon, 1995 #DM 8 . . . . . . . . . . .20.00

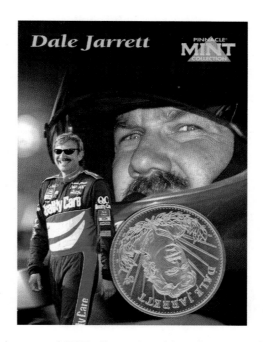

Dale Jarrett, 1997, 2 cards with coin . . . . .5.00

Mark Martin, 1997, certified . . . . . . . . . .3.00
Mark Martin, 1998, with coin . . . . . . . . .3.00
Mark Martin, 1998, without coin . . . . . . . .5.00
Ted Musgrave, 1995, Zenith Set, Helmets . .5.00
Kyle Petty, 1995 Select Set #24 . . . . . . . .3.00

Dale Earnhardt, Jr., 1999 Premium Set . . . .8.00

Ricky Rudd, 1997 Totally Certified . . . . . . .3.00
Ricky Rudd, 1997 Spellbound . . . . . . . . . .4.00

## PRESS PASS

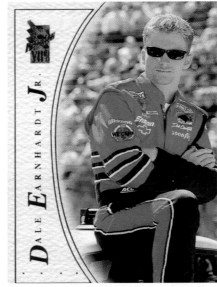

Dale Earnhardt, Jr., 2000 VIP Set . . . . . . . .5.00

1994 Promo Sheet 6⅞" x 8½" . . . . . . . . .6.00
Geoff Bodine, 1994 VIP Set, Club Member . .8.00
Jeff Burton, 1995 Optima XL Set . . . . . . .6.00
Derrike Cope, 1995 VIP Set, #4 gold foil . . .4.00
Derrike Cope, 1995 VIP Set, #4 red foil . .15.00
Dale Earnhardt, Jr., 1999 Press Pass Set . .8.00
Dale Earnhardt, Jr., 1999 Premium Set . . . .8.00
Dale Earnhardt, Jr., 2000 VIP Set . . . . . . .5.00
Harry Gant, 1994 VIP Set . . . . . . . . . . . .8.00
Harry Gant, 1994 VIP Set, gold signature 125.00
Jeff Gordon, 1994 VIP Set, Dupont Chevy . .7.00
Jeff Gordon, 1994 Optima XL Set #3 . . . .15.00
Jeff Gordon, 1995 . . . . . . . . . . . . . . . .8.00
Jeff Gordon, 1996 Clear Card #1 of 2 . . .20.00

Harry Gant, 1994 VIP Set . . . . . . . . . . . .8.00

Jeff Gordon, 1996 M-Force #1, blue . . . . . .6.00
Jeff Gordon, 1996 M-Force #2, green . . . .6.00
Jeff Gordon, 1996 M-Force #3, silver . . . . .6.00
Jeff Gordon, 1997 Premium Set #1 . . . . .6.00
Jeff Gordon, 1998 #1 . . . . . . . . . . . . .5.00
Jeff Gordon, 1998 Premium Set #1 . . . . .5.00
Jeff Gordon, 1998 Stealth Set . . . . . . . .4.00
Jeff Gordon, 1999 Press Pass Set . . . . . .4.00
Jeff Gordon, 1998 #1 . . . . . . . . . . . .5.00
Ernie Irvan, 1994 VIP Set . . . . . . . . . .4.00
Ernie Irvan, 1997 Premium Set #3 . . . . . .7.00
Dale Jarrett, 1995 VIP Set #1, gold foil . . . .3.00
Dale Jarrett, 1995 VIP Set #1, red foil . . .12.00
Dale Jarrett, 1997 . . . . . . . . . . . . . .6.00
Dale Jarrett, 1997 #2 Premium Set . . . . . .7.00
Dale Jarrett, 1997 VIP Set #1 . . . . . . . .4.00
Dale Jarrett, 1997 VIP Set #2, foil . . . . . .4.00
Dale Jarrett, 1998 #2 . . . . . . . . . . . .6.00
Dale Jarrett, 2000 Press Pass Set . . . . . .3.00
Bobby Labonte, 1995 VIP Set, #2, red foil .10.00
Bobby Labonte, 1995 VIP Set #2, gold foil . .3.00
Bobby Labonte, 1996 Premium Set . . . . . .7.00
Bobby Labonte, 1996 National Collectors Conven-
tion, gold . . . . . . . . . . . . . . . . . . .5.00

Bobby Labonte, 1995 VIP Set #2, gold foil . .3.00

Bobby Labonte, 1996 National Collectors Conven-
tion, red foil, 2,000 . . . . . . . . . . . . .10.00
Bobby Labonte, 1996 National Collectors Conven-
tion, green foil, 200 . . . . . . . . . . . .35.00
Bobby Labonte, 1997 ActionVision Set . . . .9.00
Bobby Labonte, 2000 Premium Set . . . . . .4.00
Terry Labonte, 1995 Kelloggs Chevy . . . . .3.00
Terry Labonte, 1995 Chevy #5 . . . . . . . . .3.00
Terry Labonte, 1996, #2 of 2 . . . . . . . . .4.00
Mark Martin, 1994 VIP Set, Club Member .15.00
Mark Martin, 1995 Optima XL set . . . . . .6.00
Mark Martin, 1996 VIP Set . . . . . . . . . .3.00
Mark Martin, 1998 #3 . . . . . . . . . . . .4.00
Mark Martin, 1999 VIP Set . . . . . . . . . .5.00
Mark Martin, 2000 Trackside Set . . . . . . .3.00
Jeremy Mayfield, 1998 VIP Set #1 . . . . . .4.00
Kyle Petty, 1994 Optima XL Set #1 . . . . . .8.00

Mark Martin, 1994 VIP Set, Club Member .15.00

Kyle Petty, 1995 . . . . . . . . . . . . . . .3.00
Kyle Petty, 1995, with insert shot . . . . . . .4.00
Kyle Petty, 1995 Premium Holofoil #1 . . . . .5.00
Kyle Petty, 1996 VIP Set, Club . . . . . . . . 6.00
Tony Stewart, 1999 Stealth Set . . . . . . .5.00
Rusty Wallace, 1994 VIP Set . . . . . . . . . .4.00
Rusty Wallace, 1994 Optima XL Set #2, Driver-
Owner . . . . . . . . . . . . . . . . . . . . .10.00
Rusty Wallace, 1994 Optima XL Set #2 . .10.00
Darrell Waltrip, 1995 Optima XL Set . . . . . .6.00
Michael Waltrip, 1995 VIP Set #3, gold foil .4.00

Kyle Petty, 1996 VIP Set, Club . . . . . . . . . . 6.00

Kyle Petty, 1995 Premium Holofoil #1 . . . . .5.00

Rusty Wallace, 1994 Optima XL Set #2, Driver-
Owner . . . . . . . . . . . . . . . . . . . . . . .10.00

Michael Waltrip, 1995 VIP Set #3, red foil .15.00

## PRO SET-POWER

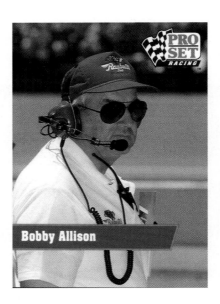

1991 Winston Cup Set, 3 card set . . . . . . .1.00
1991 NHRA Set, 3 card set . . . . . . . . . .1.00
1992 Winston Cup Set, 3 card set . . . . . . .2.00
1992 NHRA Set, 3 card set . . . . . . . . . .1.00
Junie Donlavey, 1994 Power Set, Tuff Stuff
    Show . . . . . . . . . . . . . . . . . .5.00
Dale Earnhardt, 1994 Power Set #DB1 . . .12.00
Jeff Gordon, 1994 Power Set . . . . . . . . .7.00
Bobby Hillin, 1994 Power Set, Tuff Stuff Show .7.00
Ernie Irvan, 1994 Power Set #PW1 . . . . . .3.00
Lee & Richard Petty, 1991 Petty Set, 3 card
    set . . . . . . . . . . . . . . . . . . . . . . . .1.00

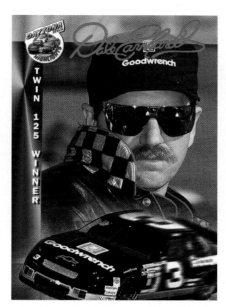

Dale Earnhardt, 1994 Power Set #DB1 . . .12.00

Junie Donlavey, 1994 Power Set, Tuff Stuff
Show . . . . . . . . . . . . . . . . . . . . . . . . .5.00

Lee & Richard Petty, 1991 Petty Set, 3 card
set . . . . . . . . . . . . . . . . . . . . . . . . .1.00

## RACING LEGENDS

Harry Gant, 1992 . . . . . . . . . . . . . . . . . . .4.00

Don Garlits, 1989 Don Garlits Museum . . . .5.00
Sammy Swindell, 1991 World of Outlaws . . .2.00
Curtis Turner, 1991 . . . . . . . . . . . . . . .5.00
Curtis Turner, 1991, car . . . . . . . . . . . .4.00
Curtis Turner Jr., 1991 . . . . . . . . . . . .4.00
Blake Wiggins, 1991 IHRA . . . . . . . . . . .2.00

### REDLINE

Harry Gant, 1991 . . . . . . . . . . . . . . . . .6.00
Rob Moroso, 1991 . . . . . . . . . . . . . . . .6.00
Ken Schrader, 1991 . . . . . . . . . . . . . . .6.00

Cale Yarborough, 1991 . . . . . . . . . . . . . .6.00

**SCORE BOARD**

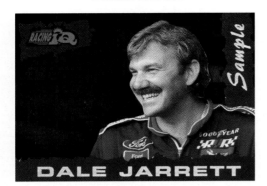

Dale Jarrett, 1997 Racing IQ Set . . . . . . . .5.00

**SKYBOX**

Jeff Gordon, 1997 ProFile . . . . . . . . . . . .4.00

Ernie Irvan, 1994 . . . . . . . . . . . . . . . . . .8.00

**TRAKS**

1995 Winston Cup Preview, 2,000 . . . . . .10.00

1995 5th Anniversary Sheet, 4 cards . . . . . . . . . . . . . . . . . . . . . . . . .1.00

Jeff Burton, 1995 #0TR14 . . . . . . . . . . .2.00

Dale Earnhardt, 1992 Racing Machines Set, Goodwrench Transporter . . . . . . . . . .12.00
Dale Earnhardt, 1992 Racing Machines Set, Goodwrench Transporter, QVC . . . . .20.00
Dale Earnhardt, 1992 Goodwrench Chevy .12.00
Ray Evernham, 1995 5th Anniversary Set . .2.00
Harry Gant, 1992 . . . . . . . . . . . . . . . . . .6.00

Jeff Gordon, 1993 . . . . . . . . . . . . . . . . .7.00

Jeff Gordon, 1995 #26 . . . . . . . . . . . . . .5.00
Alan Kulwicki, 1992 Racing Machines Set . .7.00
Steve Hmiel, 1995 #BTS1 . . . . . . . . . . . .2.00
Ernie Irvan, 1991 . . . . . . . . . . . . . . . . .4.00
Ernie Irvan, 1992 Kodak Team Set . . . . . .6.00
Ernie Irvan, 1994 Series II Havoline Racing . .3.00
Sterling Marlin, 1995 5th Anniversary Set, #4 car . . . . . . . . . . . . . . . . . . . . . . .4.00
Sterling Marlin, 1996 Review/Preview Set . .2.00
Mark Martin, 1991 . . . . . . . . . . . . . . . .4.00
Mark Martin, 1994 Series I . . . . . . . . . . .4.00
Mark Martin, 1992 Valvoline Pit Crew . . . . .4.00
Mark Martin, 1995 St. Louis Convention, 4,000 . . . . . . . . . . . . . . . . . . . . . .8.00
Mark Martin, 1995 100 Years Valvoline . . .6.00
Mark Martin, 1995 100 Years Valvoline, QVC, autographed . . . . . . . . . . . . . . . . . .35.00
Mark Martin, 1995 5th Anniversary Set . . .6.00
Mark Martin, 1995 5th Anniversary Set, #6 car . . . . . . . . . . . . . . . . . . . . . .4.00

Mark Martin, 1996 Review/Preview Set . . .2.00
Benny Parsons, 1992 . . . . . . . . . . . . . . .4.00
Kyle Petty, 1991 . . . . . . . . . . . . . . . . .3.00
Kyle Petty, 1992 . . . . . . . . . . . . . . . . .5.00
Richard Petty, 1991 The King . . . . . . . . . .5.00

Mark Martin, 1991 . . . . . . . . . . . . . . . .4.00

Richard Petty, 1991 The Racers Edge . . . . .5.00
Richard Petty, 1992, QVC . . . . . . . . . . . .6.00
Richard Petty, 1992 STP Team Set . . . . . . .5.00
Lee & Richard Petty, 1991 Lee & Richard Petty
    '72 . . . . . . . . . . . . . . . . . . . . . . . .5.00
Hut Stricklin, 1992 Raybestos Team Set . . .4.00
Rusty Wallace, 1992 . . . . . . . . . . . . . . .5.00
Rusty Wallace, 1993 . . . . . . . . . . . . . . .4.00

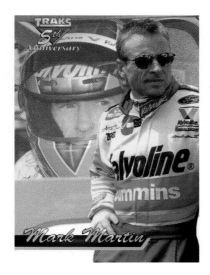

Mark Martin, 1995 St. Louis Convention,
    4,000 . . . . . . . . . . . . . . . . . . . . . . .8.00

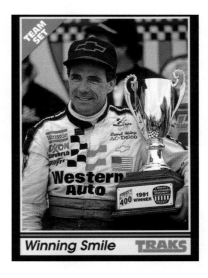

Mark Martin, 1995 100 Years Valvoline, QVC,
    autographed . . . . . . . . . . . . . . . . . .35.00

Darrell Waltrip, 1992 Western Auto Team
    Set . . . . . . . . . . . . . . . . . . . . . . . . .4.00
Michael Waltrip, 1992 Racing Machines Set,
    Country Time Transporter . . . . . . . . .3.00

## UPPER DECK

Jeff Gordon, 1995 SP Set #JG1 . . . . . . . . .9.00
Jeff Gordon, 1995 #JG1 . . . . . . . . . . . . .9.00

Jeff Gordon, 1996 SPx Set #1 . . . . . . . . .10.00
Jeff Gordon, 1997 SP Set #S24 . . . . . . . .7.00
Jeff Gordon, 1998 Maxximum . . . . . . . . .6.00

Rusty Wallace, 1995 #PR1 . . . . . . . . . . .5.00

Rusty Wallace, 1995 #RW1 . . . . . . . . . .5.00
Rusty Wallace, 1995 #PR2 . . . . . . . . . .5.00
Rusty Wallace, 1996 SP Set #S1 . . . . . . .5.00
Rusty Wallace, 1997 SPx Set #S2 . . . . . . .7.00
Rusty Wallace, 1998 Maxx Set . . . . . . . . .4.00
Rusty Wallace, 1998 SP Authentic Set . . . .6.00

## WHEELS

Davey Allison, 1993 #P5 . . . . . . . . . . . . .5.00
Assorted, 1996 Viper Set in binder, Hawaii Convention . . . . . . . . . . . . . . . . . . . . .45.00
Dale Earnhardt, 1996 Mom 'n' Pops Set . .12.00
Harry Gant, 1994 Farewell Tour Set,
  "Farewell" . . . . . . . . . . . . . . . . . . . . . .2.00

Harry Gant, 1994 Farewell Tour, "Harley
  Harry" . . . . . . . . . . . . . . . . . . . . . .2.00
Harry Gant, 1994 Farewell Tour, Harry Gant .2.00
Harry Gant, 1994 Farewell Tour #P1 . . . . .2.00
Harry Gant, 1994 Farewell Tour #P2 . . . . .3.00
Harry Gant, 1994 Farewell Tour #P3 . . . . .2.00
Harry Gant, 1994 Farewell Tour #P4 . . . . .2.00
Harry Gant, 1994 Farewell Tour #P5 . . . . .2.00
Jeff Gordon, 1993 #P2 . . . . . . . . . . . . .8.00
Jeff Gordon, 1994 High Gear Set
  #P1 . . . . . . . . . . . . . . . . . . . . . . . .10.00

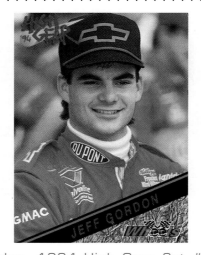

Jeff Gordon, 1994 High Gear Set #P1, gold
foil . . . . . . . . . . . . . . . . . . . . . . . . .20.00

Jeff Gordon, 1994 Farewell Tour . . . . . . . .5.00
Jeff Gordon, 1995 High Gear Set #P2 . . .8.00
Jeff Gordon, 1995 #P1, ruby, 12,000 . . .10.00
Jeff Gordon, 1995 #P1, emerald, 6,000 . .25.00

Jeff Gordon, 1995 #P1, Diamond, 3,000 .40.00
Jeff Gordon, 1996 Viper #P3 . . . . . . . . . .14.00
Jeff Gordon, 1996 Race Sharks #P1 . . . .10.00
Jeff Gordon, 1997 Predator #P1 . . . . . . . .7.00
Jeff Gordon, 1997 Predator 1st #P1 . . . . .7.00
Jeff Gordon, 1997 Red Wolf #P2 . . . . . . . .9.00
Jeff Gordon, 1997 Red Wolf 1st #P2 . . . . .9.00
Jeff Gordon, 1997 Black Wolf #P3 . . . . . . .9.00
Jeff Gordon, 1997 Black Wolf 1st #P3 . . . .9.00
Jeff Gordon, 1997 Viper #P2 . . . . . . . . . .7.00
Jeff Gordon, 1999 Wheels Set #2 of 2 . . . .4.00
Jeff Gordon, 1999 High Gear Set . . . . . . .5.00
Dale Jarrett, 1997 Viper #P1 . . . . . . . . . .5.00
Bobby Labonte, 1993 #P4 . . . . . . . . . . . .3.00
Bobby Labonte, 1996 Viper #P1 . . . . . . . .8.00
Bobby Labonte, 1996 Crown Jewels #PC1 . .6.00
Bobby Labonte, 1996 Crown Jewels #PD1 . .6.00

Bobby Labonte, 1996 Crown Jewels #PE1 . .6.00
Bobby Labonte, 1996 Crown Jewels #PS1 . .6.00

Bobby Labonte, 1998 High Gear Set . . . . .3.00
Bobby Labonte, 1999 Wheels Set #1 of 2 . .3.00
Mark Martin, 1995 High Gear Set #P3 . . . .5.00
Mark Martin, 1998 Wheels Set . . . . . . . . .4.00

Mark Martin, 1997 Jurassic Park #P1 . . . .5.00
Kyle Petty, 1994 High Gear Set #P3 . . . . . .5.00
Kyle Petty, 1994 High Gear Set #P3, gold
    Foil . . . . . . . . . . . . . . . . . . . . . . . . .10.00

Richard Petty, 1993 #P1 . . . . . . . . . . . . .3.00
Tony Stewart, 2000 High Gear Set . . . . . . .6.00
Kenny Wallace, 1993 #P3 . . . . . . . . . . . .2.00
Rusty Wallace, 1994 High Gear Set #P2 . . .5.00
Rusty Wallace, 1994 High Gear Set #P2, gold
    foil . . . . . . . . . . . . . . . . . . . . . . . . .10.00
Rusty Wallace, 1995 High Gear Set #P1 . . .5.00
Rusty Wallace, 1996 Viper #P2 . . . . . . . . .8.00

**WINNERS CHOICE**

Joe Bessey, 1992 . . . . . . . . . . . . . . . . .3.00
Ricky Craven, 1992 . . . . . . . . . . . . . . . .4.00
Joe Nemechek, 1992 . . . . . . . . . . . . . . .4.00
Shawna Robinson, 1992 . . . . . . . . . . . . .3.00
Mike Rowe, 1992 . . . . . . . . . . . . . . . . . .2.00

# SETS

### AC DELCO

1992 AC Powers The Winners, 10 card
set . . . . . . . . . . . . . . . . . . . . . . .12.00

### AC RACING

1990 AC Proven Winners, 7 card
set . . . . . . . . . . . . . . . . . . . . . . .65.00

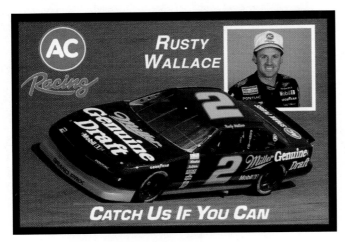

1991 AC Catch Us If You Can, 10 card
set . . . . . . . . . . . . . . . . . . . . . . .35.00
1992 AC Leaders on the Track, 8 card
set . . . . . . . . . . . . . . . . . . . . . .20.00
1993 AC Foldouts, 10 card set . . . . . . .15.00

### ACTION PACKED

Clifford, Davey & Bobby Allison, 1993 Allison
Family, 3 card set, 5,000 . . . . . . . .45.00

Dale Earnhardt, 1995 Sun Drop, 3 card
set . . . . . . . . . . . . . . . . . . . . . . . .25.00
1994 Smokin' Joes, 13 card set . . . . . . .25.00

1994 Winston Select, 24K Gold, 10
card set . . . . . . . . . . . . . . . . . . .75.00
1995 Hendricks Motorsports, 6 card set . . .6.00
1995 McDonalds, 21 card set . . . . . . . .15.00
1996 McDonalds, 29 card set . . . . . . . .15.00

### ADVANCED IMAGES

Chad Little, 1994 Bayer Racing, 5 card set .7.00
Ernie Irvan, 1994 Ernie Irvan Fan Club, 5 card
set . . . . . . . . . . . . . . . . . . . . . . . .8.00
Ted Musgrave, 1994 US Air Racing, 5 card
set . . . . . . . . . . . . . . . . . . . . . . . .5.00

### BIG LEAGUE

Ron Hornaday, 1992, 4 card set . . . . . . . .5.00

### CALIFORNIA HIGHWAY PATROL

1999 CHP, 7 card set . . . . . . . . . . . . . . .8.00

2000 CHP Sears Point, 10 cardset . . . . .10.00

## CLASSIC

1996 Speed Street . . . . . . . . . . . . . . . .10.00

## CM PRODUCTS

Harry Gant, 1991 Handsome Harry, 15 card set . . . . . . . . . . . . . . . . . . . . . . . .4.00

## DAYCO BELTS

1992 Dayco Racing, 10 card set . . . . . .12.00

NEIL BONNETT

1994 Dayco, Series III, 15 card set . . . . .10.00

Rusty Wallace, 1993 Dayco 15 card set . .10.00

## D&D RACING IMAGES

Robert Pressley, 1991 Alliance Racing, 12 card set . . . . . . . . . . . . . . . . . . . . . .6.00

## DODGE

**Bill Elliott**
35-year-old Elliott will be appearing in his fifth IROC series in the last six years. He has one victory and was runner-up to series winner Al Unser, Jr. as an IROC rookie in 1986. Bill finished third in last year's Winston Cup Series after taking the series championship in 1988.

1991 IROC (International Race of Champions), 12 card set . . . . . . . . . . . . . . . . . . . . .225.00

## EAGLE PROMOTIONS

1992 Bikers of Racing Scene, 34 card set . .5.00

## FINISH LINE

1993 Finish Line Commemorative Sheets-With binder, 30 card set . . . . . . . . . . . . .30.00

1995 Speed Street Coca-Cola 600, 65 card set . . . . . . . . . . . . . . . . . . . . . . . .10.00

## FIRST BRANDS

1991 STP 20th Anniversary, 10 card set . .20.00
1992 Daytona 500 by STP, 10 card set . . . . . . . . . . . . . . . . . . . . . . . . .17.00

## FLEER ULTRA

1997 Shoneys, 16 card set . . . . . . . . . .25.00

## FORD MOTORSPORTS

1992 NASCAR Manufacturers Champion, 10 card set . . . . . . . . . . . . . . . . . . . . . . . .14.00
1993 NASCAR Manufacturers Champion, 10 card set . . . . . . . . . . . . . . . . . . . . . . . .15.00

## GARFIELD PRESS

1st Show Car

1991 Pioneers of Racing, with numbered binder, 107 card set . . . . . . . . . . . . . . . .100.00

## GOLD CARD

Rob Moroso, 1991, 36 card set . . . . . . .15.00

## GOOD YEAR

1998 Good Year 100th Anniversary, in car tin, 50 card set . . . . . . . . . . . . . . . . . . . . .20.00

## HI-TECH

1993 Indy Tire Test, 10 card set . . . . . . . .4.00
1995 Brickyard 400, with 23k Jeff Gordon Card, 101 card set . . . . . . . . . . . . . . . .110.00
1995 Brickyard 400, in wood box, 101 card set . . . . . . . . . . . . . . . . . . . . . .300.00
1995 Lowes Team, 10 card set . . . . . . .15.00

## HOOTERS

Alan Kulwicki, 1992 Hooters Racing, 15 card set . . . . . . . . . . . . . . . . . . . . . . .8.00

## IF IT'S RACING

"Tiger" Tom Pistone, 1991, 15 card set . . .3.00

## INTERSTATE RACING

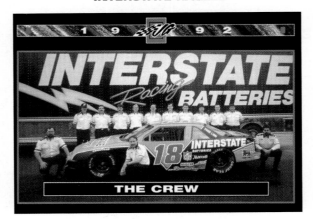

Joe Gibbs Racing, 1992, 12 card set . . . . . . . . . . . . . . . . . . . . . . . .5.00

## KELLOGGS

1992 Kelloggs, back of box, 4 card set . . . . . . . . . . . . . . . . . . . . . . . . . . .10.00
Terry Labonte, 1993 Kelloggs, 4 card set .10.00

## LIMITED EDITIONS

Chuck Bown, 1992, 15 card set . . . . . . .6.00
Harry Gant, 1992, 15 card set . . . . . . . .6.00
Jerry Glanville, 1992, 15 card set . . . . . .6.00
Jeff Gordon, 1992, 15 card set . . . . . . .14.00
Jimmy Hensley, 1992, 15 card set . . . . . .6.00
Tommy Houston, 1992, 15 card set . . . . . .6.00

Kenny Wallace, 1992, 15 card set . . . . . . .6.00

## LIPTON

1994 Lipton Tea, 4 card set . . . . . . . . . .7.00
Johnny Benson, 1995 Lipton Tea, 5 card set . . . . . . . . . . . . . . . . . . . . . . . .6.00

## LOTTERY INSTANT WIN TICKETS

2000 Virginia Drivers, unscratched, 9 card set . . . . . . . . . . . . . . . . . . . . . . . .18.00

## MAC TOOLS

1992 Mac Tools, 22 card set . . . . . . . . .25.00

## MAXX

1989 Crisco, 25 card set . . . . . . . . . . . .6.00
1990 Holly Farms, 30 card set . . . . . . . .12.00
1991 Ford Motorsports, 40 card set . . . . . . . . . . . . . . . . . . . . . . .25.00

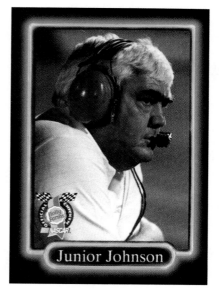

1990 Holly Farms, 30 cardset . . . . . . . .12.00

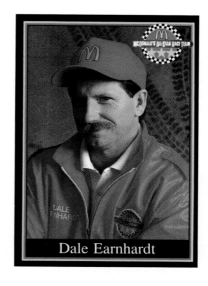

1991 Racing For Kids, 18 card set, 3 sheets . . . . . . . . . . . . . . . . . . . . . .100.00

1991 McDonalds, 30 card set . . . . . . . .25.00

1991 Racing For Kids, 18 card set, 3 sheets . . . . . . . . . . . . . . . . . . . . .100.00
1991 Winston Acrylics, 20 card set . . . . . . . . . . . . . . . . . . . . . . . . . .5.00
1992 5th Anniversary Update, red, 30 card set . . . . . . . . . . . . . . . . . . . . . . . . . .5.00
1992 5th Anniversary Update, black, 30 card set . . . . . . . . . . . . . . . . . . . . . . . . . .5.00
1992 All Pro Team Gargoles, 50 card set . .6.00
1992 Ford Motorsports, 50 card set . . . . . . . . . . . . . . . . . . . . . . . .15.00
1992 Lowe's Foods,16 sticker set . . . . . . .7.00
1992 McDonalds, 36 card set . . . . . . . .7.00
1992 McDonalds Race Team, 4 card set . . .5.00
1992 Motorsports Hall of Fame, 40 card set . . . . . . . . . . . . . . . . . . .18.00

1991 Winston Acrylics, 20 card set . . . . . . . . . . . . . . . . . . . . . . . . . .5.00
1992 Sam Bass Legends, 10 card set . . . . . . . . . . . . . . . . . . . . . . . . .6.00
1992 Sears Craftsman, 8 card set . . . . . .6.00
1992 Texaco, 20 card set . . . . . . . . . . . . .7.00
1992 The Winston, 50 card set . . . . . . . .9.00
1993 Sam Bass Acrylics, 6,000 . . . . . .62.00
1993 Case Knives, 13 card set . . . . . . .25.00
1993 Ford Motorsports, 50 card set . . . . . . . . . . . . . . . . . . . . . . . .20.00
1993 Maxx Retail Jumbos, 9 card set . . . . . . . . . . . . . . . . . . . . . . . .25.00
1993 Texaco, 20 card set . . . . . . . . . . .14.00
1993 The Winston, 51 card set . . . . . . .10.00
1993 Winnebago Motorsports, 11 card set . . . . . . . . . . . . . . . . . . . . . . . .18.00

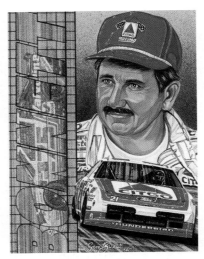

1992 Sam Bass Legends, 10 card
set . . . . . . . . . . . . . . . . . . . . . . .6.00

1994 Ford Motorsports, 3½ X 5, 25 card
set . . . . . . . . . . . . . . . . . . . . . . .28.00
1994 Maxx Premier Jumbos 5 X 7, 12 card
set . . . . . . . . . . . . . . . . . . . . . . .25.00
1996 Pepsi Daytona 500, 5 card
set . . . . . . . . . . . . . . . . . . . . . . .15.00
Jeff Burton, 1993 Baby Ruth, 4 card set . . .7.00
Bill Elliott, 1991 Melling Team, 40 card set .30.00
Bill Elliott, 1991 Bill Elliott Team, 40 card
set . . . . . . . . . . . . . . . . . . . . . . .15.00
Bill Elliott, 1992 McDonalds, dated October 10
1992, 4 card set . . . . . . . . . . . . . .7.00

Bobby Hamilton, 1992 Rookie of Year, 16 card
set . . . . . . . . . . . . . . . . . . . . . . .3.00
Ernie Irvan, 1994 Texaco Ernie Irvan Set, 50 card
set . . . . . . . . . . . . . . . . . . . . . . .12.00
Dale Jarrett, 1996 Dale Jarrett Band Aid, 4 card
set . . . . . . . . . . . . . . . . . . . . . . .10.00

## MCCORD GASKETS

1992 Michigan Engine Bearings, 12 card
set . . . . . . . . . . . . . . . . . . . . . . .11.00

## METALLIC IMPRESSIONS

1995 Winston Cup 25 years, 25 card set .45.00
1996, Racings Greats, 5 card
set . . . . . . . . . . . . . . . . . . . . . . .10.00
Dale Earnhardt, 1995, 5 card set . . . . . . .30.00
Dale Earnhardt, 1995, 20 card set,
9,950 . . . . . . . . . . . . . . . . . . . . .60.00
Jeff Gordon, 1995, 5 card set . . . . . . . .20.00
Jeff Gordon, 1995, 10 card set, 19,950 .48.00
Kyle Petty, 1995, 10 card set . . . . . . . .35.00
Richard Petty, 1995, 5 card set . . . . . . .10.00
Rusty Wallace, 1995, 5 cardset . . . . . . .10.00
Rusty Wallace, 1995, 12,500, 20 card
set . . . . . . . . . . . . . . . . . . . . . . .40.00

## MOTORCRAFT RACING

1991 Motorcraft Racing, 7 card
set . . . . . . . . . . . . . . . . . . . . . . .35.00
1992 Motorcraft Racing, 10 card
set . . . . . . . . . . . . . . . . . . . . . . .22.00
1993 Motorcraft Racing, 10 card
set . . . . . . . . . . . . . . . . . . . . . . .22.00
1993 Decade of Champions, 10 card set .15.00
1994 Quality Care Racing, 10 card
set . . . . . . . . . . . . . . . . . . . . . . .10.00

Jeff Gordon, 1994 Rookie of Year, 20 card
set . . . . . . . . . . . . . . . . . . . . . . .20.00

1993 Motorcraft Racing, 10 card set . . . . . . . . . . . . . . . . . . . . .22.00

## MW WINDOWS

1994 MW Windows, 5 card set . . . . . . .28.00
1995 MW Windows, 4 card set . . . . . . .15.00
1997 MW Windows, 5 card set . . . . . . .10.00

## MOTORSPORTS MODEL

1991 Motorsports Model, 90 card set . . . . . . . . . . . . . . . . . . . . . .5.00
1991 Motorsports Model Premier, 90 card set . . . . . . . . . . . . . . . . . . .10.00
1992 DieCards, 54 card set . . . . . . . . .10.00
1992 AM Series, 90 card set . . . . . . . .10.00

## PEPSI

1993 Daytona Pepsi, 400, 5 card set . . . . . . . . . . . . . . . . . . . . .12.00
Richard Petty, 1992, 5 card set . . . . . . . .10.00

## PINNACLE

Jeff Gordon, 1997, 3 card set . . . . . . . . .8.00
1997 Checkers, 9 card set . . . . . . . . . . .3.00

1997 Hardee's, motion cards, 6 card set . . .3.00

## PRESS PASS

1993 Press Pass Review, 34 card set . . . . . . . . . . . . . . . . . . . . . . .5.00
Bobby Labonte & Tony Stewart, 2000 Chef Boyardee, 6 card set . . . . . . . . . . . .20.00

## PRO SET

1992 Collector's World Museum, 50 card set . . . . . . . . . . . . . . . . . . . . .150.00
1992 Maxwell House, 30 card set . . . . . . . . . . . . . . . . . . . . . . .15.00
1992 Rudy Farms, 20 card set . . . . . . . .35.00
1992 Tic Tac Mints Racing, 6 card set . . . . . . . . . . . . . . . . . . . . . .14.00
1993 Maxwell House Series I, 15 card set .12.00
1993 Maxwell House Series II, 15 card set . . . . . . . . . . . . . . . . . . . . . .12.00
The Petty's, 1991 Petty Family, 50 card set .6.00
Richard Petty, 1992 Food Lion, 116 card set . . . . . . . . . . . . . . . . . . . .15.00
Richard Petty, 1992 Food Lion Petty Factory Set, 116 card set . . . . . . . . . . . . . . . . . .30.00

The Petty's, 1991 Petty Family, 50 card set .6.00

1992 Tic Tac Mints Racing, 6 card set . . . . . . . . . . . . . . . . . . . . . . . .14.00

### PROCTOR & GAMBLE

Ricky Rudd, 1995 Tide, 10 card set . . . . . .6.00
Ricky Rudd, 1996 Tide, 10th Anniversary, 10 card set . . . . . . . . . . . . . . . . . . . . . .7.50

### RACER'S CHOICE

Dale Earnhardt, 1996 Sun Drop, 3 card set .20.00

### RACING CONCEPTS

Shawna Robinson, 1992 Sparkys Racing, 9 card set . . . . . . . . . . . . . . . . . . . . . . . .7.00

## RACING LEGENDS

Geoff Bodine, 1991, 30 card set . . . . . . .15.00
Harry Gant, 1992, 33 card set . . . . . . . .20.00
Jack Ingram, 1992, 20 card set . . . . . . .10.00
Junior Johnson, 1991, 30 card set . . . . .25.00
Coo Coo Marlin, 1991, 30 card set . . . . .12.00
Sterling Marlin, 1991, 30 card set . . . . . .20.00
Curtis Turner, 1992, 20 card set . . . . . . .10.00

### REDLINE RACING

Harry Gant, 1992, 30 card set . . . . . . . . .11.00
Rob Moroso, 1992, 30 card set . . . . . . .11.00
Ken Schrader, 1992, 30 card set . . . . . . .10.00
Cale Yarborough, 1992 30 card set . . . . .10.00

### RSS MOTORSPORTS

1992 Race Car Haulers, 30 card set . . . . . . . . . . . . . . . . . . . . . . . . . . . .5.00

Fireball Roberts, 1991, Series I & II, 42 card set . . . . . . . . . . . . . . . . . . . . . . . . .15.00

## SCOREBOARD

Dale Earnhardt, 1994, National Sports Convention, 5 card set . . . . . . . . . . . . . . .50.00

## SLIM JIM

1992 Slim Jim, 30 card set . . . . . . . . . .30.00
David Green, 1994 Slim Jim, 18 card set  .13.00

## SPORTS LEGENDS

Bobby Allison, 1991, 30 card set . . . . . . . . . . . . . . . . . . . . . . . .8.00
Donnie Allison, 1991, 30 card set . . . . . . . . . . . . . . . . . . . . . . . .8.00
Buck Baker, 1992, 30 card set . . . . . . . .7.00
Neil Bonnett, 1991, 30 card set . . . . . . . . . . . . . . . . . . . . . . . .10.00
Harry Hyde, 1991, 30 card set . . . . . . . .8.00
Dale Jarrett, 1992, 30 card set . . . . . . . .8.00

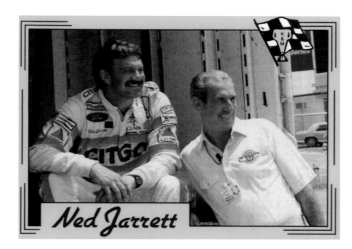

Ned Jarrett, 1991 Ned Jarrett, 30 card set  .8.00
Alan Kulwicki, 1992, 30 card set . . . . . . .10.00
Fred Lorenzen, 1993, with binder, 16 card set . . . . . . . . . . . . . . . . . . . . . . . . . .12.00
Rob Moroso, 1991, 30 card set . . . . . . .10.00
Phil Parsons, 1992, 30 card set . . . . . . .7.00
Wendell Scott, 1992, 30 card set . . . . . .7.00
Hut Stricklin, 1991, 30 card set . . . . . . . .7.00
Herb Thomas, 1991, 30 card set . . . . . . .7.00
Cale Yarborough, 1992, 30 card set . . . . .7.00

## SPORTSTAR

1986 Sportstar Photographics, 13 card set . . . . . . . . . . . . . . . . . . . . . . . .700.00
1986 Sportstar Photographics Stickers, 9 sticker complete set . . . . . . . . . . . . . . .120.00
1986 Sportstar Photographics Stickers, 6 NASCAR stickers . . . . . . . . . . . . . . .75.00

1986 Sportstar Photographics Stickers, 3 Indy Car stickers . . . . . . . . . . . . . . . . . .40.00
1992 Racing Collectibles, 16 card set . . . . . . . . . . . . . . . . . . . . . . . . . .7.00

1986 Sportstar Photographics, 13 card set . . . . . . . . . . . . . . . . . . . . . .700.00

## STOVE TOP

1993 Stove Top Stuffing Series I, 3 card set . . . . . . . . . . . . . . . . . . . . . .6.00
1993 Stove Top Stuffing Series II, 3 card set . . . . . . . . . . . . . . . . . . . . . .6.00

## SUNBELT

Harry Gant, 1992  6 card set . . . . . . . . .6.00

## T.G. RACING

GLOTZBACH'S WING

1989 Masters of Racing, 152 card set . . . . . . . . . . . . . . . . . . . . . . . .175.00
1990 Masters of Racing White Gold Series, 110 card set . . . . . . . . . . . . . . . . . . .40.00
1992 MotorArt Calendar, 12 card set . . . . .9.00
1992 Masters of Racing Update, 265 card set . . . . . . . . . . . . . . . . . . . . . . . .15.00
Tiny Lund, 1991, 55 card set . . . . . . . . .16.00

David Pearson, 1991, 6 card set . . . . . . .37.00
Wendell Scott, 1991, 6 card set . . . . . . .16.00

### TRACK PACK

Yesterday's Heroes, 48 card set . . . . . . .12.00

### TRAKS

1992 ASA Silver Anniversary, 50 card set . .8.00
1992 Country Star Racing, 14 card
    set . . . . . . . . . . . . . . . . . . . . . . . . . .6.00

1992 Goodys Invitational, 25 card
    set . . . . . . . . . . . . . . . . . . . . . . . . .25.00
1992 Preferred Collector, Traks Club, 20 card
    set . . . . . . . . . . . . . . . . . . . . . . . . .12.00
1993 Traks Trivia, 50 card set . . . . . . . . .5.00
1994 Auto Value Stores, 51 card
    set . . . . . . . . . . . . . . . . . . . . . . . . .10.00
1995 Auto Value Stores, 51 card
    set . . . . . . . . . . . . . . . . . . . . . . . . .12.00
1995 Valvoline "100 Years of Racing," in car tin,
    100 card set . . . . . . . . . . . . . . . . . .20.00
Davey Allison, 1992 Texaco Team, 25 card
    set . . . . . . . . . . . . . . . . . . . . . . . . . .9.00
Dale Earnhardt, 1991 Mom 'n' Pops Ham, 6 card
    set . . . . . . . . . . . . . . . . . . . . . . . . .25.00
Dale Earnhardt, 1991 Mom 'n' Pops Biscuits, 6
    card set . . . . . . . . . . . . . . . . . . . . .25.00
Dale Earnhardt, 1992 Mom 'n' Pops Ham, 6 card
    set . . . . . . . . . . . . . . . . . . . . . . . . .20.00
Dale Earnhardt, 1992 GM Goodwrench Team, 25
    card set . . . . . . . . . . . . . . . . . . . . .25.00
Jeff Gordon, 1992 Baby Ruth, 4 card set .20.00
Ernie Irvan, 1992 Kodak Racing, 25 card
    set . . . . . . . . . . . . . . . . . . . . . . . . .30.00
Ernie Irvan, 1992 Kodak Team, 25 card set .8.00

Dale Earnhardt, 1991 Mom 'n' Pops Ham, 6 card
    set . . . . . . . . . . . . . . . . . . . . . . . . .25.00

Ernie Irvan, 1993 Kodak Racing, 24 card
    set . . . . . . . . . . . . . . . . . . . . . . . . .25.00

Ernie Irvan, 1993 Kodak Postcards, 6 card
    set . . . . . . . . . . . . . . . . . . . . . . . . .14.00
Benny Parsons, 1992 Legendary Benny Parsons,
    50 card set . . . . . . . . . . . . . . . . . . . .8.00
Kyle Petty, 1991 Mello Yello, 13 card set . .10.00
Kyle Petty, 1992 Mello Yello Team, 25 card
    set . . . . . . . . . . . . . . . . . . . . . . . . . .9.00

COMEBACK KID

Benny Parsons, 1992 Legendary Benny Parsons, 50 card set . . . . . . . . . . . . . . . . . . . .8.00

MEAN GREEN MACHINE

Kyle Petty, 1991 Mello Yello, 13 card set . .10.00

Richard Petty, 1991 Petty STP 20th Anniversary, 50 card set . . . . . . . . . . . . . . . . . . .10.00

THE BEARD

Richard Petty, 1992 STP Team, 25 card set .8.00

Robert Pressley, 1992 Alliance Racing, 12 card set . . . . . . . . . . . . . . . . . . . . . . . .6.00
Robert Pressley, 1993 Alliance Racing, 12 card set . . . . . . . . . . . . . . . . . . . . . . .15.00
Hermie Sadler, 1994 Virginia Is for Lovers, 10 card set . . . . . . . . . . . . . . . . . . . .9.00
Hut Stricklin, 1992 Raybestos Team, 25 card set . . . . . . . . . . . . . . . . . . . . . . . .8.00
Darrell Waltrip, 1992 Western Auto Team, 25 card set . . . . . . . . . . . . . . . . . . . . .8.00
Michael Waltrip, 1992 Pennzoil Team, 25 card set . . . . . . . . . . . . . . . . . . . . . . .8.00

**UNO PLAYING CARDS**

3 Richmond With First UNO Racer

1983 UNO Racing, 30 card set . . . . . . . .150.00

**UPPER DECK**

Jeff Gordon, 1996, 20 card set . . . . . . . .20.00
Kyle Petty, 1997, Hot Wheels, 5 card set . . . . . . . . . . . . . . . . . . . . . . . . . .3.00

**VIVARIN**
Buckshot Jones, 1997, 7 card set . . . . . . .6.00

**WHEELS**

Dale Earnhardt, 1993 Mom 'n' Pops Victory Series, 6 card set . . . . . . . . . . . . . . .25.00
Dale Earnhardt, 1994 Power Pak Team Set, 20 card set . . . . . . . . . . . . . . . . . . . .25.00
Dale Earnhardt, 1994 Power Pak Team Set, gold, 20 card set . . . . . . . . . . . . . . . . . .35.00
Dale Earnhardt, 1996 Mom 'n' Pops, 3 card set . . . . . . . . . . . . . . . . . . . . . . . .30.00
Dale Earnhardt, 1996 Mom 'n' Pops Cobra Die-Cut, 3 card set . . . . . . . . . . . . . . . .45.00
Harry Gant, 1994 Power Pak Team Set, 33 card set . . . . . . . . . . . . . . . . . . . . . .10.00
Harry Gant, 1994 Power Pak Team Set, gold, 33 card set . . . . . . . . . . . . . . . . . . .17.00
Kyle Petty, 1992 Mello Yello, silver, 14 card set . . . . . . . . . . . . . . . . . . . . . . . .7.00

Dale Earnhardt, 1996 Mom 'n' Pops, 3 card set 60.00

Kyle Petty, 1992 Mello Yello, gold, 14 card set . . . . . . . . . . . . . . . . . . . . . . . . .10.00
Rusty Wallace, 1992 Pontiac Excitement, silver, 14 card set . . . . . . . . . . . . . . . . . . . .8.00
Rusty Wallace, 1992 Pontiac Excitement, gold, 14 card set . . . . . . . . . . . . . . . . . . .15.00
Rusty Wallace, 1994 Power Pak Team, 40 card set . . . . . . . . . . . . . . . . . . . . . . . .10.00
Rusty Wallace, 1994 Power Pak Team Set gold, 40 card set . . . . . . . . . . . . . . . . . .20.00

**WINNER'S CHOICE**

Ricky Craven, 1991, 30 card set . . . . . . .15.00
1992 Winners Choice, 150 card set . . . . . . . . . . . . . . . . . . . . . . . . .15.00

Harry Gant, 1994 Power Pak Team Set, gold, 33 card set . . . . . . . . . . . . . . . . . . . .17.00

# CEREAL BOXES

A decade ago, marketing gurus — inspired by the brand loyalty exhibited by race fans — realized the benefits of offering products in NASCAR-themed packaging. These products quickly earned a spot among the sport's most popular incidental collectibles.

Kellogg's introduced the first cereal box adorned with racing decor in 1991. The container featured a picture of the No. 41 Larry Hedrick Motorsports entry, a car sponsored by Kellogg's Corn Flakes.

In 1997, Dale Earnhardt made history as the first race car driver featured on the Holy Grail of sports-themed cereal containers — the Wheaties box.

It is important to note that removing the contents from a cereal box does *not* adversely affect its value as a collectible. Some collectors choose to replace the cereal with paper or styrofoam "peanuts," while others prefer to open both ends of the boxes and flatten them. Either practice is acceptable.

## GENERAL MILLS

John Andretti, #43 car, 14 oz. Lucky Charms, 2000 . . . . . . . . . . . . . . . . . . . .3.00
John Andretti, #43 car, 12 oz. Trix, 2000 . .3.00
John Andretti, #43 car, 13.75 oz. Cocoa Puffs, 2000 . . . . . . . . . . . . . . . . . . . .3.00
John Andretti, #43 car, 12 oz. Rice Chex, 2000 . . . . . . . . . . . . . . . . . . . .3.00
Johnny Benson, die-cast car offer, 15 oz. Cheerios, 1998 . . . . . . . . . . . . . . . . . . . .5.00
Johnny Benson, die-cast car offer, 20 oz. Cheerios, 1998 . . . . . . . . . . . . . . . . . . . .5.00
Johnny Benson, Kids design car offer, French Toast Crunch, 1998 . . . . . . . . . . . . .5.00
Johnny Benson, kids design car offer, Lucky Charms, 1998 . . . . . . . . . . . . . . . .5.00
Johnny Benson, poster offer, Cheerios, 1998 . . . . . . . . . . . . . . . . . . . .5.00
Johnny Benson, 2 pack with postcard, Cheerios, 1998 . . . . . . . . . . . . . . . . . . . .10.00
Johnny Benson, poster offer, 14 oz. Honey Nut Cheerios, 1998 . . . . . . . . . . . . . . . .6.00
Johnny Benson, poster offer, 20 oz. Honey Nut Cheerios, 1998 . . . . . . . . . . . . . . . .6.00
Johnny Benson, car, Cheerios, 1999 . . . . . .4.00
Johnny Benson, Race Against Drugs, Cheerios, 1999 . . . . . . . . . . . . . . . . . . . .4.00
Johnny Benson, Cheerios Racing Pals offer, Cinnamon Toast Crunch, 1999 . . . . . . . . . .4.00

Johnny Benson, Cheerios Racing Pals offer, Lucky Charms, 1999 . . . . . . . . . . . . . . . .4.00
Johnny Benson, gold foil, 14 oz. Frosted Cheerios, 1999 . . . . . . . . . . . . . . . . . . . .3.00
Johnny Benson, gold foil, 20 oz. Honey Nut Cheerios, 1999 . . . . . . . . . . . . . . . . . . . .4.00
Johnny Benson, Sure Start, Cheerios, 1999 .4.00
Jeff Burton, Frosted Cheerios, 1999 . . . . . .3.00
Kevin LePage, Multi-Grain Cheerios, 1999 . .3.00
Richard Petty, 14.25 oz. Frosted Cheerios, 2000 . . . . . . . . . . . . . . . . . . . .4.00
Richard Petty, 15 oz. Cheerios, 2000 . . . . .4.00
Richard Petty, 12 oz. Corn Chex, 2000 . . . .4.00
Richard Petty, 16 oz. Wheat Chex, 2000 . . .4.00
Richard Petty, 16 oz. Multi Grain Cheerios, 2000 . . . . . . . . . . . . . . . . . . . .4.00
Jack Roush, Win a Day at Races, Cheerios, 1999 . . . . . . . . . . . . . . . . . . . .4.00

## KELLOGG'S

Corny the Rooster, in racing uniform, Corn Flakes, 1995 . . . . . . . . . . . . . . . . . . . .10.00

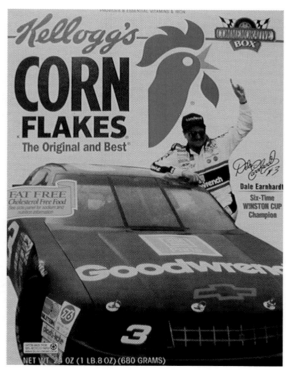

Dale Earnhardt, 1993 Champion, Corn Flakes, 1994 . . . . . . . . . . . . . . . . . . . .75.00
Dale Earnhardt, 1994 Champion, Commemorative, Corn Flakes, 1995 . . . . . . . . . . .45.00
Dale Earnhardt, 1994 Champion, Dual Pack, Corn Flakes, 1995 . . . . . . . . . . . . . . . .40.00
Dale Earnhardt Frosted Flakes, 1996 . . . .30.00
Dale Earnhardt, Jeff Gordon, Terry Labonte, Dale Jarrett, 3 Pack, 1997 . . . . . . . . . . .25.00

Bill Elliott & Joe Gibbs, Raisin Bran, 1994 .20.00
Bill Elliott, car & Tony Tiger, Frosted Flakes,
   1995 . . . . . . . . . . . . . . . . . . .15.00
Bill Elliott, Bill & Tony Tiger, Frosted Flakes,
   1995 . . . . . . . . . . . . . . . . . . .15.00
Jeff Gordon, with cereal bowl, red box, Frosted
   Mini Wheats, 1994 . . . . . . . . . . .25.00
Jeff Gordon, with cereal bowl, orange box, Frosted
   Mini Wheats, 1994 . . . . . . . . . . .25.00
Jeff Gordon, Sam Bass art, red, Frosted Mini
   Wheats, 1994 . . . . . . . . . . . . .30.00
Jeff Gordon, Sam Bass art, orange, Frosted Mini
   Wheats, 1994 . . . . . . . . . . . . .30.00
Jeff Gordon, standing by car, 1993 ROY, Frosted
   Mini Wheats, 1994 . . . . . . . . . . .30.00
Jeff Gordon, Brickyard 400 Victory Lane, Frosted
   Mini Wheats, 1995 . . . . . . . . . . .25.00

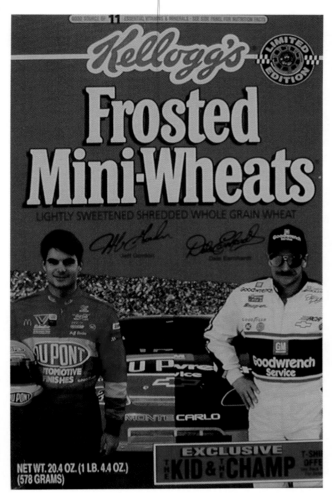

Jeff Gordon & Dale Earnhardt, Kid and the Champ,
Frosted Mini Wheats, 1995 . . . . . . . .40.00

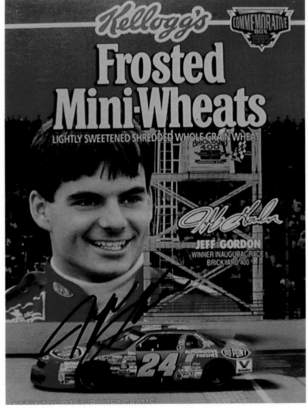

Jeff Gordon, crossing Brickyard finish line, Frosted
   Mini Wheats, 1995 . . . . . . . . . . .20.00
Jeff Gordon & Dale Earnhardt, Kid and the Champ,
   Frosted Mini Wheats, 1995 . . . . . . .40.00
Jeff Gordon, Corn Flakes, 1996 . . . . . . . .15.00
Jeff Gordon, Frosted Mini Wheats, 1996 . .15.00
Jeff Gordon, headshot with helmet, Frosted Mini
   Wheats, 1996 . . . . . . . . . . . . . .20.00
Jeff Gordon, red, Frosted Mini Wheats,
   1996 . . . . . . . . . . . . . . . . . . . .15.00
Jeff Gordon, orange, Frosted Mini Wheats,
   1996 . . . . . . . . . . . . . . . . . . . .15.00

Jeff Gordon, 1997 Champion, red, Frosted Mini
   Wheats, 1998 . . . . . . . . . . . . . . . .9.00
Jeff Gordon, 1997 Champion, orange, Frosted
   Mini Wheats, 1998 . . . . . . . . . . . . .9.00
Jeff Gordon, Fuel Up, Frosted Mini Wheats,
   1998 . . . . . . . . . . . . . . . . . . . . .7.00
Jeff Gordon, Ride with Gordon offer, Corn Pops,
   1999 . . . . . . . . . . . . . . . . . . . . .4.00
Jeff Gordon, 2 boxes with Pepsi card set, Frosted
   Mini Wheats, 1999 . . . . . . . . . . . .10.00
Jeff Gordon, 1998 Champion, Frosted Mini
   Wheats, 1999 . . . . . . . . . . . . . . . .5.00
Dale Jarrett, Fuel Up, Raisin Bran, 1998 . . .5.00
Dale Jarrett, 1999 Winston Cup Champion,
   1999 . . . . . . . . . . . . . . . . . . . . .4.00
Ned Jarrett & Dale Jarrett, Raisin Bran,
   1997 . . . . . . . . . . . . . . . . . . . . .5.00
Terry Labonte, #14 Kellogg's car, Corn Flakes,
   1993 . . . . . . . . . . . . . . . . . . . .30.00
Terry Labonte, Terry on back, Raisin Bran,
   1993 . . . . . . . . . . . . . . . . . . . .30.00
Terry Labonte, with #14 car, Corn Flakes,
   1993 . . . . . . . . . . . . . . . . . . . .30.00

Terry Labonte, #5 Kellogg's car bursting through box, Corn Flakes, 1994 . . . . . . . . . . .20.00

Terry Labonte, #5 Kellogg's car with pit crew, Corn Flakes, 1994 . . . . . . . . . . . . . . . .20.00

Terry Labonte, with cereal bowl, Corn Flakes, 1994 . . . . . . . . . . . . . . . . . . . .20.00

Terry Labonte, Kellogg's car crossing finish line, Corn Flakes, 1995 . . . . . . . . . . . . .15.00

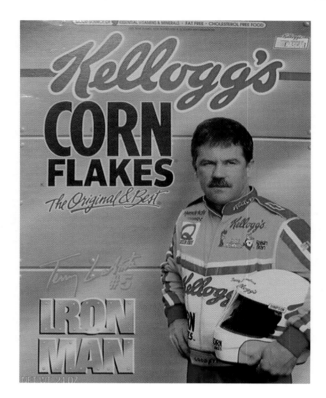

Terry Labonte, Iron Man, Corn Flakes, 1996 . . . . . . . . . . . . . . . . . . . . .15.00

Terry Labonte, Iron Man car, Corn Flakes, 1996 . . . . . . . . . . . . . . . . . . . . .15.00

Terry Labonte, Kellogg's car, Corn Flakes, 1997 . . . . . . . . . . . . . . . . . . . . .5.00

Terry Labonte, with North Wilkesboro trophy, Corn Flakes, 1995 . . . . . . . . . . . . . . . . .15.00

Terry Labonte, 2 pack die-cast cars, Honey Crunch, 1997 . . . . . . . . . . . . . . . .35.00

Terry Labonte, 1996 Champ, 3 die-cast cars, Corn Flakes, 1997 . . . . . . . . . . . . .30.00

Terry Labonte, #5 car, die-cast bank offer, Honey Crunch, 1998 . . . . . . . . . . . . . . . .5.00

Terry Labonte, with car & Corny rooster, Corn Flakes, 1997 . . . . . . . . . . . . . . . . .9.00

Terry Labonte, Fuel Up, Corn Flakes, 1998 .5.00

Terry Labonte, climbing in car, Corn Flakes, 1999 . . . . . . . . . . . . . . . . . . . . .4.00

Terry Labonte & Red Byron, Corn Flakes, 1998 . . . . . . . . . . . . . . . . . . . . .7.00

Terry Labonte & Gary Dehart, Raisin Bran, 1997 . . . . . . . . . . . . . . . . . . . . .7.00

Terry Labonte & Jeff Gordon, Team Monte Carlo, Corn Flakes, 1997 . . . . . . . . . . . . . . .7.00

Terry Labonte & Jeff Gordon, Team Monte Carlo, Frosted Mini Wheats, 1997 . . . . . . . . .7.00

Terry Labonte & Bobby Labonte, Corn Flakes, 1998 . . . . . . . . . . . . . . . . . . . . .5.00

Terry Labonte & Bobby Labonte, CD offer, Corn Flakes, 1999 . . . . . . . . . . . . . . . . .4.00

Terry Labonte & Richard Petty, Corn Flakes, 1996 . . . . . . . . . . . . . . . . . . . . .10.00

Terry Labonte, Terry & Tony Tiger, Frosted Flakes, 1997 . . . . . . . . . . . . . . . . . . . . .9.00

Terry Labonte, Terry & Tony Tiger, gold seal, Frosted Flakes, 1997 . . . . . . . . . . . . . . . . .25.00

Terry Labonte & Darrell Waltrip, Corn Flakes, 1995 . . . . . . . . . . . . . . . . . . . . .20.00

Kyle Petty, Fuel Up, Frosted Flakes, 1998 . .5.00

Kyle Petty, Corny skiing, Corn Flakes, 1998 .5.00

Kyle Petty, Corny surfing, Corn Flakes, 1998 . . . . . . . . . . . . . . . . . . . . . . . .5.00

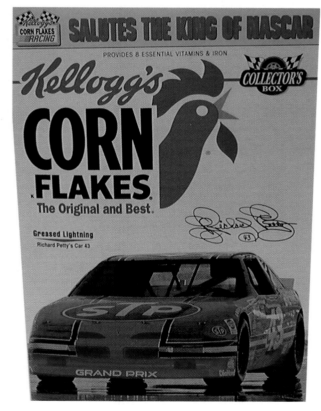

Richard Petty, jumbo box with 2 inner boxes/CF . . . . . . . . . . . . . . . . . . . . .50.00

Greg Sacks, #41 Kellogg's car, Corn Flakes, 1991 . . . . . . . . . . . . . . . . . . . . .55.00

Greg Sacks, #41 Kellogg's car, Greg Sacks & Harry Hyde, Corn Flakes, 1992 . . . . .45.00

Tony Tiger, in racing uniform, Frosted Flakes, 1995 . . . . . . . . . . . . . . . . . . . . .10.00

Tony Tiger, in car, 20 oz. Frosted Flakes, 1999 . . . . . . . . . . . . . . . . . . . . .4.00

Greg Sacks, #41 Kellogg's car, Greg Sacks, Dennis Connor & Harry Hyde, Corn Flakes, 1992 .45.00

Tony Tiger, In Car, 25 oz. Frosted Flakes, 1999 . . . . . . . . . . . . . . . . . . . . . . . . .4.00
Darrell Waltrip & Michael Waltrip, Raisin Bran, 1995 . . . . . . . . . . . . . . . . . . . . . .10.00

### WHEATIES

Dale Earnhardt, headshot, Wheaties, 1997 .50.00
Dale Earnhardt, Sam Bass art with car, Wheaties, 1997 . . . . . . . . . . . . . . . . . . . . .45.00
Dale Earnhardt, Honey Frosted Wheaties, 1997 . . . . . . . . . . . . . . . . . . . . . . . .40.00
Dale Earnhardt, Crispy Wheaties 'N' Raisins, 1997 . . . . . . . . . . . . . . . . . . . . . . .40.00
Ned Jarrett, "Legends of Racing," Wheaties, 2000 . . . . . . . . . . . . . . . . . . . . . . .10.00
Benny Parsons, "Legends of Racing," Wheaties, 2000 . . . . . . . . . . . . . . . . . . . . . .10.00
Richard Petty, Wheaties, 1998 . . . . . . . . .8.00
Richard Petty, Honey Frosted Wheaties, 1998 . . . . . . . . . . . . . . . . . . . . . . . .8.00
Richard Petty, Crispy Wheaties 'N' Raisins, 1998 . . . . . . . . . . . . . . . . . . . . . . . .8.00

Dale Earnhardt, Sam Bass art with car, Wheaties, 1997 . . . . . . . . . . . . . . . . . . . . . .45.00

Richard Petty, "Legends of Racing," Wheaties, 2000 . . . . . . . . . . . . . . . . . . . . . . .10.00
Cale Yarborough, "Legends of Racing," Wheaties, 2000 . . . . . . . . . . . . . . . . . . . . . . .10.00

### WINN DIXIE

Mark Martin, Corn Flakes . . . . . . . . . . . .5.00
Mark Martin, with #60 car, Crispy Rice . . . .5.00

## CLOCKS

### JEBCO CLOCKS

Racing-themed clocks of one type or another have been around for decades. However, these timely collectibles were released only sporadically until JEBCO introduced its ongoing series of

NASCAR clocks about 10 years ago. JEBCO has since produced over 100 driver-specific and commemorative timepieces. Production has grown from just a few releases per year to approximately two dozen issues in 2000. Production is limited and most clocks are sequentially numbered. In addition to annual issue clocks featuring standard race car graphics, other offerings commemorate special paint schemes and memorable moments.

Davey Allison, Mac Tools, 10,000 . . . . . .300.00
Todd Bodine, Tabasco, 5,000 . . . . . . . . . .75.00
Brickyard 400, Inaugural Race, 5,000 . . .95.00
Brickyard 400, 1995, 5,000 . . . . . . . . . .80.00
Brickyard 400, 1996, 5,000 . . . . . . . . . .80.00
Jeff Burton, Exide . . . . . . . . . . . . . . . . .75.00
Dale Earnhardt, 1991 Champion . . . . . .150.00
Dale Earnhardt, Magnificent 7, 10,000 . .120.00

Dale Earnhardt, 1994 Winston Cup Champion, 10,000 . . . . . . . . . . . . . . . . . . . . . . .125.00
Dale Earnhardt, 1995 Silver Winston Select Car, 5,000 . . . . . . . . . . . . . . . . . . . . . . .200.00
Dale Earnhardt – Richard Petty, 7 & 7, 10,000 . . . . . . . . . . . . . . . . . . . . . .110.00
Dale Earnhardt, Mom 'n' Pops, 2,500 . . .250.00
Dale Earnhardt, 1996, 5,000 . . . . . . . .100.00
Dale Earnhardt, Wheaties, 5,000 . . . . .245.00
Dale Earnhardt, 1997, 5,000 . . . . . . . .100.00
Dale Earnhardt, Sundrop, 5,000 . . . . . .130.00
Dale Earnhardt, Suzuka Japan, 5,000 . . .150.00
Dale Earnhardt, 1998 Daytona 500 Winner, 15,000 . . . . . . . . . . . . . . . . . . . . . .230.00
Dale Earnhardt, 1998 Goodwrench, 50th Anniversary . . . . . . . . . . . . . . . . . . . . . . .100.00
Dale Earnhardt, Bass Pro Shops, 10,000 .120.00
Dale Earnhardt, 25th Anniversary, 5,000 .130.00

Dale Earnhardt, Sundrop, 5,000 . . . . . . .130.00

Dale Earnhardt, Goodwrench – Wrangler, 2,500 . . . . . . . . . . . . . . . . . . . . . . .150.00
Dale Earnhardt, Coca-Cola Japan, 10,000 .150.00
Dale Earnhardt, The Intimidator, Snap-On .200.00
Dale Earnhardt, 1999 Last Lap of Millennium, 5,000 . . . . . . . . . . . . . . . . . . . . . . .125.00
Dale Earnhardt, Goodwrench – 2000, 5,000 . . . . . . . . . . . . . . . . . . . . . . .100.00
Dale Earnhardt, Taz, 7,500 . . . . . . . . . .130.00
Dale Earnhardt, Peter Max, 5,000 . . . . .160.00
Dale Earnhardt, Above the Rest, Sam Bass, 7,500 . . . . . . . . . . . . . . . . . . . . . . .175.00
Dale Earnhardt, Jr., AC Delco, 5,000 . . . .80.00
Dale Earnhardt, Jr., AC Delco, 1998 Busch Grand National Champion . . . . . . . . . . . . . .80.00
Dale Earnhardt, Jr., Budweiser #8 . . . . . .80.00
Bill Elliott, Budweiser, 10,000 . . . . . . . . . .85.00
Bill Elliott, McDonalds, 5,000 . . . . . . . . . .75.00
Harry Gant, Final Year, 10,000 . . . . . . . .80.00
Jeff Gordon, Sam Bass painting, 10,000 . .80.00
Jeff Gordon, Rookie of the Year, 5,000 . . .95.00
Jeff Gordon, 1995 Dupont, 5,000 . . . . . .85.00
Jeff Gordon, 1995 Winston Cup Champion, 2,400 . . . . . . . . . . . . . . . . . . . . . . .150.00
Jeff Gordon, 1997 Dupont, 5,000 . . . . . .75.00
Jeff Gordon, 1997 Daytona, 5,000 . . . . .75.00
Jeff Gordon, 1997 Jurassic Park, 5,000 . .80.00
Jeff Gordon, Winston Million, 5,000 . . . . .80.00
Jeff Gordon, 1997 Winston Cup Champion, 10,000 . . . . . . . . . . . . . . . . . . . . . . .75.00
Jeff Gordon, 1998 Dupont, 50th Anniversary . . . . . . . . . . . . . . . . . . . . .75.00
Jeff Gordon, 1998 Chromalusion . . . . . . .79.00
Jeff Gordon, Dupont, 1998 Winston Cup Champion . . . . . . . . . . . . . . . . . . . . .80.00

Jeff Gordon, Rookie of the Year, 5,000 . . .95.00

Jeff Gordon, Dupont, 1999 Daytona Winner .80.00
Jeff Gordon, Pepsi, Busch Grand National .75.00
Robby Gordon, 1997, 5,000 . . . . . . . . .75.00
Ernie Irvan, Mac Tools, 10,000 . . . . . .100.00
Ernie Irvan, 1996, #28 Car, 5,000 . . . . .85.00
Dale Jarrett, 1994 Mac Tools, 5,000 . . . .85.00
Dale Jarrett, 1995, #28 Car, 5,000 . . . . .75.00
Dale Jarrett, 1998 Ford Credit, 50th
    Anniversary . . . . . . . . . . . . . . . . . .75.00

Alan Kulwicki, 1992 Winston Cup Champion,
    10,000 . . . . . . . . . . . . . . . . . . . . .250.00

Bobby Labonte, 1998 Interstate, 50th
    Anniversary . . . . . . . . . . . . . . . .75.00
Terry Labonte, 1996 Winston Cup Champion,
    5,000 . . . . . . . . . . . . . . . . . . .75.00

Terry Labonte, Spooky Loops, 5,000 . . . . .80.00
Terry Labonte, Kellogg's, 5,000 . . . . . . .75.00
Chad Little, John Deere . . . . . . . . . . .75.00
Mark Martin, 10,000 . . . . . . . . . . . . .75.00
Mark Martin, Eagle One, 5,000 . . . . . . .75.00
Mark Martin, 1999 Valvoline . . . . . . . . .75.00
Jeremy Mayfield, Mobil 1 . . . . . . . . . .70.00
NASCAR 50th Anniversary, 10,000 . . . . .75.00
Steve Park, Burger King, 5,000 . . . . . . .85.00
Steve Park, AC Delco, 5,000 . . . . . . . .85.00
Steve Park, Pennzoil . . . . . . . . . . . . .70.00
Kyle Petty, 10,000 . . . . . . . . . . . . . .70.00
Kyle Petty, 1992 Mello Yello . . . . . . . . .70.00
Richard Petty, 1992 Fan Appreciation Tour,
    20,000 . . . . . . . . . . . . . . . . . .150.00
R.Petty – Hamilton, STP Silver Anniversary,
    5,000 . . . . . . . . . . . . . . . . . . .75.00
Morgan Shepherd, Mac Tools, 5,000 . . . .80.00
Jimmy Spencer, Smokin' Joes, 5,000 . . . .90.00
Jimmy Spencer, Winston . . . . . . . . . . .79.00
Tony Stewart, Home Depot, 2,500 . . . . . .85.00
Texas Motor Speedway, First Race, 5,000 .75.00
Rusty Wallace, Sam Bass painting, 10,000 .70.00
Rusty Wallace, 1994, 10,000 . . . . . . . .85.00
Rusty Wallace, 1996, 5,000 . . . . . . . . .80.00
Rusty Wallace, 1997, 5,000 . . . . . . . . .75.00
Rusty Wallace, 1998, 5,000 . . . . . . . . .75.00
Rusty Wallace, 1999 Miller Lite . . . . . . .75.00
Darrell Waltrip, Big K-Mart . . . . . . . . .70.00
Darrell Waltrip, Big K-Mart . . . . . . . . .75.00
Michael Waltrip, 1996, 5,000 . . . . . . . .75.00

Richard Petty, 1992 Fan Appreciation Tour,
20,000 . . . . . . . . . . . . . . . . . . . . . .150.00

## COMIC BOOKS

The vast majority of racing comic books were produced during the early years of the NASCAR collectibles craze, particularly 1991 – 92. Vortex was the primary publisher, offering comic books spotlighting such luminaries as Richard Petty, Junior Johnson, Davey Allison, Rusty Wallace, and Fred Lorenzen, to name a few. Racing comic books never quite caught on with NASCAR fans and, consequently, their value has not increased appreciably over the years. Comic books are best stored in clear plastic bags with a cardboard backing to maintain their original integrity.

### STP

Petty, 1980, art by Bob Kane (creator of
Batman) . . . . . . . . . . . . . . . . . . . . . .75.00

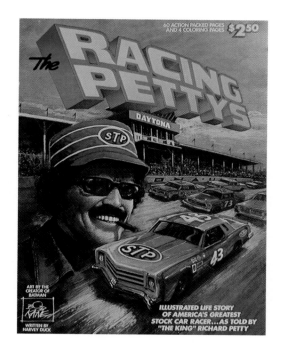

Richard Petty, 1980, art by Bob Kane (Creator of
Batman) . . . . . . . . . . . . . . . . . . . . .75.00

### VORTEX COMICS

Bobby Allison, Legends of NASCAR #4 . . . . .4.00
Bobby Allison, Legends of NASCAR #4 hologram
on cover, 10,000 . . . . . . . . . . . . . . .8.00
Davey Allison, NASCAR Adventures #4 . . . .6.00
Brett Bodine, NASCAR Adventures #8 . . . . .2.00
Darlington Speedway, NASCAR Adventures
#3 . . . . . . . . . . . . . . . . . . . . . . . . . . .2.00
Daytona Speedway, The Daytona 500 Story . .2.00
Bill Elliott, 1990 Legends of NASCAR #1, $1.50
cover price, 15,000 . . . . . . . . . . . . .25.00
Bill Elliott, 1990 Legends of NASCAR #1, $2.00
cover price, 45,000 . . . . . . . . . . . . .15.00
Bill Elliott, Legends of NASCAR #1, with four 1990
Maxx cards . . . . . . . . . . . . . . . . . . .15.00
Bill Elliott, Legends of NASCAR #6, Million
Dollar . . . . . . . . . . . . . . . . . . . . . . . .7.00
Bill Elliott, Legends of NASCAR #6, Million Dollar,
hologram on cover, 10,000 . . . . . . . .9.00
Harry Gant, Legends of NASCAR #13 . . . . .2.00
Harry Gant, Legends of NASCAR #13, hologram
on cover, 10,000 . . . . . . . . . . . . . . .5.00
Junior Johnson, Legends of NASCAR #7 . . .2.00
Junior Johnson, Legends of NASCAR #7, holo-
gram on cover, 10,000 . . . . . . . . . . .5.00
Ernie Irvan, NASCAR Adventures #5 . . . . . .2.00
Legends of NASCAR Christmas
Special . . . . . . . . . . . . . . . . . . . . . .9.00
Fred Lorenzen, NASCAR Adventures #1 . . .2.00
Sterling Marlin, Legends of NASCAR #5 . . . .2.00

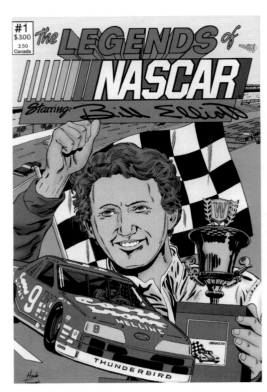

Bill Elliott, Legends of NASCAR #1, with four 1990 Maxx Cards . . . . . . . . . . . . . . . . . . .15.00

Sterling Marlin, Legends of NASCAR #5, hologram on cover, 10,000 . . . . . . . . . . . . . .5.00
Mark Martin, NASCAR Adventures #7 . . . . .4.00
Benny Parsons, Legends of NASCAR #8 . . .2.00
Benny Parsons, Legends of NASCAR #8, hologram on cover, 10,000 . . . . . . . . . . .3.00
David Pearson, NASCAR Adventures #6 . . .2.00
Richard Petty, Legends of NASCAR #2 . . . .3.00
Richard Petty, Legends of NASCAR #2, hologram on cover, 10,000 . . . . . . . . . . . . . . .8.00
Richard Petty, Legends of NASCAR #2, error hologram with #9 car . . . . . . . . . . .10.00
Richard Petty, Legends of NASCAR #12 . . .2.00
Richard Petty, Legends of NASCAR #12, hologram on cover, 10,000 . . . . . . . . . . . . . . .5.00
Richard Petty, NASCAR Adventures #2 . . . .2.00
Ken Schrader, Legends of NASCAR #3 . . . .2.00
Ken Schrader, Legends of NASCAR #3, hologram on cover, 10,000 . . . . . . . . . . . . . . .4.00
Morgan Shepherd, Legends of NASCAR #11 .3.00
Morgan Shepherd, Legends of NASCAR #11, hologram on cover, 10,000 . . . . . . . . .5.00
Talladega Speedway, Legends of NASCAR #10 . . . . . . . . . . . . . . . . . . . . . . . . . .2.00
Talladega Speedway, Legends of NASCAR #10, hologram on cover, 10,000 . . . . . . . . .4.00
Rusty Wallace, Legends of NASCAR #9 . . . .3.00
Rusty Wallace, Legends of NASCAR #9, hologram on cover, 10,000 . . . . . . . . . . . . . . .6.00

## DECANTERS

While whiskey decanters are time-honored mainstream collectibles, the pickings are relatively slim in the NASCAR category. In fact, only three pieces are widely regarded as collectibles — all of them released more than 20 years ago. The most important thing to remember about these whiskey decanters is that removing the contents decreases the value by 40 – 60 percent.

B. Allison, #15 Norris T-Bird, full . . . . . . .160.00
B. Allison, #15 Norris T-Bird, empty . . . . .60.00
Daytona 500 Pace Car, Pontiac Trans Am, full . . . . . . . . . . . . . . . . . . . .170.00
Daytona 500 Pace Car, Pontiac Trans Am, empty . . . . . . . . . . . . . . . . . . .100.00
Cale Yarborough, #11 Kar-Kare Chevrolet, full . . . . . . . . . . . . . . . . . . . . . . .160.00
Cale Yarborough, #11 Kar-Kare Chevrolet, empty . . . . . . . . . . . . . . . . . . . . . .60.00

## FIGURES

Driver figurines have been part of the NASCAR collectibles scene since Racing Champions released its Racing Superstars Series in 1991. The category didn't see much activity until 1997, when Hasbro offered 12 different driver figurines as part of it Kenner Starting Line-up collection. The series was eventually integrated into Hasbro's Winner's Circle product line. Winner's Circle continues to produce the lion's share of NASCAR figures. Other companies producing driver figures include Toy Biz and Playing Mantis/Johnny Lightning.

Sam Bobbing Head and the Coca-Cola Bobbing Head series provide a novel twist to the figurine concept.

Meanwhile, in 1998, Mattel drew worldwide attention to racing collectibles with the debut of the NASCAR 50th Anniversary Barbie.

### COCA-COLA RACING FAMILY BOBBING HEAD

Dale Jarrett, Quality Care, 5,000 . . . . . . .50.00
Bobby Labonte, Interstate, 5,000 . . . . . . .50.00
Tony Stewart, Home Depot, 5,000 . . . . . .50.00

Cola-Cola Racing Family Bobbing Heads, ea. . . . . . . 50.00

### RACING CHAMPIONS

Derrike Cope, Racing Superstars, 1991 . . .5.00
Bill Elliott, Racing Superstars, 1991 . . . . .10.00
Bobby Hamilton, Racing Superstars, 1991 . .5.00
Ernie Irvan, Racing Superstars, 1991 . . . . .9.00
Sterling Marlin, Racing Superstars, 1991 . .8.00
Richard Petty, Racing Superstars, 1991 . .12.00
Ken Schrader, Racing Superstars, 1991 . . .7.00

### SAM BOBBING HEAD

Bill Elliott, 8 doll, 5,000 . . . . . . . . . . . . .47.00
Bill Elliott, McDonald's, 1996 . . . . . . . . .35.00

### JOHNNY LIGHTNING FRONT ROW

Johnny Benson, Pennzoil . . . . . . . . . . . . .9.00
Cory McClenathan, McDonald's, NHRA Top
    Fuel . . . . . . . . . . . . . . . . . . . . . .9.00
Ernie Irvan, Texaco . . . . . . . . . . . . . . . .9.00
Sterling Marlin, Kodak . . . . . . . . . . . . . .9.00
Mark Martin, Valvoline . . . . . . . . . . . . . .9.00
Ted Musgrave, Primestar . . . . . . . . . . . . .9.00
Cruz Pedregon, McDonald's, NHRA Funny
    Car . . . . . . . . . . . . . . . . . . . . . . .9.00
Darrell Waltrip, Parts America . . . . . . . . . .9.00
Jim Yates, McDonald's, NHRA Pro Stock . . .9.00

Bill Elliott, McDonald's, 1996 . . . . . . . . .35.00

## KENNER STARTING LINEUP

Ward Burton, MBNA-1997 . . . . . . . . . . . .8.00
Ward Burton, MBNA-Series 2-1998 . . . . .8.00
Dale Earnhardt, Goodwrench, 1997 . . . . .30.00
Dale Earnhardt, Goodwrench, with Burger King, 1997 . . . . . . . . . . . . . . . . . . . . . . .25.00

Dale Earnhardt, Goodwrench, 12 Walmart Figure, 1997 . . . . . . . . . . . . . . . . . . . . . . .100.00
Earnhardt's, Dale Earnhardt Sr. & Jr. Set, 12 Sams Figures, 1998 . . . . . . . . . . . . .75.00
Dale Earnhardt, Goodwrench Plus, 1998 . .20.00
Dale Earnhardt, Goodwrench Plus, Series 2, 1998 . . . . . . . . . . . . . . . . . . . . . . . .20.00
Dale Earnhardt, Goodwrench Plus, 1999 . .20.00
Dale Earnhardt, Coca-Cola, 1999 . . . . . .20.00
Dale Earnhardt, Jr., Coca-Cola, 1999 . . . . .9.00
Dale Earnhardt, Jr., AC Delco, 1999 . . . . .10.00
Dale Earnhardt, GM Goodwrench, 2000 . .20.00
Dale Earnhardt, Goodwrench, Rooftop Celebration, 2000 . . . . . . . . . . . . . . . . . . . . . . .20.00
John Force, Castrol, 1997 . . . . . . . . . . . .10.00
John Force, Castrol, Series 2, 1998 . . . . . .9.00
John Force, Castrol Elvis, Series 2, 1998 . .9.00
Jeff Gordon, Dupont, 12 Hills Figure, 1997 .90.00
Jeff Gordon, Dupont, without Pepsi, 1997 .18.00
Jeff Gordon, Dupont, with Pepsi, 1997 . . .15.00
Jeff Gordon, Dupont, Series 2, 1998 . . . .12.00
Jeff Gordon, Jurassic Park, 1998 . . . . . . .12.00
Jeff Gordon, Dupont, 1998 Winston Cup Champion, 1999 . . . . . . . . . . . . . . . . . . . . .10.00
Jeff Gordon, Dupont, Walmart version, 1999 .12.00
Jeff Gordon, Dupont, Bascovs version, 1999 . . .12.00
Jeff Gordon, Pepsi, 1999 . . . . . . . . . . .10.00
Jeff Gordon, Dupont, 2000 . . . . . . . . . . .7.00
Jeff Gordon, Dupont, Rooftop Celebration 2000 . . . . . . . . . . . . . . . . . . . . . . . .12.00

Kenny Irwin, Texaco, Series 2, 1998 . . . . . .8.00
Dale Jarrett, Quality Care, 1997 . . . . . . .9.00
Dale Jarrett, Quality Care, 1998 . . . . . . .9.00
Dale Jarrett, Quality Care, 1999 . . . . . . .8.00
Dale Jarrett, Quality Care, 2000 . . . . . . .6.00
Dale Jarrett, Quality Care, Rooftop Celebration, 2000 . . . . . . . . . . . . . . . . . . . . . . .8.00

Bobby Labonte, Interstate, 1997 . . . . . . .8.00
Bobby Labonte, Interstate, 1998 . . . . . . .8.00
Bobby Labonte, Interstate, 1999 . . . . . . .8.00
Mike Skinner, Lowe's, 1997 . . . . . . . . . . .9.00
Darrell Waltrip, Parts America, 1997 . . . .9.00
Mike Skinner, Lowe's, 1998 . . . . . . . . . . .8.00
Tony Stewart, Home Depot, 2000 . . . . . . .7.00
Tony Stewart, Home Depot, Rooftop Celebration, 2000 . . . . . . . . . . . . . . . . . . . . . . .10.00
Kenny Wallace, Square D, Series 2, 1998 . .8.00
Rusty Wallace, Series 2, 1998 . . . . . . . . .8.00
Rusty Wallace, Elvis, Series 2, 1998 . . . . .9.00

### MATTEL BARBIE DOLL

Bill Elliott, McDonald's Uniform, 1999 . . . .35.00
50th Anniversary of NASCAR, 1998 . . . . .30.00

### TOY BIZ

Bill Elliott, McDonald's, 12" doll . . . . . . . .15.00
Bill Elliott, McDonald's, with car front . . . . .9.00
Dale Jarrett, Quality Care, 12" doll . . . . .10.00
Dale Jarrett, Quality Care, with car front . . .9.00
Mark Martin, Valvoline, 12" doll . . . . . . . .15.00
Mark Martin, Valvoline, with car front . . . . .9.00

# HELMETS

More than 100 replica helmets featuring drivers from both NASCAR and NHRA have been produced in a variety of scales. While both Ridell and Racing Champions have offered a handful of helmets between them, it was Simpson Race Products — the world's leading producer of motorsports safety equipment — that brought the concept up to full song. Simpson manufactured and sold the miniature headgear for several years before selling that segment of its operation to die-cast giant Action Performance Companies in the late 1990s. The 1:4 scale pieces represent the more affordable end of the Action/Simpson line-up, while the 1:3 and 1:2 scale reproductions have shown the most consistent appreciation in value.

Davey Allison, Texaco . . . . . . . . . . . . . . .30.00

### RACING CHAMPIONS

Davey Allison, Texaco bank . . . . . . . . . . .50.00
Brickyard 400 bank . . . . . . . . . . . .25.00
Steve Kinser, Sprint car bank . . . . . . . . .50.00

### RIDDELL

Sterling Marlin, Kodak . . . . . . . . . . . . .14.00
Brickyard 400 . . . . . . . . . . . . . . . . . .14.00

### SIMPSON 1:4 SCALE BY ACTION/RCCA

Todd Bodine, Tabasco Promo Set, red & green . . . . . . . . . . . . . . . . . . . .35.00
Dale Earnhardt, Bass Pro Shops . . . . . . .50.00
Dale Earnhardt, Coca-Cola, red . . . . . . . .50.00
Dale Earnhardt, Jr., Coca-Cola, polar bear .50.00
John Force, Castrol, Elvis . . . . . . . . . . . .35.00
Jeff Gordon, Dupont Chromalusion . . . . . .55.00
Jeff Gordon, Pepsi . . . . . . . . . . . . . . . . .40.00
Ernie Irvan, Skittles, promo . . . . . . . . . .25.00
Kenny Irwin, Texaco, Joker . . . . . . . . . . .35.00
Dale Jarrett, Ford Credit, Batman . . . . . .35.00
Bobby Labonte, Interstate, Small Soldiers . .35.00
Cruz Pedregon, Interstate, Small Soldiers . .35.00
Tony Stewart, Shell, Small Soldies . . . . . .35.00
Rusty Wallace, Miller Lite, Elvis, 10,000 . .35.00

### SIMPSON 1:4 SCALE

Davey Allison, Texaco . . . . . . . . . . . . . . .30.00
Joe Amato, Keystone . . . . . . . . . . . . . . .16.00
Shelly Anderson, Western Auto . . . . . . . .16.00
Johnny Benson, Pennzoil . . . . . . . . . . . .16.00
Kenny Berstein, Budweiser . . . . . . . . . . .16.00
Mike Bliss, Team ASE . . . . . . . . . . . . . .16.00

Brett Bodine, Lowe's . . . . . . . . . . . . . . .16.00
Jeff Burton, Exide . . . . . . . . . . . . . . . . .16.00
Ward Burton, MBNA . . . . . . . . . . . . . . .16.00
Ricky Craven, Kodiak . . . . . . . . . . . . . . .16.00
Larry Dixon, Miller . . . . . . . . . . . . . . . . .16.00
Jim Dunn, Mooneyes . . . . . . . . . . . . . . .16.00
Dale Earnhardt, Goodwrench, Black . . . . . .30.00
Dale Earnhardt, Goodwrench, Silver . . . . . .35.00
Dale Earnhardt, Goodwrench, "Olympic" . . .30.00
Bill Elliott, McDonald's . . . . . . . . . . . . . .16.00
John Force, Castrol GTX . . . . . . . . . . . . .22.00
John Force, Castrol, "Signature Edition" . . .20.00
"Big Daddy" Don Garlits . . . . . . . . . . . . .16.00
Jeff Gordon, Dupont . . . . . . . . . . . . . . .20.00
Darrell Gwynn, Coors Extra Gold . . . . . . . .16.00
Ernie Irvan, Texaco . . . . . . . . . . . . . . . .16.00
Dale Jarrett, Quality Care . . . . . . . . . . . .16.00
Blaine Johnson . . . . . . . . . . . . . . . . . . .20.00
Scott Kalitta . . . . . . . . . . . . . . . . . . . . .16.00
Chris "The Greek" Karamesines . . . . . . . .16.00
Bobby Labonte, Interstate, NFL Series . . . .20.00
Terry Labonte, Kelloggs, "Recordbreaker" . .16.00
Sterling Marlin, Kodak . . . . . . . . . . . . . .16.00
Mark Martin, Valvoline . . . . . . . . . . . . . .16.00
Jeremy Mayfield, RCA . . . . . . . . . . . . . .16.00
Cory McClenathan, McDonald's . . . . . . . . .18.00
Tom "Mongoose" McEwen . . . . . . . . . . . .16.00
Ted Musgrave, Family Channel . . . . . . . . .16.00
John Myers . . . . . . . . . . . . . . . . . . . . .16.00
Joe Nemechek, Burger King . . . . . . . . . . .16.00
Cruz Pedregon, McDonald's . . . . . . . . . . .16.00
Kyle Petty, Coors Light . . . . . . . . . . . . . .16.00
Richard Petty, STP . . . . . . . . . . . . . . . .16.00
Robert Pressley, Skoal . . . . . . . . . . . . . .16.00
Don "Snake" Prudhomme, Skoal . . . . . . . .20.00
Red Dog . . . . . . . . . . . . . . . . . . . . . . .16.00

Ricky Rudd, Tide . . . . . . . . . . . . . . . . . .16.00
Kenny Schrader, Budweiser . . . . . . . . . .16.00
Dave Schultz, Sunoco . . . . . . . . . . . . . .16.00
TNN Motorsports . . . . . . . . . . . . . . . . .16.00
Rusty Wallace, Miller . . . . . . . . . . . . . . .16.00
Darrell Waltrip, Western Auto, "Signature
    Edition" . . . . . . . . . . . . . . . . . . . . .16.00
Michael Waltrip, Citgo . . . . . . . . . . . . . .16.00
Jim Yates, McDonald's . . . . . . . . . . . . . .18.00

### SIMPSON 1:3 SCALE BY ACTION/RCCA

Dale Earnhardt, Bass Pro, 3,500 . . . . . . .80.00
Dale Earnhardt, Coca-Cola, red, 3,500 . . .70.00
Dale Earnhardt, Jr., Coca-Cola, polar bear,
    3,500 . . . . . . . . . . . . . . . . . . . . . .60.00
John Force, Castrol, Elvis, 5,000 . . . . . . .45.00
Jeff Gordon, Pepsi, 3,500 . . . . . . . . . . .45.00
Kenny Irwin, Texaco, Joker . . . . . . . . . . .45.00
Dale Jarrett, Ford Credit, Batman . . . . . . .45.00
Bobby Labonte, Interstate, Small Soldiers,
    3,500 . . . . . . . . . . . . . . . . . . . . . .45.00
Cruz Pedregon, Interstate, Small Soldiers,
    3,500 . . . . . . . . . . . . . . . . . . . . . .45.00
Tony Stewart, Shell, Small Soldies, 3,500 . .45.00
Rusty Wallace, Miller Lite, Elvis, 5,000 . . .45.00

### SIMPSON 1:3 SCALE

Dale Earnhardt, Goodwrench . . . . . . . . . .50.00
Jeff Gordon, Dupont . . . . . . . . . . . . . . .28.00
Terry Labonte, Kellogg's . . . . . . . . . . . . .26.00
Dale Jarrett, Quality Care . . . . . . . . . . . .26.00
Rusty Wallace, Miller . . . . . . . . . . . . . . .26.00

### SIMPSON 1:2 SCALE NASCAR

Davey Allison, Texaco . . . . . . . . . . . . . . .55.00

Dale Earnhardt, Goodwrench . . . . . . . . .125.00

Dale    Earnhardt,    Goodwrench,    QVC
    Autographed . . . . . . . . . . . . . . . .200.00
Bill Elliott, Budweiser . . . . . . . . . . . . . .49.00
A.J. Foyt, Copenhagen . . . . . . . . . . . . .49.00
Harry Gant, Skoal . . . . . . . . . . . . . . . .40.00
Jeff Gordon, Dupont . . . . . . . . . . . . . . .75.00
Ernie Irvan, Texaco . . . . . . . . . . . . . . .49.00
Steve Kinser, Quaker State . . . . . . . . . .49.00
Alan Kulwicki, Hooters . . . . . . . . . . . . .75.00
Alan    Kulwicki,    AK    Racing    Memorial
    1954 – 1993 . . . . . . . . . . . . . . . .75.00
Mark Martin, Valvoline . . . . . . . . . . . . .40.00
Kyle Petty, Mello Yello . . . . . . . . . . . . .40.00
Richard Petty, STP . . . . . . . . . . . . . . .49.00
Rusty Wallace, Miller . . . . . . . . . . . . . .55.00
Darrell Waltrip, Western Auto . . . . . . . .40.00

## HOODS

Plastic replica hoods are relatively new in the racing collectibles arena, just finding their way into the market in the past five years. While smaller 1:4 scale hoods are available, 1:2 scale issues have proven to be the collectors' choice. The vast majority of replica hoods have been released in extremely limited quantities. In fact, most are offered in numbers of 600 or less, with some series being individually numbered.

Replica hoods are available in both unsigned and autographed versions, with the signature series issues being worth substantially more than their bare counterparts.

### RACING DECOR 1:2 SCALE

5 Terry Labonte, Kellogg's, autographed edition,
    381 . . . . . . . . . . . . . . . . . . . . . .120.00
6 Mark Martin, Valvoline, autographed edition,
    500 . . . . . . . . . . . . . . . . . . . . . .135.00
8 Dale Earnhardt, Jr., Budweiser, autographed edi-
    tion, 579 . . . . . . . . . . . . . . . . . . .175.00
10 Ricky Rudd, Tide, autographed edition,
    300 . . . . . . . . . . . . . . . . . . . . . .120.00
20 Tony Stewart, Home Depot, autographed edi-
    tion, 1,000 . . . . . . . . . . . . . . . . . .160.00
21 Michael Waltrip, Citgo, autographed edition,
    103 . . . . . . . . . . . . . . . . . . . . . .125.00
24 Jeff Gordon, Dupont, autographed edition,
    288 . . . . . . . . . . . . . . . . . . . . . .225.00

8 Dale Earnhardt, Jr., Budweiser, autographed edition, 579 .............................175.00

20 Tony Stewart, Home Depot, autographed edition, 1,000 . . . . . . . .160.00

24 Jeff Gordon, Dupont, autographed edition, 288 ......................... 225.00

## KNIVES

Commemorative knives have enjoyed a presence on the NASCAR memorabilia scene for more than 25 years — long before the beginning of the era of collectibility we know today. The knives and knife sets that have been offered over the years run the gamut. Virtually every top driver is featured, and every manufacturer is represented in just about every style.

Production numbers start at 59 and run to over 15,000. As you might expect, the variables that dictate the value of a racing-themed knife include the subject, the brand and style of the knife, and the number of pieces produced.

Collectors should be aware that there have been a few isolated cases of unauthorized knives being produced. In those instances, knock off artists obtained blank knives from the manufacturer, then used an engraver to create an unlicensed collectible.

### ACTION

Dale Earnhardt, car, #3 Goodwrench Car, silver, 11,000 . . . . . . . . . . . . . . . . . . . . . . . .45.00
Jeff Gordon, car, #24 Dupont 1997, silver, 9,000 . . . . . . . . . . . . . . . . . . . . . . .30.00

Jeff Gordon, car, 1997 Winston Cup Champion, silver, 10,000 . . . . . . . . . . . . . . . . .30.00
Dale Jarrett, car, #88 Quality Care, silver, 5,500 . . . . . . . . . . . . . . . . . . . . . . .30.00
Rusty Wallace, car, #2 Miller, silver, 5,500 . . . . . . . . . . . . . . . . . . . . . . .30.00
Rusty Wallace, car, #2 Miller, Elvis, silver, 10,000 . . . . . . . . . . . . . . . . .30.00

### BEAR

Bristol Raceway, Trapper style, Bristol Raceway, 1,000 . . . . . . . . . . . . . . . . . . . . . . .79.00
Harry Gant, Lockback style, Farewell Tour 1994, 5,033 . . . . . . . . . . . . . . . . . . . . . . .40.00
Talladega Superspeedway, World's Fastest Speedway . . . . . . . . . . . . . . . . . . . . . . .110.00

### CASE

Bobby Allison, Trapper style, 1988 Daytona Winner, 1,000 . . . . . . . . . . . . . .200.00
Bobby Allison, Coke style, The Legend, 1,200 .215.00
Bobby Allison, Coke style, The Legend, 600 . . . . . . . . . . . . . . . . . . . . . .220.00
Bobby, Davey & Clifford Allison, Coke style, 3 knives, 100 . . . . . . . . . . . . . . . . .975.00
Davey Allison, Trapper style, Rookie of the Year, 2,000 . . . . . . . . . . . . . . . . . . . . . . .375.00
Davey Allison, Coke style, 1992 Hardcharger, 1,000 . . . . . . . . . . . . . . . . . . . . . . .650.00

Davey Allison, Trapper style, Hardcharger, 2,000 . . . . . . . . . . . . . . . . . . .175.00

Davey Allison, Trapper style, tribute to Davey, 2,000 . . . . . . . . . . . . . . . . . . . .175.00

Davey Allison, Trapper & Bowie style, mint, set 3 knives, 500 . . . . . . . . . . . . . . . . .700.00

Buddy Baker, Trapper style, 1st to Break 200 MPH, 1,200 . . . . . . . . . . . . . . . . . .100.00

Geoff Bodine, Canoe Trapper style, 1986 Daytona Winner, 1,000 . . . . . . . . . . . . . . . . .200.00

Neil Bonnett, Trapper style, Alabama Gang, 1,000 . . . . . . . . . . . . . . . . . . . .325.00

Chuck Bown, Trapper style, 1990 BGN Champion, 100 . . . . . . . . . . . . . . . . . . . . .150.00

Chevolet Racing, Lockback style . . . . . . .50.00

Dale Earnhardt, Trapper style, Winston Champ, 1980, 1986, 1987, 2,000 . . . . . . .300.00

Dale Earnhardt, Trapper style, Winston Cup Champ, 1986, 1987, 2,000 . . . . . .250.00

Dale Earnhardt, Trapper style, Winston Cup Champ, 1990, 1,500 . . . . . . . . . .250.00

Dale Earnhardt, Trapper style, Top Gun, 1,000 . . . . . . . . . . . . . . . . . . . .600.00

Dale Earnhardt, Trapper style, RCR Enterprises, 1,500 . . . . . . . . . . . . . . . . . . . .250.00

Dale Earnhardt, Trapper style, 1991 Winston Cup Champion, 2,000 . . . . . . . . . . . . . .300.00

Dale Earnhardt, Hunter style, 5-Time Champion-Marble Top, 1,500 . . . . . . . . . . .350.00

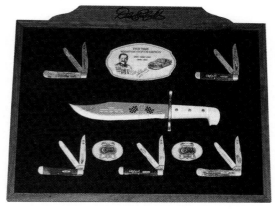

Dale Earnhardt, Trapper & Bowie style, 5 knives with Bowie, 1,000 . . . . . . . . . .1150.00

Dale Earnhardt, Trapper style, 3-Time Winston Winner, 1,000 . . . . . . . . . . . . . . . .300.00

Dale Earnhardt, Trapper Kodiak style, 7-knife wall set, 750 . . . . . . . . . . . . . . . . . .1200.00

Dale Earnhardt, Coke style, 6-Time Champion, 1,500 . . . . . . . . . . . . . . . . . . . .400.00

Dale Earnhardt, Trapper style, Top Gun #2, 1,500 . . . . . . . . . . . . . . . . . . . .340.00

Dale Earnhardt, Stag Bowie style, "Intimidator Rolls a 7," 1,000 . . . . . . . . . . . . .900.00

Dale Earnhardt, Bowie style, 7-Time Champion, 4-knife wall set, 1,000 . . . . . . . . . .1200.00

Dale Earnhardt, Trapper style, 7-Time Champ, 1,500 . . . . . . . . . . . . . . . . . . . .300.00

Dale Earnhardt – Richard Petty, Bowie style, 7-Time Champions, 1,000 . . . . . . . . . . . . .900.00

Dale Earnhardt – Richard Petty, Bowie style, 7-Time Champions, 143 . . . . . . . .1100.00

Dale Earnhardt – Richard Petty, Trapper style, 7-Time Champion, 2 knives, 1,000 . . .990.00

Dale Earnhardt, Coke style, Silver Streak, 333 . . . . . . . . . . . . . . . . . . . . .800.00

Dale Earnhardt – Richard Petty, Bowie Trapper style, 7-Time, 3 knives, 343 . . . . . . .975.00

Dale Earnhardt, Trapper style, 1995 Brickyard 400, 500 . . . . . . . . . . . . . . . . .425.00

Dale Earnhardt, Trapper style, Earnhardt Family Tree, 500 . . . . . . . . . . . . . . . . .530.00

Dale Earnhardt, Bowie style, Goodwrench, 100 . . . . . . . . . . . . . . . . . . . .1600.00

Dale Earnhardt, Trapper style, 1998 Daytona 500, 1,000 . . . . . . . . . . . . . . . . .650.00

Dale Earnhardt, Trapper style, Blast from the Past, 2,000 . . . . . . . . . . . . . . . . .225.00

Dale Earnhardt, Trapper style, IROC Champion 1999, 2,000 . . . . . . . . . . . . . . . .250.00

Dale Earnhardt, Trapper style, Earnhardt 2000, 2,000 . . . . . . . . . . . . . . . . . . . .225.00

Dale Earnhardt, Trapper style, Talladega Intimidator, 2,000 . . . . . . . . . . . . . . . . . .225.00

Dale Earnhardt – Dale Earnhardt, Jr., Trapper style, Racing into Millennium, 2,000 . . . . . . . . . . . . . . . . . . . .300.00

Dale Earnhardt, Jr., Trapper style, 1998 Busch GN Champion, 1,000 . . . . . . . . . .350.00

Dale Earnhardt, Jr., Trapper style, Rising Son, 1,000 . . . . . . . . . . . . . . . . . . . .225.00

Bill Elliott, Coke style, 2 knives, Bill & Junior Johnson, 1,500. . . . . . . . . . . . . . . . .390.00

Bill Elliott, Trapper style, Awesome Bill, 600 . . . . . . . . . . . . . . . . . . . .1000.00

Bill Elliott, Trapper style, Winston Million, 1,200 . . . . . . . . . . . . . . . . . . . .475.00

Bill Elliott, Trapper Dog Leg style, 1988, "Friends of Bill," 100 . . . . . . . . . . . . .1600.00

Bill Elliott, Trapper style, 1988 Winston Cup Champion, 3,500 . . . . . . . . . . . . . .195.00

Bill Elliott, Coke style, Driver of the Year, 1,000 . . . . . . . . . . . . . . . . . . . .365.00

Bill Elliott, Coke style, 10 Million Dollar Bill, 1,500 . . . . . . . . . . . . . . . . . . . .300.00

Bill Elliott, Coke style, 10 Million Dollar Bill, mint, 300 . . . . . . . . . . . . . . . . . . . .410.00

Harry Gant, Trapper style, Handsome Harry, 801 . . . . . . . . . . . . . . . . . . . .180.00

Harry Gant, Trapper style, Handsome Harry, 199 . . . . . . . . . . . . . . . . . . . .190.00

Harry Gant, Trapper style, Harry #33, Mr. September, 250 . . . . . . . . . . . . . . . . .200.00

Harry Gant, Trapper style, Handsome Harry, 801   . . .180.00

Harry Gant, Trapper style, Harry #7, Busch GN,
250 . . . . . . . . . . . . . . . . . . . . .200.00
Harry Gant, Trapper style, 1994 Farewell Tour,
333 . . . . . . . . . . . . . . . . . . . . .210.00
Joe Gibbs, Trapper style, Interstate – NFL,
2,500 . . . . . . . . . . . . . . . . . . . .200.00
Jeff Gordon, Trapper style, 1992 BGN Rookie of
Year, 100 . . . . . . . . . . . . . . . . .620.00
Jeff Gordon, Trapper style, 1993 Rookie of the
Year, 1,000 . . . . . . . . . . . . . . . .175.00
Jeff Gordon, Buffalo style, 1993, imitation pearl,
100 . . . . . . . . . . . . . . . . . . . . .550.00
Jeff Gordon, Trapper style, 1994 Brickyard 400
Winner, 1,500 . . . . . . . . . . . . . . .310.00
Jeff Gordon, Lightweight style, 1994 Brick-
yard 400 Winner, 15,000 . . . . . .24.00
Jeff Gordon, 1995 Winston Cup Champion, with
lighter, 1,000 . . . . . . . . . . . . . . .250.00
Jeff Gordon, Trapper style, 1995 Winston Cup
Champion, 1,000 . . . . . . . . . . . .250.00
Jeff Gordon, Trapper style, 1995 Champion, wood
box, 1,000 . . . . . . . . . . . . . . . . .275.00
Bobby Hamilton, Trapper style, Rookie of the Year,
168 . . . . . . . . . . . . . . . . . . . . .200.00
Harry Hyde, Trapper style, Days of Thunder,
1,000 . . . . . . . . . . . . . . . . . . . .180.00
Ernie Irvan, Trapper style, Natural Born, #4, Serial
#1,500 . . . . . . . . . . . . . . . . . . .210.00

Jeff Gordon, Lightweight style, 1994 Brickyard
400 Winner, 15,000 . . . . . . . . . . .24.00

Ernie Irvan, Trapper style, Natural Born, Serial
#500, 1000 . . . . . . . . . . . . . . . .170.00

Ernie Irvan, Trapper style, "We Miss You"...Ernie, with gold card, 1,000 . . .225.00

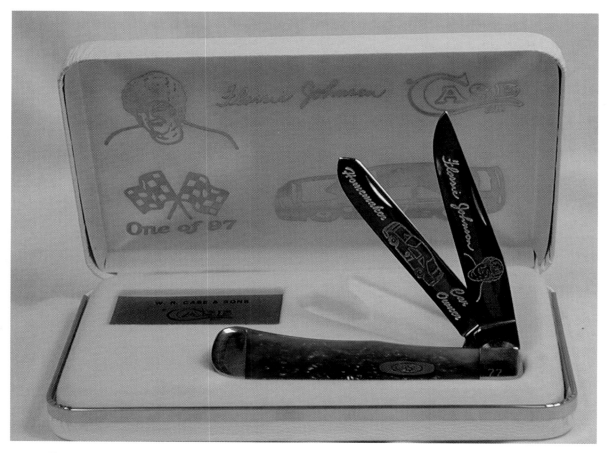

Flossie Johnson, Trapper style, Home Maker #2, 97 . . . . . . . . . . . . . . .130.00

Ernie Irvan, Trapper style, "We Miss You"...Ernie, with gold card, 1,000 . . . . . . . . . . .225.00

Ernie Irvan, Lockback style, "We Miss You...Ernie," 20,000 . . . . . . . . . . . . . . . . . .18.00

Ernie Irvan, Lockback style, "We Miss You...Ernie," 2,500 . . . . . . . . . . . . . . . . . .40.00

Dale Jarrett, Coke Stag style, Crunch car, 1,000 . . . . . . . . . . . . . . . . . . . . .220.00

Ned Jarrett, Trapper style, NASCAR Champion, 500 . . . . . . . . . . . . . . . . . . . . .200.00

Flossie Johnson, Trapper style, car owner, 97 . . . . . . . . . . . . . . . . . . . . . .200.00

Flossie Johnson, Canoe style, car owner, 97 .200.00

Flossie Johnson, Trapper style, Home Maker, 100 . . . . . . . . . . . . . . . . . . . .130.00

Flossie Johnson, Trapper style, Home Maker #2, 100 . . . . . . . . . . . . . . . . . . . .130.00

Junior Johnson, Trapper style, Ford, 1,000 . . . . . . . . . . . . . . . . . . . .140.00

Junior Johnson, Trapper style, Last American Hero, 2,000 . . . . . . . . . . . . . . .120.00

Alan Kulwicki, Trapper style, 1992 Winston Cup Champion, 1,000 . . . . . . . . . . . . .310.00

Alan Kulwicki, Trapper style, tribute to Alan, 1,000 . . . . . . . . . . . . . . . . . . .275.00

Alan Kulwicki, Gold Bowie style, tribute to Alan, 250 . . . . . . . . . . . . . . . . . . . . .600.00

Bobby Labonte, Trapper style, 1991 Busch Grand National, 100 . . . . . . . . . . . . . . . .300.00

Bobby Labonte, Trapper style, First Victory May 28, 600 . . . . . . . . . . . . . . . . . . .175.00

Terry Labonte, Trapper style, 1984 Winston Cup Champion, 100 . . . . . . . . . . . .445.00

Terry Labonte, Big Coke style, Iceman, 100 . . . . . . . . . . . . . . . . . . . . .445.00

Fred Lorenzen, Trapper style, 1960 Golden Boy, 500 . . . . . . . . . . . . . . . . . . . .140.00

Sterlin Marlin, Trapper style, 2-Time Winston Open Winner, 500 . . . . . . . . . . . . . . .125.00

Mark Martin, Trapper style, Rising Star, 1,000 . . . . . . . . . . . . . . . . . . . .250.00

Mark Martin, Trapper style, Top Flight Competitor, 450 . . . . . . . . . . . . . . . . . . . .200.00

Mark Martin, Trapper style, Top Flight Competitor, 100 . . . . . . . . . . . . . . . . . . . .500.00

J.D. McDuffie, Bull Dog style, Last Great Independent, 350 . . . . . . . . . . . . . . . . . .650.00

Jimmy Means, Trapper style, Relief Machine, 100 . . . . . . . . . . . . . . . . . . . .270.00

Billy Myers, Trapper style, 1955 National Champion, 500 . . . . . . . . . . . . . .100.00

Bobby Myers, Trapper style, NC State Champion, 500 . . . . . . . . . . . . . . . . . . . .100.00

David Pearson, Trapper style, 1960 Rookie of the Year, 1,200 . . . . . . . . . . . . . . .175.00

Richard, Lee & Kyle Petty, 3 styles, Three Pettys, 1,500 . . . . . . . . . . . . . . . . . . .800.00

Kyle Petty, Buffalo style, King of the Rock, 600 . . . . . . . . . . . . . . . . . . . . .240.00

Lee Petty, Trapper style, Stock Car Legend, 2,000 . . . . . . . . . . . . . . . . . . . .110.00

Lee Petty, Hunter style, Stock Car Legend, 500 . . . . . . . . . . . . . . . . . . . . .190.00

Richard Petty, Sod Buster style, 1976 Series, 500 . . . . . . . . . . . . . . . . . . .1300.00

Richard Petty, Grandaddy Barlow style, 1976 Series, 480 . . . . . . . . . . . . . . . .1300.00

Richard Petty, M279SS, 1976 Series, 500 . . . . . . . . . . . . . . . . . . . . .700.00

Richard Petty, Coke, Red Bone style, The King, 1,000 . . . . . . . . . . . . . . . . . . .800.00

Richard Petty, Coke, Blue Bone style, The King, 1,500 . . . . . . . . . . . . . . . . . . .800.00

Richard Petty, Coke style, The King, 32 .1900.00

Richard Petty, Coke style, Tribute to the Legend, 2,000 . . . . . . . . . . . . . . . . . . .400.00

Robert Pressley, Trapper style, Future Champion, 59 . . . . . . . . . . . . . . . . . . . .1200.00

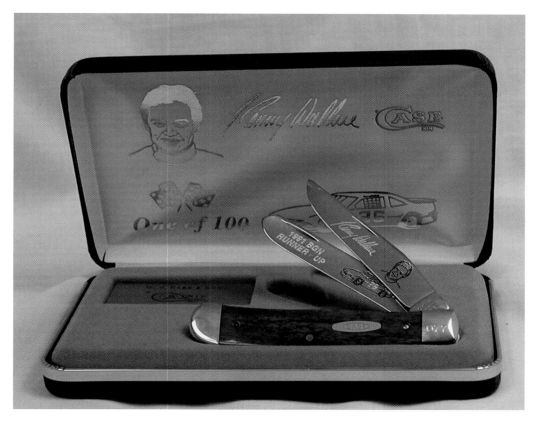

Kenny Wallace, Trapper style, 1991 BGN Runner Up, 100 . . . . . . . . . . . 225.00

Jody Ridley, Trapper style, 5-Time All Pro Champion, 600 . . . . . . . . . . . . . . . . . . . . . .140.00

Fireball Roberts, Trapper style, Purple Pontiac, 1,000 . . . . . . . . . . . . . . . . . . . . . .175.00

Wendell Scott, Trapper style , 250 . . . . .185.00

Morgan Shepherd, Trapper style, Wood Brothers, 500 . . . . . . . . . . . . . . . . . . . . . . .150.00

Smokin' Joes, Trapper style, Smokin' Joes Racing, 2,000 . . . . . . . . . . . . . . . . . . . . . . .375.00

Kenny Wallace, Trapper style, 1991 BGN Runner Up, 100 . . . . . . . . . . . . . . . . . . . .225.00

Rusty Wallace, Coke style, 1989 Winston Cup Champion, 1,000 . . . . . . . . . . . . . .250.00

Rusty Wallace, Trapper style, Rusty's Back, 300 . . . . . . . . . . . . . . . . . . . . . . .175.00

Darrell Waltrip, Trapper style, Top Money Winner 1988, 2,000 . . . . . . . . . . . . . . . . . .180.00

Darrell Waltrip, Coke style, 3-Time Winston Cup Champion, 1,000 . . . . . . . . . . . . .240.00

Glen Wood, Trapper style, The Woodchopper, 500 . . . . . . . . . . . . . . . . . . . . . . .150.00

Wood Brothers, Sod Buster style, 1976 Series, 500 . . . . . . . . . . . . . . . . . . . . . .900.00

Wood Brothers, Grandaddy Barlow style, 1976 Series, 500 . . . . . . . . . . . . . . . . . .900.00

Wood Brothers, Trapper style, 1991 Wood Brothers Racing, 500 . . . . . . . . . . . . . . . . . .130.00

Cale Yarborough, Trapper style, Tribute to a Legend, 2,000 . . . . . . . . . . . . . . . . . . . .100.00

Cale Yarborough, Sod Buster style, 1976 Grand National, 200 . . . . . . . . . . . . . . . . . .950.00

Cale Yarborough, Grandaddy Barlow style, 1976 Grand National, 200 . . . . . . . . . . . .950.00

Winston Motorsports, Coke style, 20th Anniversary, 100 . . . . . . . . . . . . . . . . . .1200.00

Winston Set, Assorted, 20th Anniversary, with chest, 20 drivers, 800 . . . .4500.00

Cale Yarborough, M279SS, 1976 Grand National,
200 . . . . . . . . . . . . . . . . . . . . . . .650.00

### FROST

Dale Earnhardt, 10 knife set, Earnhardt signature,
500 . . . . . . . . . . . . . . . . . . . . . . .900.00

Dale Earnhardt, Bowie style, Intimidator Bowie .150.00

Dale Earnhardt, Lockback style, 6-Time Series,
each set . . . . . . . . . . . . . . . . . . . . .75.00

Dale Earnhardt, Lockback style, 6-Time Champion,
2 knife set, 2,500 . . . . . . . . . . . . .150.00

Dale Earnhardt, Bowie style, 6-Time Champion,
black, 2,000 . . . . . . . . . . . . . . . .160.00

Dale Earnhardt, Lockback style, Team Set (4),
1,000 . . . . . . . . . . . . . . . . . . . . . .160.00

Dale Earnhardt, 3¾" dosed, "Intimidator Rolls A 7"
set, 2,500 . . . . . . . . . . . . . . . . . . .140.00

Dale Earnhardt, small Bowie style, "Intimidator
Rolls A 7," 5,000 . . . . . . . . . . . . . .165.00

Dale Earnhardt, Lockback style, "Intimidator Rolls
A 7" (2), 2,500 . . . . . . . . . . . . . . .135.00

Dale Earnhardt, 3¾" dosed, RCR 1994
Champions . . . . . . . . . . . . . . . . . .55.00

Dale Earnhardt, 4" dosed, Earnhardt 7-Time
Champion . . . . . . . . . . . . . . . . . . . .70.00

Dale Earnhardt, 4" dosed, RCR 1994
Champions, . . . . . . . . . . . . . . . . . . .55.00

Dale Earnhardt, Bowie style, Earnhardt 7-Time
Champion, 3,600 . . . . . . . . . . . . . .180.00

Dale Earnhardt, Bowie style, Petty – Earnhardt 7-
Time . . . . . . . . . . . . . . . . . . . . . . .160.00

Dale Earnhardt, Lockback style, Petty – Earnhardt
7-Time . . . . . . . . . . . . . . . . . . . . . .75.00

Dale Earnhardt, Bowie style, Silver Streak,
333 . . . . . . . . . . . . . . . . . . . . . . .200.00

Dale Earnhardt, K-40, Brickyard 400 . . . .45.00

Dale Earnhardt, #6542, Brickyard 400,
400 . . . . . . . . . . . . . . . . . . . . . . .220.00

Dale Earnhardt, Trapper style, 1990 IROC Championship, 333 . . . . . . . . . . . . . . . . . .250.00

Dale Earnhardt, Trapper style, 1995 IROC Championship, 333 . . . . . . . . . . . . . . . . . .280.00

Dale Earnhardt, Bowie style,1998 Daytona 500,
1,000 . . . . . . . . . . . . . . . . . . . . . .200.00

Dale Earnhardt, Jr., Rising Son . . . . . . . .55.00

Dale Earnhardt, Jr., 1st Win, Coca-Cola
300 . . . . . . . . . . . . . . . . . . . . . . .40.00

Dale Earnhardt, Jr., Busch GN Champion 1998,
1,000 . . . . . . . . . . . . . . . . . . . . . .65.00

Bill Elliott, Scrimshaw style, #9, red &
white . . . . . . . . . . . . . . . . . . . . . .125.00

Bill Elliott, Scrimshaw style, Million Dollar with face . . . . . . . . . . . . . . . . . . . .85.00
Bill Elliott, Scrimshaw style, Million Dollar with car . . . . . . . . . . . . . . . . . . . .85.00
Bill Elliott, Lockback style, #9 Steel, 10 . .200.00
Jeff Gordon, Lockback style, 1995 Winston Cup Champion . . . . . . . . . . . . . . . . . .35.00
Alan Kulwicki, Lockback style . . . . . . . .40.00
Snap-On, Lockback style, Earnhardt – Snap-On, 1994 . . . . . . . . . . . . . . . . . . . .105.00

### GERBER

Mac Tool Set, Lockback style, Earnhardt – Gant – Petty, 1992, 1,000 . . . . . . . . . . . .300.00

### HEN & ROOSTER

Dale Earnhardt, Trapper style, Winston Cup Champ. 1986 & 1987, 2,000 . . . . . . . . . . . . . . . . .180.00
Lee Petty, Trapper style, Stock Car Legend, 2,000 . . . . . . . . . . . . . . . . . . . .110.00
Cale Yarborough, Trapper style, Tribute to a Legend, 2,000 . . . . . . . . . . . . . . .120.00

### INGERSALL RAND

A. J. Foyt, #21 Purolator 1972 . . . . . . .250.00

### RCCA

Dale Earnhardt, car, #3 Goodwrench car, gold, 10,000 . . . . . . . . . . . . . . . . . . . .60.00
Jeff Gordon, car, #24 Dupont 1997, gold, 5,000 . . . . . . . . . . . . . . . . . . . .70.00
Jeff Gordon, car, 1997 Winston Cup Champion, brass, 5,000 . . . . . . . . . . . . . . . . .50.00
Dale Jarrett, car, #88 Quality Care, gold, 5,000 . . . . . . . . . . . . . . . . . . . .35.00
Rusty Wallace, car, #2 Miller, gold, 5,000 . . . . . . . . . . . . . . . . . . . .45.00
Rusty Wallace, car, #2 Miller, Elvis, brass . . . . . . . . . . . . . . . . . . . .40.00

### SCHRADE

Harry Gant, Lockback style, Gant . . . . . . .25.00
Ernie Irvan, Lockback style, #4 . . . . . . . .25.00
Dale Jarrett, Lockback style, #18 .15.00
Mac Tool Set, Lockback style, Earnhardt – Mac Tool, 1993 . . . . . . . . . . . . . . . .250.00

### UNCLE HENRY

Mac Tool Set, Lockback style, Harry Gant – Mac Tools 1990 . . . . . . . . . . . . . . . .200.00

### UTICA

Mac Tool Set, Lockback style, Irvan, Ayers & Bradham 1991 . . . . . . . . . . . . . . . . .200.00

### WENGER

Dale Earnhardt, Traveler style, Earnhardt #3, Swiss Army . . . . . . . . . . . . . . . . .75.00
Dale Earnhardt, Trail Blazer style, Earnhardt #3, Swiss Army . . . . . . . . . . . . . . . . .55.00
Dale Earnhardt, Pocket Tool style, Earnhardt #3 Swiss Army . . . . . . . . . . . . . . . . .45.00
Dale Earnhardt, Esquire style, Earnhardt #3, Swiss Army . . . . . . . . . . . . . . . . . . . .35.00

### WESTERN

Texaco, Havoline Racing . . . . . . . . . . . . .80.00

### WINCHESTER

Ward Burton, MBNA 200/500, 600 . . . . . . . . . . . . . . . . . . . .110.00
Jeff Gordon, 2 blade style, 1995 Winston Cup Champion, 1,524 . . . . . . . . . . . . .125.00
Mark Martin, 2 blade style, Dominates the Glen . . . . . . . . . . . . . . . . . . . .100.00

## MAGAZINES

Race fans have been collecting magazines and trade papers since the day the sport began. There are probably 8 – 10 publications that would rate as actually being collectible, but none more that the highly-acclaimed *Racing Pictorial*. In an era when media coverage of racing was a far cry from what we know today, publisher Ray Mann provided readers with a quarterly magazine whose photography remains the industry's benchmark. Published from 1959 through mid-1986, *Racing Pictorial* is by far one of motorsports' most popular printed collectibles.

Another favorite is the Official NASCAR Preview and Press Guide, offered by UMI Publishing. Introduced in 1986, this officially-licensed yearly magazine serves as NASCAR's annual. It provides a recap of the previous season, a look back through the history of NASCAR, and a peek at the upcoming season. It features full-color photography of virtually all of the sport's top drivers and cars.

In recent years, mainstream magazines have become more aware of NASCAR's popularity and have responded accordingly. For instance, recognizing the perfect marriage between stock car racing and television, TV Guide has released more than two dozen magazines featuring cover shots of NASCAR's top drivers. The first, featuring Jeff Gordon, made its debut in 1996.

To insure their longevity, magazines should be stored in a clear plastic bag, away from the elements. They should also be kept away from direct light, which might cause fading of the cover.

### RACING PICTORIAL

| | |
|---|---|
| 1959, first issue | 150.00 |
| 1960 – 1961 | 50.00 |
| 1961, color issue | 50.00 |
| 1961 – 1962, Annual | 50.00 |
| 1962, color issue | 50.00 |
| 1962 – 1963, Annual | 40.00 |
| 1963, color issue | 50.00 |
| 1963 – 1964, Annual | 40.00 |
| 1964, color issue | 50.00 |
| 1964 – 1965, Annual | 40.00 |
| 1965, Summer | 40.00 |
| 1965, Fall | 40.00 |
| 1965 – 1966, Annual | 50.00 |

| | |
|---|---|
| 1966, Spring | 50.00 |
| 1966, Summer | 40.00 |
| 1966, Fall | 40.00 |
| 1966 – 1967, Annual | 40.00 |
| 1967, Spring | 35.00 |
| 1967, Summer | 35.00 |
| 1967, Fall | 35.00 |
| 1967 – 1968, Annual | 40.00 |
| 1968, Spring | 30.00 |
| 1968, Summer | 30.00 |
| 1968, Fall | 30.00 |
| 1968 – 1969, error, said 1969 – 1970 | 45.00 |

| | |
|---|---|
| 1969, Spring | 30.00 |
| 1969, Summer | 30.00 |
| 1969, Fall | 30.00 |

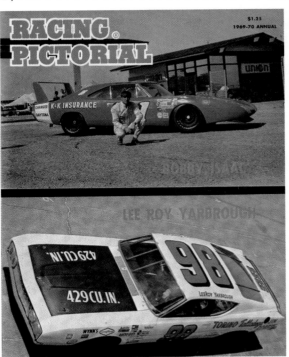

| | |
|---|---|
| 1969 – 1970, Annual | 30.00 |
| 1970, Spring, error, said Summer | 40.00 |
| 1970, Summer | 30.00 |
| 1970, Fall | 25.00 |
| 1970 – 1971, Annual | 25.00 |
| 1971, Spring | 25.00 |
| 1971, Summer | 20.00 |
| 1971, Fall | 25.00 |
| 1971 – 1972, Annual | 35.00 |
| 1972, Spring | 25.00 |
| 1972, Summer | 25.00 |
| 1972, Fall | 25.00 |
| 1972 – 1973, Annual | 30.00 |
| 1973, Spring | 20.00 |
| 1973, Summer | 25.00 |
| 1973, Fall | 25.00 |
| 1973 – 1974, Annual | 25.00 |
| 1974, Spring | 25.00 |
| 1974, Summer | 25.00 |
| 1974, Fall | 25.00 |
| 1974 – 1975, Annual | 20.00 |
| 1975, Spring | 20.00 |
| 1975, Summer | 25.00 |
| 1975, Fall | 25.00 |
| 1975 – 1976, Annual | 25.00 |
| 1976, Spring | 25.00 |
| 1976, Summer | 25.00 |
| 1976, Fall | 25.00 |
| 1976 – 1977, Annual | 25.00 |
| 1977, Spring | 20.00 |

1977, Summer . . . . . . . . . . . . . . . . . .20.00
1977, Fall . . . . . . . . . . . . . . . . . . . .20.00
1977 – 1978, Annual . . . . . . . . . . . .30.00
1978, Spring . . . . . . . . . . . . . . . . . .20.00
1978, Summer . . . . . . . . . . . . . . . . .20.00
1978, Fall . . . . . . . . . . . . . . . . . . . .20.00
1978 – 1979, Annual . . . . . . . . . . . .25.00
1979, Spring . . . . . . . . . . . . . . . . . .20.00
1979, Summer . . . . . . . . . . . . . . . . .20.00
1979, Fall . . . . . . . . . . . . . . . . . . . .20.00

Dale Earnhardt, Commemorative Issue
2/28/2001 . . . . . . . . . . . . . . . .10.00

### TV GUIDE 1996

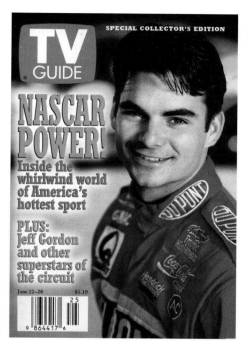

Jeff Gordon, NASCAR Power . . . . . . . . . .15.00

1979 – 1980, Annual . . . . . . . . . . . . . .25.00
1980, Spring . . . . . . . . . . . . . . . . . . .15.00
1980, Fall . . . . . . . . . . . . . . . . . . . . .15.00
1980 – 1981, Annual . . . . . . . . . . . . . .25.00
1981, Spring . . . . . . . . . . . . . . . . . . .15.00
1981, Summer . . . . . . . . . . . . . . . . . .15.00
1981, Fall . . . . . . . . . . . . . . . . . . . . .15.00
1981 – 1982, Annual . . . . . . . . . . . . . .20.00
1982, Spring . . . . . . . . . . . . . . . . . . .15.00
1982, Summer . . . . . . . . . . . . . . . . . .15.00
1982 – 1983, Annual . . . . . . . . . . . . . .20.00
1983, Spring . . . . . . . . . . . . . . . . . . .20.00
1983, Summer . . . . . . . . . . . . . . . . . .15.00
1983 – 1984, Annual . . . . . . . . . . . . . .20.00
1984, Spring . . . . . . . . . . . . . . . . . . .12.00
1985, Spring . . . . . . . . . . . . . . . . . . .12.00
1986, Spring . . . . . . . . . . . . . . . . . . .12.00
1986, Summer . . . . . . . . . . . . . . . . . .12.00

### SPORTS ILLUSTRATED

Dale Earnhardt, 2/26/2001 . . . . . . . . .20.00

### TV GUIDE 1997

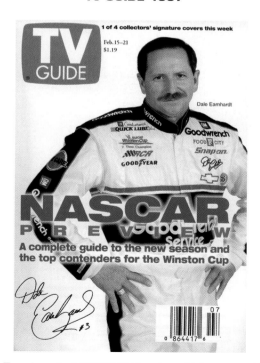

Dale Earnhardt, NASCAR Preview, February .20.00
Dale Jarrett, NASCAR Preview, February . . .5.00
Jeff Gordon, NASCAR Preview, February . . .8.00
Terry Labonte, NASCAR Preview, February . .5.00

### TV GUIDE 1998

Bobby Allison, Mark Martin, Legends of
NASCAR . . . . . . . . . . . . . . . . . . . . .5.00
Dale Earnhardt, Richard Petty, Legends of
NASCAR . . . . . . . . . . . . . . . . . . . .20.00
Dale Jarrett, Cale Yarborough, Legends of
NASCAR . . . . . . . . . . . . . . . . . . . . .5.00
Jeff Gordon, David Pearson, Legends of
NASCAR . . . . . . . . . . . . . . . . . . . . .7.00

### TV GUIDE 1999

Jeff Burton, New Stars of NASCAR, July . . .4.00

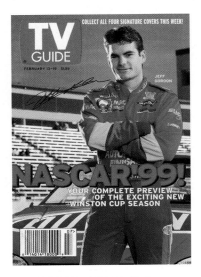

Jeff Gordon, NASCAR 1999, February . . . . .6.00
Dale Jarrett, NASCAR 1999, February . . . .5.00
Bobby Labonte, New Stars of NASCAR, July .4.00
Mark Martin, NASCAR 1999, February . . . .5.00
Jeremy Mayfield, New Stars of NASCAR, July .4.00

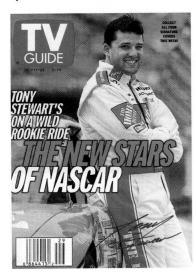

Tony Stewart, New Stars of NASCAR, July .12.00
Rusty Wallace, NASCAR 1999, February . . .5.00

### TV GUIDE 2000

Dale Earnhardt, Dale Earnhardt, Jr., All in Family,
February . . . . . . . . . . . . . . . . . . . .20.00
Dale Earnhardt, "Glory Days," August . . . . .15.00
Bill Elliott, "Glory Days," August . . . . . . . . .3.00
Ned Jarrett, Dale Jarrett, Jason Jarrett, All in
Family, February . . . . . . . . . . . . . . . .4.00
Bobby Labonte, Terry Labonte, Justin Labonte, All
in Family, February . . . . . . . . . . . . . .4.00

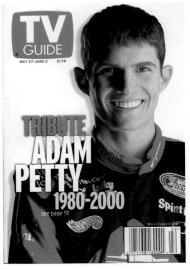

Adam Petty, Tribute 1980 – 2000 . . . . . . .14.00
Richard Petty, Kyle Petty, Adam Petty, All in Family,
February . . . . . . . . . . . . . . . . . . . .14.00
Ricky Rudd, "Glory Days," August . . . . . . . . .3.00
Rusty Wallace, "Glory Days," August . . . . . .3.00

### NASCAR YEARBOOK, RECORD BOOK,
### PRESS GUIDE

1950, 9 x 12 . . . . . . . . . . . . . . . . . . . .275.00
1951, 9 x 12 . . . . . . . . . . . . . . . . . . . .150.00
1952 . . . . . . . . . . . . . . . . . . . . . . . . .140.00
1953 . . . . . . . . . . . . . . . . . . . . . . . . .125.00
1954 . . . . . . . . . . . . . . . . . . . . . . . . .125.00
1955 . . . . . . . . . . . . . . . . . . . . . . . . .100.00
1957 . . . . . . . . . . . . . . . . . . . . . . . . .100.00
1958 . . . . . . . . . . . . . . . . . . . . . . . . . .80.00
1959 . . . . . . . . . . . . . . . . . . . . . . . . . .75.00
1960 . . . . . . . . . . . . . . . . . . . . . . . . . .50.00
1961 . . . . . . . . . . . . . . . . . . . . . . . . . .45.00
1962 . . . . . . . . . . . . . . . . . . . . . . . . . .45.00
1963 – 1966 . . . . . . . . . . . . . . . . . . . .45.00
1967 – 1969 . . . . . . . . . . . . . . . . . . . .40.00
1970 – 1975 . . . . . . . . . . . . . . . . . . . .30.00
1976 – 1979 . . . . . . . . . . . . . . . . . . . .25.00
1980 – 1985 . . . . . . . . . . . . . . . . . . . .15.00
1986, First Newsstand Edition, 8½ x 11 . . .9.00
1987 – 1989, 8½ x 11 . . . . . . . . . . . . . .8.00
1990 – 1995, 8½ x 11 . . . . . . . . . . . . . .8.00

1996 – 1998, 8½ x 11 . . . . . . . . . . . . . .8.00
1999 – 2000, 8½ x 11 . . . . . . . . . . . . .8.00

# MEDALLIONS

More than six dozen different NASCAR-themed collectible medallions and coins have been introduced over the past two decades. Most feature a particular driver, while others commemorate specific events like the Daytona 500 or Brickyard 400.

Enviromint has been the most active in the category, producing nearly 50 different pieces using a variety of precious metals. Quantities are always extremely limited, and appraisals run the gamut depending on the subject and the material used.

Another much sought-after series is the nine-medallion Winston 20th Anniversary collection. This ensemble pays tribute to the nine men who captured NASCAR championships during Winston's first two decades as title sponsor of NASCAR's top division.

## ENVIROMINT

1995 Brickyard 400, Pace Truck, silver, 10,000 . . . . . . . . . . . . . . . . . . . . . .20.00
1995 Brickyard 400, Pace Truck, 24k gold, 500 . . . . . . . . . . . . . . . . . . . . . .65.00
1995 Brickyard 400, Pace Truck, bronze, 1,995 . . . . . . . . . . . . . . . . . . . . . .20.00
1996 Brickyard 400, silver, 1,996 . . . . .35.00
1996 Brickyard 400, 24k gold, 500 . . . .55.00
1996 Brickyard 400, bronze, 1,996 . . . .20.00
1997 Brickyard 400, silver, 1,996 . . . . .35.00
1997 Brickyard 400, gold, 500 . . . . . . .55.00
Dale Earnhardt, 15,000 . . . . . . . . . . .45.00
Dale Earnhardt, 24k gold, 5,000 . . . . . .150.00
Dale Earnhardt, 1998 Daytona 500 Win, silver, 5,000 . . . . . . . . . . . . . . . . . . . . . .100.00
Dale Earnhardt, 50th Anniversary NASCAR, silver, 10,000 . . . . . . . . . . . . . . . . . . . . . .75.00
Dale Earnhardt – Richard Petty, 7&7 Set, 7,000 . . . . . . . . . . . . . . . . . . . . . .110.00
Dale Earnhardt – Richard Petty, 7&7 Set, 24k gold, 1,995 . . . . . . . . . . . . . . . . .175.00
Jeff Gordon, 1995 Winston Cup Champion, 1,510 . . . . . . . . . . . . . . . . . . . . . .50.00
Jeff Gordon, 1995 Winston Cup Champion, 24k gold, 100 . . . . . . . . . . . . . . . . . .250.00
Jeff Gordon, 1995 Winston Cup Champion, silver card, 72 . . . . . . . . . . . . . . . . . . . . . .350.00
Jeff Gordon, 1995 Winston Cup Champion, 24k card, 27 . . . . . . . . . . . . . . . . . . . . . .475.00

Jeff Gordon, 1995 Winston Cup Champion, 1,510 . . . . . . . . . . . . . . . . . . . . . .50.00

Jeff Gordon, Brickyard 400 Winner, 1,823 .45.00
Jeff Gordon, Brickyard 400 Winner, 24k, 180 . . . . . . . . . . . . . . . . . . . . . .250.00
Jeff Gordon, Hendricks Motorsports, silver, 582 . . . . . . . . . . . . . . . . . . . . . .85.00
Jeff Gordon, Hendricks Motorsports, 24k gold, 90 . . . . . . . . . . . . . . . . . . . . . .250.00
Jeff Gordon, Hendricks Motorsports, bronze, 200 . . . . . . . . . . . . . . . . . . . . . .65.00
Jeff Gordon, 1997 Winston Cup Champion, silver . . . . . . . . . . . . . . . . . . . . . .55.00
Jeff Gordon, 50th Anniversary NASCAR, silver, 10,000 . . . . . . . . . . . . . . . . . . . . . .50.00
Mark Martin, 1995, 5,000 . . . . . . . . . .35.00
Mark Martin, 1995, 24k gold, 500 . . . . .75.00
Mark Martin, 50th Anniversary of NASCAR, silver, 10,000 . . . . . . . . . . . . . . . . . . . . . .50.00
Richard Petty, silver, 9,077 . . . . . . . . . .45.00
Richard Petty, silver & gold set, 98 . . . . 950.00
Richard Petty, pure gold, 39 . . . . . . . . 1000.00
Richard Petty, 7-Time Champ, silver, 5,000 . . . . . . . . . . . . . . . . . . . . . .29.00
Richard Petty, 7-Time Champ, 24k gold, 500 . . . . . . . . . . . . . . . . . . . . . .49.00
Richard Petty, 50th Anniversary of NASCAR, silver, 10,000 . . . . . . . . . . . . . . . . . . . . . .50.00
Rusty Wallace, 1995, silver, 535 . . . . . . .75.00
Rusty Wallace, 1995, 24k gold, 50 . . . .150.00
Rusty Wallace, 1995, bronze, 40 . . . . . .100.00
Rusty Wallace, Penske Racing 1996, silver, 1,996 . . . . . . . . . . . . . . . . . . . . . .35.00
Rusty Wallace, Penske Racing 1996, 24k gold, 500 . . . . . . . . . . . . . . . . . . . . . .75.00
Rusty Wallace, Penske Racing 1996, bronze, 1,996 . . . . . . . . . . . . . . . . . . . . . .20.00
Rusty Wallace, Penske Racing 1996, 3-piece set, 96 . . . . . . . . . . . . . . . . . . . . . .155.00

## MINT COLLECTIBLES

Bill Elliott, 1988 Winston Cup Champion, 10,000 . . . . . . . . . . . . . . . . . . . . . .10.00
Harry Gant, Mr. September, 10,000 . . . . .10.00

## KEN SCHRADER

Ken Schrader, Daytona Pole Winner, 10,000 . . . . . . . . . . . . . . . . . . . . . .10.00

### RACING CENTENNIAL

Ernie Irvan, with 4 x 6 Traks card . . . . . . .15.00
Mark Martin, with 4 x 6 Traks card . . . . . .15.00

### SUPERSTAR COLLECTION

Bobby Allison, 1982 . . . . . . . . . . . . . . .40.00
Geoff Bodine, 1988 . . . . . . . . . . . . . . .35.00
Dale Earnhardt, 1987 . . . . . . . . . . . . . .75.00
Bill Elliott, 1984 . . . . . . . . . . . . . . . . .45.00
Harry Gant, 1985 . . . . . . . . . . . . . . . . .40.00
Ernie Irvan, 1991 . . . . . . . . . . . . . . . . .40.00
Junior Johnson, 1981 . . . . . . . . . . . . . .40.00
Rob Moroso, 1989 . . . . . . . . . . . . . . . .40.00
Richard Petty, 1986 . . . . . . . . . . . . . . .40.00

Tim Richmond, 1987 . . . . . . . . . . . . . . .60.00
Rusty Wallace, 1990 . . . . . . . . . . . . . . .45.00
Cale Yarborough, 1983 . . . . . . . . . . . . .35.00

### WINSTON 20TH ANNIVERSARY

9 Medallion Set . . . . . . . . . . . . . . . . . .425.00
9 Medallion Set, with cherry case & poster
    set . . . . . . . . . . . . . . . . . . . . . . . . .550.00
Bobby Allison, 1983 Winston Cup
    Champion . . . . . . . . . . . . . . . . . . . .40.00

Dale Earnhardt, 1980, 1986, 1987, 1990, 1991
Winston Cup Champion . . . . . . . . .100.00

Bill Elliott, 1988 Winston Cup Champion . .50.00
Terry Labonte, 1984 Winston Cup
    Champion . . . . . . . . . . . . . . . . . . . .55.00
Benny Parsons, 1973 Winston Cup
    Champion . . . . . . . . . . . . . . . . . . . .40.00
Richard Petty, 1971, 1972, 1974, 1975, 1979
    Winston Cup Champion . . . . . . . . . . .50.00
Rusty Wallace, 1989 Winston Cup
    Champion . . . . . . . . . . . . . . . . . . . .65.00
Darrell Waltrip, 1981, 1982, 1985 Winston Cup
    Champion . . . . . . . . . . . . . . . . . . . .45.00
Cale Yarborough, 1976, 1977, 1978 Winston
    Cup Champion . . . . . . . . . . . . . . . . .45.00

## MODEL KITS

Scale modeling has been a part of Americana for a half century. Just as many enthusiasts enjoy building plastic models, a comparable number prefer to collect unbuilt kits. NASCAR models first started gaining popularity about 30 years ago. At first, they were merely customizing options for street car kits. Then, in 1971, MPC released a series of "true" stock car kits. Within a few years, other model manufacturers — most notably AMT-ERTL and Revell-Monogram — had developed their own NASCAR product lines.

From a standpoint of collectibility, unbuilt kits are worth far more than built models. Building a kit actually decreases the value by 70 – 90%. It should also be noted that, on older kits, removing the shrink wrap from the box does *not* negatively effect the value. In fact, some potential buyers actually see it as a plus because it allows them to inspect the body shell for heat-induced distortion.

### AMT, ERTL 1:16 SCALE

7 Kyle Petty, 7-Eleven, Kit 6718, 1985 T-
    Bird . . . . . . . . . . . . . . . . . . . . . . . .110.00
28 Cale Yarborough, Hardee's, Kit 6717, 1985
    T-Bird . . . . . . . . . . . . . . . . . . . . . . .110.00

43 Richard Petty, STP, Kit 6741, 1985 Pontiac . . . . . . . . . . . . . . . . . . . . . .120.00

75 Lake Speed, Nationwise, Kit 6746, 1985 Pontiac . . . . . . . . . . . . . . . . . . . . . .100.00

### AMT, ERTL 1:25 SCALE

Kit 6372, Generic Chevy Monte Carlo Stock Car . . . . . . . . . . . . . . . . . . . . . . . . . .10.00

Kit 1895, 1975 Chevelle Malibu Stock Car .18.00

Kit 3688, 1972 – 1976 Chevelle & Malibu Generic Kit . . . . . . . . . . . . . . . . . . . . . .50.00

Kit 6296, Generic Ford T-Bird Stock Car . . . . . . . . . . . . . . . . . . . . . . . . . .10.00

3 Goodwrench, Kit 8451, 1997 Supertruck .10.00

3 Mike Skinner, Goodwrench, Kit 8243, Chevrolet Supertruck . . . . . . . . . . . . . . . . .11.00

4, 43, 22 Kodak, STP, Maxwell House, Kit 8910 . . . . . . . . . . . . . . . .65.00

4 Bobby Hamilton, Kodak, Kit 6299, 1998 Monte Carlo . . . . . . . . . . . . . . . . . . . . . . .9.00

4 Ernie Irvan, Kodak, Kit 6802, Hauler . . .40.00

4 Ernie Irvan, Kodak, Kit 6727, 1991 Lumina . . . . . . . . . . . . . . . . . . . . .16.00

4 Rick Wilson, Kodak, Kit 6731, 1990 Oldsmobile . . . . . . . . . . . . . . . . . . . .20.00

5 Terry Labonte, Kelloggs, Kit 8187, 1995 Monte Carlo . . . . . . . . . . . . . . . . . . . . . .12.00

5 Terry Labonte, Kellogg's, Kit 8090, 1997 Monte Carlo . . . . . . . . . . . . . . . . . . . .9.00

5 Terry Labonte, Kellogg's, Kit 6297, 1998 Monte Carlo . . . . . . . . . . . . . . . . . . . .10.00

6 Mark Martin, Valvoline, Kit 8189, 1995 T-Bird . . . . . . . . . . . . . . . . . . . . . .9.00

6 Mark Martin, Valvoline, Kit 8403, 1996 T-Bird . . . . . . . . . . . . . . . . . . . . . .12.00

6 Mark Martin, Valvoline, Kit 8756, 1992 T-Bird . . . . . . . . . . . . . . . . . . . . . .20.00

7 Alan Kulwicki, Zerex, Kit 6739, 1990 T-Bird . . . . . . . . . . . . . . . . . . . . . .75.00

7 Geoff Bodine, QVC, Kit 8161, 1997 T-Bird . . . . . . . . . . . . . . . . . . . . . .9.00

7 Geoff Bodine, QVC, Kit 8406, 1996 T-Bird . . . . . . . . . . . . . . . . . . . . . .12.00

7 Geoff Bodine, QVC, Kit 8706, 1996 T-Bird . . . . . . . . . . . . . . . . . . . . . .9.00

7 Kyle Petty, 7-Eleven, Kit 8047, 1983 Pontiac . . . . . . . . . . . . . . . . . . . . . .75.00

8 Jeff Burton, Raybestos, Kit 8191, 1995 T-Bird . . . . . . . . . . . . . . . . . . . . . .9.00

9 Bill Elliott, Coors, Kit 6019, Hauler . . . . . . . . . . . . . . . . . . . . . .60.00

9 Bill Elliott, Coors, Kit 6962, 1990 T-Bird . . . . . . . . . . . . . . . . . . . . . .46.00

9 Bill Elliott, Coors Light, Kit 6740, 1991 T-Bird . . . . . . . . . . . . . . . . . . . . . .25.00

11 Darrell Waltrip, Pepsi, Kit 8043, 1983 Chevrolet . . . . . . . . . . . . . . . . . . . . .75.00

12 Bobby Allison, Coca-Cola, Kit T421, 1973 Chevrolet . . . . . . . . . . . . . . . . . . . . .125.00

12 Bobby Allison, Kit 3030, 1973 Matador Sportsman . . . . . . . . . . . . . . . . . . . .35.00

12 Bobby Allison, Kit T373, 1973 Chevy Malibu . . . . . . . . . . . . . . . . . . . . .125.00

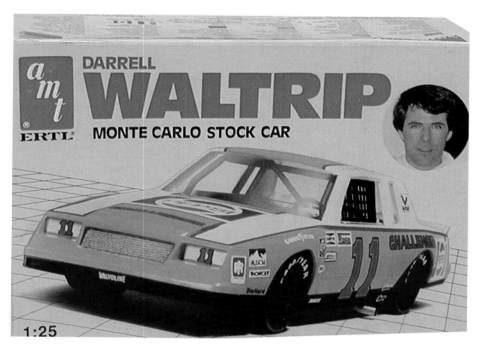

11 Darrell Waltrip, Pepsi, Kit 8043, 1983 Chevrolet . . . .75.00

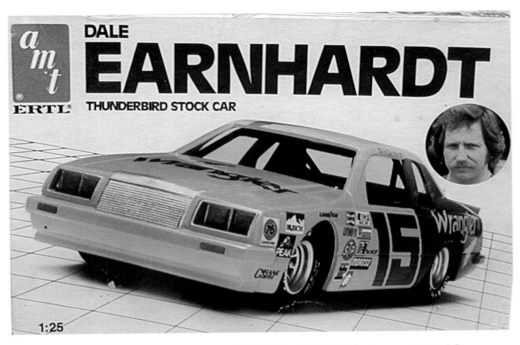

15 Dale Earnhardt, Wrangler, Kit 8046, 1984 T-Bird . . .150.00

15 Dale Earnhardt, Wrangler, Kit 8046, 1984 T-Bird . . . . . . . . . . . . . . . . . . . .150.00

15 Geoff Bodine, Motorcraft, Kit 6162, 1992 T-Bird . . . . . . . . . . . . . . . . . . . .11.00

15 Morgan Shepherd, Motorcraft, Kit 6730, 1991 T-Bird . . . . . . . . . . . . . . . . . .15.00

16 Bobby Allison, Coca-Cola, Kit T430, 1975 Matador . . . . . . . . . . . . . . . . . .120.00

16 Bobby Allison, Coca-Cola, Kit 8116, 1975 Matador . . . . . . . . . . . . . . . . . .15.00

16 Bobby Allison, Penske, Kit T430, 1975 Matador . . . . . . . . . . . . . . . . . .120.00

16 Bobby Allison, Penske, Kit T565, 1976 van & trailor . . . . . . . . . . . . . . . .190.00

17 Bill Sedgwick, DieHard, Kit 8244, Chevrolet Supertruck . . . . . . . . . . . . . . . .11.00

17 Darrell Waltrip, Parts America, Kit 8163, 1997 Monte Carlo . . . . . . . . . . . . . .9.00

17 Darrell Waltrip, Western Auto, Kit 8404, 1996 Monte Carlo . . . . . . . . . . . . . .12.00

17 Die Hard, Kit 8453, 1997 Super-truck . . . . . . . . . . . . . . . . . . . . .9.00

18 Bobby Labonte, Interstate, Kit 8186, 1995 Monte Carlo . . . . . . . . . . . . . . . .12.00

18 Dale Jarrett, Interstate, Kit 8752, 1991 Chevrolet . . . . . . . . . . . . . . . . . .12.00

21 Buddy Baker, Valvoline, Kit 8042, 1983 T-Bird . . . . . . . . . . . . . . . . . . . .70.00

21 Neil Bonnett & Dale Jarrett, Citgo, Kit 6733, 1990 T-Bird . . . . . . . . . . . . . . .25.00

21 Toby Butler, Ortho, Kit 8304, Ford Super-truck . . . . . . . . . . . . . . . . . . . .11.00

22 Sterling Marlin, Maxwell House, Kit 6457, 1991 T-Bird . . . . . . . . . . . . . . . . .20.00

24 Jack Sprague, Quaker State, Kit 8406, Chevrolet Supertruck . . . . . . . . . . . .11.00

24 Jeff Gordon, Dupont, Kit 6852, 1993 Lumina . . . . . . . . . . . . . . . . . . . .40.00

24 Jeff Gordon, Dupont, Kit 8190, 1995 Monte Carlo . . . . . . . . . . . . . . . . . . .10.00

26 Brett Bodine, Quaker State, Kit 6894, 1993 T-Bird . . . . . . . . . . . . . . . . . . .15.00

27 Rusty Wallace, Miller, Kit 6961, 1990 Pontiac . . . . . . . . . . . . . . . . . . . .46.00

28 Gordon Johncock, Kit T395, 1973 Chevelle . . . . . . . . . . . . . . . . . .115.00

28 Cale Yarborough, Hardee's, Kit 8045, 1983 Chevrolet . . . . . . . . . . . . . . . .75.00

30 Michael Waltrip, Country Time, Kit 6732, 1990 Pontiac . . . . . . . . . . . . . . . .19.00

42 Kyle Petty, Mello Yello, Kit 8106, 1991 Pontiac . . . . . . . . . . . . . . . . . . . .14.00

43 Richard Petty, Kit T229, 1976 Dodge Dart . . . . . . . . . . . . . . . . . . . .130.00

43 Richard Petty, Kit T569, 1976 Dodge & Ford Truck Set . . . . . . . . . . . . . . . .180.00

43 Richard Petty, STP, Kit 6728, 1990 Pontiac . . . . . . . . . . . . . . . . . . . . .25.00

43 Richard Petty, STP, Kit 8044, 1984 Pontiac . . . . . . . . . . . . . . . . . . . . .55.00

44 Rick Wilson, STP, Kit 6892, 1993 Pontiac . . . . . . . . . . . . . . . . . . . . .17.00

52 Kenny Schrader, AC Delco, Kit 8305, Chevrolet Supertruck . . . . . . . . . . . . .11.00

54 Lennie Pond, Kit T443, 1975 Chevy
Malibu . . . . . . . . . . . . . . . . . . . .110.00

66 Chad Little, Phillips 66, Kit 8754, 1992
T-Bird . . . . . . . . . . . . . . . . . . .12.00

68 Bobby Hamilton, Country Time, Kit 6819,
1991 Oldsmobile . . . . . . . . . . . .15.00

72 Benny Parsons, Kings Row, Kit T429, 1974
Chevrolet . . . . . . . . . . . . . . . . .100.00

88 Dale Jarrett, Ford Credit, Kit 8160,
T-Bird . . . . . . . . . . . . . . . . . . .10.00

88 Donnie Allison, Kit T380, 1974 Digard
Chevelle . . . . . . . . . . . . . . . . . .80.00

90 Kit T391, 1972 Jo Han Rebox . . . . .52.00

94 Bill Elliott, McDonalds, Kit 8200, 1997
T-Bird . . . . . . . . . . . . . . . . . . .9.00

94 Bill Elliott, McDonalds, Kit 8402, 1996
T-Bird . . . . . . . . . . . . . . . . . . .12.00

94 Bill Elliott, McDonalds, Kit 8188, 1995
T-Bird . . . . . . . . . . . . . . . . . . .10.00

94 Sterling Marlin, Sunoco, Kit 6738, 1990
Oldsmobile . . . . . . . . . . . . . . . .18.00

98 Kenny Irwin, Jr., Raybestos, Kit 8242, Ford
Supertruck . . . . . . . . . . . . . . . . .15.00

### AMT, ERTL 1:32 SCALE SNAP

4 Ernie Irvan, Kodak, Kit 8707, 1992
Lumina . . . . . . . . . . . . . . . . . . .14.00

6 Mark Martin, Valvoline, Kit 8729, 1992
T-Bird . . . . . . . . . . . . . . . . . . .14.00

10 Derrike Cope, Purolator, Kit 8722, 1992
Lumina . . . . . . . . . . . . . . . . . . .13.00

15 Geoff Bodine, Motorcraft, Kit 8730, 1992
T-Bird . . . . . . . . . . . . . . . . . . .13.00

18 Dale Jarrett, Interstate, Kit 8728, 1992
Lumina . . . . . . . . . . . . . . . . . . .13.00

21 Morgan Shepherd, Citgo, Kit 8712, 1993
T-Bird . . . . . . . . . . . . . . . . . . .13.00

22 Sterling Marlin, Maxwell House, Kit 8708,
1992 T-Bird . . . . . . . . . . . . . . . .13.00

26 Brett Bodine, Quaker State, Kit 8723, 1993
T-Bird . . . . . . . . . . . . . . . . . . .13.00

42 Kyle Petty, Mello Yello, Kit 8727, 1992
Pontiac . . . . . . . . . . . . . . . . . . .13.00

43 Richard Petty, STP, Kit 8709, 1992
Pontiac . . . . . . . . . . . . . . . . . . .13.00

44 Rick Wilson, STP, Kit 8712, 1993
Pontiac . . . . . . . . . . . . . . . . . . .14.00

66 Chad Little, Phillips 66, Kit 8799, 1992
T-Bird . . . . . . . . . . . . . . . . . . .13.00

### JO HAN 1:25 SCALE

22 Kit GC2200, 1969 Oval Track . .39.00
27 Kit GC3372, 1972 Oval Track . .39.00
43 Richard Petty, Kit GC964, 1964
Plymouth . . . . . . . . . . . . . . . . . .55.00

43, 40 Richard Petty & Pete Hamilton, Kit
GC1470, 1970 Superbird . . . . . . . .65.00

43 Richard Petty, Kit GC1970, 1970
Superbird . . . . . . . . . . . . . . . . . .65.00

### LINDBERG 1:25 SCALE

43 Richard Petty, Kit 72164, 1964 Plymouth .9.00

### MPC 1:16 SCALE

43 Richard Petty, STP, Kit 3053, 1973
Charger . . . . . . . . . . . . . . . . . . .190.00

71 Buddy Baker, K & K Insurance, Kit 3055,
1973 Charger . . . . . . . . . . . . . . .190.00

### MPC 1:25 SCALE KITS

1 Donnie Allison, Hawaiian Tropic, Kit 681, 1976
Malibu . . . . . . . . . . . . . . . . . . .110.00

2 Rusty Wallace, Alugard, Kit 6367, 1985 Pontiac . . . . . . . . . . . . . . . . . . . . .80.00

11 Buddy Baker, Kit 1702, 1971 NASCAR
Charger . . . . . . . . . . . . . . . . . . .139.00

11 Coo Coo Marlin, Kit 1707, 1972 Monte
Carlo . . . . . . . . . . . . . . . . . . . .110.00

15 Bobby Isaac, 1972 Ford Torino . . . . .165.00

16 David Pearson, Chattanooga Chew, Kit 6365,
1985 Chevrolet . . . . . . . . . . . . . .95.00

20 Kit 846, 1982 Super Stocker Grand
Prix . . . . . . . . . . . . . . . . . . . . .32.00

21 Donnie Allison, Kit 1704, 1971 NASCAR
Mercury . . . . . . . . . . . . . . . . . . .115.00

22 Cale Yarborough, Kit 1709, 1973
Chevrolet . . . . . . . . . . . . . . . . . .115.00

22 Dick Brooks, Kit 1705, 1971 NASCAR
Charger . . . . . . . . . . . . . . . . . . .115.00

25 Bobby Isaac, Kit 1710, 1973 Ford
Torino . . . . . . . . . . . . . . . . . . . .105.00

33 David Pearson, Kit 1706, 1971 NASCAR
GTO . . . . . . . . . . . . . . . . . . . . .115.00

37 Kit 738, 1983 Super Stocker Monte
Carlo . . . . . . . . . . . . . . . . . . . .35.00

39 Jim Hurtubise, Kit 1712, 1977 Chevelle .90.00

43 Richard Petty, Kit 1701, 1971 Daytona
Charger . . . . . . . . . . . . . . . . . . .165.00

43 Richard Petty, Kit 1708, 1973 NASCAR
Charger . . . . . . . . . . . . . . . . . . .175.00

43 Richard Petty, Kit 1713, 1978 NASCAR
Charger . . . . . . . . . . . . . . . . . . .165.00

55 Benny Parsons, Copenhagen, Kit 6366, 1985
Chevrolet . . . . . . . . . . . . . . . . . .80.00

56 Jim Hurtubise, Kit 1703, 1971 NASCAR
Chevelle . . . . . . . . . . . . . . . . . .100.00

58 Kit 845, 1982 Super Stocker Buick . .32.00

66 Phil Parsons, Skoal, Kit 6368, 1985
Chevrolet . . . . . . . . . . . . . . . . . .85.00

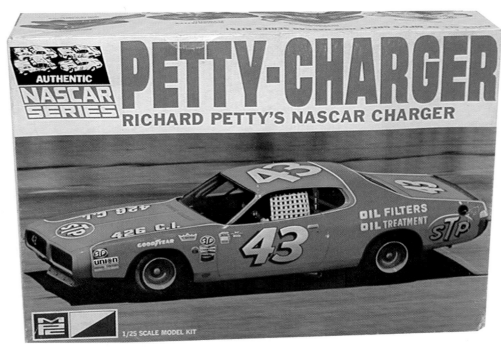

43 Richard Petty, Kit 1708, 1973 NASCAR Charger . . . . . . . . . .175.00

71 Buddy Baker, Kit 1711, 1973 Charger . . . . . . . . . . . . . . . . . . . . . .140.00
71 Bobby Isaac, K & K Insurance, Kit 731, 1971 Dodge . . . . . . . . . . . . . . . . . . . . . .175.00

## POLAR LIGHTS 1:24 SCALE

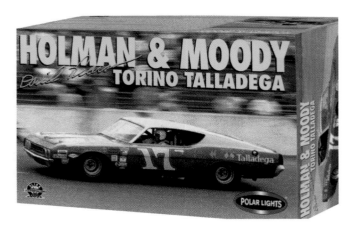

17 David Pearson, Holman & Moody, Torino, Talladega . . . . . . . . . . . . . . . . . . .10.00
21 Cale Yarborough, Wood Brothers, Mercury Cyclone . . . . . . . . . . . . . . . . . . . . .10.00
27 Donnie Allison, Sunny King, Ford Talladega . . . . . . . . . . . . . . . . . . . . .10.00
98 Lee Roy Yarbrough, Junior Johnson, Mercury Cyclone . . . . . . . . . . . . . . . . . . . .10.00

## REVELL-MONOGRAM 1:24 SCALE

Kit 664, 1981 – 1983 Buick Regal Generic Kit, 5,000 . . . . . . . . . . . . . . . . . . . . . .30.00
Kit 664, 1981 – 1983 Buick Regal Generic Kit, 2,500 . . . . . . . . . . . . . . . . . . . . . .45.00
Kit 6182, 1983, 86 T-Bird Generic Kit . . .50.00
NASCAR, Kit 4130, 50th Anniversary of NASCAR, gold . . . . . . . . . . . . . . . . . . . . .26.00
1 Buddy Baker, UNO, Kit 2205, 1982 Buick Regal . . . . . . . . . . . . . . . . . . . . . .68.00
1 Mike Chase, DieHard, Kit 2474, Chevrolet Truck . . . . . . . . . . . . . . . . . . . . . .9.00
1 Coca-Cola Parade Car, Kit 2550, 1997 Monte Carlo . . . . . . . . . . . . . . . . . . . . . .9.00
2 Mike Bliss, Team ASE, Kit 2547, Ford Truck . . . . . . . . . . . . . . . . . . . . . .9.00
2 Rusty Wallace, Pontiac Excitement, Kit 2960, 1992 Pontiac . . . . . . . . . . . . . . . . . .15.00
3 Dale Earnhardt, AC Delco, Kit 035, 1996 Monte Carlo . . . . . . . . . . . . . . . . . . . .60.00
3 Dale Earnhardt, Goodwrench, Kit 663, 1994 Lumina . . . . . . . . . . . . . . . . . . . . .35.00
3 Dale Earnhardt, Goodwrench Plus, Kit 036, 1997 Monte Carlo . . . . . . . . . . . . .35.00
3 Dale Earnhardt, Goodwrench, Kit 0763, silver, 1996 Monte Carlo . . . . . . . . . . . . .85.00
3 Dale Earnhardt, Goodwrench, Kit 2447, 1995 Monte Carlo . . . . . . . . . . . . . . . . . .25.00
3 Dale Earnhardt, Goodwrench, Kit 2585, 2000 Monte Carlo . . . . . . . . . . . . . . . . . .20.00

3 Dale Earnhardt, Goodwrench, Kit 2900, 1988 Monte Carlo . . . . . .55.00

3 Dale Earnhardt, Goodwrench, Kit 4137, 1998
Monte Carlo, in tin . . . . . . . . . . . . . .60.00
3 Dale Earnhardt, Goodwrench, Kit 2900, 1988
Monte Carlo . . . . . . . . . . . . . . . . . .55.00
3 Dale Earnhardt, Goodwrench, Kit 2900, 1988
Monte Carlo Re-issue . . . . . . . . . . . .40.00
3 Dale Earnhardt, Goodwrench, Kit 2927, 1990 –
1992 Lumina . . . . . . . . . . . . . . . . .30.00
3 Dale Earnhardt, Goodwrench, Kit 4131, clear
body, 15,000 . . . . . . . . . . . . . . . .75.00
3 Dale Earnhardt, Olympics, Kit 2483, 1996
Monte Carlo . . . . . . . . . . . . . . . . .35.00
3 Dale Earnhardt, Pro Bass, Kit 4134, 1998
Monte Carlo . . . . . . . . . . . . . . . . .30.00
3 Dale Earnhardt, Jr., AC Delco, Kit 2587, 1998
Monte Carlo . . . . . . . . . . . . . . . . .10.00
3 Mike Skinner, Goodwrench, Kit 2458, Chevrolet
Truck . . . . . . . . . . . . . . . . . . . . . .9.00
4 Sterling Marlin, Kodak, Kit 2448, 1995 Monte
Carlo . . . . . . . . . . . . . . . . . . . . . .9.00
5 Ricky Rudd, Tide, Kit 2440, 1993 Lumina .20.00
5 Terry Labonte, Kellogg's, Kit 2479, Monte
Carlo . . . . . . . . . . . . . . . . . . . . . .10.00
5 Terry Labonte, Kellogg's, Kit 2974, 1994
Lumina . . . . . . . . . . . . . . . . . . . .15.00
5 Terry Labonte, Kellogg's, Kit 4139, 1998
Monte Carlo, in tin . . . . . . . . . . . . .21.00
5 Terry Labonte, Spooky Fruit Loops, Kit 4127,
Monte Carlo . . . . . . . . . . . . . . . . .15.00
5 Terry Labonte, Tony Tiger, Kit 4114, 1997
Monte Carlo, 10,000 . . . . . . . . . . . .12.00

6 Mark Martin, Valvoline, Kit 031, 1997
T-Bird . . . . . . . . . . . . . . . . . . . . .19.00
6 Mark Martin, Valvoline, Kit 2477, T-Bird .11.00
6 Mark Martin, Valvoline, Kit 2477, Taurus .11.00
6 Mark Martin, Valvoline, Kit 2586, 2000
Taurus . . . . . . . . . . . . . . . . . . . . .9.00
6 Mark Martin, Folgers, Kit 2928, 1990 – 1992
T-Bird . . . . . . . . . . . . . . . . . . . . .18.00
6 Mark Martin, Valvoline, Kit 2959, 1992
T-Bird . . . . . . . . . . . . . . . . . . . . .15.00
6 Mark Martin, Valvoline, Kit 4140, 1998 Taurus,
in tin . . . . . . . . . . . . . . . . . . . . . .21.00
6 Rick Carelli, Total, Kit 2475, Chevrolet
Truck . . . . . . . . . . . . . . . . . . . . . .9.00
7 Alan Kulwicki, AK Racing, Kit 0760, 1993
T-Bird, 5,000 . . . . . . . . . . . . . . . .25.00
7 Alan Kulwicki, Hooters, Kit 0762, T-Bird,
5,000 . . . . . . . . . . . . . . . . . . . . .30.00
7 Alan Kulwicki, Zerex, Kit 2908, 1989
T-Bird . . . . . . . . . . . . . . . . . . . . .75.00
7 Darrell Waltrip, Western Auto, Kit 2949, 1991
Lumina . . . . . . . . . . . . . . . . . . . .23.00
7 Geoff Bodine, Exide, Kit 2450, 1994
T-Bird . . . . . . . . . . . . . . . . . . . . . .9.00
7 Harry Gant, Mac Tools, Kit HG124, 1993
Lumina . . . . . . . . . . . . . . . . . . . .35.00
7 Harry Gant, Mac Tools, Kit 898, 1993
Lumina . . . . . . . . . . . . . . . . . . . .70.00
8, 84, 12 Miller, Kit 2915, 1989 Buick . . .60.00
8 Rick Wilson & Bobby Hillin, Snickers, Kit 2940,
1990 – 1991 Buick . . . . . . . . . . . .14.00

9 Bill Elliott, Coors, Kit 2244, 1985 T-Bird . .70.00

9 Bill Elliott, Coors, Kit 2244, 1984 T-Bird . . . . . . . . . . . . . . . . . . .85.00

9 Bill Elliott, Coors, Kit 2244, Winston 1984 T-Bird . . . . . . . . . . . . . . . . . .95.00

9 Bill Elliott, Melling, Kit 2207, 1983 T-Bird . . . . . . . . . . . . . . . . . . . .75.00

9 Bill Elliott, Melling, Kit 2244, 1984 T-Bird Speedway . . . . . . . . . . . . . . . . . .90.00

9 Lake Speed, Cartoon Network, Kit 4133, 1998 Birthday. . . . . . . . . . . . . . . . . . .15.00

9 Lake Speed, Cartoon Network, Kit 2563, 1998 Taurus . . . . . . . . . . . . . . . . . . .9.00

9 Zombie Island, Kit 4146, 1998 Taurus . .14.00

9 Cartoon Network, Kit 7619, 1998 Taurus . . . . . . . . . . . . . . . . . . . .10.00

10 Derrike Cope, Purolator, Kit 2941, 1991 Lumina . . . . . . . . . . . . . . . . . . .15.00

10 Ricky Rudd, Tide, Kit 2478, T-Bird . . . .10.00

10 Ricky Rudd, Tide, Kit 2449, 1994 T-Bird . . . . . . . . . . . . . . . . . . . .9.00

11 Brett Bodine, Lowe's Gold, Kit 032, 1997 T-Bird . . . . . . . . . . . . . . . . . . .19.00

11 Darrell Waltrip, Mountain Dew, Kit 2204, 1983 Buick . . . . . . . . . . . . . . . . .74.00

11, 12 Darrell Waltrip & Neil Bonnett, Budweiser, Kit 2245, 1984 Monte Carlo . . . . . .115.00

12 Hut Stricklin, Raybestos, Kit 2431, 1991 Buick . . . . . . . . . . . . . . . . . . . .15.00

15 Dale Earnhardt, Wrangler, Kit 2206, 1983 T-Bird . . . . . . . . . . . . . . . . . . .125.00

15 Dale Earnhardt, Wrangler, Kit 3150, T-Bird . . . . . . . . . . . . . . . . . . . .60.00

15 Lake Speed, Quality Care, Kit 2451, 1994 T-Bird . . . . . . . . . . . . . . . . . . . .9.00

15 Ricky Rudd, Motorcraft, Kit 2723, 1986 T-Bird . . . . . . . . . . . . . . . . . . . .56.00

16 Ron Hornaday, NAPA, Kit 2519, Chevrolet Truck . . . . . . . . . . . . . . . . . . . .9.00

16 Ted Musgrave, Family Channel, Kit 2465, 1995 T-Bird . . . . . . . . . . . . . . . . .9.00

17 Darrell Waltrip, Budweiser Colors, Kit 041, 1997 Monte Carlo . . . . . . . . . . . .20.00

17 Darrell Waltrip, Chrome, Kit 038, 1997 Monte Carlo . . . . . . . . . . . . . . . . .22.00

17 Darrell Waltrip, Gatorade Colors, Kit 045, 1997 Monte Carlo . . . . . . . . . . . .20.00

17 Darrell Waltrip, Mountain Dew Colors, Kit 039, 1997 Monte Carlo . . . . . . . . .20.00

17 Darrell Waltrip, Parts America, Kit 042, 1997 Monte Carlo . . . . . . . . . . . .20.00

17 Darrell Waltrip, Parts America, Kit 4112, Chrome, 5,000 . . . . . . . . . . . . . .15.00

17 Darrell Waltrip, Pepsi Colors, Kit 046, 1997 Monte Carlo . . . . . . . . . . . .20.00

17 Darrell Waltrip, Tide, Kit 2755, 1987 Chevrolet . . . . . . . . . . . . . . . . .85.00

18 Hardees, Kit 2920, Days of Thunder, 1990 Lumina . . . . . . . . . . . . . . . . . . . .25.00

18 Bobby Labonte, Interstate, Kit 2987, 2000 Pontiac . . . . . . . . . . . . . . . . . . . .9.00

20 Tony Stewart, Home Depot, Kit 2986, 2000 Pontiac . . . . . . . . . . . . . . . . . . .10.00

21 Morgan Shepherd, Cheerwine, Kit 646, 1994 T-Bird . . . . . . . . . . . . . . . . . . . .25.00

21 Morgan Shepherd, Citgo, Kit 2961, 1992 T-Bird . . . . . . . . . . . . . . . . . . . .22.00

21 Michael Waltrip, Citgo Dog, Kit 4113, 1997 T-Bird, 10,000 . . . . . . . . . . . . . . . .12.00

22 Bobby Allison, Miller, Kit 2298, 1984 Buick GN . . . . . . . . . . . . . . . . . . . . .35.00

22 Bobby Allison, Miller, Kit 2298, 1984 Buick Speedway . . . . . . . . . . . . . . . . .50.00

22 Sterling Marlin, Maxwell House, Kit 2942, 1991 T-Bird . . . . . . . . . . . . . . . .13.00

22 Ward Burton, Caterpillar, Kit 2992, 2000 Pontiac . . . . . . . . . . . . . . . . . . .10.00

23 Chad Little, John Deere, Kit 2492, 1996 Pontiac . . . . . . . . . . . . . . . . . . . .9.00

24 Jack Sprague, Quaker State, Kit 2499, Chevrolet Truck . . . . . . . . . . . . . .9.00

24 Jeff Gordon, Dupont Chroma Premier, Kit 044, 1997 Monte Carlo . . . . . . . . . . .35.00

24 Jeff Gordon, Dupont, Kit 2476, Monte Carlo . . . . . . . . . . . . . . . . . . . .10.00

24 Jeff Gordon, Dupont, Kit 2441, 1993 Lumina . . . . . . . . . . . . . . . . . . .25.00

24 Jeff Gordon, Dupont, Kit 4138, 1998 Monte Carlo, in tin . . . . . . . . . . . . . . .21.00

24 Jeff Gordon, Dupont, Kit 1704, Hauler .35.00

24 Jeff Gordon, Dupont, Kit 2568, 2000 Monte Carlo . . . . . . . . . . . . . . . . . . . .9.00

24 Jeff Gordon, Jurassic Park, Kit 047, 1997 Monte Carlo . . . . . . . . . . . . . . . .22.00

24 Jeff Gordon, Jurassic Park, Kit 2525, 1997 Monte Carlo . . . . . . . . . . . . . . . .10.00

25 Tim Richmond, Folgers, Kit 2734, 1987 Monte Carlo . . . . . . . . . . . . . . . . .30.00

26 Johnny Benson, Cheerios, Kit 2553, 1998 Taurus . . . . . . . . . . . . . . . . . . . .11.00

26 Ricky Rudd, Quaker State, Kit 2786, 1989 Buick . . . . . . . . . . . . . . . . . . . .25.00

27 Hut Stricklin, McDonald's, Kit 2442, 1993 T-Bird . . . . . . . . . . . . . . . . . . . .20.00

28 Davey Allison, Havoline, Kit 2990, black & white, with figure, 1987 T-Bird . . . . . .20.00

28 Davey Allison, Mac Tools, Kit DA124, 1993 T-Bird . . . . . . . . . . . . . . . . . . . .81.00

28 Davey Allison, Texaco, Kit 2430, 1991 T-Bird . . . . . . . . . . . . . . . . . . . .10.00

28 Davey Allison, Texaco, Kit 2916, 1989 T-Bird . . . . . . . . . . . . . . . . . . . .85.00

28 Cale Yarborough, Hardee's, Kit 3153, 1984 Monte Carlo . . . . . . . . . . . . . . . .12.00

28 Davey Allison, Havoline, Kit 2990, black & white, with figure,1987 T-Bird . . . . . . .20.00

28 Ernie Irvan, Mac Tools, Kit EI124, 1994 T-Bird . . . . . . . . . . . . . . . . . . . . . .40.00

28 Ernie Irvan, Texaco, Kit 2471, 1996 T-Bird . . . . . . . . . . . . . . . . . . . . . . . .9.00

28 Ernie Irvan, Texaco Black & White, Kit 052, 1997 T-Bird . . . . . . . . . . . . . . . . . . .21.00

29 Cale Yarborough, Hardee's, Kit 2754, 1987 Oldsmobile . . . . . . . . . . . . . . . . . .50.00

29 Cartoon Network, Kit 2484, Monte Carlo . . . . . . . . . . . . . . . . . . . . . . .10.00

29 Kit 4128, Tom & Jerry Monte Carlo . . . . . . . . . . . . . . . . . . . . . . . .14.00

29 WCW, Kit 2485, Monte Carlo . . . . . . .10.00

30 Michael Waltrip, Countrytime & Kool Aid, Kit 2932, Pontiac . . . . . . . . . . . . . . . .18.00

30 Michael Waltrip, Pennzoil, Kit 2939, 1991 Pontiac . . . . . . . . . . . . . . . . . . . . . .15.00

31 Dale Earnhardt, Jr., Wrangler, Kit 054, Monte Carlo . . . . . . . . . . . . . . . . . . . . . . .45.00

31 Mike Skinner, Lowe's, Kit 053, 1997 Monte Carlo . . . . . . . . . . . . . . . . . . . . . . .20.00

31 Mike Skinner, Lowe's, Kit 2523, 1997 Monte Carlo . . . . . . . . . . . . . . . . . . . . . . .9.00

31 Mike Skinner, Lowe's, Kit 2991, 2000 Monte Carlo . . . . . . . . . . . . . . . . . . . . . . .9.00

32 Dale Jarrett, Mac Tools, Kit DJ125, 1995 T-Bird . . . . . . . . . . . . . . . . . . . . . .35.00

33 Harry Gant, Skoal, Kit 2706, 1985 Monte Carlo . . . . . . . . . . . . . . . . . . . . . . .85.00

35 Todd Bodine, Tabasco, Kit 4129, Pontiac . . . . . . . . . . . . . . . . . . . . . .14.00

35 Alan Kulwicki, Quincys, Kit 0761, T-Bird, 5,000 . . . . . . . . . . . . . . . . . . . . . . .25.00

37 Jeremy Mayfield, K-Mart, Kit 2552, Taurus . . . . . . . . . . . . . . . . . . . . . .12.00

40 Kenny Wallace, Dirt Devil, Kit 2973, 1994 Pontiac . . . . . . . . . . . . . . . . . . . . . .11.00

42 Kyle Petty, Mello Yello, Kit 2428, 1991 Pontiac . . . . . . . . . . . . . . . . . . . . . . . .16.00

42 Kyle Petty, Peak, Kit 2906, 1989 Pontiac . . . . . . . . . . . . . . . . . . . . . .35.00

43 Bobby Hamilton, STP, Kit 2493, 1997 Pontiac . . . . . . . . . . . . . . . . . . . . . .9.00

43 Richard Petty, STP, Curb, Kit 2722, 1985 Pontiac . . . . . . . . . . . . . . . . . . . . . . .90.00

43 Richard Petty, STP, Kit 3151, Legends, 1984 Pontiac . . . . . . . . . . . . . . . . . . . . . .12.00

44 Kyle Petty, Hot Wheels, in tin, Kit 4117, 10,000 . . . . . . . . . . . . . . . . . . . . .20.00

44 Kyle Petty, Hot Wheels, Kit 4136, 1998 Blues Brothers Pontiac . . . . . . . . . . . . . . .15.00

44 Kyle Petty, Hot Wheels, Kit 2524, 1997 Pontiac . . . . . . . . . . . . . . . . . . . . . .9.00

44 Terry Labonte, Piedmont, Kit 3152, 1984 Monte Carlo . . . . . . . . . . . . . . . . . .11.00

44 Terry Labonte, Piedmont, Kit 2299, 1984 Chevrolet . . . . . . . . . . . . . . . . . . . .88.00

46 City Chevrolet, Kit 2917, Days of Thunder, 1990 Lumina . . . . . . . . . . . . . . . . . .25.00

46 Wally Dallenbach, Kit 4132, Woody Woodpecker . . . . . . . . . . . . . . . . . . . . . .17.00

47 Ron Bouchard, Valvoline, Kit 2707, 1984 Buick . . . . . . . . . . . . . . . . . . . . . .79.00

51 Mello Yello, Kit 2921, Days of Thunder, 1990 Lumina . . . . . . . . . . . . . . . . . . . . . .25.00

52 Ken Schrader, AC Delco, Kit 2473, Chevrolet Truck . . . . . . . . . . . . . . . . . . . . . . .9.00

57 Hut Stricklin & Jimmy Spencer, Heinz, Kit 2914, 1990 Pontiac . . . . . . . . . . . . .18.00

60 Mark Martin, Winn Dixie, Kit 9460, 1994 T-Bird . . . . . . . . . . . . . . . . . . . . . .40.00

60 Mark Martin, Winn Dixie, Kit CHD9460, 1994 T-Bird . . . . . . . . . . . . . . . . . . . . . .40.00

66 Dick Trickle, Trop Artic, Kit 2930, 1990 Pontiac . . . . . . . . . . . . . . . . . . . . . .16.00

71 Dave Marcis, Olive Garden, Kit CHD9571, 1995 Monte Carlo, 5,000 . . . . . . . . .30.00

75 Neil Bonnett, Valvoline, Kit 2787, 1989 Pontiac . . . . . . . . . . . . . . . . . . . . . .60.00

75 Rick Mast, Remington Camouflage, Kit 028, 1997 T-Bird . . . . . . . . . . . . . . . . . .19.00

75 Joe Ruttman, Dinner Bell, Kit 2432, 1991 Oldsmobile . . . . . . . . . . . . . . . . . . .15.00

75 Todd Bodine, Factory Stores, Kit 2466, 1995 T-Bird . . . . . . . . . . . . . . . . . . . . . .9.00

75 Rick Mast, Remington, Kit 2518, 1997 T-Bird . . . . . . . . . . . . . . . . . . . . . .9.00

80 Joe Ruttman, LCI, Kit 2529, Ford Truck .9.00

83 Lake Speed, K-Mart, Kit 2779, 1987 Oldsmobile . . . . . . . . . . . . . . . . . . . . . .18.00

87 Joe Nemechek, Burger King, Kit 2468, 1995 Monte Carlo . . . . . . . . . . . . . . . . . . .9.00

87 Joe Nemechek, Burger King, Kit 027, 1997 Monte Carlo . . . . . . . . . . . . . . . . . .19.00

88 Dale Jarrett, Quality Care, Kit 2472, 1996 T-Bird . . . . . . . . . . . . . . . . . . . . . .9.00

94 Bill Elliott, Mac Tonite, Kit 4124, 1997 T-Bird, 10,000 . . . . . . . . . . . . . . . . .12.00

94 Bill Elliott, McDonald's, Kit 2469, 1995 T-Bird . . . . . . . . . . . . . . . . . . . . . .9.00
94 Bill Elliott, McDonald's, Kit 2486, T-Bird .10.00
94 Bill Elliott, McDonald's, Kit 4145, gold plated . . . . . . . . . . . . . . . . . . . . . .25.00
97 Chad Little, John Deere, Kit 2492, 1997 Pontiac . . . . . . . . . . . . . . . . . . . . . .9.00
99 Jeff Burton, Exide, Kit 2556, Taurus . .10.00
99 Jeff Burton, Exide, Kit 035, 1997 T-Bird . . . . . . . . . . . . . . . . . . . . . .19.00
99 Joe Ruttman, Exide, Kit 2529, 1998 Supertruck . . . . . . . . . . . . . . . . . . . . .9.00

### REVELL-MONOGRAM 1:24 PROFINISH GLUE KITS

3 Dale Earnhardt, Goodwrench Plus, Kit 1640, 2000 Monte Carlo . . . . . . . . . .25.00
17 Matt Kenseth, DeWalt Tools, Kit 1657, 2000 Taurus . . . . . . . . . . . . . . . . . .15.00
18 Bobby Labonte, Interstate, Kit 1645, 2000 Pontiac . . . . . . . . . . . . . . . . . . .15.00
20 Tony Stewart, Home Depot, Kit 1646, 2000 Pontiac . . . . . . . . . . . . . . . . . .15.00
24 Jeff Gordon, Dupont, Kit 1641, 2000 Monte Carlo . . . . . . . . . . . . . . . . . . .15.00
28 Ricky Rudd, Texaco Havoline, Kit 1651, 2000 Taurus . . . . . . . . . . . . . . . . .15.00
88 Dale Jarrett, Quality Care, Kit 1642, 2000 Taurus . . . . . . . . . . . . . . . . . . .15.00

### REVELL-MONOGRAM 1:24 SCALE COMBO SETS

3, 24 Dale Earnhardt & Jeff Gordon, Kit 0780, Brickyard Wins . . . . . . . . . . . . . . . .60.00
3 Dale Earnhardt, Wrangler, Kit 6298 . . . .80.00
4 Ernie Irvan & Rick Wilson, Kodak, Kit 6367 . . . . . . . . . . . . . . . . . . . . . . .27.00
7, 90 Alan Kulwicki & Ken Schrader, Zerex, Red Baron, Kit 6392 . . . . . . . . . . . . . . .28.00
7, 90 Alan Kulwicki & Ken Schrader, Kit 6368, Rookie of the Year . . . . . . . . . .28.00
11 Darrell Waltrip, Pepsi, Mountain Dew, Kit 6391 . . . . . . . . . . . . . . . . . . . . . .26.00
15, 21 Benny Parsons & Neil Bonnett, Kit 6857, T-Bird Legends . . . . . . . . . . . . .29.00
42, 43 Kit 6389, Racing Pettys . . . . . . .25.00

### REVELL-MONOGRAM 1:24 PROFINISH SNAPTITE

3 Dale Earnhardt, Goodwrench Plus, Kit 1346 . . . . . . . . . . . . . . . . . . . . .15.00
3 Dale Earnhardt, Goodwrench, Kit 1311, 1998 Monte Carlo . . . . . . . . . . . . . . .25.00
5 Terry Labonte, Kellogg's, Kit 1317, 1998 Monte Carlo . . . . . . . . . . . . . . . . .14.00
6 Mark Martin, Valvoline, Kit 1343, 2000 Taurus . . . . . . . . . . . . . . . . . . . . . .14.00

6 Mark Martin, Valvoline, Kit 1312, 1998 Taurus . . . . . . . . . . . . . . . . . . . . . .14.00
9 Cartoon Network, Kit 1315, 1998 Taurus . . . . . . . . . . . . . . . . . . . . . .14.00
24 Jeff Gordon, Dupont, Kit 1310, 1998 Monte Carlo . . . . . . . . . . . . . . . . . . .15.00
24 Jeff Gordon, Dupont, Kit 1341, 2000 Monte Carlo . . . . . . . . . . . . . . . . . . .14.00
26 Johnny Benson, Cheerios, Kit 1316, 1998 Taurus . . . . . . . . . . . . . . . . . . .14.00
94 Bill Elliott, McDonald's, Kit 1313, 1998 Taurus . . . . . . . . . . . . . . . . . . . . . .14.00
99 Jeff Burton, Exide, Kit 1314, 1998 Taurus . . . . . . . . . . . . . . . . . . . . . .14.00

### REVELL-MONOGRAM 1:32 SCALE SNAPTITE

2 Rusty Wallace, Penske Racing, Kit 1700, 1994 T-Bird . . . . . . . . . . . . . . . . . . .9.00
3 Dale Earnhardt, Goodwrench, Kit 1088, 1992 Lumina . . . . . . . . . . . . . . . . . .30.00
3 Dale Earnhardt, Goodwrench, Kit 1090, Race Set . . . . . . . . . . . . . . . . . . . . .52.00
3 Dale Earnhardt, Goodwrench, Kit 1705, Monte Carlo . . . . . . . . . . . . . . . . . . .9.00
3 Dale Earnhardt, Goodwrench, Kit 1706, Monte Carlo, Olympics . . . . . . . . . . . . . .10.00
3 Dale Earnhardt, Goodwrench, Kit 1709, Hauler . . . . . . . . . . . . . . . . . . . . . .18.00
5 Terry Labonte, Spooky Fruit Loops, Kit 1713, Monte Carlo . . . . . . . . . . . . . . .8.00
6 Mark Martin, Valvoline, Kit 1087, 1992 T-Bird . . . . . . . . . . . . . . . . . . . . . . .9.00
12 Hut Stricklin, Raybestos, Kit 1089, 1992 Lumina . . . . . . . . . . . . . . . . . . . . . .9.00
18 Bobby Labonte, Interstate, Kit 1703, Monte Carlo . . . . . . . . . . . . . . . . . . .9.00
24 Jeff Gordon, Dupont, Kit 1702, Monte Carlo . . . . . . . . . . . . . . . . . . . . . .10.00
24 Jeff Gordon, Dupont, Kit 1704, Hauler . . . . . . . . . . . . . . . . . . . . . .20.00
24 Jeff Gordon, Jurassic Park, Kit 1710, 1997 Monte Carlo . . . . . . . . . . . . . . .7.00
26 Brett Bodine, Quaker State, Kit 1095, 1993 T-Bird . . . . . . . . . . . . . . . . . . .8.00
26 Steve Kinser, Quaker State, Kit 1095, 1995 T-Bird . . . . . . . . . . . . . . . . . . .8.00
27 Jimmy Spencer, McDonald's, Kit 1701, 1994 T-Bird . . . . . . . . . . . . . . . . . . .8.00
28 Davey Allison, Texaco, Kit 1086, 1992 T-Bird . . . . . . . . . . . . . . . . . . . . . .12.00
28 Davey Allison, Texaco, Kit 1091, Race Set . . . . . . . . . . . . . . . . . . . . . .25.00
29 Cartoon Network, Kit 1707, Monte Carlo . . . . . . . . . . . . . . . . . . . . . . .9.00
44 Kyle Petty, Hot Wheels, Kit 1712, Hauler . . . . . . . . . . . . . . . . . . . . . .13.00

68 Bobby Hamilton, Country Time, Kit 1094,
   1993 T-Bird . . . . . . . . . . . . . . . . . .9.00
88 Dale Jarrett, Quality Care, Kit 1708, 1997
   T-Bird . . . . . . . . . . . . . . . . . . .7.00
94 Bill Elliott, Thunderbat, Kit 1701, 1995
   T-Bird . . . . . . . . . . . . . . . . . . .9.00

## ORNAMENTS

Decorative ornaments constitute a relatively new category of NASCAR collectibles. Hallmark — internationally known as a leader in the greeting card and gift industry — introduced the first NASCAR driver ornament in 1997. That Jeff Gordon issue was part of Hallmark's three-piece Stock Car Champions ensemble. The company offered a Richard Petty edition the following year, and concluded the series with a Bill Elliott piece in 1999. A Dale Earnhardt commemorative ornament was released last season. Hallmark has also produced a few other NASCAR-themed ornaments.

Last year, Coca-Cola joined the fray with a collection of ornaments done as a cross promotion with Circle K Stores. Both the Coca-Cola and Hallmark brand names have attracted a huge following of collectors — folks who collect anything and everything with either logo on it. Hence, these ornaments are an item of interest to both NASCAR fans and Coca-Cola and Hallmark collectors.

### COCA-COLA

Dale Earnhardt, porcelain . . . . . . . . . . . .30.00
Bobby Labonte, porcelain . . . . . . . . . . . .10.00
Santa Claus, Porcelain . . . . . . . . . . . . . .10.00

### HALLMARK

Jeff Gordon, Stock Car Champions, 1997 .60.00
Richard Petty, Stock Car Champions, 1998 . .30.00
Bill Elliott, Stock Car Champions, 1999 . . .25.00

Jeff Gordon, Stock Car Champions, 1997 .60.00

Dale Earnhardt, Stock Car Champions, 2000 . . . . . . . . . . . . . . . . . . . . .60.00

## PORCELAIN CARS

Two years ago, porcelain race car replicas made their NASCAR debut with the introduction of Integrity Collectibles' 1:12 scale IPM Series. Less than a dozen different IPM cars have been produced to date. Quantities have been extremely limited — usually 1000 or less. Collectors should note that of the 410 No. 23 Jimmy Spencer Winston cars produced, only 205 made their way into circulation due to a factory defect.

### IPM 1:12 CAR

2 Rusty Wallace, Miller Lite . . . . . . . . .250.00

24 Jeff Gordon, Dupont . . . . . . . . . . . .250.00

3 Dale Earnhardt, Goodwrench, 1,000 . . .400.00
5 Terry Labonte, Kellogg's, 500 . . . . . . .250.00
6 Mark Martin, Valvoline, 1,200 . . . . . . .250.00
8 Dale Earnhardt, Jr. . . . . . . . . . . . . . .250.00
23 Jimmy Spencer, Winston . . . . . . . .250.00
24 Jeff Gordon, Dupont . . . . . . . . . . . .250.00
88 Dale Jarrett, Quality Care, 1999 Winston Cup
   Champion, 500 . . . . . . . . . . . . . .250.00
99 Jeff Burton, Exide . . . . . . . . . . . . .250.00

## POSTCARDS

Few racing collectibles enjoy the widespread appeal of driver postcards, also known as hand-outs or autograph cards. Nearly every NASCAR fan owns at least a couple of postcards of his or her favorite driver.

The first known NASCAR driver postcard appeared in 1952 and featured legendary Fonty Flock. Only a handful of different postcards were released during the remainder of the 1950s. Then, in 1962, *Racing Pictorial Magazine* began mass producing postcards for many of NASCAR's top stars. *Racing Pictorial* published the majority of all driver postcards released over the next dozen years.

When corporate sponsors started arriving on the scene in the mid-1970s, they quickly recognized the value of postcards as a public relations tool. Today, at least one postcard per year is produced on every driver competing regularly in NASCAR's Winston Cup, Busch Grand National, and Craftsman Truck series. In fact, most drivers release several postcards per year, promoting a variety of primary and associate sponsors.

## NASCAR BUSCH GRAND NATIONAL SERIES

### 1968

13 Charles St. John, St. John's Motors,
   3½ x 5½ . . . . . . . . . . . . . . . . . . .25.00

### 1970

12 Frank Sessoms, Chevelle, #521049,
   4¼ x 6 . . . . . . . . . . . . . . . . . . . . .30.00
97 Red Farmer, Long-Lewis Ford, 1967 Fairlane,
   #R11695, 3½ x 5½ . . . . . . . . . . . .35.00
97 Red Farmer, Long-Lewis Ford, 1963 Fairlane,
   #270197, 3½ x 5½ . . . . . . . . . . . .35.00

### 1971

97 Red Farmer, Long-Lewis Ford, 5½ x 7 . .35.00

### 1972

40 Tom Collela, Gallavan, Chevelle, #97693,
   5 x 7 . . . . . . . . . . . . . . . . . . . . . .20.00
48 Darrell Waltrip, Sterling Beer, Chevelle,
   3½ x 5 . . . . . . . . . . . . . . . . . . . .150.00

### 1973

2 L. D. Ottinger, Black Diamond Coal Co., Chevelle,
   5 x 7 . . . . . . . . . . . . . . . . . . . . . .25.00
11 Jack Ingram, J.W. Hunt, 5 x 7 . . . . . .25.00

### 1974

88 Dave Mader, Digard, Chevelle,
   3½ x 5 . . . . . . . . . . . . . . . . . . . . .25.00

### 1975

3 Boyce Eckerd, Nova, B & W, 5 x 7 . . . . .12.00
83 Bubba Tatum, Fidelity American Bank,
   4 x 6 . . . . . . . . . . . . . . . . . . . . . .20.00

### 1976

02 Dave Marcis, Shoney's, Chevelle, 5 x 7 .18.00
83 Bubba Tatum, Fidelity American Bank,
   4 x 6 . . . . . . . . . . . . . . . . . . . . . .20.00

### 1977

83 Charlie Ford, Central Fidelity Bank,
   4 x 6 . . . . . . . . . . . . . . . . . . . . . .20.00

### 1978

50 Jay Hedgecock, Hot Rod Barns, Pontiac,
   5½ x 7 . . . . . . . . . . . . . . . . . . . . .30.00
50 Morgan Shepherd, Hot Rod Barns, Pontiac,
   #P3425, 5½ x 7 . . . . . . . . . . . . . .20.00

### 1979

4 Bob Pressley, Buck Stove, blank back,
   5½ x 7 . . . . . . . . . . . . . . . . . . . . .25.00

### 1980

12 Tommy Ellis, thin stock, B & W,
   8½ x 11 . . . . . . . . . . . . . . . . . . . .10.00
16 Butch Lindley, Pontiac, #481354,
   5½ x 7 . . . . . . . . . . . . . . . . . . . . .25.00

## 1982

21 David Pearson, Chattanooga Chew, pavement, 6 x 9 . . . . . . . . . . . . . . . . . . . . . . . .15.00
21 David Pearson, Chattanooga Chew, grass, 6 x 9 . . . . . . . . . . . . . . . . . . . . . . . . .12.00
21 Morgan Shepherd, Thunderbird, 4 x 6 . . . . . . . . . . . . . . . . . . . . . .15.00

## 1983

28 Phil Parsons, Skoal, #MF-201, 5 x 7 . .15.00

## 1984

11 Jack Ingram, Skoal Bandit, 5 x 7½ . . . .15.00

## 1985

00 Sam Ard, Thomas Brothers Ham, 5 x 7 .15.00
6 Tommy Houston, Southern Biscuit, #P21171, 5 x 7 . . . . . . . . . . . . . . . . . . . . . . .10.00
6 Tommy Houston, Southern Biscuit, B & W thin stock, 5½ x 8½ . . . . . . . . . . . . . . . . .8.00
11 Jack Ingram, Skoal, 5 x 7 . . . . . . . . .12.00
14 Ronnie Silver, Coors Light, 6 x 9 . . . . .10.00
21 Larry Pearson, Chattanooga Chew, 6 x 9 .8.00

32 Dale Jarrett, Pet Dairy, 5 x 7 . . . . . . .30.00
45 Charlie Luck, Luck Stone Co., 5 x 7 . . . .7.00
63 Jimmy Hensley, Cloverdale Lumber, 4 x 7 . . . . . . . . . . . . . . . . . . . . . . .12.00
75 Brad Teague, Food Country, 6 x 9 . . . . .8.00

## 1986

00 Jimmy Hensley, Thomas Brothers Ham, 4 x 7 . . . . . . . . . . . . . . . . . . . . . . . .12.00
6 Tommy Houston, Southern Biscuit, B & W, 6 x 9 . . . . . . . . . . . . . . . . . . . . . . . .8.00
23 Donnie Allison, Jerzees, thin stock, 8½ x 11 . . . . . . . . . . . . . . . . . . . . . . .5.00
32 Dale Jarrett, Nationwide Insurance, 5 x 7 . . . . . . . . . . . . . . . . . . . . . . . .25.00

## 1987

5 Jimmy Hensley, Advance Auto Parts, 5 x 7 .8.00
6 Tommy Houston, Southern Biscuit, B & W, 6 x 9 . . . . . . . . . . . . . . . . . . . . . . . .6.00
7 Chuck Bown, Skoal, 6 x 9 . . . . . . . . . .12.00
11 Jack Ingram, Skoal, 6 x 9 . . . . . . . . .12.00
21 Larry Pearson, Chattanooga Chew, 6 x 9 .8.00
23 Donnie Allison, Jerzees, 5 x 7 . . . . . . .10.00
27 Elton Sawyer, Bill Davis Racing, B & W headshot, 7 x 5 . . . . . . . . . . . . . . . . .6.00
37 Patty Moise, Red Roof Inns, 6 x 9 . . . .10.00
77 Morgan Shepherd, Winner's Circle, 6 x 9 . . . . . . . . . . . . . . . . . . . . . . . .10.00
89 Mike Swain, Winner's Circle, 6 x 9 . . . . .8.00
89 Mike Swain, Bull Frog Knits, B & W, blank back, 5 x 7 . . . . . . . . . . . . . . . . . . . . .7.00

## 1988

2 L.D. Ottinger, Detroit Gasket, 6 x 9 . . . . .6.00
5 Jimmy Hensley, Advance Auto Parts, 7 x 5 .6.00
6 Tommy Houston, Southern Biscuit, 5½ x 8½ . . . . . . . . . . . . . . . . . . . . . . .5.00
7 Chuck Bown, Skoal, 6 x 9 . . . . . . . . . . .8.00
11 Jack Ingram, Skoal, 6 x 9 . . . . . . . . . .8.00
11 Jack Ingram, Skoal, blank back, 6 x 9 . .10.00
12 Bobby Allison, Piper, 6 x 9 . . . . . . . . .12.00
21 Larry Pearson, Chattanooga Chew, 6 x 9 .6.00
22 Rick Mast, 6 x 9 . . . . . . . . . . . . . . .6.00
5 Rob Moroso, Moroso, 8 x 10 . . . . . . . .15.00
32 Dale Jarrett, Port-A-Lube, 5½ x 7 . . . .10.00
37 Patty Moise, Crisco, 5 x 8 . . . . . . . . . .7.00
37 Patty Moise, Crisco, with coupon, 5 x 8 .7.00
56 Ronald Cooper, Speedway Sanitation, 6 x 9 . . . . . . . . . . . . . . . . . . . . . . . .6.00
63 Mike Swain, Texas Pete, #P36187, 5 x 7 .5.00
71 Dave Marcis, Gasohol, B & W, paper, 8½ x 11 . . . . . . . . . . . . . . . . . . . . . . .3.00
75 Brad Teague, Food Country, 3½ x 9 . . . .5.00

25 Rob Moroso, Moroso, 8 x 10 . . . . . .15.00

32 Dale Jarrett, Port-A-Lube, 5½ x 7 . . . . .10.00

84 Mike Alexander, Action Vans, 7 x 5 . . . .15.00
90 Ed Berrier, Cox Lumber, 5 x 7 . . . . . . .6.00
99 Tommy Ellis, 6 x 9 . . . . . . . . . . . . . . .8.00

## 1989

1 Mark Martin, Carolina Ford Dealers, 11 x 7 . . . . . . . . . . . . . . . . . . . . . .15.00
2 L.D. Ottinger, Detroit Gasket, #P45944, 5 x 7 . . . . . . . . . . . . . . . . . . . . . .5.00
5 Jimmy Hensley, Advance Auto Parts, with head-shots, 5 x 7 . . . . . . . . . . . . . . . . . . . .5.00
6 Tommy Houston, Southern Biscuit, paper, 6 x 9 . . . . . . . . . . . . . . . . . . . . . . . .5.00
7 Billy Clark, Skoal, BGN North, 6 x 9 . . . . .6.00
9 Steve Grissom, Texas Pete, 6 x 9 . . . . . . .7.00
11 Jack Ingram, Skoal, headshots left side, 6 x 9 . . . . . . . . . . . . . . . . . . . . . . .7.00
11 Jack Ingram, Skoal, headshot right side, 6 x 9 . . . . . . . . . . . . . . . . . . . . . . .7.00
17 Darrell Waltrip, Superflo, 6 x 9 . . . . . .10.00
17 Darrell Waltrip, Superflo, 10 x 8 . . . . . .15.00
25 Rob Moroso, Swisher Sweets, 6 x 9 . . .15.00
25 Rob Moroso, Swisher Sweets, different logo on back, 6 x 9 . . . . . . . . . . . . . . . . . .20.00

30 Michael Waltrip, Post Cereal, coupon paper, 9 x 6 . . . . . . . . . . . . . . . . . . . . . .5.00
30 Michael Waltrip, Post Cereal, paper, 8 x 10 . . . . . . . . . . . . . . . . . . . . . .5.00
30 Michael Waltrip, Post Cereal, thick stock, 8 x 10 . . . . . . . . . . . . . . . . . . . . . . .5.00
32-56 Robert Powell, Coca-Cola, with late model stock car, 6 x 9 . . . . . . . . . . . . . . . .5.00
36 Kenny Wallace, Cox Lumber, 6 x 9 . . . . .7.00
41 Jamie Aube, BGN North, 5 x 7 . . . . . . .8.00
42 Kyle Petty & Todd Bodine, Uniden-Ames, 6 x 4 . . . . . . . . . . . . . . . . . . . . . .5.00

44 Bobby Labonte, Winner's Circle, with late model stock car, 6 x 9 . . . . . . . . . . . . .7.00
45 Patty Moise, Freedom, 6 x 9 . . . . . . . .5.00
52 Ken Schrader, Red Baron Pizza, 5½ x 8 . . . . . . . . . . . . . . . . . . . . . .8.00
52 Ken Schrader, Red Baron Pizza, with ASA car, 6 x 11 . . . . . . . . . . . . . . . . . . . .12.00
60 Dale Shaw, Budweiser, BGN North, 5½ x 8 . . . . . . . . . . . . . . . . . . . . . .5.00
63 Chuck Bown, Nescafe, 8 x 10 . . . . . . .4.00
75 Rick Wilson, Food Country, B & W, with Shields Electronic's logo, 5 x 8 . . . . . .5.00
75 Rick Wilson, Food Country, B & W, without Shields logo, 5 x 8 . . . . . . . . . . . . . .5.00
75 Rick Wilson, Food Country, 8½ x 12½ . . .5.00
81 Bobby Hillin, Rose's, 8 x 10 . . . . . . . . .7.00
81 Bobby Hillin, Rose's, 5 x 7 . . . . . . . . . .5.00
96 Tom Peck, Silkens, 6 x 9 . . . . . . . . . . .5.00
97 Morgan Shepherd, Winner's Circle, 6 x 9 . . . . . . . . . . . . . . . . . . . . . . .7.00
99 Tommy Ellis, Goo-Goo Clusters, 6 x 9 . . .5.00
99 Tommy Ellis, Goo-Goo Clusters, 8 x 10 . .7.00

## 1990

2 L.D. Ottinger, Detroit Gasket, #P55326, 5 x 7 . . . . . . . . . . . . . . . . . . . . . .4.00
2 L.D. Ottinger, Detroit Gasket, #P52400, 5 x 7 . . . . . . . . . . . . . . . . . . . . . .4.00

6 Tommy Houston, Rose's, 6 x 9 . . . . . . . .3.00
6 Tommy Houston, B & W, headshot, 5 x 7 .3.00
7 Billy Clark, Skoal, BGN North, front view,
   6 x 9 . . . . . . . . . . . . . . . . . . . . . . . . .5.00
7 Billy Clark, Skoal, BGN North, side view,
   6 x 9 . . . . . . . . . . . . . . . . . . . . . . . . .5.00
7 Harry Gant, Skoal, Buick LeSabre, paper stock,
   8½ x 11 . . . . . . . . . . . . . . . . . . . . . . .5.00
7 Harry Gant, Skoal, Buick Regal, paper stock,
   8½ x 11 . . . . . . . . . . . . . . . . . . . . . . .5.00

8 Bobby Hamilton, 6 x 9 . . . . . . . . . . . . .40.00
9 Ben Hess, Texas Pete, without Western Steer
   logo, 6 x 9 . . . . . . . . . . . . . . . . . . . .3.00
9 Ben Hess, Texas Pete, with Western Steer logo,
   6 x 9 . . . . . . . . . . . . . . . . . . . . . . . . .3.00
9 Ben Hess, Texas Pete, printed autograph &
   Western Steer logo, 6 x 9 . . . . . . . . . .3.00
9 Morgan Shepherd & Ward Burton, Texas Pete,
   6 x 9 . . . . . . . . . . . . . . . . . . . . . . . . .3.00
11 Jack Ingram, Skoal, 6 x 9 . . . . . . . . . .4.00
12 Jeff Burton, Armour, blank back, 6 x 9 . .8.00
12 Jeff Burton, Armour, printed back, 6 x 9 .5.00
12 Jeff Burton, Armour, 8½ x 11 . . . . . . .15.00
22 Rick Mast, Raven Boats, B & W, 8 x 10 .8.00
25 Jimmy Hensley, Fast Fare, 6 x 9 . . . . . .3.00
25 Jimmy Hensley, Fast Fare, headshot,
   11 x 8 ½ . . . . . . . . . . . . . . . . . . . . . .3.00
26 Davey Johnson, Dailey's, 6 x 9 . . . . . . .3.00
26 Davey Johnson, Dailey's, B & W, headshot,
   11 x 8½ . . . . . . . . . . . . . . . . . . . . . .3.00
27 Elton Sawyer, Gwaltney, with coupon,
   5½ x 6 ¼ . . . . . . . . . . . . . . . . . . . . .3.00
31 Steve Grissom, Big Mama, 6 x 9 . . . . . .4.00
32 Dale Jarrett, Nestle's Crunch, 6 x 9 . . . .5.00
36 Kenny Wallace, Cox Lumber, 11 x 7 . . . .3.00
36 Kenny Wallace, Cox Lumber & Mac Tools,
   6 x 9 . . . . . . . . . . . . . . . . . . . . . . . . .3.00
41 Jamie Aube, Mountain Racing Buick, BGN
   North, 6 x 9 . . . . . . . . . . . . . . . . . . .4.00
44 Bobby Labonte, Penrose, blank back thin
   stock, 7 x 11 . . . . . . . . . . . . . . . . . . .7.00
44 Bobby Labonte, Penrose, blank back,
   7 x 11 . . . . . . . . . . . . . . . . . . . . . . . .7.00

44 Bobby Labonte, Penrose, printed back,
   7 x 11 . . . . . . . . . . . . . . . . . . . . . . . .5.00
46 Rick Carelli, Chesrown Racing, 6 x 9 . . .5.00
47 Kelly Moore, Jordan Lumber, BGN North, B &
   W, 4 x 6 . . . . . . . . . . . . . . . . . . . . . .3.00
59 Robert Pressley, Alliance, with tear-off,
   6 x 9 . . . . . . . . . . . . . . . . . . . . . . . . .3.00
59 Robert Pressley, Alliance, with tear-off,
   5½ x 9 . . . . . . . . . . . . . . . . . . . . . . .4.00
63 Chuck Bown, Nescafe, 8 x 10 . . . . . . .3.00
63 Chuck Bown, Nescafe, with printed autograph,
   8 x 10 . . . . . . . . . . . . . . . . . . . . . . . .3.00
72 Tracy Leslie, Detroit Gasket, 5 x 7 . . . .3.00
72 Ken Bouchard, ADAP, BGN North, 6 x 9 .3.00
75 Brad Teague, U-Can Rent, 6 x 9 . . . . . .3.00
75 Ernie Irvan, U-Can Rent, 6 x 9 . . . . . . .5.00
79 Dave Rezendes, KRR, 6 x 9 . . . . . . . . .3.00
85 Bobby Moon, 6 x 9 . . . . . . . . . . . . . .3.00
86 Dana Patten, Just Say No To Drugs, BGN
   North, 6 x 9 . . . . . . . . . . . . . . . . . . .4.00
96 Tom Peck, thin stock, 8 x 10 . . . . . . . .3.00
99 Tommy Ellis, Goo-Goo Clusters, 6 x 9 . . .3.00

## 1991

03 Peter Sospenzo, Bojangle's, 4 x 6 . . . . .5.00
05 Richard Lasater, Eclipse Racing, 5 x 7 . .3.00

JEFF GORDON AND CAROLINA FORD DEALERS THUNDERBIRD

1 Jeff Gordon, Carolina Ford Dealers, 5 x 7 .70.00
1 Tony Hirschman, Jr., SKF, BGN North,
   5 x 7 . . . . . . . . . . . . . . . . . . . . . . . .5.00
5 Jay Fogleman, Inn Keeper, 5 x 7 . . . . . . .3.00
6 Tommy Houston, Rose's, 6 x 9 . . . . . . . .3.00
7 Harry Gant, Skoal, 6 x 9 . . . . . . . . . . . .4.00
7 Billy Clark, Skoal, BGN North, 6 x 9 . . . . .4.00
7 Curtis Markham, Skoal, BGN North,
   6 x 9 . . . . . . . . . . . . . . . . . . . . . . . . .3.00
8 David Green, TIC Financial, 5 x 7 . . . . . .3.00
9 Troy Beebe, Taco Bell, 9 x 6 . . . . . . . . .3.00
10 Ernie Irvan, Mac Tools, 8 x 10 . . . . . . .5.00
10 Ernie Irvan, Mac Tools, B & W,
   6 x 3½ . . . . . . . . . . . . . . . . . . . . . . .2.00

11 Jack Ingram, Skoal Commerative, 10 x 12 . . . . . . . . . . . . . . . . . . . .4.00
12 Tommy Ellis, Wings To Go, 6 x 9 . . . . .3.00
15 Ken Schrader, Exxon Superflo, 10 x 8 . . . . . . . . . . . . . . . . . . . .10.00
18 Mike Wallace, Dailey's, 6 x 9 . . . . . . .3.00
19 Cecil Eunis, Levine Racing, 6 x 8 . . . . .4.00
23 Kenny Gragg, Hale-Holbrook, 6 x 9 . . . .4.00
23 Kenny Gragg, Hale-Holbrook, 8½ x 11 . . .4.00
25 Ricky Craven, SpeeDee Tune-up, BGN North, 5½ x 8 . . . . . . . . . . . . . . . . .3.00
25 Ricky Craven, SpeeDee Tune-up, BGN North, more info back, 5½ x 8 . . . . . . . . . . .3.00
27 Elton Sawyer, Gwaltney, 6 x 9 . . . . . . .3.00
27 Ward Burton, Gwaltney, 9 x 6 . . . . . . .4.00
29 Phil Parsons, Diamond Ridge Racing, thin stock, 10 x 8 . . . . . . . . . . . . . . . . .2.00
31 Steve Grissom, Channellock, 5¼ x 8¼ . . . . . . . . . . . . . . . . . . .3.00
31 Steve Grissom, Roddenberry's, 5½ x 8 . .4.00
32 Dale Jarrett, Nestle's Crunch, 8 x 10 . . .5.00
34 Todd Bodine, Hungry Jack Pancakes, 9 x 6 . . . . . . . . . . . . . . . . . . . . .3.00
36 Kenny Wallace, Cox Lumber, 6 x 9 . . . .3.00
36 Kenny Wallace, Cox Lumber, 7 x 12 . . . .4.00
37 Rich Burgess, R. B. Racing, 6 x 9 . . . . .3.00
38 Brad Teague, CJR Products, 6 x 9 . . . . .3.00
41 Jamie Aube, Budweiser, BGN North, 6 x 9 . . . . . . . . . . . . . . . . . . . . .4.00
41 Jamie Aube, Citgo, BGN North, 5 x 9 . . .4.00
44 Bobby Labonte, Penrose, 7 x 11 . . . . . .4.00
47 Frank Bumgardner, JFG Coffee, 6 x 9 . . .3.00
49 Ed Ferree, Ferree Racing, 6 x 9 . . . . . .3.00
51 Mike McLaughlin, Coors Extra Gold, BGN North, 5¼ x 8¼ . . . . . . . . . . . . . . .4.00
59 Robert Pressley, Alliance, with tear-off, 5½ x 8½ . . . . . . . . . . . . . . . . . . .3.00
63 Chuck Bown, Nescafe, without printed autograph, 8 x 10 . . . . . . . . . . . . . . . .3.00
63 Chuck Bown, Nescafe, with printed autograph, 8 x 10 . . . . . . . . . . . . . . . . . .3.00
69 Jeff Spraker, BGN North, thin stock, 6¼ x 10 . . . . . . . . . . . . . . . . . . .2.00
72 Tracy Leslie, Detroit Gasket, 6 x 9 . . . . .3.00
72 Mark Reed, Havoline, BGN North, B & W, 4 x 6 . . . . . . . . . . . . . . . . . . . . .3.00
75 Butch Miller, Food Country, paper stock, 8 x 10 . . . . . . . . . . . . . . . . . . . .3.00
75 Butch Miller, Food Country, paper stock, 8¼ x 12½ . . . . . . . . . . . . . . . . . .3.00
77 Shawna Robinson, Sparkey's, 6 x 9 . . . .4.00
79 Dave Rezendes, KRR Enterprises, 6 x 8 .3.00
81 Davey Johnson, Dailey's, 6 x 9 . . . . . . .3.00
83 Jeff McClure, SurfAir, 5 x 7 . . . . . . . .3.00
87 Joe Nemechek, Mother's Polish, 6 x 9 . .5.00
87 Joe Nemechek, Lozito's, blank back, 6 x 9 . . . . . . . . . . . . . . . . . . . . .7.00

87 Joe Nemechek, Lozito's, printed back, 6 x 9 . . . . . . . . . . . . . . . . . . . . .5.00
96 Tom Peck, paper stock, 8 x 10 . . . . . . .2.00
96 Tom Peck, paper stock, with Ott Brothers Logo, 8 x 10 . . . . . . . . . . . . . . . . .2.00
97 Morgan Shepherd, Texas Pete, 6 x 9 . . .3.00
98-16 Hal Goodson, Downtown Radio, with late model stock car, 5 x 7 . . . . . . . . . . .3.00

DRIVER - JEFF BURTON

99 Jeff Burton, Armour, B & W, blank back, 6 x 9 . . . . . . . . . . . . . . . . . . . .12.00
99 Jeff Burton, Armour, inset with black background, 6 x 9 . . . . . . . . . . . . . . . .5.00
99 Jeff Burton, Armour, inset with blue background, 6 x 9 . . . . . . . . . . . . . . . . .7.00

## 1992

01 Randy McDonald, GM Parts Pro Shop, BGN North, 6 x 9 . . . . . . . . . . . . . . . . .4.00
08 Bobby Dotter, 6 x 9 . . . . . . . . . . . . .3.00
08 Bobby Dotter, Jeno's Pizza, 6 x 9 . . . . .3.00
O Dick McCade, Fisher Racing, BGN North, 8 x 10 . . . . . . . . . . . . . . . . . . . .3.00
1 Jeff Gordon, Baby Ruth, 8 x 10 . . . . . .20.00
1 Jeff Gordon, Baby Ruth, with Bill Davis, B & W, 8½ x 11 . . . . . . . . . . . . . . . . . .12.00
5 Richard Lasater, Inn Keeper, 7 x 5 . . . . .2.00
5 Richard Lasater, Ranch Steak & Seafood House, 4 x 6 . . . . . . . . . . . . . . . . . . . . .3.00
6 Tommy Houston, Rose's, 6 x 9 . . . . . . .2.00
7 Harry Gant, Mac Tools, 8 x 10 . . . . . . .3.00
7 Harry Gant, Mac Tools & Shields Electric, blank back, 6½ x 9½ . . . . . . . . . . . . . . . .4.00
7 Curtis Markham, Skoal, BGN North, 6 x 9 . . . . . . . . . . . . . . . . . . . . .3.00
8 Jeff Burton, TIC Financial, 5¾ x 8 . . . . .3.00
9 Clifford Allison, QVC Memorial Card, 4 x 6 . . . . . . . . . . . . . . . . . . . .10.00
9 Joe Bessey, AC Delco, BGN North, two different backs, 6 x 9 . . . . . . . . . . . . . . . . .3.00
14 Mike Stefanik, Auto Palace, BGN North, 6 x 9 . . . . . . . . . . . . . . . . . . . . .3.00
15 Ken Schrader, AC Delco, 5½ x 8 . . . . . .4.00

CLIFFORD LAWERANCE ALLISON
October 20, 1964 - August 13, 1992

9 Clifford Allison, QVC Memorial Card, 4 x 6 . . . . . . . . . . . . . . . . . .10.00

19 Tom Peck, Ott Brothers, at Martinsville, 6 x 9 . . . . . . . . . . . . . .3.00
19 Tom Peck, Ott Brothers, 6 x 9 . . . . . . .3.00
20 Mike Wallace, 1st Ade, 6 x 9 . . . . . . .4.00
20 Jimmy Spencer, 1st Ade, 6 x 8 . . . . . .3.00
22 Ed Berrier, Greased Lighting, 6 x 9 . . . .3.00
22 Ed Berrier, Greased Lighting, paper, 11 x 8½ . . . . . . . . . . . . . . . . . .2.00
23 Kenny Gragg, Hale-Holbrook, 6 x 9 . . . .4.00
25 Shawna Robinson, Polaroid, 5½ x 8 . . . .3.00
25 Shawna Robinson, Polaroid, photo stock, 5 x 7 . . . . . . . . . . . . . . . . . . . . .2.00
Shawna Robinson, Dry Dene, B & W, headshot, 7 x 5 . . . . . . . . . . . . . . . . . . .3.00
27 Ward Burton, Gwaltney, 5¾ x 8¼ . . . . .3.00
31 Steve Grissom, Channellock, 8 x 6 . . . . .3.00
31 Steve Grissom, Roddenberry's, 6 x 8¼ . .3.00
32 Bobby Gahan, C & H Motorsports, 3½ x 6½ . . . . . . . . . . . . . . . . . . .3.00
32 Bobby Gahan, C & H Motorsports, 5½ x 8½ . . . . . . . . . . . . . . . . . . .4.00
34 Todd Bodine, Hungry Jack, in grass, 9 x 6 . . . . . . . . . . . . . . . . . . . . .2.00
34 Todd Bodine, Hungry Jack, 9 x 7 . . . . .3.00
36 Kenny Wallace, Dirt Devil, headshot, 9 x 7 . . . . . . . . . . . . . . . . . . . .3.00
36 Kenny Wallace, Dirt Devil, on top of car, 8½ x 6 . . . . . . . . . . . . . . . . . . . . . .3.00
37 Rich Burgess, Henry James BBQ, blank back, 5¼ x 8 . . . . . . . . . . . . . . . . . . . .3.00
37 Rich Burgess, Henry James BBQ, 6 x 9 .3.00
44 Bobby Labonte, Slim Jim, without printed autograph, 8 x 10 . . . . . . . . . . . . . . . .4.00
44 Bobby Labonte, Slim Jim, with printed autograph, 8 x 10 . . . . . . . . . . . . . . . .4.00
44 Bobby Labonte, Slim Jim, with books beside car, 8 x 10 . . . . . . . . . . . . . . . .6.00
47 Kelly Moore, Jordan, paper, BGN North, 4 x 6 . . . . . . . . . . . . . . . . . . . . .2.00
48 Jack Sprague, Staff America, 5 x 7 . . . .2.00

51 Mike McLaughlin, Coors Extra Gold, BGN North, 5½ x 8½ . . . . . . . . . . . . . . . .4.00
59 Robert Pressley, Alliance, with coupon, 5½ x 9 . . . . . . . . . . . . . . . . . . . .2.00
60 Mark Martin, Winn-Dixie, 8 x 10 . . . . .3.00
63 Chuck Bown, Nescafe, 6 x 9 . . . . . . . .2.00
72 Tracy Leslie, Detroit Gasket, 6 x 9 . . . .2.00
75 Butch Miller, Food Country USA, 6 x 9 . .4.00
87 Joe Nemechek, Texas Pete, 6 x 9 . . . . .3.00
92 Hut Stricklin, Stanley Tools, 6 x 9 . . . . .2.00
99 Ricky Craven, Dupont, 8¼ x 6 . . . . . . .3.00

## 1993

02 Michael Ritch, blank back, 8 x 10 . . . . .5.00
02 Michael Ritch, Hardee's, 8 x 10 . . . . . .5.00
02 Michael Ritch, photo stock, blank back, 6 x 9 . . . . . . . . . . . . . . . . . . . . . .3.00
05 Bobby Hamilton, Moen Faucets, 5 x 7 . .2.00
08 Bobby Dotter, DeWalt Tools, inset, street clothes, 8 x 10 . . . . . . . . . . . . . . . .2.00
08 Bobby Dotter, DeWalt Tools, inset, uniform, 8 x 10 . . . . . . . . . . . . . . . . . . . . .2.00
0 Dick McCabe, Fisher Snowplows, 6¼ x 9 .3.00
0 Dick McCabe, Long Pontiac & GMC Trucks, 5½ x 8½ . . . . . . . . . . . . . . . . . . . .3.00
1 Rodney Combs, Jebco Clocks, 5 x 7 . . . .4.00
1 Rodney Combs, Luxaire, 8¼ x 6 . . . . . . .3.00
1 Rodney Combs, Luxaire, 8 x 10 . . . . . . .3.00

Proudly Sponsors Ward Burton
& The #2 Hardee's Race Car In The
1993 NASCAR Busch Grand National Series

2 Ward Burton, Hardee's, 6½ x 9½ . . . . .2.00
2 Ward Burton, Hardee's, with two cars & crew, 6½ x 9½ . . . . . . . . . . . . . . . . . . . .2.00
5 Richard Lasater, Eclipse Racing, 8 x 10 . .2.00
6 Tommy Houston, Rose's, 6 x 9 . . . . . . . .1.00
6 Mike Stefanik, Valvoline / Auto Palace, BGN North, 8½ x 11 . . . . . . . . . . . . . . . .2.00
6 Mike Stefanik, headshot, BGN North, 8 x 5 . . . . . . . . . . . . . . . . . . . . . . .2.00
6 Robbie Crouch, Auto Palace, BGN North, 8½ x 11 . . . . . . . . . . . . . . . . . . . .2.00
7 Harry Gant, French's, dark version, 6 x 9 . . . . . . . . . . . . . . . . . . . . .2.00

7 Harry Gant, French's, light version, 6 x 9 . . . . . . . . . . . . . . . . . . . . . . . .2.00

7 Curtis Markham, Skoal, BGN North, 5½ x 8½ . . . . . . . . . . . . . . . . . . .3.00

8 Jeff Burton, Baby Ruth, 8 x 10 . . . . . . .3.00

9 Mike Wallace, FDP Brakes, without printed autograph, 8½ x 11 . . . . . . . . . . . . . . .2.00

9 Mike Wallace, FDP Brakes, with printed autograph, 8½ x 11 . . . . . . . . . . . . . . .2.00

14 Terry Labonte, M&W Windows, print date 8-31-92, 8 x 10 . . . . . . . . . . . . . . . .2.00

14 Terry Labonte, M&W Windows, print date 10-22-93, 8 x 10 . . . . . . . . . . . . . .2.00

14 Terry Labonte, M&W Windows, in uniform, 8 x 10 . . . . . . . . . . . . . . . . . . . . .2.00

14 Terry Labonte, M&W Windows, Carolina Builders Invitation, 4 x 6 . . . . . . . . . .7.00

14 Terry Labonte, M&W Windows, Carolina Builders, different date, 4 x 6 . . . . . . .8.00

15 Mike Rowe, O'Conner, paper, BGN North, 6 x 9 . . . . . . . . . . . . . . . . . . . . . . .2.00

15 Andy Santerre, O'Conner, BGN North, 6 x 9 . . . . . . . . . . . . . . . . . . . . . . . .2.00

19 Tom Peck, S-K Tools, without Ott Brothers logo, 6 x 9 . . . . . . . . . . . . . . . . .2.00

19 Tom Peck, S-K Tools, with Ott Brothers logo, 6 x 9 . . . . . . . . . . . . . . . . . . .2.00

20 Randy LaJoie, FinaLube, 5½ x 8½ . . . . .2.00

22 Ed Berrier, Greased Lighting, 6 x 9 . . . . .2.00

22 Ed Berrier, Greased Lighting, update sticker on back, 6 x 9 . . . . . . . . . . . . . . . . .3.00

23 Chad Little, If It's Paper, 5 x 7 . . . . . . .2.00

23 Chad Little, Bayer, 5 x 7 . . . . . . . . . . .2.00

24 Troy Beebe, Banana Boat, blank back, 8 x 10 . . . . . . . . . . . . . . . . . . . . . .4.00

25 Hermie Sadler, Virginia Is For Lovers, 5½ x 8½ . . . . . . . . . . . . . . . . . . . . .1.00

25 Hermie Sadler, Virginia Is For Lovers, 8 x 10 . . . . . . . . . . . . . . . . . . . . . .2.00

25 Hermie Sadler, Virginia Is For Lovers, fan club, 4 x 6 . . . . . . . . . . . . . . . . . . .3.00

25 Hermie Sadler, Virginia Is For Lovers, photo, 5 x 7 . . . . . . . . . . . . . . . . . . . . . .1.00

25 Hermie Sadler, Shell, photo, 5 x 7 . . . . .1.00

25 Shawna Robinson, Polaroid, photo, 5 x 7 .1.00

26 Sammy Swindell, Bull & Hanna's, 6¾ x 9¾ . . . . . . . . . . . . . . . . . . . . .3.00

27 Roy Payne, Hyde, without driver & crew chief listed on front, 8 x 10 . . . . . . . . . .2.00

27 Roy Payne, Hyde, with driver & crew chief on front, 8 x 10 . . . . . . . . . . . . . . . . .3.00

27 Dave Dion, Berlin City Ford, BGN North, 8½ x 11 . . . . . . . . . . . . . . . . . . . . .2.00

28 Tim Steele, Havoline, 5 x 7 . . . . . . . . .4.00

29 Phil Parsons, Matchbox, 5½ x 8¼ . . . . .1.00

31 Steve Grissom, Channellock, without blue border, 9 x 7 . . . . . . . . . . . . . . . . .2.00

31 Steve Grissom, Channellock, with blue bordor, 10 x 8 . . . . . . . . . . . . . . . . . . . . .3.00

31 Steve Grissom, Channellock, Color of Performance, blank back, 10 x 7 . . . . . . . . . .5.00

32 Dale Jarrett, Pic'-N-Pay Shoes, photo, 5 x 7 . . . . . . . . . . . . . . . . . . . . . . .1.00

32 Dale Jarrett, Pic'-N-Pay Shoes, 5½ x 7 . .2.00

34 Todd Bodine, Fiddle Faddle, 8 x 10 . . . . .1.00

35 Shawna Robinson, Polaroid, 9 x 7 . . . . .1.00

35 Shawna Robinson, Polaroid, with Aaron Tippin, blank back, 11 x 8½ . . . . . . . . . . . . .5.00

35 Shawna Robinson, Polaroid, Captiva Camera foldover, 3½ x 7 . . . . . . . . . . . . . . .1.00

36 Kenny Wallace, Dirt Devil, comes with Peachstate die-cast hauler, 6 x 9 . . . . . . . .10.00

38 Babe Branscombe, Central-Racing Capital, BGN North, 5½ x 8½ . . . . . . . . . . . .2.00

40 Kenny Wallace, T.G.I. Fridays, BGN North, 6 x 9¼ . . . . . . . . . . . . . . . . . . . . .2.00

41 Jamie Aube, Budweiser, BGN North, 5½ x 8 . . . . . . . . . . . . . . . . . . . . .3.00

42 Andy Hillenburg, Budget Gourmet, 6 x 9 . . . . . . . . . . . . . . . . . . . . . . .1.00

44 David Green, Slim Jim, with printed autograph, 8 x 10 . . . . . . . . . . . . . . . . . . . . .1.00

44 David Green, Slim Jim, without printed autograph, 8 x 10 . . . . . . . . . . . . . . . . .1.00

46 Steve Hoddick, Classics Inc., blank back, BGN North, 10 x 8 . . . . . . . . . . . . . . . . .2.00

48 Sterling Marlin, Cappio Iced Cappuccino, blank back, 8 x 10 . . . . . . . . . . . . . . . . .3.00

51 Mike McLaughlin, Coors Extra Gold, BGN
   North, 8 x 10 . . . . . . . . . . . . . . . . .3.00
52 Ken Schrader, AC-Delco, 8½ x 11 . . . .2.00
54 Gerald Gravel, MARC Motorsports, BGN
   North, 4 x 6 . . . . . . . . . . . . . . . . . .2.00
55 Tim Fedewa, 5 x 7 . . . . . . . . . . . . . .2.00
57 Jason Keller, Air Products, 6 x 9 . . . . .3.00
59 Robert Pressley, Alliance, 5½ x 8½ . . . .1.00
59 Robert Pressley, Alliance, photo, beside car,
   8 x 10 . . . . . . . . . . . . . . . . . . . . .2.00
59 Robert Pressley, Alliance, photo, in front of
   car, 8 x 10 . . . . . . . . . . . . . . . . . .2.00
60 Mark Martin, Winn-Dixie, 5 x 7 . . . . . .1.00
60 Mark Martin, Winn-Dixie, 8 x 10 . . . . .1.00
60 Mark Martin, Winn-Dixie, shelf talker,
   5½ x 7 . . . . . . . . . . . . . . . . . . . . .2.00
62 Larry Carroll, Wilmington Trust, BGN North,
   5½ x 7½ . . . . . . . . . . . . . . . . . . . .2.00
62 Larry Carroll, Wilmington Trust & Masters Inn,
   BGN North, 5 x 7½ . . . . . . . . . . . . .2.00
63 Chuck Bown, Nescafe, 6 x 9 . . . . . . . .1.00
63 Chuck Bown, Nescafe, 8 x 10 . . . . . . .5.00
66 Nathan Buttke, Buttke Diary, 8 x 10 . . . .1.00
66 Dan Ferri, Somerville Lumber, BGN North,
   4 x 6 . . . . . . . . . . . . . . . . . . . . . .2.00
69 Jeff Spraker, WFE, BGN North,
   6½ x 10 . . . . . . . . . . . . . . . . . . . .2.00
72 Tracy Leslie, Detroit Gasket, 6 x 9¼ . . . .1.00
72 Mark Reed, Havoline, BGN North,
   3½ x 5 . . . . . . . . . . . . . . . . . . . . .2.00
74 Jack Sprague, Staff America, without fan club
   address, 5¾ x 8 . . . . . . . . . . . . . . .1.00
74 Jack Sprague, Staff America, with fan club
   address, 5¾ x 8 . . . . . . . . . . . . . . .1.00
79 Dave Rezendes, Lipton Tea, 6 x 9 . . . . .1.00
87 Joe Nemechek, Dentyne, without fan club
   address, 5¾ x 8¼ . . . . . . . . . . . . . .1.00
87 Joe Nemechek, Dentyne, with fan club
   address, 5¾ x 8¼ . . . . . . . . . . . . . .1.00
87 Joe Nemechek, Dentyne, comes with Peachstate die-cast hauler, 5¾ x 8¾ . . . . . .8.00
92 Larry Pearson, Stanley Tools, 6 x 9 . . . .1.00
92 Larry Pearson, Stanley Tools, headshot,
   6 x 4 . . . . . . . . . . . . . . . . . . . . . .2.00
92 Larry Pearson, Stanley Tools, comes with
   Peachstate die-cast hauler, 5¾ x 8¾ . . .8.00
93 Troy Beebe, Banana Boat, 8½ x 11 . . . .3.00
93 Troy Beebe, Banana Boat, blank back,
   8½ x 11 . . . . . . . . . . . . . . . . . . . .5.00
97 Joe Bessey, Auto Palace & AC-Delco,
   5 x 7 . . . . . . . . . . . . . . . . . . . . . .2.00
97 Joe Bessey, Auto Palace & AC-Delco,
   6 x 9 . . . . . . . . . . . . . . . . . . . . . .2.00
97 Joe Bessey, Auto Palace & AC-Delco, hauler,
   6 x 9 . . . . . . . . . . . . . . . . . . . . . .3.00
98 Jim Bown, Rose Auto Wrecking, 6 x 9 . .2.00
99 Ricky Craven, Dupont, 8 x 10 . . . . . . . .2.00

## 1994

03 David Bonnett, Voyager, error Bonnet,
   5½ x 8½ . . . . . . . . . . . . . . . . . . . .7.00
03 David Bonnett, Voyager, correct Bonnett,
   5½ x 8½ . . . . . . . . . . . . . . . . . . . .3.00
04 Kenny Wallace, T.G.I. Fridays, BGN North,
   6½ x 8¾ . . . . . . . . . . . . . . . . . . . .3.00
04 Kenny Wallace, T.G.I. Fridays, with coupon,
   BGN North, 6½ x 8¾ . . . . . . . . . . . .7.00
05 Tommy Ellis, Moen, 5 x 7 . . . . . . . . . .2.00
06 Clay Brown, Stone Litho, 6 x 9 . . . . . . .2.00
07 George Crenshaw, Campbells, 6½ x 9½ .2.00
08 Bobby Dotter, Hyde Tools, single, 8 x 10 .1.00
08 Bobby Dotter, Hyde Tools, engaged,
   8 x 10 . . . . . . . . . . . . . . . . . . . . .2.00
08 Bobby Dotter, Hyde Tools, Engine Doctor, 8 x 10 .5.00
09 Jabe Jones, RP Racing To Fight Blindness,
   5 x 7 . . . . . . . . . . . . . . . . . . . . . .2.00
09 Tom Rosati, Tic Tac, BGN North,
   8½ x 11 . . . . . . . . . . . . . . . . . . . .2.00
0 Mike Garvey, UniFirst Uniforms, 5 x 7 . . . .3.00
0 Dick McCabe, Fisher Snowplows, BGN North,
   6¼ x 9 . . . . . . . . . . . . . . . . . . . . .2.00
0 Dick McCabe, Long Pontiac-GMC, BGN North,
   5½ x 8½ . . . . . . . . . . . . . . . . . . . .2.00
1 Mike Stefanik, Luxaire, 8 x 10 . . . . . . . .3.00
1 Jeff Neal, Luxaire, 8 x 10 . . . . . . . . . .2.00
2 Ricky Craven, Dupont, 8 x 10 . . . . . . . .2.00
2 Ricky Craven, Dupont & SpeeDee, 5 x 7½ .2.00
4 Bryan Goewey, Primetime Vans, BGN North,
   8½ x 10 . . . . . . . . . . . . . . . . . . . .3.00
5 Richard Lasater, Key Alert, 7 x 9½ . . . . .2.00
6 Tommy Houston, Red Devil Paints, 6 x 9 . .2.00
6 Robbie Crouch, Auto Palace, BGN North,
   6 x 9 . . . . . . . . . . . . . . . . . . . . . .3.00
6 Robbie Crouch, Valvoline, BGN North, 6 x 9 .3.00
7 Harry Gant, Team Manheim, without printed
   autograph, 7 x 5 . . . . . . . . . . . . . . .3.00
7 Harry Gant, Team Manheim, with printed autograph, 7 x 5 . . . . . . . . . . . . . . . . . .3.00
7 Harry Gant, Team Manheim, color, 8 x 10 .5.00
7 Harry Gant, Team Manheim, B & W,
   8 x 10 . . . . . . . . . . . . . . . . . . . . .5.00
7 Curtis Markham, Skoal, BGN North,
   5½ x 8½ . . . . . . . . . . . . . . . . . . . .2.00
7 Dale Shaw, Skoal, BGN North, 5½ x 8½ . .2.00
8 Kenny Wallace, TIC Financial, 7½ x 10. . . .2.00
8 Kenny Wallace, Square D, blank back,
   7½ x 10 . . . . . . . . . . . . . . . . . . . .2.00
8 Kenny Wallace, Red Dog, 8 x 10 . . . . . . .5.00
8 Mike Zuidema, Ocean Spray, side view,
   4 x 6 . . . . . . . . . . . . . . . . . . . . . .1.00
8 Mike Zuidema, Ocean Spray, angled view,
   4 x 6 . . . . . . . . . . . . . . . . . . . . . .1.00
9 Mike Wallace, FDP Brakes & Fred Beck Pontiac,
   blue ink, 6 x 9 . . . . . . . . . . . . . . . .3.00

9 Mike Wallace, FDP Brakes & Fred Beck Pontiac, black ink, 6 x 9 . . . . . . . . . . . . . . .3.00

14 Terry Labonte, MW Windows, 8 x 10 . . .2.00

14 Terry Labonte, MW Windows, 6 x 9 . . . .3.00

14 Mike Stefanik, Auto Palace & Sunoco, BGN North, 5½ x 8½ . . . . . . . . . . . . . . .2.00

15 Dirk Stephens, Greased Lighting, 6 x 9 . .2.00

15 Dirk Stephens, headshot, 6 x 9 . . . . . . .2.00

15 Dirk Stephens, 6 x 9 . . . . . . . . . . .2.00

15 Andy Santerre, O'Conner, BGN North, 6 x 9 . . . . . . . . . . . . . . . . . . . .2.00

16 Chad Chaffin, 31-W Insulation, Action, 5 x 7 . . . . . . . . . . . . . . . . . . . .3.00

16 Chad Chaffin, 31-W Insulation, posed, 5 x 7 . . . . . . . . . . . . . . . . . . . .3.00

16 Stub Fadden, NAPA, BGN North, 5¼ x 8 .3.00

17 Robbie Reiser, error, name misspelled, 5 x 7 . . . . . . . . . . . . . . . . . . . .4.00

17 Robbie Rieser, correct, 5 x 7 . . . . . . . .2.00

18 Scott Deware, Pace Trailers, BGN North, 5½ x 8½ . . . . . . . . . . . . . . . . . .2.00

19 Kirk Shelmerdine, 5½ x 8½ . . . . . . . . . .2.00

19 Rich Fogal, Jr., Burnham, 5½ x 8½ . . . .3.00

21 Morgan Shepherd, Techna Lube, blank back, 10 x 8 . . . . . . . . . . . . . . . . . .15.00

21 Morgan Shepherd, Cheerwine, printed autograph, 8 x 10 . . . . . . . . . . . . . . . . . .1.00

21 Morgan Shepherd, Cheerwine, without printed autograph, 8 x 10 . . . . . . . . . . . . . . . .1.00

21 Eric Bodine, Great American, BGN North, 5 x 7 . . . . . . . . . . . . . . . . . . . .2.00

22 Ed Berrier, Embers Charcoal, photo stock, 10 x 8 . . . . . . . . . . . . . . . . . . . .1.00

22 Ed Berrier, Embers Charcoal, photo stock, car only, 8 x 10 . . . . . . . . . . . . . . . .1.00

22 Jeff Berry, TAD Technical Institute, BGN North, 5½ x 8½ . . . . . . . . . . . . . . . .2.00

23 Chad Little, Bayer Select, 8 x 10⅛ . . . . .1.00

23 Chad Little, Harris-Teeter, blank back, 5½ x 8½ . . . . . . . . . . . . . . . . . .2.00

23 Chad Little, Harris-Teeter, printed back, 5½ x 8½ . . . . . . . . . . . . . . . . . .1.00

23 Jerry Marguis, BGN North, 5½ x 8½ . . .2.00

25 Hermie Sadler, Virginia Is For Lovers, 8 x 10 .1.00

25 Hermie Sadler, Virginia Is For Lovers, white border, thin stock, 8½ x 11 . . . . . . . .2.00

25 John Swanson, New England Pontiac Dealers, BGN North, 5½ x 8½ . . . . . . . . . . .2.00

27 Roy Payne, Motorsports Designs, 5 x 7 .2.00

28 Ernie Irvan, Mac Tools, 5½ x 8½ . . . . .3.00

28 Ernie Irvan, Mac Tools, art card by Sam Bass, 5¾ x 4¾ . . . . . . . . . . . . . . . . . .2.00

29 Steve Grissom, Channellock, 9 x 6 . . . . .2.00

29 Steve Grissom, Channellock, blank back, 8 x 10 . . . . . . . . . . . . . . . . . . . .5.00

29 Phil Parsons, Matchbox, 5½ x 8 . . . . . .1.00

31 Tom Peck, Channellock, 9 x 6 . . . . . . . .2.00

32 Dale Jarrett, Pic-N-Pay Shoes, 5½ x 7 . .2.00

33 Bobby Labonte, Dentyne, light version, 6 x 9 . . . . . . . . . . . . . . . . . . . .2.00

33 Bobby Labonte, Dentyne, dark version, 6 x 9 . . . . . . . . . . . . . . . . . . . .2.00

34 Mike McLaughlin, Fiddle-Faddle, B & W, blank back, 10 x 7 . . . . . . . . . . . . . . . .7.00

34 Mike McLaughlin, Fiddle-Faddle, 8 x 10 . .1.00

34 Mike McLaughlin, Hyde Tools, with logo on back, 8 x 10 . . . . . . . . . . . . . . . .3.00

34 Mike McLaughlin, Hyde Tools, with hat on back, 8 x 10 . . . . . . . . . . . . . . . .2.00

34 Glenn Sullivan, Christy's, BGN North, 5½ x 8½ . . . . . . . . . . . . . . . . . .2.00

35 No Driver, Milacron, 8 x 10 . . . . . . . . . .1.00

38 Elton Sawyer, Red Carpet Lease, fold-over, 11 x 8½ . . . . . . . . . . . . . . . . . .10.00

38 Elton Saywer, Red Carpet Lease, 5½ x 8½ . . . . . . . . . . . . . . . . . .2.00

38 Elton Saywer, Red Carpet Lease, drawing, 8 x 10 . . . . . . . . . . . . . . . . . . . .1.00

38 Babe Branscombe, Central, BGN North, by hauler, 5½ x 8½ . . . . . . . . . . . . . . .3.00

38 Babe Branscombe, Central, BGN North, on track, 5½ x 8½ . . . . . . . . . . . . . . .3.00

40 Patty Moise, Dial & Purex, Hickory Preview, paper, 4 x 6 . . . . . . . . . . . . . . . .4.00

40 Patty Moise, Dial & Purex, at Speedway Club, 6 x 9 . . . . . . . . . . . . . . . . . . . .2.00

40 Patty Moise, Dial & Purex, with crew chief, 6 x 9 . . . . . . . . . . . . . . . . . . . .2.00

40 Patty Moise, Dial & Purex, in victory lane, schedule back, 6 x 9 . . . . . . . . . . .2.00

38 Elton Sawyer, Red Carpet Lease, fold-over, 11 x 8½ . . . . . . . . . . . . . . . . . . . . . .10.00

40 Patty Moise, Dial & Purex, In Victory Lane, info back, 6 x 9 . . . . . . . . . . . . . . . . . . . . .4.00

40 Patty Moise, Dial & Purex, headshot, paper, 7½ x 5 . . . . . . . . . . . . . . . . . . . . . . . .3.00

41 Johnny Smith, White House, B & W, 8 x 10 . . . . . . . . . . . . . . . . . . . .3.00
41 Johnny Smith, White House, 5½ x 8½ . . .2.00
41 Joey McCarthy, Rent-A-Wreck, BGN North, 4 x 6 . . . . . . . . . . . . . . . . . . . . . .2.00
42 Andy Hillenburg, Budget Gourmet, 6 x 9 . . . . . . . . . . . . . . . . . . . . . . . .1.00
42 Andy Hillenburg, Budget Gourmet, with crew chief on back, 10 x 8 . . . . . . . . . . .1.00
42 Andy Hillenburg, Budget Gourmet, without crew chief on back, 10 x 8 . . . . . . . . .3.00
43 Rodney Combs, French's, Black Flag, Charlotte on wall, 5¼ x 10¼ . . . . . . . . . . . . . .1.00
43 Rodney Combs, French's, Black Flag, no Charlotte on wall, 5¼ x 10¼ . . . . . . . . . . .1.00
44 David Green, Slim Jim, with printed autograph, 8 x 10 . . . . . . . . . . . . . . . . . . . . . .1.00
44 David Green, Slim Jim, without printed autograph, 8 x 10 . . . . . . . . . . . . . . . . . . . .1.00
46 Shawna Robinson, Polaroid, 6 x 9 . . . . .1.00
46 Marty Noll, Qik Joe & Milazzo, BGN North, 8 x 10 . . . . . . . . . . . . . . . . . . . . . .2.00
47 Kerry Teague, Gals, 5 x 8½ . . . . . . . . .2.00
51 Eddie Goodson, RE Goodson Construction, 5 x 7 . . . . . . . . . . . . . . . . . . . . . . . .3.00
52 Ken Schrader, AC-Delco, printed back, 8½ x 11 . . . . . . . . . . . . . . . . . . . . . .2.00
52 Ken Schrader, AC-Delco, blank back, 8½ x 11 . . . . . . . . . . . . . . . . . . . . . .3.00
52 Ken Schrader, Eastman, photo, 8 x 10 . .2.00
53 Greg Clark, paper stock, 7 x 5 . . . . . . .1.00
54 Gerald Gravel, Downeast Drilling, BGN North, 5 x 7 . . . . . . . . . . . . . . . . . . . . . . . .2.00
55 Tim Fedewa, 1993 front, 1994 back, 5 x 7 . . . . . . . . . . . . . . . . . . . . . . . .2.00
55 Tim Fedewa, 6 x 9 . . . . . . . . . . . . . .2.00
56 Martin Truex, Blount Seafood, BGN North, 5½ x 8½ . . . . . . . . . . . . . . . . . . . . . . . .3.00
57 Jason Keller, Budget Gourmet, 8 x 10 . .1.00
59 Dennis Setzer, Alliance, blank back, white name, 5½ x 8½ . . . . . . . . . . . . . . . . .3.00
59 Dennis Setzer, Alliance, white name with coupon, 5½ x 8½ . . . . . . . . . . . . . . . .1.00
59 Dennis Setzer, Alliance, red name with coupon, 5½ x 8½ . . . . . . . . . . . . . . . . .3.00
60 Mark Martin, Winn-Dixie, 5 x 7 . . . . . . .1.00
60 Mark Martin, Winn-Dixie, 8 x 10 . . . . . .1.00
61 Mike Olsen, BGN North, 5½ x 8½ . . . . .2.00
61 Mike Olsen, NAPA, BGN North, 4½ x 7¼ .2.00
63 Jim Bown, Luck's, 6 x 9 . . . . . . . . . . .1.00
63 Jim Bown, Lysol, 6 x 9 . . . . . . . . . . .1.00
64 Jimmy Spencer, Dura Lube, blank back, 8½ x 11 . . . . . . . . . . . . . . . . . . . . . .3.00
69 Brad Noffsinger, Robbie Stanley Tribute, 8¼ x 10 . . . . . . . . . . . . . . . . . . . . . .2.00
69 Jeff Spraker, WFE Challenge, BGN North with border, 5½ x 8½ . . . . . . . . . . . . . . . .1.00

69 Jeff Spraker, WFE Challenge, BGN North without border, 5½ x 8½ . . . . . . . . . .1.00
71 Kevin LePage, Vermont Teddy Bear, 6 x 9 .1.00
71 Bobby Dragon, Talarico, BGN North, 5½ x 8½ . . . . . . . . . . . . . . . . .2.00
72 Tracy Leslie, Detroit Gasket, 7 x 9 . . . . .1.00
73 Brian Ross, BGN North, 6½ x 9 . . . . . .2.00
74 Johnny Benson, Staff America, 8 x 10 . .3.00
75 Doug Heveron, Food Country, 5¾ x 9 . . .1.00
76 Tom Bolles, BGN North, two cars, 5½ x 8½ . . . . . . . . . . . . . . . . .1.00
76 Tom Bolles, BGN North, on track, 5½ x 8½ . . . . . . . . . . . . . . . . .1.00
79 Dave Rezendes, Lipton, 6½ x 9½ . . . . . .1.00
82 Derrike Cope & Mike Laws, Sports World, 11 x 8½ . . . . . . . . . . . . . . . . .10.00
82 Derrick Cope, Sports World, 11 x 8½ . . .3.00
86 Tim Steele, H. S. Die, 5 x 7 . . . . . . . .3.00
87 Joe Nemechek, BellSouth, 11 x 8½ . . . .2.00
87 Joe Nemechek, Mighty Auto Parts, 11 x 8½ . . . . . . . . . . . . . . . . .3.00
88 Mike Skinner, Kentucky Fried Chicken, 10 x 12 . . . . . . . . . . . . . . . . .3.00
91 Stanton Barrett, Wendy's, 5½ x 7 . . . . .2.00
92 Larry Pearson, Stanley Tools, 5 x 7 . . . .1.00
92 Larry Pearson, Stanley Tools, with gloss, 8 x 10 . . . . . . . . . . . . . . . . .1.00
92 Larry Pearson, Stanley Tools, without gloss, 8 x 10 . . . . . . . . . . . . . . . . .1.00
95 Jack Baldwin, Royal Oak, 5½ x 8½ . . . . .3.00
95 Brian Donley, BGN North, 3½ x 5½ . . . .2.00
96 Stevie Reeves, Clabber Girl, 8 x 10 . . . .1.00
97 Joe Bessey, BellSouth, BGN North, 6 x 9 .2.00
99 Robert Pressley, Luxaire, 8½ x 11 . . . . .3.00

## 1995

00 Buckshot Jones, Crown-Fiber, 8 x 10 . . .3.00
00 Buckshot Jones, Longhorn Steakhouse, Zip Code 320136, 8 x 10 . . . . . . . . . . .3.00
00 Buckshot Jones, Longhorn Steakhouse, Zip Code 30136, 8 x 10 . . . . . . . . . . . .2.00
03 David Bonnett, Hummingbird, 5½ x 8½ . .2.00
03 Gary Green, BGN North, 5½ x 8½ . . . . .1.00
03 Gary Green, BGN North, paper, 8½ x 11 .1.00
07 George Crenshaw, Badcock Home Furnishings, 6½ x 9½ . . . . . . . . . . . . . . . . .2.00
08 Bobby Dotter, Hyde Tools, 8 x 10 . . . . .1.00
08 Bobby Dotter, Hyde Tools, 10 x 8 . . . . .1.00
09 Jabe Jones, Zeebs Racing, 5 x 7 . . . . .2.00
09 Mike Stefanik, Burnham Racing, BGN North, 5½ x 8½ . . . . . . . . . . . . . . . . .2.00
1 Hermie Sadler, DeWalt Tools, photo, 6 x 8 .1.00
1 Hermie Sadler, DeWalt Tools, No #, 8 x 10 .2.00
1 Hermie Sadler, DeWalt Tools, #LDWRACEPC, 8 X 10 . . . . . . . . . . . . . . . . .1.00
1 Hermie Sadler, Peebles, 11 x 8½ . . . . . . .3.00

1 Hermie Sadler, Peebles, 10 x 8 . . . . . . .2.00
1 Joe Bessey, Delco-Remy, BGN North, 8½ x 11 . . . . . . . . . . . . . . . . .3.00
2 Ricky Craven, Dupont, 8 x 10 . . . . . . .2.00
2 Ricky Craven, Krytox By Dupont, 8 x 10 . .2.00
2 Dan Meservey Jr., Mobil 1, BGN North, 5 x 8 . . . . . . . . . . . . . . . . .3.00
3 Jeff Green, GM Goodwrench, 6 x 9 . . . . .3.00
4 Jeff Purvis, Kodak, with coupon, 5½ x 8¾ .2.00
5 Brad Teague, Food Country, B & W, blank back, 5½ x 8¼ . . . . . . . . . . . . . . . . .2.00
6 Tommy Houston, Red Devil Paint, 6 x 9 . . .1.00
7 Stevie Reeves, Clabber Girl, error, blue car, 8 x 10 . . . . . . . . . . . . . . . . .7.00
7 Stevie Reeves, Clabber Girl, correct, teal car, 8 x 10 . . . . . . . . . . . . . . . . .2.00
7 Dale Shaw, Skoal, BGN North, 8 x 10 . . . .3.00
7 Dale Shaw, Skoal, BGN North, 8½ x 11 . .2.00
8 Kenny Wallace, Red Dog, 8 x 10 . . . . . .1.00
8 Kenny Wallace, Red Dog & Square D, yellow writing, 8 x 10 . . . . . . . . . . . . . . . . .4.00
8 Kenny Wallace, Red Dog & Square D, blue & yellow writing, 8 x 10 . . . . . . . . . . . . . . . . .3.00
8 Kenny Wallace, Red Dog & Square D, blue & yellow writing, 4 x 6 . . . . . . . . . . . . . . . . .3.00
8 Tom Rosati, Ocean Spray, BGN North, 8½ x 11 . . . . . . . . . . . . . . . . .3.00
8 Beaver Dragon, Ocean Spray, BGN North, 8½ x 11 . . . . . . . . . . . . . . . . .3.00
8 Kim Baker, Ocean Spray, BGN North, paper, 8½ x 11 . . . . . . . . . . . . . . . . .2.00
9 Russ Galindo, Behind the Wheel Video, car only, 5½ x 8½ . . . . . . . . . . . . . . . . .1.00
9 Russ Galindo, Behind the Wheel Video, with driver, 5½ x 8½ . . . . . . . . . . . . . . . . .1.00
9 Russ Galindo, Behind the Wheel Video, 8 x 10 . . . . . . . . . . . . . . . . .1.00
10 Bill Duggan, Polaris, BGN North, paper, 8½ x 11 . . . . . . . . . . . . . . . . .1.00
12 Mike Dillion, Kennametal, 6 x 8½ . . . . .3.00
12 Mike Dillion, Kennametal, tri-fold, 4½ x 6 . .5.00
12 Mike Dillion, Kennametal, fold-over, 5½ x 8½ . . . . . . . . . . . . . . . . .10.00
12 Mike Dillion, Kennametal, tri-fold, 5½ x 8½ . . . . . . . . . . . . . . . . .8.00
14 Terry Labonte, MW Windows, 10 x 8 . . .2.00
15 Jerry Nadeau, Buss Fuse, 5 x 7¼ . . . . .3.00
15 Derek Lynch, O'Conner, BGN North, 6 x 9 .2.00
15 Derek Lynch, GMC Truck, BGN North, 5¼ x 8½ . . . . . . . . . . . . . . . . .2.00
16 Stub Fadden, NAPA, BGN North, 5 x 7½ .2.00
17 Robbie Reiser, FDP Brakes, 4½ x 7 . . . .2.00
18 L.W. Miller, UniFirst Uniforms, 6 x 9 . . . .2.00
18 Todd Bodine & Sammy Kershaw, UniFirst Uniforms, 6 x 9 . . . . . . . . . . . . . . . . .2.00
18 Todd Bodine & Randy Porter, UniFirst Uniforms, 6 x 9 . . . . . . . . . . . . . . . . .2.00

**NASCAR All Pro 300**

*Charlotte Motor Speedway
October 7, 1995
TV: TBS, 12:45pm EST*

12 Mike Dillion, Kennametal, fold-over, 5½ x 8½ . . . . . . . . . . . . . . . . . . . . . . .10.00

18 Randy Porter, UniFirst Uniforms, 6 x 9 . .2.00
18 Scott DeWare, Pace Trailers, BGN North, 5¼ x 8¼ . . . . . . . . . . . . . . . . . . . . . . .2.00
20 Jimmy Spencer, FINA, No Gloss, 5½ x 8½ .3.00
20 Jimmy Spencer, FINA, with gloss, 5½ x 8½ . . . . . . . . . . . . . . . . . . . . . . .2.00
20 Jimmy Spencer, FINA, with Fina logo, 5½ x 8½ . . . . . . . . . . . . . . . . . . . . . . .2.00
20 Jimmy Spencer, FINA & Lance, error, car cut off, 5½ x 8½ . . . . . . . . . . . . . . . . . . .3.00
20 Jimmy Spencer, FINA & Lance, whole car, 5½ x 8½ . . . . . . . . . . . . . . . . . . . . . . .2.00
21 Morgan Shepherd, Cheerwine, 8½ x 11 .2.00
21 Eric Bodine, Great American, thin stock, BGN North, 5 x 7 . . . . . . . . . . . . . . . . . . .3.00
22 Jeff Barry, TAD Resources, BGN North, 5 x 8 . . . . . . . . . . . . . . . . . . . . . . . . .2.00
23 Chad Little, Bayer, without coupon, 8 x 10 . . . . . . . . . . . . . . . . . . . . . . . . .1.00
23 Chad Little, Bayer, with coupon, 8 x 10 . .1.00
23 Chad Little, Bayer, 5 x 7 . . . . . . . . . . .3.00
23 Chad Little, Harris Teeter, 6 x 9 . . . . . .1.00
23 Jerry Marquis, BGN North, 5½ x 8½ . . .2.00
25 Kirk Shelmerdine, Big Johnson, 5½ x 8½ .2.00
25 Johnny Rumley, Big Johnson, B & W, photo stock, 6 x 8 . . . . . . . . . . . . . . . . . . . .1.00
25 Johnny Rumley, Big Johnson, with coupon, 5½ x 8½ . . . . . . . . . . . . . . . . . . . . . .1.00
25 John Swanson, New England Pontiac Dealers, BGN North, 5½ x 8½ . . . . . . . . . . . . . .2.00
26 Kenny Kagle, Suburban Propane, 5½ x 8½ . . . . . . . . . . . . . . . . . . . . . . .2.00
29 Steve Grissom, Channellock, 6 x 8 . . . .2.00
30 Denny Dole, BGN North, 6 x 9 . . . . . . .3.00
32 Dale Jarrett, Mac Tools, 8 x 10 . . . . . .1.00
34 Mike McLaughlin, French's & Black Flag, fold-over, 4 x 10 . . . . . . . . . . . . . . . . . .1.00
34 Mike McLaughlin, French's & Black Flag, fold-over, blank back, 4 x 10 . . . . . . . . . . .3.00

34 Mike McLaughlin, Wheels Auto Stores, 5¼ x 8⅛ . . . . . . . . . . . . . . . . . . . . . .2.00
34 Glenn Sullivan, Christy's, BGN North, 8½ x 11 . . . . . . . . . . . . . . . . . . . . . .3.00
35 Doug Heveron, Cincinnati Milacron, 8½ x 11 . . . . . . . . . . . . . . . . . . . . . .1.00
36 Shawna Robinson, CPR Motorsports, blank back, 8 x 10 . . . . . . . . . . . . . . . . . . .8.00
36 Shawna Robinson, CPR Motorsports, printed back, 8 x 10 . . . . . . . . . . . . . . . . . . .1.00
38 Elton Sawyer, Red Carpet Lease, 6¼ x 11 .1.00
38 Babe Branscombe, Racing Capital, BGN North, 7½ x 11 . . . . . . . . . . . . . . . . . . . .2.00
39 Tim Bender, Carstar, paper, 8½ x 11 . . .1.00
40 Patty Moise, Purex & Dial, 6 x 9 . . . . . .1.00
41 Mark Green, Brewco, 6 x 8 . . . . . . . . .3.00
41 Green Brothers, Brewco, 6 x 8 . . . . . . .3.00
42 Bobby Hamiltom & Kyle Petty, Band & Shower to Shower, 6 x 9 . . . . . . . . . . . . . . . . .2.00
43 Rodney Combs, Hulk Hogan, 6 x 9 . . . . .2.00
43 Rodney Combs, Snapper, with NASCAR truck, 6 x 9 . . . . . . . . . . . . . . . . . . . . . . .2.00
44 David Green, Slim Jim, without printed autograph, 8 x 10 . . . . . . . . . . . . . . . . . .1.00
44 David Green, Slim Jim, with printed autograph, 8 x 10 . . . . . . . . . . . . . . . . . . . . . .1.00
44 Andy Santerre, Lube Plus, BGN North, 5½ x 8½ . . . . . . . . . . . . . . . . . . . . . .2.00
46 Elliott Sadler, Veeder-Root, photo, 6 x 8 .3.00
47 Jeff Fuller, Sunoco, photo, 5 x 7 . . . . . .1.00
47 Jeff Fuller, Sunoco, 8½ x 11 . . . . . . . .1.00
47 Kelly Moore, Tic-Tac, BGN North, 5¼ x 8 .2.00
47 Kelly Moore, Tic-Tac, BGN North, flag background, 5¼ x 8 . . . . . . . . . . . . . . . . .2.00
49 Scott Kilby, Arndt-Herman, error, 6 x 8½ .3.00
49 Scott Kilby, Arndt-Herman, sticker, 6 x 8½ . . . . . . . . . . . . . . . . . . . . . . .2.00
49 Scott Kilby, Arndt-Herman, correct, 6 x 8½ . . . . . . . . . . . . . . . . . . . . . . .1.00
51 Jim Bown, Luck's, 6 x 9 . . . . . . . . . . .1.00
51 Jerry Marquis, Wheels & Castrol, BGN North, 8⅛ x 10½ . . . . . . . . . . . . . . . . . . . .3.00
51 Jerry Marquis, Wheels & Castrol, BGN North, flag background, 8⅛ x 10½ . . . . . . . . .3.00
52 Ken Schrader, AC Delco, 8 x 10 . . . . . .1.00
53 Marc Madison, S-Line, BGN North without headshot insert, 5½ x 8¼ . . . . . . . . . .7.00
53 Marc Madison, S-Line, BGN North with headshot insert, 5½ x 8¼ . . . . . . . . . . . . . .3.00
54 Gerald Gravel, S & J Transportion, BGN North, 5¼ x 8¼ . . . . . . . . . . . . . . . . . . . .2.00
55 Tim Fedewa, Lemon Chill, paper, 8½ x 11 .1.00
55 Tim Fedewa, paper, 8½ x 11 . . . . . . . .1.00
55 Tim Fedewa, paper, name on side, 8½ x 11 . . . . . . . . . . . . . . . . . . . . . .1.00
55 Tim Fedewa, white, green, yellow car, paper, 8½ x 11 . . . . . . . . . . . . . . . . . . . . . .1.00

55 Tim Fedewa, Dynamark Security Centers, paper, 8½ x 11 . . . . . . . . . . . . . . .1.00
55 Tim Fedewa, Meijer, blank back, 5½ x 8½ .1.00
55 Tim Fedewa, Meijer, printed back, 5½ x 8½ . . . . . . . . . . . . . . . . . .1.00
55 Tim Fedewa, D-R Racing, 5½ x 8½ . . . . .1.00
55 Tim Fedewa, D-R Racing, 5½ x 8½ . . . . .1.00
55 Tim Fedewa, Florida State University, Seminoles, 6 x 9 . . . . . . . . . . . . . . . .2.00
56 Martin Truex, Blount Seafoods, BGN North, 8 x 10 . . . . . . . . . . . . . . . . . . . .2.00
56 Martin Truex, Wynn's, BGN North, 5½ x 8½ . . . . . . . . . . . . . . . . . . .2.00
57 Jason Keller, Budget Gourmet, B & W, 10 x 8 . . . . . . . . . . . . . . . . . . . .3.00
57 Jason Keller, Budget Gourmet, 8 x 10 . .1.00
59 Dennis Setzer, Alliance, with coupon, 5½ x 8½ . . . . . . . . . . . . . . . . . .1.00
59 Lou Rettenmeier, BGN North, 5 x 7 . . . .2.00
60 Mark Martin, Winn-Dixie, 5 x 7 . . . . . .1.00
60 Mark Martin, Winn-Dixie, 10 x 8 . . . . . .1.00
60 Mark Martin, Winn-Dixie, Shelftalker, 7 x 11 . . . . . . . . . . . . . . . . . . . .1.00
61 Danny Edwards, headshot, 6 x 4 . . . . . .1.00
63 Curtis Markham, Lysol, 6 x 8¾ . . . . . . .1.00
64 Dirk Stephens, Dura Lube, B & W, 5¼ x 7¼ . . . . . . . . . . . . . . . . . . .2.00
64 Dirk Stephens, Dura Lube, 6 x 9 . . . . . .1.00
64 Randy LaJoie, Dura Lube, 6 x 9 . . . . . .2.00
65 Rob Wilson, Scituate Concrete Pipe, BGN North, 5 x 7½ . . . . . . . . . . . . . . . . .2.00
66 Johnny Chapman, NC State University, 6 x 9 . . . . . . . . . . . . . . . . . . . .2.00
67 Tom Peck, Spartan, paper, 8½ x 11 . . . .1.00
67 Tom Peck, Spartan, 6 x 8 . . . . . . . . . .2.00
67 Tom Peck, Dave Marcis Day, 5½ x 8½ . .5.00
68 Chris Diamond, J & L Motors, 6 x 8½ . .1.00
69 Jeff Spraker, WFE Challenge, BGN North, 5 x 8 . . . . . . . . . . . . . . . . . . . .2.00
71 Kevin LePage, Vermont Teddy Bear, 6 x 9 .1.00
71 Bobby Dragon, Talarico, BGN North, 5½ x 8½ . . . . . . . . . . . . . . . . . .2.00
72 Tracy Leslie, Detroit Gasket, 7¼ x 10 . . .1.00
74 Johnny Benson, Lipton, 10 x 8 . . . . . .2.00
74 Johnny Benson, Lipton, fold-over, 5 x 8 . .1.00
75 Rick Wilson, Food Country, 5½ x 8½ . . . .1.00
76 Tom Bolles, BGN North, 5½ x 8½ . . . . .2.00
80 Toby Porter, Greased Lighting, 6 x 9 . . . .1.00
82 Derrick Cope, FDP Brakes, photo stock, 8 x 10 . . . . . . . . . . . . . . . . . . . .3.00
87 Joe Nemechek, BellSouth Mobility, 6 x 9 .2.00
87 Ron Thiel, Jr., Levitz Furniture, BGN North, 8 x 10 . . . . . . . . . . . . . . . . . . . .3.00
88 Pete Orr, Farmer's Choice, photo, 5 x 7 .1.00
88 Pete Orr, Farmer's Choice, 8 x 10 . . . .2.00
90 Mike Wallace, Duron Paints, 8 x 10 . . . .2.00
92 Larry Pearson, Stanley Tools, 5 x 7 . . . .1.00

82 Derrick Cope, FDP Brakes, photo stock, 8 x 10 . . . . . . . . . . . . . . . . . . . .3.00

92 Larry Pearson, Stanley Tools, revised May 1, 1995, 5 x 7 . . . . . . . . . . . . . . .1.00
93 Troy Beebe, Taco Bell, 5½ x 8½ . . . . . . .1.00
95 John Tanner, Cat Motorsports, 8½ x 10¼ .3.00
95 No Driver, Cat Motorsports, 8½ x 10¼ . .2.00
98 Keith Lamell, Lamell Lumber, BGN North, 5¼ x 8⅛ . . . . . . . . . . . . . . . . . . .3.00
98 Brian Donley, BGN North, 8½ x 11 . . . . .3.00
99 Phil Parsons, Luxaire, with coupon, 8½ x 10 . . . . . . . . . . . . . . . . . . . .1.00

## 1996

00 Buckshot Jones, Aquafresh, 8 x 10 . . . .1.00
00 Buckshot Jones, Aquafresh, 10 x 8 . . . .3.00
00 Buckshot Jones, Aquafresh, art card by Jeanne Barnes, 6 x 4 . . . . . . . . . . . . .2.00
02 Michael Ritch, East Carolina University Pirates, photo stock, 8 x 10 . . . . . . . . . . . . . . .3.00

1 Hermie Sadler, DeWalt Tools & Buckeye Do-It Center 4 x 6 . . . . . . . . . . . . . . . . . .1.00
1 Hermie Sadler, DeWalt Tools & Don Cox, color, 8 x 10 . . . . . . . . . . . . . . . . . . . .5.00
1 Hermie Sadler, DeWalt Tools & Don Cox, B & W, 8 x 10 . . . . . . . . . . . . . . . . . . . .2.00

1 Hermie Sadler, DeWalt Tools & Don Cox, B & W,
5½ x 4 . . . . . . . . . . . . . . . . . . . . . .1.00
1 Hermie Sadler, DeWalt Tools & Peebles,
6 x 4¼ . . . . . . . . . . . . . . . . . . . . . . .1.00
1 Hermie Sadler, DeWalt Tools & Peebles,
10 x 8¼ . . . . . . . . . . . . . . . . . . . . . .2.00
1 Hermie Sadler, DeWalt Tools, 10 x 8 . . . .1.00
2 Ricky Craven, Dupont, Krytox, large Dupont logo,
8 x 10 . . . . . . . . . . . . . . . . . . . . . . .1.00
2 Ricky Craven, Dupont, Krytox, small Dupont
logo, 8 x 10 . . . . . . . . . . . . . . . . . . . .1.00
3 Jeff Green, GM Goodwrench, 8 x 10 . . . .2.00
4 Jeff Purvis, Phoenix Racing, 8 x 10 . . . . .1.00
4 Brad Bennett, BGN North, without headshot
insert, 6 x 9 . . . . . . . . . . . . . . . . . . . .3.00
4 Brad Bennett, BGN North, with headshot insert,
6 x 9 . . . . . . . . . . . . . . . . . . . . . . . .4.00
5 Terry Labonte, Bayer & Actron, 8 x 10 . . .2.00
5 Terry Labonte, Bayer & Actron, Virginia Lottery,
11 x 8½ . . . . . . . . . . . . . . . . . . . . . .5.00
5 Brad Teague, Food Country, B & W, printed
back, 5½ x 8¼ . . . . . . . . . . . . . . . .1.00
6 Tommy Houston, Suburban Propane,
8 x 10 . . . . . . . . . . . . . . . . . . . . . . .1.00
6 Tommy Houston, Suburban Propane, with
coupon, 8 x 10 . . . . . . . . . . . . . . . . .2.00
6 Robbie Crouch, Auto Palace, BGN North,
8½ x 11 . . . . . . . . . . . . . . . . . . . . . .3.00
7 Brandon Butler, Skoal, BGN North, posed, no
car, 8¼ x 5¼ . . . . . . . . . . . . . . . . .2.00
7 Brandon Butler, Skoal, BGN North,
5¼ x 8¼ . . . . . . . . . . . . . . . . . . . . .2.00
8 Kenny Wallace, Red Dog Beer, 8 x 10 . . .1.00
9 Joe Bessey, Delco, Remy, car & hauler,
8½ x 11 . . . . . . . . . . . . . . . . . . . . . .1.00
10 Phil Parsons, Channellock, 6 x 8 . . . . . .2.00
10 Phil Parsons, Channellock, with tear-off,
6 x 8 . . . . . . . . . . . . . . . . . . . . . . . .1.00
10 Phil Parsons, Channellock, without tear-off,
6 x 8 . . . . . . . . . . . . . . . . . . . . . . . .1.00
10 Phil Parsons, Channellock, 5 x 5 . . . . . .5.00
12 Michael Waltrip, MW Windows,
8 x 10 . . . . . . . . . . . . . . . . . . . . . . .1.00
13 Ted Christopher, LesCare, BGN North,
6 x 9 . . . . . . . . . . . . . . . . . . . . . . . .1.00
14 Patty Moise, Dial & Purex, missing glad on
back, 6 x 9 . . . . . . . . . . . . . . . . . . . .1.00
14 Patty Moise, Dial & Purex, corrected,
6 x 9 . . . . . . . . . . . . . . . . . . . . . . . .2.00
15 Tony Stewart, Mariah Vision 3, 8 x 10 .25.00
15 Jerry Marquis, O'Conner GMC-Buick, BGN
North, 5 x 8 . . . . . . . . . . . . . . . . . . .2.00
16 Stub Fadden, NAPA, BGN North,
8 x 10 . . . . . . . . . . . . . . . . . . . . . . .1.00
17 Robbie Reiser, Triton Trailers, 4½ x 7 . . .1.00
17 Bob Brunell, Brunell Asphalt, BGN North,
5 x 8 . . . . . . . . . . . . . . . . . . . . . . . .2.00

15 Tony Stewart, Mariah Vision 3, 8 x 10 .25.00

21 Eric Bodine, Glacier Ridge, BGN North,
5¼ x 8¼ . . . . . . . . . . . . . . . . . . . . .2.00
23 Chad Little, John Deere, 8 x 10 . . . . . . .1.00
23 Chad Little, John Deere, Spokane Hoopfest,
7 x 10 . . . . . . . . . . . . . . . . . . . . . . .4.00
24 Mike Harmon, MedPartners, 8½ x 11 . .2.00
26 Derrike Cope, Badcock, fan club, Cornelius,
NC, 8½ x 11 . . . . . . . . . . . . . . . . . . .1.00
26 Derrike Cope, Badcock, fan club, Jamestown,
NC, 8½ x 11 . . . . . . . . . . . . . . . . . . .1.00
26 Derrike Cope, Badcock, glossy, different back,
8½ x 11 . . . . . . . . . . . . . . . . . . . . . .1.00
28 Hut Stricklin, Smokey Mountain Chew,
6 x 9 . . . . . . . . . . . . . . . . . . . . . . . .1.00
28 Bill Penfold, BGN North, 5¼ x 8¼ . . . . .2.00
29 Steve Grissom, World Championship
Wrestling, Diamond Ridge, teal, 8 x 10 .1.00
29 Steve Grissom, World Championship Wrestling,
Diamond Ridge, yellow, 8 x 10 . . . . . . . .1.00
29 Steve Grissom, World Championship
Wrestling, 8½ x 11 . . . . . . . . . . . . . . .1.00
29 No Driver, World Championship Wrestling,
8½ x 11 . . . . . . . . . . . . . . . . . . . . . .1.00
29 No Driver, World Championship Wrestling With
Sting, photo stock, 10 x 8 . . . . . . . . . .2.00
29 Dave Dion, 1996 BGN North Champion,
8¼ x 10¼ . . . . . . . . . . . . . . . . . . . .3.00
32 Dale Jarrett, Band-Aid, 8 x 9 . . . . . . . .1.00
32 Dale Jarrett, Band-Aid, 4 x 6 . . . . . . . .1.00
34 Mike McLaughlin, Royal Oak, Stocks For Tots
photo, 8 x 10 . . . . . . . . . . . . . . . . . . .1.00
34 Mike McLaughlin, Royal Oak, thin red stripe on
front, 8 x 10 . . . . . . . . . . . . . . . . . . .1.00
34 Mike McLaughlin, Royal Oak, thick red stripe
on front, 8 x 10 . . . . . . . . . . . . . . . . .1.00
34 Mike McLaughlin, Team Goulds, printed back,
8 x 10 . . . . . . . . . . . . . . . . . . . . . . .1.00

23 Chad Little, John Deere, Spokane Hoopfest, 7 x 10   .4.00

34 Mike McLaughlin, Team Goulds, Hospitality
Pass – Dover, 8 x 13 . . . . . . . . . . . . .4.00
34 Mike McLaughlin, Team Goulds, Hospitality
Pass – Bristol, 8 x 13 . . . . . . . . . . .4.00
34 Mike McLaughlin, Team Goulds, Hospitality
Pass – Watkins Glen, 8 x 13 . . . . . . .4.00
34 Mike McLaughlin, Team Goulds, Hospitality
Pass – Richmond, 8 x 13 . . . . . . . . .4.00
34 Glenn Sullivan, Brioschi, BGN North,
6 x 9 . . . . . . . . . . . . . . . . . . . . . .2.00
35 Mike Laughlin Jr., NWTF, with coupon,
8 x 10 . . . . . . . . . . . . . . . . . . . .1.00
37 Mark Green, Timber Wolf, 6 x 9 . . . . .2.00
37 Mark Green, Timber Wolf, 8 x 10 . . . .1.00
38 Dennis Setzer, Lipton Tea, 8 x 10 . . . . .1.00
38 No Driver, Lipton Tea, blank back, 8 x 10  .1.00
40 Tim Fedewa, Kleenex, no Tim on front,
6 x 9 . . . . . . . . . . . . . . . . . . . . . .3.00
40 Tim Fedewa, Kleenex, Tim on front, 6 x 9 .1.00
43 Rodney Combs, Lance, purple car,
5½ x 8½ . . . . . . . . . . . . . . . . . . .2.00
43 Rodney Combs, Lance, blue car, name in big
letters, 5½ x 8½ . . . . . . . . . . . . . . .1.00
43 Rodney Combs, Lance, blue car, name in small
letters, 5½ x 8½ . . . . . . . . . . . . . . .1.00
44 Bobby Labonte, Shell, 8 x 10 . . . . . . . .1.00
44 Andy Santerre, Wynn's, BGN North,
5¾ x 8¼ . . . . . . . . . . . . . . . . . . .2.00
46 Elliott Sadler, DeWalt Tools, photo, 6 x 8 .1.00
47 Jeff Fuller, Sunoco, 8 x 10 . . . . . . . . . .1.00
47 Kelly Moore, Tic Tac, BGN North, 8 x 10 .2.00
48 Randy Porter, UniFirst Uniforms, 6 x 9 . .1.00
49 Kyle Petty, National Wrestling Organization,
8 x 10 . . . . . . . . . . . . . . . . . . . . .2.00
50 Jimmy Kitchens, Healthsource, fold-over,
5½ x 8½ . . . . . . . . . . . . . . . . . . .5.00
51 Jim Bown, Luck's, 6 x 9 . . . . . . . . . . .1.00

51 Jim Bown, Barbasol, 6 x 9 . . . . . . . . . .1.00
51 Mike Stefanik, Burnham, BGN North,
8 x 10 . . . . . . . . . . . . . . . . . . . . .1.00
52 Ken Schrader & Andy Hillenburg, AC-Delco,
8 x 10 . . . . . . . . . . . . . . . . . . . . .1.00
53 Greg Clark, 8 x 6 . . . . . . . . . . . . . . .1.00
55 Brad Leighton, Coed Naked with tear-off, BGN
North, 5½ x 8½ . . . . . . . . . . . . . . . .1.00
56 Martin Truex, Blount Seafood, BGN North,
8 x 10 . . . . . . . . . . . . . . . . . . . . .1.00
57 Jason Keller, Slim Jim, B & W photo,
5 x 7 . . . . . . . . . . . . . . . . . . . . . .1.00
57 Jason Keller, Slim Jim, with printed autograph,
8 x 10 . . . . . . . . . . . . . . . . . . . . .1.00
57 Jason Keller, Slim Jim, without printed autograph, 8 x 10 . . . . . . . . . . . . . . . . .1.00
57 Jason Keller, Slim Jim, with printed autograph,
dark red car, 8 x 10 . . . . . . . . . . . . .1.00
57 Jason Keller, Slim Jim, without printed autograph, dark red car, 8 x 10 . . . . . . . . .1.00
60 Mark Martin, Winn-Dixie, 5 x 7 . . . . .1.00
60 Mark Martin, Winn-Dixie, 8 x 10 . . . . . .1.00
60 Dale Shaw, R.D. Roy Transport, paper, BGN
North, 5 x 8½ . . . . . . . . . . . . . . . . .1.00
60 Dale Shaw, Ocean Spray, BGN North,
5¼ x 8¼ . . . . . . . . . . . . . . . . . . .1.00
61 Mike Olsen, Little Trees, BGN North,
8 x 10 . . . . . . . . . . . . . . . . . . . . .1.00
61 Mike Olsen, Little Trees, with green e-mail
number, BGN North, 8 x 10 . . . . . . . . .1.00
61 Mike Olsen, Little Trees, with black e-mail
number, BGN North, 8 x 10 . . . . . . . . .1.00
63 Curtis Markham, Lysol, 6 x 8½ . . . . . . .1.00
64 Bobby Dotter, Dura Lube, 6 x 9 . . . . . .4.00
64 Dick Trickle, Dura Lube, 6 x 9 . . . . . . .1.00
65 Dean Chrystal, CRE-Graphix, BGN North,
5¼ x 7½ . . . . . . . . . . . . . . . . . . .1.00

66 Nathan Buttke, Duragloss, 7 x 9 . . . . . .2.00
66 Nathan Buttke, Duragloss, Car Quest Auto Parts, 7 x 9 . . . . . . . . . . . . . . . . . . .2.00
67 Tom Peck, Spartan Motors, Dave Marcis Day, 5½ x 8½ . . . . . . . . . . . . . . . . . . . . .4.00
69 Jeff Spraker, Mariah Vision 3, BGN North, 5¼ x 8¼ . . . . . . . . . . . . . . . . . . . .2.00
70 Dale Fischlein, Murphy Motorsports, B & W, 5½ x 8½ . . . . . . . . . . . . . . . . . . . .2.00
70 Dale Fischlein, Hummingbird, 5½ x 8½ . .2.00
72 Mike Dillion, Detroit Gaskets, 7¼ x 10 . .1.00
72 Mike Dillion, Detroit Gaskets, without Vic Kangas, crew chief, 7¼ x 10 . . . . . . .1.00
74 Randy LaJoie, FINA, 6 x 9 . . . . . . . . . .1.00
75 Doug Heveron, Food Country, 5½ x 8½ . .1.00
75 Brad Teague, Food Country, 6 x 9 . . . . .1.00
76 Tom Bolles, BGN North, 6 x 9 . . . . . . . .2.00
77 Bryan Wall, Mountaineer, BGN North, 5 x 8 . . . . . . . . . . . . . . . . . . . . . . . .2.00
81 Todd Bodine, Pro Motion, photo stock, 8 x 10 . . . . . . . . . . . . . . . . . . . . . .2.00
81 Todd Bodine, Cape Canaveral, photo stock, 8 x 10 . . . . . . . . . . . . . . . . . . . . . .2.00
81 Todd Bodine, Cape Canaveral, with tear-off, 8½ x 11 . . . . . . . . . . . . . . . . . . . .1.00
81 Todd Bodine, Cape Canaveral, with tear-off, 7 x 8½ . . . . . . . . . . . . . . . . . . . . .1.00
81 Dan Maservey, Mobil 1, color copy, BGN North, 5 x 7½ . . . . . . . . . . . . . . . . .1.00
81 Dan Maservey, Mobil 1, color copy, BGN North, 8¼ x 10¼ . . . . . . . . . . . . . . .1.00
83 Sterling Marlin, Trane, color paper copy, two different, 8 x 10 . . . . . . . . . . . . . . . .1.00
83 Keith Lamell, Auto Solutions, BGN North, 5¼ x 8¼ . . . . . . . . . . . . . . . . . . . .2.00
85 Shane Hall, 6 x 9 . . . . . . . . . . . . . . .1.00
87 Joe Nemechek, BellSouth Mobility, 1995 front with NOKIA added, 6¼ x 8¾ . . . . . . . .2.00
88 Kevin LePage, Farmer's Choice, 8¼ x 10 .1.00

88 Kevin LePage, Farmer's Choice, Hydro logo on front, 8¼ x 10 . . . . . . . . . . . . . . . .3.00
88 Kevin LePage, Farmer's Choice, name added to front, 8¼ x 10 . . . . . . . . . . . . . . .1.00

90 Mike Wallace, Duron Paints, 8 x 10 . . . .1.00
90 Herb Drugg, BGN North, 5¼ x 8¼ . . . . .2.00
92 Larry Pearson, Stanley Tools, 5 x 7 . . .1.00
93 Troy Beebe, ILOCO Mart, 5½ x 8½ . . . . .1.00

93 Troy Beebe, J.B. Hunt, flatbed, 4¼ x 6 . .5.00
94 Ron Barfield, New Holland, 8½ x 11 . . . .1.00
94 Ron Barfield, New Holland, car only, 3 x 6 . . . . . . . . . . . . . . . . . . . . . . . .1.00
94 Ron Barfield, New Holland, with Ron, 3 x 6 . . . . . . . . . . . . . . . . . . . . . . . .1.00
94 Ron Barfield, New Holland, cars on track, 3 x 6 . . . . . . . . . . . . . . . . . . . . . . . .1.00
94 Ron Barfield, New Holland, photo stock, five different, 8 x 10 . . . . . . . . . . . . . . . . .1.00
95 David Green, Caterpillar, 8 x 10 . . . . . . .1.00
96 Stevie Reeves, Clabber Girl, blank back, 8 x 10 . . . . . . . . . . . . . . . . . . . . . .3.00
96 Stevie Reeves, Clabber Girl, printed back, 8 x 10 . . . . . . . . . . . . . . . . . . . . . .1.00
96 Stevie Reeves, Clabber Girl, with coupon, 8 x 10 . . . . . . . . . . . . . . . . . . . . . .1.00
99 Glenn Allen, Luxaire, tear-off with drawings, 8½ x 10 . . . . . . . . . . . . . . . . . . . . .1.00
99 Glenn Allen, Luxaire, tear-off with photos, 8½ x 10 . . . . . . . . . . . . . . . . . . . . .1.00

## 1997

00 Buckshot Jones, Aquafresh, 10 x 8 . . . .1.00
00 Buckshot Jones, Aquafresh, headshot, 10 x 8 . . . . . . . . . . . . . . . . . . . . . .1.00
00 Buckshot Jones, Aquafresh, Shelftalker, 9 x 12 . . . . . . . . . . . . . . . . . . . . . .2.00
00 Buckshot Jones, Aquafresh, with coupons, 8 x 6 . . . . . . . . . . . . . . . . . . . . . . .1.00
06 Chuck Lachance, BGN North, 5¾ x 8¼ . .1.00
08 Bobby Dotter, Lube Tech, with #68 NASCAR Truck, 8 x 10 . . . . . . . . . . . . . . . . . .1.00
1 Hermie Sadler, DeWalt Tools, 8 x 10 . . . .1.00
1 Hermie Sadler, DeWalt Tools, 4¼ x 5½ . . .4.00
1 Hermie Sadler, Peebles, 10 x 8 . . . . . . .2.00
2 Ricky Craven, Raybestos, 8 x 10 . . . . . . .1.00

3 Steve Park, AC Delco, 1 of 5,000, 8 x 10   . .12.00

2   Ricky Craven, Raybestos, checkered sleeve jacket, 8 x 10 . . . . . . . . . . . . . . . . . .1.00
3   Steve Park, AC Delco, 1 of 5,000, 8 x 10 . . . . . . . . . . . . . . . . . . . . . . . .12.00
3 Steve Park, AC Delco, 8 x 10 . . . . . . . . .1.00

3 Steve Park, Thunder Valley, "Race Steve Park," 4 x 6 . . . . . . . . . . . . . . . . . . . . . . . . . .15.00
4 Dale Shaw, Phoenix, 8 x 10 . . . . . . . . .1.00
5 Terry Labonte, Alka-Seltzer & Bayer, 8 x 10 .1.00
5 Terry Labonte, Alka-Seltzer & Bayer, different crew Info, 8 x 10 . . . . . . . . . . . . . . . .1.00
5 Steve Holzhausen, Howes, BGN North, 5½ x 7 . . . . . . . . . . . . . . . . . . . . . .2.00
6 Joe Bessey, Power Team, 8 x 10 . . . . . . .1.00
6 Robbie Crouch, Auto Palace, BGN North, 8 x 10 . . . . . . . . . . . . . . . . . . . . . .2.00
7 Bobby Dragon, Skoal, BGN North, 8 x 10 .1.00
8 Jeff Green, photo, 8 x 10 . . . . . . . . . . .2.00
8 Jeff Green, 8 x 10 . . . . . . . . . . . . . . . .1.00

9 Jeff Burton, Track Gear, thin stock, 8½ x 11 . . . . . . . . . . . . . . . . . . . . . .1.00
9 Jeff Burton, Track Gear, thick stock, 8½ x 11 . . . . . . . . . . . . . . . . . . . . . .1.00
10 Phil Parsons, Channellock, with coupon, 6 x 8 . . . . . . . . . . . . . . . . . . . . . . . .1.00
10 Phil Parsons, Channellock, Honeywell, 7 x 9 . . . . . . . . . . . . . . . . . . . . . . . .2.00
11 Jimmy Foster, photo, 7 x 5 . . . . . . . . . .1.00
11 Jimmy Foster, Outdoor Life & SpeedVision, 6 x 9 . . . . . . . . . . . . . . . . . . . . . . . .1.00
11 Jimmy Foster, Northeastern Supply, 6 x 9 . . . . . . . . . . . . . . . . . . . . . . . .2.00
12 Kenny Wallace, Gray Bar & St. Louis Post Dispatch, 8½ x 11 . . . . . . . . . . . . . . .3.00
13 Ted Christopher, LesCare, BGN North, 8 x 10 . . . . . . . . . . . . . . . . . . . . . .1.00
14 Patty Moise, Pure Silk, photo, 5 x 7 . . . .2.00
15 Jerry Marquis, O'Conner GMC, BGN North, 5 x 8 . . . . . . . . . . . . . . . . . . . . . . . .1.00
16 Stub Fadden, NAPA, BGN North, 10 x 8 .1.00
17 Tim Bender, Kraft, 6 x 9 . . . . . . . . . . . .1.00
17 Tim Bender, Kraft & Bull's Eye, 6 x 9 . . .2.00
17 Bob Brunell, Brunell Asphalt & Camoplast, BGN North, 5 x 8 . . . . . . . . . . . . . . . .1.00
17 Matt Kenseth, Kraft & Bull's Eye, 6 x 9 . .4.00
20 Blaise Alexander, Rescue Engine Formula, 5½ x 8½ . . . . . . . . . . . . . . . . . . . . . .2.00
21 Michael Waltrip, Band-Aid, 8 x 10 . . . . .1.00
21 Eric Bodine, Bully Hill Vineyards, BGN North, 6 x 9 . . . . . . . . . . . . . . . . . . . . . . . .2.00
21 Eric Bodine, Bully Hill Vineyards, name in block letters, BGN North, 6 x 9 . . . . . . . . .4.00

17 Matt Kenseth, Kraft & Bull's Eye, 6 x 9 . . . . . . .4.00

22 Scott Lagasse', Super Sports Racing, B & W, headshot, 5½ x 8½ . . . . . . . . . . . . . .2.00
22 Scott Lagasse', Pest OFFense, 5½ x 8½ .1.00
25 Jamie Aube, New England Pontiac Dealers, BGN North, 8½ x 11 . . . . . . . . . . . . . .1.00
26 Blaise Alexander, Rescue Engine Formula, 5½ x 8½ . . . . . . . . . . . . . . . . . . . . .2.00
29 Elliott Sadler, photo, 8 x 10 . . . . . . . . .2.00
29 Elliott Sadler, 8 x 10 . . . . . . . . . . . . . .1.00
29 Elliott Sadler, Phillips 66 Performance Team, paper stock, 5 x 7 . . . . . . . . . . . . . . .2.00
29 Elliott Sadler, Phillips 66 Performance Team, 8 x 10 . . . . . . . . . . . . . . . . . . . . . .1.00
29 Elliott Sadler, Phillips 66 & Trop Artic, 8½ x 11½ . . . . . . . . . . . . . . . . . . . . .1.00
29 Dave Dion, Berlin City Ford, BGN North, 8 x 10 . . . . . . . . . . . . . . . . . . . . . . .1.00
30 Denny Doyle, Sta-Rite Pumps, BGN North, 6 x 9 . . . . . . . . . . . . . . . . . . . . . . . .1.00
32 Dale Jarrett, White Rain, 8½ x 11 . . . . .1.00
33 Tim Fedewa, Kleenex, 6 x 9 . . . . . . . . .1.00
34 Mike McLaughlin, Royal Oak, 621 Victories, 8 x 10 . . . . . . . . . . . . . . . . . . . . . . .1.00
34 Mike McLaughlin, Royal Oak, 62 Victories, 8 x 10 . . . . . . . . . . . . . . . . . . . . . . .2.00
34 Mike McLaughlin, Team Goulds, 8 x 10 . .1.00
35 Lyndon Amick, Team Amick, Daytona 300, photo stock, 10 x 8 . . . . . . . . . . . . . . .2.00
35 Lyndon Amick, Team Amick, photo stock, 10 x 8 . . . . . . . . . . . . . . . . . . . . . . .2.00
36 Todd Bodine, Stanley Tools, with coupon, 6¼ x 9½ . . . . . . . . . . . . . . . . . . . . .1.00
37 Mark Green, Timber Wolf, 1996 front, 1997 back, 8 x 10 . . . . . . . . . . . . . . . . . . .1.00
37 Mark Green, Timber Wolf, 1996 front, 1997 back, more info, 8 x 10 . . . . . . . . . . .2.00

38 Elton Sawyer, Barbasol, 10 x 12 . . . . . .1.00
38 Babe Branscombe, Polaris, BGN North, 5¼ x 8¼ . . . . . . . . . . . . . . . . . . . . .2.00
40 David Bonnett, Dunlop Golf, 8 x 10 . . . . .3.00
41 Joey McCarth, Rent-A-Wreck, 4 x 6 . . . .1.00
42 Tom Cary Jr., Aircraft Supply Co., BGN North, 4 x 9 . . . . . . . . . . . . . . . . . . . . . . . .2.00
43 Rodney Combs, Lance, 6 x 9 . . . . . . . .1.00
43 Dennis Setzer, Lance, 6 x 9 . . . . . . . . .1.00
44 Bobby Labonte, Shell, 8 x 10 . . . . . . . .1.00
44 Tony Stewart, Shell, 8 x 10 . . . . . . . . . .3.00
44 Andy Santerre, Monro Muffler-Brake, BGN North, 8½ x 11 . . . . . . . . . . . . . . . . .1.00
44 Andy Santerre, Monro Muffler-Brake, left side, BGN North, 8 x 10 . . . . . . . . . . . . . . .1.00
44 Andy Santerre, Monro Muffler-Brake, right side, BGN North, 8 x 10 . . . . . . . . . . . .1.00
45 Greg Sacks, Hunter's Specialties, 5½ x 8½ . . . . . . . . . . . . . . . . . . . . .1.00
45 Greg Sacks, Hunter's Specialties, coupon and different front, 5½ x 8½ . . . . . . . . . . .1.00
45 Jeff Fuller, Hunter's Specialties, with tear-off, 5½ x 8¾ . . . . . . . . . . . . . . . . . . . . .1.00
45 Franklin Butler, BGN North, 5 x 8 . . . . . .1.00
47 Jeff Fuller, Sunoco, 8 x 10 . . . . . . . . . .1.00
47 Jeff Fuller, Sunoco, 360 Communications, 7½ x 11 . . . . . . . . . . . . . . . . . . . . . .1.00
47 Robert Pressley, 360 Racing & The Cellular Store, 7¼ x 9 . . . . . . . . . . . . . . . . . .1.00
47 Kelly Moore, Tic Tac, BGN North, 8 x 10 . . . . . . . . . . . . . . . . . . . . . .2.00
48 Randy Porter, UniFirst Uniforms, 6 x 9 . .1.00
49 Kyle Petty, National Wrestling Organization, with coupon, 8 x 10 . . . . . . . . . . . . . .1.00
51 Mike Stefanik, Burnham Boilers, BGN North, 8 x 10 . . . . . . . . . . . . . . . . . . . . . . .1.00

55 Brett Roubiniek, Best Cigar, BGN North, 5 x 8 . . . . . . . . . . . . . . . . . . . .2.00
57 Jason Keller, Slim Jim, 8 x 10 . . . . . . .1.00
59 Lou Rettenmeier, Mobil, BGN North, 5 x 7¼ . . . . . . . . . . . . . . . . . . .1.00
60 Mark Martin, Winn Dixie, 8 x 10 . . . . . .1.00
60 Mark Martin, Winn Dixie, 5 x 7 . . . . . .1.00
60 Dale Shaw, Ocean Spray, BGN North, 5½ x 8 . . . . . . . . . . . . . . . . . . .1.00
61 Mike Olsen, Little Trees, name in thin letters, 8 x 10 . . . . . . . . . . . . . . . . . . .2.00
61 Mike Olsen, Little Trees, name in thick letters, 8 x 10 . . . . . . . . . . . . . . . . . . .2.00
63 Tracy Leslie, Lysol, 7 x 9½ . . . . . . . . .1.00
63 Jake Raudabaugh, Squeezit Racing, BGN North, 5 x 7 . . . . . . . . . . . . . . . . .1.00
64 Dick Trickle, Dura Lube, headshot, 9 x 6 .1.00
66 Perry Tripp, 5 x 7½ . . . . . . . . . . . . .3.00
72 Mike Dillon, Detroit Gasket, 7¼ x 10 . . .1.00
74 Randy LaJoie, FINA, 6 x 9 . . . . . . . . .1.00
74 Randy LaJoie, FINA, St. Louis Post Dispatch, 8½ x 11 . . . . . . . . . . . . . . . . . .5.00
74 Tracy Gordon, Merit Motorsports, BGN North, 5½ x 8 . . . . . . . . . . . . . . . . . . .2.00
74 Tracy Gordon, Balance, BGN North, 5 x 8 .2.00
75 Rick Wilson, Food Country, without gloss, 6 x 9 . . . . . . . . . . . . . . . . . . . .2.00
75 Rick Wilson, Food Country, with gloss, 6 x 9 . . . . . . . . . . . . . . . . . . . .1.00
77 Dennis Setzer, Mark III Financial Group, 6 x 9 . . . . . . . . . . . . . . . . . . . .4.00
77 Jeff McClure, Team Lear, light color, 6¼ x 9 . . . . . . . . . . . . . . . . . .4.00
77 Jeff McClure, Team Lear, dark color, 6¼ x 9 . . . . . . . . . . . . . . . . . .2.00
77 No Driver, Team Lear, 6¼ x 9 . . . . . . .3.00
77 Bryan Wall, Mercury Mountaineer, BGN North, 5 x 8 . . . . . . . . . . . . . . . . . . . .3.00
77 Bryan Wall, Auto City, BGN North, 8 x 10 .1.00
77 Bryan Wall, Auto City, blank back, BGN North, 8 x 10 . . . . . . . . . . . . . . . . . .1.00
77 Bryan Wall, Player's, BGN North, 8 x 10 . . . . . . . . . . . . . . . . . .2.00
78 Nathan Buttke, CarQuest Auto Parts, 7 x 9 . . . . . . . . . . . . . . . . . . . .1.00
78 Nathan Buttke, CarQuest, St. Louis Post Dispatch, 8½ x 11 . . . . . . . . . . . . . .5.00
81 Dan Meservey, Mobil 1, BGN North, 8½ x 11 . . . . . . . . . . . . . . . . . .2.00
83 Wayne Grubb, Link-Belt Racing, 5 x 7 . . .1.00
85 Shane Hall, Luck's, with coupon, 8 x 10 .1.00
85 Shane Hall, Bama Jams & Jellies, 8 x 10 .1.00
87 Joe Nemechek, BellSouth Mobility, 6 x 9 . . . . . . . . . . . . . . . . . . . .2.00
87 Joe Nemechek, BellSouth Mobility, more info, 6 x 9 . . . . . . . . . . . . . . . . . . . .1.00
88 Kevin LePage, Hype Energy, 8 x 10 . . . .1.00

88 Kevin LePage, Hype Energy, Busch preview, 8½ x 11 . . . . . . . . . . . . . . . . . .25.00

88 Kevin Schwantz, Ryder, blank back, 8 x 10 . . . . . . . . . . . . . . . . . . .3.00
89 Johnny Chapman, Alarm South, 7 x 9 . . .2.00
90 Herb Drugg, BGN North, As Fast As You D.A.R.E., 5¼ x 8 . . . . . . . . . . . .1.00
90 Herb Drugg, BGN North, goracing.com, 5¼ x 8 . . . . . . . . . . . . . . . . . . .1.00
94 Ron Barfield, New Holland, 8½ x 11 . . . .1.00
95 Tim Zock, Showcar Express, BGN North, 5¼ x 8¼ . . . . . . . . . . . . . . . . . .1.00
95 Tim Zock, 1-888-Team-LCI, BGN North, 5¼ x 8¼ . . . . . . . . . . . . . . . . . .1.00
96 Stevie Reeves, Big A Auto Parts, B & W, photo, 8 x 10 . . . . . . . . . . . . . .1.00
96 Stevie Reeves, Big A Auto Parts, 10 x 8 .1.00
96 Tom Peck, Dave Marcis Day, 6 x 9 . . . . .3.00
97 Doug Reid III, MedPartners, 8 x 10 . . . .1.00
97 Adam Friend, New Hampshire College, BGN North, 8½ x 11 . . . . . . . . . . . . . .1.00
99 Glenn Allen, Luxaire, 8½ x 10 . . . . . . .1.00
99 Glenn Allen, Luxaire, St. Louis Post Dispatch, 8½ x 11 . . . . . . . . . . . . . . . . . .5.00
99 Rick Hauser, QuicShine, paper, BGN North, 8½ x 11 . . . . . . . . . . . . . . . . . .1.00

## 1998

00 Buckshot Jones, headshot, 7½ x 5½ . . .1.00
00 Buckshot Jones, Bayer & Alka-Seltzer, 8 x 10 . . . . . . . . . . . . . . . . . . .1.00
00 Buckshot Jones, Bayer & Alka-Seltzer, lower air ducts, 8 x 10 . . . . . . . . . . . . . .3.00
00 Buckshot Jones, Bayer & Alka-Seltzer, lower air ducts with bullet holes, 8 x 10 . . . . .3.00
0 Bill Penfold, Hewitts, BGN North, 5½ x 8½ .3.00
01 John Barber, Makita, BGN North, 5½ x 8½ . . . . . . . . . . . . . . . . . .2.00
06 Paul Richardson, NAPA, BGN North, 5½ x8½ . . . . . . . . . . . . . . . . . .2.00
1 Sterling Marlin, Ray O Vac, 8 x 10 . . . . .2.00

**Dale Earnhardt Jr. Debuts with ACDelco**

3 Dale Earnhardt, Jr., AC Delco, 1,200 produced, 8 x 10 . . 75.00

1 Sterling Marlin, Ray O Vac, Talladega on wall, 8 x 10 . . . . . . . . . . . . . . . . . . . . . . . . .2.00

2 Ron Barfield, New Holland, 8 x 10 . . . . . .1.00

2 Ron Barfield, New Holland, angled view, 8 x 10 . . . . . . . . . . . . . . . . . . . . . . . . .1.00

2 Ron Barfield, New Holland, with tractor, 8 x 10 . . . . . . . . . . . . . . . . . . . . . . . .2.00

2 Joe Barnes, BGN North, 5 x 7½ . . . . . . .3.00

2 Joe Barnes, BGN North, 6 x 8 . . . . . . . .3.00

3 Dale Earnhardt, Jr., AC Delco, 1,200 produced, 8 x 10 . . . . . . . . . . . . . . . . . . . . . . . . .75.00

3 Dale Earnhardt, Jr., AC Delco, 8 x 10 . . . .3.00

3 Dale Earnhardt, Jr., AC Delco & Food City, 8 x 10 . . . . . . . . . . . . . . . . . . . . . . . .5.00

4 Jeff Purvis, Lance, 8½ x 11 . . . . . . . . . .1.00

4 Jeff Purvis, Lance, different print on back, 8½ x 11 . . . . . . . . . . . . . . . . . . . . . . .2.00

4 Jeff Purvis, Lance, Bull & Hannah's, 8½ x 11 . . . . . . . . . . . . . . . . . . . . . . . .1.00

4 Jeff Purvis, Lance, David Lee Murphy, 8½ x 11 . . . . . . . . . . . . . . . . . . . . . . . .2.00

4 Glenn Sullivan, LesCare, BGN North, 8½ x 11 . . . . . . . . . . . . . . . . . . . . . . . .3.00

4 Brad Bennett, Dura Lube, BGN North, 6 x 9 . . . . . . . . . . . . . . . . . . . . . . . . . .3.00

6 Joe Bessey, Power Team, 8 x 10 . . . . . . .1.00

6 Joe Bessey, Power Team, 8¼ x 10¼ . . . .2.00

6 Joe Bessey, Power Team, sheet with A. J. Foyt, 5 x 7 . . . . . . . . . . . . . . . . . . . . . . . . . .5.00

6 Martin Truex, Auto Zone, BGN North, 8½ x 11 . . . . . . . . . . . . . . . . . . . . . . . .2.00

6 Brad Bennett, Auto Palace, BGN North, 8 x 10 . . . . . . . . . . . . . . . . . . . . . . . . . .2.00

7 No Driver, Team Shields, with #04 truck & #20 late model stock, 6½ x 9½ . . . . . . . . . .1.00

7 Bobby Dragon, Skoal, BGN North, 8¼ x 10¼ . . . . . . . . . . . . . . . . . . . . . . .2.00

8 Bobby Hillin, Yahoo Sports, 8 x 10 . . . . .3.00

8 Bobby Hillin, Clean Shower, 8 x 10 . . . . . .1.00

9 Jeff Burton, Track Gear, 8½ x 11 . . . . . . .1.00

10 Phil Parsons, Dura Lube, 6 x 9 . . . . . . .1.00

10 Phil Parsons, Dura Lube, Honeywell, 7 x 9 . . . . . . . . . . . . . . . . . . . . . . . . . .1.00

12 Jimmy Spencer, Zippo, 5½ x 8 . . . . . . . .1.00

12 Jimmy Spencer, All Pro, bumber on back, error, with crew, 5 x 7 . . . . . . . . . . . . .7.00

12 Jimmy Spencer, All Pro, bumper on back, with crew, 5 x 7 . . . . . . . . . . . . . . . . . . . . .4.00

12 Jimmy Spencer, All Pro, without crew, 5½ x 8½ . . . . . . . . . . . . . . . . . . . . . . .5.00

12 Scott Hansen, Graybar & Bussmann, 8½ x 11 . . . . . . . . . . . . . . . . . . . . . . . .3.00

13 Ted Christopher, Whelen Engineering, BGN North, 8 x 10 . . . . . . . . . . . . . . . . . . . .1.00

13 Ted Christopher, Whelen Engineering, BGN North, 8½ x 11 . . . . . . . . . . . . . . . . . . .2.00

14 Patty Moise, Rhodes, 8 x 10 . . . . . . . . .1.00

14 Tracy Gordon, R & L Enterprises, BGN North, 8½ x 11 . . . . . . . . . . . . . . . . . . . . . . . .2.00

14 Tracy Gordon, Certain Teed, BGN North, 8½ x 11 . . . . . . . . . . . . . . . . . . . . . . . .2.00

15 Ken Schrader, Oakwood Homes, red writing, 4 x 6 . . . . . . . . . . . . . . . . . . . . . . . . . .2.00

15 Ken Schrader, Oakwood Homes, blue writing, 4¼ x 6 . . . . . . . . . . . . . . . . . . . . . . . .2.00

15 Ken Schrader, Oakwood Homes, 8½ x 11 . .1.00

15 Ken Schrader, Oakwood Homes, checkered flag sale, 4 x 6 . . . . . . . . . . . . . . . . . .1.00
15 Ken Schrader, Oakwood Homes, Racing Sellabration, 4 x 6 . . . . . . . . . . . . . . .2.00
16 Stub Fadden, NAPA, BGN North, 10¼ x 8 . . . . . . . . . . . . . . . . . . .1.00
17 Matt Kenseth, LYCOS, B & W, 8 x 10 . .3.00
17 Matt Kenseth, LYCOS, color, 8 x 10 . . . .2.00
17 Matt Kenseth, LYCOS, color, 8½ x 12½ .2.00
17 Matt Kenseth, LYCOS, 5½ x 8½ . . . . . . .5.00
20 Blaise Alexander, Rescue, headshot, photo, 7 x 5 . . . . . . . . . . . . . . . . . . .1.00
20 Blaise Alexander, Rescue, yellow background, 6 x 9 . . . . . . . . . . . . . . . . . . .3.00
20 Blaise Alexander, Rescue, 8½ x 11 . . . . .1.00
20 Blaise Alexander, Rescue, 6¾ x 8¾ . . . .1.00
21 Michael Waltrip, Band-Aid, 8 x 9 . . . . . .1.00
21 Eric Bodine, Bully Hills Vineyards, BGN North, 6 x 9 . . . . . . . . . . . . . . . . . . .1.00
22 Scott Lagassé, Red Sale, B & W, 6 x 9 . .3.00
23 Lance Hooper, World Championship Wrestling, 8 x 10 . . . . . . . . . . . . . . . . . . .1.00
26 Scott Bolbouley, Buyer Choice, BGN North Car, facing left, 8½ x 11 . . . . . . . . . . . . .2.00
26 Scott Bolbouley, Buyer Choice, BGN North Car, facing right, 8½ x 11 . . . . . . . . . . . . .2.00
27 James Brown, BGN North, 6 x 8 . . . . . .4.00

28 Casey Atwood, LAR Motorsports, 8½ x 11 . . . . . . . . . . . . . . . . . . . . . .3.00
29 Hermie Sadler, Peebles, headshot, 10 x 8 . . . . . . . . . . . . . . . . . . . . .2.00
29 Hermie Sadler, DeWalt Tools, wall shown on top right corner, 8 x 10 . . . . . . . . . . .3.00
29 Hermie Sadler, DeWalt Tools, 8 x 10 . . .1.00
30 Mike Cope, Slim Jim, 10 x 8 . . . . . . . .1.00
30 Todd Bodine, Slim Jim, 8 x 10 . . . . . . .1.00
32 Jason Jarrett, White Rain, headshot, blank back, 7 x 5 . . . . . . . . . . . . . . . . . . .1.00
32 Jason Jarrett, photo stock, blank back, 8 x 10 . . . . . . . . . . . . . . . . . . .1.00
32 Dale Jarrett, White Rain, thin stock, 8½ x 11 . . . . . . . . . . . . . . . . . . .1.00
32 Dale Jarrett, White Rain, 8½ x 11 . . . . .1.00

32 Dale Jarrett, White Rain, with tear-off, 8½ x 10¾ . . . . . . . . . . . . . . . . . . .1.00
33 Tim Fedewa, Kleenex, 6 x 9 . . . . . . . .1.00
34 Mike McLaughlin, Goulds Pumps, 8 x 10 .1.00
34 Mike McLaughlin, Goulds Pumps, light blue background, 8 x 10 . . . . . . . . . . . . . .1.00
34 Mike McLaughlin, Trident Pump, 8½ x 11 .3.00
35 Lyndon Amick, SCANA, behind car, 9 x 9 .2.00
35 Lyndon Amick, SCANA, behind car with NASCAR, 9 x 9 . . . . . . . . . . . . . . . .1.00
35 Lyndon Amick, SCANA, in front of car, 9 x 9 . . . . . . . . . . . . . . . . . . . . .1.00
36 Matt Hutter, Stanley Tools, headshot, blank back, 7 x 5 . . . . . . . . . . . . . . . . . .1.00
36 Matt Hutter, Stanley Tools, 8¼ x 9½ . . . .1.00
36 David Green, Stanley Tools, 8¼ x 9½ . . .1.00
36 David Green, Stanley Tools, more info on tear-off, 8¼ x 9½ . . . . . . . . . . . . . . . . . .1.00
37 Mark Green, Timber Wolf, 8 x 10 . . . .1.00
38 Elton Sawyer, Barbasol, 8 x 10 . . . . . .1.00
39 Eddie Beahr, Fidelity Printing, 8 x 10 . . . .2.00
40 Rick Fuller, Channellock, 6 x 8 . . . . . . .1.00
40 Kevin LePage, Channellock, 6 x 8 . . . . .2.00
40 No Driver, Channellock, 6 x 8 . . . . . . . .1.00
42 J.D. Gibbs, Carolina Turkey, 6½ x 8 . . . .2.00
42 Tom Cary Jr., AAA Aircraft Supply, red & white, BGN North, 5 x 8 . . . . . . . . . .2.00
42 Tom Cary Jr., AAA Aircraft Supply, black & green, BGN North, 5 x 8 . . . . . . . . . .2.00
43 Stevie Reeves, Curb Records, 8 x 10 . . .2.00
43 Brad Noffsinger, Curb Records, 8 x 10 . .2.00
44 Tony Stewart, Shell, 8 x 10 . . . . . . . . .3.00
45 Brad Loney, Hunter's Specialties, with tear-off, 5½ x 9 . . . . . . . . . . . . . . . . . . .3.00
45 Franklin Butler, BGN North, 5 x 8 . . . . . .2.00

46 Gary Laton, Tampico, blank back, 8 x 10 . .7.00
46 Gary Laton, Tampico, 6 x 8 . . . . . . . . .2.00
47 Andy Santerre, Monro, with tear-off, 8½ x 10 . . . . . . . . . . . . . . . . . . . .1.00
48 Dale Shaw, UniFrist, 6 x 9 . . . . . . . . . .1.00

50 Jimmy Foster, Dr Pepper, facing right, 9 x 7 . . . . . . . . . . . . . . . . . . . .1.00

50 Jimmy Foster, Dr Pepper, facing left, 9 x 7 . . . . . . . . . . . . . . . . . . .1.00

50 Jimmy Foster, Dr Pepper, photocopy, 11 x 8½ . . . . . . . . . . . . . . . . . .1.00

51 Mike Stefaink, Burnham, BGN North, 8 x 10 . . . . . . . . . . . . . . . . . . .1.00

52 Kevin Grubb, Crestar, 5½ x 8½ . . . . . .1.00

54 Kathryn Teasdale, IGA Racing, 6 x 9 . . . .1.00

54 Kathryn Teasdale, IGA Racing, different logos on back, 6 x 9 . . . . . . . . . . . . . . . .2.00

54 Kathryn Teasdale, IGA Racing, blank back, 6 x 9 . . . . . . . . . . . . . . . . . . .3.00

54 No Driver, IGA Racing, 6 x 9 . . . . . . . .2.00

54 Gege Gravel, Profit Tools, BGN North, 5½ x 8½ . . . . . . . . . . . . . . . . . .3.00

56 Jeff Krogh, Clearwater, 6¼ x 9¼ . . . . .1.00

57 Jason Keller, Justin Boots, thin stock, blank back, 10 x 8 . . . . . . . . . . . . . . . . .3.00

57 Jason Keller, 5 x 7 . . . . . . . . . . . . . .3.00

58 Hank Parker, Jr., B.A.S.S., 5 x 8 . . . . . .1.00

59 Robert Pressley, Kingsford Charcoal, 8 x 10 . . . . . . . . . . . . . . . . . . . .1.00

59 Robert Pressley, 360 Communications, 8 x 10 . . . . . . . . . . . . . . . . . . . .1.00

60 Mark Martin, Winn-Dixie, 5 x 7 . . . . . . .1.00

60 Mark Martin, Winn-Dixie, 8 x 10 . . . . . .1.00

60 Dale Shaw, Ocean Spray, blank back, BGN North, 5 x 8 . . . . . . . . . . . . . . . . .1.00

61 Mike Olsen, Little Trees, BGN North, 8 x 10 . . . . . . . . . . . . . . . . . . . .1.00

63 Tracy Leslie, Lysol, 7 x 9½ . . . . . . . . . .1.00

64 Dick Trickle, SCHNEIDER National, 7 x 9 .1.00

64 Dick Trickle, Freightliner, 7 x 9 . . . . . . .3.00

64 No Driver, SCHNEIDER National, blank back, 10 x 8 . . . . . . . . . . . . . . . . . . . .3.00

66 Elliott Sadler, TropArtic, #3650-98A01, 8½ x 11½ . . . . . . . . . . . . . . . . . .1.00

66 Elliott Sadler, TropArtic, #3650-98A02, 8½ x 11½ . . . . . . . . . . . . . . . . . .1.00

67 Jamie Aubie, AirGas, BGN North, whole car, 5 x 8 . . . . . . . . . . . . . . . . . . . .3.00

67 Jamie Aubie, AirGas, BGN North, driver close-up, 5 x 8 . . . . . . . . . . . . . . . . . .3.00

70 Dale Fischlein, Adrian Carriers, 5¼ x 7¾ .2.00

70 Dale Fischlein, Adrian Carriers, blank back, 8½ x 11 . . . . . . . . . . . . . . . . . . .3.00

72 Mike Dillon, Detroit Gaskets, 7¼ x 9½ . .1.00

72 Mike Dillon, Detroit Gaskets, 7¼ x 10 . . .1.00

72 Mike Dillon, MGM Brakes, 7¼ x 10 . . . .1.00

74 Randy LaJoie, FINA, Gray, info on card back, 6 x 9 . . . . . . . . . . . . . . . . . . . .1.00

74 Randy LaJoie, FINA, color, info on card back, correct, 6 x 9 . . . . . . . . . . . . . . . .1.00

74 Randy LaJoie, FINA, color, info card back, error, 6 x 9 . . . . . . . . . . . . . . . . . .2.00

64 No Driver, SCHNEIDER National, blank back, 10 x 8 . . . . . . . . . . . . . . . . . . . .3.00

74 Randy LaJoie, FINA, Piggly Wiggly added, 6 x 9 . . . . . . . . . . . . . . . . . . . .3.00

74 Randy LaJoie, Sears, B & W, 11 x 8½ . .2.00

74 Ben Rowe, BGN North, 5½ x 8½ . . . . . .3.00

75 Kelly Denton, Food Country, 6 x 9 . . . .2.00

76 Tom Bolles, BGN North with modified, 6 x 9 . . . . . . . . . . . . . . . . . . . .2.00

77 Ed Berrier, Lear, 6½ x 9 . . . . . . . . . . .1.00

77 Bryan Wall, Woodworks, Wall's, BGN North, 8 x 10 . . . . . . . . . . . . . . . . . . . .2.00

77 Bryan Wall, Wall's, fold-over, BGN North, 5½ x 4¼ . . . . . . . . . . . . . . . . . .2.00

77 Bryan Wall, Players, BGN North, 8 x 10 .2.00

77 Bryan Wall, Players, Pennzoil, BGN North, 8 x 10 . . . . . . . . . . . . . . . . . . . .1.00

78 Hank Parker Jr., Synergyn, 5½ x 8½ . . . .2.00

78 Hank Parker Jr., 5 x 8 . . . . . . . . . . . .3.00

78 Loy Allen, blank back, 5¼ x 8 . . . . . . . .5.00

80 Mark Krogh, blank back, 9¼ x 6¼ . . . . .1.00

80 John Lesniak, Team Ocean Spray, BGN North, 5 x 8 . . . . . . . . . . . . . . . . . . . .1.00

82 Mark McFarland, Carolina Shoe, with tear-off, 8 x 10 . . . . . . . . . . . . . . . . . . . .1.00

82 Mark McFarland, Carolina Shoe, with white background, 8½ x 11 . . . . . . . . . . . .4.00

83 Wayne Grubb, Link-Belt, 8½ x 11 . . . . . .1.00

84 Rick Fuller, 1-877-Lexcomm, BGN North, 8½ x 11 . . . . . . . . . . . . . . . . . . .3.00

85 Shane Hall, Bama Jams & Jellies, 8 x 10 .1.00

85 Shane Hall, Big A Auto Parts, 8 x 10 .1.00

85 Shane Hall, Big A Auto Parts, extra writing on bottom, 8 x 10 . . . . . . . . . . . . . . . . . .2.00

87 Joe Nemechek, Ericsson Racing, 8 x 10 .1.00

87 Joe Nemechek, BellSouth, fan club, 5½ x 8½ . . . . . . . . . . . . . . . . . . . .5.00

88 Kevin Schwantz, Ryder, blank back, barn background, 8 x 10 . . . . . . . . . . . . . . . . . . .1.00

88 Jeff Taylor, Kemp Enterprises, BGN North, 5¼ x 8¼ . . . . . . . . . . . . . . . .1.00

89 Stanton Barrett, Allerest, thin stock, 8½ x 11 . . . . . . . . . . . . . . . . . .3.00

89 Stanton Barrett, headshot, B & W, 10 x 8 . . . . . . . . . . . . . . . . . . . . .2.00

89 Jeff Fuller, Allerest, 8 x 10 . . . . . . . . .1.00

89 Ashton Lewis, Allerest, 8 x 10 . . . . . . .2.00

89 Glenn Berhio, Ocean Spray, BGN North, 5 x 8 . . . . . . . . . . . . . . . . . . . . . .3.00

90 Herb Drugg, Ocean Spray, BGN North, 5 x 8 . . . . . . . . . . . . . . . . . . . . . .1.00

92 Derrike Cope, Kraft, 6 x 9 . . . . . . . . .1.00

92 No Driver, Kraft, 6 x 9 . . . . . . . . . . . .1.00

92 Mike Gallo, University Rubber, BGN North, 5 x 8 . . . . . . . . . . . . . . . . . . . . . .1.00

93 Dave Blaney, Amoco, thin stock, 8½ x 11 . . . . . . . . . . . . . . . . . . . .2.00

93 Dave Blaney, Amoco, thick stock, 8½ x 11 . . . . . . . . . . . . . . . . . . . .2.00

94 Gene Haddick, BGN North, 5 x 7 . . . . .3.00

95 Tim Zock, BGN North, 5½ x 8½ . . . . . . .2.00

96 No Driver, Big A Auto Parts, blank back, 5 x 7 . . . . . . . . . . . . . . . . . . . . . .3.00

96 No Driver, Big A Auto Parts, blank back, 6 x 9 . . . . . . . . . . . . . . . . . . . . . .4.00

99 Glenn Allen, Luxaire, 8½ x 10 . . . . . . .1.00

## 1999

00 Larry Pearson, Cheez-It, bust shot, 10 x 8 . . . . . . . . . . . . . . . . . . . . .1.00

00 Larry Pearson, Cheez-it, 8 x 10 . . . . . .1.00

01 Philip Morris, PMI Racing, 8 x 10 . . . . .1.00

01 Philip Morris, LLumar Window Film, 8 x 10 . . . . . . . . . . . . . . . . . . . . .1.00

05 Mike Stefanik, Prime Motorsports, bust shot, 10 x 8 . . . . . . . . . . . . . . . . . . . . .1.00

06 Paul Richardson, NAPA, right side, BGN North, 5½ x 8½ . . . . . . . . . . . . . . . . . .2.00

06 Paul Richardson, NAPA, left side, BGN North, 5½ x 8½ . . . . . . . . . . . . . . . . . .2.00

06 Paul Richardson, NAPA, with coupon, left side, BGN North, 5½ x 8½ . . . . . . . . . . . .2.00

09 Mike Garvey, Emerald First, BGN North, 8 x 10 . . . . . . . . . . . . . . . . . . . . .2.00

0 Bill Penfold, Hewitt's Auto Body, BGN North, 5 x 8 . . . . . . . . . . . . . . . . . . . . .2.00

1 Randy LaJoie, Phoenix Racing, 8 x 10 . . .2.00

1 Randy LaJoie, Bob Evans, phone number on back, 8 x 10 . . . . . . . . . . . . . . . . . .1.00

1 Randy LaJoie, Bob Evans, website on back, 8 x 10 . . . . . . . . . . . . . . . . . . . . .1.00

2 Joe Barnes, BGN North, 4 x 6 . . . . . . .2.00

3 Dale Earnhardt, Jr., AC Delco, error back, wrong zip code, 8 x 10 . . . . . . . . . .2.00

3 Dale Earnhardt, Jr., AC Delco, blank back, 8 x 10 . . . . . . . . . . . . . . . . . . . . .3.00

3 Dale Earnhardt, Jr., AC Delco, light print back, 8 x 10 . . . . . . . . . . . . . . . . . . . . .1.00

3 Dale Earnhardt, Jr., AC Delco, dark print back, 8 x 10 . . . . . . . . . . . . . . . . . . . . .1.00

3 Dale Earnhardt, Jr., Nabisco, with tear-off blank back, 8 x 10 . . . . . . . . . . . . . . . .3.00

3 Dale Earnhardt, Jr., Nabisco, with tear-off printed back, 8 x 10 . . . . . . . . . . . . .2.00

3 Mike Bruno, Summit, BGN North, 8 x 10 .2.00

4 Jeff Purvis, Lance Snacks, Lance logo on front, 8 x 10 . . . . . . . . . . . . . . . . . . . . .1.00

4 Jeff Purvis, Lance Snacks, Bull & Hannah's logo on front, 8 x 10 . . . . . . . . . . . . . . .1.00

5 Dick Trickle, Schneider Motorsports, 7 x 9 .1.00

5 Dick Trickle, Schneider Motorsports, Romo decal added to car, 7 x 9 . . . . . . . . . .1.00

5 Dick Trickle, Deka Batteries, 7 x 9 . . . . .2.00

6 Joe Bessey, Power Team, 8½ x 11 . . . . .1.00

6 Joe Bessey, Power Team, embossed, 8½ x 11 . . . . . . . . . . . . . . . . . . . .1.00

7 Dale Shaw, Steenbeke, BGN North, 5 x 8 . . . . . . . . . . . . . . . . . . . . . .2.00

9 Jeff Burton, Track Gear, 8½ x 11 . . . . . .1.00

9 Kenny White Jr., logo Log, BGN North, 8½ x 11 . . . . . . . . . . . . . . . . . . . .2.00

9 Kenny White Jr., Ted Williams, BGN North, 8 x 10 . . . . . . . . . . . . . . . . . . . . .1.00

10 Phil Parsons, Alltel, B & W, 8½ x 11 . . .2.00

10 Phil Parsons, Alltel, 8 x 10 . . . . . . . . . .1.00

10 Phil Parsons, Alltel, website added, 8 x 10 . . . . . . . . . . . . . . . . . . . . .1.00

10 Phil Parsons, Alltel, Special Olympics, blank back, 6 x 9 . . . . . . . . . . . . . . . . . . .3.00

10 Phil Parsons, Alltel, thin stock fold-over, 6 x 9 . . . . . . . . . . . . . . . . . . . . . .1.00

11 Kenny Irwin, Ray-O-Vac, 8 x 10 . . . . . .1.00

12 Jimmy Spencer, Zippo, 8 x 10 . . . . . . .1.00

12 Carey Heath, BGN North, 5¼ x 8¼ . . . .2.00

13 Ted Christopher, Whelen, BGN North, 8½ x 11 . . . . . . . . . . . . . . . . . . . .1.00

14 Sterling Marlin, University of Tenn, blank back, 8 x 10 . . . . . . . . . . . . . . . . . . . . .3.00

14 Tracy Gordon, Tic-Tac, BGN North, 8½ x 11 . . . . . . . . . . . . . . . . . . . .1.00

15 Ken Schrader, Oakwood Homes, with #52 truck, 8½ x 11 . . . . . . . . . . . . . . . .1.00

15 Ken Schrader, Oakwood Homes, thin stock, with #52 truck, 8½ x 11 . . . . . . . . . .1.00

14 Sterling Marlin, University of Tenn, blank back, 8 x 10 . .3.00

15 Ken Schrader, Oakwood Homes, with #52 truck, 4¼ x 6 . . . . . . . . . . . . . . . . . . . .1.00

17 Matt Kenseth, DeWalt, non glossy back, 8 x 10 . . . . . . . . . . . . . . . . . . . . . . . .1.00

17 Matt Kenseth, DeWalt, glossy back, 8 x 10 . . . . . . . . . . . . . . . . . . . . . . . .1.00

17 Matt Kenseth, Luxaire, with Andy Hillenburg, 8 x 10 . . . . . . . . . . . . . . . . . . . . . . . .2.00

17 Matt Kenseth, Kraft, 7 x 5 . . . . . . . . .3.00

18 Bobby Labonte, MBNA, 8 x 10 . . . . . . .1.00

18 J.D. Gibbs, MBNA, facing right, 8 x 10 . .1.00

18 J.D. Gibbs, MBNA, facing left, 8 x 10 . .1.00

18 Jason Leffler, MBNA, one headshot, 8 x 10 . . . . . . . . . . . . . . . . . . . . . . . .1.00

18 Jason Leffler, MBNA, two headshots, 8 x 10 . . . . . . . . . . . . . . . . . . . . . . . .1.00

18 No Driver, Land O'Lakes, BGN North, 5 x 8 . . . . . . . . . . . . . . . . . . . . . . . . .1.00

19 Mike Skinner, Yellow Freight, thin stock, blank back, 8½ x 11 . . . . . . . . . . . . . . . . . . .3.00

19 Mike Skinner, Yellow Freight, 8½ x 11 . . .1.00

19 Mike Skinner, Yellow Freight, with tear-off, 8½ x 11 . . . . . . . . . . . . . . . . . . . . . . . .1.00

19 Mike Skinner, Yellow Freight, Haldex, 8½ x 11 . . . . . . . . . . . . . . . . . . . . . . . .1.00

19 Jamie Skinner, Yellow Freight, blank back, 8½ x 11 . . . . . . . . . . . . . . . . . . . . . . . .2.00

21 Michael Waltrip, Band-Aid, blank back, 9 x 8 . . . . . . . . . . . . . . . . . . . . . . . . .1.00

21 Michael Waltrip, Band-Aid, with tear-off, 9 x 8 . . . . . . . . . . . . . . . . . . . . . . . . .1.00

21 Eric Bodine, Bully Hill Vineyards, BGN North, 6 x 9 . . . . . . . . . . . . . . . . . . . . . . . . .1.00

22 Jimmy Kitchens, AIR Jamaica Vacations, 8 x 10 . . . . . . . . . . . . . . . . . . . . . . . .1.00

23 Lance Hooper, World Championship Wrestling, 8½ x 11 . . . . . . . . . . . . . . . . . . . . . . . .1.00

24 Jeff Gordon, Pepsi, Team Hendrick, 6 x 4 .1.00

24 Ray Evernham, Pepsi, Team Hendrick, 6 x 4 . . . . . . . . . . . . . . . . . . . . . . . . .1.00

24 Jeff Gordon, Pepsi, Team Garden-Evernham, 6 x 4 . . . . . . . . . . . . . . . . . . . . . . . . .1.00

24 Ray Evernham, Pepsi, Team Garden-Evernham, 6 x 4 . . . . . . . . . . . . . . . . . . . . . . . . .1.00

24 Ricky Hendrick, Dupont, 8½ x 11 . . . . . .1.00

25 Jeff Finley, Dura Lube, blank back, 6 x 9 .1.00

25 Kenny Wallace, DuraLube, 8 x 10 . . . . .1.00

25 Kenny Wallace, DuraLube, not for sale added on front, 8 x 10 . . . . . . . . . . . . . . . .1.00

26 Scott Bouley, Plastic Coat, BGN North, 4 x 6 . . . . . . . . . . . . . . . . . . . . . . . . .1.00

27 Casey Atwood, Castrol, blank back, 8 x 10 . . . . . . . . . . . . . . . . . . . . . . . .2.00

27 Casey Atwood, Castrol, 8½ x 11 . . . . . .1.00

28 Andy Kirby, Williams Travelcenters, photo, 5 x 7 . . . . . . . . . . . . . . . . . . . . . . . . .1.00

28 Andy Kirby, Williams Travelcenters, blank back, 8 x 10 . . . . . . . . . . . . . . . . . . . . . . . .3.00

28 Andy Kirby, Williams Travelcenters, 8½ x 11 . . . . . . . . . . . . . . . . . . . . . . . .1.00

29 Curtis Markham, Graybar, 8½ x 11 . . . .2.00

29 Dave Dion, Berlin City, BGN North, 8¼ x 10¼ . . . . . . . . . . . . . . . . . . . . .1.00

30 Denny Doyle, Sta-Rite, BGN North, 8½ x 11 . . . . . . . . . . . . . . . . . . . . . . . .2.00

32 Jeff Green, Kleenex, 10 x 8 . . . . . . . . .1.00

32 Dale Quarterly, Bollegraaf & Lubo USA, BGN North, 5½ x 8 . . . . . . . . . . . . . . . . . .3.00

33 Jason Jarrett, Bayer headshot, B & W photo, 7 x 5 . . . . . . . . . . . . . . . . . . . . . . .1.00

33 Jason Jarrett, Bayer & Alka Seltzer, headshot, B & W photo, 7 x 5 . . . . . . . . . . . . . .1.00

33 Jason Jarrett, Bayer & Alka Seltzer, blank back, 8 x 10 . . . . . . . . . . . . . . . . . .2.00

33 Jason Jarrett, Bayer & Alka Seltzer, Bayer on hood, 8 x 10 . . . . . . . . . . . . . . . . .1.00

33 Jason Jarrett, Bayer & Alka Seltzer, Alka Seltzer on hood, 8 x 10 . . . . . . . . . . . .1.00

33 Jason Jarrett, Coca-Cola Racing Family, 5½ x 8½ . . . . . . . . . . . . . . . . . . . . . .6.00

34 Mike McLaughlin, Goulds Pumps, Busch on uniform, 8 x 10 . . . . . . . . . . . . . . . . .2.00

34 Mike McLaughlin, Goulds Pumps, Little Trees on uniform, 8 x 10 . . . . . . . . . . . . .1.00

34 Mike McLaughlin, Little Trees, 8 x 10 . . .1.00

35 Lyndon Amick, Powertel, SCANA, blank back, 10¼ x 8 . . . . . . . . . . . . . . . . .3.00

35 Lyndon Amick, SCANA, 7 x 9 . . . . . . . .1.00

35 Lyndon Amick, SCANA, without Barry Dodson & Reddog Barnes on back, 7 x 9 . . . . .1.00

36 Tim Fedewa, Stanley Tools, 8 x 10 . . . .1.00

37 Kevin Grubb, Timber Wolf, blank back, 8 x 10 . . . . . . . . . . . . . . . . . . . . . . .2.00

37 Kevin Grubb, Timber Wolf, 8 x 10 . . . . .1.00

38 Glenn Allen, Barbasol, leaning on car, photo, 5 x 7 . . . . . . . . . . . . . . . . . . . . . . .1.00

38 Glenn Allen, Barbasol, standing by car, photo, 5 x 7 . . . . . . . . . . . . . . . . . . . . . . .1.00

38 Glenn Allen, Barbasol, 8 x 10 . . . . . . . .1.00

38 Babe Branscombe, BGN North, 5½ x 8 .1.00

39 Eddie Beahr, Fidelity Printing, 8 x 10 . . . .1.00

39 Chad Beahr, Fidelity Printing, 8 x 10 . . . .1.00

40 Kerry Earnhardt, Channellock, 10 x 8 . . .1.00

40 Stanton Barrett, Channellock, 10 x 8 .2.00

40 No Driver, Channellock, 8 x 10 . . . . . . .1.00

40 Matt Kobyluck, Mohegan Sun, BGN North, 8 x 10 . . . . . . . . . . . . . . . . . . . . . .1.00

41 David Green, AFG, 8 x 10 . . . . . . . . . . .1.00

42 Tom Cary Jr, AAA Aircraft Supply, BGN North, 5 x 8 . . . . . . . . . . . . . . . . . . . . . . .1.00

43 Shane Hall, CT-Tecumseh, blank back, 8½ x 11 . . . . . . . . . . . . . . . . . . .3.00

43 Shane Hall, CT-Tecumseh, B & W, car on back, 8½ x 11 . . . . . . . . . . . . . . . . . . .2.00

43 Shane Hall, CT-Tecumseh, color car on back, 8½ x 11 . . . . . . . . . . . . . . . . . . .2.00

43 Shane Hall, CT-Tecumseh, American on back, 8½ x 11 . . . . . . . . . . . . . . . . . . .2.00

43 Shane Hall, CT-Tecumseh, without American on back, 8½ x 11 . . . . . . . . . . . . . . . .2.00

44 Slim Jim, The Labonte's, 8 x 10 . . . . . .1.00

44 Justin Labonte, Slim Jim, 8 x 10 . . . . . .1.00

45 Adam Petty, Spree, 5½ x 4¼ . . . . . . . .2.00

45 Adam Petty, Spree, 11 x 8½ . . . . . . . .1.00

45 Adam Petty, Coca-Cola Racing Family, 5½ x 8½ . . . . . . . . . . . . . . . . . . . . . .6.00

47 Andy Santerre, Monro Muffler & Brakes, 8 x 10 . . . . . . . . . . . . . . . . . . . . . . .1.00

47 Andy Santerre, Monro Muffler & Brakes, 11 x 8½ . . . . . . . . . . . . . . . . . . . . .1.00

47 Andy Santerre, Monro Muffler & Brakes Speedy logo, 8 x 10 . . . . . . . . . . . .2.00

47 Kelly Moore, LesCare Kitchens, BGN North, 8 x 10 . . . . . . . . . . . . . . . . . . . . . .1.00

40 Kerry Earnhardt, Channellock, 8 x 10 . . 4.00

49 Gus Wasson, 5 x 7 . . . . . . . . . . . .1.00

50 Mark Green, Dr. Pepper, 8 x 10 . . . . . .1.00

50 Brett Roubinek, Crystal Rock, BGN North, 5 x 8 . . . . . . . . . . . . . . . . . . . . . .1.00

50 Brett Roubinek, Crystal Rock, side view, BGN North, 5 x 8 . . . . . . . . . . . . . . . . . .1.00

52 Jeff Finley, Dura Lube, blank back, 6 x 9 .2.00

53 Hank Parker Jr, Team Marines, 8 x 10 . .1.00

53 Dan Koonmen, Secrephone, BGN North, 8½ x 11 . . . . . . . . . . . . . . . . . . . . .2.00

54 Brett Bodine, Gold Bond Powder, 8½ x 11 . . . . . . . . . . . . . . . . . . . . .1.00

54 Gerald Gravel, Profit Tools, BGN North, 5 x 8 . . . . . . . . . . . . . . . . . . . . . .1.00

55 Michael Ritch, Fla. State Univ. Gators, #55, with Gator logo on back , 7½ x 10 . . . .3.00

55 Michael Ritch, Fla. State Univ. Gators, Team Gator logo on back, 7½ x 10 . . . . . . .3.00

55 Michael Ritch, Fla. State University Gators, 6¼ x 8¼ . . . . . . . . . . . . . . . . . . . .1.00

55 Michael Ritch, Fla. State Univ. Gators, 5¼ x 6¾ . . . . . . . . . . . . . . . . . . . .1.00

55 Brad Leighton, Sheraton, BGN North, 5½ x 8½ . . . . . . . . . . . . . . . . . . . . .2.00

55 Brad Leighton, Foxwoods, thin stock, BGN North, 8 x 10 . . . . . . . . . . . . . . . . . .2.00

56 Jeff Krogh, CFI & Clearwater, blank back, 6¼ x 8¼ . . . . . . . . . . . . . . . . . . . .3.00

56 Jeff Krogh, CFI & Clearwater, printed back, 6 x 8 . . . . . . . . . . . . . . . . . . . . . .2.00

57 Jason Keller, IGA, 13 x 8 . . . . . . . . . .1.00

57 Jason Keller, Excedrin, 10 x 8 . . . . . . .2.00

59 Mike Dillon, Match Light, B & W, card stock, 8½ x 11 . . . . . . . . . . . . . . . . . . . .2.00

59 Mike Dillon, Match Light & Rockwell, 4 x 11 . . . . . . . . . . . . . . . . . . . . . .1.00

59 Mike Dillon, Match Light & Rockwell, 6 x 10½ . . . . . . . . . . . . . . . . . . . .1.00

60 Mark Martin, Winn Dixie, 5 x 7 . . . . . . .1.00

60 Mark Martin, Winn Dixie, 8 x 10 . . . . . .1.00

61 Mike Olsen, Little Trees, BGN North, 8 x 10 . . . . . . . . . . . . . . . . . . . . . .1.00

63 Chuck Bown, Exxon Superflo, 8 x 10 . . . .1.00

65 No Driver, Overtons.com, 6 x 9 . . . . . .1.00

66 Todd Bodine, Trop Artic, 8½ x 11¾ . . . .1.00

67 Joe Buford, Town & Country Ford, 11 x 8½ . . . . . . . . . . . . . . . . . . . .1.00

67 Jamie Aube, BGN North, 5 x 7 . . . . . . .2.00

72 Hermie Sadler, MGM Brakes, 7¼ x 10 . .1.00

72 Hermie Sadler, Detroit Gaskets, 7¼ x 10 . . . . . . . . . . . . . . . . . . . .1.00

72 Hermie Sadler, Peebles, 10 x 8 . . . . . . .2.00

72 No Driver, MGM Brakes, 7½ x 10 . . . . .1.00

74 Tony Raines, headshot, 6 x 9 . . . . . . . .2.00

76 Kerry Earnhardt, Marines, blank back, 8 x 10 . . . . . . . . . . . . . . . . . . . . . .2.00

76 Tom Bolles, Kendell, BGN North, 6 x 9 . .2.00

77 Ed Berrier, Lear, 6¼ x 9 . . . . . . . . . . .1.00

77 Bryan Wall, Burnham Boilers, BGN North, 8 x 10 . . . . . . . . . . . . . . . . . . . . . .3.00

77 Bryan Wall, Burnham Boilers, BGN North, 10 x 8 . . . . . . . . . . . . . . . . . . . . . .1.00

79 R.D. Smith, 6 x 9 . . . . . . . . . . . . . . .1.00

80 Mark Krogh, CFI & Clearwater, blank back, 9¼ x 6¼ . . . . . . . . . . . . . . . . . . . .3.00

80 Mark Krogh, CFI & Clearwater, 6 x 9 . . .2.00

80 Bobby Hamilton, Hot Tamales, 8½ x 11 .1.00

81 Jerry Glanville, UniFirst, with tear-off, 7 x 9¼ . . . . . . . . . . . . . . . . . . . . . .2.00

82 Rick Beebe, Mejjer, blank back, 8½ x 11 .2.00

83 Wayne Grubb, Link-Belt, 8 x 10 . . . . . .1.00

87 Joe Nemechek, BellSouth, SEND, 5 x 7 .3.00

88 Jeff Taylor, Kemp, BGN North, 5 x 8 . . . .2.00

89 Jeff Fuller, Fiberall, wrong phone number, 8 x 10 . . . . . . . . . . . . . . . . . . . . . .1.00

89 Jeff Fuller, Fiberall, sticker phone number, 8 x 10 . . . . . . . . . . . . . . . . . . . . . .1.00

89 Jeff Fuller, Fiberall, different team members, 8 x 10 . . . . . . . . . . . . . . . . . . . . . .1.00

90 Brad Loney, Coyne Textile Services, insert, street clothes, 8½ x 11 . . . . . . . . . . .1.00

90 Brad Loney, Coyne Textile Services, insert, uniform, 8½ x 11 . . . . . . . . . . . . . . .1.00

91 Rich Bickle, Aqua Velva, 8½ x 11 . . . . .1.00

93 Dave Blaney, Amoco, 8½ x 11 . . . . . . .1.00

93 Dave Blaney, Amoco, thin stock, 8½ x 11 .1.00

96 Gus Wasson, Island Oasis, 8 x 10 . . . . .1.00

98 Elton Sawyer, Lysol, headshot, color photo, 7 x 5 . . . . . . . . . . . . . . . . . . . . . .1.00

98 Elton Sawyer, Lysol, with coupons, thin stock, 8½ x 8½ . . . . . . . . . . . . . . . . . . . .1.00

98 Elton Sawyer, Lysol, owners Akins and Sutton, 8½ x 11 . . . . . . . . . . . . . . . . . . . .1.00

98 Elton Sawyer, Lysol, owner Brad Akins, 8½ x 11 . . . . . . . . . . . . . . . . . . . .1.00

99 Kevin Lepage, Redman, blank back, 8 x 10 . . . . . . . . . . . . . . . . . . . . . .2.00

99 Kevin Lepage, Redman, printed back, 8 x 10 . . . . . . . . . . . . . . . . . . . . . .1.00

## 2000

00 Buckshot Jones, Cheez-it, 7 x 11 . . . . . .1.00

09 Bryon Chew, Buzz Chew Auto Group, BGN North, 5 x 8 . . . . . . . . . . . . . . . . . .2.00

0 Shane Hall, Ohio State Univ., 8 x 10 . . . . .1.00

1 Randy LaJoie, Bob Evans Restaurant, 8 x 10 . . . . . . . . . . . . . . . . . . . . . .1.00

2 Kevin Harvick, AC Delco, 10 x 8 . . . . . . .3.00

3 Ron Hornaday, NAPA, with tear-off, 8 x 10 . . . . . . . . . . . . . . . . . . . . . .2.00

4 Jeff Purvis, Porter Cable, 8½ x 11 . . . . . .1.00

4 Jeff Purvis, Porter Cable, blank back, 8 x 10 . . . . . . . . . . . . . . . . . . . . . .2.00

2 Kevin Harvick, AC Delco, 10 x 8 . . . . . . .8.00

5 Dick Trickle, Schneider Trucking, 8 x 10 . .1.00
5 Dick Trickle, Deka Batteries, 7 x 9 . . . . . .2.00
7 Michael Waltrip, Band-Aid, 8 x 9 . . . . . . .1.00
8 Bobby Hillin, Jr., Kleenex, 10 x 8 . . . . . . .1.00
9 Jeff Burton, Northern Light, with tear off,
   8½ x 11 . . . . . . . . . . . . . . . . . . . . . . .1.00
10 Jeff Green, NesQuik, 8½ x 11 . . . . . . . .2.00
10 Jeff Green, NesQuik, with tear off,
   11 x 8½ . . . . . . . . . . . . . . . . . . . . . .1.00
11 Jason Jarrett, Rayovac, blank back,
   5½ x 8½ . . . . . . . . . . . . . . . . . . . . .2.00
11 Jason Jarrett, Rayovac, printed back,
   5½ x 8½ . . . . . . . . . . . . . . . . . . . . .2.00
15 Derrick Gilchrist, Hot Tamales, 8 x 10 . .2.00
17 Matt Kenseth, Visine, 8 x 10 . . . . . . . .1.00
17 Jason Schuler, Visine, 8 x 10 . . . . . . . .1.00
19 Mike & Jamie Skinner, PAMECO Racing,
   8½ x 11 . . . . . . . . . . . . . . . . . . . . .2.00
19 Mike Skinner, Kobalt Tools, photo stock,
   8 x 10 . . . . . . . . . . . . . . . . . . . . . . .2.00
19 P.J. Jones & Jamie Skinner, PAMECO Racing,
   8½ x 11 . . . . . . . . . . . . . . . . . . . . .1.00
20 Mike Borkowski, AT&T, headshot, 8 x 10 .2.00
20 Mike Borkowski, AT&T, 8 x 10 . . . . . . .1.00
21 Mike Dillon, Rockwell Automation, thin stock,
   11 x 8½ . . . . . . . . . . . . . . . . . . . . .1.00
21 Mike Dillon, Rockwell Automation, card stock,
   11 x 8½ . . . . . . . . . . . . . . . . . . . . .1.00
24 Jeff Gordon, Pepsi, 8 x 10 . . . . . . . . . .1.00
25 Kenny Wallace & Andy Santerre, Lance,
   www.lance.com, 8 x 10 . . . . . . . . . . . .1.00
25 Kenny Wallace & Andy Santerre, Lance,
   www.lancesnacks.com, 8 x 10 . . . . . . .1.00
26 Bobby Hamilton, Jr., AllCar Motorsports,
   6 x 9 . . . . . . . . . . . . . . . . . . . . . . . .1.00
30 Hermie Sadler, Little Trees, 8 x 10 . . . . .1.00
31 Steve Park, Whelen, 8½ x 11 . . . . . . . .1.00

33 Tony Raines, headshot, B & W, photo stock,
   7 x 5 . . . . . . . . . . . . . . . . . . . . . . . .1.00
33 Tony Raines, Bayer/ Alka-Seltzer Plus,
   8½ x 11 . . . . . . . . . . . . . . . . . . . . .1.00
34 David Green, AFG Glass, car angled view,
   10 x 8 . . . . . . . . . . . . . . . . . . . . . . .2.00
34 David Green, AFG Glass, printed autograph on
   bottom, 10 x 8 . . . . . . . . . . . . . . . . .1.00
34 David Green, AFG Glass, leaning on car,
   printed autograph on bottom, 10 x 8 . . .1.00
34 David Green, AFG Glass, printed autograph on
   top, 10 x 8 . . . . . . . . . . . . . . . . . . .1.00

35 Lyndon Amick, Mitsubishi, 6 x 6 . . . . . . .2.00
35 Lyndon Amick, Mitsubishi, 7 x 9 . . . . . . .1.00
36 Tim Fedewa, Stanley Tools, 8 x 10 . . . . .1.00
42 Kenny Irwin, BellSouth, 8 x 10 . . . . . . . .2.00
43 Jay Sauter, Quality Farm & Country, inset, rear
   of car, 8½ x 11 . . . . . . . . . . . . . . . . .1.00
43 Jay Sauter, Quality Farm & Country, inset,
   headshot, 8½ x 11 . . . . . . . . . . . . . .1.00
44 Slim Jim, The Labontes, 8 x 10 . . . . . .1.00
45 Adam Petty, Sprint, blank back,
   8½ x 11 . . . . . . . . . . . . . . . . . . . . .3.00
45 Adam Petty, Sprint, 8½ x 11 . . . . . . . . .1.00
45 Adam Petty, Sprint, B & W, sweepstakes
   entry, 8½ x 5½ . . . . . . . . . . . . . . . . .1.00
48 Mike McLaughlin, Goulds Pumps, white
   uniform, 8 x 10 . . . . . . . . . . . . . . . . .2.00
48 Mike McLaughlin, Goulds Pumps, red & blue
   uniform, 8 x 10 . . . . . . . . . . . . . . . . .2.00
50 Tony Roper, Dr. Pepper, 8 x 10 . . . . . . .1.00
53 Hank Parker, Jr., Team Marines, 8 x 10 .1.00
55 Michael Ritch, Florida State Univ. Gators,
   8 x 10 . . . . . . . . . . . . . . . . . . . . . . .1.00
57 Jason Keller, Excedrin, front, without gloss,
   8 x 10 . . . . . . . . . . . . . . . . . . . . . . .2.00
57 Jason Keller, Excedrin, front, with gloss,
   8 x 10 . . . . . . . . . . . . . . . . . . . . . . .2.00

59 Phil Parsons, Kingsford Matchlight, 5½ x 8½ . . . . . . . . . . . . . . . . . . . . . .1.00
60 Mark Martin, Winn-Dixie, 7 x 5 . . . . . . .1.00
63 Mark Green, Exxon Superflo, 8 x 10 . . . .1.00
75 Kelly Denton, Food Country, 8½ x 5½ . . .1.00
77 Chad Chaffin, Lear, 9 x 6¼ . . . . . . . . .1.00
81 Blaise Alexander, Tracfone, artwork, 8 x 10 .1.00
81 Blaise Alexander, Tracfone, with tear-off, 8 x 10 . . . . . . . . . . . . . . . . . . . . . . .1.00
82 Dave Steele, Channellock, with tear-off, 8 x 10 . . . . . . . . . . . . . . . . . . . . . . .1.00
87 Joe Nemechek, Cellular One, 8 x 10 . . . .1.00
91 Rich Bickle, Aqua Velva, 8 x 10 . . . . . . .1.00
92 Jimmy Johnson, Alltel, blue background, 8 x 10 . . . . . . . . . . . . . . . . . . . . . . .1.00
92 Jimmy Johnson, Alltel, yellow background, 8 x 10 . . . . . . . . . . . . . . . . . . . . . . .1.00
96 Gus Wasson, Island Oasis, 8 x 10 . . . . .1.00
98 Elton Sawyer, Lysol, white rear spoiler, 8½ x 11 . . . . . . . . . . . . . . . . . . . . . .1.00
98 Elton Sawyer, Lysol, yellow rear spoiler, 8½ x 11 . . . . . . . . . . . . . . . . . . . . . .1.00
99 Greg Schaefer, Rite-Way Electric, BGN North, 8½ x 11 . . . . . . . . . . . . . . . . . . . . . .2.00

## NASCAR CRAFTSMAN TRUCK SERIES

### 1995

04 Wayne Lowery, Carolina Celluar Paging, 3½ x 5½ . . . . . . . . . . . . . . . . . . . . . . .1.00
1 P. J. Jones, Sears DieHard, error, PJ upside-down, 8 x 10 . . . . . . . . . . . . . . . . . . . .1.00
1 P. J. Jones, Sears DieHard, correct, 8 x 10 . . . . . . . . . . . . . . . . . . . . . . .2.00

1 Mike Chase, Sears DieHard, 8 x 10 . . . . .1.00
2 Mike Bliss, Ultra Wheels, 8½ x 11 . . . . .1.00
3 Mike Skinner, GM Goodwrench, blank back, 8 x 10 . . . . . . . . . . . . . . . . . . . . . . .5.00
3 Mike Skinner, GM Goodwrench, black shirt, 8 x 10 . . . . . . . . . . . . . . . . . . . . . . .1.00
3 Mike Skinner, GM Goodwrench, blue shirt, 8 x 10 . . . . . . . . . . . . . . . . . . . . . . .2.00
6 Rick Carelli, Total Racing, 8½ x 11 . . . . .2.00
16 Ron Hornaday, Papa John's Pizza, paper, 8½ x 11 . . . . . . . . . . . . . . . . . . . . . .2.00
16 Ron Hornaday, Papa John's Pizza, paper, 8½ x 11 . . . . . . . . . . . . . . . . . . . . . .2.00
16 Ron Hornaday, Papa John's Pizza, green border, 5½ x 8½ . . . . . . . . . . . . . . . .2.00
16 Ron Hornaday, Papa John's, black border, fan club in California, 5½ x 8½ . . . . . . . . .2.00
16 Ron Hornaday, Papa John's, black border, fan club in North Carolina, 5½ x 8½ . . . . . .3.00
21 Toby Butler, Ortho, 8½ x 11 . . . . . . . . .1.00
21 Toby Butler, Ortho, with coupon, 8½ x 11 1.00
23 T.J. Clark, MTX, black borders, 8 x 10 . .1.00
23 T.J. Clark, MTX, gray borders, 8 x 10 . . .1.00
24 Scott Lagassé, DuPont, 8 x 10 . . . . . . .1.00
28 Ernie Irvan, NAPA, 8 x 10 . . . . . . . . . .2.00
30 No Driver, Grand Daddy Racing, The Rules Have Change, B & W, 6 x 4 . . . . . . . . .2.00
37 Bob Strait, Target Expediting, 6 x 9 . . . .4.00
38 Sammy Swindell, Channellock, 6 x 8 . . . .1.00
43 Rodney Combs, Comfrey Corner, 7 x 5 . .2.00
52 Ken Schrader, AC-Delco, with BGN, ARCA & Dirt, 8½ x 11 . . . . . . . . . . . . . . . . . .1.00
54 Steve McEachern, McEachern Racing, with fan club address, 5¼ x 6¾ . . . . . . . . . . .3.00
54 Steve McEachern, McEachern Racing, 4¾ x 6¾ . . . . . . . . . . . . . . . . . . . . . .1.00
63 Ron Esau, Mega Power, 8½ x 11 . . . . . .2.00

63 Ron Esau, Mega Power, 8½ x 11, . . . . 2.00

65 Ken Allen, OnSat, thick border, 5½ x 8½ .1.00
65 Ken Allen, OnSat, thin border, fold-over,
   5½ x 8½ . . . . . . . . . . . . . . . . . .1.00
71 Kenji Momoto, Marukatsu, 6 x 4 . . . . .3.00
75 Ron Hornaday, Spears, 8 x 10 . . . . . . .1.00

Jerry Glanville and the "Fanasaurus" posing with the new #81 NASCAR Supertruck sponsored by Race Fans Unlimited."

Printed by BSC Litho, Harrisburg, PA. 1-800-272-5484

81 Jerry Glanville, Race Fans Unlimited,
   8 x 10 . . . . . . . . . . . . . . . . . . .3.00
83 Steve Portenga, Coffee Critic, photo,
   4 x 6 . . . . . . . . . . . . . . . . . . . .1.00
87 John Nemechek, paper, 8½ x 11 . . . . . .3.00
87 John Nemechek, Burger King, 5 x 7 . . . .3.00
87 John Nemechek, Delco-Remy, 8 x 10 . . .5.00
98 Butch Miller, Raybestos, 5½ x 8½ . . . . .1.00

## 1996

0 Frank Davis, Teamers Local #71, paper stock,
   8½ x 11 . . . . . . . . . . . . . . . . . . .1.00

DRIVER PROFILE
EDWARD HOWELL

0 Edward Howell, 5½ x 8 . . . . . . . . . . . .3.00
2 Mike Bliss, Ultra Wheels, 8½ x 11 . . . . . .1.00
2 Mike Bliss, Ultra Wheels, reformatted back,
   8½ x 11 . . . . . . . . . . . . . . . . . . .1.00
3 Mike Skinner, GM Goodwrench, desert background on front, 8 x 10 . . . . . . . . . . .3.00

3 Mike Skinner, GM Goodwrench, gold background
   on front, 8 x 10 . . . . . . . . . . . . . .1.00
6 Rick Carelli, Total, 8½ x 11 . . . . . . . . . .2.00
6 Rick Carelli, ReMax, 8½ x 11 . . . . . . . . .1.00
7 Dave Rezendes, QVC, B & W, blank back,
   5 x 7 . . . . . . . . . . . . . . . . . . . . .2.00
7 Dave Rezendes, QVC, with tear-off,
   8 x 10 . . . . . . . . . . . . . . . . . . . .1.00
8 John Nemechek, 6½ x 8½ . . . . . . . . . . .1.00
8 John Nemechek, Not For Sale on back,
   6½ x 8½ . . . . . . . . . . . . . . . . . . .1.00
9 Joe Bessey, New Hampshire, photo stock,
   8 x 10 . . . . . . . . . . . . . . . . . . . .2.00
10 Mike Colabucci, Visa, 8½ x 11 . . . . . . .2.00
12 David Smith, Blake Racing, paper stock,
   5½ x 8½ . . . . . . . . . . . . . . . . . . .1.00
12 David Smith, Blake Racing, paper stock,
   8½ x 11 . . . . . . . . . . . . . . . . . . .1.00

15 Mark Gibson, Blue Bandits Motorsports,
   6 x 10 . . . . . . . . . . . . . . . . . . . .3.00
16 Ron Hornaday, NAPA, blank back,
   8 x 10 . . . . . . . . . . . . . . . . . . .3.00
16 Ron Hornaday, NAPA/without Teresa's picture,
   8 x 10 . . . . . . . . . . . . . . . . . . . .2.00
16 Ron Hornaday, NAPA, with Teresa's picture,
   8 x 10 . . . . . . . . . . . . . . . . . . . .1.00
17 Bill Sedgwick, Sears DieHard, battery shaped,
   8½ x 8 . . . . . . . . . . . . . . . . . . . .1.00
19 Lance Norick, Macklanburg-Duncan,
   8 x 10 . . . . . . . . . . . . . . . . . . . .1.00
19 Lance Norick, 1-800-4PRO RACE, 8 x 10 .2.00
20 Walker Evans, Dana, 8 x 10 . . . . . . . . .1.00
20 Walker Evans, Dana, truck at different angle,
   8 x 10 . . . . . . . . . . . . . . . . . . . .1.00
20 Walker Evans, Dana, with New Dodge logo on
   front, 8 x 10 . . . . . . . . . . . . . . . . .1.00
21 Doug George, Ortho, 8½ x 11 . . . . . . . .1.00
21 Doug George, Ortho, with tear-off,
   8½ x 11 . . . . . . . . . . . . . . . . . . .1.00
22 Rusty Wallace, Miller, 8 x 10 . . . . . . . .2.00
22 Kenny Wallace & Rick Johnson, Red Dog,
   8 x 10 . . . . . . . . . . . . . . . . . . . .1.00
23 T. J. Clark, J & H Car-Lectibles, 8 x 10 . .1.00

23 T. J. Clark, CRG Motorsports & J&H Car-Lectibles, 3 x 4 . . . . . . . . . . . . . . .1.00

23 T. J. Clark, CRG Motorsports & J&H Car-Lectibles, 8½ x 11 . . . . . . . . . . . . .1.00

24 Jack Sprague, Quaker State, dark green background, 8 x 10 . . . . . . . . . . . . . . .2.00

24 Jack Sprague, Quaker State, light green background, 8 x 10 . . . . . . . . . . . . . . .1.00

24 Jack Sprague, Quaker State, light green background, 2nd headshot, 8 x 10 . . . . . .1.00

25 Andy Genzman, DE's LP Gas, 5¼ x 8¼ . .1.00

25 Andy Genzman, DE's LP Gas, Mississippi B-B-Q on back, 5¼ x 8¼ . . . . . . . . . . . . .1.00

29 Bob Keselowski, Winnebago, 8 x 10 . . . .1.00

29 Bob Keselowski, Winnebago, New Dodge logo on front, 8 x 10 . . . . . . . . . . . . .1.00

30 Jimmy Hensley, Mopar, 8 x 10 . . . . . .1.00

30 Jimmy Hensley, Mopar, New Dodge logo on front, 8 x 10 . . . . . . . . . . . . . . .1.00

31 Bob Brevak, Concor, 8½ x 11 . . . . . . .2.00

33 Harry Gant, Westview Capital, 8 x 10 . . .1.00

34 Bob Brevak, Concor, 8½ x 11 . . . . . . .1.00

43 Rich Bickle, Cummins & Georgia Pacific, blank back, 8 x 10 . . . . . . . . . . . . . .3.00

43 Rich Bickle, Cummins, with tear-off, 8½ x 8 . . . . . . . . . . . . . . . . . . . . .1.00

43 Rich Bickle, Georgia Pacific, with tear-off, 8½ x 8 . . . . . . . . . . . . . . . . . . . .1.00

43 Rich Bickle, Cummins & Georgia Pacific, Dodge Motorsports, 8 x 10 . . . . . . . . . . . .1.00

43 Rich Bickle, Cummins, art card, 4 x 6 . .2.00

53 Dan Press, Advantage Memory Corp., 8 x 10 . . . . . . . . . . . . . . . . . . . . .1.00

72 Kevin Harvick, Baja Grill, 8½ x 11 . . . . .2.00

75 Nathan Buttke, Spears, 7 x 9 . . . . . . .1.00

78 Mike Chase, Petron Plus, 8½ x 11 . . . . .3.00

83 Mike Portenga, The Coffee Critic, headshot on right side, 5 x 8 . . . . . . . . . . . . . .1.00

83 Mike Portenga, The Coffee Critic, headshot on left side, 5½ x 8½ . . . . . . . . . . . . .1.00

88 Terry Cook, Pave Pro-Seal Master, 8½ x 11 . . . . . . . . . . . . . . . . . . . .1.00

90 Lance Norwick, Oklahoma City, with tear-off, 8½ x 11 . . . . . . . . . . . . . . . . . . . .2.00

92 Charlie Cragan, Rotary, B & W, 8 x 10 . .1.00

98 Butch Miller, Raybestos, 8 x 10 . . . . . .1.00

98 Kenny Irwin Jr., Raybestos, 8 x 10 . . . . .2.00

## 1997

04 Brad Teague, MR Motorsports, blank back, 6 x 9 . . . . . . . . . . . . . . . . . . . . . .1.00

05 John Blewett III, Bob McGuire Chevrolet, 5¼ x 8⅛ . . . . . . . . . . . . . . . . . . .1.00

06 Billy Pauch, Greenfield Racing, 8 x 10 . . .1.00

09 Tim Buckley, Soff-Cut, thin stock, 5 x 7½ . . . . . . . . . . . . . . . . . . . .1.00

09 Tim Buckley, Soff-Cut, thin stock, 7½ x 10½ . . . . . . . . . . . . . . . . . . .1.00

2 Mike Bliss, Team ASE Racing, 8½ x 11 . . .1.00

3 Jay Sauter, GM Goodwrench, blank back, 8 x 10 . . . . . . . . . . . . . . . . . . . . .3.00

3 Jay Sauter, GM Goodwrench, 8 x 10¼ . . .1.00

4 Wayne Grubb, Link-Belk Construction, 5 x 7 . . . . . . . . . . . . . . . . . . . . .2.00

4 Wayne Grubb, Link-Belk Construction, cranes added on back, 5 x 7 . . . . . . . . . . . . .2.00

6 Rick Carelli, Re Max, 8½ x 11 . . . . . . .1.00

7 Tammy Jo Kirk, Lovable Bras, 8 x 10 . . . .1.00

9 Ron Esau, Rhino Linings, 8½ x 11 . . . . .2.00

11 Andy Hillenburg, Gravy Train, 6 x 9 . . . .1.00

13 Mike Colabucci, Vista, 8 x 10 . . . . . . .1.00

13 Jimmy Lynn Davis, White Cloud, fold-over, 5 x 7½ . . . . . . . . . . . . . . . . . . . .2.00

14 Rick Crawford, Circle Bar Motel, 8 x 10 .1.00

15 Mike Cope, Penrose, 8 x 10 . . . . . . . .1.00

16 Ron Hornaday, NAPA Brakes, 10¼ x 8 . .1.00

17 Rich Bickle, Sears DieHard, battery shaped, 9 x 8½ . . . . . . . . . . . . . . . . . . . .1.00

17 Rich Bickle, Sears DieHard, Fort Worth Star-Telegram, 8½ x 11 . . . . . . . . . . . . . .3.00

18 Michael Dokken, Dana, B & W, 10 x 8 . .1.00

18 Michael Dokken, Dana, 1996 truck, 8 x 10 . . . . . . . . . . . . . . . . . . . . .1.00

18 Michael Dokken, Dana, 1997 truck, 8 x 10 . . . . . . . . . . . . . . . . . . . . .1.00

18 No Driver, Dana, 8 x 10 . . . . . . . . . .1.00

19 Tony Raines, Pennzoil, 1996 truck, 8 x 10 . . . . . . . . . . . . . . . . . . . . .1.00

19 Tony Raines, Pennzoil, 1997 truck, 8 x 10 . . . . . . . . . . . . . . . . . . . . .1.00

20 Butch Miller, The Orleans, 8½ x 11 . . . .1.00

23 T.J. Clark, Borg-Warner Select, 6½ x 9½ . . . . . . . . . . . . . . . . . . .2.00

24 Jack Sprague, Quaker State & Slick 50, 8½ x 11 . . . . . . . . . . . . . . . . . . . .1.00

24 Jack Sprague, Quaker State, 8½ x 11 . .1.00

53 Ken Schrader, Penda, paper stock, posed on track, 8 x 10, . .1.00

24 Jack Sprague, Quaker State, Fort Worth Star-Telegram, 8½ x 11 . . . . . . . . . . . . . . .3.00
25 Andy Genzman, 1-800-GRILL-OUT, 5¼ x 8¼ . . . . . . . . . . . . . . . . . . . . . . .1.00
26 Andy Belmont, 5¼ x 7¼ . . . . . . . . . . .1.00
26 Andy Belmont, with headshot, 5¼ x 7¼ .2.00
27 Mike Rizzo, Hydro-Stop Roofing, blank back, 7 x 10 . . . . . . . . . . . . . . . . . . . . . . .2.00
27 Mike Rizzo, Hydro-Stop Roofing, printed back, 7¼ x 10 . . . . . . . . . . . . . . . . . . . . .2.00
27 Mike Rizzo, Baldwin Filters, blank back, 8 x 10 . . . . . . . . . . . . . . . . . . . . . . .2.00
27 Mike Rizzo, Hastings Filters, blank back, 8 x 10 . . . . . . . . . . . . . . . . . . . . . . .2.00
28 Ernie Irvan, Federated, blank back, 8 x 10 . . . . . . . . . . . . . . . . . . . . . . .2.00
29 Bob Keselowski, Mopar, art work, 8 x 10 .1.00
29 Bob Keselowski, Mopar, 1996 truck, 8 x 10 . . . . . . . . . . . . . . . . . . . . . . .1.00
29 Bob Keselowski, Mopar, 1997 truck, 8 x 10 . . . . . . . . . . . . . . . . . . . . . . .1.00
31 Tony Roper, ConCor Tools And Machine, 8 x 10 . . . . . . . . . . . . . . . . . . . . . . .1.00
32 Kenny Hendrick, Ultra Shield, with white border, 11 x 8½ . . . . . . . . . . . . . . . . .1.00
32 Kenny Hendrick, Ultra Shield, 2nd back, 11 x 8½ . . . . . . . . . . . . . . . . . . . .1.00
32 Kenny Hendrick, Ultra Shield, 3rd back, 11 x 8½ . . . . . . . . . . . . . . . . . . . .1.00
32 Curtis Markham, Boomer's Team Heroes, 5½ x 8½ . . . . . . . . . . . . . . . . . . . . .1.00
35 Lonnie Rush Jr., Ortho, with coupon, 8½ x 11 . . . . . . . . . . . . . . . . . . . . . .1.00
35 Dave Rezendes, Ortho, with coupon, 8½ x 11 . . . . . . . . . . . . . . . . . . . . . .1.00
35 Ortho, 8½ x 11 . . . . . . . . . . . . . . . . .1.00

37 David Green – Scott Walters, Red Man Racing, 8 x 10 . . . . . . . . . . . . . . . . . . . . . .1.00
39 Jeff Spraker, M.J. Software, with Reymore Chevrolet, 5 x 8 . . . . . . . . . . . . . . . .1.00
39 Jeff Spraker, M.J. Software, without Reymore Chevrolet, 5 x 8 . . . . . . . . . . . . . . .1.00
42 Ken Bouchard, Touch 1, 8 x 10 . . . . . .1.00
43 Jimmy Hensley, Cummins, 1996 truck, 8 x 10 . . . . . . . . . . . . . . . . . . . . . . .1.00
43 Jimmy Hensley, Cummins, 1997 truck, 8 x 10 . . . . . . . . . . . . . . . . . . . . . . .1.00
43 Jimmy Hensley, Cummins, 1972 Petty Charger on back, 8½ x 11 . . . . . . . . . . . . . . .1.00
43 Jimmy Hensley, International Trucks, 6 x 9 . . . . . . . . . . . . . . . . . . . . . . .1.00
44 Boris Said, 1-800-COLLECT, fold-over, 4 x 6 . . . . . . . . . . . . . . . . . . . . . . .1.00
44 Boris Said, Federated, blank back, 10 x 8 .1.00
45 Michael Cohen, 8½ x 11 . . . . . . . . . .1.00
51 Richie Petty, paper stock, 8½ x 11 . . . . .1.00
52 Toby Butler, Purolator Pure One, 8 x 10 .1.00
52 Toby Butler, Purolator Pure One, fan club sticker, 8 x 10 . . . . . . . . . . . . . . . . .1.00
52 Pure One, 8 x 10 . . . . . . . . . . . . . . .1.00
52-53 Ken Schrader and Wallace, Penda, paper stock, action, 8 x 10 . . . . . . . . . . . . .1.00
53 Ken Schrader, Penda, paper stock, printed autograph, 8 x 10 . . . . . . . . . . . . . . .1.00
53 Ken Schrader, Penda, paper stock, without autograph, 8 x 10 . . . . . . . . . . . . . .1.00
53 Ken Schrader, Penda, paper stock, posed on track, 8 x 10 . . . . . . . . . . . . . . . . .1.00
54 Jon Leavy, thick stock, 8½ x 11 . . . . . .1.00
54 Jon Leavy, thin stock, 8½ x 11 . . . . . . .1.00
55 Kevin Grubb, Virginia Is For Lovers, 5½ x 7 . . . . . . . . . . . . . . . . . . . . . . .2.00

56 Darin Brassfield, Husky Tools, 8 x 10 . . .2.00
56 Brandon Butler, Husky Tools, 8 x 10 . . . .1.00
60 Andy Houston, Addington Racing, 6 x 9 .1.00
61 Randy Tolsma, Xpress & IWX Motor Freight,
    8 x 10 . . . . . . . . . . . . . . . . . . .1.00
65 Ken Allen, Ultra Shield, 5 x 7 . . . . . . . .1.00
66 No Driver, Carlin Oil Heat, Winning With Oil-
    Heat, 5½ x 8½ . . . . . . . . . . . . . . . .1.00
66 No Driver, Carlin Oil Heat, The Heat Is On,
    5½ x 8½ . . . . . . . . . . . . . . . . . . .1.00
66 Bryan Reffner, Carlin Oil Heat, 8½ x 11 . .1.00
66 Bryan Reffner, Carlin Oil Heat, standing by
    truck, 8½ x 11 . . . . . . . . . . . . . . .1.00
68 Bobby Dotter, Downey Tonneaus Truck Covers,
    5½ x 8½ . . . . . . . . . . . . . . . . . . .2.00
75 Dan Press, Spears, 7 x 9 . . . . . . . . . .1.00
75 Kevin Harvick, Spears, 5½ x 8½ . . . . . .1.00
75 Kevin Harvick, Spears, lighting background,
    5½ x 8½ . . . . . . . . . . . . . . . . . . .2.00
80 Joe Ruttman, LCI, paper, 8½ x 11 . . . . .1.00
80 Joe Ruttman, LCI, with coupon, 7¼ x 8½ .1.00
86 Stacy Compton, Valvoline Instant Oil Change,
    6½ x 9½ . . . . . . . . . . . . . . . . . . .1.00
88 Terry Cook, Seal Master, B & W, blank back,
    11 x 8½ . . . . . . . . . . . . . . . . . . .2.00
88 Terry Cook, PBA / Seal Master Racing,
    8½ x 11 . . . . . . . . . . . . . . . . . . .1.00
88 Terry Cook, Stone Construction, 5½ x 4 .1.00
90 Lance Norick, NHL, with coupon,
    8½ x 11 . . . . . . . . . . . . . . . . . . .1.00
90 Lance Norick, NHL, Dodge, 8 x 10 . . . .1.00
92 Mark Kinser, Rotary, 5½ x 8½ . . . . . . .1.00
92 Doug George, Rotary, 5½ x 8½ . . . . . . .1.00
93 Mike Skinner, LLumar, 7 x 9 . . . . . . . .1.00

94 Ron Barfield, Super 8 Motels, B & W,
    8½ x 11 . . . . . . . . . . . . . . . . . . .2.00
98 Kenny Irwin, Raybestos, 8 x 10 . . . . . .1.00
98 Kenny Irwin, Raybestos, Ford Trucks,
    8 x 10 . . . . . . . . . . . . . . . . . . . .2.00

## 1998

00 Ryan McGlynn, Buyer's Choice,
    11 x 8½ . . . . . . . . . . . . . . . . . . .1.00
2 Mike Bliss, Team ASE, 8 x 10 . . . . . . . .1.00
3 Jay Sauter, GM Goodwrench, 8 x 10 . . . .1.00
5 Mike & Jamie Skinner, Llumar, 8 x 10 . . . .1.00
5 Jamie Skinner, Llumar, truck only, photo stock,
    8 x 10 . . . . . . . . . . . . . . . . . . . .1.00
6 Rick Carelli, ReMax, 8½ x 11 . . . . . . . .1.00
6 Rick Carelli, ReMax, different back,
    8½ x 11 . . . . . . . . . . . . . . . . . . .1.00
7 Barry Bodine, 10 x 8 . . . . . . . . . . . . .1.00
10 Lonnie Rush, A & G Coal Corp., 8½ x 11 .1.00
10 Lonnie Rush, A & G Coal Corp., 8 x 11½ .1.00
10 Lonnie Rush, Ohio State, 8½ x 11 . . . . .1.00
14 Rick Crawford, Circle Bar, 1997 front, 1998
    info on back, 8 x 10 . . . . . . . . . . . . .1.00
16 Ron Hornaday, NAPA, 8 x 10 . . . . . . . .1.00
16 Ron Hornaday, NAPA / Fort Worth Star,
    8½ x 11 . . . . . . . . . . . . . . . . . . .1.00
18 Butch Miller, Dana, blank back, 8 x 10 . .1.00
18 Butch Miller, Dana Racing, 8 x 10 . . . . .1.00
18 Butch Miller, Dana, Team Mopar, 8 x 10 .1.00
19 Tony Raines, Pennzoil, 8 x 10 . . . . . . .1.00
24 Jack Sprague, 1-800-MARROW2, Fort Worth
    Star, 8½ x 11 . . . . . . . . . . . . . . . .1.00
24 Jack Sprague, GMAC, 8½ x 11 . . . . . . .1.00

16 Ron Hornaday, NAPA / Fort Worth Star, 8½ x 11 . . .1.00

24 Jack Sprague, Quaker State, with trophy, 11 x 8½ . . . . . . . . . . . . . . . . . . .2.00
26 No Driver, Auto Trim Design, 8 x 10 . . . 2.00
29 Bob Keselowski, Team Mopar, 8 x 10 . . .1.00
31 Tony Roper, Concor, 8 x 10 . . . . . . . . .1.00
31 Kevin Cywinski, Bendix, 8 x 10 . . . . . . .1.00
35 Ron Barfield, Ortho, 8½ x 11 . . . . . . .1.00
35 Ron Barfield, Ortho-New Holland, 8½ x 11 . . . . . . . . . . . . . . . . . . . .1.00
37 Scot Walters, Red Man, 8 x 10 . . . . . . .1.00
42 Rick McCray, 11 x 8½ . . . . . . . . . . . .1.00
42 Rick McCray, Sylvania, 8 x 10 . . . . . . .2.00
43 Jimmy Hensley, Cummins, Team Mopar, 8 x 10 . . . . . . . . . . . . . . . . . . . . . .1.00
44 Boris Said, Federated Auto Parts, 8½ x 6 .1.00
44 Boris Said, Federated Auto Parts, with tear-off, 10 x 8 . . . . . . . . . . . . . . . . . . . . . .2.00
50 Greg Biffle, Grainger, schedule on back 8 x 10 . . . . . . . . . . . . . . . . . . . . . .1.00
50 Greg Biffle, Grainger, racing gear on back, 8 x 10 . . . . . . . . . . . . . . . . . . . . . .1.00
50 Greg Biffle, Grainger, Open House, 7 x 5 .3.00
52 Mike Wallace, Pure One, street clothes, 8 x 10 . . . . . . . . . . . . . . . . . . . . . .1.00
52 Mike Wallace, Pure One, driver's suit, 8 x 10 . . . . . . . . . . . . . . . . . . . . . .1.00
55 Dave Rezendes, Icehouse Beer, 8 x 10 . .1.00
55 No Driver, Icehouse Beer, 10 x 8 . . . . .2.00
60 Andy Houston, Addington, 1997 front, 1998 back, 6 x 9 . . . . . . . . . . . . . . . . . . .1.00
61 Randy Tolsma, IWX Motor Freight, with fan club address, 8 x 10 . . . . . . . . . . . . .1.00
61 Randy Tolsma, IWX Motor Freight, without fan club address, 8 x 10 . . . . . . . . . . . . .1.00
63 Bobby Myers, Car-Mate, 5½ x 8½ . . . . .1.00
66 Bryan Reffner, Carlin Oil Heat, 8½ x 11 . .1.00
75 Kevin Harvick, Spears, 5½ x 8½ . . . . . .2.00
78 No Driver, MCI, blank back, 5½ x 8½ . . .1.00
78 Dominic Dobson, MCI, Team Mopar, 8 x 10 . . . . . . . . . . . . . . . . . . . . . .1.00
81 Jerry Glanville, UniFirst Uniforms, 6 x 9 .1.00
82 Randy Nelson, Rhino Linings / Viejas, 8 x 10 . . . . . . . . . . . . . . . . . . . . . .1.00
84 Wayne Anderson, Porter-Cable Racing, 8½ x 11 . . . . . . . . . . . . . . . . . . . .1.00
84 Wayne Anderson, Porter-Cable Racing, black border, 8½ x 11 . . . . . . . . . . . . . . . .1.00
86 Stacy Compton, Royal Crown Cola, white uniform, 8½ x 11 . . . . . . . . . . . . . . .1.00
86 Stacy Compton, Royal Crown Cola, blue uniform, 8½ x 11 . . . . . . . . . . . . . . .1.00
86 Stacy Compton, Royal Crown, blue uniform, different back, 8½ x 11 . . . . . . . . . . .1.00
88 Terry Cook, PBA Tour & Seal Master, 8½ x 11 . . . . . . . . . . . . . . . . . . . .1.00
90 Lance Norick, NHL, 8 x 10 . . . . . . . . .1.00
90 Lance Norick, Team Mopar, 8 x 10 . . . .1.00

93 Joe Madore, Big Daddy's BBQ Sauce, blank back, 8½ x 11 . . . . . . . . . . . . . . . . .1.00
98 Rob Rizzo, Hastings Filters, 8½ x 10½ . .1.00
99 Joe Ruttman, Exide, with tear-off, 11 x 8½ . . . . . . . . . . . . . . . . . . . .1.00

## 1999

00 Ryan McGlynn, Buyer's Choice, 11 x 8½ .1.00
00 Ryan McGlynn, Buyer's Choice, 5½ x 8½ .3.00
1 Dennis Setzer, Mopar, fold-over, 7½ x 11 .1.00
2 Mike Wallace, ASE, 8 x 10 . . . . . . . . . .1.00
3 Jay Sauter, GM Goodwrench, 8 x 10 . . . .1.00
4 Bobby Hamilton, Dana, 8 x 10 . . . . . . . .1.00
4 Bobby Hamilton, Dana / Coastal, 8 x 10 . .3.00
6 Rick Carrelli, ReMax, 8½ x 11 . . . . . . . .1.00
14 Rick Crawford, Circle Bar, 8½ x 11 . . . .1.00
16 Ron Hornaday, NAPA, 8 x 10 . . . . . . . .1.00
18 Butch Miller, Dana, fold-over, 7½ x 11 . . .1.00
18 Joe Ruttman, Dana, fold-over, 7½ x 11 . . .1.00
21 Tim Steele, headshot, blank back, 11 x 8½ . . . . . . . . . . . . . . . . . . . .2.00
21 Tim Steele, H. S. Die, blank back, 6 x 9 .2.00
24 Jack Sprague, Team GMAC, 8½ x 11 . . .1.00
25 Randy Tolsma, Supergrad Motor Oil, fold-over, 7½ x 11 . . . . . . . . . . . . . . . . . . . .1.00
26 Jamie McMurray, Mittler Brothers Machine & Tool, 8 x 10 . . . . . . . . . . . . . . . . . .1.00
27 Lonnie Rush & Rob Rizzo, Hastings Filters, 8½ x 10½ . . . . . . . . . . . . . . . . . . .1.00
31 Kevin Cywinski, Auto Trim Design, 8 x 10 .1.00
40 Brad Bennett, 6 x 9 . . . . . . . . . . . . . .1.00
41 Randy Renfrow, blank back, 8 x 10 . . . . .2.00
42 Rick McCray, Burn Care, 8½ x 11 . . . . .1.00
43 Jimmy Hensley, Dodge, fold-over, 7½ x 11 . . . . . . . . . . . . . . . . . . . .1.00
46 Rob Morgan, Acxiom, thin stock, 8½ x 11 . . . . . . . . . . . . . . . . . . . .2.00
46 Rob Morgan, Acxiom, 7½ x 11 . . . . . . .1.00
50 Greg Biffle, Grainger, 8 x 10 . . . . . . . .1.00
52 Scott Hansen, Pena, 8½ x 11 . . . . . . . .2.00
54 Brian Sockwell, Maddux, 5½ x 8½ . . . . .3.00
54 Brian Sockwell, Maddux, without name on front, 5½ x 8½ . . . . . . . . . . . . . . . . .3.00
55 No Driver, Icehouse Beer, 5 x 8½ . . . . .2.00
55 Ron Barfield, Icehouse Beer, 8 x 10 . . . .1.00
59 Mark Gibson, CornWell Tools, 8 x 10 . . .1.00
60 Andy Houston, Cat — The Rental Store, 8 x 10 . . . . . . . . . . . . . . . . . . . . . .1.00
66 Mike Stefanik, Carlin Oil Heat, with Andrea Bonda, 8½ x 11 . . . . . . . . . . . . . . . .1.00
66 Mike Stefanik, Carlin Oil Heat, without Andrea Bonda, 8½ x 11 . . . . . . . . . . . . . . . .1.00
66 Mike Stefanik, Carlin Oil Heat, 11 x 8½ . .1.00
69 Jeff Spraker, National Parts Peddler, 8 x 10 . . . . . . . . . . . . . . . . . . . . . .1.00
73 David Starr, 8½ x 11 . . . . . . . . . . . . .2.00

75 No Driver, Spears, blank back, 3½ x 5 . .2.00
75 No Driver, Spears, blank back, 4½ x 7 . .2.00
75 Andy Houston, Spears, headshot on back, 5½ x 8½ . . . . . . . . . . . . . . . . . . . . . .2.00
75 Andy Houston, Spears, headshot on front, 5½ x 8½ . . . . . . . . . . . . . . . . . . . . . .2.00
86 Stacy Compton, RC Cola, postcard back, 7 x 5½ . . . . . . . . . . . . . . . . . . . . . . .2.00
86 Stacy Compton, RC Cola, info back, 7 x 5½ . . . . . . . . . . . . . . . . . . . . . . .2.00
86 Stacy Compton, RC Cola, fold-over, 7½ x 11 . . . . . . . . . . . . . . . . . . . . .1.00
88 Terry Cook, Seal Master, 8½ x 11 . . . . .1.00
89 Stan Boyd, Precision Automotive, 5½ x 8½ . . . . . . . . . . . . . . . . . . . . . .2.00
90 Lance Norick, Centeon, 8½ x 11 . . . . .1.00
93 Joe Madore, Big Daddy's BBQ, blank back, 5½ x 8½ . . . . . . . . . . . . . . . . . . . . . . .2.00
98 Kevin Harvick, Porter Cable, 8½ x 11 . . .1.00
99 Mike Bliss, Exide, without coupon, 8½ x 11 . . . . . . . . . . . . . . . . . . . . . .1.00
99 Mike Bliss, Exide, without coupon, 8½ x 11 . . . . . . . . . . . . . . . . . . . . . .1.00
99 Mike Bliss, Exide, with coupon, 8½ x 11 .1.00

## 2000

00 Ryan McGlynn, Howes Lubricator Products, blank back, 8½ x 11 . . . . . . . . . . . . . . .1.00
00 Ryan McGlynn, Howes Lubricator Products, blank back, 8 x 4 . . . . . . . . . . . . . . .1.00
00 Ryan McGlynn, Howes Lubricator Products, blank back, 6 x 4 . . . . . . . . . . . . . . .1.00
1 Dennis Setzer, Mopar, fold-over, 7½ x 11 . .1.00
2 Mike Wallace, Team ASE, 8 x 10 . . . . . . .1.00
3 Bryan Reffner, Team Menard, side view, 8½ x11 . . . . . . . . . . . . . . . . . . . . . .2.00
3 Bryan Reffner, Team Menard, angled view, 8½ x 11 . . . . . . . . . . . . . . . . . . . . . .1.00
12 Carlos Contreras, Hot Wheels, fold-over, 7½ x 11 . . . . . . . . . . . . . . . . . . . . . .1.00
14 Rick Crawford, Milwaukee Tools, with tear-off, 8½ x 11 . . . . . . . . . . . . . . . . . . . . . .1.00
16 Jimmy Hensley, Team Rensi, blank back, 8 x 10 . . . . . . . . . . . . . . . . . . . . . .2.00
18 Joe Ruttman, Dana, fold-over, 7½ x 11 . .1.00
25 Randy Tolsma, Citgo Supergard Motor Oil, fold-over, 7½ x 11 . . . . . . . . . . . . . . . . .1.00
26 Jamie McMurray, Mittler Brothers Machine & Tool, blank back, 5 x 7 . . . . . . . . . . .1.00
41 Randy Renfrow, fold-over, 7½ x 11 . . . . .1.00
43 Steve Grissom, Dodge, fold-over, 7½ x 11 . . . . . . . . . . . . . . . . . . . . . .1.00
46 Rob Morgan, Acxiom, fold-over, 7½ x 11 .1.00
50 Greg Biffle, Grainger, 10 x 8 . . . . . . . . .2.00
54 Brian Sockwell, Maddux, thin stock, 5¼ x 8 . . . . . . . . . . . . . . . . . . . . . .1.00

60 Andy Houston, Cat Rental, 8 x 10 . . . . .1.00
66 Rick Carelli, Carlin Oil Heat, blank back, 8½ x 11 . . . . . . . . . . . . . . . . . . . . . .2.00
66 Rick Carelli, Carlin Oil Heat, 8½ x 11 . . .1.00
73 B.A. Wilson, www.sonntagracing.com, 8½ x 11 . . . . . . . . . . . . . . . . . . . . . .2.00
73 B.A. Wilson, www.sonntagracing.net, 8½ x 11 . . . . . . . . . . . . . . . . . . . . . .1.00
75 Marty Houston, Spears, 8½ x 11 . . . . . .1.00
86 Mike Cope, RC Cola, fold-over, 7½ x 11 . .1.00
87 John Nemechek, In Memory, blank back, 10 x 8 . . . . . . . . . . . . . . . . . . . . . .1.00
88 Terry Cook, TTC Transmissions, 8½ x 11 .1.00
90 Lance Norrick, Aventis, 8½ x 11 . . . . . .1.00
93 Wayne Edwards, WorldBestBuy.com, 8 x 10 . . . . . . . . . . . . . . . . . . . . . .1.00
99 Kurt Busch, Exide, 8½ x 11 . . . . . . . . .1.00

## NASCAR WINSTON CUP SERIES

### 1952

14 Fonty Flock, Air Lift Special, Oldsmobile .125.00

### 1953

Frank Mundy, B & W, posed, 3½ x 5½ . . . .45.00

### 1955

149 Ray Crawford, Crawford's Markets, Lincoln, 3½ x 5 . . . . . . . . . . . . . . . . . . . . . .50.00
300 Tim Flock, Mercury Outboard, Chrysler 300, 3½ x 5 . . . . . . . . . . . . . . . . . . . . . .75.00

## 1956

30 Frank Mundy, Mercury Outboard, Chrysler 300, 3½ x 5 . . . . . . . . . . . . . . . . . . .75.00

503 Frank Mundy, Mercury Outboard, Dodge Convertible, 3½ x 5½ . . . . . . . . . . . . . .50.00

## 1962

4 Rex White, Rathman, #38,091F, 5½ x 7  .30.00

8 Joe Weatherly, Hollman Pontiac, #38,093F, 5½ x 7 . . . . . . . . . . . . . . . . . . . . . .35.00

11 Ned Jarrett, Rathman Chevrolet, #38,090F, 5½ x 7 . . . . . . . . . . . . . . . . . . . . . .35.00

22 Fireball Roberts, Stephens Pontiac, #38,087F, 5½ x 7 . . . . . . . . . . . . . . . . . . . . . .45.00

28 Fred Lorenzen, Lafayette Ford, #38,088F, 5½ x 7 . . . . . . . . . . . . . . . . . . . . . .45.00

42-43 Lee & Richard Petty, Plymouths, #38,089F, 5½ x 7 . . . . . . . . . . . . . .60.00

87-88 Buck & Buddy Baker, Chryslers, #38,092F, 5½ x 7 . . . . . . . . . . . . . . . . . . . . .45.00
87 Buck Baker, Chrysler, 8 x 10 . . . . . . . .35.00

## 1963

22 Fireball Roberts, S.E. Ford Dealers, #42,221F, 5½ x 7 . . . . . . . . . . . . . . . . . . . . .75.00

28 Fred Lorenzen, Lafayette Ford, #41,813F, 5½ x 7 . . . . . . . . . . . . . . . . . . . . .55.00
29 Nelson Stacy, Ron's Ford Sales, #41,812F, 5½ x 7 . . . . . . . . . . . . . . . . . . . . .45.00

## 1964

1 Billy Wade, Bristol Lincoln-Mercury, #46,148F, 3 x 5 . . . . . . . . . . . . . . . . . . . . .50.00

6 David Pearson, Dodge, 3 x 5 . . . . . . . . .45.00
11 Ned Jarrett, Courtesy Ford, #44,702F, 5 x 7 . . . . . . . . . . . . . . . . . . . . .85.00
15 Parnelli Jones, Bill Stroppe Mercury, #45,280F, 5 x 7 . . . . . . . . . . . . . .50.00

16 Darel Dieringer, Bill Stroppe Mercury, #45,279F, 5 x 7 . . . . . . . . . . . . . . .40.00

**1965**

6 David Pearson, Dodge, 3 x 5 . . . . . . . . .40.00

21 Marvin Panch, English Motors, B & W,
8 x 10 . . . . . . . . . . . . . . . . . . . . . .30.00

7 Bobby Johns, Bunnell Motor Co., Ford,
#48,518F, 5 x 7 . . . . . . . . . . . . . .30.00

22 Fireball Roberts, Young Ford, #44701F,
5 x 7 . . . . . . . . . . . . . . . . . . . . . .50.00
25 Paul Goldsmith, Plymouth, #44,903F,
5 x 7 . . . . . . . . . . . . . . . . . . . . . .30.00
26 Bobby Isaac, Dodge, #46,147F, 3 x 5 .40.00
26 Curtis Turner, Ed Martin Ford, thin stock, B & W
8 x 10 . . . . . . . . . . . . . . . . . . . . . .30.00

11 Ned Jarrett, Richmond Motors, Ford,
#48,175F, 5 x 7 . . . . . . . . . . . . . .85.00
19 J.T. Putney, Chevrolet, #55062, 3 x 5 .30.00

28 Fred Lorenzen, Lafayette Ford, #44,700F,
5¼ x 7 . . . . . . . . . . . . . . . . . . . . . .35.00
47 A.J. Foyt, Texas Dealers, Dodge, #46,076,
3 x 5 . . . . . . . . . . . . . . . . . . . . . .35.00

21 Marvin Panch, Augusta Motor Sales, Ford,
#49,076F, 5 x 7 . . . . . . . . . . . . . .30.00

## 1966

26 Jr. Johnson, Holly Farms, Ford, 3 x 5 . . .30.00
26 Jr. Johnson, Holly Farms, Ford, with Herb Nab, 3 x 5 . . . . . . . . . . . . . . . . . . .35.00

6 David Pearson, S.E. Dodge Dealers, #51,855F, 3 x 5 . . . . . . . . . . . . . . . . . . . . . . .35.00

27 Cale Yarborough, Abingdon Motor Co., Ford, #49,682F, 5 x 7 . . . . . . . . . . . . . . .35.00

11 Ned Jarrett, Richmond Ford, #51,856F, 3 x 5 . . . . . . . . . . . . . . . . . . . . . . .30.00

28 Fred Lorenzen, Lafayette Ford, #48,172F, 5 x 7 . . . . . . . . . . . . . . . . . . . . . . .35.00
29 Dick Hutcherson, East Tenn. Motor Co., Ford, #48,519F, 5 x 7 . . . . . . . . . . . . . . .25.00

12 Lee Roy Yarbrough, Dodge, 3 x 5 . . . . .40.00

David Pearson & Cotton Owens, Cotton Picker Drag Car, 3 x 5 . . . . . . . . . . . . . .75.00

21 Marvin Panch, Harvest Motors, Ford, #52,181F, 3 x 5 . . . . . . . . . . . . . . .30.00

26 Bobby Isaac, Holly Farms, Ford, action, #52,182F, 3 x 5 . . . . . . . . . . . . . . .30.00
26 Bobby Isaac, Holly Farms, posed with Herb, Jr., 3 x 5 . . . . . . . . . . . . . . . . . . . . .35.00

27 Cale Yarborough, Abingdon Motor Co., Ford, #52,183F, 3 x 5 . . . . . . . . . . . . . . .25.00

28 Fred Lorenzen, Lafayette Ford, #51,857F, 3 x 5 . . . . . . . . . . . . . . . . .30.00
28 Fred Lorenzen, Lafayette Ford, #53,258F, 5 x 7 . . . . . . . . . . . . . . . . .30.00

29 Dick Hutcherson, East Tenn. Motor Co., Ford, #52,184F, 3 x 5 . . . . . . . . . . . . . . .25.00

41 Curtis Turner, Harvest Motors, Ford, #52,185F, 3 x 5 . . . . . . . . . . . . . . .30.00

47 A.J. Foyt, Holly Farms Poultry, Ford, #52,186F, 3 x 5 . . . . . . . . . . . . . . .25.00
48 James Hylton, 1965 Dodge, #57,232F, 3 x 5 . . . . . . . . . . . . . . . . . . . . .35.00

55 Tiny Lund, 1964 Ford, #52,179F, 5½ x 7 . . . . . . . . . . . . . . . . . . . . .35.00

64 Elmo Langley, Quality Plumbing, 1964 Ford,
#17745-C, 3 x 5 . . . . . . . . . . . . . . . .30.00

98 Sam McQuagg, Dodge, 3 x 5 . . . . . . .35.00

99 Paul Goldsmith, Plymouth, posed, Daytona,
#6DK-342, 3 x 5 . . . . . . . . . . . . . . .30.00

### 1967

3 Buddy Baker, Dodge with Ray Fox, palm trees,
#57,200F, 5 x 7 . . . . . . . . . . . . . . .45.00

11 Mario Andretti, Bunnell Motor, Ford,
#56,384F, 5 x 7 . . . . . . . . . . . . . . .30.00

13 Curtis Turner, Chevelle, #17719-C,
3 x 5 . . . . . . . . . . . . . . . . . . . . . . .45.00
16 Bobby Allison, Mercury, B & W, 5 x 7 . .45.00

17 David Pearson, Lafayette Ford, #24627-C,
5 x 7 . . . . . . . . . . . . . . . . . . . . . . .35.00

21 Cale Yarborough, Ron's Ford, #56,381F,
5 x 7 . . . . . . . . . . . . . . . . . . . . . . .30.00

26 Darel Dieringer, Abingdon Motor Co., Ford,
#56,382F, 5 x 7 . . . . . . . . . . . . . .30.00

27 A.J. Foyt, Sheraton Thompson, Ford,
#56,673F, 5 x 7 . . . . . . . . . . . . . .30.00

28 Fred Lorenzen, Lafayette Ford, #56,385F,
    5 x 7 . . . . . . . . . . . . . . . . . . . . . . . . .30.00

29 Dick Hutcherson, East Tenn. Motor Co., Ford,
    #56,383F, 5 x 7 . . . . . . . . . . . . . . .30.00
43 Richard Petty, Plymouth, 5 x 7 . . . . . . .30.00
43 Richard Petty, Plymouth, Pines For Praise,
    B & W, 5 x 7 . . . . . . . . . . . . . . . . . . .45.00

43 Richard Petty, Plymouth, posed in field,
    #96922, 3 x 5 . . . . . . . . . . . . . . . . . .75.00

43 Richard Petty, Plymouth, B & W, fan club,
    8 x 10 . . . . . . . . . . . . . . . . . . . . . . . .30.00

43 Richard Petty, fan club, B & W, headshot,
    8 x 10 . . . . . . . . . . . . . . . . . . . . . . . .30.00

55 Tiny Lund, Hallmark Homes, Ford, #3687, 3 x
    5 . . . . . . . . . . . . . . . . . . . . . . . . . . .30.00

99 Paul Goldsmith, Plymouth, posed, shop, #7DK-
    576, 3 x 5 . . . . . . . . . . . . . . . . . . . . .30.00

## 1968

0 Ramo Stott, Plymouth, 3½ x 5½ . . . . . .30.00
1 Bud Moore, King Enterprises, Dodge, #38092-
    C, 3 x 5 . . . . . . . . . . . . . . . . . . . . . . .35.00

2 Bobby Allison, 1966 Chevelle, #40874-C,
    3 x 5 . . . . . . . . . . . . . . . . . . . . . . . . .35.00

2  Bobby Allison, Chevelle, #66-238,
    3 x 5 . . . . . . . . . . . . . . . . . .45.00
2  Andy Hampton, Dodge, 3½ x 5½ . . . . .30.00

3  Buddy Baker, Royal Dodge, #44587-C,
    3 x 5 . . . . . . . . . . . . . . . . . . .30.00
3  Buddy Baker, Dodge with truck, 4 x 6 . . .40.00
3  Buddy Baker, Lenox Dodge, #106706,
    3 x 5 . . . . . . . . . . . . . . . . . . . . .45.00
3  Buddy Baker, Royal Dodge, 3½ x 5 . . . . .35.00
3  Don White, Dodge, posed at Nichels,
    3½ x 5½ . . . . . . . . . . . . . . . . . . .30.00

6  Charlie Glotzbach, Dodge, #106705,
    3 x 5 . . . . . . . . . . . . . . . . . . . . .35.00
8  Bob Watson, Dodge, ARCA, 3½ x 5½ . . .30.00
11  Mario Andretti, Bunnell Motor Co., Mercury,
    #61,318, 5 x 7 . . . . . . . . . . . . . .30.00
12  Terry Nickles, Allied Auto Supply, 3 x 5 .35.00
14  Jerry Grant, Plymouth, #66,237,
    5 x 7 . . . . . . . . . . . . . . . . . . . .40.00
16  Tiny Lund, Mercury, #61,326, 5 x 7 . .35.00
16  Tiny Lund, Mercury, 5 x 7 . . . . . . . . .45.00
16  Tiny Lund, Mercury, #66,222, 5 x 7 . .35.00
16  Tiny Lund, Mercury Cougar, B & W,
    3½ x 5 . . . . . . . . . . . . . . . . . . .100.00
17  David Pearson, East Tenn. Motor, Ford,
    #61,317, 5 x 7 . . . . . . . . . . . . . . .35.00
17  David Pearson, East Tenn. Motor, Ford, blank
    back, 5 x 7 . . . . . . . . . . . . . . . . .30.00
17  David Pearson, East Tenn. Motor, Torino, blank
    back, 5 x 8 . . . . . . . . . . . . . . . . .30.00
21  Cale Yarborough, 60 Minute Cleaners, Mer-
    cury, B & W, 3 x 5 . . . . . . . . . . . . .35.00

21  Cale Yarborough, 60 Minute Cleaners, auto-
    graph, #68,264, 5 x 7 . . . . . . . . . .30.00
21  Cale Yarborough, 60 Minute Cleaners, Mer-
    cury, #61,323, 5 x 7 . . . . . . . . . . .30.00
21  Cale Yarborough, 60 Minute Cleaners, Mer-
    cury, #66,215, 5 x 7 . . . . . . . . . . .30.00
21  Cale Yarborough, 60 Minute Cleaners, Mer-
    cury, blank back, 5 x 7 . . . . . . . . . .30.00
22  Darel Dieringer, Plymouth with inset, #69,253,
    5 x 7 . . . . . . . . . . . . . . . . . . . . .30.00
22  Darel Dieringer, Plymouth, no inset, #66,221,
    5 x 7 . . . . . . . . . . . . . . . . . . . . .30.00
26  Lee Roy Yarbrough, Winebarger Motor, Mer-
    cury, #61,322, 5 x 7 . . . . . . . . . . .30.00

27  Donnie Allison, Dick Brannan, Ford, #66,213,
    5 x 7 . . . . . . . . . . . . . . . . . . . .45.00
27  Donnie Allison, Dick Brannan, Ford, action,
    #41605-C, 5 x 7 . . . . . . . . . . . . . .30.00
27  A.J. Foyt, Ford, #61,319, 5½ x 7 . . . .30.00
29  Bobby Allison, Long-Lewis Ford, #61,321,
    5 x 7 . . . . . . . . . . . . . . . . . . . . .40.00
29  Bud Moore, Long-Lewis Ford, #42719-C,
    5½ x 7 . . . . . . . . . . . . . . . . . . . .40.00
37  Don Tarr, 1967 Dodge, 5 x 7 . . . . . .45.00
43  Richard Petty, Plymouth, vinyl top,
    8 x 10 . . . . . . . . . . . . . . . . . . . .40.00
43  Richard Petty, Plymouth, vinyl top, #66,214,
    5 x 7 . . . . . . . . . . . . . . . . . . . . .40.00

43 Richard Petty, Plymouth, vinyl, top, #61,327,
3 x 5 . . . . . . . . . . . . . . . . . . . . . .40.00

Richard Petty NASCAR'S winningest driver says:
Men who know autos **best** recommend GRAYSON ROSE

43 Richard Petty, Grayson Rose, #43954-C,
6 x 9 . . . . . . . . . . . . . . . . . . . . . .45.00
48 James Hylton, Brooks Massey, Dodge, action,
#66,218, 5 x 7 . . . . . . . . . . . . . . .45.00
48 James Hylton, Dodge "Leading the Pack,"
4 x 6 . . . . . . . . . . . . . . . . . . . . . .30.00
66 Donnie Allison, Don Wagner Ford, #61,320,
5 x 7 . . . . . . . . . . . . . . . . . . . . . .45.00

BOBBY ISAAC

71 Bobby Isaac, K & K Insurance Dodge, blank
back, #61,325, 5 x 7 . . . . . . . . . . .35.00
71 Bobby Isaac, K & K Insurance, 2 different
insets, #61,325, 5 x 7 . . . . . . . . . .30.00
98 Lee Roy Yarbrough, Winebarger, Mercury,
posed, 5 x 7 . . . . . . . . . . . . . . . . .35.00
98 Lee Roy Yarbrough, Winebarger, Ford, action,
#41,606-C, 5 x 7 . . . . . . . . . . . . . .35.00

98 Lee Roy Yarbrough, Winebarger, Mercury,
autograph, #66,216, 5 x 7 . . . . . . .35.00

LeROY YARBOROUGH

98 Lee Roy Yarbrough, Winebarger, Mercury,
name bottom, blank back, 5 x 7 . . . . .35.00
99 Paul Goldsmith, Valleydale Meats, Plymouth,
#61,324, 5 x 7 . . . . . . . . . . . . . . .40.00
99 Paul Goldsmith, Valleydale Meats, Plymouth,
printed back, 5 x 7 . . . . . . . . . . . . .40.00
99 Paul Goldsmith, Valleydale Meats, Plymouth,
blank back, 5 x 7 . . . . . . . . . . . . . .35.00
99 Paul Goldsmith, Frosty Morn Meats, Plymouth,
5 x 7 . . . . . . . . . . . . . . . . . . . . . .45.00

## 1969

6 Buddy Baker, Addy, Dodge Daytona, #60319-C,
5½ x 7 . . . . . . . . . . . . . . . . . . . . .25.00
6 Buddy Baker, Addy, Dodge Daytona, blank back,
5½ x 7 . . . . . . . . . . . . . . . . . . . . .25.00
9 Roy Tyner, Pepsi, Pontiac, #49080-C,
6 x 9 . . . . . . . . . . . . . . . . . . . . . .30.00

11 A.J. Foyt, Don Wagner, Ford, #113707,
5½ x 7 . . . . . . . . . . . . . . . . . . . . .20.00

17 David Pearson, East Tenn. Motor, Ford,
#113705, 5½ x 7 . . . . . . . . . . . . .25.00
21 Cale Yarborough, 60 Minute Cleaners, Mercury, #113706, 5½ x 7 . . . . . . . . . .25.00

22 Bobby Allison, Burnside, Dodge Daytona,
#60318-C, 5½ x 7 . . . . . . . . . . . . .30.00
22 Bobby Allison, Dodge, blue & gold, 5 x 7 .35.00
27 Donnie Allison, East Point, Ford, #113708,
5½ x 7 . . . . . . . . . . . . . . . . . . . . .20.00

30 Dave Marcis, DeWitt, Dodge Daytona,
#60317-C, 5½ x 7 . . . . . . . . . . . . .25.00

43 Richard Petty, East Tenn. Motor, Ford,
#113710, 5½ x 7 . . . . . . . . . . . . .30.00
48 James Hylton, Welch, Dodge Daytona,
#60316-C, 5½ x 7 . . . . . . . . . . . . .30.00
67 Buddy Arrington, Auto Sales & Body, Dodge,
blank back, 3½ x 5½ . . . . . . . . . . . .18.00
71 Bobby Isaac, K & K Ins., Dodge, #73516,
5 x 7½ . . . . . . . . . . . . . . . . . . . . .20.00

98 Lee Roy Yarbrough, Jim Robbins, Mercury,
#113709, 5½ x 7 . . . . . . . . . . . . .25.00

99 Paul Goldsmith, Dodge, #113767,
3½ x 5½ . . . . . . . . . . . . . . . . . . . .25.00

## 1970

5 Buddy Arrington, Dodge Daytona, #83807,
5½ x 7 . . . . . . . . . . . . . . . . . . . . . .25.00
6 Neil Castles, Stewart Mathena, Dodge Daytona,
5 x 7 . . . . . . . . . . . . . . . . . . . . . .30.00

10 Bill Champion, 1969 Ford, #84351,
5 x 7 . . . . . . . . . . . . . . . . . . . . . .25.00
13 Eddie Yarboro, 1969 Plymouth, #85624,
5½ x 7 . . . . . . . . . . . . . . . . . . . . .20.00
17 David Pearson, East Tenn. Motor, 1969 Ford,
#83805, 5½ x 7 . . . . . . . . . . . . . .25.00

18 Joe Frasson, Dodge Daytona, #84350,
5½ x 7 . . . . . . . . . . . . . . . . . . . . .25.00
22 Bobby Allison, Joe Britt, Dodge Daytona,
#83,806, 4½ x 7 . . . . . . . . . . . . . .30.00
22 Bobby Allison, Coca-Cola, Dodge Daytona,
#85,621, 5½ x 7 . . . . . . . . . . . . . .25.00
25 Jabe Thomas, Star City Body Shop, #83811,
5½ x 7 . . . . . . . . . . . . . . . . . . . . .20.00
26 Earl Brooks, SOS, 1969 Ford, #85630,
5½ x 7 . . . . . . . . . . . . . . . . . . . . .25.00
28 Fred Lorenzen, Piper T.C. Liners, Dodge,
#83802, 5½ x 7 . . . . . . . . . . . . . .25.00
28 Fred Lorenzen, Dodge Daytona, #67256-C,
3 x 5 . . . . . . . . . . . . . . . . . . . . . .35.00

30 Dave Marcis, Welch, Dodge Daytona,
#85626, 5½ x 7 . . . . . . . . . . . . . .18.00
32 Dick Brooks, Bestline, Plymouth Superbird,
#63029-C, 5 x 7 . . . . . . . . . . . . . .35.00

34 Wendell Scott, 1969 Ford, #85623,
5½ x 7 . . . . . . . . . . . . . . . . . . . . .75.00
36 Don Tarr, Coca-Cola, Plymouth Superbird,
#83815, 5½ x 7 . . . . . . . . . . . . . .30.00
36 Butch Hirst, Plymouth Superbird, #85268,
5 x 7 . . . . . . . . . . . . . . . . . . . . . .35.00

40 Pete Hamilton, 7-UP, Plymouth Superbird,
5 x 7 . . . . . . . . . . . . . . . . . . . . . .30.00

42 Marty Robbins, Dodge Daytona, #85627,
5½ x 7 . . . . . . . . . . . . . . . . . . . . .25.00

43 Richard Petty, Plymouth Superbird,
   5 x 7 . . . . . . . . . . . . . . . . . . . . . . .30.00
46 Roy Mayne, Ralph Kimsey, 1969 Chevelle,
   #85629, 5½ x 7 . . . . . . . . . . . . .25.00
47 Raymond Williams, Ford, #85622, 5x7 .25.00
48 James Hylton, Mullins Ford, 1969 Ford,
   #83801, 5½ x 7 . . . . . . . . . . . . .25.00
55 Tiny Lund, Baughman, Dodge Daytona,
   #67884-C, 5 x 7 . . . . . . . . . . . . .30.00
64 Elmo Langley, Woodfield, 1969 Mercury,
   #83809, 5½ x 7 . . . . . . . . . . . . .20.00

67 Dick May, Costner-Eagleton, 1969 Ford,
   #85633, 5½ x 8 . . . . . . . . . . . . .20.00
68 Larry Baumel, Ford, #83928, 5 x 7 . . .25.00
70 J.D. McDuffie, 1969 Mercury, #85632,
   5½ x 7 . . . . . . . . . . . . . . . . . . . . . .30.00

71 Bobby Isaac, K & K Insurance, Dodge Daytona,
   #60801-C, 5½ x 7 . . . . . . . . . . . . .30.00
71 Bobby Isaac, K & K Insurance, Dodge Daytona,
   #83813, 6 x 9 . . . . . . . . . . . . . . . .25.00

72 Benny Parsons, Montgomery Motors, 1969
   Ford, #83814, 5 x 7 . . . . . . . . . . .25.00
74 Bill Shirey, 1969 Plymouth, #83927,
   5 x 7 . . . . . . . . . . . . . . . . . . . . . .25.00
76 Ben Arnold, 1969 Ford, #85634,
   5½ x 7 . . . . . . . . . . . . . . . . . . . . . .25.00
79 Frank Warren, 1969 Plymouth, no sponsor,
   #85625, 5 x 7 . . . . . . . . . . . . . . . .30.00
88 Bill Hollar, 1969 Ford, #85631, 5½ x 7 .20.00
96 Ray Elder, Hargis Engineers, Dodge, #83810,
   5½ x 7 . . . . . . . . . . . . . . . . . . . . . .25.00

99 Charlie Glotzbach, Dodge Daytona, #0EK-5,
   3½ x 5½ . . . . . . . . . . . . . . . . . . . . .25.00
99 Charlie Glotzbach, Dow, Dodge Daytona,
   #84251, 6 x 9 . . . . . . . . . . . . . . . .25.00
99 Charlie Glotzbach, Dow, Dodge Daytona,
   B & W, thick stock, 8 x 10 . . . . . . . .20.00

## 1971

3 Charlie Glotzbach, Monte Carlo, at Charlotte,
   5 x 7 . . . . . . . . . . . . . . . . . . . . . . .25.00

3 Charlie Glotzbach, Monte Carlo, at Michigan,
   #92826, 5½ x 7 . . . . . . . . . . . . . .25.00

4 John Sears, J. Marvin Mills, Dodge, #R22933,
   4 x 6 . . . . . . . . . . . . . . . . . . . .25.00

8 Ed Negre, 1969 Ford, #92828, 5 x 7 . .25.00
11 Buddy Baker, Dodge by Petty, 5 x 7 . . .25.00
12 Bobby Allison, Coca-Cola, Dodge, #89,623,
   5½ x 7 . . . . . . . . . . . . . . . . . . . .30.00
12 Bobby Allison, Coca-Cola, Mercury, #91357,
   5½ x 7 . . . . . . . . . . . . . . . . . . . .30.00

24 Cecil Gordon, Jet Glaze, 1969 Mercury,
   5½ x 7 . . . . . . . . . . . . . . . . . . . .45.00

43 Richard Petty, Southern Plymouth,
   5 x 7 . . . . . . . . . . . . . . . . . . . .35.00
43 Richard Petty, Southern Plymouth,
   8½ x 11 . . . . . . . . . . . . . . . . . . . .25.00
71 Bobby Isaac, K & K Insurance, Dodge,
   5 x 7 . . . . . . . . . . . . . . . . . . . .25.00

90 Bill Dennis, Teleprompter, Mercury, #87920,
   5½ x 7 . . . . . . . . . . . . . . . . . . . .20.00
97 Red Farmer, Long-Lewis Ford, #87,917,
   5½ x 7 . . . . . . . . . . . . . . . . . . . .25.00

99 Fred Lorenzen, STP, Plymouth, #85198,
   5½ x 7 . . . . . . . . . . . . . . . . . . . .25.00

## 1972

1 Winston Show Car, Plymouth, angle view,
   5 x 7 . . . . . . . . . . . . . . . . . . . .15.00

1 Winston Show Car, Plymouth, side view, 5 x 7 . . . . . . . . . . . . . . . . . .15.00

1 Winston Show Car, Monte Carlo, 5 x 7 . . . . . . . . . . . . . . . . . . . . .15.00

1 Winston Show Car, Plymouth, 3½ x 5 . . .15.00

11 Buddy Baker, STP, Dodge, 5 x 7 . . . . .25.00

12 Bobby Allison, Coca-Cola, Monte Carlo, side view, 5 x 7 . . . . . . . . . . . . . . . . . . . . .25.00

12 Bobby Allison, Coca-Cola, Monte Carlo, angle view, 5 x 7 . . . . . . . . . . . . . . . . . . . . .25.00

18 Joe Frasson, Frasson Cement, Dodge, 5 x 7 . . . . . . . . . . . . . . . . . .20.00

21 A.J. Foyt, Purolator, Mercury, 5½ x 7 . .25.00

21 A.J. Foyt, Purolator, Mercury, Valvoline can on back, #97084, 5½ x 7 . . . . . . . . . .25.00

21 David Pearson, Purolator, Mercury, #95976, 5 x 7 . . . . . . . . . . . . . . . . . . . . .20.00

43 Richard Petty, STP, Plymouth, posed, 5 x 7 . . . . . . . . . . . . . . . . . .20.00

43 Richard Petty, STP, Plymouth, action, over-head, 5 x 7 . . . . . . . . . . . . . . . . . .25.00

48 James Hylton, Pop Kola, 1971 Mercury, blank back, 8 x 10 . . . . . . . . . . . . . . . . . .35.00

72 Benny Parsons, Pop Kola, blank back, 8 x 10 . . . . . . . . . . . . . . . . . . . . .30.00

92 Larry Smith, Carling Ford, #94596-C, 3 x 5 . . . . . . . . . . . . . . . . . . . . .35.00

96 Ray Elder, Olympia Beer, Dodge, #4509, 8 x 10 . . . . . . . . . . . . . . . . . . . . .30.00

96 Ray Elder, Hargis Engineers Dodge, posed, pit road, 5 x 7 . . . . . . . . . . . . . . . . . .25.00

97 Red Farmer, Long-Lewis Ford, #R28574, 3½ x 5½ . . . . . . . . . . . . . . . . . . . . .35.00

## 1973

O Eddie Bond, Dodge, STP, 5 x 7 . . . . . . .12.00

00 Bobby Mausgrover, Monte Carlo, STP, 5 x 7 . . . . . . . . . . . . . . . . . .10.00

01 Earl Canavan, Buanno Trans., Plymouth, STP, 5 x 7 . . . . . . . . . . . . . . . . . .12.00

02 L.D. Ottinger, Thundercraft Boats, Chevelle, STP, 5 x 7 . . . . . . . . . . . . . . . . . .12.00

03 Tommy Gale, Mercury, STP, 5 x 7 . . . . .12.00

04 Hershel McGriff, Precision Eng., Plymouth, STP, 5 x 7 . . . . . . . . . . . . . . . . . .12.00

05 Dave Sisco, LOF Glass, Monte Carlo, STP, 5 x 7 . . . . . . . . . . . . . . . . . .12.00

06 Neil Castles, Howard Furniture, Dodge, STP, 5 x 7 . . . . . . . . . . . . . . . . . .12.00

09 Charlie Barnett, Dahlonega Ford Sales, STP, 5 x 7 . . . . . . . . . . . . . . . . . .12.00

1 Winston Show Car, Dodge, angle view, 5 x 7 . . . . . . . . . . . . . . . . . .10.00

1 Slick Gardner, Mercury, STP, 5 x 7 . . . . .12.00

2 Dave Marcis, Atlanta Speedway, Dodge, STP, 5 x 7 . . . . . . . . . . . . . . . . . .12.00

2 Dave Marcis, AMC, Matador, 8 x 10 . . .25.00

4 John Sears, J. Marvin Mills, Dodge, STP, 5 x 7 . . . . . . . . . . . . . . . . . . . . .15.00

15 Bobby Isaac, Sta-Power, Ford with printed autograph, 5 x 7, . . . . . . . . .150.00

6 Dick Brooks, John Naughton Insurance, Dodge, STP, 5 x 7 . . . . . . . . . . . . . . . . . .12.00

7 Dean Dalton, Belden Asphalt, Mercury, STP, 5 x 7 . . . . . . . . . . . . . . . . . . . .12.00

8 Ed Negre, Dodge, STP, 5 x 7 . . . . .12.00

9 Pete Hamilton, Plymouth, STP, 5 x 7 . . . .12.00

10 Bill Champion, Mercury, with sunglasses, STP, 5 x 7 . . . . . . . . . . . . . . . . . .12.00

10 Bill Champion, Mercury, no sunglasses, STP, 5 x 7 . . . . . . . . . . . . . . . . . .12.00

11 Cale Yarborough, Kar-Kare, Chevelle, with printed autograph, 5 x 7 . . . . . . . . . .18.00

11 Cale Yarborough, Kar-Kare, Chevelle, action, STP, 5 x 7 . . . . . . . . . . . . . . . .15.00

11 Cale Yarborough, Kar-Kare, Chevelle, posed, 5 x 7 . . . . . . . . . . . . . . . . . . . .20.00

12 Bobby Allison, Coca-Cola, Chevelle, grass, 5 x 7 . . . . . . . . . . . . . . . . . . . .30.00

12 Bobby Allison, Coca-Cola, pit road, #744-6-73, 5 x 7 . . . . . . . . . . . . . . . . . . .30.00

12 Bobby Allison, Coca-Cola, garage, #R28428, 3½ x 5½ . . . . . . . . . . . . . . . . . .25.00

12 Bobby Allison, Coca-Cola, Chevelle, 5 x 7 . . . . . . . . . . . . . . . . . . . .25.00

12 Bobby Allison, Victory Lane, head shot, 10 x 8 . . . . . . . . . . . . . . . . . . . .25.00

14 Coo Coo Marlin, Cunningham-Kelley, Monte Carlo, STP, 5 x 7 . . . . . . . . . . . . . . .25.00

15 Bobby Isaac, Sta-Power, Ford, 5 x 7 . .100.00

15 Bobby Isaac, Sta-Power, Ford, with printed autograph, 5 x 7 . . . . . . . . . . . . .150.00

17 Bill Dennis, Emrick Chevrolet, Monte Carlo, STP, 5 x 7 . . . . . . . . . . . . . . . . . .12.00

18 Joe Frasson, Dodge, STP, 5 x 7 . . . . .12.00

19 Henley Gray, Lindsey Lincoln-Mercury, Mercury, STP, 5 x 7 . . . . . . . . . . . . . . . .12.00

20 Rick Newsom, Holbrook Waterproofing, Ford, STP, 5 x 7 . . . . . . . . . . . . . . . . . .12.00

22 Jimmy Crawford, Eastern Airlines, 3½ x 4½ . . . . . . . . . . . . . . . . . . . .30.00

23 Roy Mayne, Dodge, STP, 5 x 7 . . . . . .12.00

24 Cecil Gordon, Monte Carlo, STP, 5 x 7 .12.00

25 Jabe Thomas, Dodge, STP, 5 x 7 . . . . .12.00

26 Earl Brooks, H.J. Drummond, Ford, STP, 5 x 7 . . . . . . . . . . . . . . . . . . . .15.00

28 Gordon Johncock, Monte Carlo, STP, 5 x 7 . . . . . . . . . . . . . . . . . . . .12.00

28 Gordon Johncock, Pylon Wiper Blades, Chevelle, STP, 5 x 7 . . . . . . . . . . . . .15.00

29 Bill Hollar, Mercury, STP, 5 x 7 . . . . . .12.00

30 Walter Ballard, Heikmian, Monte Carlo, STP, 5 x 7 . . . . . . . . . . . . . . . . . . . .18.00

31 Jim Vandiver, Bradford Enterprises, Dodge, STP, 5 x 7 . . . . . . . . . . . . . . . . . .12.00

34 Wendell Scott, Ford, STP, 5 x 7 . . . . . .45.00

35 Dick May & Walter Ballard, Heikmian, Mercury, STP, 5 x 7 . . . . . . . . . . . . . . .15.00

36 H.B. Bailey, Pontiac Grand AM, STP, 5 x 7 . . . . . . . . . . . . . . . . . . . .12.00

38 Tony Bettenhausen, Vita, Fresh, Chevelle, STP, 5 x 7 . . . . . . . . . . . . . . . . . .12.00

40 D.K. Ulrich, Noel's Auto Sales, Ford, STP, 5 x 7 . . . . . . . . . . . . . . . . . . . .12.00

42 Marty Robbins, Dodge, two different head shots, STP, 5 x 7 . . . . . . . . . . . . . .15.00

43 Richard Petty, STP, Dodge, STP, 5 x 7 . .25.00

43 Richard Petty, STP, Dodge, #R28337, 3½ x 5½ . . . . . . . . . . . . . . . . . . . .30.00

RICHARD PETTY - NASCAR GRAND NATIONAL CHAMPION
PART OF THE UNITED MOBILE HOMES SALES TEAM

43 Richard Petty, United Mobile Home, Dodge, 3½ x 5 . . . . . . . . . . . . . . . . . .100.00

43 Richard Petty, STP, B & W, fan club, 8 x 10 . . . . . . . . . . . . . . . . . . . .25.00

44 Richard Brown, Monte Carlo, STP, 5 x 7 . . . . . . . . . . . . . . . . . . . .12.00

45 Vic Parsons, Mercury, STP, 5 x 7 . . . . .12.00

47 Raymond Williams, Jet Way Products, 2 different head shots, STP, 5 x 7 . . . . . . . .15.00

48 James Hylton, Mercury, STP, 5 x 7 . . . .18.00

49 John Utsman, Dodge, STP, 5 x 7 . . . . .12.00

52 Earl Ross, Red Cap Beer, Monte Carlo, action, STP, 5 x 7 . . . . . . . . . . . . . . . .15.00

52 Earl Ross, Red Cap Beer, Monte Carlo, black ink, STP, 5 x 7 . . . . . . . . . . . . . .15.00

52 Earl Ross, Red Cap Beer, Monte Carlo, posed, STP, 4½ x 7 . . . . . . . . . . . . . . . .18.00

53 David Ray Boggs, Hopper, Crews Ford, STP, 5 x 7 . . . . . . . . . . . . . . . . . . . .12.00

54 Lennie Pond, Master Chevrolet Sales, Chevelle, STP, 5 x 7 . . . . . . . . . . . . . . . .15.00

55 Jerry Barnett, Winston West, 6 x 9 . . .20.00

60 Maynard Troyer, Nagle, Ford, STP, 5 x 7 .12.00

61 Ed Sczech, Chevelle, STP, 5 x 7 . . . . . .12.00

64 Elmo Langley, Ford, STP, 5 x 7 . . . . . .15.00

67 Buddy Arrington, Kentucky Fried Chicken, Plymouth, STP, 5 x 7 . . . . . . . . . . . .15.00

68 Alton Jones, Crimsondale Nursery, Chevelle, STP, 5 x 7 . . . . . . . . . . . . . . . . . .12.00

70 J.D. McDuffie, Monte Carlo, STP, 5 x 7 .20.00

95 Darrell Waltrip, Terminal Transport, STP, two different head shots, 5 x 7 . . .75.00

71 Buddy Baker, K & K Insurance, Dodge, 5 x 7 . . . . . . . . . . . . . . . . . . . . . . .18.00
72 Benny Parsons, Monte Carlo, STP, 5 x 7 .15.00
72 Benny Parsons, Russell Bennett Chevrolet, 5 x 7 . . . . . . . . . . . . . . . . . . . . . . .18.00
72 Benny Parsons, Union 76, 5 x 7 . . . . .20.00
76 Ben Arnold, Taylor Speed Sport, Ford, STP, 5 x 7 . . . . . . . . . . . . . . . . . . . . . . .12.00
77 Charlie Roberts, Sunny King, Ford, STP, 5 x 7 . . . . . . . . . . . . . . . . . . . . . . .12.00
79 Frank Warren, Dodge, 2 different head shots, STP, 5 x 7 . . . . . . . . . . . . . . . . . . . .15.00
82 Bill Ward, Bama Auto Sales, Monte Carlo, STP, 5 x 7 . . . . . . . . . . . . . . . . . . . . . . . .15.00
83 Paul Tyler, Smithville Farms, Mercury, STP, 5 x 7 . . . . . . . . . . . . . . . . . . . .12.00
84 Bob Davis, Socar, Dodge, STP, 5 x 7 . . .12.00
85 Ronnie Daniel, Chevelle, STP, 5 x 7 . . . .12.00
86 Bob Greeley, Morris Auto Parts, Plymouth, STP, 5 x 7 . . . . . . . . . . . . . . . . . . . .12.00
88 Donnie Allison, Digard Racing Team, Chevelle, STP, 5 x 7 . . . . . . . . . . . . . . . . . . . . .15.00
89 Johnny Barnes, Hopper, Crews Mercury, STP, 5 x 7 . . . . . . . . . . . . . . . . . . . . . .15.00
90 No Driver, Rent-A-Racer Truxmore, Mercury, STP, 5 x 7 . . . . . . . . . . . . . . . . . . . . .12.00
90 No Driver, Truxmore, Mercury, 5 x 7 . .15.00
92 Larry Smith, Carling Black Label Beer, Mercury, action, STP, 5 x 7 . . . . . . . . . .20.00
92 Larry Smith, Carling Black Label Beer, Mercury, #99650-C, 6 x 9 . . . . . . . . . .30.00
95 Darrell Waltrip, Terminal Transport, STP, two different head shots, 5 x 7 . . . . . . . .75.00

96 Richard Childress, L.C. Newton, two different head shots, STP, 5 x 7 . . . . . . . . . . .12.00
96 Ray Elder, Olympia Beer, Dodge, 5 x 7 . .12.00
97 Red Farmer, Long-Lewis Ford, STP, 5 x 7 .12.00
98 Mel Larson, Therma Sol, Chevelle, STP, 5 x 7 . . . . . . . . . . . . . . . . . . . . . . . .12.00
99 Ron Keslowski, General Kinetics Cams, Dodge, STP, 5 x 7 . . . . . . . . . . . . . . . . . . . .12.00

## 1974

01 Sonny Hutchins, Dominion Oxygen, Monte Carlo, 3 x 7 . . . . . . . . . . . . . . . . .18.00
05 David Sisco, Reliable Plumbing, Chevelle, 5 x 7 . . . . . . . . . . . . . . . . . . . . . . . .15.00
1 Winston Show Car, Dodge, angle view, 5 x 7 . . . . . . . . . . . . . . . . . . . . . . . .10.00
1 Winston Show Car, Dodge, side view, 5 x 7 . . . . . . . . . . . . . . . . . . . . . . . .10.00
1 Winston Show Car, Chevelle, side view, 5 x 7 . . . . . . . . . . . . . . . . . . . . . . . .10.00
2 Dave Marcis, Deppe Enterprises, Dodge, STP, 5 x 7 . . . . . . . . . . . . . . . . . . . . . . . .15.00
2 Ramo Stott, Housby Mack Inc., 3½ x 5 . .20.00
11 Cale Yarborough, Carling Black Label Beer, Chevelle, STP, 5 x 7 . . . . . . . . . . . . . .35.00
11 Cale Yarborough, Kar Kare, Chevelle, STP, 5 x 7 . . . . . . . . . . . . . . . . . . . . . . . .20.00
12 Bobby Allison, Coca-Cola, Chevelle, action, 5 x 7 . . . . . . . . . . . . . . . . . . . . . . . .18.00
12 Bobby Allison, Matador with Penske, 6 x 9 . . . . . . . . . . . . . . . . . . . . . . .21.00
15 Buddy Baker, B & W, headshot, 7 x 5½ .15.00

05 David Sisco, Reliable Plumbing, Chevelle, 5 x 7 . . . . . . . . . . . . . . . .15.00

21 David Pearson, Purolator, Mercury, action,
#10607-D, 4 x 6 . . . . . . . . . . . . . .15.00
22 Jimmy Crawford, Plymouth, 3 x 5 . . . .25.00
30 Tighe Scott, Ballard Racing, Chevelle,
3 x 7 . . . . . . . . . . . . . . . . . . .20.00
41 Grant Adcox, Adcox-Kirby, Chevelle,
5 x 7 . . . . . . . . . . . . . . . . . . . .25.00
42 Marty Robbins, Dodge, 5 x 7 . . . . . . .25.00

43 Richard Petty, STP Dodge, front pose, pits,
3 x 5 . . . . . . . . . . . . . . . . . . . .20.00
43 Richard Petty, STP Dodge, on top of car, STP,
5 x 7 . . . . . . . . . . . . . . . . . . . .20.00
43 Richard Petty, STP Dodge, beside car, STP, two
different backs, 5 x 7 . . . . . . . . . . .20.00
43 Richard Petty, STP, Rays Kingburgers, Dodge,
beside car, 5 x 7 . . . . . . . . . . . . . . .30.00

2 Ramo Stott, Housby Mack Inc., 3½ x 5 . . . . . .20.00

43 Richard Petty, STP, Dodge, posed, 6 x 9 . . . . . . . . . . . . . . . . . . . .15.00

48 James Hylton, Bob Stott Chevrolet, Chevelle, 5 x 7 . . . . . . . . . . . . . . . . . . . .25.00

48 James Hylton, Nitro Nine, Chevelle, 5 x 7 . . . . . . . . . . . . . . . . . . . .25.00

54 Lennie Pond, Master Chevrolet Sales, Chevelle, STP, 5 x 7 . . . . . . . . . . . . . . . . . .15.00

61 Johnny Rutherford, Chevelle, 5 x 7 . . . .18.00

72 Benny Parsons, Kings Row, Chevelle, 5 x 8 . . . . . . . . . . . . . . . . . . . .20.00

79 Frank Warren, Native Tan, Dodge, 5 x 7 . . . . . . . . . . . . . . . . . . . .20.00

83 Ramo Stott, Smithville Farms, Chevelle, 5 x 7 . . . . . . . . . . . . . . . . . . . .20.00

88 Donnie Allison, Digard Racing, Chevelle, 4 x 6 . . . . . . . . . . . . . . . . . . . .25.00

90 Charlie Glotzbach, Truxmore, Ford, #781217, 6 x 9 . . . . . . . . . . . . . . . . . . . .25.00

90 Junie Donlavey, Truxmore, Ford, Junie in car, #781218, 6 x 9 . . . . . . . . . . . . . . .15.00

90 Charlie Glotzbach, Truxmore, Ford, #781220, 6 x 9 . . . . . . . . . . . . . . . . . . . .25.00

90 Miss Truxmore, Truxmore, Ford, #781221, 6 x 9 . . . . . . . . . . . . . . . . . . . .25.00

90 No Driver, Truxmore, Ford, pit stop, #781222, 6 x 9 . . . . . . . . . . . . . . . .20.00

95 Darrell Waltrip, Terminal Transport, Chevelle, 5 x 7 . . . . . . . . . . . . . . . . . . . .35.00

## 1975

1 Winston Show Car, 1974 Dodge, with logos on bottom, 5 x 7 . . . . . . . . . . . . . . . .10.00

1 Winston Show Car, Chevelle, glossy & dull finish, 5 x 7 . . . . . . . . . . . . . . . . . . . .10.00

06 Neil Castles, Del Reeves Special, Chevrolet, 8 x 10 . . . . . . . . . . . . . . . . . . .20.00

11 Cale Yarborough, Chevelle, red & white, 5 x 7 . . . . . . . . . . . . . . . . . . . .25.00

11 Cale Yarborough, Ethyl Gas, Chevelle, 5 x 7 . . . . . . . . . . . . . . . . . . . .25.00

11 Cale Yarborough, Holly Farms, Chevelle, white car, 8 x 10 . . . . . . . . . . . . . . . . .20.00

12 Bobby Allison, Matador, posed, 5 x 7 . .20.00

12 Bobby Allison, Coca-Cola, Matador, posed, 6 x 9 . . . . . . . . . . . . . . . . . . . .20.00

15 Buddy Baker, Ford, 6 x 9 . . . . . . . . .20.00

15 Buddy Baker, art headshot, 5 x 4 . . . . .12.00

16 Bobby Allison, Coca-Cola, Matador, #I45415, 3½ x 5½ . . . . . . . . . . . . . . . . . . .20.00

16 Bobby Allison, Coca-Cola, Matador, beside car, 10 x 8 . . . . . . . . . . . . . . . . . . . .20.00

17 Darrell Waltrip, Terminal Transport, Chevelle, 5 x 7 . . . . . . . . . . . . . . . . . . . .18.00

21 David Pearson, Purolator, Mercury, blank back, 8½ x 11 . . . . . . . . . . . . . . . . . . .15.00

21 David Pearson, Purolator, Mercury, #AM, 75-33, 3 x 5 . . . . . . . . . . . . . . . . . . .15.00

28 A.J. Foyt, Gilmore, Chevelle, in car, 5 x 7 . . . . . . . . . . . . . . . . . . . .15.00

28 A.J. Foyt, Gilmore, Chevelle, beside car, 10 x 7½ . . . . . . . . . . . . . . . . . . .15.00

28 A.J. Foyt, Gilmore, Chevelle, kneeling, 5 x 7 . . . . . . . . . . . . . . . . . . . .18.00

30 Tighe Scott, Ballard Racing, Chevelle, 8½ x 3½ . . . . . . . . . . . . . . . . . . .18.00

35 Dan Daughtry, Ford, 5 x 7 . . . . . . . .20.00

43 Richard Petty, STP, Dodge, 5 x 7 . . . . .15.00

43 Richard Petty, STP, Dodge, Grand National Champion, 5 x 7 . . . . . . . . . . . . . . .15.00

48 James Hylton, Nitro Nine, Chevelle, 5 x 7 . . . . . . . . . . . . . . . . . . . .15.00

60 Joe Mihalic, Pittsburgh, Chevelle, 5 x 7 . . . . . . . . . . . . . . . . . . . .35.00

64 Elmo Langley, Independent Auto Salvage, Ford, 5 x 7 . . . . . . . . . . . . . . . . . . . .15.00

65 Carl Adams, Travelodge, Ford, 5 x 7 . . .25.00

66 Terry Link, Subtropic, Pontiac, 5 x 7 . . .25.00

70 J.D. McDuffie, Glen's Landscaping, Chevelle, 5 x 7 . . . . . . . . . . . . . . . . . . . .18.00

71 Dave Marcis, K & K Insurance, Dodge, 5 x 7 . . . . . . . . . . . . . . . . . . . .15.00

72 Benny Parsons, Kings Row, Chevelle, 6 x 9 .15.00

74 Randy Tissot, Tilitco Enterprises, Chevelle, 5 x 7 . . . . . . . . . . . . . . . . . . . .15.00

79 Frank Warren, Massey Dodge, 5 x 7 . .18.00

82 Ferrell Harris, Cougar Coal, Dodge, 5 x 7 . . . . . . . . . . . . . . . . . . . .18.00

83 Ramo Stott, Smithville Farms, Chevelle, 5 x 7 . . . . . . . . . . . . . . . . . . . .15.00

88 Donnie Allison, Chevelle, blank back, 5 x 7 . . . . . . . . . . . . . . . . . . . .12.00

88 Donnie Allison, Chevelle with strips, posed, 6 x 9 . . . . . . . . . . . . . . . . . . . .15.00

90 Dick Brooks, Truxmore, Ford, 6 x 9 . . .15.00

96 Richard Childress, Chevelle, 5 x 7 . . . .15.00

98 Richie Panch, Grey Rock, Monte Carlo, 5 x 7 . . . . . . . . . . . . . . . . . . . .25.00

## 1976

2 Bobby Allison, Penske, Cam 2, Mercury, posed, 5 x 8 . . . . . . . . . . . . . . . . . . . .15.00

2 Bobby Allison, Penske, Cam 2, Mercury, action, 5 x 8 . . . . . . . . . . . . . . . . . . . .15.00

11 Cale Yarborough, Holly Farms, Chevelle, 5 x 7 . . . . . . . . . . . . . . . . . . . .15.00

11 Cale Yarborough, Holly Farms, Chevelle, 2 Shots, 5 x 7 . . . . . . . . . . . . . . .10.00

11 Cale Yarborough, Holly Farms, Chevelle, 8 x 10 . . . . . . . . . . . . . . . . . .10.00

11 Cale Yarborough, Holly Farms, 2 shots, full view, 6½ x 7½ . . . . . . . . . .15.00

11 Cale Yarborough, Holly Farms, Chevelle, 3 shots, B & W, 8 x 10 . . . . . . . . . . .12.00

11 Cale Yarborough, Ethyl, Chevelle, 5 x 7 . . . . . . . . . . . . . . . . . . . .18.00

15 Buddy Baker, Norris, Ford, 2 shots with printed autograph, 5 x 7½ . . . . . . . . .15.00

15 Buddy Baker, Norris Industries, Ford, 2 shots, 5 x 7 . . . . . . . . . . . . . . . . . . .12.00

15 Buddy Baker, printed autograph, 5 x 8 . . . . . . . . . . . . . . . . . . . .15.00

18 Joe Frasson, Mr. Zip, Chevelle, dark color, #134318, 5½ x 7 . . . . . . . . . . . . .12.00

18 Joe Frasson, Mr. Zip, Chevelle, light color, #131711, 5½ x 7 . . . . . . . . . .12.00

21 David Pearson, Purolator, Mercury, 2 Shots, 5½ x 7 . . . . . . . . . . . . . . . . . .10.00

24 Cecil Gordon, Purette, Chevelle, #32733-D, 3½ x 5½ . . . . . . . . . . . . . . . . . .15.00

31 Jim Vandiver, H. B. Ranier, Dodge, 5 x 7 .12.00

43 Richard Petty, STP Dodge, 2 shots, posed, STP, 5 x 7 . . . . . . . . . . . . . . . . . .15.00

43 Richard Petty, STP Dodge, posed, STP, 5 x 7 . . . . . . . . . . . . . . . . . . . .15.00

43 Richard Petty, STP Dodge, bio on back, posed, STP, 3½ x 5½ . . . . . . . . . . . . . .15.00

43 Richard Petty, STP Dodge, Welcome Back, STP, 3½ x 5½ . . . . . . . . . . . . . .15.00

47 Bruce Hill, Hill Racing, Chevelle, 5 x 7 . . . . . . . . . . . . . . . . . . . .15.00

54 Lennie Pond, Pepsi, Monte Carlo, 7 x 5 . . . . . . . . . . . . . . . . . . . .12.00

66 Terry Link, Subtropic, Pontiac, 3 x 5 . . .18.00

72 Benny Parsons, King Row, Chevelle, action, 5 x 7 . . . . . . . . . . . . . . . . . . . .12.00

## 1977

1 Donnie Allison, Hawaiian Tropic, Monte Carlo, action, 5 x 7 . . . . . . . . . . . . . . . . . .15.00

3 Richard Childress, L.C. Newton, Monte Carlo, #061036, 5½ x 7 . . . . . . . . . . . . .15.00

5 Neil Bonnett, Jim Stacy Dodge, color, thin stock, 8 x 10 . . . . . . . . . . . . . . . . . . . .20.00

11 Cale Yarborough, Holly Farms, Chevelle, 2 shots, 5 x 7 . . . . . . . . . . . . . . . . . .10.00

11 Cale Yarborough, Holly Farms, Chevelle, trophy, 5 x 7 . . . . . . . . . . . . . . . . . .10.00

12 Bobby Allison, FNCTC, Matador with headshot, blank back, 8 x 10 . . . . . . . . . .25.00

12 Bobby Allison, Matador, opposite side of car, fan club, 3 x 5 . . . . . . . . . . . . . . .18.00

14 CooCoo Marlin, Cunningham – Kelley, Chevelle, #091063, 5½ x 7 . . . . . . . . . . . . .15.00

16 Dave Sisco, Reliable Plumbing, Chevelle, #121334, 5½ x 7 . . . . . . . . . . . . .15.00

21 David Pearson, Purolator, Mercury, 2 shots, 5 x 7 . . . . . . . . . . . . . . . . . .10.00

22 Ricky Rudd, NAPA, B & W, thin stock, fan club, 8½ x 11 . . . . . . . . . . . . . . . . . .15.00

27 Sam Sommers, M.C. Anderson, Chevelle, 5 x 7 . . . . . . . . . . . . . . . . . . . .15.00

36 Ron Hutcherson, Brittanica, Chevrolet, #111200, 5½ x 7 . . . . . . . . . . . . .18.00

43 Richard Petty, STP, Dodge, on top of car, 5 x 7 . . . . . . . . . . . . . . . . . . . .15.00

72 Benny Parsons, FNCTC, Monte Carlo, 5 x 7 . . . . . . . . . . . . . . . . . . . .12.00

72 Benny Parsons, FNCTC, Champion, Chevelle, pits, 5½ x 7½ . . . . . . . . . . . . .12.00

79 Frank Warren, Native Tan, Dodge, #111205, 5 x 7 . . . . . . . . . . . . . . . . . . . .15.00

88 Darrell Waltrip, Gatorade, Chevelle, head shot, blank back, 5 x 7 . . . . . . . . . . . . . .15.00

88 Darrell Waltrip, Gatorade, head shot, printed back, 5 x 7 . . . . . . . . . . . . . .15.00

88 Darrell Waltrip, Gatorade, Chevelle, head shot, blank back, 8 x 10 . . . . . . . . . . . . . .15.00

## 1978

1 Winston Show Car, Dodge, with logo on bottom, 5 x 7 . . . . . . . . . . . . . . . . . .10.00

1 Donnie Allison, Hawaiian Tropic, Monte Carlo, pits, 5 x 8 . . . . . . . . . . . . . . . . . .15.00

2 Dave Marcis, Shoney's, Chevelle, 5 x 7 . .12.00

15 Bobby Allison, Norris Industries, Ford, 5½ x 7¼ . . . . . . . .15.00

3 Richard Childress, Kansas Jack, Oldsmobile, blank back, 8 x 10 . . . . . . . . . . . . .20.00

3 Richard Childress, Kansas Jack, Oldsmobile, printed back, 8 x 10 . . . . . . . . . . . .20.00

11 Cale Yarborough, FNCTC, Oldsmobile, 5 x 8 . . . . . . . . . . . . . . . . . . . . . .15.00

15 Bobby Allison, Norris Industries, Ford, 5½ x 7¼ . . . . . . . . . . . . . . . . . . . .15.00

27 Buddy Baker, Oldsmobile, #211136, 5 x 7 . . . . . . . . . . . . . . . . . . . . . .15.00

28 Jerry Jolly, Ski Machine, 8½ x 11 . . . . .20.00

43 Richard Petty, STP, Dodge, 5½ x 8½ . . . . . . . . . . . . . . . . . . . .25.00

48 Al Holbert, Southland Industries, Oldsmobile, #251082, 5 x 7 . . . . . . . . . . . . . . .18.00

54 Lennie Pond, Win Inc., Monte Carlo, #221125, 5½ x 9 . . . . . . . . . . . .15.00

54 Lennie Pond, Win Inc., Monte Carlo, B & W, blank back, 5 x 7 . . . . . . . . . . . . . .12.00

72 Benny Parsons, FNCTC, Monte Carlo, 5 x 7 . . . . . . . . . . . . . . . . . . . . . .12.00

88 Darrell Waltrip, Gatorade, Monte Carlo, head shot, 5 x 7 . . . . . . . . . . . . . . . . .12.00

88 Darrell Waltrip, Gatorade, Monte Carlo, B & W, 8 x 10 . . . . . . . . . . . . . . . . . .15.00

92 Skip Manning, Strat-A-Graph, Monte Carlo, 5½ x 7 . . . . . . . . . . . . . . . . . . . .15.00

## 1979

1 Winston Show Car, 1976 Mercury, logos on bottom, 5 x 7 . . . . . . . . . . . . . . . . .12.00

1 Winston Show Car, 1977 Oldsmobile, logos on bottom, 5 x 7 . . . . . . . . . . . . . . . .10.00

2 Dale Earnhardt, Monte Carlo, #P4481, 6 x 9 . . . . . . . . . . . . .75.00

40 D.K. Ulrich, Army, Monte Carlo, #361243, 6 x 9 . . . . .15.00

1 Donnie Allison, Hawaiian Tropic, Oldsmobile, posed, 5 x 7 . . . . . . . . . . . . . . . .18.00

2 Dale Earnhardt, Monte Carlo, #P4481, 6 x 9 . . . . . . . . . . . . . . . . . . . . . . .75.00

2 Dale Earnhardt, B & W head shot, fan club, thin stock, 8 x 10 . . . . . . . . . . . . . .100.00

2 Dale Earnhardt, B & W action shot, fan club, thin stock, 8 x 10 . . . . . . . . . . . .80.00

3 Richard Childress, CRC, Oldsmobile, 5 x 7 . . . . . . . . . . . . . . . . . . . . . . .15.00

11 Cale Yarborough, Busch Beer, Oldsmobile, with Junior, 5 x 7 . . . . . . . . . . . .15.00

11 Cale Yarborough, Busch Beer, Oldsmobile, with Junior, 5 x 7½ . . . . . . . . . . . .15.00

12 Childers Racing, Ken Coal Racing, Oldsmobile, #431316, 5½ x 7 . . . . . . . . . . . . .15.00

15 Bobby Allison, Hodgdon, Ford, 5 x 7 . . .15.00

15 Bobby Allison, Hodgdon, Ford, printed autograph, 5 x 7 . . . . . . . . . . . . . . . . .15.00

17 Roger Hamby, Kings Inn, Oldsmobile, #381412, 3 x 8 . . . . . . . . . . . . . . . .15.00

21 Neil Bonnett, Purolator, Mercury, 5 x 7½ . . . . . . . . . . . . . . . . . . . . . .15.00

21 Neil Bonnett, Purolator, Mercury, thin stock, 8 x 10 . . . . . . . . . . . . . . . . . . . . .15.00

24 Cecil Gordon, Sadler Oldsmobile, #471005, 5 x 7 . . . . . . . . . . . . . . . . . . . . . . .15.00

27 Benny Parsons, Oldsmobile, #341113, 5½ x 7 . . . . . . . . . . . . . . . . . . . . .12.00

27 Benny Parsons, Griffin Marine, Oldsmobile, 5 x 7 . . . . . . . . . . . . . . . . . . . . . . .12.00

28 Buddy Baker, Spectra, Oldsmobile, #7039 & #P4609, 6 x 9 . . . . . . . . . . . . . . .15.00

30 Tighe Scott, RRRRRus Togs, Buick, 5 x 7 . . . . . . . . . . . . . . . . . . . . . . .15.00

40 D.K. Ulrich, Midwestern Farm Lines, Buick, #301231, 5½ x 7 . . . . . . . . . . . . .12.00

40 D.K. Ulrich, Army, Monte Carlo, #361243, 6 x 9 . . . . . . . . . . . . . . . . . . . . . .15.00

42 Kyle Petty, B & W, head shot, 7 x 5 . . .15.00

43 Richard Petty, STP, Monte Carlo, 2 shots, two backs, 5 x 7½ . . . . . . . . . . . . . . . .15.00

43 Richard Petty, Southern Pride, large logo on back, 8 x 10 . . . . . . . . . . . . . . . .20.00

43 Richard Petty, Southern Pride, small logo on back, 8 x 10 . . . . . . . . . . . . . . . . .20.00

43 Richard Petty, Southern Pride, no logo on back, 8 x 10 . . . . . . . . . . . . . . . . .30.00

43 Richard Petty, Southern Pride, fan club, B & W, 5 x 7 . . . . . . . . . . . . . . . . . . . .12.00

43 Richard Petty, leaning on car, fan club, B & W, 7 x 5 . . . . . . . . . . . . . . . . . . . . .12.00

44 Terry Labonte, Strat-A-Graph, Buick, #341052, 5½ x 7 . . . . . . . . . . . . . .25.00

## 1980

48 James Hylton, Palatine Auto Parts, Caprice,
 5 x 7 . . . . . . . . . . . . . . . . . . . . . . . . .20.00
51 A. J. Foyt, Valvoline, Oldsmobile,
 5½ x 7½ . . . . . . . . . . . . . . . . . . . .15.00
53 Slick Johnson, Zoom, Monte Carlo,
 5 x 7 . . . . . . . . . . . . . . . . . . . . . . . .20.00
67 Buddy Arrington, Reid's Trailer Sales, Dodge,
 #381210, 5½ x 7 . . . . . . . . . . . . .15.00
72 Joe Millikan, Appliance Wheels, Oldsmobile,
 5 x 7 . . . . . . . . . . . . . . . . . . . . . . . .18.00
72 Joe Millikan, L. G. DeWitt, Monte Carlo,
 5 x 7 . . . . . . . . . . . . . . . . . . . . . . . .18.00
88 Darrell Waltrip, Gatorade, Monte Carlo, 2
 different backs, 5 x 7 . . . . . . . . . . .15.00
88 Darrell Waltrip, Gatorade, Monte Carlo,
 8 x 10 . . . . . . . . . . . . . . . . . . . . . . .18.00
88 Darrell Waltrip, Gatorade, Monte Carlo,
 8 x 10 . . . . . . . . . . . . . . . . . . . . . . .18.00

1 Donnie Allison, Hawaiian Tropic, Oldsmobile,
 wins, 5 x 7 . . . . . . . . . . . . . . . .15.00

90 Ricky Rudd, Truxmore, Mercury, #361208,
 6 x 9 . . . . . . . . . . . . . . . . . . . . . . . .20.00

1 Donnie Allison, Hawaiian Tropic, Oldsmobile,
 printed autograph, 5 x 7 . . . . . . . . . .15.00
1 David Pearson, Hawaiian Tropic, Monte Carlo,
 #481074, 5½ x 9 . . . . . . . . . . . . . .20.00

2 Dale Earnhardt, Oldsmobile, 6 x 8 . . . .140.00

3 Richard Childress, CRC, Oldsmobile, with crew, 5 x 7 . . . . . . . . . . . . . . . . . . . . . . . .20.00

28 Buddy Baker, NAPA Shocks, Oldsmobile, hand on car, #451097, 6 x 9 . . . . . . . . .20.00

9 Bill Elliott, Mercury, #391358, 5 x 7 . . .75.00
11 Cale Yarborough, Busch Beer, Oldsmobile, with Junior, Ned, & Roy, 5 x 7½ . . . . . . .18.00
11 Cale Yarborough, Honda-Mazda, Holmes Wreckers, 6 x 9 . . . . . . . . . . . . . .25.00
15 Bobby Allison, Hodgdon, B & W, pit road, 5 x 6 . . . . . . . . . . . . . . . . . . . . . . .15.00
15 Bobby Allison, Hodgdon, B & W, with crew, 5 x 7 . . . . . . . . . . . . . . . . . . . . . . .20.00
15 Bobby Allison, head shot, 5½ x 4½ . . . .20.00
16 Rusty Wallace, Penske, Caprice, B & W, thick stock, blank back, 8 x 10 . . . . . . . . .30.00
16 Rusty Wallace, Headshot, B & W, thick stock, blank back, 8 x 10 . . . . . . . . . . . . .15.00
27 Benny Parsons, Melling Pumper, Oldsmobile, 5 x 7 . . . . . . . . . . . . . . . . . . . . . . .12.00
27 Benny Parsons, World 600 Winner, 4¼ x 5½ . . . . . . . . . . . . . . . . . . . . .12.00
27 Benny Parsons, NAPA Promo, leaning against car, 4¼ x 5½ . . . . . . . . . . . . . . . . . .12.00
27 Benny Parsons, NAPA, waving, 8½ x 5½ . . . . . . . . . . . . . . . . . . . . .12.00

28 Buddy Baker, NAPA Shocks, Oldsmobile, hand on hood, #451098, 6 x 9 . . . . . . . . .20.00
30 Tighe Scott, RRRRRuss, Oldsmobile, #481237, 5½ x 9 . . . . . . . . . . . . .18.00
42,43 Pettys, STP, cars in background, two different backs, 5 x 7½ . . . . . . . . . .20.00
66 Lake Speed, Monte Carlo, #481236, 5½ x 7 . . . . . . . . . . . . . . . . . . . .20.00
71 Dave Marcis, Buck Stoves, Oldsmobile, #481037, 5½ x 9 . . . . . . . . . . . . .18.00
88 Darrell Waltrip, Gatorade, Oldsmobile, posed, #461226, 5 x 7 . . . . . . . . . . . . . . .18.00
90 Jody Ridley, Truxmore, Mercury, #451286, 6 x 9 . . . . . . . . . . . . . . . . . . . . . .18.00
Richard & Kyle Petty, B & W, posed, fan club, 6½ x 5 . . . . . . . . . . . . . . . . . . . . .15.00

## 1981

1 Buddy Baker, B & W, 11 x 8½ . . . . . . . .12.00
1 Buddy Baker, art card, B & W, George Paylor, 11 x 8½ . . . . . . . . . . . . . . . . . .12.00
2 Dale Earnhardt, Wrangler, Pontiac, blank back, 5½ x 9 . . . . . . . . . . . . . . . . . . . . . .50.00

2 Dale Earnhardt, Wrangler, with cargo plane, 6 x 9 . . .325.00

5 Morgan Shepherd, Performance Connection, Pontiac, with late model, #P7569, 6 x 9 . . . . . . . . . . . . . . . . . . .20.00

5 Morgan Shepherd, Performance Connection, Pontiac, pit road, blank back, 6 x 9 . . . . . . . . . . . . . . . . . . .20.00

9 Bill Elliott, Mell Gear, Ford, blue, 5 x 7 . . .25.00

11 Darrell Waltrip, Mountain Dew, Buick, 5 x 7 . . . . . . . . . . . . . . . . . . . .18.00

13 Dick Brooks, Carolina Tool, Ford, 5 x 7 . . . . . . . . . . . . . . . . . . . . .35.00

15 Benny Parsons, Melling, Ford, posed, 5 x 7 . . . . . . . . . . . . . . . . . . . .12.00

15 Benny Parsons, Melling, Ford, with crew, 5 x 7 . . . . . . . . . . . . . . . . . . . .12.00

16 David Pearson, Halpern Enterprises, Pontiac, #641372, 5½ x 9 . . . . . . . . . . . . .20.00

17 Roger Hamby, Kings Inn, Oldsmobile, 7½ x 3½ . . . . . . . . . . . . . . . . . . .15.00

21 Neil Bonnett, Purolator, Ford, blank back, 8½ x 11 . . . . . . . . . . . . . . . . . .15.00

21 Neil Bonnett, Hodgdon, Ford, blank back, 8 x 10 . . . . . . . . . . . . . . . . . . .15.00

21 Neil Bonnett, Hodgdon, Ford, blank back, 5 x 7 . . . . . . . . . . . . . . . . . . . .15.00

22 Stan Barrett, Skoal Bandit, Pontiac, blank back, 5 x 7 . . . . . . . . . . . . . . . . .150.00

27 Cale Yarborough, Valvoline, Buick, with crew, 5 x 7½ . . . . . . . . . . . . . . . . . .15.00

28 Bobby Allison, Hardee's, Buick, posed, blank back, 5 x 7 . . . . . . . . . . . . . . . . .15.00

28 Bobby Allison, Hardee's, Buick, action, 5 x 7 . . . . . . . . . . . . . . . . . . . .12.00

28 Bobby Allison, Hardee's, Buick, B & W, action, blank back, 8 x 10 . . . . . . . . . . . . .12.00

28 Bobby Allison, Tuflon, Pontiac Tempest, 5 x 7 . . . . . . . . . . . . . . . . . . . .85.00

28 Bobby Allison, Tuflon, Pontiac, Ranier Racing, 5 x 7 . . . . . . . . . . . . . . . . . . . .40.00

28 Bobby Allison, Tuflon, Pontiac, Winning Combination, 5 x 7 . . . . . . . . . . . . . . . . .25.00

33 Harry Gant, Skoal Bandit, Pontiac, blank back, 5 x 7 . . . . . . . . . . . . . . . . . . . .15.00

42 Kyle Petty, STP, Buick, #STP 1-42, 5 x 6½ . . . . . . . . . . . . . . . . . . .15.00

42 Kyle Petty, STP, Buick, 6 x 9 . . . . . . . .25.00

**Ranier Racing 1981**

28 Bobby Allison, Tuflon, Pontiac, Ranier Racing 5 x 7          40.00

43 Richard Petty, STP, Buick, #STP 1-42,
   5 x 6½ . . . . . . . . . . . . . . . . . . . .15.00
43 Richard Petty, STP, Buick, 5 x 7½ . . . . .25.00
44 Terry Labonte, Strat-A-Graph, Buick,
   #581289, 5½ x 7 . . . . . . . . . . . . . .15.00
66 Lake Speed, Oldsmobile, #581255,
   5½ x 9 . . . . . . . . . . . . . . . . . . . .15.00
67 Buddy Arrington, Hills Racing, Dodge,
   #581281, 5½ x 7 . . . . . . . . . . . . .15.00

Kyle & Richard Petty, STP, no cars, posed, #STP
   1-42, 5 x 7½ . . . . . . . . . . . . . . . .15.00

## 1982

1 Buddy Baker, UNO, Buick, 5½ x 8½ . . . .18.00
1 Buddy Baker, UNO, B & W, head shot,
   11 x 8½ . . . . . . . . . . . . . . . . . . .15.00
1 Kyle Petty, UNO, STP, Buick, #P11032,
   6 x 9 . . . . . . . . . . . . . . . . . . . . .20.00

71 Dave Marcis, Norton, Buick, 6 x 8½ . . .20.00
71 Dave Marcis, Norton, Buick, B & W, thick
   stock, blank back, 3 x 5 . . . . . . . . . .18.00
88 Ricky Rudd, Gatorade, Buick, #581194,
   5½ x 7 . . . . . . . . . . . . . . . . . . . .18.00
90 Jody Ridley, Truxmore, Mercury,
   6 x 9 . . . . . . . . . . . . . . . . . . . . .15.00
98 Johnny Rutherford, Levi Garrett, Pontiac, blank
   back, 5 x 7 . . . . . . . . . . . . . . . . .15.00
99 Tim Richmond, UNO, B & W, head shot,
   11 x 8½ . . . . . . . . . . . . . . . . . . .30.00

02 Mark Martin, Apache Stove, Buick,
   5 x 7 . . . . . . . . . . . . . . . . . . . . .20.00
02 Mark Martin, AMS Oil Racing, thin stock,
   8 x 10 . . . . . . . . . . . . . . . . . . . .20.00

2 Joe Ruttman, J.D. Stacy, Buick, #P9404,
5½ x 8½ . . . . . . . . . . . . . . . . . . . . .15.00
2 Tim Richmond, Stacy Pak, Buick, #P10412,
8 x 10 . . . . . . . . . . . . . . . . . .30.00
3 Ricky Rudd, Piedmont Airlines, Pontiac,
#P10046, 3½ x 5½ . . . . . . . . . . .15.00
3 Ricky Rudd, Piedmont Airlines, Pontiac,
5½ x 7 . . . . . . . . . . . . . . . . . . .15.00
9 Bill Elliott, Melling, Ford, 5 x 7 . . . . . . .18.00
11 Darrell Waltrip, Mountain Dew, Buick, with
order form, 5 x 7 . . . . . . . . . . . .15.00
11 Darrell Waltrip, Mountain Dew, fan club,
8 x 10 . . . . . . . . . . . . . . . . . . . .15.00

15 Dale Earnhardt, Wrangler, Ford, 5½ x 9 .45.00
16 David Pearson, Chattanooga Chew, Buick,
4 x 6 . . . . . . . . . . . . . . . . . . . . . .12.00
17 Lake Speed, Yazoo, Buick, #P10409 &
#P11463, 5 x 7 . . . . . . . . . . . . . .10.00
20 Rick Newson, Bull Frog Knits, 3 x 5 . . .18.00
27 Cale Yarborough, Valvoline, Buick,
5 x 7½ . . . . . . . . . . . . . . . . . . . .10.00
27 Cale Yarborough, Valvoline, Buick, blue, printed
autograph, 5 x 7½ . . . . . . . . . . .10.00
33 Harry Gant, Skoal Bandit, Buick, #MF, 200,
5 x 7 . . . . . . . . . . . . . . . . . . . . . .10.00
35 Morgan Shepherd, 4 x 5½ . . . . . . . .18.00
36 H.B. Bailey, Alemeda Auto Parts, Pontiac,
#P10418, 5½ x 7 . . . . . . . . . . . .10.00
42 Kyle Petty, STP, Pontiac, oval, 4 x 7 . . .15.00

42 Kyle Petty, STP Collector's Series,
3½ x 5½ . . . . . . . . . . . . . . . . . . .12.00
43 Richard Petty, STP, Pontiac, oval, 5½ x 7 .15.00
43 Richard Petty, STP, Collectors Series,
3½ x 5 . . . . . . . . . . . . . . . . . . . .12.00
44 Terry Labonte, J.D. Stacy, Buick,
5½ x 8½ . . . . . . . . . . . . . . . . . . .12.00
44 Terry Labonte, Texas Jeans, Buick, paper
stock, 8 x 10 . . . . . . . . . . . . . . .12.00
44 Terry Labonte, Strat-A-Graph, Texas Jeans,
5½ x 8½ . . . . . . . . . . . . . . . . . . .12.00
47 Ron Bouchard, J.D. Stacy, Buick, #P9514 &
#P10150, 5½ x 7 . . . . . . . . . . . . .10.00
50 Joe Millikan, Performance Connection, Pontiac, 6 x 9 . . . . . . . . . . . . . . . . . . .12.00
55 Benny Parsons, Skoal, Buick, 5 x 7 . . .10.00
75 Joe Ruttman, Pet Dairy, Buick, 5 x 7 . .15.00
88 Bobby Allison, Gatorade, Daytona Win,
#P10204, 5½ x 7 . . . . . . . . . . . . .12.00
88 Bobby Allison, Gatorade, action, #P9859,
5½ x 7 . . . . . . . . . . . . . . . . . . . .12.00
88 Bobby Allison, Gatorade, B & W, 8 x 10 .10.00
88 Bobby Allison, Gatorade, posed, #P9515 &
#P9716, 5½ x 7 . . . . . . . . . . . . . .12.00
90 Jody Ridley, J.D. Stacy, Ford, 5½ x 8 . .10.00
98 Morgan Shepherd, Levi Garrett, Buick,
#P19176, 5½ x 7 . . . . . . . . . . . . .10.00
98 Morgan Shepherd, Levi Garrett, thin stock,
8½ x 11 . . . . . . . . . . . . . . . . . . . .8.00
Horst Fischer, STP, Saunders Leasing, hauler,
5 x 7 . . . . . . . . . . . . . . . . . . . . . .10.00
Richard & Kyle Petty, STP, Saunders Leasing,
hauler, 5 x 7 . . . . . . . . . . . . . . . .15.00

# 1983

0 Delma Cowart, Coastal Transmissions, Buick,
#741310, 5½ x 9 . . . . . . . . . . . . .10.00
1 Lake Speed, UNO, Bullfrog Knits, Chevrolet,
#P13522, 6 x 9 . . . . . . . . . . . . . .10.00

**Owner: Hoss Ellington — Driver: Lake Speed**

**Sponsors: Uno and Bullfrog Knits**

1 Lake Speed, UNO, Bullfrog Knits, Chevrolet, B &
W, 3½ x 5 . . . . . . . . . . . . . . . . . . .8.00

**MARK MARTIN
VALVRING RACING BUICK**

2 Mark Martin, Valvring, Buick, #P12914, 5½ x 7 . . .25.00

2 Morgan Shepherd, ACM Equipment Sales, Buick, 6 x 9 . . . . . . . . . . . . . . . . . . . .15.00

2 Morgan Shepherd, "My Car," 8 x 10 . . . .25.00

3 Ricky Rudd, Piedmont Airlines, Chevrolet, 5½ x 7 . . . . . . . . . . . . . . . . . . . . . . .12.00

4 Lake Speed, UNO, Chevrolet, B & W, 4 x 6 .10.00

7 Kyle Petty, 7-Eleven, Pontiac, 5 x 7 . . . . .12.00

9 Bill Elliott, Melling, Ford, 5 x 7 . . . . . . .15.00

11 Darrell Waltrip, Pepsi, Chevrolet, thick outline around head shots, 6 x 9 . . . . . . . . .10.00

11 Darrell Waltrip, Pepsi, Chevrolet, thin outline around head shots, 6 x 9 . . . . . . . . .10.00

16 David Pearson, Chattanooga Chew, Buick, 4 x 6 . . . . . . . . . . . . . . . . . . . . . .10.00

16 David Pearson, Chattanooga Chew, 6 x 9 . . . . . . . . . . . . . . . . . . . . . . . .10.00

16 David Pearson, Chattanooga Chew, 8 x 10 . . . . . . . . . . . . . . . . . . . . . .10.00

16 David Pearson, Chattanooga Chew, 7½ x 9½ . . . . . . . . . . . . . . . . . . . . .10.00

17 Sterling Marlin, HESCO Exhaust, Chevrolet, #86013-D, 6 x 9 . . . . . . . . . . . . . . .18.00

20 Rick Newsome, Bull Frog Knits, 5½ x 7 . . . . . . . . . . . . . . . . . . . . . .10.00

2 Morgan Shepherd, ACM Equipment Sales, Buick, 6 x 9 .15.00

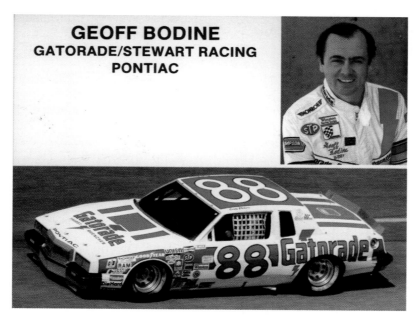

**GEOFF BODINE**
**GATORADE/STEWART RACING**
**PONTIAC**

88 Geoff Bodine, Gatorade, Pontiac, #P13256, 5 x 7 . .10.00

21 Buddy Baker, Valvoline, Ford, 5 x 7½ . . . . . . . . . . . . . . . . . . . .10.00
22 Bobby Allison, Miller, Buick, 5½ x 7 . . . . .8.00
28 Cale Yarborough, Hardee's, Chevrolet, 5½ x 7 . . . . . . . . . . . . . . . . . . . . .10.00
33 Harry Gant, Skoal Bandit, Buick, #P13114, 5½ x 7 . . . . . . . . . . . . . . . . . . . . .10.00
33 Harry Gant, Skoal Bandit, Buick, #P14858, 5½ x 7 . . . . . . . . . . . . . . . . . . . . .10.00
33 Harry Gant, Skoal Bandit, Buick, #P13358, 5½ x 7 . . . . . . . . . . . . . . . . . . . . .10.00
33 Harry Gant, Skoal Bandit, Buick, #MF-200, 5½ x 7 . . . . . . . . . . . . . . . . . . . . .10.00
36 H.B. Bailey, Pontiac, 5 x 7 . . . . . . . .10.00
43 Richard Petty, STP, Texas Jeans, Pontiac, 8 x 6 . . . . . . . . . . . . . . . . . . . . . .20.00
43 Richard Petty, STP, Pontiac, logo on top, 5 x 7½ . . . . . . . . . . . . . . . . . . . . .10.00
43 Richard Petty, STP, Pontiac, logo on bottom, 6 x 8 . . . . . . . . . . . . . . . . . . . . . .15.00
43 Richard Petty, Sealed Power Card, 6 x 9 . . . . . . . . . . . . . . . . . . . . . .15.00
44 Terry Labonte, Budweiser, Chevrolet, solid red, 6 x 9 . . . . . . . . . . . . . . . . . . . . .10.00
44 Terry Labonte, Budweiser, Chevrolet, red & white, 6 x 9 . . . . . . . . . . . . . . . . . .10.00
47 Ron Bouchard, Foster Grant, Buick, #P13092, 5½ x 7 . . . . . . . . . . . . .10.00
48 Trevor Boys, Hylton, McCaig Chevrolet, #P14284, 5 x 7 . . . . . . . . . . . . . . .10.00
55 Benny Parsons, Copenhagen, "Cope" car, Chevrolet, #PI4I52, 5½ x 7 . . . . . . . . .8.00
55 Benny Parsons, Copenhagen, "Cope" car, Chevrolet, #P15870, 5½ x 7 . . . . . . . . .10.00
64 Tommy Gale, Sunny King, Ford, 5 x 7 . . .8.00

67 Buddy Arrington, Chrysler, #871160, 5½ x 7 . . . . . . . . . . . . . . . . . . . . . .8.00
75 Neil Bonnett, Hodgdon, Chevrolet, 8 x 10 . . . . . . . . . . . . . . . . . . . . . .10.00
75 Neil Bonnett, headshot, fan club, 8 x 10 .15.00
77 Ken Ragan, Clinomint, Chevrolet, #881594, 5½ x 7 . . . . . . . . . . . . . . . . . . . . .12.00
82 Mark Stahl, Autobell Car Wash, 1982 Ford, #P14234, 4 x 6 . . . . . . . . . . . . . .15.00
84 Jody Ridley, Cumberland Carpet, Buick, #P13399, 3½ x 8 . . . . . . . . . . . . . .12.00
88 Geoff Bodine, Gatorade, Pontiac, #P13256, 5 x 7 . . . . . . . . . . . . . . . . . . . . .10.00
88 Geoff Bodine, Gatorade, Pontiac, Darlington, #P12915, 5 x 7 . . . . . . . . . . . . . . .10.00
90 Dick Brooks, Sunny King, Ford, 5 x 7 . .10.00
90 Dick Brooks, Chameleon, Ford, orange front, 9 x 6 . . . . . . . . . . . . . . . . . . . . .10.00
96 Jimmy Walker, 1982 Ford, 4 x 6 . . . . .15.00
98 Joe Ruttman, Levi Garrett, #P12549, 5½ x 7 . . . . . . . . . . . . . . . . . . . . .10.00
98 Joe Ruttman, Levi Garrett, #P14452, 5½ x 7 . . . . . . . . . . . . . . . . . . . . .10.00
98 Joe Ruttman, Levi Garrett, #P12808, 5½ x 7 . . . . . . . . . . . . . . . . . . . . .10.00
98 Joe Ruttman, Levi Garrett, Buick, 3½ x 5 . . . . . . . . . . . . . . . . . . . . .10.00

## 1984

01 Doug Heveron, Syracuse Classic, Chevrolet, #P17363, 5½ x 7 . . . . . . . . . . . . . .15.00
01 Doug Heveron, Syracuse Classic, hauler, #P17264, 6 x 9 . . . . . . . . . . . . . . .15.00
1 Winston Show Car, Monte Carlo, 4 x 6 . . .6.00

1 Winston Show Car, Monte Carlo, 8 x 10 .5.00
1 Lake Speed, Bullfrog Knits, Chevrolet, #PI5868,
   5½ x 7 . . . . . . . . . . . . . . . . . .12.00
1 Lake Speed, Bullfrog, Chevrolet, Darlington Win,
   #P17265, 5¼ x 7 . . . . . . . . . . . .12.00
3 Dale Earnhardt, Wrangler, Chevrolet, 9 x 6 .35.00
4 Tommy Ellis, Morrell Datsun, Chevrolet,
   #P18579, 3½ x 5½ . . . . . . . . . . . .15.00
5 Geoff Bodine, All Star Racing, Chevrolet,
   5 x 7½ . . . . . . . . . . . . . . . . . .12.00
5 Geoff Bodine, All Star Racing, Chevrolet,
   5 x 7 . . . . . . . . . . . . . . . . . . . .10.00
6 D.K. Ulrich, California Cooler, Chevrolet,
   5 x 7 . . . . . . . . . . . . . . . . . . . .10.00
7 Kyle Petty, Ford MotorSport, art,
   8½ x 11 . . . . . . . . . . . . . . . . . .10.00
8 Bobby Hillin, Buick, #P17266, 5½ x 7 . .12.00
9 Bill Elliott, Coors, Melling, #P16727,
   5½ x 7 . . . . . . . . . . . . . . . . . .15.00
9 Bill Elliott, Coors, Melling, #P18774,
   5½ x 7 . . . . . . . . . . . . . . . . . .15.00
9 Bill Elliott, Coors, Melling, #P17924,
   5½ x 7 . . . . . . . . . . . . . . . . . .15.00
11 Darrell Waltrip, Budweiser, Chevrolet, Daytona,
   6 x 8½ . . . . . . . . . . . . . . . . . .12.00
11 Darrell Waltrip, Budweiser, Chevrolet,
   6 x 9 . . . . . . . . . . . . . . . . . . . .12.00

11 Darrell Waltrip, Budweiser, Chevrolet, fan club,
   8 x 10 . . . . . . . . . . . . . . . . . . .18.00
12 Neil Bonnett, Budweiser, Chevrolet, Daytona,
   6 x 9 . . . . . . . . . . . . . . . . . . . .12.00
12 Neil Bonnett, Budweiser, Chevrolet,
   6 x 9 . . . . . . . . . . . . . . . . . . . .12.00
12 Neil Bonnett, Budweiser, Chevrolet, fan club,
   8 x 10 . . . . . . . . . . . . . . . . . . .18.00
11, 12 Darrell Waltrip & Neil Bonnett, Kentucky
   Fried Chicken, 6 x 11½ . . . . . . . . . .15.00
15 Ricky Rudd, Wrangler, Ford, 6 x 9 . . . .12.00
16, 21 David & Larry Pearson, Chattanooga
   Chew, 6 x 9 . . . . . . . . . . . . . . . .10.00
16, 21 David & Larry Pearson, Chattanooga
   Chew, 8 x 10 . . . . . . . . . . . . . . .10.00
17 Clark Dwyer, Hesco Exhaust, Chevrolet,
   #P16783, 5½ x 7 . . . . . . . . . . . .12.00
21 Buddy Baker, Valvoline, Ford, #V-1029,
   5 x 7½ . . . . . . . . . . . . . . . . . .12.00
22 Bobby Allison, Miller, Buick,
   5½ x 7 . . . . . . . . . . . . . . . . . .12.00
22 Bobby Allison, Miller, Buick, Favorite Driver,
   5½ x 7 . . . . . . . . . . . . . . . . . .12.00
22 Bobby Allison, Miller, Quaker State, Buick,
   9 x 12 . . . . . . . . . . . . . . . . . . .15.00
27 Tim Richmond, Old Milwaukee, Pontiac,
   #89480, 5 x 7½ . . . . . . . . . . . . . .15.00

27 Tim Richmond, Old Milwaukee, B & W, 2 shots,
   11 x 8½ . . . . . . . . . . . . . . . . . . .18.00

27 Tim Richmond, Old Milwaukee, B & W, 3
shots, 11 x 8½ . . . . . . . . . . . . . . . . . .25.00
28 Cale Yarborough, Hardee's, Chevrolet, Restaurant, 9 x 6 . . . . . . . . . . . . . . . . . . .12.00
28 Cale Yarborough, Hardee's, Chevrolet, Daytona, 5 x 7 . . . . . . . . . . . . . . . . . . .8.00
28 Cale Yarborough, Hardee's, Chevrolet,
enlarged, 6 x 9 . . . . . . . . . . . . . . . .8.00
33 Harry Gant, Skoal Bandit, Chevrolet,
5½ x 7 . . . . . . . . . . . . . . . . . . . . .12.00
41 Ronnie Thomas, Advance Auto, Pontiac, blank
back, 8 x 10 . . . . . . . . . . . . . . . . . .8.00
43 Richard Petty, STP, Pontiac, with lighthouse,
9 x 6 . . . . . . . . . . . . . . . . . . . . . .10.00
44 Terry Labonte, Piedmont, Chevrolet, black
name on front, 6 x 9 . . . . . . . . . . . .10.00
44 Terry Labonte, Piedmont, Chevrolet, white
name on front, 6 x 9 . . . . . . . . . . . .10.00
47 Ron Bouchard, Foster Grant, Buick,
5 x 7 . . . . . . . . . . . . . . . . . . . . . .12.00
48 Trevor Boys, Hylton, McCaig, Chevrolet,
#P16399, 5 x 7 . . . . . . . . . . . . . . . .12.00
55 Benny Parsons, Copenhagen, Chevrolet,
5½ x 7 . . . . . . . . . . . . . . . . . . . . .10.00
66 Phil Parsons, Skoal Bandit, age 26,
5½ x 7 . . . . . . . . . . . . . . . . . . . . .10.00
70 J.D. McDuffie, Rumple Furniture, #P18268,
5½ x 7 . . . . . . . . . . . . . . . . . . . . .15.00
70 J.D. McDuffie, Rumple Furniture, #P16333,
5½ x 7 . . . . . . . . . . . . . . . . . . . . .15.00
71 Mike Alexander, Action Vans, Oldsmobile,
#P18134, 5½ x 7 . . . . . . . . . . . . . . .18.00

77 Ken Ragan, McCord Gaskets, Cherolet, B &
W, 5 x 7 . . . . . . . . . . . . . . . . . . . .10.00
77 Ken Ragan, McCord Gaskets, Chevrolet,
5 x 7 . . . . . . . . . . . . . . . . . . . . . .10.00
77 Ken Ragan, McCord Gaskets, Chevrolet, B &
W, 8 x 10 . . . . . . . . . . . . . . . . . . .12.00
84 Jody Ridley, Cumberland, Chevrolet,
6 x 9 . . . . . . . . . . . . . . . . . . . . . .12.00
87 Randy Baker, Dominos Pizza, Buick,
6 x 9 . . . . . . . . . . . . . . . . . . . . . .12.00

**RUSTY WALLACE**
GATORADE®/STEWART RACING
PONTIAC

88 Rusty Wallace, Gatorade, Pontiac,
5½ x 7 . . . . . . . . . . . . . . . . . . . . .12.00
90 Dick Brooks, Chameleon, Ford, #P17002,
5½ x 7 . . . . . . . . . . . . . . . . . . . . .10.00
97 Dean Combs, Best Products, Oldsmobile, B &
W, 5 x 7 . . . . . . . . . . . . . . . . . . . .12.00
98 Joe Ruttman, Levi Garrett, Chevrolet,
#P17267, 5½ x 7 . . . . . . . . . . . . . . .10.00

## 1985

00 Phil Barkdoll, Helen Rae Special, Chevrolet,
#P22739, 5½ x 7 . . . . . . . . . . . . . . .10.00

12 Neil Bonnett, Budweiser, Chevrolet, fan club, 8 x 10 . . .15.00

07 Randy LaJoie, Snellman Const., Chevrolet, #P21095, 5 x 7 . . . . . . . . . . . . . . .10.00

1 Winston Show Car, Monte Carlo, 4 x 6 . . .5.00

1 Winston Show Car, T-Bird, 4 x 6 . . . . . .5.00

2 Rusty Wallace, Alugard, Pontiac, posed, 5½ x 7 . . . . . . . . . . . . . . . . . .18.00

2 Rusty Wallace, Alugard, Pontiac, action, 5½ x 7 . . . . . . . . . . . . . . . . . .18.00

3 Dale Earnhardt, Wrangler, Chevrolet, blank back, 9 x 6 . . . . . . . . . . . . . . . .30.00

4 Joe Ruttman, Folger's Coffee, Chevrolet, 6 x 9 . . . . . . . . . . . . . . . . . . . . .10.00

4 Joe Ruttman, Folger's Coffee, Chevrolet, with concert ad, 6 x 9 . . . . . . . . . . . . .12.00

5 Geoff Bodine, Levi Garrett, Chevrolet, 5 x 7 . . . . . . . . . . . . . . . . . . . .8.00

6 Eddie Bierschwale, Mission, Chevrolet, #P21492, 5½ x 7 . . . . . . . . . . . .8.00

6 Trevor Boys, US Racing, hauler & 4 cars, B & W, 8 x 10 . . . . . . . . . . . . . . . . . .10.00

7 Kyle Petty, 7-Eleven, Ford, 9½ x 6½ . . . .12.00

7 Kyle Petty, 7-Eleven, Ford, color drawing, 11 x 8½ . . . . . . . . . . . . . . . . . .10.00

8 Bobby Hillin, Chevrolet, #P19715, 5½ x 7 .10.00

9 Bill Elliott, Coors, Ford, action, #P20164, 5½ x 7 . . . . . . . . . . . . . . . . . .10.00

9 Bill Elliott, Coors, Ford, thumbs up, #P20164, 5½ x 7 . . . . . . . . . . . . . . . . . .15.00

9 Bill Elliott, Coors, Ford, stopped on track, 5 x 7 . . . . . . . . . . . . . . . . . . .10.00

11 Darrell Waltrip, Budweiser, Chevrolet, 6 x 9 . . . . . . . . . . . . . . . . . . . . .10.00

11 Darrell Waltrip, Budweiser, Chevrolet, wife inset, blank back, 8 x 10 . . . . . . . . . .15.00

11 Darrell Waltrip, Budweiser, Chevrolet, fan club, 8 x 10 . . . . . . . . . . . . . . . . . .12.00

12 Neil Bonnett, Budweiser, Chevrolet, 6 x 9 . . . . . . . . . . . . . . . . . . . . .10.00

12 Neil Bonnett, Budweiser, Chevrolet, fan club, 8 x 10 . . . . . . . . . . . . . . . . . .15.00

11, 12 No Driver, Budweiser, Budweiser Racing Team, 5 x 7½ . . . . . . . . . . . . . . . . .12.00

14 A.J. Foyt, Valvoline, NASCAR, Indy, IMSA, #V-1205, 5 x 7½ . . . . . . . . . . . . . . . . .12.00

15 Ricky Rudd, Motorcraft, Ford, 8 x 10 . .12.00

17 Ken Ragan, McCord Gaskets, Chevrolet, 5 x 7 . . . . . . . . . . . . . . . . . . . . .10.00

21 David Pearson, Chattanooga Chew, Chevrolet, car only, 6 x 9 . . . . . . . . . . . . . . . .10.00

21 David Pearson, Chattanooga Chew, car, truck, van, 6 x 9 . . . . . . . . . . . . . . . . . .10.00

22 Bobby Allison, Miller, Buick, 5 x 7½ . . . .10.00

28 Cale Yarborough, Hardee's, Ford, Go With A Winner, 9 x 6 . . . . . . . . . . . . . . . .10.00

28 Cale Yarborough, Hardee's, Ford, with trailer, 5½ x 9 . . . . . . . . . . . . . . . . . . .12.00

28 Cale Yarborough, Hardee's, Ford, drawing, blank back, 5½ x 8 . . . . . . . . . . . . .10.00

33 Harry Gant, Skoal Bandit, Chevrolet, 5½ x 7 . . . . . . . . . . . . . . . . . . . .10.00

41 Ronnie Thomas, Chevrolet, on hill, #P19586, 6 x 9 . . . . . . . . . . . . . . . . . . . . .10.00

43 Richard Petty, STP, Pontiac, 200 Wins, 6½ x 9 . . . . . . . . . . . . . . . . . . .12.00

43 Richard Petty, STP, Pontiac, Smithsonian, blank back, 5 x 7 . . . . . . . . . . . . . . . .10.00

44 Terry Labonte, Piedmont Airlines, Chevrolet, 1984 Champion, 6 x 9 . . . . . . . . . .14.00

44 Terry Labonte, Piedmont Airlines, Playcraft Charger Boats, 6 x 9 . .10.00

47 Ron Bouchard, Valvoline, Buick, #V-1154,
   5 x 7½ . . . . . . . . . . . . . . . . . . . . . . . .10.00
52 Jimmy Means, Broadway Motors, Chevrolet,
   5 x 7 . . . . . . . . . . . . . . . . . . . . . . . . .10.00
64 Clark Dwyer, Sunny King Ford, #P20132, 5½ x
   7 . . . . . . . . . . . . . . . . . . . . . . . . . . . .10.00
66 Phil Parsons, Skoal Bandit, Chevrolet, Blue,
   5½ x 7 . . . . . . . . . . . . . . . . . . . . . . . .10.00
67 Buddy Arrington, Motorsports Designs, Ford,
   #P24062, 5½ x 7 . . . . . . . . . . . . . .8.00
70 J.D. McDuffie, Rumple Furniture, Pontiac,
   #P19110, 5½ x 7 . . . . . . . . . . . .12.00

70 J.D. McDuffie, Rumple Furniture, Pontiac,
   #P22645, 5½ x 7 . . . . . . . . . . . . . .12.00
75 Lake Speed, Nationwise, 2 different backs,
   5 x 7 . . . . . . . . . . . . . . . . . . . . . . . . .10.00
77 Greg Sacks, Miller, Buick, 5 x 7 . . . . . .15.00
88 Buddy Baker, Bullfrog, Oldsmobile, #P19798,
   5½ x 9 . . . . . . . . . . . . . . . . . . . . . . . .10.00
88 Buddy Baker, Liquid Wrench, Oldsmobile,
   8 x 10 . . . . . . . . . . . . . . . . . . . . . . . . .10.00
90 Ken Schrader, Ultra Seal, Ford, 6 x 9 . .12.00
98 Trevor Boys, McCaig Racing, Chevrolet,
   #P20348, 5½ x 7 . . . . . . . . . . . . . .10.00

## 1986

70 J.D. McDuffie, Rumple Furniture, Pontiac,
#P21029, 5½ x 7 . . . . . . . . . . .12.00

1 Sterling Marlin, Bulls, Eye BBQ Sauce,
   Chevrolet, 5 x 8 . . . . . . . . . . . . . . . .10.00

4 Rick Wilson, Kodak Films, Oldsmobile, 4 x 8½ . . . . .12.00

3 Dale Earnhardt, Wrangler, Chevrolet, 9 x 6 . . . . . . . . . . . . . . . . . . . . . .30.00
3 Dale Earnhardt, Wrangler, Unocal, paper stock, 8 x 10 . . . . . . . . . . . . . . . . . . . .25.00
4 Rick Wilson, Kodak Films, Oldsmobile, 4 x 8½ . . . . . . . . . . . . . . . . . . . . .12.00

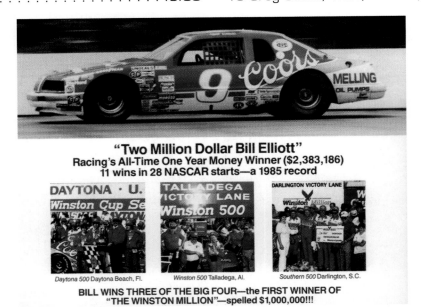

4 Rick Wilson, Kodak Films, Oldsmobile, inset, 4 x 8½ . . . . . . . . . . . . . . . . . . . .10.00
5 Geoff Bodine, Levi Garrett, Chevrolet, 6 x 4½ . . . . . . . . . . . . . . . . . . . . .8.00

5 Geoff Bodine, Levi Garrett, Chevrolet, 500 Win, blank back, 5½ x 8½ . . . . . . . . . . . . .8.00
5 Geoff Bodine, Levi Garrett, Chevrolet, paper stock, 5½ x 8½ . . . . . . . . . . . . . . .5.00
7 Kyle Petty, 7-Eleven, Ford, 8½ x 11 . . . .10.00
8 Bobby Hillin, Miller, Buick, #P26288, 5½ x 7 . . . . . . . . . . . . . . . . . . . .8.00
9 Bill Elliott, Coors, Ford, #P20164, 7 x 5½ . . . . . . . . . . . . . . . . . . .10.00
9 Bill Elliott, Coors, Ford, 2 Million Dollar Winner, 5½ x 7 . . . . . . . . . . . . . . . .12.00
9 Bill Elliott, Coors, Ford, Go With A Winner, 5 x 8½ . . . . . . . . . . . . . . . . . . .20.00
9 Bill Elliott, Coors, Ford, action, 8½ x 11 . .12.00
9 Bill Elliott, Coors, Unocal 76, paper stock, 8½ x 11 . . . . . . . . . . . . . . . . . .12.00
9 Bill Elliott, Snap-On, art, blank back, 10 x 8 . . . . . . . . . . . . . . . . . . . .10.00
10 Greg Sacks, TRW, Pontiac, #X-1025, 5 x 7 . . . . . . . . . . . . . . . . . . . .12.00
10 Greg Sacks, TRW, Pontiac, 8 x 10 . . . .25.00

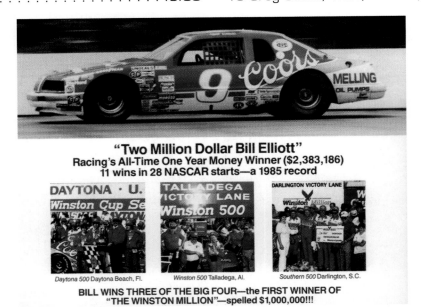

9 Bill Elliott, Coors, Ford, 2 Million Dollar Winner, 5½ x 7 . . .12.00

26 Joe Ruttman, Quaker State, Buick Motorsports, 8½ x 11 . .12.00

11 Darrell Waltrip, Budweiser, Chevrolet, with order form, 6 x 9 . . . . . . . . . . . . .10.00

11 Darrell Waltrip, Budweiser, Chevrolet, no order form, 6 x 9 . . . . . . . . . . . . . . . . . .10.00

11, 17 Darrell Waltrip, Daltrip Waltrip Fan Club, blank back, 8 x 10 . . . . . . . . . . .15.00

11, 12 No Driver, Budweiser, Budweiser Racing Team, 6 x 9 . . . . . . . . . . . . . .12.00

12 Neil Bonnett, Budweiser, Chevrolet, with order form, 6 x 9 . . . . . . . . . . . . . . .10.00

12 Neil Bonnett, Budweiser, Chevrolet, no order form, 6 x 9 . . . . . . . . . . . . . . . . . .10.00

12 Neil Bonnett, Budweiser, Chevrolet, fan club, 8 x 10 . . . . . . . . . . . . . . . . . . . .15.00

15 Ricky Rudd, Motorcraft, Ford, 8½ x 11 . . . . . . . . . . . . . . . . . . . .8.00

17 Eddie Bierschwale, K-Mart/Wynn's, Oldsmobile, #P27633, 5½ x 7 . . . . . . . . . .10.00

17 Eddie Bierschwale, K-Mart/Wynn's, Chevrolet, #P28400, 6 x 9 . . . . . . . . . . . . . . .10.00

18 Tommy Ellis, Freedlander, Chevrolet, blank back, 5½ x 7 . . . . . . . . . . . . . . . . . .12.00

21 Larry Pearson, Chattanooga Chew, Chevrolet, GN & LMS, 6 x 9 . . . . . . . . . . . . . . .8.00

22 Bobby Allison, Miller, Buick, #P26287, 5½ x 7 . . . . . . . . . . . . . . . . . . .10.00

22, 8 No Driver, Miller, Miller Racing Team, 8 x 10 . . . . . . . . . . . . . . . . . . . . .8.00

23 Michael Waltrip, Hawaiian Punch, Pontiac, 5 x 7 . . . . . . . . . . . . . . . . . . . . . .10.00

23 Michael Waltrip, Days Inn Racing Team, Pontiac, #P27633, 5 x 7 . . . . . . . . . . . .10.00

25 Tim Richmond, Folger's, Chevrolet, paper stock, 7 x 5½ . . . . . . . . . . . . . . . .10.00

26 Joe Ruttman, Quaker State, Buick, 11 x 8½ . . . . . . . . . . . . . . . . . . . .8.00

26 Joe Ruttman, Quaker State, Buick Motorsports, 8½ x 11 . . . . . . . . . . . . . . .12.00

27 Rusty Wallace, Alugard, Pontiac, 5½ x 7 . . . . . . . . . . . . . . . . . . . . . .15.00

28 Cale Yarborough, Hardee's, Ford, 6 x 9 .10.00

33 Harry Gant, Skoal Bandit, Chevrolet, #P24351, 5½ x 7 . . . . . . . . . . . . . . .10.00

33 Harry Gant, Skoal Bandit, Chevrolet, #P24908, 5½ x 7 . . . . . . . . . . . . . . .10.00

33 Harry Gant, Skoal, with Indy car, 8 x 10 . .20.00

**ALAN KULWICKI**
**QUINCY'S FAMILY STEAK HOUSE RACING TEAM**

35 Alan Kulwicki, Quincy's Steakhouse, Ford, #P25715, 5½ x 7 . . . . . . . . . . . . . .80.00

43 Richard Petty, STP, Pontiac, blue carpet, 6 x 9 . . . . . . . . . . . . . . .15.00

43 Richard Petty, STP, Pontiac, brown carpet, 6 x 9 . . . . . . . . . . . . . . .10.00

43 Richard Petty, Oakwood Homes, Charlotte locations on back, 5½ x 8½ . . . . . . . .10.00

43 Richard Petty, Oakwood Homes, 5½ x 8½ . . . . . . . . . . . . . . .10.00

43 Richard Petty, STP, Unocal 76, paper stock, 8½ x 11 . . . . . . . . . . . . . . .12.00

44 Terry Labonte, Piedmont Airlines, Oldsmobile, 6 x 9 . . . . . . . . . . . . . . .8.00

55 Benny Parsons, Copenhagen, Oldsmobile, #P24350, 5½ x 7 . . . . . . . . . . .8.00

55 Benny Parsons, Copenhagen, Oldsmobile, #P24910, 5½ x 7 . . . . . . . . . . .8.00

64 Rodney Combs, Sunny King Ford, #56730, 3 x 5 . . . . . . . . . . . . . . .12.00

66 Phil Parsons, Skoal, Oldsmobile, #P24909, 5½ x 7 . . . . . . . . . . . . . . .8.00

66 Phil Parsons, Skoal, Oldsmobile, #P24349, 5½ x 7 . . . . . . . . . . . . . . .8.00

67 Buddy Arrington, Pannell Sweatshirts, Ford, 5½ x 7 . . . . . . . . . . . . . . .10.00

70 J.D. McDuffie, Rumple Furniture, Pontiac, #P24886, 5½ x 7 . . . . . . . . . .10.00

70 J.D. McDuffie, Winkle Pontiac, #P27806, 5½ x 7 . . . . . . . . . . . . . . .12.00

71 Dave Marcis, Helen Rae Special, Pontiac, #P25719, 4¾ x 6 . . . . . . . . . .10.00

71 Dave Marcis, Helen Rae Special, Pontiac, #P25719, 3¼ x 5¾ . . . . . . . . . .8.00

73 Phil Barkdoll, Helen Rae Special, Ford, #P25717, 4¾ x 6 . . . . . . . . . .10.00

73 Phil Barkdoll, Helen Rae Special, Ford, #P25717, 3¼ x 5¾ . . . . . . . . . .8.00

75 Rahmoc, Nationwise Insurance, Pontiac, haulers, 6 x 9 . . . . . . . . . . . . . . .8.00

77 Ken Ragan, McCord Gaskets, Chevrolet, 5 x 7 . . . . . . . . . . . . . . .8.00

79 Derrike Cope, Western Peterbilt, Ford, blank back, 8 x 10 . . . . . . . . . . .15.00

81 Chet Fillip, Circle Bar Truck Corral, Ford, 5 x 7 . . . . . . . . . . . . . . .10.00

88 Buddy Baker, Crisco, Oldsmobile, 7 x 5 . .8.00

88 Buddy Baker, Crisco, Oldsmobile, printed autograph, 7 x 5 . . . . . . . . . . .8.00

88 Buddy Baker, Crisco, Oldsmobile, headshot, B & W, 7 x 5 . . . . . . . . . . .8.00

88 Buddy Baker, B & W, headshot, thin stock, 10 x 8 . . . . . . . . . . . . . . .6.00

90 Ken Schrader, Red Baron Pizza, Ford, 6 x 9 . . . . . . . . . . . . . . .8.00

90 Ken Schrader, Red Baron Pizza, Red Baron logo on front, 6 x 9 . . . . . . . . . . .8.00

94 Eddie Bierschwale, Kodak Film, Pontiac, #P24,348, 5½ x 7 . . . . . . . . . .15.00

94 Eddie Bierschwale, Kodak Film, Pontiac, with crew, 4 x 8½ . . . . . . . . . . .25.00

98 Ron Bouchard, Valvoline, Pontiac, in grass, #V1311, 5 x 7½ . . . . . . . . . . .8.00

98 Ron Bouchard, Valvoline, Pontiac, at Daytona, #V1311, 5 x 7½ . . . . . . . . . . .8.00

## 1987

1 Ron Bouchard, Bull's Eye BBQ Sauce, Chevrolet, 6 x 9 . . . . . . . . . . . . . . .10.00

3 Dale Earnhardt, Wrangler, Chevrolet, 8 x 6 . . . . . . . . . . . . . . .25.00

3 Dale Earnhardt, Wrangler, Chevrolet, 6 x 9 . . . . . . . . . . . . . . .50.00

3 Dale Earnhardt, Top Gun, paper stock, 6 x 9 . . . . . . . . . . . . . . .85.00

4 Rick Wilson, Kodak Film, Oldsmobile, 5 x 9 .6.00

5 Geoff Bodine, Levi Garrett, Chevrolet, 5½ x 8½ . . . . . . . . . . . . . . .6.00

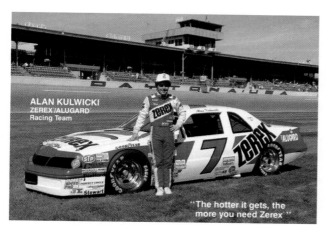

7 Alan Kulwicki, Zerex, Ford, 5½ x 7 . . . . .12.00
8 Bobby Hillin, Miller, Buick, 6 x 9 . . . . . . .8.00
9 Bill Elliott, Coors, Ford, #P20164, 7 x 5½ . . . . . . . . . . . . . . . . . . .8.00
9 Bill Elliott, Coors, Ford, 8½ x 11 . . . . . . .8.00
11 Terry Labonte, Budweiser, Chevrolet, Bud card, 6 x 9 . . . . . . . . . . . . . . . . . . . .6.00
11 Terry Labonte, Budweiser, Chevrolet, KFC card, 6 x 9 . . . . . . . . . . . . . . . . .6.00
15 Ricky Rudd, Motorcraft, Ford, 8½ x 11 . .5.00
17 Darrell Waltrip, Tide, Chevrolet, 5½ x 8½ . . . . . . . . . . . . . . . . . . . . .8.00
18 Dale Jarrett, Freedlander, Chevrolet, blank back, 5½ x 8½ . . . . . . . . . . . . . . .12.00
21 Kyle Petty, Citgo, Ford, 8½ x 11 . . . . . .8.00
22 Bobby Allison, Miller, Buick, 6 x 9 . . . . .10.00
22 Bobby Allison, Miller, headshot, 7 x 5 . . .4.00
26 Morgan Shepherd, Quaker State, Buick, 8 x 10 . . . . . . . . . . . . . . . . . . . . . . . .5.00

26 Morgan Shepherd, Quaker State, Buick Motorsports, 8½ x 11 . . . . . . . . . . . . . . .10.00
27 Rusty Wallace, Kodiak, Pontiac, 5 x 8 . . .6.00
28 Davey Allison, Havoline, Ford, 11 x 8½ . . . . . . . . . . . . . . . . . . . .12.00
22, 8 Miller, Miller Racing, Buicks, 8 x 10 . .5.00
28 Davey Allison, Havoline, First Win, Talladega, hand numbered only 500 produced for Texaco VIPs, 8 x 10 . . . . . . . . . . . . . . . . .500.00
29 Cale Yarborough, Hardee's, Ford, Fast Lane, 9 x 6 . . . . . . . . . . . . . . . . . . . . . .10.00
30 Michael Waltrip, All Pro, Chevrolet, 8 x 10 . . . . . . . . . . . . . . . . . . . . . . .8.00
33 Harry Gant, Skoal Bandit, Chevrolet, 6 x 9 .8.00
33 Harry Gant, Skoal Bandit, Food Lion & Citgo stickers added, 6 x 9 . . . . . . . . . . . . .8.00
43 Richard Petty, STP, Pontiac, with space shuttle, 6 x 8½ . . . . . . . . . . . . . . . . . . . . .8.00
43 Richard Petty, STP, Pontiac, with space shuttle, blank back, 8 x 10 . . . . . . . . . .10.00
43 Richard Petty, Wheeled Coach, thin stock, 8½ x 11 . . . . . . . . . . . . . . . . . . . . .8.00
44 Sterling Marlin, Piedmont, Oldsmobile, 6 x 9 . . . . . . . . . . . . . . . . . . . . . . . .6.00
50 Greg Sacks, Valvoline, Pontiac, #V-1502, 5 x 7 . . . . . . . . . . . . . . . . . . . . . . . .8.00
55 Phil Parsons, Copenhagen, Oldsmobile, 6 x 9 . . . . . . . . . . . . . . . . . . . . . . . .6.00
64 Rodney Combs, Jim Testa Ford, blank back, 5 x 7 . . . . . . . . . . . . . . . . . . . . .10.00
71 Dave Marcis, Lifebuoy, Chevrolet, #2106-E, 4 x 6 . . . . . . . . . . . . . . . . . . . . . . .8.00
75 Neil Bonnett, Valvoline, Pontiac, #V-1471, 5 x 7 . . . . . . . . . . . . . . . . . . . . . .10.00

18 Dale Jarrett, Freedlander, Chevrolet, blank back, 5½ x 8½ . . 12.00

"The dramatic scene behind me took place on May 3, 1987 at Talladega, Alabama...the day I won my first 500 mile Winston Cup Series race! My crew got a free ride to victory lane and a share of the excitement that comes with a *winning ride!*"

Together, we know what it's like to *Ride with a Winner*... Havoline Motor Oil and Texaco Anti-Freeze/Coolant.

Davey Allison

Special Limited Edition    121/500

28 Davey Allison, Havoline, First Win, Talladega, hand numbered only 500 produced for Texaco VIPs, 8 x 10 . . . . . . . . . . . . . . . . . . . . . . . . . . .500.00

82 Mark Stahl, Auto Bell Car Wash, Ford, blank back, 5 x 7 . . . . . . . . . . . . . . . . . . .10.00

83 Lake Speed, K-Mart Wynn's, Oldsmobile, 5 x 7 . . . . . . . . . . . . . . . . . . . . . . . . .8.00

86 Buddy Baker, Crisco, Oldsmobile, 5½ x 8½ . . . . . . . . . . . . . . . . . . . . .8.00

89 Jim Sauter, Evinrude, Pontiac, 5 x 7 . . . .8.00

90 Ken Schrader, Red Baron Pizza, Ford, 7½ x 6 . . . . . . . . . . . . . . . . . . . . . .8.00

90 Ken Schrader, Red Baron Pizza, Ford, 8 x 10 . . . . . . . . . . . . . . . . . . . . . . .8.00

90 Ken Schrader, Red Baron, Ford, Victory Lane, blank back, 7 x 11 . . . . . . . . . . . . . . .8.00

95 Chad Little, Coors, Winston West, 8½ x 11 . . . . . . . . . . . . . . . . . . . . .12.00

98 Ed Pimm, Curb & Cannon Village, Buick, #P34051, 5½ x 7 . . . . . . . . . . . . . . .8.00

## 1988

04 Hershel McGriff, U.S. Bank, Pontiac, 4 x 6 . . . . . . . . . . . . . . . . . . . . . . .6.00

2 Ernie Irvan, Kroger, Chevrolet, 6 x 10 . . .10.00

2 Ernie Irvan, Kroger, Pontiac, 6 x 10 . . . .10.00

3 Dale Earnhardt, Goodwrench, Chevrolet, at shop, 6 x 9 . . . . . . . . . . . . . . . . . .18.00

3 Dale Earnhardt, Goodwrench, Chevrolet, at Daytona, 6 x 9 . . . . . . . . . . . . . . . .18.00

4 Rick Wilson, Kodak Films, Oldsmobile, 5 x 9 . . . . . . . . . . . . . . . . . . . . . . .3.00

5 Geoff Bodine, 1987 IROC Champion, 5½ x 8½ . . . . . . . . . . . . . . . . . . . . .5.00

5 Geoff Bodine, Levi Garrett, Chevrolet, 5½ x 8½ . . . . . . . . . . . . . . . . . . . . .4.00

6 Mark Martin, Stroh Light, Ford, 5½ x 8 . . . . . . . . . . . . . . . . . . . . . .35.00

6 Mark Martin, Stroh Light, Ford, with bonus pack logo, 5½ x 8 . . . . . . . . . . . . . . . .10.00

7 Alan Kulwicki, Zerex, Ford, 5½ x 7 . . . . .12.00

8, 81 Bobby Hillin, Miller, Buick, with BGN, 7 x 9 . . . . . . . . . . . . . . . . . . . . . . .7.00

9 Bill Elliott, Coors, Ford, #L910312160, 5½ x 7 . . . . . . . . . . . . . . . . . . . . . .5.00

9 Bill Elliott, Coors, Ford, action, 8½ x 11 . .5.00

9 Bill Elliott, Thunder Road, 4 x 6 . . . . . .5.00

10 Ken Bouchard, Ford, #P37722, 5½ x 7 . . . . . . . . . . . . . . . . . . . . . .10.00

11 Terry Labonte, Budweiser, Chevrolet, 6 x 9 .5.00

11 Terry Labonte, Banquet Foods, blank back, 5½ x 8½ . . . . . . . . . . . . . . . . . . . . .5.00

11 Terry Labonte, Baby Ruth, Terry only, 9 x 6 .5.00

14 A.J. Foyt, Copenhagen, 3 cars, 8 x 10 . . . . . . . . . . . . . . . . . . . . . .8.00

15 Brett Bodine, Crisco, Ford, 5 x 8 . . . . . .5.00

17 Darrell Waltrip, Tide, Chevrolet, 5½ x 8½ . . . . . . . . . . . . . . . . . . . . . .5.00

2 Ernie Irvan, Kroger, Pontiac, 6 x 9 . . . . .10.00

6 Mark Martin, Stroh Light, Ford, 5½ x 8 . . .35.00

17 Darrell Waltrip, Tide, Superflo card, 8 x 10 . . . . . . . . . . . . . . . . . . . . . .12.00

19 Chad Little, Coors, Ford, on left side, 8½ x 11 . . . . . . . . . . . . . . . . . . . . .10.00

19 Chad Little, Coors, Ford, on right side, 8½ x 11 . . . . . . . . . . . . . . . . . . . . .10.00

21 Kyle Petty, Citgo, Ford, 8½ x 11 . . . . . . .6.00

24 John McFadden, Alliance, Chevrolet, fold-up, 4 x 7 . . . . . . . . . . . . . . . . . . . . . . . .4.00

25 Ken Schrader, Folgers, Chevrolet, 5½ x 7 . . . . . . . . . . . . . . . . . . . . . . .5.00

26 Ricky Rudd, Quaker State, Buick, 8 x 10 .4.00

26 Ricky Rudd, Quaker State, Buick, blank back, 8 x 10 . . . . . . . . . . . . . . . . . . . . . .8.00

27 Rusty Wallace, Kodiak, Pontiac, 5 x 8 . . .5.00

27 Rusty Wallace, Kodiak, Pontiac, with extra decals, 5 x 8 . . . . . . . . . . . . . . . . . .5.00

28 Davey Allison, Havoline, Ford, 8½ x 11 . . . . . . . . . . . . . . . . . . . . . . .7.00

28 Davey Allison, Havoline, Ford, fan club, 4 x 7 . . . . . . . . . . . . . . . . . . . . . . . .5.00

28 Davey Allison, Havoline Star, with pit crew, B & W, 8½ x 11 . . . . . . . . . . . . . . . . . .15.00

28 Robert Yates, TRW, 6 x 9 . . . . . . . . . .10.00

29 Cale Yarborough & Ned Jarrett, Hardee's, Oldsmobile, 6 x 9 . . . . . . . . . . . . . . .10.00

30 Michael Waltrip, Countrytime, Pontiac, left side, 5½ x 8 . . . . . . . . . . . . . . . . . . .5.00

30 Michael Waltrip, Countrytime, Pontiac, right side, 5½ x 8 . . . . . . . . . . . . . . . . . .10.00

31 Brad Teague, Slender You, Oldsmobile, 8 x 10 . . . . . . . . . . . . . . . . . . . . . . .6.00

31 Joe Ruttman, Slender You, Oldsmobile, 8 x 10 . . . . . . . . . . . . . . . . . . . . . . .8.00

31 No Driver, Slender You, Clark Motorsports, Oldsmobile, 5 x 7 . . . . . . . . . . . . . . .10.00

32, 77 J. D. McDuffie & Ken Ragan, Bob Beard Racing, 5 x 7 . . . . . . . . . . . . . . . . . .10.00

33 Harry Gant, Skoal Bandit, Chevrolet, 6 x 9 . . . . . . . . . . . . . . . . . . . . . .10.00

36 H.B. Bailey, National Motors Racing, #P38102, 5½ x 7 . . . . . . . . . . . . .7.00

43 Richard Petty, STP, Pontiac, 6 x 9 . . . . .8.00

43 Richard Petty, STP, Pontiac, 30th Anniversary, 6 x 9 . . . . . . . . . . . . . . . . . . . .10.00

44 Sterling Marlin, Piedmont Airlines, Oldsmobile, 6 x 9 . . . . . . . . . . . . . . . . . . . .5.00

55 Phil Parsons, Crown/Skoal, Oldsmobile, 6 x 9 . . . . . . . . . . . . . . . . . . . .5.00

57 Morgan Shepherd, Heinz, Buick, #P39840, 5½ x 7 . . . . . . . . . . . . . . . . . . . .8.00

57 Morgan Shepherd, Heinz, Buick, #P40428, 5½ x 7 . . . . . . . . . . . . . . . . . . . .8.00

57 Morgan Shepherd, Heinz, B & W, fan club, blank back, 8 x 10 . . . . . . . . . . . . .10.00

68 Derrike Cope, Purolator, Ford, 9 x 6 . . . .8.00

70 J.D. McDuffie, Rumple Furniture, Pontiac, #P37210, 5½ x 7 . . . . . . . . . . . . .10.00

71 Dave Marcis, Lifebuoy, Chevrolet, 6 x 9 . .6.00

73 Phil Barkdoll, Helen Rae Special, Ford, 4 x 6 .6.00

75 Neil Bonnett, Valvoline, Pontiac, #V-1713, 5 x 7 . . . . . . . . . . . . . . . . . . . .8.00

77 Ken Ragan, All Pro Bumper-To-Bumper, Ford, 5 x 7 . . . . . . . . . . . . . . . . . . . .8.00

78 Jay Sommers, Doe Chevrolet, 6 x 9 . . .10.00

83 Lake Speed, K-Mart Wynn's, Oldsmobile, 5 x 7 . . . . . . . . . . . . . . . . . . . .6.00

83 Lake Speeed, K-Mart Wynn's, Oldsmobile, with trophy, 5 x 7 . . . . . . . . . . . . . . .6.00

88 Buddy Baker, Red Baron, Oldsmobile, 5 x 8 . . . . . . . . . . . . . . . . . . . .8.00

88 Buddy Baker, NASCAR Legend, blank back, 8½ x 11 . . . . . . . . . . . . . . . . . . . .8.00

88 Buddy Baker, "Baker," Red Baron Promotion, blank back, 7½ x 11 . . . . . . . . . . . . .8.00

89 Jim Sauter, Evinrude, Pontiac, 5 x 7 . . . .6.00

90 Benny Parsons, Bull's Eye, Ford, 8 x 5 . .8.00

90 Benny Parsons, Bull's Eye, Ford, coupon, 7½ x 6 . . . . . . . . . . . . . . . . . . . .10.00

90 Benny Parsons, Bull's Eye, Ford, car only, 7½ x 6 . . . . . . . . . . . . . . . . . . . .12.00

97 Rodney Combs, GM Tech, AC Buick, #7991-E, 3½ x 5½ . . . . . . . . . . . . . . . . . . . .8.00

98 Ed Pimm, Sunoco, Buick, blank back, 5 x 7  8.00

98 Brad Noffsinger, Sunoco, Buick, #RP-1000, 5½ x 7 . . . . . . . . . . . . . . . . . . . .8.00

98 Curb Motorsports, Sunoco, Buick, photo, blank back, 5 x 7 . . . . . . . . . . . . . . . . . . . .5.00

8, 12, Miller, Miller Racing, Buicks, 8 x 10 . .4.00

## 1989

3 Dale Earnhardt, Goodwrench, Lumina, full back, 6 x 9 . . . . . . . . . . . . . . . . . . . .15.00

3 Dale Earnhardt, Goodwrench, Lumina, half back, 6 x 9 . . . . . . . . . . . . . . . . . . . .30.00

4 Rick Wilson, Kodak Films, Oldsmobile, 1988 front, 5 x 9 . . . . . . . . . . . . . . . . . . . .3.00

04 Hershel McGriff, U.S. Bank, Pontiac, West, 5 x 7 . . . . . . . . . . . . . . . . . . . .8.00

5 Geoff Bodine, Levi Garrett, Monte Carlo, 5½ x 8 . . . . . . . . . . . . . . . . . . . .5.00

5 Geoff Bodine, Levi Garrett, Monte Carlo, 8 x 10 . . . . . . . . . . . . . . . . . . . .5.00

8/81 Bobby Hillin, Miller, Rose's, error, blank back 7 x 9 . .10.00

5 Geoff Bodine, Exxon Super Flo, Monte Carlo, 10 x 8 . . . . . . . . . . . . . . . . . . . . .6.00
6 Mark Martin, Stroh's Light, Ford, 5 x 8 . .12.00
6 Mark Martin, Stroh's Light, Ford, printed autograph, 5 x 8 . . . . . . . . . . . . . . . . . .10.00
7 Alan Kulwicki, Zerex, Ford, 5½ x 7 . . . . .10.00
8, 81 Bobby Hillin, Miller, Rose's, error, blank back, 7 x 9 . . . . . . . . . . . . . . . . . .10.00

BOBBY HILLIN, JR.

8, 81 Bobby Hillin, Miller, Rose's, Correct, blank back, 7 x 9 . . . . . . . . . . . . . . . . . .8.00
8, 81 Bobby Hillin, Miller, Rose's, printed back, 7 x 9 . . . . . . . . . . . . . . . . . . . . . . .5.00
8 Rodney Pickler, Miller, hauler driver, blank back, 6 x 9 . . . . . . . . . . . . . . . . . . . . .10.00
8, 84 Bobby Hillin & Mike Alexander, Miller, Buicks, #01-81453, 8 x 10 . . . . . . . .4.00
9 Bill Elliott, Coors, Ford, #8148, 5½ x 7 . . .5.00
9 Bill Elliott, Coors, Ford, action, 8½ x 11 . .5.00
9 Bill Elliott, Melling Racing, Ford, posed, 8½ x 11 . . . . . . . . . . . . . . . . . . . . . . .7.00
9 Bill Elliott, Parma International, Ford, 8½ x 11 . . . . . . . . . . . . . . . . . . . . . .10.00
10 Derrike Cope, Purolator, Pontiac, 6 x 9 . .4.00
11 Terry Labonte, Budweiser, Ford, 6 x 9 . .4.00
11 Terry Labonte, Baby Ruth, Ford, 6 x 9 . .4.00
11 Terry Labonte, Banquet, Ford, 2 different thick & paper, blank, 5½ x 8½ . . . . . . . . . .4.00
14 A.J. Foyt, Copenhagen, Oldsmobile, 3 shots, 8 x 10 . . . . . . . . . . . . . . . . . . . . . . .7.00
15 Brett Bodine, Motorcraft, Ford, 8½ x 11 .4.00
16 Larry Pearson, Chattanooga Chew, Buick, 5½ x 8½ . . . . . . . . . . . . . . . . . . . . . .4.00
17 Darrell Waltrip, Tide, Lumina, 5 x 7 . . . .7.00
17 Darrell Waltrip, B & W, headshot, fan club, 7 x 5 . . . . . . . . . . . . . . . . . . . . . . . .7.00
17 Darrell Waltrip, Exxon Superflo, with car, 10 x 8 . . . . . . . . . . . . . . . . . . . . . .12.00
17 Darrell Waltrip, Exxon Superflo, holding oil bottle, 10 x 8 . . . . . . . . . . . . . . . . .10.00

21 Neil Bonnett, Citgo, Ford, 8½ x 11 . . . . .8.00
23 Eddie Bierschwale, One Grand Pit Kit, Oldsmobile, 5½ x 8½ . . . . . . . . . . . . . . . . . . .5.00
24 Johnny McFadden, Alliance, 1988 update sticker, fold-up, 4 x 7 . . . . . . . . . . . . .4.00
25 Ken Schrader, Folgers, Lumina, 5 x 7 . . .5.00
25 Ken Schrader, Folgers, Lumina, coupon, 6 x 9 . . . . . . . . . . . . . . . . . . . . . . . .3.00
25 Ken Schrader, Exxon Superflo, with car, 10 x 8 . . . . . . . . . . . . . . . . . . . . . .12.00
26 Ricky Rudd, Quaker State, white writing "Racing," 8 x 10 . . . . . . . . . . . . . . . .5.00
26 Ricky Rudd, Quaker State, green writing "Racing," 8 x 10 . . . . . . . . . . . . . . . .8.00
26 Ricky Rudd, Quaker State, error, sticker flapping, 8 x 10 . . . . . . . . . . . . . . . .12.00
26 Ricky Rudd, Quaker State, Buick, blank back, 8 x 10 . . . . . . . . . . . . . . . . . . . . . .8.00
27 Rusty Wallace, Kodiak, Pontiac, #22-183, 6½ x 9½ . . . . . . . . . . . . . . . . . . . . .5.00
28 Davey Allison, Havoline, Ford, 8½ x 11 . .5.00
28 Davey Allison, Havoline, Ford, grandstands on front, 8½ x 11 . . . . . . . . . . . . . . . .5.00
28 Davey Allison, Havoline, Ford, 5½ x 8½ .15.00
29 Dale Jarrett, Hardee's, Pontiac, 5½ x 8 .5.00
29 Dale Jarrett, Hardee's Deluxe, Pontiac, 5½ x 8 . . . . . . . . . . . . . . . . . . . . . . .6.00
30 Michael Waltrip, Country Time, Pontiac, 8½ x 6 . . . . . . . . . . . . . . . . . . . . . . .5.00
33 Harry Gant, Skoal Bandit, Oldsmobile, 1988 Front, 6 x 9 . . . . . . . . . . . . . . . . . . .5.00

NASCAR WINSTON CUP

40 Ben Hess, Oldsmobile, 6 x 9 . . . . . . . .5.00
42 Kyle Petty, Peak, Pontiac, 6 x 8½ . . . . . .5.00
42 Kyle Petty, Peak, B & W, headshot, 10 x 8 . . . . . . . . . . . . . . . . . . . . . . . .7.00
43 Richard Petty, STP, Pontiac, 6 x 9 . . . . .7.00
43 Richard Petty, Goody's, 1970 Plymouth, 6 x 9 . . . . . . . . . . . . . . . . . . . . . . . .3.00
48 Greg Sacks, Dinner Bell, Pontiac, posed, 8 x 10 . . . . . . . . . . . . . . . . . . . . . . . .6.00
48 Greg Sacks, Dinner Bell, Pontiac, action, 8 x 10 . . . . . . . . . . . . . . . . . . . . . . . .6.00

48 No Driver, Dinner Bell, blank back, 6 x 9 . . . . .20.00

52 Jimmy Means, Alka-Seltzer, Pontiac, 5 x 7 . . . . . . . . . . . . . . . . . . . .4.00
55 Phil Parsons, Crown/Skoal Classic, Oldsmobile,1988 front, 6 x 9 . . . . . . . . .5.00
55 Phil Parsons, Crown/Skoal Classic, Oldsmobile, 6 x 9 . . . . . . . . . . . . . . . .5.00
55 Phil Parsons, Crown/Skoal Classic, Oldsmobile, 8½ x 11 . . . . . . . . . . . . . .5.00
57 Hut Stricklin, Heinz, Pontiac, 5½ x 8½ . .4.00
68 Derrike Cope, Purolator, Pontiac, B & W head shot, 11 x 8½ . . . . . . . . . . . . . . . .8.00
71 Dave Marcis, Lifebuoy, Monte Carlo, 1988 Front, 6 x 9 . . . . . . . . . . . . . . . .5.00
75 Morgan Shepherd, Valvoline, Pontiac, #V1947, 7 x 9 . . . . . . . . . . . . . . .5.00
83 Lake Speed, Bull's Eye, Oldsmobile, 9 x 5 .5.00
84 Dick Trickle, Miller, Buick, 5 x 7 . . . . . .5.00
84 Eddie Vogt, Miller, hauler driver, blank back, 6 x 9 . . . . . . . . . . . . . . . . . . . .10.00
88 Greg Sacks, Crisco, Pontiac, 5 x 8 . . . . .5.00
88 Jimmy Spencer, Crisco, Pontiac, #BRMH1226, 5 x 8 . . . . . . . . . . . . .5.00
88 Jimmy Spencer, Crisco Fleetwood, Pontiac, 6 x 9 . . . . . . . . . . . . . . . . . . . .7.00
89 Rodney Combs, Evinrude, Pontiac, 6 x 9 .5.00
90 Chad Little, Pelco, Ford, B & W, 5 x 7 .10.00
94 Sterling Marlin, Sunoco, Oldsmobile, yellow outline around number, #RP1003, 5 x 7 . . .5.00
94 Sterling Marlin, Sunoco, Oldsmobile, red outline around number, #RP1003, 5 x 7 . .5.00

## 1990

01 Mickey Gibbs, Days Inn, Ford, #P53014, 6 x 9. . . . . . . . . . . . . . . . . . . . .4.00
04 Herschel McGriff, U.S. Bank, Pontiac, 5 x 7. . . . . . . . . . . . . . . . . . . . .7.00

1 Terry Labonte, Skoal Classic, Oldsmobile, 6 x 9 . . . . . . . . . . . . . . . . . . . .5.00
1 Terry Labonte, Skoal Classic, Oldsmobile, 7 x 11 . . . . . . . . . . . . . . . . . . .4.00
3 Dale Earnhardt, Goodwrench, Lumina, 6 x 9 . . . . . . . . . . . . . . . . . . . .9.00
4 Ernie Irvan, Kodak, Oldsmobile, car cut-off, 5 x 9 . . . . . . . . . . . . . . . . . . . .4.00
4 Ernie Irvan, Kodak, Oldsmobile, 5 x 9 . . . .4.00
4 Ernie Irvan, Kodak, Oldsmobile, 12 x 12 . .4.00
5 Ricky Rudd, Levi Garrett, Lumina, #16-036, 6½ x 9½ . . . . . . . . . . . . . . . . . . . .4.00

5 Ricky Rudd, Superflo card, 10 x 8 . . . . .10.00
6 Mark Martin, Folgers, Ford, 5 x 7 . . . . . .4.00

"TAKE IT FROM THE ONES WHO KNOW. SEAT BELTS SAVE LIVES."

MARK MARTIN, #6

Sponsored by the Arizona Department of Public Safety and the Ford Motor Company.

Thanks to Phoenix International Raceway

6 Mark Martin, Buckle Up America, with sheriff, 8 x 10  . . .7.00

7 Alan Kulwicki, Zerex, Ford, 5½ x 7 . . . . . .4.00
8 Bobby Hillin, Snickers, Buick, with inset, 6 x 9 . . . . . . . . . . . . . . . . . . . . . . . . . .3.00
8 Bobby Hillin, Snickers, Buick, no inset, 6 x 9 . . . . . . . . . . . . . . . . . . . . . . . . .25.00
9 Bill Elliott, Coors, Ford, Legends, 7 x 5½ . . . . . . . . . . . . . . . . . . . . . . . .5.00
9 Bill Elliott, Melling, Ford, with order form, 5½ x 8½ . . . . . . . . . . . . . . . . . . . . . .5.00
9 Bill Elliott, Coors, Ford, with dog sticker, 6 x 9 . . . . . . . . . . . . . . . . . . . . . . . . .5.00
9 Bill Elliott, Coors, Ford, with farm tractor, 8 x 10 . . . . . . . . . . . . . . . . . . . . . . . .4.00
9 Bill Elliott, One Grand Car Products, 4 x 6 . . . . . . . . . . . . . . . . . . . . . . . . .5.00
9 Bill Elliott, Daytona 500 card, 4 x 6 . . . . .3.00
9 Bill Elliott, B & W headshot, 7 x 5 . . . . . .4.00
10 Derrike Cope, Purolator, Lumina, 6 x 9 . .3.00
11 Geoff Bodine, Budweiser, Ford, posed, 4 x 6 . . . . . . . . . . . . . . . . . . . . . . . . .3.00
11 Geoff Bodine, Budweiser, Ford, action, 4½ x 6¾ . . . . . . . . . . . . . . . . . . . . . . .3.00
11 Geoff Bodine, Banquet, rear shot, 6 x 9 .3.00
11 Geoff Bodine, Baby Ruth, 6 x 9 . . . . . .5.00
12 Hut Stricklin, Raybestos, Buick, glossy version, 6 x 9 . . . . . . . . . . . . . . . . . . . . . . . . .5.00
12 Hut Stricklin, Raybestos, Buick, non-glossy version, 6 x 9 . . . . . . . . . . . . . . . . . .5.00
12 Hut Stricklin, Raybestos, B & W, 5 x 7 . .7.00
12 Hut Stricklin, Raybestos, B & W, car only, 5 x 7 . . . . . . . . . . . . . . . . . . . . . . . . .7.00

14 A.J. Foyt, Copenhagen, Oldsmobile, 3 shots, 8 x 10 . . . . . . . . . . . . . . . . . . . . . . . .6.00
15 Morgan Shepherd, Motorcraft, Ford, 8½ x 11 . . . . . . . . . . . . . . . . . . . . . .4.00
17 Darrell Waltrip, Tide, Lumina, 5 x 7 . . . .5.00
17 Darrell Waltrip, B & W headshot, 7 x 5 .4.00
17 Darrell Waltrip, Tide, Lumina, video ad, 7 x 4 . . . . . . . . . . . . . . . . . . . . . . . . .5.00
17 Darrell Waltrip, Exxon Superflo, Winston Cup, blank back, 10 x 8 . . . . . . . . . . . . . .12.00
17 Darrell Waltrip, Exxon Superflo, ASA, 10 x 8 . . . . . . . . . . . . . . . . . . . . . . .12.00
17 Darrell Waltrip, fan club card, 8 x 10 . . .8.00
17 Darrell Waltrip, Winning On Empty, fold-over art ad, 5 x 7 . . . . . . . . . . . . . . . . . .5.00
18 Greg Sacks & Stan Barrett, Ultra Slim Fast, Sacks with hat, 6 x 9 . . . . . . . . . . . . . .4.00
18 Greg Sacks & Stan Barrett, Ultra Slim Fast, Sacks without hat, 6 x 9 . . . . . . . . . . .5.00
19 Chad Little, Bull's Eye, Ford, 5 x 7 . . . . .4.00
19 Chad Little, Bull's Eye, Ford, 6 x 9 . . . . .8.00
20 Rob Moroso, Crowns, Oldsmobile, 6 x 9 . . . . . . . . . . . . . . . . . . . . . . . . .8.00
20 Rob Moroso, thick stock, blank back, 8½ x 11 . . . . . . . . . . . . . . . . . . . . . .5.00
20 Rob Moroso, headshot, thick stock, 6 x 9 . . . . . . . . . . . . . . . . . . . . . . . . .4.00
21 Neil Bonnett, Citgo, Ford, 8½ x 11 . . . . .5.00
21 Dale Jarrett, Citgo, Ford, 8½ x 11 . . . . .5.00
25 Ken Schrader, Kodiak, Lumina, #22-183, 6½ x 9½ . . . . . . . . . . . . . . . . . . . . . .4.00

25 Ken Schrader, Superflo, Winston Cup, 8 x 10 . . . . . . . . . . . . . . . . . . . .10.00
26 Brett Bodine, Quaker State, Buick, 8 x 10 .4.00
26 Brett Bodine, Quaker State, Buick, front shot, 8 x 10 . . . . . . . . . . . . . . . . . . . . .4.00
27 Rusty Wallace, Miller Genuine Draft, #1783486BA, 8 x 10 . . . . . . . . . .3.00
27 Rusty Wallace, Miller, Pontiac, pit stop, 8 x 10 . . . . . . . . . . . . . . . . . . .10.00
27 Rusty Wallace, Miller, Pontiac, B & W, 6 x 9 . . . . . . . . . . . . . . . . . . . . . .5.00

*From one Winston winner to another*

Rusty Wallace
1989 NASCAR Winston Cup Champion

27 Rusty Wallace, Winston Winner's Circle, 8½ x 5½ . . . . . . . . . . . . . . . . . .10.00
28 Davey Allison, Havoline, Ford, #Z-1475, 11 x 8½ . . . . . . . . . . . . . . . . . . .4.00
30 Michael Waltrip, Country Time, Pontiac, 5½ x 8 . . . . . . . . . . . . . . . . . . . . .4.00
33 Harry Gant, Skoal Bandit, Oldsmobile, 6 x 9 . . . . . . . . . . . . . . . . . . . . . .4.00
33 Harry Gant, Skoal Bandit, Oldsmobile, 7 x 11 . . . . . . . . . . . . . . . . . . . . .4.00
38 Dick Johnson, Red Kote, Ford, 6 x 9 . . .8.00
40 Tom Kendall, EDS, Lumina, 8½ x 11 . . . .8.00
42 Kyle Petty, Peak, Pontiac, 6 x 8½ . . . . .5.00
42 Kyle Petty, Peak, Pontiac, no tear, off, 6 x 9 . . . . . . . . . . . . . . . . . . . . . .5.00
42 Kyle Petty, Uniden, 5 x 7 . . . . . . . . . . .4.00
43 Richard Petty, STP, Pontiac, 9 x 6 . . . . .5.00
57 Jimmy Spencer, Heinz 57, Pontiac, 6 x 8½ . . . . . . . . . . . . . . . . . . . . .3.00

66 Dick Trickle, Trop-Artic, still shot, #102990HO1, 5½ x 8 . . . . . . . . . .3.00
66 Dick Trickle, Trop-Artic, Pontiac with Cale, blank back, 11 x 8½ . . . . . . . . . .5.00
66 Dick Trickle, Trop-Artic, Pontiac, action, #722-90GO1, 5½ x 8 . . . . . . . . . .5.00
71 Dave Marcis, Big Apple Market, Lumina, #P52900, 6 x 9 . . . . . . . . . . . . .3.00
75 Rick Wilson, Dinner Bell, Oldsmobile, no Food Lion, blank back, 8 x 10 . . . . . . . . . .3.00
75 Rick Wilson, Dinner Bell, Oldsmobile, right side, blank back, 8 x 10 . . . . . . . . . .3.00
77 Ken Ragan, Jasper Engines, Ford, B & W, 5 x 7 . . . . . . . . . . . . . . . . . . . . .4.00
83 Lake Speed, Prestone, Oldsmobile, 6 x 9 .3.00
94 Sterling Marlin, Sunoco, 5 x 7 . . . . . . .3.00
97 Chuck Bown, Kellogg's, Lumina, 6 x 9 . . .3.00
98 Butch Miller, Banquet, Lumina, blank back, 6 x 9 . . . . . . . . . . . . . . . . . . . . . .3.00
98 Butch Miller, Planters Nuts, Lumina, 6 x 9 . . . . . . . . . . . . . . . . . . . . . .3.00

# 1991

OO Scott Gaylord, One Grand, Oldsmobile, 4½ x 5 . . . . . . . . . . . . . . . . . . . . .4.00
O3 Kerry Teague, Gunk Green Cleaner, 8½ x 10¼ . . . . . . . . . . . . . . . . . . . .2.00
1 No Driver, Winston Cup Showcars, 5½ x 7 .2.00
1 Rick Mast, Skoal, Oldsmobile, 7 x 11 . . . .2.00
2 Rusty Wallace, Miller, Pontiac, 8 x 10 . . . .2.00
2 Rusty Wallace, Pit Stop, 8 x 10 . . . . . . . .8.00
3 Dale Earnhardt, Western Steer, thin stock, 3 x 4 . . . . . . . . . . . . . . . . . . . . . .9.00
3 Dale Earnhardt, Goodwrench, Sam Bass card, thick stock, 3 x 4 . . . . . . . . . . . . . .8.00
3 Dale Earnhardt, McCord Gaskets, blank back, 5 x 7 . . . . . . . . . . . . . . . . . . . . .15.00
3 Dale Earnhardt, Sam Bass, promo, 4 fingers, 3 x 4 . . . . . . . . . . . . . . . . . . . . .8.00
3 Dale Earnhardt, Goodwrench, Chevy, 8 x 10 . . . . . . . . . . . . . . . . . . . . . .6.00
3 Dale Earnhardt, Goodwrench, Chevy, with printed autograph, 8 x 10 . . . . . . . . .6.00
3 Dale Earnhardt, Goodwrench, Cedar Ridge RV Center, 8 x 10 . . . . . . . . . . . . . . .10.00
3 Richard Childress, RCR Enterprises, 6 x 9 .8.00
4 Ernie Irvan, Kodak, Chevy, at speed, 4½ x 9 .4.00
4 Ernie Irvan, Kodak, Daytona 500 Champion, 4½ x 9 . . . . . . . . . . . . . . . . . . . . .3.00
5 Ricky Rudd, Tide, Chevy, 5 x 7 . . . . . . . .3.00
5 Ricky Rudd, Superflo, 8½ x 4 . . . . . . . .10.00
6 Mark Martin, Folgers, Ford, 5 x 7 . . . . .4.00
7 Alan Kulwicki, Hooters, Ford, 8 x 10 . . . .8.00
7 Alan Kulwicki, Hooters, Ford, 5 x 7 . . . . .5.00
7 Alan Kulwicki, Hooters, Ford, with girls, 4¼ x 6 . . . . . . . . . . . . . . . . . . . . .5.00

1/500                    *"The Intimidator"*                    Sam Bass '91

3 Dale Earnhardt, Goodwrench, Sam Bass card, thick stock, 3 x 4 . . 8.00

8 Rick Wilson, Snickers, Buick, 6 x 9 . . . . .3.00
8 Rick Wilson, Snickers, without Harry Hyde on front, 6 x 9 . . . . . . . . . . . . . . . . . . .3.00
9 Bill Elliott, Coors Light, Ford, 7 x 5 . . . . . .4.00
9 Bill Elliott, Melling, 5 x 7 . . . . . . . . . . . .4.00
10 Derrike Cope, Purolator, Chevy, 6 x 9 . . .3.00
11 Ned Jarrett, Richmond Motors, reprint of 1965 postcard, 5 x 7 . . . . . . . . . . . . .5.00
11 Geoff Bodine, Budweiser, Ford, 4¼ x 6¾ . .3.00
12 Bobby Allison, Raybestos, Buick, B & W, with head shot inset, 6 x 9 . . . . . . . . . . .10.00
12 Hut Stricklin, Raybestos, Buick, 6 x 9 . . .4.00
17 Darrell Waltrip, Western Auto, Chevy, art card, 9 x 6 . . . . . . . . . . . . . . . . . . . .4.00
17 Darrell Waltrip, Western Auto, faded front, car on back, 9 x 6 . . . . . . . . . . . . . . . .10.00

17 Darrell Waltrip, Western Auto, holding trophy, 8 x 5½ . . . . . . . . . . . . . . . . . . . . .10.00
17 Darrell Waltrip, Western Auto, car only, 8 x 10 . . . . . . . . . . . . . . . . . . . . . . . .8.00
17 Darrell Waltrip, Western Auto, Chevy, with hauler, 8 x 10 . . . . . . . . . . . . . . . . . .8.00
17 Darrell Waltrip, Western Auto, Chevy, with crew, 5 x 8 . . . . . . . . . . . . . . . . . .8.00
17 Darrell Waltrip, Western Auto, Chevy, 3 views, 6 x 9 . . . . . . . . . . . . . . . . . . . . . . .3.00
17 Darrell Waltrip, Superflo, 8½ x 11 . . . .10.00
19 Chad Little, Bulls Eye, Ford, 5 x 7 . . . . .3.00
19 Chad Little, Bulls Eye, Ford, fold-over, 5¾ x 8¾ . .5.00
19 Chad Little, Tyson, Ford, 6 x 9 . . . . . . .5.00
21 Dale Jarrett, Contract For Life, fold-over, 5 x 7 . . . . . . . . . . . . . . . . . . . . . . . .3.00

3 Dale Earnhardt, McCord Gaskets, blank back, 5 x 7, 15.00

94 Terry Labonte, Sunoco, blank back, 6 x 9 . . .10.00

21 Dale Jarrett, Citgo, Ford, 8½ x 11 . . . . .3.00

22 Sterling Marlin, Maxwell House, Ford, 5¼ x 8¼ . . . . . . . . . . . . . . . . . . . . . . .3.00

23 Eddie Bierschwale, Autofinders, Oldsmobile, 6 x 9 . . . . . . . . . . . . . . . . . . . . . . . . .4.00

23 Mike Chase, Freymiller, Winston West, 5 x 7 . . . . . . . . . . . . . . . . . . . . . . . .5.00

24 Mickey Gibbs, Team III, headshots, 7 x 5 .5.00

24 Mickey Gibbs, Team III, color headshots, 8 x 10 . . . . . . . . . . . . . . . . . . . . . . .5.00

25 Ken Schrader, Superflo, 8½ x 11 . . . . .12.00

25 Ken Schrader, Kodiak, Chevy, 6 x 9 . . . .2.00

25 Ken Schrader, Kodiak, Chevy, bear logo on back, 6 x 9 . . . . . . . . . . . . . . . . . . . .2.00

25 Ken Schrader, Buckle Up With Crash Dummies, 5 x 7 . . . . . . . . . . . . . . . . .3.00

26 Brett Bodine, Quaker State, Buick, 8 x 10 . . . . . . . . . . . . . . . . . . . . . .2.00

26 Brett Bodine, Quaker State, Buick, crown logo on front, 8 x 10 . . . . . . . . . . . . . . .3.00

28 Davey Allison, Havoline, Ford, 11 x 8½ . . . . . . . . . . . . . . . . . . . . .5.00

29 Phil Parsons, Diamond Ridge, paper stock, 8 x 10 . . . . . . . . . . . . . . . . . . . . . . . .5.00

30 Michael Waltrip, Pennzoil, Pontiac, 8 x 10 . . . . . . . . . . . . . . . . . . . . . . . .3.00

30 Michael Waltrip, Pennzoil, with fan club address, 8 x 10 . . . . . . . . . . . . . . . .2.00

30 Michael Waltrip, Pennzoil, black background, 8 x 10 . . . . . . . . . . . . . . . . . . . . . . .2.00

30 Michael Waltrip, Pennzoil, black background without Ken Wilson, 8 x 10 . . . . . . . .2.00

33 Harry Gant, Skoal, Oldsmobile, 6 x 12 . .3.00

41 Larry Pearson, headshot, B & W, 8½ x 5½ . . . . . . . . . . . . . . . . . . . . .4.00

41 Larry Pearson, Kellogg's, Chevy, 6 x 9 . .5.00

42 Kyle Petty, Mello Yello, Pontiac, 6 x 12 . .3.00

43 Richard Petty, STP, Pontiac, 10 x 8 . . . . .5.00

47 Greg Sacks, Kanawha Insurance, 5½ x 7½ . . . . . . . . . . . . . . . . . . . . .3.00

52 Jimmy Means, Alka Seltzer, 5 x 7 . . . . .2.00

55 Ted Musgrave, Jasper, 5 x 7 . . . . . . . .3.00

65 Dave Mader, Jasper, Chevy, action, 5 x 7 . . . . . . . . . . . . . . . . . . . . . . .5.00

65 Dave Mader, Jasper, posed on pit road, 5 x 7 . . . . . . . . . . . . . . . . . . . . . . .5.00

66 Cale Yarborough, Phillips 66, Pontiac, 6 x 9 . . . . . . . . . . . . . . . . . . . . . . .3.00

66 Lake Speed, Phillips 66, Pontiac, 6 x 9 . .5.00

66 No Driver, action shot, Winston Cup schedule back, 11 x 8½ . . . . . . . . . . . . . . . . . .3.00

68 Bobby Hamilton, Country Time, Pontiac, 6 x 9 . . . . . . . . . . . . . . . . . . . . . . .3.00

73 Bill Schmitt, Motorcraft Fast Lube, Winston West, 5 x 7 . . . . . . . . . . . . . . . . . . . .4.00

75 Joe Ruttman, Dinner Bell, Oldsmobile, 8 x 10 . . . . . . . . . . . . . . . . . . . . . . .3.00

89 Jim Sauter, Evinrude, Pontiac, 6 x 9 . . . .5.00

94 Terry Labonte, Sunoco, blank back, 6 x 9 . . . . . . . . . . . . . . . . . . . . . . .10.00

94 Terry Labonte, Sunoco, 8 x 10 . . . . . . .3.00

98 Jimmy Spencer, Planters Peanuts, 6 x 9 .2.00

98 Jimmy Spencer, Banquet Chicken, 6 x 9 .2.00

## 1992

00 Scott Gaylord, One Grand, Oldsmobile, 5 x 7 . . . . . . . . . . . . . . . . . . . . . . . . .3.00

04 Hershel McGriff, U.S. Bank, Pontiac, 5 x 7 . . . . . . . . . . . . . . . . . . . . . . . . .4.00

2 Rusty Wallace, Miller, car only, blank back, 7 x 10 . . .7.00

0 Delma Cowart, Masters Economy Inn, Ford, #P71707, 3½ x 5½ . . . . . . . . . . . . .3.00

1 No Driver, Winston, Winston Cup Showcars, 8 x 6½ . . . . . . . . . . . . . . . . . . . . .2.00

1 Rick Mast, Skoal, 8¾ x 8¾ . . . . . . . . . .3.00

2 Rusty Wallace, Tom Johnson Camping Center, 8¾ x 5¾ . . . . . . . . . . . . . . . . .4.00

2 Rusty Wallace, Miller Genuine Draft, 8 x 10 . . . . . . . . . . . . . . . . . . . . . . . .2.00

2 Rusty Wallace, Miller, 6 card promo set, 3½ x 5½ . . . . . . . . . . . . . . . . . . . .20.00

2 Rusty Wallace, Miller, car only, blank back, 7 x 10 . . . . . . . . . . . . . . . . . . . . . .7.00

2 Rusty Wallace, Team Penske, with Indy Car, blank back, 8 x 10 . . . . . . . . . . . . . .6.00

3 Dale Earnhardt, Goodwrench, 5-Time Champion, 8 x 10 . . . . . . . . . . . . . . . . .5.00

3 Dale Earnhardt, Goodwrench, with printed autograph, 8 x 10 . . . . . . . . . . . . . . . . .5.00

3 Dale Earnhardt, Goodwrench, blank back, 8 x 10 . . . . . . . . . . . . . . . . . . . .11.00

3 Dale Earnhardt, with Warren Johnson, 8 x 10 . . . . . . . . . . . . . . . . . . . . .21.00

4 Ernie Irvan, Kodak, Daytona 500 Champion, #A4-3, 5 x 9 . . . . . . . . . . . . . . . . . . .2.00

4 Ernie Irvan, Kodak, pit stop, with printed autograph, 5 x 9 . . . . . . . . . . . . . . . . . . .3.00

4 Ernie Irvan, Kodak, pit stop, 5 x 9 . . . . . .2.00

4 Ernie Irvan, Kodak, Chevrolet, 5 x 7 . . . . .2.00

4 Ernie Irvan, Kodak, Chevrolet, blank back, 8 x 10 . . . . . . . . . . . . . . . . . . . . . .8.00

5 Ricky Rudd, Tide, Chevrolet, 5 x 7 . . . . . .2.00

6 Mark Martin, Valvoline, Ford, #V-2954, 4 x 6 . . . . . . . . . . . . . . . . . . . . . . . .2.00

6 Mark Martin, Valvoline, headshot, SCN-9257, 7 x 5 . . . . . . . . . . . . . . . . . . . . . . .3.00

6 Mark Martin, Valvoline, Ford, #V-3093, 8½ x 11 . . . . . . . . . . . . . . . . . . . . . .2.00

3 Dale Earnhardt, with Warren Johnson, 8 x 10 . . 21.00

6 Mark Martin, McDonald's All, Stars, #V-3274, 8½ x 11 . . . . . . . . . . . . . . . .3.00

7 Alan Kulwicki, Hooter's, Ford, 5 x 7 . . . . .8.00

8 Rick Wilson, Snickers, Ford, 6 x 9 . . . . .4.00

8 No Driver, Snickers, Ford, 2 different backs, 6 x 9 . . . . . . . . . . . . . . . . . . .3.00

9 Phil Parsons, Melling, Ford, 5½ x 7 . . . . .3.00

9 Chad Little, Melling, Ford, B & W, blank back, 8½ x 11 . . . . . . . . . . . . . . . . .5.00

10 Derrike Cope, Purolator, Chevrolet, #92-1, 6 x 9 . . . . . . . . . . . . . . . . . . . .3.00

11 Bill Elliott, Budweiser, 5½ x 8 . . . . . . .3.00

11 Bill Elliott, Budweiser, 8½ x 11 . . . . . . .4.00

11 Bill Elliott, Budweiser, small Bud logo with beer Wagon, 6 x 9 . . . . . . . . . . . . . .5.00

11 Bill Elliott, Budweiser, large Bud logo with beer Wagon, 6 x 9 . . . . . . . . . . . . . .4.00

11 Bill Elliott, Show Offs, 5½ x 8¼ . . . . . .10.00

12 Hut Stricklin, Raybestos, without gloss, #2870-R, 6 x 9 . . . . . . . . . . . . . . .3.00

12 Hut Stricklin, Raybestos, with gloss, #2870-R, 6 x 9 . . . . . . . . . . . . . . . . . . . .3.00

12 Hut Stricklin, Raybestos, action, #2870-R, 6 x 9 . . . . . . . . . . . . . . . . . . . .3.00

12 Hut Stricklin, Raybestos, Meineke back, 6 x 9 . . . . . . . . . . . . . . . . . . . .5.00

12 Bobby Allison, Raybestos, Chevrolet, #2871-R, 6 x 9 . . . . . . . . . . . . . . . . . . . .4.00

13 Mike Skinner, Glidden, Chevrolet, blank back, thin stock, 8½ x 11 . . . . . . . . . . . .4.00

14 A.J. Foyt, Copenhagen, 10 x 8 . . . . . .6.00

15 Geoff Bodine, Motorcraft, 4½ x 7 . . . . .4.00

15 Geoff Bodine, Motorcraft, fold-out poster, 8 x 10 . . . . . . . . . . . . . . . . . . . .2.00

15 Rick Scribner, All-Pro Auto Parts, Oldsmobile, Winston West, 4 x 9 . . . . . . . . . . . . .4.00

16 Wally Dallenbach Jr., Keystone, #L910379850, 5 x 7 . . . . . . . . . . . .2.00

17 Darrell Waltrip, Western Auto, 6 x 9 . . .3.00

17 Darrell Waltrip, Western Auto, fan club, 6 x 9 . . . . . . . . . . . . . . . . . . .10.00

18 Dale Jarrett, Interstate Batteries, Chevrolet, 6 x 9 . . . . . . . . . . . . . . . . . . . .3.00

19 Chad Little, Red Baron Pizza, Ford, 5 x 7 5.00

20 Mike Wallace, Orkin, Oldsmobile, 5 x 7 . .5.00

21 Morgan Shepherd, Citgo, headshot, SCN-9258, 7 x 5 . . . . . . . . . . . . . . . .3.00

21 Morgan Shepherd, Citgo, Ford, 8½ x 11 .3.00

21 Morgan Shepherd, headshot, 11 x 8½ . .4.00

21 Wood Brothers, headshots, 8½ x 11 . . .4.00

22 Sterling Marlin, Maxwell House, Ford, fold-over, 5¼ x 8¼ . . . . . . . . . . . . . . .2.00

22 Sterling Marlin, Maxwell House, fold-over with Junior, 5¼ x 8¼ . . . . . . . . . . .2.00

22 Sterling Marlin, Maxwell House, blank back, 6 x 8½ . . . . . . . . . . . . . . . . . . .4.00

22 Sterling Marlin, Maxwell House, blank back, 8 x 10 . . . . . . . . . . . . . . . . . . .4.00

24 Kenny Wallace, Dirt Devil, blank back, 5 x 7 . . . . . . . . . . . . . . . . . . . .6.00

25 Ken Schrader, Kodiak, Chevrolet, 7½ x 10 .2.00

26 Brett Bodine, Quaker State, Ford, 8 x 10 .2.00

27 Jeff McClure, Race For Life, blank back, 4 x 6½ . . . . . . . . . . . . . . . . . . .2.00

27 Jeff McClure, Race For Life, blank back, 6 x 8½ . . . . . . . . . . . . . . . . . . .2.00

27 Jeff McClure, Race For Life, blank back, 8 x 10 . . . . . . . . . . . . . . . . . . .2.00

28 Davey Allison, Texaco Havoline, Ford, 11 x 8½ . . . . . . . . . . . . . . . . . . .8.00

28 Davey Allison, Krispy Kreme, 11 x 8½ .15.00

28 Davey Allison, Havoline, headshot, printed autograph, 10 x 8 . . . . . . . . . . . . . .12.00

28 Davey Allison, Long, Lewis Ford, 6½ x 10 .30.00

29 Andy Hillenburg, Gowen Oldsmobile, light & dark front, 5 x 7 . . . . . . . . . . . . .4.00

30 Michael Waltrip, Pennzoil, 3 different backs, #2950, 8 x 10 . . . . . . . . . . . . . . .2.00

31 Bobby Hillin, Martin Birrane, headshot, SCN-9311, 7 x 5 . . . . . . . . . . . . . . . . .3.00

32 Jimmy Horton, Active Racing, left Horton off back, 6 x 9 . . . . . . . . . . . . . . . . .7.00

32 Jimmy Horton, Active Racing, Chevrolet, 6 x 9 . . . . . . . . . . . . . . . . . . . .3.00

27 Jeff McClure, Race For Life, blank back, 4 x 6½ . . . . . . . . . . . . . . . . . . .2.00

33 Harry Gant, Skoal, Oldsmobile, 7¾ x 8½ .3.00
33 Harry Gant, Old Timer, Schrade, 8 x 10 .8.00
37 Richard Carelli, Chesrown Racing, Chevrolet, 8½ x 11 . . . . . . . . . . . . . . . . .5.00
41 Greg Sacks, Kellogg's, Chevrolet, 2 different insets on back, 6 x 9 . . . . . . . . . . . . .3.00
42 Kyle Petty, Mello Yello, blank back, 6 x 12 .2.00
42 Kyle Petty, Stalker Radar Detectors, blank back, 5 x 7 . . . . . . . . . . . . . . . . .10.00
43 Richard Petty, The Ride Of A Life Time, #STP-1610, 6 x 9 . . . . . . . . . . . . . . . . .8.00
43 Richard Petty, STP, 5 different printings, 6 x 9 . . . . . . . . . . . . . . . . . . . . . .5.00

43 Richard Petty, Mickey Truck Bodies, blank back, 8½ x 11 . . . . . . . . . . . . . . . .8.00
43 Richard Petty, Louisville Speedway, headshot, 7 x 5 . . . . . . . . . . . . . . . . . . . . .8.00
43 Richard Petty, Bristol's Salute To Richard Petty, 5 x 7 . . . . . . . . . . . . . . . . . . . .7.00
43 Richard Petty, STP, leaning on car, SCN-9256, 7 x 5 . . . . . . . . . . . . . . . . . . . . .3.00
43 Richard Petty, STP, posed on pit road, SCN-9229, 5 x 7 . . . . . . . . . . . . . . . . . . .3.00
43 Richard Petty, STP, headshot, SCN-9230, 5 x 7 . . . . . . . . . . . . . . . . . . . .3.00
43 Richard Petty, STP, pit stop, SCN-9259, 5 x 7 . . . . . . . . . . . . . . . . . . . . .3.00
43 Richard Petty, International Trucks, AD-43181X, 6 x 9 . . . . . . . . . . . .10.00
43 Richard Petty, Gwaltney, 5 x 8½ . . . . . .8.00
22 Sterling Marlin, Maxwell House, blank back, 8 x 10 . . . . . . . . . . . . . . . . . . . .4.00
22 Sterling Marlin, Maxwell House, blank back, 6 x 8½ . . . . . . . . . . . . . . . . . . . .4.00
43 Richard Petty, The Daytona News, Journal, 6 x 11 . . . . . . . . . . . . . . . . . . . . .7.00
43 Richard Petty, The Charlotte Observer, 11 x 8½ . . . . . . . . . . . . . . . . . . . . .6.00
43 Richard Petty, Reynolds Aluminum Recycling, 8 x 10 . . . . . . . . . . . . . . . .10.00

47 Buddy Baker, Kanawha Insurance Co., 5½ x 8½ . . . . . . . . . . . . . . . . . . . . .3.00
48 James Hylton, Hard Racing, Pontiac, #P70668, 5½ x 7 . . . . . . . . . . . . .5.00
49 Stanley Smith, FMC, 5½ x 8½ . . . . . . .3.00
49 Stanley Smith, Ameritron Batteries, 5½ x 8½ . . . . . . . . . . . . . . . . . . . . .3.00
55 Ted Musgrave, Jasper, Pontiac, no wall on front, 5 x 7 . . . . . . . . . . . . . . . . .3.00
55 Ted Musgrave, Jasper, Ford, no crew chief, 5 x 7 . . . . . . . . . . . . . . . . . . . . .2.00
55 Ted Musgrave, Jasper, Ford, crew chief Sandy Jones, 5 x 7 . . . . . . . . . . . . . . . . .2.00
57 Dick May, McClure Trucking Co., blank back, 4 x 6 . . . . . . . . . . . . . . . . . . . . .5.00
59 Andy Belmont, FDP Brakes, 5½ x 8½ . . .4.00
66 Chad Little, Trop Artic, Ford, #1208-92, 5 x 8 . . . . . . . . . . . . . . . . . . . . .3.00
66 Chad Little, Trop Artic, Ford, #1207-92, 8½ x 11 . . . . . . . . . . . . . . . . .3.00
66 Cale Yarborough, Trop Artic, Ford, #1208-92, 5 x 8 . . . . . . . . . . . . . . . . . . . . .2.00
66 Jimmy Hensley, Trop Artic, Ford, #1505-92, 5 x 8 . . . . . . . . . . . . . . . . . . . . .2.00
68 Bobby Hamilton, Country Time, Oldsmobile, Preview, blank back, 5½ x 8¼ . . . . . . .5.00
68 Bobby Hamilton, Country Time, Oldsmobile, 2 different backs, 5½ x 14 . . . . . . . . . .2.00
68 Bobby Hamilton, Country Time, headshot, SCN-9260, 7 x 5 . . . . . . . . . . . . . . . . .3.00
71 Jim Sauter, Big Apple Market, B & W, blank back, 5½ x 8½ . . . . . . . . . . . . . . . . .6.00
71 Dave Marcis, Wehrs, Chevrolet, 5 x 7 . .3.00
71 Dave Marcis, K & K Insurance, Dodge, 8 x 10 . . . . . . . . . . . . . . . . . . . . .5.00
73 Bill Schmitt, Nevada City Water, Winston West, 4 x 9 . . . . . . . . . . . . . . . . . . .5.00
77 Mike Potter, Kenova, Chevrolet, 2 backs, 5½ x 8½ . . . . . . . . . . . . . . . . . . . . .5.00
83 Lake Speed, Purex, Oldsmobile, 6 x 8 . . .3.00
83 Lake Speed, Purex, Ford, 6 x 8 . . . . . . .2.00
92 Ron Hornaday Jr., Palmdale Chiropractic, 8½ x 11 . . . . . . . . . . . . . . . . . . . .4.00
94 Terry Labonte, Sunoco, Oldsmobile, 8 x 10 . . . . . . . . . . . . . . . . . . . . .3.00
97 Flossie Johnson, Budweiser, car owner, 5 x 7 . . . . . . . . . . . . . . . . . . . . .4.00
98 Jimmy Spencer, Moly Black Gold, 6 x 9 . .5.00
98 Jimmy Spencer, Food City, 6 x 9 . . . . . .6.00
98 Jimmy Spencer, Food City, headshot, 6 x 9 . . . . . . . . . . . . . . . . . . . . .6.00

## 1993

02 T. W. Taylor, Children's Miracle Network, 6 x 9 . . . . . . . . . . . . . . . . . . . . .3.00
1 Rick Mast, Skoal, 7 x 12 . . . . . . . . . . .1.00

2 Rusty Wallace, 1992 front, 1993 back, 8 x 10 . . . . . . . . . . . . . . . . .2.00
2 Rusty Wallace, Brickyard 400 ad, 6 x 9 . .5.00
2 Rusty Wallace, fan club, headshot, 5¾ x 4¾ . . . . . . . . . . . . . . . . . .3.00
2 Rusty Wallace, Licensed To Fly, Jeanne Barnes, 6 x 4 . . . . . . . . . . . . . . . . .2.00
2 Rusty Wallace, Miller, 6 card promo set, 3¾ x 5½ . . . . . . . . . . . . . .15.00
3 Richard Childress, Back In Black, crew card, 8½ x 11 . . . . . . . . . . . . . . .2.00
3 Dale Earnhardt, Goodwrench, 1992 front, 1993 back, 8 x 10 . . . . . . . . . . . . . .5.00
3 Dale Earnhardt, Sun Drop Promo, 8 x 5½ . . . . . . . . . . . . . . . . . .10.00
3 Dale Earnhardt, fan club, posed by car, 10 x 8 . . . . . . . . . . . . . . . . .12.00
4 Ernie Irvan, Kodak, drawing, 9 x 13 . . . . .4.00
4 Ernie Irvan, Kodak, with order form, 5½ x 8 . . . . . . . . . . . . . . . . . .3.00
4 Ernie Irvan, Kodak, 6 card set, 3½ x 4½ .18.00
5 Ricky Rudd, Tide, 5 x 7 . . . . . . . .1.00
6 Mark Martin, Valvoline, 8½ x 11 . . . . . . .2.00
6 Mark Martin, Oil Change Reminder, V-2954-93, 3½ x 5 . . . . . . . . . . . . . . . . . .3.00
7 Alan Kulwicki, Hooter's, with girls, 5 x 7 . .5.00

7 Jimmy Hensley & Tommy Kendell, Family Channel, Accentuate The Positive, 8½ x 11 30.00
7 Jimmy Hensley & Tommy Kendall, Family Channel, Road Course, 8½ x 11 . . . . . . . . .3.00
7 Jimmy Hensley, Cellular One, photo, 8 x 10 .3.00
7 Jimmy Hensley, Purolator, paper, 8½ x 11 .2.00
7 Jimmy Hensley, 1992 Rookie, Watson Promotions, 5 x 7 . . . . . . . . . . . . . . . . . .2.00
8 Sterling Marlin, Raybestos, blank back, 5¾ x 8¾ . . . . . . . . . . . . . . . . . .6.00
8 Sterling Marlin, Raybestos, by truck, 5½ x 8½ . . . . . . . . . . . . . . . . . .2.00
8 Sterling Marlin, Douglas Battery, 5½ x 7 . .5.00
9 No Driver, Orkin, 6 x 9 . . . . . . . . . . . .3.00
9 Chad Little, Orkin, 6 x 9 . . . . . . . . . . . .3.00

9 Chad Little, Mayflower, headshot, 9 x 6 . .25.00
9 Chad Little, Orkin, action, 6 x 9 . . . . . . .3.00
9 P.J. Jones, Melling, B & W, headshot, 8½ x 5½ . . . . . . . . . . . . . . . . . .3.00
9 P.J. Jones, Melling, 4 x 6 . . . . . . . . . .3.00
11 Bill Elliott, Clevite Engine Parts, 5 x 7 . . .3.00
11 Bill Elliott, Budweiser, 5½ x 8 . . . . . . . .2.00
11 Bill Elliott, The Racing Collection Watches, 4 x 6 . . . . . . . . . . . . . . . . . . .2.00
12 Jimmy Spencer, Meineke, 8 x 10 . . . . .2.00
12 Jimmy Spencer, Meineke, no owner or driver names under insets, 8 x 10 . . . . . . . .1.00
12 Jimmy Spencer, Meineke, pit stop, photo stock, 8 x 10 . . . . . . . . . . . . . . .3.00
14 Terry Labonte, Kellogg's & M W Windows, fan club, 8 x 10 . . . . . . . . . . . . . . .6.00
14 Terry Labonte, Kellogg's, with order form, 8½ x 11½ . . . . . . . . . . . . . . .1.00
15 Geoff Bodine, Motorcraft, standup postcard, 8½ x 11 . . . . . . . . . . . . . . . . .1.00
16 Wally Dallenbach, Jr., Keystone, 6½ x 8¼ .1.00
17 Darrell Waltrip, Western Auto, 6 x 8½ . .1.00
17 Darrell Waltrip, Western Auto, fan club, headshot, 8 x 10 . . . . . . . . . . . . . . .5.00
17 Darrell Waltrip, Western Auto, fan club, action shot, 5½ x 8½ . . . . . . . . . . . . . .5.00
18 Dale Jarrett, Interstate Batteries, 7½ x 11 . . . . . . . . . . . . . . . . . .1.00
19 Chad Little, Harris Teeter, 5 x 7 . . . . . . .3.00
20 Joe Ruttman, Fina Lube, 8½ x 5½ . . . . .2.00
20 Bobby Hamilton, Fina Lube, 8 x 10 . . . . .2.00
20 Randy LaJoie, Fina Lube, photo stock, 8 x 10 . . . . . . . . . . . . . . . . . . .1.00
20 Dirk Stepens, Pepsi, Winston West, 5 x 7 . . . . . . . . . . . . . . . . . . .2.00
21 Morgan Shepherd, Citgo, 8½ x 11 . . . .1.00
22 Bobby Labonte, Maxwell House, 8½ x 10½ . . . . . . . . . . . . . . . . .5.00
23 Eddie Bierschwale, Splitfire, Oldsmobile, 4 x 6 . . . . . . . . . . . . . . . . . . .2.00

24 Jeff Gordon, Dupont, 6 x 9 . . . . . . . . .35.00
24 Jeff Gordon, Dupont, headshot, 8 x 10 . .5.00

24 Jeff Gordon, Dupont, standing by car, 8 x 10 . . . . . . . . . . . . . . . . . .5.00
24 Jeff Gordon, Old Hickory Credit Union, fold-over, 4 x 10 . . . . . . . . . . . . . .5.00
25 Ken Schrader, Kodiak, 7½ x 10 . . . . . .1.00
25 Ken Schrader, Brewco, 8½ x 11 . . . . .4.00
26 Brett Bodine, Quaker State, 8 x 10 . . . .1.00
27 Hut Stricklin, McDonald's, headshot, photo, 10 x 8 . . . . . . . . . . . . . . . . .2.00
27 Hut Stricklin, McDonald's, with printed autographs, 5½ x 8 . . . . . . . . . . . . .3.00
27 Hut Stricklin, McDonald's, no printed autographs, 5½ x 8 . . . . . . . . . . . . .1.00
27 Hut Stricklin, McDonald's, 8 x 10 . . . . .2.00
28 Davey Allison, Texaco, Havoline, 11 x 8½ .3.00
28 Davey Allison, Rising Star, Jeanne Barnes art, 6 x 4 . . . . . . . . . . . . . . . . .2.00
28 Lake Speed, Texaco, headshot, B & W, 7 x 5 . . . . . . . . . . . . . . . . . . .1.00
28 No Driver, Texaco, car shot, B & W, 5 x 7 . . . . . . . . . . . . . . . . . . .1.00
30 Michael Waltrip, old front without Purolator decal, 8 x 10 . . . . . . . . . . . . .1.00
31 Neil Bonnett, Mom 'N' Pops, 5 x 7 . . . .12.00
32 Jimmy Horton, Active Racing, 8 x 10 . . .2.00
33 Harry Gant, Skoal, 6 x 9 . . . . . . . . .2.00
33 Harry Gant, Pro Cal, 6 x 9 . . . . . . . .2.00
37 Loy Allen, Naturally Fresh, 5 x 7 . . . . .2.00
37 Rick Carelli, Chesrown Racing, Winston West, 8½ x 11 . . . . . . . . . . . . . . .2.00
40 Kenny Wallace, Dirt Devil, headshot, 7 x 5 . . . . . . . . . . . . . . . . . . .3.00
40 Kenny Wallace, Dirt Devil, 9 x 6 . . . . . .1.00
41 Phil Parsons, Hedrick Motorsports, B & W headshot, 8½ x 5½ . . . . . . . . . . .2.00
41 Doug Richert, Hedrick Motorsports, B & W headshot, 8½ x 5½ . . . . . . . . . . .2.00
41 Harry Hyde, Hedrick Motorsports, B & W headshot, 8½ x 5½ . . . . . . . . . . .2.00
41 Larry Hedrick, Hedrick Motorsports, B & W headshot, 8½ x 5½ . . . . . . . . . . .2.00
41 No Driver, Hedrick Motorsports, group shot, B & W, 5½ x 8½ . . . . . . . . . . .10.00
41 Phil Parsons, Manheim Auctions, 5½ x 8½ . . . . . . . . . . . . . . . . .2.00
41 Phil Parsons, Manheim Auctions, fold-over, 5½ x 8½ . . . . . . . . . . . . . . .2.00
42 Kyle Petty, Caterpillar, Cat, 5½ x 12 . . . .3.00
42 Kyle Petty, Caterpillar, Cat, paper stock, 9 x 11 . . . . . . . . . . . . . . . . .2.00
42 Kyle Petty, The Tradition Continues, Jeanne Barnes, 6 x 4 . . . . . . . . . . . . .2.00
42 Kyle Petty, Fast Times 1993, B & W, 5 x 8 . . . . . . . . . . . . . . . . . . .3.00
42 Kyle Petty, Sparks Will Fly, 8½ x 11 . . . .4.00
42 Kyle Petty, No Fear, blank back, 9½ x 7¼ .6.00
42 Kyle Petty, Mello Yello, 6 x 12½ . . . . . .1.00

43 Richard Petty, "Randleman Rocket," 6 x 5 .3.00
43 Richard Petty, Start To Finish, Jeanne Barnes, 6 x 4 . . . . . . . . . . . . . . . . .2.00
43 Richard Petty, Embers Charcoal, posed, 4 x 5 . . . . . . . . . . . . . . . . . . .3.00
44 Richard Petty, STP, with car, 6 x 9 . . . . .2.00
44 Rick Wilson & Richard Petty, STP, with car, 6 x 9 . . . . . . . . . . . . . . . . .2.00
45 Rich Bickle, Terminal Trucking, 8 x 10 . . .1.00
45 Rich Bickle, Kraft, 3½ x 4 . . . . . . . . . .2.00
45 Rich Bickle, Kraft, 6 x 9 . . . . . . . . . . .2.00
45 Rich Bickle, Kraft, Chevrolet, with Ford Decals, 3½ x 4 . . . . . . . . . . . . . .3.00
45 Rich Bickle, Kraft, Chevrolet, with Ford Decals, 6 x 9 . . . . . . . . . . . . . .4.00
48 James Hylton, Dial Page, paper stock, 8½ x 11 . . . . . . . . . . . . . . . . .2.00
48 James Hylton, Rumple, 5 x 7 . . . . . . .2.00
50 Greg Sacks, Slick 50, 8¼ x 10¾ . . . . .25.00
50 P. J. Jones, Slick 50, 8½ x 11½ . . . . . .3.00
50 Bobby Jones, Slick 50, owner, 8½ x 11½ . . . . . . . . . . . . . . . . .1.00
52 Jimmy Means, Hurley Limo, 4 x 6 . . . . .4.00
52 Jimmy Means, NAPA, B & W, Dave Marcis Day, 5¾ x 8¾ . . . . . . . . . . . . . .5.00
53 Richie Petty, STG, Winston Cup Water, 6 x 9 . . . . . . . . . . . . . . . . . . .2.00
55 Ted Musgrave, Jasper & US Air, 5 x 8 . .2.00
55 Ted Musgrave, Jasper & US Air, 2 different backs, 5 x 7 . . . . . . . . . . . . . .2.00
56 Tony Hunt, Shaver-Boring, Winston West, 6 x 9 . . . . . . . . . . . . . . . . . . .3.00
66 Mike Wallace, Duron Paint, 6 x 9 . . . . .1.00
68 Bobby Hamilton, Country Time, t-shirt offer, thick stock, 8¼ x 10¾ . . . . . . . . . . .1.00
68 Bobby Hamilton, "Stove Top Stuffing," 7 x 4½ . . . . . . . . . . . . . . . . . . .2.00
68 Bobby Hamilton, Country Time, with order form, Outline "C.T." back, 6 x 9 . . . . . . .1.00
68 Bobby Hamilton, Country Time, with order form, color "C.T." back, 6 x 9 . . . . . . . .1.00
71 Dave Marcis, Freeman's Car Stereo, B & W, 8½ x 11 . . . . . . . . . . . . . . . . .5.00
71 Dave Marcis, Raines Kennels, 6 x 9 . . . .3.00
75 Dick Trickle, Factory Stores of America, blank back, 6 x 9 . . . . . . . . . . . . . . .5.00
75 Dick Trickle, Factory Stores of America, B & W, 5 x 7 . . . . . . . . . . . . . . . . .5.00
75 Dick Trickle, Factory Stores of America, blank back, 6 x 9 . . . . . . . . . . . . . . .2.00
75 Todd Bodine, Factory Stores of America, 6 x 9 . . . . . . . . . . . . . . . . . . .2.00
75 Bill Sedgwick, Spears, Winston West, 5¾ x 8½ . . . . . . . . . . . . . . . . .3.00
90 Bobby Hillin, Heilig Meyers, Jimmy Spencer over door, 5 x 7 . . . . . . . . . . . . .7.00
90 Bobby Hillin, Heilig Meyers, 5 x 7 . . . . . .1.00

90 Bobby Hillin, Heilig Meyers, with Luke,
5 x 7 . . . . . . . . . . . . . . . . . . . . . .3.00
98 Derrike Cope, Bojangles, 6 x 9½ . . . . .2.00
98 Cale Yarborough, Bojangles, 6 x 9½ . . . .2.00
98 Derrike Cope, Bojangles, 8 x 10 . . . . . .3.00

## 1994

02 T. W. Taylor, Children's Miracle Network,
6 x 9 . . . . . . . . . . . . . . . . . . . .3.00
02 Curtis Markham, Advil, 9 x 6 . . . . . . . .2.00
02 Derrike Cope, Advil, 6 x 9 . . . . . . . . .3.00
1 Rick Mast, Skoal, 6 x 9 . . . . . . . . . .2.00
1 Rick Mast, Skoal, fan club, 5 x 7½ . . . . .5.00
2 Rusty Wallace, Miller Genuine Draft, "The Cold
One," 8 x 10 . . . . . . . . . . . . . . . .2.00
2 Rusty Wallace, Miller Genuine Draft, with transporter, 8 x 10 . . . . . . . . . . . . . .4.00
2 Rusty Wallace, Miller Genuine Draft, car only,
8 x 10 . . . . . . . . . . . . . . . . . . . .5.00
2 Rusty Wallace, Miller Genuine Draft, victory
lane, blank back, 8 x 10 . . . . . . . . . .5.00
2 Rusty Wallace, Miller Genuine Draft, action shot,
8¼ x 11 . . . . . . . . . . . . . . . . . . . .8.00
2 Rusty Wallace, Rusty Wallace Dealership,
6 x 8 . . . . . . . . . . . . . . . . . . . . . .5.00
2 Rusty Wallace, Tom Johnson Camping Center,
9 x 6 . . . . . . . . . . . . . . . . . . . . . .2.00
2 Rusty Wallace, MGD, Sam Bass, 9¼ x 7½ .5.00
2 Rusty Wallace, art card by Jeanne Barnes,
4¾ x 6 . . . . . . . . . . . . . . . . . . . .2.00
2 Rusty Wallace, art card by Sam Bass, "Fly It,"
5¾ x 4¾ . . . . . . . . . . . . . . . . . .3.00
2 Rusty Wallace, art card by Jeanne Barnes,
"Second to None," 4¾ x 6 . . . . . . . . .3.00
2 Rusty Wallace, art card, headshot,
7 x 5½ . . . . . . . . . . . . . . . . . . . .5.00
2 Rusty Wallace, art card, action, 5½ x 7 . .5.00
2 Roger Penske, art card by Sam Bass,
5¾ x 4¾ . . . . . . . . . . . . . . . . . . .3.00
2 Bill McAnally, Mega Power, Winston West,
5 x 7 . . . . . . . . . . . . . . . . . . . . . .3.00
3 Dale Earnhardt, GM Goodwrench, error, crew
members with wrong names, 8 x 10 . . .8.00
3 Dale Earnhardt, GM Goodwrench, correct,
8 x 10 . . . . . . . . . . . . . . . . . . . .5.00
3 Dale Earnhardt, Winston Cup Champion, Winston Cup preview, 8 x 10 . . . . . . . . .40.00
3 Dale Earnhardt, GM Goodwrench, glossy front,
8 x 10 . . . . . . . . . . . . . . . . . . . .10.00
3 Dale Earnhardt, GM Goodwrench, headshot, fan
club, 8 x 10 . . . . . . . . . . . . . . . . .15.00
3 Dale Earnhardt, collector's ring, 6 x 9 . . . .4.00
3 Dale Earnhardt, Western Steer, blank back
7 x 5 . . . . . . . . . . . . . . . . . . . . .5.00
3 Dale Earnhardt, Western Steer, printed back,
7 x 5 . . . . . . . . . . . . . . . . . . . . .18.00

3 Dale Earnhardt, Winston Cup Champion, Winston Cup preview, 10 x 8 . . . . . . . . .40.00

3 Dale Earnhardt, art card by Jeanne Barnes,
"Earnhardt VI," 4 x 6 . . . . . . . . . . . .3.00
3 Dale Earnhardt, Collector's World, "Earnhardt
VI," 7½ x 4¾ . . . . . . . . . . . . . . . .3.00
3 Dale Earnhardt, Collector's World, "The Golden
Touch," 4 x 5¼ . . . . . . . . . . . . . . .3.00
3 Dale Earnhardt, Collector's World, "Eye of the
Storm," 4 x 5¼ . . . . . . . . . . . . . . .3.00
3 Dale Earnhardt, art card by Sam Bass, "Six
Shooter," 5¾ x 4¾ . . . . . . . . . . . . .8.00
3 Dale Earnhardt, art card by Sam Bass, "6 Time
Champion," 5¾ x 4¾ . . . . . . . . . . . .8.00
3 Dale Earnhardt, Chevrolet, Gambler Package,
paper, 8½ x 11 . . . . . . . . . . . . . . .8.00
3 Dale Earnhardt, GM Goodwrench, 3 card set,
8 x 10 . . . . . . . . . . . . . . . . . . . .130.00
4 Sterling Marlin, Kodak, 1st version, highlights,
5½ x 8½ . . . . . . . . . . . . . . . . . . .4.00
4 Sterling Marlin, Kodak, Daytona Win, with gloss,
5½ x 8½ . . . . . . . . . . . . . . . . . . .2.00
4 Sterling Marlin, Kodak, Daytona Win, without
gloss, 5½ x 8½ . . . . . . . . . . . . . . .2.00
4 Sterling Marlin, Kodak / Delco Remy,
5½ x 8½ . . . . . . . . . . . . . . . . . . .4.00
4 Sterling Marlin, art card by Jeanne Barnes,
4¾ x 6 . . . . . . . . . . . . . . . . . . . .2.00
5 Terry Labonte, Kellogg's, 8¼ x 12½ . . . . .2.00
5 Terry Labonte, Kellogg's, Goodyear Day, B & W,
8 x 4¾ . . . . . . . . . . . . . . . . . . . .5.00
5 Terry Labonte, art card by Sam Bass, paper,
4¾ x 5¾ . . . . . . . . . . . . . . . . . . .1.00
6 Mark Martin, Valvoline, #V-3093-94,
8 x 10 . . . . . . . . . . . . . . . . . . . .3.00

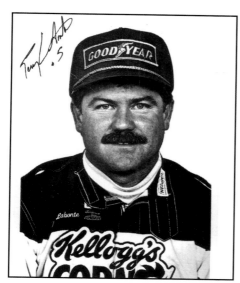

5 Terry Labonte, Kellogg's, Goodyear Day, B & W, 8 x 4¾ . . . . . . . . . . . . . . . . . .5.00

6 Mark Martin, Reese's, 7½ round . . . . . . .2.00
6 Mark Martin, Valvoline, with coupon, #94-VMO-046-1, 8½ x 11 . . . . . . . . . . . . . . .2.00
6 Mark Martin, Valvoline, Oil Change Reminder, #V-3674-94, 4 x 6 . . . . . . . . . . . . . . .3.00
6 Mark Martin, Valvoline, Oil Change Reminder, #V-2954-94, 4 x 7 . . . . . . . . . . . . . . .3.00
6 Mark Martin, Valvoline, artist card by Jeanne Barnes, 4¾ x 6 . . . . . . . . . . . . . .2.00
6 Mark Martin, Buckle Up, color, 8 x 10 . . .5.00
6 Mark Martin, Buckle Up, B & W, 8 x 10 . .5.00
6 Mark Martin, Valvoline, Collector's World Paper Show, 1 of 5000, 5 x 7 . . . . . . . . . . .6.00
6 Mark Martin, Valvoline, action shot, 8¼ x 11 . . . . . . . . . . . . . . . . . . . . .8.00
6 Mark Martin, Cummins Diesel, 8½ x 11 . .5.00
6 Mark Martin, art card, headshot, 5½ x 7 .5.00
6 Mark Martin, art card, action, 5½ x 7 . . .5.00
6 Dennis Ritchie, Valvoline, transporter driver, #94-VOLI-2, 4¼ x 6¼ . . . . . . . . . .4.00
7 Geoff Bodine, Exide Batteries, 5½ x 8½ . . .2.00
7 Alan Kulwicki, art card by Jeanne Barnes, 6 x 4 . . . . . . . . . . . . . . . . . . . . . . . .2.00
7 Alan Kulwicki, Collector's World ad card by Jeanne Barnes, 8 x 5 . . . . . . . . . . .2.00
7 Peter Jellen, Exide, transporter driver, 4¼ x 6¼ . . . . . . . . . . . . . . . . . . .3.00
8 Jeff Burton, Douglas Battery, 7 x 9 . . . . .5.00
8 Jeff Burton, Raybestos, without window net, 5½ x 8½ . . . . . . . . . . . . . . . . . . .2.00
8 Jeff Burton, Raybestos, with window net, 5½ x 8½ . . . . . . . . . . . . . . . . . . .2.00
9 Rich Bickle, Orkin, 6 x 9 . . . . . . . . . . .2.00
09 Stan Fox, Jack's Tool Rental, 8½ x 11 . . .4.00
10 Ricky Rudd, Tide, with Bill Ingle, 5 x 7 . . .2.00

10 Ricky Rudd, Tide, without Bill Ingle, 5 x 7 . . . . . . . . . . . . . . . . . . . . . .2.00
10 Ricky Rudd, Tide, Race Against Drugs, 5 x 7 . . . . . . . . . . . . . . . . . . . . . .3.00
10 Ricky Rudd, Tide, show car promo, 8 x 10 . . . . . . . . . . . . . . . . . . . .15.00
10 Tom Brown, Tide, transporter driver, #94 Vol.2-2, 4¼ x 6¼ . . . . . . . . . . . .3.00
11 Bill Elliott, Budweiser, 5½ x 8 . . . . . . . . .3.00
11 Bill Elliott, Budweiser, 8 x 10 . . . . . . . .3.00
11 Brett Bodine, Lowes, 1995 Team, 8 x 10 . . . . . . . . . . . . . . . . . . . .10.00
12 Bobby Allison, Brigadier, blank back, 8 x 10 . . . . . . . . . . . . . . . . . . . . .5.00
12 Bobby Allison, Mansion Homes, blank back, 8 x 10 . . . . . . . . . . . . . . . . . . . . .5.00
12 Bobby Allison, Buccaneer, blank back, 8 x 10 . . . . . . . . . . . . . . . . . . . . .5.00
12 Bobby Allison, Cavalier Homes, blank back, 8 x 10 . . . . . . . . . . . . . . . . . . . . .5.00
12 Derrike Cope, Straight Arrow, 8 x 10 . . .5.00
12 Derrike Cope, Straight Arrow, car only, 8 x 10 . . . . . . . . . . . . . . . . . . . .10.00
14 John Andretti, Grand Piano, 5 x 7 . . . . .3.00
14 John Andretti, Grand Piano, blank back, 5 x 7 . . . . . . . . . . . . . . . . . . . . . .4.00
14 John Andretti, Grand Piano, with coupon, 5 x 10 . . . . . . . . . . . . . . . . . . . . .5.00
14 John Andretti, art card by Bart Heldman, 3½ x 5½ . . . . . . . . . . . . . . . . . .10.00
14 Bobby Hillin, Grand Piano, 5 x 7 . . . . . .5.00
14 Phil Parsons, Grand Piano, 5 x 7 . . . . . .5.00
15 Lake Speed, Quality Care, car shaped, 5¾ x 11 . . . . . . . . . . . . . . . . . . . .2.00
15 Lake Speed, Quality Care, 4 x 6 . . . . . . .4.00
15 Lake Speed, Quality Care, 6 x 9 . . . . . .20.00
15 Terry Orr, Quality Care, transporter driver, #94 Vol. 2-6, 4¼ x 6¼ . . . . . . . . . .3.00
16 Ted Musgrave, Family Channel, photo, 8 x 10 . . . . . . . . . . . . . . . . . . . . .2.00
16 Ted Musgrave, Family Channel, 6 x 9 . . .3.00
16 Ted Musgrave, Family Channel, action shot, 8¼ x 11 . . . . . . . . . . . . . . . . . . . .8.00
16 Craig Phillips, Family Channel, transporter driver, #94 Vol 2-3, 4¼ x 6¼ . . . . . . .3.00
17 Darrell Waltrip, Western Auto, 2 different headshots, 8 x 10 . . . . . . . . . . . .3.00
17 Darrell Waltrip, Western Auto, art card by Jeanne Barnes, 4 x 6 . . . . . . . . . . . .2.00
17 Darrell Waltrip, Western Auto, action shot, 8¼ x 11 . . . . . . . . . . . . . . . . . . . .8.00
18 Dale Jarrett, Interstate Batteries, 8 x 10 .2.00
18 Dale Jarrett, art card by Jeanne Barnes, 4¾ x 6 . . . . . . . . . . . . . . . . . . . . .2.00
18 Dale Jarrett, Fire & Ice, 8 x 10 . . . . . . .5.00
18 Dale Jarrett, art card, headshot, 8 x 6 . .5.00
18 Dale Jarrett, art card, action, 6 x 8 . . . .5.00

19 Loy Allen, Hooters, large printed autograph on back, 8 x 10 . . . . . . . . . . . . . . .4.00
19 Loy Allen, Hooters, small printed autograph on back, 8 x 10 . . . . . . . . . . . . . . .3.00
19 Loy Allen, Hooters, in restaurant, 8 x 10 .2.00
20 Randy LaJoie, FINA, 5½ x 8½ . . . . . . . .2.00
20 Randy LaJoie, FINA & Lance, 5½ x 8½ . .2.00
20 Randy LaJoie, FINA & Kool, Aid, 5½ x 8½ 4.00
20 Buddy Baker, FINA, car only, 5½ x 8½ . . .3.00
20 Buddy Baker, FINA, 5½ x 8½ . . . . . . . .3.00
20 Bobby Hillin, FINA & Lance, 5½ x 8½ . . .3.00
21 Morgan Shepherd, Citgo, blank back, 8¼ x 10¾ . . . . . . . . . . . . . . . . . . .4.00
21 Morgan Shepherd, Citgo, 8¼ x 10¾ . . . .2.00
21 Morgan Shepherd, Citgo, 5 card set, 3½ x 5½ . . . . . . . . . . . . . . . . . .10.00
21 Morgan Shepherd, art card by Jeanne Barnes, 4¾ x 6 . . . . . . . . . . . . . . . . . . . . . .2.00
21 Ricky Simmons, Citgo, transporter driver, #94 Vol. 1-3, 4¼ x 6¼ . . . . . . . . . . . . . . .3.00
22 Bobby Labonte, Maxwell House, 8¼ x 10½ . . . . . . . . . . . . . . . . . . . .3.00
23 Hut Stricklin, Smokin' Joe's, yellow door numbers, 8 x 10¼ . . . . . . . . . . . . . .2.00
23 Hut Stricklin, Smokin' Joe's, green door numbers, 8 x 10¼ . . . . . . . . . . . . . .2.00
23 Wayne Jenks, Smokin' Joe's, Transporter Driver, 4¼ x 6¼ . . . . . . . . . . . . . . .3.00
24 Jeff Gordon, DuPont, 8 x 10 . . . . . . .4.00
24 Jeff Gordon, Snickers, 6¼ x 8½ . . . . . .5.00
24 Jeff Gordon, Circle Track, 10½ x 7¼ . . .3.00
24 Jeff Gordon, art card by Jeanne Barnes, 4¾ x 6 . . . . . . . . . . . . . . . . . . . . . .2.00
24 Jeff Gordon, art card by Jeanne Barnes, "New Horizons," 4 x 6 . . . . . . . . . . . . . . . .3.00
24 Jeff Gordon, Collector's World ad card by Sam Bass, 4 x 5¼ . . . . . . . . . . . . . . . .2.00
24 Jeff Gordon, art card, headshot, 5½ x 7 .5.00
24 Jeff Gordon, art card, action, 5½ x 7 . . .5.00
24 Jeff Gordon, Dupont & FMC, blank back, 8½ x 11 . . . . . . . . . . . . . . . . . . . .8.00
24 Jeff Gordon, Dupont & FMC, paper stock, 8½ x 11 . . . . . . . . . . . . . . . . . . . .4.00
24 Jeff Gordon, Dupont & FMC, printed back, 8½ x 11 . . . . . . . . . . . . . . . . . . . .5.00
24, 2 Jeff Gordon & Ricky Craven, Dupont, fold-over, 5 x 6½ . . . . . . . . . . . . . . . . . .4.00
24, 2 Jeff Gordon & Ricky Craven, Dupont, fold-over, Bruce's Body Shop, 5 x 6½ . . . . . .4.00
25 Ken Schrader, Kodiak, 7 3/16 x 10 . . . .2.00
26 Brett Bodine, Quaker State, 8 x 10 . . . .2.00
27 Jimmy Spencer, McDonald's, 5½ x 8 . . .2.00
28 Fred Lorenzen, LaFayette Ford, authorized reprint, 5¼ x 7 . . . . . . . . . . . . . . .5.00
28 Davey Allison, Art Card, "The Prayer" by Skipper, 7 x 9 . . . . . . . . . . . . . . .20.00
28 Ernie Irvan, Havoline, blank back, 8¼ x 5 .7.00

28 Ernie Irvan, Havoline, 8½ x 11 . . . . . . .3.00
28 Ernie Irvan, art card by Jeanne Barnes, 4¾ x 6 . . . . . . . . . . . . . . . . . . . . . .2.00
28 Steve Foster, Texaco, transporter driver, #94 Vol.2-1, 4¼ x 6¼ . . . . . . . . . . . . . . .4.00
28 Ken Collins, Collins Racing, Winston West, 5¾ x 9 . . . . . . . . . . . . . . . . . . . . .5.00
29 Steve Grissom, Diamond Ridge, photo stock, 5 x 7 . . . . . . . . . . . . . . . . . . . . . .3.00
29 Steve Grissom, Diamond Ridge, green car, 5 x 7 . . . . . . . . . . . . . . . . . . . . .20.00
29 Steve Grissom, Diamond Ridge, teal car, 5 x 7 . . . . . . . . . . . . . . . . . . . . . .1.00
29 John Krebs, Channellock, Winston West, 10 x 8 . . . . . . . . . . . . . . . . . . . . .7.00
29 John Krebs, Channellock, Winston West, 9 x 6 . . . . . . . . . . . . . . . . . . . . . .3.00
30 Michael Waltrip, Pennzoil, 8 x 10 . . . . .5.00
31 Ward Burton, Hardee's, gray background, 8 x 10 . . . . . . . . . . . . . . . . . . . . .2.00
31 Ward Burton, Hardee's, 8 x 10 . . . . . . .2.00
32 Dick Trickle, Active, 5 x 7 . . . . . . . . .2.00
32 Dick Trickle, Skybox, 4½ x 7 . . . . . . . .2.00
33 Harry Gant, Farewell Tour, B & W, 4 x 5½ .1.00
33 Harry Gant, Skoal, 8½ x 12 . . . . . . . .3.00
33 Harry Gant, art card by Jeanne Barnes, 4¾ x 6 . . . . . . . . . . . . . . . . . . . . . .2.00
34 Mike McLaughlin, Coors, gray background, 8½ x 11 . . . . . . . . . . . . . . . . . . . .3.00
34 Mike McLaughlin, Coors, blue background, 8½ x 11 . . . . . . . . . . . . . . . . . . . .5.00
37 Rodney Orr, Church Street Station, 8 x 10 . . . . . . . . . . . . . . . . . . . .15.00
40 Bobby Hamilton, Kendall, 8 x 10 . . . . .2.00
40 Bobby Hamilton, Kendall, photo stock, 5 x 7 . . . . . . . . . . . . . . . . . . . . . .2.00
40 Bobby Hamilton, Lane, B & W, blank back, 8½ x 11 . . . . . . . . . . . . . . . . . . . .5.00
41 Joe Nemechek, Meineke, 8 x 10 . . . . .2.00
41 Joe Nemechek, Hedrick Meineke, blank back, 6 x 9 . . . . . . . . . . . . . . . . . . . . . .4.00
42 Kyle Petty, No Fear, 9 x 7 . . . . . . . . .5.00
42 Kyle Petty, NASCAR World, 7 x 5 . . . . .10.00
42 Kyle Petty, No Fear, photo stock, 10 x 8 .4.00
42 Kyle Petty, International Trucks, 6 x 9 . . .5.00
43 Wally Dallenbach Jr., STP, 6 x 9 . . . . . .2.00
43 Richard Petty, International Trucks, 6 x 9 .5.00
43 Richard Petty, STP, 6 x 9 . . . . . . . . .3.00
43 Richard Petty, Craftsman Racing, with John Force & Mark Smith, 8 x 10 . . . . . . . . .7.00
44 Richard Petty, International Trucks, 6 x 9 .5.00
44 Bobby Hillin, Buss Fuse, side shot, 5 x 7 .3.00
44 Bobby Hillin, Buss Fuse, angle shot, 5 x 7 .4.00
45 Rich Bickle, Orkin, 6 x 9 . . . . . . . . . .2.00
49 Stanley Smith, Kresto, 5½ x 8½ . . . . . .3.00
50 Mike Chase, Star Race, Winston West, 5 x 7 . . . . . . . . . . . . . . . . . . . . . .3.00

51 Neil Bonnett, Country Time, 10 x 8 . . .20.00
51 Neil Bonnett, Country Time, 5½ x 8 . . . .3.00
51 Jeff Purvis, Country Time, 5½ x 8 . . . . .3.00
52 Jimmy Means, NAPA, 5½ x 8½ . . . . . .7.00
52 Kirk Shelmerdine, NAPA, 5½ x 8½ . . . .7.00
54 Robert Pressley & Harry Gant, Team Manheim, with #7 Harry Gant BGN, 5 x 7 . . . . . . . . . . . . . . . . . . . .3.00
55 Jimmy Hensley, 6 x 9 . . . . . . . . . . . . .3.00
57 Dick May, McClure Motors, autograph space added, 5 x 7 . . . . . . . . . . . . . . . . .2.00
61 Rick Carelli, Chesrown Total, 8½ x 11 . . .3.00
61 Rick Carelli, Total Racing, on pit road, 8½ x 11 . . . . . . . . . . . . . . . . . . . .3.00
61 Rick Carelli, Total Racing, 2 cars & truck, 8½ x 11 . . . . . . . . . . . . . . . . . . . .3.00
62 No Driver, 1-800-MY-DIXIE, 3 x 5½ . . . .11.00
66 Mike Wallace, Duron, 10 x 8 . . . . . . . .4.00
66 Mike Wallace, Duron, Fred Beck Pontiac, GMC, 5½ x 8½ . . . . . . . . . . . . . .3.00
66 Mike Wallace, Duron, "Hottest Colors At The Race!," 11 x 8½ . . . . . . . . . . . . .15.00
71 Dave Marcis, STG, 6 x 9 . . . . . . . . . .3.00
71 Dave Marcis, Olive Garden, 6 x 9 . . . . .3.00
71 Dave Marcis, Terrimite, 6 x 9½ . . . . . .4.00
71 Dave Marcis, Prodigy, Health Management System, 5¾ x 9 . . . . . . . . . . . . . . .3.00
75 Todd Bodine, Factory Stores of America, 7 x 10 . . . . . . . . . . . . . . . . . . . . .2.00
75 Ron Hornaday Jr., Spears, color background, 5½ x 8½ . . . . . . . . . . . . . . . . . .2.00
75 Ron Hornaday Jr., Spears, sky background, 5½ x 8½ . . . . . . . . . . . . . . . . . .2.00
77 Greg Sacks, US Air, car only, 5 x 7¾ . . .2.00
77 Greg Sacks, Jasper, 2 different backs, car only, 5 x 7¾ . . . . . . . . . . . . . . . .2.00
77 Greg Sacks, US Air, 5 x 7¾ . . . . . . . .2.00
77 Greg Sacks, Jasper, 5 x 7¼ . . . . . . . .2.00
78 Jay Hedgecock, 6 x 9 . . . . . . . . . . . .3.00
80 Joe Ruttman, Park, Ohio, paper stock, 8½ x 11 . . . . . . . . . . . . . . . . . . . .2.00
89 Jim Sauter, Kraft/ Bullseye, 6 x 9 . . . . .3.00
89 Jim Sauter, Kraft/ Bullseye, blank back, 3½ x 5 . . . . . . . . . . . . . . . . . . . . .1.00
89 Jim Sauter, Kraft/ Bullseye, schedule, 3½ x 5 . . . . . . . . . . . . . . . . . . . . .1.00
90 Bobby Hillin, Heilig Meyers, 6 x 9 . . . . .5.00
90 Mike Wallace, Heilig Meyers, headshot, 10 x 8 . . . . . . . . . . . . . . . . . . . .10.00
90 Mike Wallace, Heilig Meyers, 6 x 9 . . . .2.00
98 Derrike Cope, Fingerhut, 5½ x 8½ . . . . .2.00
98 Derrike Cope, Fingerhut, Masterbuilt logo on back, 5½ x 8½ . . . . . . . . . . . . . . .2.00
98 Jeremy Mayfield, Fingerhut, 5½ x 8½ . . .2.00
98 Jeremy Mayfield, Fingerhut, ACME logo on back, 5½ x 8½ . . . . . . . . . . . . . . .2.00
98 Cale Yarborough, Masterbuilt, 10 x 8 . . .4.00

98 Jeremy Mayfield, Campbell, Hausfeld, with order form, 3¼ x 5½ . . . . . . . . . . . . .2.00
98 Jeremy Mayfield, Campbell, Hausfeld, 5½ x 8½ . . . . . . . . . . . . . . . . . . .4.00
99 Danny Sullivan, Checker's, photo stock, 8 x 10 . . . . . . . . . . . . . . . . . . . . .4.00
99 Danny Sullivan, The Corporate Car, 6 x 9 .5.00

## 1995

0 Delma Cowart, Masters Inn, #P95131, 5½ x 3¾ . . . . . . . . . . . . . . . . . . .2.00
1 Rick Mast, Skoal, 9¼ x 6¾ . . . . . . . . . .1.00
2 Rusty Wallace, Miller Genuine Draft, 8 x 10 . . . . . . . . . . . . . . . . . . . . .1.00
2 Rusty Wallace, Miller Genuine Draft, 5¾ x 4¾ . . . . . . . . . . . . . . . . . . .2.00
2 Rusty Wallace, Team Penske, Mobil 1, 8½ x 11 . . . . . . . . . . . . . . . . . . .4.00
2 Rusty Wallace, Chevy Chase Bank, 11 x 8½ . . . . . . . . . . . . . . . . . . .4.00
2 Rusty Wallace, Fleetwood Recreational Vehicles, 11 x 8½ . . . . . . . . . . . . . . . . . . .3.00
2 Rusty Wallace, Fleetwood Recreational Vehicles, with red autograph, 11 x 8½ . . . . . . .3.00
2 Rusty Wallace, Fleetwood Recreational Vehicles, red autograph, no coupon, 11 x 8½ . . .4.00
2 Rusty Wallace, Mazak, 8½ x 11 . . . . . . .3.00
2 Rusty Wallace, Midnight Pilot, art card, 6 x 4 . . . . . . . . . . . . . . . . . . . . . .2.00
2 Rusty Wallace, MGD, Race art card, 8 x 10 . . . . . . . . . . . . . . . . . . . . .5.00
2 Rusty Wallace, Traks Cartoons, 10 x 8 . . .5.00
2 Rusty Wallace, Miller Racing, 1996 preview card, 10 x 8 . . . . . . . . . . . . . . . . .12.00
2 Rusty Wallace, fan club, 10 x 8 . . . . . . .5.00

3 Dale Earnhardt, Goodwrench, error, Earnhardt on left, 8 x 10¼ . . . . . . . . . . . . . . . .30.00
3 Dale Earnhardt, Goodwrench, correct, Earnhardt on right, 8 x 10¼ . . . . . . . . . . .5.00

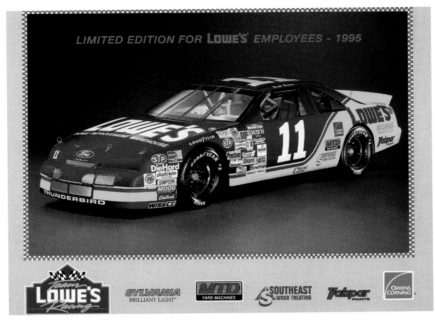

11 Brett Bodine, Lowes, employee's card, 8 x 10 . . .5.00

3 Dale Earnhardt, Winston Cup preview,
 8½ x 12 . . . . . . . . . . . . . . . . . .25.00
3 Dale Earnhardt, Goodwrench, blank back,
 10 x 8 . . . . . . . . . . . . . . . . . . . .22.00
3 Dale Earnhardt, Food City, error, Earnhardt on
 left, 8 x 10¼ . . . . . . . . . . . . . .30.00
3 Dale Earnhardt, Food City, correct, Earnhardt on
 right, 8 x 10¼ . . . . . . . . . . . . . .5.00
3 Dale Earnhardt, Choose To Be Drug Free,
 8 x 10 . . . . . . . . . . . . . . . . . . .20.00
3 Dale Earnhardt, fan club, blank back,
 10 x 8 . . . . . . . . . . . . . . . . . . . .8.00
4 Sterling Marlin, Kodak, 6½ x 8¾ . . . . . .1.00
4 Sterling Marlin, Kodak, Back to Back Daytona
 500 Winner, 6½ x 8¾ . . . . . . . . . . .1.00
4 Sterling Marlin, Kodak, blank back, 8 x 10 .5.00
4 Sterling Marlin, Bill Plemmons RV World, paper,
 11 x 8½ . . . . . . . . . . . . . . . . . . .1.00
4 Sterling Marlin, Traks Cartoons, 10 x 8 . .5.00
4 Sterling Marlin & Jeff Purvis, AC Delco,
 6 x 9 . . . . . . . . . . . . . . . . . . . . .4.00
4 Sterling Marlin, Choose To Be Drug Free,
 8 x 10 . . . . . . . . . . . . . . . . . . . .8.00
5 Terry Labonte, Kelloggs, with Winston logo on
 uniform, 5½ x 8½ . . . . . . . . . . . .1.00
5 Terry Labonte, Kelloggs, without Winston logo
 on uniform, 5½ x 8½ . . . . . . . . . . .1.00
5 Terry Labonte, Choose To Be Drug Free,
 8 x 10 . . . . . . . . . . . . . . . . . . . .8.00
5 Terry Labonte, Kelloggs, Ron Crawford art card,
 6 x 4 . . . . . . . . . . . . . . . . . . . . .3.00
6 Mark Martin, Valvoline, 8½ x 11 . . . . . .1.00
6 Dennis Ritchie, Valvoline, transporter driver,
 #95 Vol. 4-2, 4¼ x 6 . . . . . . . . . . .3.00
6 Mark Martin, Valvoline, race art, 8 x 10 . .5.00

6 Mark Martin, Valvoline, Ron Crawford, art card,
 5¾ x 4¾ . . . . . . . . . . . . . . . . . .3.00
6 Mark Martin, Valvoline, Oil Change Reminder,
 #V-3674-95, 4 x 6 . . . . . . . . . . . . .3.00
6 Mark Martin, Valvoline, Oil Change Reminder,
 #V-2953-95, 4 x 6 . . . . . . . . . . . . .3.00
6 Mark Martin, Valvoline, fan club, 4 x 6 . . .2.00
6 Mark Martin, Traks Cartoons, 10 x 8 . . . .5.00
6 Mark Martin, Valvoline, race art card,
 8 x 10 . . . . . . . . . . . . . . . . . . . . .5.00
6 Mark Martin, Valvoline, race art card, B & W,
 8 x 10 . . . . . . . . . . . . . . . . . . . . .5.00
7 Geoff Bodine, Exide Batteries, 5½ x 8½ . . .1.00
7 Geoff Bodine, Choose To Be Drug Free,
 8 x 10 . . . . . . . . . . . . . . . . . . . .7.00
7 Alan Kulwicki, Hooters, Ron Crawford, art card,
 5¾ x 4¾ . . . . . . . . . . . . . . . . . .2.00
8 Jeff Burton, Raybestos, 5½ x 8½ . . . . . .2.00
8 Jeff Burton, Douglas Batteries, 7 x 9 . . . .4.00
8 Jeff Burton, Grand Piano & Furniture,
 5 x 7 . . . . . . . . . . . . . . . . . . . . .2.00
9 Lake Speed, Spam, age 46, 6 x 9 . . . . . .1.00
9 Lake Speed, Spam, age 47, 6 x 9 . . . . . .1.00
9 Lake Speed, Spam, show car promo,
 5 x 4 . . . . . . . . . . . . . . . . . . . . .3.00
9 Bill Elliott, Collector's World of Racing insert,
 5¼ x 8 . . . . . . . . . . . . . . . . . . .4.00
10 Ricky Rudd, Tide, 5½ x 8½ . . . . . . . . . .1.00
10 Ricky Rudd, Tide, with race gear,
 5½ x 8½ . . . . . . . . . . . . . . . . . .1.00
10 Ricky Rudd, Tide, show car promo,
 8 x 10 . . . . . . . . . . . . . . . . . . . .10.00
10 Ricky Rudd, Choose To Be Drug Free,
 8 x 10 . . . . . . . . . . . . . . . . . . . .8.00
11 Brett Bodine, Lowes, 8 X 10 . . . . . . . .2.00

11 Brett Bodine, Lowes, employee's card, 8 X 10 . . . . . . . . . . . . . . . . .15.00
111 Brett Bodine, Lowes, 10 x 8 . . . . . . .1.00
11 Brett Bodine, Hill's Dept. Store, B & W, 8½ x 11 . . . . . . . . . . . . . . . . .5.00
11 Brett Bodine, Choose To Be Drug Free, 8 x 10 . . . . . . . . . . . . . . . . .7.00
12 Derrike Cope, Straight Arrow, white car numbers, 8 x 10 . . . . . . . . . . . . .1.00
12 Derrike Cope, Straight Arrow, blue car numbers, 8 x 10 . . . . . . . . . . . . .1.00
12 Derrike Cope, Straight Arrow, art card, 8 x 10 . . . . . . . . . . . . . . . . .2.00
12 Derrike Cope, Straight Arrow, Florida Air National Guard, 8 x 10 . . . . . . . . . .2.00
15 Dick Trickle, Quality Care, 6 x 11 . . . . . .1.00
15 Dick Trickle, Quality Care, fan club, 8½ x 10¾ . . . . . . . . . . . . . . . . .5.00
16 Ted Musgrave, Family Channel, #MS3098, 8 x 11 . . . . . . . . . . . . . . . . .1.00
16 Ted Musgrave, Family Channel, #MS3505, 8 x 11 . . . . . . . . . . . . . . . . .1.00
16 Ted Musgrave, Speed Stick, black writing on front, 6 x 9 . . . . . . . . . . . . .3.00
16 Ted Musgrave, Speed Stick, yellow writing on front, 6 x 9 . . . . . . . . . . . . .3.00
16 Ted Musgrave, Speed Stick, blank back, 3¾ x 5¼ . . . . . . . . . . . . . . . . .2.00
17 Darrell Waltrip, Western Auto, Winston Cup preview, blank back, 7 x 9 . . . . . . .5.00
17 Darrell Waltrip, Western Auto, 7 x 9 . . .1.00
17 Darrell Waltrip, Western Auto, fan club, 5½ x 8 . . . . . . . . . . . . . . . . .3.00
18 Dale Jarrett, Wix Filters, 2 different backs, 4¼ x 6¼ . . . . . . . . . . . . . . . . .3.00
18 Bobby Labonte, Interstate Batteries, 1-95, 8 x 10 . . . . . . . . . . . . . . . . .2.00
18 Bobby Labonte, Interstate Batteries, 7-95, 8 x 10 . . . . . . . . . . . . . . . . .2.00
18 Bobby Labonte, Choose To Be Drug Free, 8 x 10 . . . . . . . . . . . . . . . . .10.00
19 Loy Allen, Healthsource, 6 x 9 . . . . . . .1.00
19 Loy Allen, Healthsource, 9 x 6 . . . . . . .2.00
19 Loy Allen, Healthsource, Ron Crawford, art card, 11 x 8½ . . . . . . . . . . . . .3.00
20 Bobby Hillin, FINA, Winston Cup & Busch Grand National, 5½ x 8½ . . . . . . . . . .3.00
20 Bobby Hillin, Lance, Winston Cup & Busch Grand National, 5½ x 8½ . . . . . . . . .3.00
21 Morgan Shepherd, Citgo, 8 x 10 . . . . . .1.00
21 Morgan Shepherd, Golden Eye, 4 x 5 . . .5.00
22 Randy LaJoie, MBNA, photo stock, headshot, 10 x 8 . . . . . . . . . . . . . . . . .2.00
22 Randy LaJoie, MBNA, in street clothes, 8 x 10 . . . . . . . . . . . . . . . . .1.00
22 Randy LaJoie, MBNA, in driver's suit, 8 x 10 . . . . . . . . . . . . . . . . .2.00

22 No Driver, MBNA, blank back, 8 x 10 . . .5.00
22 No Driver, MBNA, printed back, 8 x 10 . .2.00
22 Ward Burton, MBNA, 8 x 10 . . . . . . . .2.00
23 Jimmy Spencer, Smokin' Joes, 8 x 10 . . .1.00
24 Jeff Gordon, Dupont, 8 x 10 . . . . . . . .2.00
24 Jeff Gordon, Dupont, Ron Crawford, art card, 4¾ x 5¾ . . . . . . . . . . . . . .3.00
24 Jeff Gordon, Brickyard 400, Ron Crawford, art card, 6 x 4 . . . . . . . . . . . . . .2.00
24 Jeff Gordon, Traks Cartoons, 8 x 10 . . .6.00
24 Jeff Gordon, race art, Rolling Thunder, B & W, 8 x 10 . . . . . . . . . . . . . . . . .5.00
24 Jeff Gordon, Choose To Be Drug Free, 8 x 10 . . . . . . . . . . . . . . . . .12.00
24 Ray Evernham, Skittles, 5 x 7 . . . . . . .3.00
25 Ken Schrader, Budweiser, 5½ x 8¼ . . . .3.00

25 Ken Schrader, Budweiser, driver in car, 8 x 10 . . . . . . . . . . . . . . . . .8.00
25 Ken Schrader, Budweiser, without personal information, 8 x 10 . . . . . . . . . . . . .8.00
25 Ken Schrader, Budweiser, with personal information, 8 x 10 . . . . . . . . . . . . .1.00
25 Ken Schrader, Pedigree, 8 x 10 . . . . . . .5.00
25 Ken Schrader, Thumbs Up, David Poole, art card, 4 x 6 . . . . . . . . . . . . . . . . .2.00
26 Steve Kinser, Quaker State, photo, 8½ x 11 . . . . . . . . . . . . . . . . .3.00
26 Steve Kinser, Quaker State, 8 x 10 . . . . .2.00
26 Hut Stricklin, Quaker State, B & W photo, 7 x 5 . . . . . . . . . . . . . . . . .1.00
27 Loy Allen, Hooters, 8 x 10 . . . . . . . . .1.00
28 Ernie Irvan, Havoline, 8½ x 11 . . . . . . .2.00
28 Ernie Irvan, Havoline, photo stock, 7 x 5 .2.00
28 Dale Jarrett, Havoline, 8½ x 11 . . . . . . .1.00
28 Dale Jarrett, Mac Tools, 6½ x 8½ . . . . .5.00
28 Dale Jarrett, Havoline, High Performance Products, 8½ x 11 . . . . . . . . . . . . .4.00
28 Dale Jarrett, Choose To Be Drug Free, 8 x 10 . . . . . . . . . . . . . . . . .10.00

29 Steve Grissom & Buddy Parrott, Meineke, photo stock, 5 x 7 . . . . . . . . . . . . .1.00
29 Steve Grissom, Meineke, 2 different fan club addresses, 8 x 10 . . . . . . . . . . . . .1.00
29 Steve Grissom, Meineke, with crew chief B. Frazier, 8 x 10 . . . . . . . . . . . . . .1.00
30 Michael Waltrip, Pennzoil, 8 x 10 . . . . .1.00
31 Ward Burton, Hardee's, 8 x 10 . . . . . . .1.00
31 Ward Burton, Hardee's, Ferguson Tub, logo on top, 8 x 10 . . . . . . . . . . . . .1.00
31 Ward Burton, Hardee's, Ferguson Tub, logo on bottom, 8 x 10 . . . . . . . . . . .1.00
31 Greg Sacks, Hardee's, 5½ x 8½ . . . . . .3.00
31 Ward Burton, race art, 8 x 10 . . . . . . .5.00
31 Greg Sacks, Choose To Be Drug Free, 8 x 10. . . . . . . . . . . . . . . . . . . . . . .8.00
32 Mike Chase, active, photo stock, 7 x 5 . . . .2.00
32 Chuck Brown, active, error, 5½ x 8½ . . . .10.00
32 Chuck Bown, active, correct, 5½ x 8½ . .2.00
33 Robert Pressley, Skoal, 6 x 9 . . . . . . . .1.00
33 Robert Pressley, Skoal, fan club, 6 x 9 . .4.00
33 Robert Pressley, Sears, B & W, paper stock, 10 x 8 . . . . . . . . . . . . . . . . . . . . .3.00
33 Robert Pressley, Asheville Racer, Jeanne Barnes, art card, 6 x 4 . . . . . . . . . . .2.00
37 John Andretti, Kranefuss, Haas, B & W, headshot, 8 x 10 . . . . . . . . . . . . . . . .5.00
37 John Andretti, K-Mart, art card, 8½ x 11 .2.00
37 John Andretti, K-Mart, 8½ x 11 . . . . . . .2.00
40 Greg Sacks, Kendall, 8½ x 11 . . . . . . .2.00
41 Ricky Craven, Kodiak, 7 x 9 . . . . . . . . .1.00
41 Ricky Craven, Kodiak, fan club, headshot, 8 x 10. . . . . . . . . . . . . . . . . . . . . .7.00
42 Kyle Petty, Rock 101 WROQ, B & W, 10 x 8 . . . . . . . . . . . . . . . . . . . . . .5.00
42 Kyle Petty, Coors Light, 10 x 8 . . . . . . .1.00
42 Kyle Petty, Traks Cartoons, 10 x 8 . . . . .4.00
43 Bobby Hamilton, STP, 6 x 9 . . . . . . . . .1.00
43 Richard Petty, STP, 6 x 9 . . . . . . . . . . .1.00
43 Richard Petty, International Trucks, blank back, 6 x 9 . . . . . . . . . . . . . . . . . . . . . .6.00
43 Richard Petty, International Trucks, printed back, 6 x 9 . . . . . . . . . . . . . . . . . .3.00
44 Jeff Purvis, Jackaroo, 2 different backs, 5 x 7 . . . . . . . . . . . . . . . . . . . . . .2.00
47 Billy Standridge, World Championship Wrestling, B & W, 8 x 10 . . . . . . . .2.00
49 Steve Sellers, Coke, Winston West, 5 x 7 .3.00
50 A.J. Foyt, Copenhagen, 8 x 10 . . . . . . .3.00
54 Rich Bickle, Kleenex, with soft touch on back, 6 x 9 . . . . . . . . . . . . . . . . . . . . . .2.00
54 Rich Bickle, Kleenex, with cause on back, 6 x 9 . . . . . . . . . . . . . . . . . . . . . .2.00
62 No Driver, 1-800-MY-DIXIE, N.C. Division, 3 x 5½ . . . . . . . . . . . . . . . . . . . . .5.00
66 Ben Hess, headshot, paper stock, 11 x 8½ . . . . . . . . . . . . . . . . . . . .2.00

71 Dave Marcis, Olive Garden, Lumina, 8 x 10 . . . . . . . . . . . . . . . . . . . . . .2.00
71 Dave Marcis, Olive Garden, Monte Carlo, 8 x 10 . . . . . . . . . . . . . . . . . . . . . .2.00
71 Dave Marcis, STG, 10 x 8 . . . . . . . . . .3.00
75 Todd Bodine, Factory Stores of America, 10 x 7 . . . . . . . . . . . . . . . . . . . . . .1.00
77 Davey Jones, US Air, car only, 5 x 7¾ . . .2.00
77 Davey Jones, US Air, 5 x 7¾ . . . . . . . .2.00
77 Davey Jones, Jasper, 5 x 7¾ . . . . . . . .2.00
77 Bobby Hillin, Jasper, 6 x 9 . . . . . . . . . .2.00
77 Mike Chase, Old Milwaukee, Winston West, paper stock, 8½ x 11 . . . . . . . . . . .3.00
77 Mike Chase, Old Milwaukee, Winston West, 8½ x 11 . . . . . . . . . . . . . . . . . . . .3.00
78 Pancho Carter, Equipment Supply Co., 6 x 9 . . . . . . . . . . . . . . . . . . . . . .2.00
78 Jay Hedgecock, Diamond Rio, photo stock, 8 x 10 . . . . . . . . . . . . . . . . . . . . .3.00
81 Kenny Wallace, T.I.C., 8 x 10 . . . . . . . .2.00
87 Joe Nemechek, Burger King, yellow letters on car, 8 x 10 . . . . . . . . . . . . . . . . .2.00
87 Joe Nemechek, Burger King, white letters on car, 8 x 10 . . . . . . . . . . . . . . . . .1.00
87 Joe Nemechek, Mighty Auto Parts, 8 x 10 . . . . . . . . . . . . . . . . . . . . . .3.00
87 Joe Nemechek, Cintas Uniforms, 8½ x 11 .3.00
87 Joe Nemechek, Burger King, car only, action, 8 x 10 . . . . . . . . . . . . . . . . . . . . .3.00
87 Joe Nemechek, Burger King, Joe & car, posed, 8 x 10 . . . . . . . . . . . . . . . .3.00
87 Joe Nemechek, Burger King, Joe only, 8 x 10 . . . . . . . . . . . . . . . . . . . . . .3.00
87 Joe Nemechek, Burger King, car only, 8 x 10 . . . . . . . . . . . . . . . . . . . . . .3.00
87 Joe Nemechek, Delco Remy, blank back, 8 x 10 . . . . . . . . . . . . . . . . . . . . . .3.00
90 Mike Wallace, Heilig Meyers, 6 x 9 . . . .1.00
94 Bill Elliott, McDonald's, 3 different Kudzu phone #'s, 8 x 10 . . . . . . . . . . . . . . . . . . .1.00
94 Bill Elliott, Reese's, small headshot on back, 8 x 8 . . . . . . . . . . . . . . . . . . . . . . .2.00
94 Bill Elliott, Reese's, large headshot on back, 8 x 8 . . . . . . . . . . . . . . . . . . . . . . .2.00
94 Bill Elliott, Amoco, 5½ x 8¼ . . . . . . . .1.00
94 Bill Elliott, fan club, 8 x 10 . . . . . . . . .10.00
94 Bill Elliott, Choose To Be Drug Free, 8 x 10 . . . . . . . . . . . . . . . . . . . . . .10.00
94 Bill Elliott, Sam Bass promo, 5¼ x 4¼ . . .2.00
98 Jeremy Mayfield, RCA, with Cale, 5½ x 8½ . . . . . . . . . . . . . . . . . . . .2.00
98 Jeremy Mayfield, Campbell – Hausfeld, 8½ x 11 . . . . . . . . . . . . . . . . . . . .2.00
98 Jeremy Mayfield, RCA, DSS logo on back, 5½ x 8½ . . . . . . . . . . . . . . . . . . . .2.00
98 Jeremy Mayfield, RCA, Masterbuilt logo on back, 5½ x 8½ . . . . . . . . . . . . . . .2.00

98 Jeremy Mayfield, Masterbuilt, 5½ x 8½ . .2.00
98 Jeremy Mayfield, Campbell, Hausfeld, with
    tear-off, 6½ x 8½ . . . . . . . . . . . . . .2.00
98 Jeremy Mayfield, RCA, standing by car, 5½ x
    8½ . . . . . . . . . . . . . . . . . . . . . . .2.00
98 Jeremy Mayfield, Campbell, Hausfeld, send-off,
    8½ x 11 . . . . . . . . . . . . . . . . .10.00
98 Cale Yarborough, Campbell, Hausfeld, send-off,
    8½ x 11 . . . . . . . . . . . . . . . . .10.00
98 Cale Yarborough, Campbell, Hausfeld, no logo
    on front, 8½ x 11 . . . . . . . . . . .10.00
99 Shawna Robinson, Tombstone Pizza,
    6 x 9 . . . . . . . . . . . . . . . . . . . . . .3.00

### 1996

07 Lance Hooper, Firebird Oil, Winston West,
    8½ x 11 . . . . . . . . . . . . . . . . . . . .3.00
1 Rick Mast, Hooters, 1st printed back,
    8 x 10 . . . . . . . . . . . . . . . . . . . 6.00
1 Rick Mast, Hooters, 2nd blank back,
    8 x 10 . . . . . . . . . . . . . . . . . . . .5.00
1 Rick Mast, Hooters, 3rd printed back,
    8 x 10 . . . . . . . . . . . . . . . . . . . 1.00
1 Rick Mast, Hughs Network, insight, races 185,
    11 x 8½ . . . . . . . . . . . . . . . . . . .2.00
1 Rick Mast, Hughs Network, insight, races 201,
    11 x 8½ . . . . . . . . . . . . . . . . . . .2.00
2 Rusty Wallace, Miller, circle track,
    10¼ x 7½ . . . . . . . . . . . . . . . . . .4.00
2 Rusty Wallace, Miller, slanted, 8 x 10 . . . .1.00
2 Rusty Wallace, Miller, Mazak,
    8½ x 11 . . . . . . . . . . . . . . . . . . 4.00
2 Rusty Wallace, Miller, 4½ x 5¾ . . . . . . .2.00
2 Rusty Wallace, Miller, fan club, 10 x 8 . . . 5.00
2 Rusty Wallace, Miller, fan club,
    7½ x 9½ . . . . . . . . . . . . . . . . . . .5.00
2 Rusty Wallace, Mead Coated Papers, Color,
    7 x 5 . . . . . . . . . . . . . . . . . . . . 2.00
2 Rusty Wallace, Mead Coated Papers, B & W,
    7 x 5 . . . . . . . . . . . . . . . . . . . . 2.00
3 Dale Earnhardt, GM Goodwrench, blank back,
    8 x 10 . . . . . . . . . . . . . . . . . . . 30.00
3 Dale Earnhardt, GM Goodwrench, printed back,
    8 x 10 . . . . . . . . . . . . . . . . . . . .5.00
3 Dale Earnhardt, GM Goodwrench, Gargoyles,
    4 x 6 . . . . . . . . . . . . . . . . . . . . .8.00
3 Dale Earnhardt, GM Goodwrench, Sam Bass
    promo, 3 x 5 . . . . . . . . . . . . . . . 5.00
3 Dale Earnhardt, GM Goodwrench, Sam Bass
    promo, 4¾ x 5¾ . . . . . . . . . . . . . .5.00
3 Dale Earnhardt, GM Goodwrench, Circle Track,
    7¼ x 10¼ . . . . . . . . . . . . . . . . .10.00
3 Dale Earnhardt, Sam Bass art card, Blaze Of
    Glory, 4 x 9 . . . . . . . . . . . . . . . . 5.00
3 Dale Earnhardt, David Peeler art card, Atlanta
    1996, 10¼ x 8 . . . . . . . . . . . . . . 5.00

NASCAR のトップチーム、日本でデビュー

3 Dale Earnhardt, AC Delco, 1 of 5000,
    8 x 10, . . . . . . . . . . . . . . .45.00

4 Sterling Marlin, Kodak Film, two different fan
    club prices, 8½ x 11 . . . . . . . . . . . 1.00
4 Sterling Marlin, Parts Plus, 5 x 8½ . . . . . 3.00
4 Sterling Marlin, Parts Plus, blank back,
    8 x 10 . . . . . . . . . . . . . . . . . . . . 5.00
5 Terry Labonte, Kellogg's, 8½ x 11 . . . . . . 1.00
5 Terry Labonte, Kellogg's, Iron Man logo on front,
    8½ x 11 . . . . . . . . . . . . . . . . . . .2.00
6 Mark Martin, Valvoline, 1st no tear-off, on sand,
    8½ x 11 . . . . . . . . . . . . . . . . . . . 4.00
6 Mark Martin, Valvoline, 2nd with tear-off, on
    sand, 8½ x 11 . . . . . . . . . . . . . . .6.00
6 Mark Martin, Valvoline, action, with tear-off,
    8½ x 11 . . . . . . . . . . . . . . . . . . .3.00
6 Mark Martin, Valvoline, 3rd Roush logo on back,
    8½ x 11 . . . . . . . . . . . . . . . . . . .1.00
6 Mark Martin, Valvoline, press pass, back to
    Back Charlotte Wins, 4 x 6 . . . . . . . .6.00
6 Mark Martin, Valvoline, Winning Lap game,
    4 x 5 . . . . . . . . . . . . . . . . . . . . .1.00
6 Mark Martin, Valvoline, Oil Change Reminder,
    3½ x 5 . . . . . . . . . . . . . . . . . . . .3.00
6 Mark Martin, "Re-Mark-Able," art card,
    6 x 4 . . . . . . . . . . . . . . . . . . . . .2.00
7 Geoff Bodine, QVC, 1st no tear-off,
    10 x 8 . . . . . . . . . . . . . . . . . . . .3.00
7 Geoff Bodine, QVC, 2nd with tear-off,
    10 x 8 . . . . . . . . . . . . . . . . . . . .2.00
7 Geoff Bodine, QVC, 3rd different headshot,
    10 x 8 . . . . . . . . . . . . . . . . . . . .2.00
7 Geoff Bodine, QVC, 8½ x 10 . . . . . . . . .1.00
8 Hut Stricklin, Stavola Brothers, preview,
    7 x 9 . . . . . . . . . . . . . . . . . . . . .5.00
8 Hut Stricklin, Circuit City, 7 x 9 . . . . . . . .1.00
8 Hut Stricklin, Kendall Motor Oil,
    8 x 10 . . . . . . . . . . . . . . . . . . . .2.00

21 Michael Waltrip, Citgo, The Art of Racing, 8 x 10 . .30.00

9 Lake Speed, Spam, LUV, SPAM on back, 6 x 9 . . . . . . . . . . . . . . . . . .1.00

9 Lake Speed, Spam, 686, SPAM on back, 6 x 9 . . . . . . . . . . . . . . . . . .1.00

10 Ricky Rudd, Tide, 5¾ x 10 . . . . . . . . .1.00

10 Ricky Rudd, Tide, show car promo, 8 x 10 . . . . . . . . . . . . . . . . . . . .10.00

11 Brett Bodine, Lowe's, 8 x 10 . . . . . . . .1.00

11 Brett Bodine, Lowe's, Ron Crawford art card, 6 x 4 . . . . . . . . . . . . . . . . . . . . .1.00

12 Derrike Cope, Mighty Auto Parts, 8 x 10 . . . . . . . . . . . . . . . . . . . . .3.00

12 Derrike Cope, Badcock Furniture, 8½ x 11 . . . . . . . . . . . . . . . . . . . . .3.00

12 Derrike Cope, Badcock Furniture, with Bobby Allison insert, 8½ x 11 . . . . . . . . . . .2.00

14 A.J. Foyt, Copenhagen, with Indy cars, 8 x 11 . . . . . . . . . . . . . . . . . . . . .4.00

15 Wally Dallenbach, Hayes, action shot, 8 x 10 . . . . . . . . . . . . . . . . . . . . .3.00

15 Wally Dallenbach, Hayes, art card, 8 x 10 . . . . . . . . . . . . . . . . . . . . .3.00

15 Wally Dallenbach, Hayes, 8 x 10 . . . . . .1.00

16 Ted Musgrave, The Family Channel, 6 x 9 .3.00

16 Ted Musgrave, Primestar, 6 x 9 . . . . . . .1.00

16 Ted Musgrave, Primestar, with Aquafresh coupon, 6 x 11 . . . . . . . . . . . . . . . .2.00

17 Darrell Waltrip, Parts America, B & W, blank back, thick stock, 8 x 10 . . . . . . . . . .1.00

17 Darrell Waltrip, Parts America, blank back, 7 x 9 . . . . . . . . . . . . . . . . . . . . .4.00

17 Darrell Waltrip, Parts America, printed back, 7 x 9 . . . . . . . . . . . . . . . . . . . . .1.00

17 Darrell Waltrip, fan club, headshot, 8½ x 11 . . . . . . . . . . . . . . . . . . . .7.00

18 Bobby Labonte, Interstate Batteries, 1st fourth season, 6 x 10 . . . . . . . . . . . . . . . .3.00

18 Bobby Labonte, Interstate Batteries, 2nd fifth season, 6 x 10 . . . . . . . . . . . . . . . .1.00

18 Bobby Labonte, Shell Fire & Ice, 8 x 10 .2.00

18 Bobby Labonte, Wix Filters, no gloss, 6 x 9 . . . . . . . . . . . . . . . . . . . . .3.00

18 Bobby Labonte, Wix Filters, glossy, 6 x 9 . . . . . . . . . . . . . . . . . . . . .3.00

18 Joe Gibbs, Champion Spark Plugs, 8½ x 11 . . . . . . . . . . . . . . . . . . . .3.00

19 Loy Allen, Healthsource, Ron Crawford art card, 11 x 8½ . . . . . . . . . . . . . . . . .3.00

19 Loy Allen, Healthsource, blank back, 6 x 9 . . . . . . . . . . . . . . . . . . . . .3.00

19 Loy Allen, Healthsource, printed back, 6 x 9 . . . . . . . . . . . . . . . . . . . . .2.00

19 Loy Allen, Healthsource, blank back, 7 x 9 . . . . . . . . . . . . . . . . . . . . .3.00

19 Loy Allen, Healthsource, printed back, 7 x 9 . . . . . . . . . . . . . . . . . . . . .2.00

21 Michael Waltrip, Citgo, The Art Of Racing, 8 x 10 . . . . . . . . . . . . . . . . . . . .30.00

21 Michael Waltrip, Citgo, 8 x 10 . . . . . . .1.00

21 Michael Waltrip, Grand Piano & Furniture, 8 x 10 . . . . . . . . . . . . . . . . . . . . .2.00

21 Michael Waltrip, A Winning Combination, 21, Jeanne Barnes art card, 6 x 4 . . . . . . .2.00

22 Ward Burton, MBNA, Preview, 1995 front, 1996 back, 8 x 10 . . . . . . . . . . . . . . .7.00

22 Ward Burton, MBNA, 8 x 10 . . . . . . . .1.00

22 Ward Burton, Award Winning Day, Jeanne Barnes art card, 6 x 4 . . . . . . . . . .2.00
23 Jimmy Spencer, Smokin' Joe's, 8½ x 11½ .1.00
24 Jeff Gordon, Dupont, 8 x 10 . . . . . . . .1.00
24 Jeff Gordon, Pit Boss, blank back, thick stock, 11 x 8½ . . . . . . . . . . . . . . . .5.00
24 Jeff Gordon, Pit Boss, blank back, thin stock, 11 x 8½ . . . . . . . . . . . . . . . .2.00
24 Jeff Gordon, Coye Consultants, 9 x 6 . . .3.00
24 Jeff Gordon, Skittles, shelf hanger, 5½ x 9 . . . . . . . . . . . . . . . . . . . . .3.00
24 Ray Everham, Pocono, blank back, 7 x 5 . .3.00
24 Ray Everham, Skittles, information added to front, 5 x 7 . . . . . . . . . . . . . . . .1.00
25 Ken Schrader, Budweiser, 1995 front, 1996 back, 8 x 10 . . . . . . . . . . . . . . . . .7.00
25 Ken Schrader, Budweiser, 8 x 10 . . . . .1.00
25 Ken Schrader, Pedigree, with puppy, 8 x 10 . . . . . . . . . . . . . . . . . . . . .5.00
27 Elton Sawyer, David Blair Motorsports, 6 x 9 . . . . . . . . . . . . . . . . . . . . .2.00
28 Ernie Irvan, Havoline, 11 x 8½ . . . . . . .2.00

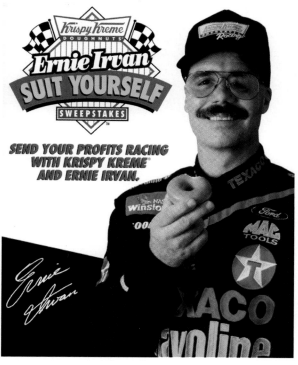

28 Ernie Irvan, Krispy Kreme, fold-over, 11 x 8½ . . . . . . . . . . . . . . . . . . .12.00
28 Ernie Irvan, Raybestos, 8 x 10 . . . . . . .3.00
28 Ernie Irvan, headshot, photo, 7½ x 5 . . .1.00
28 Ernie Irvan, Mac Tools, 5 x 8 . . . . . . . .3.00
28 Robert Yates, Plastic Kote, 5½ x 8 . . . . .3.00
29 Steve Grissom, Cartoon Network, preview, 8 x 10 . . . . . . . . . . . . . . . . . . . .3.00
29 Steve Grissom, Cartoon Network, First In Family Racing, 8 x 10 . . . . . . . . . . . .1.00
29 No Driver, Cartoon Network, 8 x 10 . . . .2.00

30 Johnny Benson, Pennzoil, blank back, 8 x 10 . . . . . . . . . . . . . . . . . . . . .8.00
30 Johnny Benson, Pennzoil, printed back, 8 x 10 . . . . . . . . . . . . . . . . . . . . .1.00
30 Johnny Benson, Pennzoil, blank back, 4 x 5 . . . . . . . . . . . . . . . . . . . . .4.00
30 Johnny Benson, Pontiac Motorsports, 8½ x 11 . . . . . . . . . . . . . . . . . . . .6.00

31 Mike Skinner, Realtree, 8 x 10 . . . . . . .15.00

31 Mike Skinner, Snap-On Racing, 1 of 5,000, 8 x 10 . . . . . . . . . . . . . . . . . . .20.00
33 Robert Pressley, Skoal, 6 x 9 . . . . . . . .1.00
34 Mike McLaughlin, Hardinge Inc., 8 x 10 .5.00
37 John Andretti, K-Mart / Little Caesars, 11 x 8½ . . . . . . . . . . . . . . . . . . . .2.00
37 Jeremy Mayfield, K-Mart / Little Caesars, 11 x 8½ . . . . . . . . . . . . . . . . . . . .3.00
37 Jeremy Mayfield, K-Mart / Little Caesars, photo stock, 10 x 8 . . . . . . . . . . . . . .3.00
38 Butch Gilliland, Stroppe Motorsports, Winston West, 8 x 11 . . . . . . . . . . . . . . . . . .3.00

50 A. J. Foyt, Kennametal, no decals, 5 x 8   .5.00    50 A. J. Foyt, Kennametal, with decals, 5 x 8   . .4.00

41 Ricky Craven, Kodiak, 8 x 10 . . . . . . . .1.00
41 Ricky Craven, Kodiak, fan club, headshot,
   10 x 8 . . . . . . . . . . . . . . . . . . . .7.00
41 Ricky Craven, Kodiak, without Waddell Wilson,
   8 x 10 . . . . . . . . . . . . . . . . . . . .2.00
42 Kyle Petty, Coors Light, fold-over, 6 x 8 . .2.00
42 Robby Gordon, Team Sabco, B & W photo,
   10 x 8 . . . . . . . . . . . . . . . . . . . .2.00
43 Bobby Hamilton, STP, 6 x 9 . . . . . . . . .2.00
43 Richard Petty, STP, 6 x 9 . . . . . . . . . .2.00
43 Richard Petty, International Truck, 6 x 9 .4.00
43 Richard Petty, International Truck, thin stock,
   7½ x 11½ . . . . . . . . . . . . . . . . . . .2.00
43 Richard Petty, Vectra, thin stock,
   11½ x 8½ . . . . . . . . . . . . . . . . . . .2.00
43 Richard Petty, 25th Anniversary, Ron Crawford
   art card, 6 x 4 . . . . . . . . . . . . . . . .2.00
43 Bobby Hamilton & Richard Petty, 25th Anniversary, Jeanne Barnes art card, 6 x 4 . . .2.00
43 Richard Petty, fan club, headshot, thin stock,
   8½ x 11 . . . . . . . . . . . . . . . . . . .3.00
43 Richard Petty, The Race Is On, Secretary of
   State, 7 x 5 . . . . . . . . . . . . . . . . . .7.00
43 Richard Petty, Pepsi shelf tanker, 6 x 11 .2.00
44 Jeff Purvis, Phoenix Racing, 8 x 10 . . . .3.00
44 Jeff Purvis, David Lee Murphy, with tear-off
   schedule, 5½ x 8¼ . . . . . . . . . . . . . .2.00
46 Stacy Compton, Virginia 13 WSET, B & W,
   posed, 8½ x 5½ . . . . . . . . . . . . . . . .4.00
50 A. J. Foyt, Kennametal, no decals, 5 x 8 .5.00
50 A. J. Foyt, Kennametal, with decals,
   5 x 8 . . . . . . . . . . . . . . . . . . . . .4.00
50 A. J. Foyt, Kennametal, with tear-off,
   8½ x 11 . . . . . . . . . . . . . . . . . . .4.00
50 A. J. Foyt, Kennametel, 7½ x 10½ . . . . .4.00
50 A. J. Foyt, Kennametel & Grainger,
   8½ x 11 . . . . . . . . . . . . . . . . . . .4.00
63 Dick Trickle, Purina Hi Pro, 6 x 9 . . . . .2.00
71 Dave Marcis, Prodigy, 7 x 10 . . . . . . .2.00
75 Morgan Shepherd, Remington, 1st dog logo on
   front, 8 x 10 . . . . . . . . . . . . . . . . .3.00

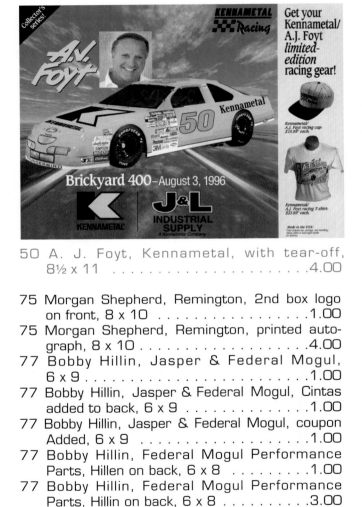

50 A. J. Foyt, Kennametal, with tear-off,
   8½ x 11 . . . . . . . . . . . . . . . . . . .4.00

75 Morgan Shepherd, Remington, 2nd box logo
   on front, 8 x 10 . . . . . . . . . . . . . . .1.00
75 Morgan Shepherd, Remington, printed autograph, 8 x 10 . . . . . . . . . . . . . . . . .4.00
77 Bobby Hillin, Jasper & Federal Mogul,
   6 x 9 . . . . . . . . . . . . . . . . . . . . .1.00
77 Bobby Hillin, Jasper & Federal Mogul, Cintas
   added to back, 6 x 9 . . . . . . . . . . . .1.00
77 Bobby Hillin, Jasper & Federal Mogul, coupon
   Added, 6 x 9 . . . . . . . . . . . . . . . . .1.00
77 Bobby Hillin, Federal Mogul Performance
   Parts, Hillen on back, 6 x 8 . . . . . . . .1.00
77 Bobby Hillin, Federal Mogul Performance
   Parts, Hillin on back, 6 x 8 . . . . . . . .3.00
77 Bobby Hillin, faded front, 5 x 8 . . . . . . .3.00
78 Randy McDonald, Diamond RIO, photo stock,
   10 x 8 . . . . . . . . . . . . . . . . . . . .2.00
78 Randy McDonald, Diamond RIO, card stock,
   printed back, 10 x 8 . . . . . . . . . . . .7.00
80 Joe Ruttman, David Lee Murphy, blank back,
   8 x 10 . . . . . . . . . . . . . . . . . . . .4.00
81 Kenny Wallace, T.I.C. & Square D, Brittany age
   6, 8 x 10 . . . . . . . . . . . . . . . . . . .10.00

81 Kenny Wallace, T.I.C. & Square D, Brittany Age 5, 8 x 10 . . . . . . . . . . . . . . . . . . . . .1.00
81 Kenny Wallace, Square D, 8 x 10 . . . . .1.00
81 Kenny Wallace, T.I.C. & Red Dog, with #8 BGN car, 8 x 10 . . . . . . . . . . . . . . . . . . .5.00
87 Joe Nemechek, Burger King, 6½ x 8½ . .2.00
87 Joe Nemechek, Burger King, 8 x 10 . . .2.00
87 Joe Nemechek, Cintas, 8½ x 11 . . . . . .2.00
87 Joe Nemechek, Mighty Auto Parts, 8 x 10 . . . . . . . . . . . . . . . . . . . . . . .4.00
88 Dale Jarrett, Quality Care & Red Carpet Lease, tri-fold, 8½ x 11 . . . . . . . . . . . . . .2.00
88 Dale Jarrett, Quality Care & Red Carpet, Daytona 500, 8½ x 11 . . . . . . . . . . . . .2.00
90 Mike Wallace, Heilig-Meyers, 6 x 9 . . . .2.00
90 Mike Wallace, Heilig-Meyers, paper stock, 8½ x 11 . . . . . . . . . . . . . . . . . . . .1.00
90 Dick Trickle, Heilig-Meyers, 6 x 9 . . . . .2.00
94 Bill Elliott, McDonald's, without speedline on back, 10 x 8 . . . . . . . . . . . . . . . . . .1.00
94 Bill Elliott, McDonald's, with speedline on back, 10 x 8 . . . . . . . . . . . . . . . . . . .1.00
94 Bill Elliott, New Holland, 6 x 3 . . . . . . .5.00
94 Bill Elliott, Elliott Museum, 6 x 8 . . . . . .10.00
94 Bill Elliott, Reese's, 6½ x 8 . . . . . . . . .2.00
94 Bill Elliott, Fan's Favorite, Jeanne Barnes art card, 6 x 4 . . . . . . . . . . . . . . . . . . .2.00
94 Bill Elliott, New Holland Oil, 8 x 10 . . . . .5.00
95 Gary Bradberry, Shoney's, without printed autograph, 6 x 9 . . . . . . . . . . . . . . . . . . .2.00
95 Gary Bradberry, Shoney's, with printed autograph, 6 x 9 . . . . . . . . . . . . . . . . . . .2.00
97 Chad Little, Sterling Cowboy, blank back, 8 x 10 . . . . . . . . . . . . . . . . . . . . . .7.00
97 Chad Little, Sterling Cowboy, printed back, 8 x 10 . . . . . . . . . . . . . . . . . . . . . .2.00
98 Jeremy Mayfield, RCA, 8 x 10 . . . . . . .1.00
98 Jeremy Mayfield, Campbell – Hausfeld, paper stock, 8½ x 11 . . . . . . . . . . . . . . . .1.00
98 Jeremy Mayfield, RCA, Masterbuilt, 5½ x 8½ . . . . . . . . . . . . . . . . . . . .3.00
98 Jeremy Mayfield, RCA & Husqvarna, blank back, 5½ x 8½ . . . . . . . . . . . . . . . .5.00
98 John Andretti, RCA, 8 x 10 . . . . . . . . .2.00
99 Jeff Burton, Exide, 5½ x 8½ . . . . . . . .1.00
99 Jeff Burton, Mayflower Transit, 5½ x 8½ .5.00

## 1997

07 Sean Woodside, Cinema Services, Winston West, 8½ x 11 . . . . . . . . . . . . . . . . . .2.00
1 No Driver, Winston, Blue Miller & Band, photo stock, 8 x 10 . . . . . . . . . . . . . . . . . .2.00
1 Morgan Shepherd, Delco Remy America, 8 x 10 . . . . . . . . . . . . . . . . . . . . . .1.00
1 Morgan Shepherd, Delco Remy 2nd solid blue background on front, 8 x 10 . . . . . . . . .1.00

1 Richard Jackson, R & L Carriers, 8 x 10 .1.00
1 Morgan Shepherd, R & L Carriers, 8 x 10 . . . . . . . . . . . . . . . . . . . . . .1.00
2 Rusty Wallace, Miller Lite, 10 x 8 . . . . . .1.00
2 Rusty Wallace, Miller Lite & Stevens Aviation, Ford Taurus, 8 x 10 . . . . . . . . . . . . .2.00
2 Rusty Wallace, Miller Lite, fan club with #22 truck, 10 x 8 . . . . . . . . . . . . . . . . . .4.00
2 Rusty Wallace, Miller Lite, Ron Crawford, white border, 6 x 4 . . . . . . . . . . . . . . . . .2.00
2 Rusty Wallace, Miller Lite, Ron Crawford, black border, 6 x 4 . . . . . . . . . . . . . . . . .2.00
2 Rusty Wallace, Mead, headshot, color, 7 x 5 . . . . . . . . . . . . . . . . . . . . . .1.00
2 Rusty Wallace, Mead, headshot, B & W, 7 x 5 . . . . . . . . . . . . . . . . . . . . . .1.00
2 Rusty Wallace, Fort Worth Star, Telegram, 11 x 8½ . . . . . . . . . . . . . . . . . . . .7.00
2 Rusty Wallace, autograph card, 7 x 5 . . . .1.00
2 Rusty Wallace, Tom Johnson Camping Center, 6 x 9 . . . . . . . . . . . . . . . . . . . . . .1.00
3 Dale Earnhardt, GM Goodwrench, blank back, red border, 8 x 10 . . . . . . . . . . . . .20.00
3 Dale Earnhardt, GM Goodwrench, 8 x 10 . . . . . . . . . . . . . . . . . . . . . .5.00
3 Dale Earnhardt, GM Goodwrench, blank back, black border, 8 x 10 . . . . . . . . . . . . .20.00
3 Dale Earnhardt, GM Goodwrench & Food City, 8 x 10 . . . . . . . . . . . . . . . . . . . . . .5.00
3 Dale Earnhardt, GM Goodwrench & Fort Worth Star, 11 x 8½ . . . . . . . . . . . . . . . . .7.00

NASCARウィンストンカップで7回の優勝

3 Dale Earnhardt, AC Delco, Japan Race, 8 x 10 . . . . . . . . . . . . . . . . . . . . . .45.00
3 Joe Bean, C & R Transport, Winston West, 8½ x 11 . . . . . . . . . . . . . . . . . . . . .3.00
4 Sterling Marlin, Kodak, 8½ x 11 . . . . . . .1.00
4 Sterling Marlin, Kodak Gold, 8½ x 11 . . . .1.00
5 Terry Labonte, Kellogg's, with helmet on front, 8½ x 11 . . . . . . . . . . . . . . . . . . . .2.00
5 Terry Labonte, Kellogg's, 8½ x 11 . . . . . .1.00
5 Terry Labonte, Kellogg's, fan club, 8 x 10 .5.00
5 Terry Labonte, Fort Worth Star, Telegram, 11 x 8½ . . . . . . . . . . . . . . . . . . . .7.00

6 Mark Martin, Valvoline, 8½ x 11 . . . . . . .1.00
6 Mark Martin, Valvoline, Oil Change Reminder with printer tabs, 4 x 6 . . . . . . . . . . .1.00
6 Mark Martin, Valvoline, with Cummins order form, 8½ x 11 . . . . . . . . . . . . . . . . .2.00
6 Mark Martin, Valvoline, Ron Crawford, 6 x 4 . . . . . . . . . . . . . . . . . . . . . . .2.00
7 Geoff Bodine, QVC, 7¼ x 10 . . . . . . . . . .1.00
7 Geoff Bodine, QVC, Lincoln Tech with tear-off, 8½ x 10½ . . . . . . . . . . . . . . . . . . .1.00
7 Geoff Bodine, fan club, waving, 5 x 7 . . . .4.00
7 Geoff Bodine, fan club, action, 5 x 7 . . . . .4.00
8 Hut Strickland, Circuit City, 9 x 7 . . . . . .1.00
9 Lake Speed, Melling, blank back, 4 x 6 . . .1.00
10 Ricky Rudd, Tide, 5½ x 8 . . . . . . . . . .1.00
10 Ricky Rudd, Tide, 10th Anniversary, 5 x 7 . . . . . . . . . . . . . . . . . . . . . . . .1.00
10 Ricky Rudd, Tide & Buddy's Home Furnishings, 4 x 6 . . . . . . . . . . . . . . . . . . . . . . .5.00
10 Ricky Rudd, Tide & FSP High Performance Parts, 10 x 8 . . . . . . . . . . . . . . . . . .5.00
11 Brett Bodine, Close Call, photo stock, 8 x 10 . . . . . . . . . . . . . . . . . . . . . . .2.00
11 Brett Bodine, Close Call, 8½ x 11 . . . . .1.00
11 Brett Bodine, blank back, 5½ x 7 . . . . .5.00
14 Steve Park, Burger King, 8 x 10 . . . . . .3.00
16 Ted Musgrave, Family Channel & Primestar, 6 x 9 . . . . . . . . . . . . . . . . . . . . . . .1.00
16 Ted Musgrave, Family Channel & Primestar, with coupon, 6 x 9 . . . . . . . . . . . . . . .1.00
16 Ted Musgrave, Family Channel & Primestar, with satelite dish offer, 6 x 9 . . . . . . . . .5.00
16 Bill McAnally, NAPA, Winston West, 6 x 9 .3.00
17 Darrell Waltrip, Parts America, name off center on back, 8 x 10 . . . . . . . . . . . .2.00
17 Darrell Waltrip, Parts America, name centered on back, 8 x 10 . . . . . . . . . . .1.00
17 Darrell Waltrip, Parts America, printed autograph, on logo on front, 8 x 10 . . . . . . .1.00
17 Darrell Waltrip, Silver Anniversary Tribute with Darrell, 8½ x 11 . . . . . . . . . . . . . . . .2.00
17 Darrell Waltrip, Silver Anniversary Tribute with Rifle, blank back, 8½ x 11 . . . . . . . . . .2.00
17 Darrell Waltrip, Parts America & Okuma, with tear-off, 8½ x 8¾ . . . . . . . . . . . . . . .1.00
18 Bobby Labonte, Interstate Batteries, 6½ x 8¼ . . . . . . . . . . . . . . . . . . . .1.00
18 Bobby Labonte, Interstate Batteries, Texas card, 6¼ x 8½ . . . . . . . . . . . . . . . . .3.00
18 Bobby Labonte, Shell Motorsports, 8 x 10 . . . . . . . . . . . . . . . . . . . . . . .2.00
18 Bobby Labonte, Cintas, 11 x 8½ . . . . . .2.00
18 Bobby Labonte, Ditch Witch, blank back, 8 x 10 . . . . . . . . . . . . . . . . . . . . . . .3.00
19 Loy Allen, Child Support Recovery, 6 x 9 .1.00
19 Loy Allen, Child Support Recovery, different phone number, 6 x 9 . . . . . . . . . . . . .1.00

19 Gray Bradbery, Child Support Recovery, 8 x 10 . . . . . . . . . . . . . . . . . . . . . . .1.00
21 Michael Waltrip, Citgo, 8 x 10 . . . . . . . .1.00
21 Michael Waltrip, Citgo & Grand Furniture, 8 x 10 . . . . . . . . . . . . . . . . . . . . . . .1.00
22 Ward Burton, MBNA, 8 x 10 . . . . . . . . .1.00
23 Jimmy Spencer, Camel, 8½ x 11 . . . . . .1.00
23 Jimmy Spencer, Camel, 7 x 10 . . . . . . . .1.00
24 Jeff Gordon, Dupont, with crew, 8 x 10 . .1.00
24 Jeff Gordon, Dupont, with Jeff only, 8 x 10 . . . . . . . . . . . . . . . . . . . . . . .2.00
24 Jeff Gordon, Dupont & Edy's Ice Cream, 7½ x 8½ . . . . . . . . . . . . . . . . . . . . .2.00
24 Jeff Gordon, Edys Ice Cream, sweepstakes, 8 x 8 . . . . . . . . . . . . . . . . . . . . . . .2.00

24 Jeff Gordon, Dupont & Dreyer's Ice Cream, 8½ x 8½ . . . . . . . . . . . . . . . . . . . . .2.00
24 Jeff Gordon, Dupont & Pepsi, 7 x 5 . . . .3.00
24 Jeff Gordon, Milk, thin stock, blank back, 8 x 10 . . . . . . . . . . . . . . . . . . . . . . .2.00
24 Jeff Gordon, Fort Worth Star-Telegram, 11 x 8½ . . . . . . . . . . . . . . . . . . . . .7.00
25 Ricky Craven, Budweiser & Pedigree, blank back, 8 x 10 . . . . . . . . . . . . . . . . . . .5.00
25 Ricky Craven, Budweiser & Pedigree, printed back, 8 x 10 . . . . . . . . . . . . . . . . . . .3.00
25 Ricky Craven, Budweiser, 8 x 10 . . . . . .1.00
25 Ricky Craven, Budweiser, St. Louis Post Dispatch, 8½ x 11 . . . . . . . . . . . . . . . . .3.00
26 Rich Bickle, Team Twister, with #93 truck & #98 BGN, 8¼ x 11 . . . . . . . . . . . . . . .3.00
28 Davey Allison, Ron Crawford, 6 x 4 . . . . .2.00
28 Ernie Irvan, Havoline, with coupon, 11 x 8½ . . . . . . . . . . . . . . . . . . . . .1.00
28 Ernie Irvan, Havoline, without coupon, 11 x 8½ . . . . . . . . . . . . . . . . . . . . .1.00
28 Ernie Irvan, Raybestos, 8 x 10 . . . . . . .4.00

28 Ernie Irvan, Texaco, with lower printed auto-graph, 11 x 8½ . . . . . . . . . . . . . . . .2.00
28 Ernie Irvan, Texaco, with elbow high printed autograph, 11 x 8½ . . . . . . . . . . . . .3.00
28 Ernie Irvan, America Remembers, Colt .45 Tribute, 8½ x 11 . . . . . . . . . . . . . . .2.00
28 Robert Yates, Havoline, with coupon, 11 x 8½ . . . . . . . . . . . . . . . . . . . . . .1.00
28 Kenny Irwin, Havoline, 8½ x 11 . . . . . . .3.00
29 Robert Pressley, Cartoon Network, blank back, 8 x 10 . . . . . . . . . . . . . . . . . .3.00
29 Robert Pressley, Cartoon Network, arms crossed, 8 x 10 . . . . . . . . . . . . . .2.00
29 Robert Pressley, Cartoon Network & First Plus, arms crossed, 8 x 10 . . . . . . . .2.00
29 Robert Pressley, Cartoon Network, hands on hip, 8 x 10 . . . . . . . . . . . . . . . .1.00
29 Robert Pressley, Cartoon Network & First Plus, hands on hip, blank back, 8 x 10 .3.00
29 Robert Pressley, Cartoon Network & First Plus, hands on hip, red back, 8 x 10 . .3.00
29 Robert Pressley, Cartoon Network & First Plus, hands on hip, black back, 8 x 10 . . . . . . . . . . . . . . . . . . . . . .3.00
29 Jeff Green, Cartoon Network & General Mills, blank back, 8 x 10 . . . . . . . . . . . . . .4.00
29 Jeff Green, Cartoon Network, photo stock, 6 x 8 . . . . . . . . . . . . . . . . . . . .3.00
29 Jeff Green, Cartoon Network & First Plus, 8 x 10 . . . . . . . . . . . . . . . . . . . . .2.00
29 Cale Yarborough, RCA & Campbell, Hausfeld, send off, 8½ x 11 . . . . . . . . . . . . . .5.00

29 Jeff Green, Cartoon Network, Green on front, 8 x 10 . . . . . . . . . . . . . . . . . . . . . .1.00

30 Johnny Benson, Pennzoil, preview, 8 x 10 . . . . . . . . . . . . . . . . . . . . .3.00
30 Johnny Benson, Pennzoil, 8 x 10 . . . . . .1.00
31 Mike Skinner, Lowe's, 8½ x 11 . . . . . . . .1.00
31 Mike Skinner, Lowe's, without Steve Allen, 8½ x 11 . . . . . . . . . . . . . . . . . . . .1.00
31 Mike Skinner, Piedmont Aviation, 7 x 11 .2.00
33 Ken Schrader, Skoal, 7¾ x 9½ . . . . . . . .1.00
33 Ken Schrader, Skoal, APR added to back, 7¾ x 9½ . . . . . . . . . . . . . . . . . . . . .1.00

29 Jeff Green, Cartoon Network, 8 x 10 . . . 5.00

33 Ken Schrader, Skoal, in uniform, 7¾ x 9½ .1.00
33 Ken Schrader, International Trucks, 6 x 9 .2.00
33 Ken Schrader, Adams International, 6 x 9 .3.00
34 Todd Bodine, Hardinge, Inc., 8 x 10 . . . .3.00

**1997 Race Car**

35 Todd Bodine, Tabasco, art card, blank back,
7 x 10 . . . . . . . . . . . . . . . . . .5.00
35 Todd Bodine, Tabasco, 6 x 9 . . . . . . .1.00
36 Derrick Cope, Skittles, 8 x 10 . . . . . . .1.00
36 Derrick Cope, Skittles, 2nd back,
8 x 10 . . . . . . . . . . . . . .1.00
37 Jeremy Mayfield, K-Mart & RC Cola, headshot, thin stock, 10 x 8 . . . . . . . . . . .1.00
37 Jeremy Mayfield, K-Mart & RC Cola,
11 x 8½ . . . . . . . . . . . . . . . . . .1.00
37 Jeremy Mayfield, International Trucks,
6 x 9 . . . . . . . . . . . . . . . . . . . .3.00
38 Butch Gilliland, Stroppe Motorsports, Winston
West, 8½ x 11 . . . . . . . . . . . . . .1.00
40 Robby Gordon, Coors Lite, thin stock,
8½ x 11 . . . . . . . . . . . . . . . . . .2.00
40 Robby Gordon, Coors Lite, 12 x 9 . . . . .2.00

41 Steve Grissom, Kodiak, headshot,
10 x 8 . . . . . . . . . . . . . . . . .2.00
41 Steve Grissom, Kodiak, headshot, blank back,
11 x 8½ . . . . . . . . . . . . . . . . . .3.00
41 Steve Grissom, Kodiak, 8 x 10 . . . . . . .1.00
42 Joe Nemecheck, BellSouth, employees only,
6¼ x 9 . . . . . . . . . . . . . . . . . .12.00
42 Joe Nemecheck, BellSouth, photo stock,
5 x 7 . . . . . . . . . . . . . . . . . . . .3.00
42 Joe Nemecheck, BellSouth, 9 x 6¼ . . . .1.00
42 Joe Nemecheck, BellSouth, car, side view on
back, 8 x 10 . . . . . . . . . . . . . . .1.00
42 Joe Nemecheck, BellSouth, car, angled view on
back, 8 x 10 . . . . . . . . . . . . . . .1.00
43 Bobby Hamilton, STP, 6 x 9 . . . . . . . . .1.00
43 Bobby Hamilton, Parkway Margarine,
5 x 8 . . . . . . . . . . . . . . . . . .4.00
43 Bobby Hamilton, STP, Hughes, with Richard
Petty, coupon, 8½ x 8 . . . . . . . . . . .1.00
43 Richard Petty, International Trucks,
6 x 9 . . . . . . . . . . . . . . . . . . .3.00
43 Richard Petty, International Trucks,
11 x 8½ . . . . . . . . . . . . . . . . . .3.00
43 Richard Petty, Cellular One, thin stock,
11 x 8½ . . . . . . . . . . . . . . . . . .1.00
43 Richard Petty, Cellular One, Petty Driving Expe-
rience, 8½ x 11 . . . . . . . . . . . . . .1.00
43 Richard Petty, STP, 6 x 9 . . . . . . . . . .1.00
44 Kyle Petty, Hot Wheels, photo stock,
7 x 5 . . . . . . . . . . . . . . . . . .1.00
44 Kyle Petty, Hot Wheels, headshot, blank back,
11 x 8½ . . . . . . . . . . . . . . . . . .4.00
44 Kyle Petty, Hot Wheels, 8½ x 11 . . . . .1.00
44 Kyle Petty, Spree, 8 x 10 . . . . . . . . . .2.00
44 Kyle Petty, Hot Wheels, action shot,
8½ x 11 . . . . . . . . . . . . . . . . . .2.00

42 Joe Nemecheck, BellSouth, employees only, 6¼ x 9 . . .12.00

44 Kyle Petty, International Trucks, 6 x 9 . . .3.00
45 Ron Hornaday, Tootsietoy, Winston West, 8 x 10 . . . . . . . . . . . . . . . . . . . .4.00
45 Ron Hornaday, Xtreme j, 6 x 9 . . . . . .10.00
45 Gary Smith, Tootsietoy, Winston West, 6¼ x 9¼ . . . . . . . . . . . . . . . . . . . . . .2.00
46 Wally Dallenbach Jr., First Union, photo stock, 5 x 7 . . . . . . . . . . . . . . . . . . . . . . .1.00
46 Wally Dallenbach Jr., First Union, inset, tan shirt, 8 x 10 . . . . . . . . . . . . . . . . . .1.00
46 Wally Dallenbach Jr., First Union, inset, in uniform, 8 x 10 . . . . . . . . . . . . . . . . . .1.00
46 Wally Dallenbach, First Union, show car, Springfield,TN, 8½ x 5½ . . . . . . . . . .5.00
46 Wally Dallenbach, First Union, show car, Nashville, TN, 8½ x 5½ . . . . . . . .5.00 46 Wally Dallenbach, First Union, show car, Hendersonville, 8½ x 5½ . . . . . . . . .5.00
55 Joe Ruttman, Sealy Furniture, blank back, 8 x 10 . . . . . . . . . . . . . . . . . . . .2.00
55 Joe Ruttman, Sealy Furniture, blank back with Michael Waltrip, 8 x 10 . . . . . . . . . . .2.00
65 Sammy Potashnick, PTI Racing, B & W, Winston West, 5½ x 8½ . . . . . . . . . . . . . .2.00
65 Sammy Potashnick, PTI Racing, Color, Winston West, 5½ x 8½ . . . . . . . . . . . . . . .2.00
71 Dave Marcis, Realtree, 8½ x 11 . . . . . .1.00
71 Dave Marcis, Realtree, without crew chief, 8½ x 11 . . . . . . . . . . . . . . . . . . . .1.00
75 Rick Mast, Remington, 8½ x 11 . . . . . .1.00
75 Rick Mast, Remington, with coupon, 8½ x 11 . . . . . . . . . . . . . . . . . . . .1.00
77 Bobby Hillin, Jasper, 5½ x 8½ . . . . . . .1.00
77 Bobby Hillin, Jasper & Federal Mogul, 6 x 9 . . . . . . . . . . . . . . . . . . . . . . .1.00
77 No Driver, Jasper, 5½ x 8½ . . . . . . . . .1.00
77 Morgan Shepherd, Jasper, 5½ x 8½ . . . .1.00
77 Morgan Shepherd, Jasper & Federal Mogul, 5½ x 8½ . . . . . . . . . . . . . . . . . . . . .1.00
78 Billy Standridge, Diamond Rio, 5½ x 8½ .1.00
78 Billy Standridge, Hanes, 5½ x 8½ . . . . . .3.00

78 No Driver, Triad Motorsports, blank back, 8½ x 11 . . . . . . . . . . . . . . . . . . . .2.00
78 Gary Bradberry, Hanes, blank back, thick stock, 8 x 10 . . . . . . . . . . . . . . . . .3.00
78 Gary Bradberry, Hanes, blank back, thin stock, 8 x 10 . . . . . . . . . . . . . . . . . . . .3.00
81 Kenny Wallace, Square D, 8 x 10 . . . . .1.00
81 Kenny Wallace, Square D, without E. Jones & G. Martin, 8 x 10 . . . . . . . . . . . . . . .1.00
81 Kenny Wallace, Square D, fan day, 7 x 8 . . . . . . . . . . . . . . . . . . . . . . .3.00
81 Kenny Wallace, Square D, #102DM9701, 5½ x 8½ . . . . . . . . . . . . . . . . . . . .3.00
81 Kenny Wallace, Square D, #102DM9702, 5½ x 8½ . . . . . . . . . . . . . . . . . . . .3.00
81 Kenny Wallace, Square D, #102DM9703, 5½ x 8½ . . . . . . . . . . . . . . . . . . . .3.00
81 Kenny Wallace, Square D, #102DM9704, 5½ x 8½ . . . . . . . . . . . . . . . . . . . .3.00
81 Kenny Wallace, Square D, #102DM9705, 5½ x 8½ . . . . . . . . . . . . . . . . . . . .3.00
88 Dale Jarrett, Quality Care & Ford Credit, bifold, 9 x 11 . . . . . . . . . . . . . . . . . .1.00
88 Dale Jarrett, TranSouth 400 Winner's Circle, 8 x 10 . . . . . . . . . . . . . . . . . . . . .4.00
90 Dick Trickle, Heilig-Meyers, tape on uniform, 7 x 9 . . . . . . . . . . . . . . . . . . . . . . .3.00
90 Dick Trickle, Heilig-Meyers, correct, 7 x 9 .1.00
91 Mike Wallace, Spam, photo stock without speakers on roof, 8 x 10 . . . . . . . . . .3.00
91 Mike Wallace, Spam, photo stock with speakers on roof, 8 x 10 . . . . . . . . . . . . . .1.00
91 Mike Wallace, Spam, with coupon error, 6 x 9 . . . . . . . . . . . . . . . . . . . . . . .1.00
91 Mike Wallace, Spam, 2nd back with coupon correct, 6 x 9 . . . . . . . . . . . . . . . . .1.00
91 Mike Wallace, Spam, 3rd back with coupon correct, T. Twister, 6 x 9 . . . . . . . . . .1.00
94 Bill Elliott, McDonald's, 8 x 10 . . . . . . .1.00
94 Bill Elliott, Reese's, B & W back, 8 x 6½ . . . . . . . . . . . . . . . . . . . . . . .1.00
94 Bill Elliott, Reese's, color back, 8 x 6½ . .1.00
95 Gary Bradberry, Feed The Children, 6 x 9 .1.00
96 David Green, Caterpillar, without printed autograph, 8 x 10 . . . . . . . . . . . . . . . . .1.00
96 David Green, Caterpillar, without printed autograph, without Butch Enders, 8 x 10 . . . . . . . . . . . . . . . . . . . . . .1.00
96 David Green, Caterpillar, without printed autograph, ICI Paints Logo, 8 x 10 . . . . . . .2.00
96 David Green, Caterpillar Tractor, printed autograph, 8 x 10 . . . . . . . . . . . . . . . . . .1.00
96 David Green, Caterpillar Tractor, printed autograph without Butch Enders, 8 x 10 . . . . . . . . . . . . . . . . . . . . . .1.00
96 David Green, Caterpillar, Cat Financial logo, 8 x 10 . . . . . . . . . . . . . . . . . . . . . .1.00

**#78 Hanes Thunderbird**
*Driven by Bobby Hillin Jr.*

78 Bobby Hillin, Hanes, blank back, 8½ x 11 .3.00

97 Chad Little, John Deere, Miller Motorsports Show, 8½ x 11 . . . . . . . . . . . . . .7.00
97 Chad Little, John Deere, 8 x 10 . . . . . . .1.00
98 John Andretti, RCA, 8 x 10 . . . . . . . . . .1.00
98 John Andretti, RCA, with more information on back, 8 x 10 . . . . . . . . . . . . . . . . . .1.00
98 John Andretti, RCA & Campbell-Hausfeld, thin stock, 8½ x 11 . . . . . . . . . . . . . .1.00
98 John Andretti, RCA & Mighty Auto Parts, 8 x 10 . . . . . . . . . . . . . . . . . . . .1.00
98 John Andretti, RCA & Campbell-Hausfeld, send-off, 8½ x 11 . . . . . . . . . . . . .5.00
98 John Andretti, RCA & Radio Shack, 8 x 10 . . . . . . . . . . . . . . . . . . . .3.00
99 Jeff Burton, Exide, 8½ x 11 . . . . . . . . .2.00
99 Jeff Burton, Exide, printed autograph large, different back, 8½ x 11 . . . . . . . . . . .1.00
99 Jeff Burton, Exide, printed autograph small, different back, 8½ x 11 . . . . . . . . .1.00
99 Jeff Burton, Parts Plus, 5 x 8 . . . . . . .2.00
99 Jeff Burton, Exide, Mayflower back, 8½ x 11 . . . . . . . . . . . . . . . . . . .3.00
99 Jeff Burton, Exide, printed autograph small, blank back, 8½ x 11 . . . . . . . . . . . .3.00

## 1998

00 Buckshot Jones, Aquafresh, 00 shaped die-cut, 10 x 8 . . . . . . . . . . . . . . . . . . .1.00
00 Buckshot Jones, Aquafresh, with coupon, 8 x 6 . . . . . . . . . . . . . . . . . . . . .1.00
07 Dan Pardus, MidWest Transit, red & white car, 8 x 10 . . . . . . . . . . . . . . . . . . . .2.00
07 Dan Pardus, MidWest Transit, red & yellow car, 8 x 10 . . . . . . . . . . . . . . . . . .1.00
08 John Kinder, Winston West, 8 x 10 . . . .2.00
1 Steve Park, Pennzoil, 8 x 10 . . . . . . . . .1.00
1 Steve Park, Pennzoil, 5 x 7 . . . . . . . . . .2.00
1 Darrell Waltrip, Pennzoil, blank back, 10 x 8 . . . . . . . . . . . . . . . . . . . . .4.00
2 Rusty Wallace, Miller, 8½ x 11 . . . . . . .1.00
2 Rusty Wallace, Miller & Mobil 1, 8½ x 11 .2.00
2 Rusty Wallace, Stevens Aviation, 8 x 10 . .2.00
2 Rusty Wallace, Miller & Lennox, 8½ x 11 .3.00
2 Rusty Wallace, fan club with airplane, 8 x 10 . . . . . . . . . . . . . . . . . . . . .2.00
2 Rusty Wallace, Mead, headshot, color, 7 x 5 . . . . . . . . . . . . . . . . . . . . .1.00
2 Rusty Wallace, Mead, headshot, B & W, 7 x 5 . . . . . . . . . . . . . . . . . . . . .1.00
2 Rusty Wallace, Mead, show car, 5 x 7 . . .1.00
3 Dale Earnhardt, GM Goodwrench, 1 of 8,000, small print, preview, 6 x 9 . . . . . . . .20.00
3 Dale Earnhardt, GM Goodwrench, 1 of 8,000, large print, 6 x 9 . . . . . . . . . . . . .20.00
3 Dale Earnhardt, GM Goodwrench, 1 of 28,000, show car, 6 x 9 . . . . . . . . . . . . . .15.00

## The 1998 Goodwrench Team

3 Dale Earnhardt, GM Goodwrench, 1 of 8,000, small print, preview, 6 x 9 . . . . . . . .20.00

3 Dale Earnhardt, GM Goodwrench, 8 x 10 .5.00
3 Dale Earnhardt, Fort Worth Star, Telegram, 11 x 8½ . . . . . . . . . . . . . . . . . .7.00
3 Dale Earnhardt, Bass Pro Shops, 5 x 7 . . .6.00
3 Dale Earnhardt, Bass Pro Shops & Jebco Clocks, 5 x 10½ . . . . . . . . . . . . . .4.00
3 Dale Earnhardt, Bass Pro & Tracker Boats, 5 x 7 . . . . . . . . . . . . . . . . . . . . .6.00
3 Dale Earnhardt, GM Goodwrench & Food City, 8 x 10 . . . . . . . . . . . . . . . . . . . .5.00
3 Dale Earnhardt, art with Dale Jr., 5 x 6 . .7.00
3 Dale Earnhardt, art with Dale Jr., 8 x 10 .10.00
4 Bobby Hamilton, Kodak Flim, Preview, photo stock, 5 x 7 . . . . . . . . . . . . . . . . .1.00
4 Bobby Hamilton, Kodak Flim, 11 x 8½ . . . .1.00
5 Terry Labonte, Kellogg's, 11 x 8½ . . . . . .1.00

5 Terry Labonte, Kellogg's, fan club, headshot with car, 11 x 8½ . . . . . . . . . . . . . . . .5.00
6 Mark Martin, Valvoline, 11 x 8½ . . . . . . .1.00
7 Geoff Bodine, Philips Lucent Technologies, 8 x 10 . . . . . . . . . . . . . . . . . . . . .2.00
7 Geoff Bodine, Philips Lucent Technologies, kneeling, 8 x 10 . . . . . . . . . . . . . . . . . .7.00

7 Geoff Bodine, Philips Lucent Technologies, Geoff on front, 8 x 10 . . . . . . . . . . . . . . . .3.00

7 Geoff Bodine, Philips Lucent Technologies, leaning on car, 8 x 10 . . . . . . . . . . . . . . . .1.00

7 Geoff Bodine, Philips Lucent Technologies, leaning on car, 5 x 7 . . . . . . . . . . . . . . . .2.00

7 Geoff Bodine, Lincoln Tech, 8 x 10 . . . . .2.00

8 Hut Stricklin, Circuit City, 7 x 9 . . . . . . .1.00

9 Lake Speed, Cartoon Network, blank back, 8 x 10 . . . . . . . . . . . . . . . . . . . .3.00

9 Lake Speed, Cartoon Network, printed back, 8 x 10 . . . . . . . . . . . . . . . . . . . .1.00

9 Lake Speed, Cartoon Network, Happy Birthday NASCAR, 8 x 10 . . . . . . . . . . . . . . .1.00

9 No Driver, Cartoon Network, 8 x 10 . . . .1.00

9 Gary Blackley, Winston West, 3 x 4 . . . .3.00

10 Ricky Rudd, Tide, 5 x 7 . . . . . . . . . . .1.00

12 Jeremy Mayfield, Mobil 1, with printed auto, 11 x 8½ . . . . . . . . . . . . . . . . . . . .1.00

15 Ted Musgrave, Rescue, white writing on front, 5½ x 8½ . . . . . . . . . . . . . . . . . . . . . .5.00

11 Brett Bodine, PAYCHEX, preview, 8½ x 11 . . . . . . . . . . . . . . . . . . . .10.00

11 Brett Bodine, PAYCHEX, blue & silver background, 8½ x 11 . . . . . . . . . . . . . . .2.00

11 Brett Bodine, PAYCHEX, blue background, 8½ x 11 . . . . . . . . . . . . . . . . . . . .3.00

11 Brett Bodine, PAYCHEX, blue & silver background without Doug Richardson, 8½ x 11 . . . . . . . . . . . . . . . . . . . .1.00

12 Jeremy Mayfield, Mobil 1, blank back, 8½ x 11 . . . . . . . . . . . . . . . . . . . .7.00

12 Jeremy Mayfield, Mobil 1, without printed auto, 11 x 8½ . . . . . . . . . . . . . . . . . . . .1.00

12 Jeremy Mayfield, Mobil 1, with printed auto, 11 x 8½ . . . . . . . . . . . . . . . . . . . .1.00

12 Austin Cameron, Neal Electric, Winston West, 8 x 10 . . . . . . . . . . . . . . . . . . . .3.00

13 Jerry Nadeau, First Plus, 8 x 10 . . . . .1.00

13 Jerry Nadeau, First Plus, with Bill Elliott & Dan Marino, 8 x 10 . . . . . . . . . . . . . . . . .1.00

13 Jerry Nadeau, First Plus, with Bill Elliott & Dan Marino, phone number 1-888, 8 x 10 . . . . . . . . . . . . . . . . . . . .1.00

14 Neville Lance, AutoPro, Australian NASCAR, 8¼ x 11¾ . . . . . . . . . . . . . . . . . . . .5.00

15 Ted Musgrave, Rescue, yellow writing on front, 5½ x 8½ . . . . . . . . . . . . . . . . . . . . . .5.00

15 Rick Scriber, Winston West, 5½ x 8½ . . .2.00

16 Ted Musgrave, PrimeStar, with tear-off, 6 x 9 . . . . . . . . . . . . . . . . . . . .1.00

16 Ted Musgrave, PrimeStar, without tear-off, 6 x 9 . . . . . . . . . . . . . . . . . . . .1.00

16 Bill McAnally, NAPA, Winston West, 8 x 10 . . . . . . . . . . . . . . . . . . . .2.00

16 Kevin LePage, Primestar, 8 x 10 . . . . .1.00

17 Darrell Waltrip, preview, headshot, photo, 10 x 8 . . . . . . . . . . . . . . . . . . . . . .4.00

17 Darrell Waltrip, Speedblock & Builders Square, 10½ x 7 . . . . . . . . . . . . . . . . . . . . .2.00

18 Bobby Labonte, Interstate Batteries, 6 x 8 . . . . . . . . . . . . . . . . . . . . . .1.00

18 Bobby Labonte, Wix Filters, fold-over, 8½ x 5½ . . . . . . . . . . . . . . . . . . . .1.00

18 Bobby Labonte, Ditch Witch, with tear-off, 8½ x 11 . . . . . . . . . . . . . . . . . . . . .2.00

18 Bobby Labonte, Shell Motorsports, 8 x 10 . . . . . . . . . . . . . . . . . . . . .3.00

18 Bobby Labonte, Cintas, 8½ x 11 . . . . . .3.00

19 Tony Raines, Yellow Freight, 8 x 10 . . . .1.00

19 Tony Raines, Yellow Freight, bio & schedule, 8 x 10 . . . . . . . . . . . . . . . . . . . . .3.00

19 Tony Raines, Yellow Freight, with coupon, 8½ x 11 . . . . . . . . . . . . . . . . . . . .1.00

19 Tony Raines, Yellow Freight, printed autograph with coupon, 8½ x 11 . . . . . . . . . .1.00

21 Michael Waltrip, Citgo, 8 x 10 . . . . . . .1.00

21 Michael Waltrip, Grand Home Furniture, oil bottle decal, 8 x 10 . . . . . . . . . . . . .1.00

21 Michael Waltrip, Grand Home Furniture, without oil bottle decal, 8 x 10 . . . . . . . . .1.00

22 Ward Burton, MBNA, 8 x 10 . . . . . . . .1.00

22 Ward Burton, MBNA, AMOCO sticker on car, front, 8 x 10 . . . . . . . . . . . . . . . . .1.00

23 Jimmy Spencer, Winston, white numbers, 11 x 8½ . . . . . . . . . . . . . . . . . . . .5.00

23 Jimmy Spencer, Winston, red numbers, 11 x 8½ . . . . . . . . . . . . . . . . . . . .1.00

24 Jeff Gordon, Dupont, 10 x 8 . . . . . . . .1.00

24 Jeff Gordon, Fort Worth Star, Telegram, 11 x 8½ . . . . . . . . . . . . . . . . . . . .7.00

24 Jeff Gordon, Philadelphia Daily News, 8 x 10 . . . . . . . . . . . . . . . . . . . . .4.00

25 Kevin Culver, Winston West, 5½ x 8½ . .3.00

26 Johnny Benson, Cheerios, preview, headshot, 7 x 5 . . . . . . . . . . . . . . . . . . . . .3.00

26 Johnny Benson, Cheerios, with car, 7 x 5 . . . . . . . . . . . . . . . . . . . . .5.00

26 Johnny Benson, Cheerios, 8½ x 11 . . . .1.00

26 Johnny Benson, General Mills, kid car, blank back, 11 x 8½ . . . . . . . . . . . . . . . .1.00

28 Kenny Irwin, Havoline, with tear-off, 8½ x 11 . . . . . . . . . . . . . . . . . . . .1.00

28 Kenny Irwin, Raybestos, 8 x 10 . . . . . . .2.00

28 Kenny Irwin, Havoline, Joker with trademark on front, 8½ x 11 . . . . . . . . . . . . . .2.00

28 Kenny Irwin, Havoline, Joker without trademark on front, 8½ x 11 . . . . . . . . . . . . . .3.00

28 Robert Yates, Havoline, with tear-off, 8½ x 11 . . . . . . . . . . . . . . . . . . . .1.00

29 Jeff Green, 8 x 10 . . . . . . . . . . . . . .1.00

30 Derrike Cope, Gumout, blank back, 8 x 10 .2.00

30 Derrike Cope, Gumout, 8 x 10 . . . . . . .1.00

30 Derrike Cope, Gumout & Pony Computer, paper stock, 5½ x 8½ . . . . . . . . . . .1.00

30 Derrike Cope, Gumout & Pony Computer, card stock, 5½ x 8½ . . . . . . . . . . . . . .2.00

30 Derrike Cope, Rudy's Farm, with coupon, 11 x 8½ . . . . . . . . . . . . . . . . . . . .1.00

31 Mike Skinner, Lowe's, 8 x 10 . . . . . . . .1.00

33 Ken Schrader, Skoal, 8 x 10 . . . . . . . .1.00

35 Todd Bodine, Tabasco, preview, 5½ x 8¼ .5.00

35 Todd Bodine, Tabasco, with tear-off, 8 x 10 . . . . . . . . . . . . . . . . . . . . .1.00

36 Ernie Irvan, Skittles, with tear-off, 8 x 10 .1.00

36 Ernie Irvan, Screen Saver, thin stock, 8½ x 11 . . . . . . . . . . . . . . . . . . . .1.00

40 Sterling Marlin, Coors, 11 x 8½ . . . . . .1.00

41 Steve Grissom, Kodiak, 8 x 10 . . . . . . .1.00

42 Joe Nemechek, BellSouth, preview, photo stock, 5 x 7 . . . . . . . . . . . . . . . . . .2.00

42 Joe Nemechek, BellSouth, 8 x 10 . . . . .1.00

42 Joe Nemechek, Lucent Technologies, 8½ x 11 . . . . . . . . . . . . . . . . . . . .3.00

43 John Andretti, STP, 6 x 9 . . . . . . . . .1.00

43 Richard Petty, STP, 6 x 9 . . . . . . . . . .1.00

43 Richard Petty, GoodYear, 1970 Plymouth, 1998 Pontiac, 8½ x 11 . . . . . . . . . . .3.00

43 Richard Petty, International Truck, 6 x 9 .3.00

43 Richard Petty & John Andretti, International Truck, 6 x 9 . . . . . . . . . . . . . . . . .3.00

44 Kyle Petty, Hot Wheels, B & W, 8 x 10 . .4.00

44 Kyle Petty, Hot Wheels, 8½ x 11 . . . . . .1.00

43 Kyle Petty, International Truck, 6 x 9 . . . .3.00

46 Wally Dallenbach Jr., First Union, preview, photo stock, 5 x 7 . . . . . . . . . . . . . .1.00

46 Wally Dallenbach Jr., First Union, 8 x 10 .2.00

46 No Driver, First Union, 8 x 10 . . . . . . .2.00

46 Jeff Green, The Money Store, 8 x 10 . . .2.00

47 Billy Standridge, Team FCR, photo stock, 4 x 6 . . . . . . . . . . . . . . . . . . . . .2.00

47 Billy Standridge, Team FCR, 8 x 10 . . . .1.00

50 Ricky Craven, Budweiser, 8 x 10 . . . . . .1.00

50 Ricky Craven, Pedigree, 8 x 10 . . . . . . .2.00
50 Wally Dallenbach, Budweiser, 11 x 8½ . .1.00
65 Sammy Potashnick, PTI Racing, thin stock, color, Winston West, 8 x 10 . . . . . . . .1.00
65 Sammy Potashnick, PTI Racing, Winston West, 8 x 10 . . . . . . . . . . . . . . . . . .2.00
70 Davey Manthis, Star Nursey, Winston West, 8½ x 11 . . . . . . . . . . . . . . . . . . . . . .3.00
71 Dave Marcis, Team RealTree, 8½ x 11 . .1.00
75 Rick Mast, Remington, with tear-off, 8½ x 11 . . . . . . . . . . . . . . . . . . . . . .1.00
77 Robert Pressley, Jasper, 8 x 10 . . . . . .1.00
77 Robert Pressley, Jasper, sponsors added to back, 8 x 10 . . . . . . . . . . . . . . . . .1.00
77 Robert Pressley, Jasper, more information on back, 8 x 10 . . . . . . . . . . . . . . . . .1.00
78 Gary Bradberry, Triad Motorsports, headshot, blank back, 5 x 7 . . . . . . . . . . . . . .1.00
78 Gary Bradberry, Pilot Travel Centers, photo stock, 8 x 10 . . . . . . . . . . . . . . . . .1.00
78 Gary Bradberry, Pilot Travel Centers, 8 x 10 . . . . . . . . . . . . . . . . . . . . . .1.00
78 Gary Bradberry, Pilot Travel Centers, without Richard Broome, 8 x 10 . . . . . . . . . .1.00
81 Kenny Wallace, Square D, 8 x 10 . . . . .1.00
85 Kevin Richards, Monaco Enterprises, Winston West, on pit road, 5½ x 8½ . . . . . . .3.00
85 Kevin Richards, Monaco Enterprises, Winston West with transporter, 5½ x 8½ . . . . .3.00
88 Dale Jarrett, Quality Care & Ford Credit, 11 x 8½ . . . . . . . . . . . . . . . . . . . . .1.00
88 Dale Jarrett, Quality Care & Ford Credit, car different angle, 11 x 8½ . . . . . . . . . .1.00
88 Dale Jarrett, Quality Care, Batman, 8½ x 11 . . . . . . . . . . . . . . . . . . . . . .1.00
88 Dale Jarrett, Quality Care & Ford Credit, blank back, 8½ x 11 . . . . . . . . . . . . . . . . .4.00

89 Dennis Setzer, McRib, blank back, 8 x 10 . . . . . . . . . . . . . . . . . . . . . .12.00

90 Dick Trickle, Heilig-Meyers, 6¾ x 9 . . . . .1.00
91 Kevin Lepage, Pionite, 6 x 9 . . . . . . . . .1.00

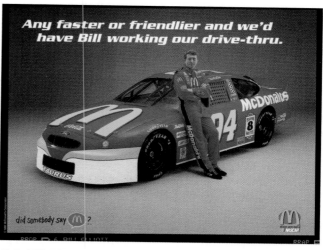

94 Bill Elliott, McDonald's, with printer's marks, 8 x 10 . . . . . . . . . . . . . . . . . . . . . .7.00
94 Bill Elliott, McDonald's, without printer's marks, 8 x 10 . . . . . . . . . . . . . . . . . . . . . .1.00
94 Bill Elliott, Reese's, 8 x 6½ . . . . . . . . .1.00
94 Bill Elliott, Drive Thru Crew, 8 x 10 . . . . .2.00

94 Bill Elliott, McDonald's Big Mac, blank back, 10 x 8 . . . . . . . . . . . . . . . . . . . . . .5.00
96 David Green, Caterpillar, 8 x 10 . . . . . . .1.00
96 David Green, Caterpillar & Siemens, 8 x 10 . . . . . . . . . . . . . . . . . . . . . .1.00

96 David Green, Caterpillar & Cat Financial,
   8 x 10 . . . . . . . . . . . . . . . . . . . . .2.00
96 David Green, Caterpillar & ICI Delux Paints,
   8 x 10 . . . . . . . . . . . . . . . . . . . . .2.00
96 No Driver, Caterpillar, 8 x 10 . . . .1.00
97 Chad Little, John Deere, 8½ x 11 . . . . .1.00
97 Chad Little, Haulmark Race Trailers,
   8½ x 11 . . . . . . . . . . . . . . . . . .3.00
98 Greg Sacks, Thorn Apple Valley, 11 x 8½ .1.00
98 Greg Sacks, Thorn Apple Valley, with tear-off,
   8½ x 11 . . . . . . . . . . . . . . . . .1.00
98 Greg Sacks, Mighty Auto Parts, 8½ x 11 .2.00
98 Rich Bickle, Thorn Apple Valley, with tear-off,
   8½ x 11 . . . . . . . . . . . . . . . . .1.00
99 Jeff Burton, Exide, with tear-off, 11 x 8½ 1.00
99 Jeff Burton, Exide, with tear-off & with 3-98,
   11 x 8½ . . . . . . . . . . . . . . . . .1.00
99 Jeff Burton, Exide, Mayflower, without tear-off,
   11 x 8½ . . . . . . . . . . . . . . . . . .3.00
99 Jeff Burton, Exide & Parts Plus, 6 x 9 . .2.00

# 1999

00 Buckshot Jones, headshot, color photo stock,
   7 x 5 . . . . . . . . . . . . . . . . . . . . 1.00
00 Buckshot Jones, headshot, color photo stock,
   8 x 10 . . . . . . . . . . . . . . . . . . . . .1.00

00 Buckshot Jones, Buckshot Racing, pink writing
   on front, 7 x 11 . . . . . . . . . . . . . . .3.00
00 Buckshot Jones, Buckshot Racing, purple writing on front, 7 x 11 . . . . . . . . . . . . .1.00
01 Jeff Green, Tracfone, 8 x 10 . . . . . . . .2.00
05 John Metcalf, ReMax, Winston West,
   8½ x 11 . . . . . . . . . . . . . . . . . . . .3.00
1 Steve Park, Philadelphia News & The Inquirer,
   blank back, 8¼ x 12 . . . . . . . . . . . . .3.00
1 Steve Park, Philadelphia News & The Inquirer,
   11 x 5¾ . . . . . . . . . . . . . . . . . . . .2.00
1 Steve Park, Pennzoil, fold-over, 11 x 8½ . .1.00
1 Steve Park, Pennzoil, 7 x 6 . . . . . . . . . .3.00
1 Steve Park, Coca-Cola Racing Family,
   5½ x 8½ . . . . . . . . . . . . . . . . . . . .6.00

1 Dale Earnhardt Jr., Coca-Cola Racing Family,
   5½ x 8½ . . . . . . . . . . . . . . . . . . .6.00
1 Butch Gilliland, Ralphs Food 4 Less, Winston
   West, 8½ x 11 . . . . . . . . . . . . . . . .3.00
1 Butch Gilliland, Ralphs Food 4 Less, with tear-
   off, Winston West, 8 x 10 . . . . . . . . .3.00
2 Rusty Wallace, Miller Lite, 8 x 10 . . . . . .1.00
2 Rusty Wallace, Mead Coated Papers,
   8 x 10 . . . . . . . . . . . . . . . . . . . . .1.00
2 Rusty Wallace, headshot, fan club, 7 x 5 . .1.00
2 Rusty Wallace, with hot rod, fan club,
   8 x 10 . . . . . . . . . . . . . . . . . . . . .3.00
2 Rusty Wallace, Lennox, 8½ x 11 . . . . . . .2.00
2 Rusty Wallace, Miller Lite, with Indy car,
   5½ x 8½ . . . . . . . . . . . . . . . . . . . .1.00
2 Rusty Wallace, Oakley, 6 x 4 . . . . . . . . .3.00
3 Dale Earnhardt, GM Goodwrench, blank back,
   8 x 10 . . . . . . . . . . . . . . . . . . . .10.00
3 Dale Earnhardt, GM Goodwrench, 8 x 10 .5.00
3 Dale Earnhardt, GM Goodwrench & Burger
   King, 8 x 10 . . . . . . . . . . . . . . . . .12.00
3 Dale Earnhardt, Coca-Cola, Go 220,
   8 x 5½ . . . . . . . . . . . . . . . . . . . .10.00
3 Dale Earnhardt, Coca-Cola, without Go 220,
   8 x 5½ . . . . . . . . . . . . . . . . . . . . .5.00
3 Dale Earnhardt, Star Telegram, Sam Bass art,
   8½ x 11 . . . . . . . . . . . . . . . . . . . .5.00
3 Dale Earnhardt, Jebco Clocks, 10½ x 5 . .4.00
3 Dale Earnhardt, Coca-Cola Racing Family,
   5½ x 8½ . . . . . . . . . . . . . . . . . . . .9.00
4 Bobby Hamilton, Kodak Max, 8½ x 11 . . .1.00
4 Bobby Hamilton, Kodak Max, with tear-off,
   8½ x 11 . . . . . . . . . . . . . . . . . . . .3.00
5 Terry Labonte, Kellogg's, 11 x 8½ . . . . . .1.00
6 Mark Martin, Valvoline, with coupon,
   11 x 8½ . . . . . . . . . . . . . . . . . . . .1.00
6 Mark Martin, Eagle One, United States,
   3¾ x 8 . . . . . . . . . . . . . . . . . . . . .2.00
6 Mark Martin, Eagle One, Canada, 3¾ x 8 .2.00
6 Mark Martin, Platinum Stock Car Series,
   10¾ x 8¾ . . . . . . . . . . . . . . . . . . .2.00
7 Michael Waltrip, Philips, bust shot, Birthday,
   April 18, 1963, 10 x 8 . . . . . . . . . . .2.00
7 Michael Waltrip, Philips, bust shot, Birthday,
   April 30, 1963, 10 x 8 . . . . . . . . . . .2.00
7 Michael Waltrip, Philips, with car, 8 x 10 .1.00
7 Michael Waltrip, Philips & Lucent Technologies,
   8 x 10 . . . . . . . . . . . . . . . . . . . . .2.00
7 Michael Waltrip, Williams Electrical Supply,
   7 x 5 . . . . . . . . . . . . . . . . . . . . . .2.00
7 Michael Waltrip, with coupon, 8 x 10 . . . .1.00
7 Michael Waltrip, Sealy, 8 x 10 . . . . . . . .3.00
8 Dale Earnhardt Jr., Bud Racing, 8 x 10 . . .2.00
8 Dale Earnhardt Jr., Outlaw, without Additives
   with Attitude logo, 8 x 10 . . . . . . . . .3.00
8 Dale Earnhardt Jr., Outlaw, Additives with
   Attitude logo, 8 x 10 . . . . . . . . . . . .3.00

7 Michael Waltrip, Williams Electrical Supply,
7 x 5 . . . . . . . . . . . . . . . . . . . . . . . . . . .2.00

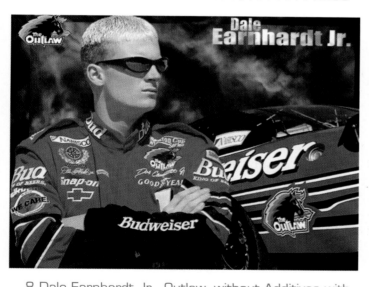

8 Dale Earnhardt Jr., Outlaw, without Additives with
Attitude logo, 8 x 10 . . . . . . . . . . . . . .3.00

8 Dale Earnhardt Jr., Outback Steakhouse 200,
6 x 4½ . . . . . . . . . . . . . . . . . . . . . . . . .3.00

9 Jerry Nadeau, Cartoon Network & Dexter's
Labratory, 8 x 10 . . . . . . . . . . . . . . . .1.00

9 Jerry Nadeau, Cartoon Network, Jetsons,
8 x 10 . . . . . . . . . . . . . . . . . . . . . . . . . .1.00

9 Jerry Nadeau, TBS, Braves, 8 x 10 . . . . .1.00

9 Jerry Nadeau, World Championship Wrestling,
wearing helmet, 8 x 10 . . . . . . . . . . . .1.00

9 Jerry Nadeau, World Championship Wrestling,
without helmet, 8 x 10 . . . . . . . . . . .1.00

10 Ricky Rudd, Tide, 5 x 7 . . . . . . . . . . .1.00

10 Ricky Rudd, Coca-Cola, Go 220, 8 x 5½ .3.00

10 Ricky Rudd, Coca-Cola, without Go 220,
8 x 5½ . . . . . . . . . . . . . . . . . . . . . . . . .2.00

10 Ricky Rudd, Outback Steakhouse, blank back, 6
x 4½ . . . . . . . . . . . . . . . . . . . . . . . . . .4.00

10 Ricky Rudd, Outback Steakhouse, Invitation,
6 x 4½ . . . . . . . . . . . . . . . . . . . . . . . . .5.00

10 Ricky Rudd, Tide, show car promo,
8½ x 11 . . . . . . . . . . . . . . . . . . . . . . . .3.00

10 Ricky Rudd, Coca-Cola Racing Family,
5½ x 8½ . . . . . . . . . . . . . . . . . . . . . . . .6.00

11 Brett Bodine, Paychex, 8½ x 11 . . . . . .1.00

11 Brett Bodine, Click It Or Ticket, 5 x 7 . . .2.00

12 Jeremy Mayfield, Mobil 1, Haulmark trailers,
11 x 8½ . . . . . . . . . . . . . . . . . . . . . . . .3.00

12 Jeremy Mayfield, Mobil 1, color car on back,
8½ x 11 . . . . . . . . . . . . . . . . . . . . . . . .1.00

12 Jeremy Mayfield, Mobil 1, B & W car on back,
8½ x 11 . . . . . . . . . . . . . . . . . . . . . . . .1.00

12 Jeremy Mayfield, Outback Steakhouse, blank
back, 6 x 4½ . . . . . . . . . . . . . . . . . . . .4.00

12 Jeremy Mayfield, Outback Steakhouse,
invitation, 6 x 4½ . . . . . . . . . . . . . . . . .5.00

12 Jeremy Mayfield, Coca-Cola Racing Family,
5½ x 8½ . . . . . . . . . . . . . . . . . . . . . . . .6.00

14 Boris Said, Federated Auto Parts, with #44
truck, 8 x 10 . . . . . . . . . . . . . . . . . . . .1.00

16 Kevin Lepage, Primestar, 8½ x 11 . . . . .1.00

16 Kevin Lepage, TV Guide, 8½ x 11 . . . . . .3.00

16 Kevin Lepage, TV Guide, more info on back,
8½ x 11 . . . . . . . . . . . . . . . . . . . . . . . .1.00

16 Kevin Lepage, TV Guide Sweepstakes,
7½ x 5 . . . . . . . . . . . . . . . . . . . . . . . . .1.00

16 Sean Woodside, NAPA, Winston West,
9 x 12 . . . . . . . . . . . . . . . . . . . . . . . . .2.00

18 Bobby Labonte, Wix, 6 x 8¾ . . . . . . . . .2.00

18 Bobby Labonte, Interstate Batteries,
5¾ x 8¾ . . . . . . . . . . . . . . . . . . . . . . . .1.00

18 Bobby Labonte, Outback Steakhouse, blank
back, 6 x 4½ . . . . . . . . . . . . . . . . . . . .4.00

18 Bobby Labonte, Outback Steakhouse, invitation,
6 x 4½ . . . . . . . . . . . . . . . . . . . . . . . . .5.00

18 Bobby Labonte, Daewoo, Race Winner, MBNA
400, 5 x 4 . . . . . . . . . . . . . . . . . . . . . .2.00

18 Bobby Labonte, Daewoo, Race Winner, Pocono
500, 5 x 4 . . . . . . . . . . . . . . . . . . . . . .2.00

18 Bobby Labonte, Daewoo, Race Winner, Penn-
sylvania 500, 5 x 4 . . . . . . . . . . . . . . .2.00

18 Bobby Labonte, Daewoo, Race Winner, Pepsi
400, 5 x 4 . . . . . . . . . . . . . . . . . . . . . .2.00

18 Bobby Labonte, Daewoo, Race Winner, NAPA
500, 5 x 4 . . . . . . . . . . . . . . . . . . . . . .2.00

18 Bobby Labonte, Coca-Cola Racing Family,
5½ x 8½ . . . . . . . . . . . . . . . . . . . . . . . .6.00

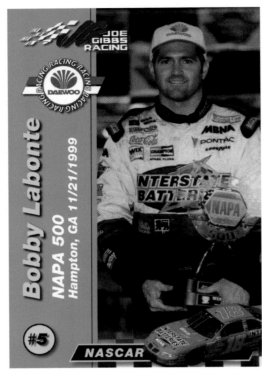

18 Bobby Labonte, Daewoo, Race Winner, NAPA 500, 5 x 4 . . . . . . . . . . . . . . . . . . . . . . .2.00

19 Tom Hubert, Bradford White Corp, 7 x 10 . . . . . . . . . . . . . . . . . . . . . . . .2.00

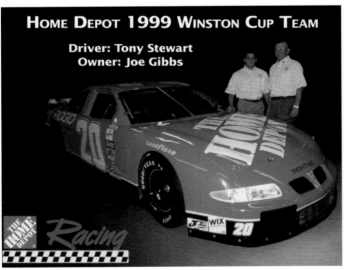

20 Tony Stewart, Home Depot, blank back, 8 x 10 . . . . . . . . . . . . . . . . . . . . . . . . .3.00

20 Tony Stewart, Home Depot, error, Stuart on back, 8 x 10 . . . . . . . . . . . . . . . . . .2.00

20 Tony Stewart, Home Depot, correct, Stewart on back, 8 x 10 . . . . . . . . . . . . . . . .1.00

20 Tony Stewart, Home Depot, behind car in uniform, 8 x 10 . . . . . . . . . . . . . . . . . . .1.00

20 Tony Stewart, Outback Steakhouse, blank back, 6 x 4½ . . . . . . . . . . . . . . . . . . . .4.00

20 Tony Stewart, Outback Steakhouse, invitation, 6 x 4½ . . . . . . . . . . . . . . . . . . . . .5.00

20 Tony Stewart, Outback Steakhouse 200, blank back, 6 x 4½ . . . . . . . . . . . . . . . . .3.00

20 Tony Stewart, Coca-Cola Racing Family, 5½ x 8½ . . . . . . . . . . . . . . . . . . . . .6.00

20 Tony Stewart, Daewoo, Race Winner, Exide 400, 5 x 4 . . . . . . . . . . . . . . . . . . . .2.00

20 Tony Stewart, Daewoo, Race Winner, Dura Lube 500K, 5 x 4 . . . . . . . . . . . . . . . .2.00

20 Tony Stewart, Daewoo, Race Winner, Jiffy Lube Miami 400, 5 x 4 . . . . . . . . . . .2.00

21 Elliott Sadler, Citgo, preview, 8½ x 11 . . .5.00
21 Elliott Sadler, Citgo, 8 x 10 . . . . . . . . . .1.00
21 Elliott Sadler, Citgo, with tear-off, 8 x 10 . . . . . . . . . . . . . . . . . . . . . . . .1.00
21 Elliott Sadler, Grand Racing, 8 x 10 . . . .1.00
22 Ward Burton, Caterpillar, in street clothes, 8 x 10 . . . . . . . . . . . . . . . . . . . . . . . .2.00
22 Ward Burton, Caterpillar, in uniform, www.Cat.com.racing on back, 8 x 10 . . .1.00
22 Ward Burton, Caterpillar, in uniform, cat merchandise on back, 8 x 10 . . . . . . . . . . .1.00
22 Ward Burton, Cat Financial, 8 x 10 . . . .2.00
22 Ward Burton, Siemens Racing, 8 x 10 . .2.00
23 Jimmy Spencer, Winston, 8½ x 11 . . . . .1.00
23 Ricky Craven, Hollywood Video, with tear-off, 8½ x 11 . . . . . . . . . . . . . . . . . . . . . . .3.00
24 Jeff Gordon, Dupont, 7¾ x 10 . . . . . . . .1.00
24 Jeff Gordon, Star Telegram, Sam Bass art, 8½ x 11 . . . . . . . . . . . . . . . . . . . . . . .3.00
24 Jeff Gordon, Ray-Ban, #55026, 4 x 6 . .3.00
24 Jeff Gordon, Ray-Ban, #55031, 4 x 6 . .3.00
25 Wally Dallenbach, Budweiser, Schrader on car, 8 x 10 . . . . . . . . . . . . . . . . . . . . . . . .1.00
25 Wally Dallenbach, Budweiser, 8 x 10 . . .2.00
25 Wally Dallenbach, Budweiser, with 1999 car, 8 x 10 . . . . . . . . . . . . . . . . . . . . . . . .1.00
26 Johnny Benson, Cheerios, Betty Crocker Series 1, 8½ x 11 . . . . . . . . . . . . . . . . .1.00
26 Johnny Benson, Cheerios, Betty Crocker Series 2, 8½ x 11 . . . . . . . . . . . . . . . . .1.00

26 Johnny Benson, Cheerios, Betty Crocker Series 2, 5½ x 8½ . . . . . . . . . . . . . .1.00
26 Johnny Benson, Pop-Secret 400, 8½ x 11 . . . . . . . . . . . . . . . . . . .2.00
28 Kenny Irwin, Havoline, with tear-off, 8½ x 11 . . . . . . . . . . . . . . . . . . .1.00
28 Kenny Irwin, Raybestos, 8 x 10 . . . . . .2.00
28 Kenny Irwin, Outback Steakhouse, blank back, 6 x 4½ . . . . . . . . . . . . . . . . . . .4.00
28 Kenny Irwin, Outback Steakhouse, invitation, 6 x 4½ . . . . . . . . . . . . . . . . . . .5.00
28 Kenny Irwin, Outback Steakhouse 200, blank back, 6 x 4½ . . . . . . . . . . . . . . .3.00
28 Kenny Irwin, Coca-Cola Racing Family, 5½ x 8½ . . . . . . . . . . . . . . . . . . .6.00
30 Derrike Cope, State Fair, Rudy's Farm, Jimmy Dean & Bryan, with tear-off, 8 x 10 . . . . . . . . . . . . . . . . . . .1.00
30 Derrike Cope, State Fair, thin stock, 8½ x 11 . . . . . . . . . . . . . . . . . . .1.00
30 Derrike Cope, Bryan, with tear-off, 10 x 8 . . . . . . . . . . . . . . . . . . .1.00
30 Derrike Cope, Harris Teeter Race Festival, blank back, 9 x 6 . . . . . . . . . . . . .2.00
30 Derrike Cope, State Fair, Rudy's Farm, Jimmy Dean & Bryan, die-cast offer, 8 x 10 . . .1.00
31 Mike Skinner, Lowe's, 8 x 10 . . . . . . . .1.00
32 Eric Norris, JaniKing, Winston West, 8 x 10 . . . . . . . . . . . . . . . . . . .2.00
33 Ken Schrader, ARP on car, 8 x 10 . . . . .1.00
33 Ken Schrader, Skoal on car, 8 x 10 . . . .2.00
33 Ken Schrader, Miller Towing Equipment, 8½ x 11 . . . . . . . . . . . . . . . . . . .2.00
36 Ernie Irvan, M&M's, black & yellow jackets on tear-off, 8 x 10 . . . . . . . . . . . . . . . . .2.00
36 Ernie Irvan, M&M's, red & yellow jackets on tear-off, 8 x 10 . . . . . . . . . . . . . . . . .1.00
36 Ernie Irvan, Mighty Auto Parts, 8 x 10 . .3.00
36 Ernie Irvan, Pedigree, 10 x 8 . . . . . . . .2.00
36 Ernie Irvan, Spy Sunglasses, 6 x 4½ . . . .2.00
40 Sterling Marlin, Coors, with tear-off, 8 x 10 . . . . . . . . . . . . . . . . . . .1.00
41 David Green, Kodiak, color photo, 7 x 5 . . . . . . . . . . . . . . . . . . .1.00
41 David Green, Kodiak, kneeling with helmet, 11 x 8½ . . . . . . . . . . . . . . . . . . .3.00
41 David Green, Kodiak, 8 x 10 . . . . . . . . .1.00
42 Joe Nemechek, Bellsouth, blank back, 8 x 10 . . . . . . . . . . . . . . . . . . .3.00
42 Joe Nemechek, Bell South, with BGN & with tear-off, 8½ x 11 . . . . . . . . . . . . . . .1.00
43 John Andretti, STP, blank back, 10 x 8 . .5.00
43 John Andretti, STP, 6 x 9 . . . . . . . . . . .1.00
43 Richard Petty, STP, 6 x 9 . . . . . . . . . . .1.00
43, 44 Richard Petty, Kyle Petty & John Andretti, Red Lobster, 10 x 8 . . . . . . . . . . .3.00
44 Kyle Petty, Coca-Cola, Go 220, 8 x 5½ . .4.00

44 Kyle Petty, Coca-Cola, without Go 220, 8 x 5½ . . . . . . . . . . . . . . . . . . .3.00
44 Kyle Petty, Hot Wheels, on track, 8½ x 11 . . . . . . . . . . . . . . . . . . .1.00
44 Kyle Petty, Hot Wheels, posed, 8½ x 11 .2.00
44 Kyle Petty, Coca-Cola Racing Family, 5½ x 8½ . . . . . . . . . . . . . . . . . . .6.00
45 Rich Bickle, 10-10-345 Lucky Dog, bust shot, 10 x 8 . . . . . . . . . . . . . . . . . . .1.00
45 Rich Bickle, 10-10-345 Lucky Dog, bust shot, more information on back, 10 x 8 . . . . .2.00
45 Rich Bickle, 10-10-345 Lucky Dog, sweepstakes card, 11 x 8½ . . . . . . . . . . . . .1.00
45 Rich Bickle, 10-10-345 Lucky Dog, thin stock, 5½ x 8½ . . . . . . . . . . . . . . . . . . .1.00
45 Rich Bickle, 10-10-345 Lucky Dog, bust shot, 11 x 8½ . . . . . . . . . . . . . . . . . . .3.00
45 Rich Bickle, 10-10-345 Lucky Dog, without pictures on back, 10 x 8 . . . . . . . . . . .1.00
45 Rich Bickle, 10-10-345 Lucky Dog, with pictures on back, 10 x 8 . . . . . . . . . . .1.00
47 Billy Standridge, Team FCR, 8 x 10 . . . .1.00
50 Dan Pardus, MidWest Transit, crew chief John McQueen, 8 x 10 . . . . . . . . . . . . . .1.00
50 Dan Pardus, MidWest Transit, crew chief Jay Born, 8 x 10 . . . . . . . . . . . . . . . . .1.00
50 Ricky Craven, MidWest Transit, 8 x 10 . .1.00
55 Kenny Wallace, Square D, 8 x 10 . . . . .1.00
58 Ricky Craven, Turbine Solutions Racing, 8 x 10 . . . . . . . . . . . . . . . . . . .1.00
59 Ricky Craven, Hollywood Video, with tear-off, 8½ x 11 . . . . . . . . . . . . . . . . . . .1.00
59 Ricky Craven, Hollywood Video, with tear-off, different logo on back, 8½ x 11 . . . . . . .1.00
59 Ricky Craven, Hollywood Video, with different tear-off, 8½ x 11 . . . . . . . . . . . . . . .1.00

59 Ricky Craven, Hollywood Video, without tear-off, 8½ x 11 . . . . . . . . . . . . . . . . . . .1.00
59 Hut Stricklin, Turbine Solutions, 8 x 10 . .1.00
59 Mark Gibson, Hollywood Video, with tear-off, 8½ x 11 . . . . . . . . . . . . . . . . . . .1.00

60 Geoffrey Bodine, Power Team, with Joe Bessey & #6 BGN, 8 x 10 . . . . . . . . . . .3.00

60 Geoffrey Bodine, Power Team, with Joe Bessey #6 BGN & #14 IRL A. J. Foyt, 8 x 10. . . . . . . . . . . . . . . . . . . .1.00

60 Geoffrey Bodine, Power Team, 8 x 10 . . .1.00

60 Geoffrey Bodine, Power Team, embossed, 8 x 10 . . . . . . . . . . . . . . . . . . . . . .1.00

60 Geoffrey Bodine, Power Team, embossed, more information on back, 8 x 10 . . . . .1.00

66 Darrell Waltrip, Big K-Mart, no Route 66 logo on front, 8 x 10 . . . . . . . . . . . . . . . .3.00

66 Darrell Waltrip, Big K-Mart, Route 66, 8 x 10. . . . . . . . . . . . . . . . . . . . . . . .1.00

66 Darrell Waltrip, Big K-Mart, 5½ x 10½ . .3.00

66 Darrell Waltrip, Big K-Mart, Route 66 on hood, 8 x 10 . . . . . . . . . . . . . . . . . . . . .1.00

71 Dave Marcis, Realtree, blank back, photo stock, 8 x 10 . . . . . . . . . . . . . . . . . .3.00

71 Dave Marcis, Realtree, 8½ x 11 . . . . . .2.00

73 Ken Bouchard, Three Stooges Beer, 6 x 9 .3.00

75 Ted Musgrave, Remington, with tear-off, 8½ x 11 . . . . . . . . . . . . . . . . . . . . .1.00

75 Ted Musgrave, Polaris, 8½ x 11 . . . . . .2.00

77 Robert Pressley, Jasper, with tear-off, ATV on back, 8 x 10 . . . . . . . . . . . . . . . . .1.00

77 Robert Pressley, Jasper, with tear-off, show car on back, 8 x 10 . . . . . . . . . . . . . .1.00

77 Robert Pressley, Federal Mogul, with tear-off, 8 x 10. . . . . . . . . . . . . . . . . . . . . . .2.00

77 Robert Pressley, Federal Mogul, without tear-off, 8 x 10 . . . . . . . . . . . . . . . . . . .2.00

77 Doug Bawel, Wheels On Fire, 7 x 9 . . . .1.00

77 Joe Bean, Rudolph Foods, Winston West, 8½ x 11 . . . . . . . . . . . . . . . . . . . . .2.00

85 Kevin Richards, Monaco Enterprises, Winston West, 8½ x 11 . . . . . . . . . . . . . . . . .3.00

85 Kevin Richards, Monaco Enterprises, Las Vegas, Winston West, 8½ x 11 . . . . . .3.00

87 Ron Fellows, Bully Hill Vineyards, 6 x 9 . .3.00

88 Dale Jarrett, Quality Care, fold-over, 11 x 8½ . . . . . . . . . . . . . . . . . . . . .1.00

88 Dale Jarrett, Fleetwood, 11 x 8½ . . . . .2.00

88 Dale Jarrett, Coca-Cola, Go 220, 8 x 5½ . . . . . . . . . . . . . . . . . . . . . . .4.00

88 Dale Jarrett, Coca-Cola, without Go 220, 8 x 5½ . . . . . . . . . . . . . . . . . . . . . .2.00

88 Dale Jarrett, Outback Steakhouse 200, fold-over, 6 x 4 . . . . . . . . . . . . . . . . . . . . .2.00

88 Dale Jarrett, Outback Steakhouse 200, blank back, 6 x 4 . . . . . . . . . . . . . . . . . . .2.00

88 Dale Jarret, Coca-Cola Racing Family, 5½ x 8½ . . . . . . . . . . . . . . . . . . . . .6.00

90 Hut Srricklin, Hills Brothers, 8 x 10 . . . .2.00

90 Junie Donlavey, NesQuik, 8 x 10 . . . . . .1.00

91 Steve Grissom, 8 x 10 . . . . . . . . . . . .2.00

94 Bill Elliott, McDonald's, 8 x 10 . . . . . . . .1.00

94 Bill Elliott, McDonald's, merchandise sticker, 8 x 10 . . . . . . . . . . . . . . . . . . . . . .1.00

94 Bill Elliott, Coca-Cola, Go 220, 8 x 5½ . . .4.00

94 Bill Elliott, Coca-Cola, without Go 220, 8 x 5½ . . . . . . . . . . . . . . . . . . . . . .2.00

94 Bill Elliott, Reese's, 8 x 6½ . . . . . . . . .1.00

94 Bill Elliott, Team Stihl, 8½ x 11 . . . . . . .2.00

94 Bill Elliott, Coca-Cola Racing Family, 5½ x 8½ . . . . . . . . . . . . . . . . . . . . .6.00

94 Bill Elliott, Platinum Stock Car Collectible Series, 10¾ x 8¾ . . . . . . . . . . . . . . .2.00

97 Chad Little, John Deere, Haulmark trailers, 8½ x 11 . . . . . . . . . . . . . . . . . . . . .3.00

97 Chad Little, John Deere, 8½ x 11 . . . . .1.00

98 Rick Mast, Hobas Pipe, 6 x 9 . . . . . . .2.00

98 Rick Mast, Universal, photo stock, 8 x 10 .1.00

98 Rick Mast, CFW, Intelos, 8 x 10 . . . . . .2.00

98 Rick Mast, Intelos, 8 x 10 . . . . . . . . . .1.00

99 Jeff Burton, Exide Batteries, with merchandise tear-off, 8½ x 11 . . . . . . . . . . . . . . .1.00

99 Jeff Burton, Exide Batteries, with sweepstakes tear-off, 8½ x 11 . . . . . . . . . . . . . . .1.00

99 Jeff Burton, Coca-Cola, Go 220, 8 x 5½ .4.00

99 Jeff Burton, Coca-Cola, without Go 220, 8 x 5½ . . . . . . . . . . . . . . . . . . . . . .2.00

99 Jeff Burton, Mayflower Racing, 8½ x 11 .2.00

99 Jeff Burton, Parts Plus, 8½ x 11 . . . . . .2.00

99 Jeff Burton, SKF Motorsports, with tear-off, 8½ x 11 . . . . . . . . . . . . . . . . . . . . .2.00

99 Jeff Burton, Coca-Cola Racing Family, 5½ x 8½ . . . . . . . . . . . . . . . . . . . . .6.00

## 2000

1 Steve Park, Pennzoil, fold-over, 8½ x 11 . .1.00

2 Rusty Wallace, Miller Lite, 8 x 10 . . . . . .1.00

3 Dale Earnhardt, GM Goodwrench, Childress in white shirt, 8 x 10 . . . . . . . . . . . . . .10.00

3 Dale Earnhardt, GM Goodwrench, Childres in black shirt, 8 x 10 . . . . . . . . . . . . . . .5.00

3 Dale Earnhardt, GM Goodwrench, Childress, black shirt, 8 x 10 . . . . . . . . . . . . . . .5.00

3 Dale Earnhardt, Team Monte Carlo, Taz, 8½ x 11 . . . . . . . . .15.00

3 Dale Earnhardt, Purdue Chicken, with tear-off, 11 x 8½ . . . . . . . . . . . . . . . . . . . . . .8.00
4 Bobby Hamilton, Kodak Max, 8½ x 11 . . .1.00
5 Terry Labonte, Kellogg's, 11 x 8½ . . . . . .1.00
6 Mark Martin, Valvoline, 8½ x 12 . . . . . . .1.00
6 Mark Martin, NASCAR For Dummies, 6½ x 5 . . . . . . . . . . . . . . . . . . . . . . . .2.00
7 Michael Waltrip, Philips, Nations Rent, with tear-off, 8 x 10 . . . . . . . . . . . . . . . .1.00
7 Michael Waltrip, Philips, Alto, 6 x 8 . . . . .1.00

8 Dale Earnhardt, Jr, Budweiser, Born To Run, 8 x 10 . . . . . . . . . . . . . . . . . . . . . . .4.00
8 Dale Earnhardt, Jr, Budweiser, 8 x 10 . . .1.00
9 Stacy Compton, Kodiak, thin stock, 8½ x 11 . . . . . . . . . . . . . . . . . . . . . . . .1.00
9 Stacy Compton, Kodiak, 8 x 10 . . . . . . .1.00
9 Stacy Compton, Cougar Racing, 8 x 10 . . .2.00
11 Brett Bodine, Ralphs, Coca-Cola, 8½ x 11 1.00
12 Jeremy Mayfield, Mobil One, 8½ x 11 . . .1.00
13 Robby Gordon, body shot, 9 x 7 . . . . . . .2.00

13 Robby Gordon, Duracell, 8½ x 11 . . . . . .1.00
14 A. J. Foyt, Conseco, headshot, 4 x 6¼ . .1.00
14 Mike Bliss, Conseco, headshot, 4 x 6¼ . .2.00
14 Mike Bliss & A. J. Foyt, Conseco, with tear-off, 8½ x 11 . . . . . . . . . . . . . . . . . . . .1.00
14 No Driver, Conseco, car only, 4 x 6 . . . .1.00
16 Kevin Lepage, bust shot, card stock, 7 x 5 . . . . . . . . . . . . . . . . . . . . . . . .2.00
16 Kevin Lepage, For Sale By Owner, thin stock, 8 x 10 . . . . . . . . . . . . . . . . . . . . . .2.00
17 Matt Kenseth, DeWalt Tools, 8 x 10 . . .1.00
18 Bobby Labonte, Interstate Batteries, 5¾ x 8¾ . . . . . . . . . . . . . . . . . . . . . .1.00
20 Tony Stewart, Home Depot, 8½ x 11 . . .2.00
21 Elliott Sadler, Citgo, 11 x 14 . . . . . . . .1.00
21 Elliott Sadler, Goldfish, 8 x 10 . . . . . . .2.00
22 Ward Burton, Caterpillar, 8 x 10 . . . . . .1.00
22 Ward Burton, Caterpillar, more patches on uniform, 8 x 10 . . . . . . . . . . . . . . . . . .1.00
22 Ward Burton, Hobas Pipe, 8 x 10 . . . . .2.00
24 Jeff Gordon, Dupont, 8 x 10 . . . . . . . .1.00

24 Jeff Gordon, Team Monte Carlo, 8½ x 11  5.00

24 No Driver, NASCAR Cafe, car only, 9 x 4 . . 1.00
25 Jerry Nadeau, Michael Holigan, 8 x 10 . . 1.00
25 Jerry Nadeau, Michael Holigan, website added on front, 8 x 10 . . . . . . . . . . . . . . . 1.00
26 Jimmy Spencer, Big K-Mart, 8 x 10 . . . . 1.00
26 Jimmy Spencer, Big K-Mart, thin stock, 10 x 8 . . . . . . . . . . . . . . . . . . . 2.00
27 Jeff Fuller, Viagra, 5¾ x 8¾ . . . . . . . . . 1.00
28 Ricky Rudd, Texaco Havoline, 11 x 8½ . . 1.00
28 Ricky Rudd, Havoline, 8½ x 11 . . . . . . . 3.00
28 Ricky Rudd, Raybestos, 8 x 10 . . . . . . 2.00
31 Mike Skinner, Lowe's, LOWES.COM, 8 x 10 . . . . . . . . . . . . . . . . . . . . 1.00
31 Mike Skinner, Lowe's, LOWES.com, 8 x 10 . . . . . . . . . . . . . . . . . . . . 2.00
32 Scott Pruett, Tide, 5 x 7 . . . . . . . . . 2.00
32 Scott Pruett, Tide, with #97 BGN car, 8 x 10 . . . . . . . . . . . . . . . . . . . 3.00
32 Scott Pruett, Tide, 8½ x 11 . . . . . . . . 1.00
33 Joe Nemechek, Oakwood Homes, without fan club, 8 x 10 . . . . . . . . . . . . . . 2.00
33 Joe Nemechek, Oakwood Homes, with fan club, 8 x 10 . . . . . . . . . . . . . . . 1.00
34 David Green, Kendall, 8 x 10 . . . . . 1.00
36 Ken Schrader, M & M's, 8 x 10 . . . . 1.00
36 Ken Schrader, M & M's, with tear-off, 8 x 10 . . . . . . . . . . . . . . . . . . . . 1.00
40 Sterling Marlin, Coors Light, with tear-off, 8 x 10 . . . . . . . . . . . . . . . . . . . . 1.00
42 Kenny Irwin, BellSouth, with tear-off back, picture on left, 11 x 8½ . . . . . . . . . . . . 1.00
42 Kenny Irwin, BellSouth, with tear-off back, picture on right, 11 x 8½ . . . . . . . . . . . 1.00
42 Kenny Irwin, BellSouth, with tear-off writing on front, 11 x 8½ . . . . . . . . . . . . . . . 1.00
43 John Andretti, STP, blank back, 6 x 9 . . . 4.00
43 John Andretti, STP, printed back, 6 x 9 . . 1.00
43 Richard Petty, STP, 6 x 9 . . . . . . . . . . 1.00
43-44 Richard Petty, John Andretti, Kyle Petty & Adam Petty, Red Wing Shoes, 8½ x 11 . 1.00
44 Kyle Petty, Hot Wheels, 8 x 10 . . . . . . . 1.00
50 Ricky Craven, MidWest Transit, 8 x 10 . . 1.00
55 Kenny Wallace, Square D, with tear-off, 8 x 10 . . . . . . . . . . . . . . . . . . . . 1.00
55 Kenny Wallace, Cooper Lighting, 8 x 10 . 1.00
60 Geoffery Bodine, Power Team, 8 x 10 . . . 1.00
66 Darrell Waltrip, Big K-Mart, 8 x 10 . . . . 1.00
66 Darrell Waltrip, Big K-Mart, thin stock, 8 x 10 . . . . . . . . . . . . . . . . . . . . . 2.00
75 Wally Dallenbach, TBS-WCW, Cartoon Network, 8 x 10 . . . . . . . . . . . . . . . . 1.00
75 Wally Dallenbach, Red Cell Batteries, 8½ x 11 . . . . . . . . . . . . . . . . . . . 1.00
77 Robert Pressley, Jasper Engines, fold-over, 8½ x 11 . . . . . . . . . . . . . . . . . . . 1.00
88 Dale Jarrett, Quality Care & Ford Credit, fold-over, 11 x 8½ . . . . . . . . . . . . . . 1.00

90 Ed Berrier, Hills Brothers Coffee, 8 x 10 . 1.00
93 Dave Blaney, Amoco Ultimate, 8½ x 11 . . 1.00
93 Dave Blaney, Siemens, 11 x 8½ . . . . . . . 1.00
94 Bill Elliott, McDonald's Drive Thru, 8 x 10 . 1.00
94 Bill Elliott, Team Stihl, 8 x 10 . . . . . . . . 2.00
97 Chad Little, John Deere, 8½ x 11 . . . . . 1.00
99 Jeff Burton, Exide Batteries, without gloss, 8½ x 11 . . . . . . . . . . . . . . . . . . . 2.00
99 Jeff Burton, Exide Batteries, with gloss, 8½ x 11 . . . . . . . . . . . . . . . . . . . 1.00
99 Jeff Burton, Mayflower, 8½ x 11 . . . . . . 2.00
99 Jeff Burton, Parts Plus, 8½ x 11 . . . . . 2.00
99 Jeff Burton, OnSite, 8½ x 11 . . . . . . . . 2.00

## 2001

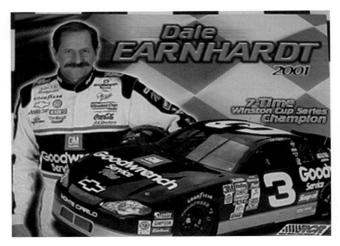

3 Dale Earnhardt, Goodwrench, 8 x 10 . . . 50.00
3 Dale Earnhardt, Hershey's Racing, with tear-off, 6½ x 11½ . . . . . . . . . . . . . . . . . . . 35.00
3 Dale Earnhardt, Bud Shootout, with Dale Jr, 8 x 10 . . . . . . . . . . . . . . . . . . . . . 50.00

3 Dale Earnhardt, Goodwrench, GMAC, yellow Corvette . . . . . . . . . . . . . . . . . . . . 40.00

# POSTERS

Posters, like driver handouts, have proven to be an invaluable marketing and public relations tool over the years. Most NASCAR posters are created with the intent to promote a sponsor, commemorate an event, or both.

More than 300 collector, worthy NASCAR posters have been printed over the years. Leading the way in terms of collectibility is the series of posters commemorating NASCAR's all-star race, The Winston. R. J. Reynolds has produced one poster per year since the race's inception in 1985. This collection is easily the most sought-after of all racing posters. Other valuable issues include posters featuring top drivers like Dale Earnhardt, Richard Petty, Jeff Gordon, etc.

Unfortunately, posters are relatively inexpensive to produce, which makes them a favorite source of income for counterfeiters. There have been quite a few reports of some of the more desirable posters — especially The Winston posters — being counterfeited. It is very important to be certain of a poster's authenticity before making a purchase — particularly if it is a big ticket item.

## ASSORTED

1989 AC Sparkplug, All Fired Up To Win, 17 x 22 . . . . . . . . . . . . . . . . . . . . . . .25.00
1990 AC Racing, "Proven Winners," 13 x 30 . . . . . . . . . . . . . . . . . . . . . . .20.00
1991 AC Racing, "Catch Us If You Can," 26 x 11 . . . . . . . . . . . . . . . . . . . . . . .15.00
1995 Atlanta, "Road To The Winston Cup," 34 x 23 . . . . . . . . . . . . . . . . . . . . . . .8.00
1995 Beauty of Speed, six girls doing pit stop on #63 car, 18 x 24 . . . . . . . . . . . . . . . . .6.00
1996 Brickyard 400, shows top 3 in 1995, 36 x 24 . . . . . . . . . . . . . . . . . . . . . . .20.00
1998 Bud Shootout, #50 car & 16 drivers, 27 x 19 . . . . . . . . . . . . . . . . . . . . . . .5.00
1999 Bud Shootout, 15 drivers, 27 x 19 . .4.00
2000 Bud Shootout, 14 drivers, 27 x 19 . .4.00
1999 Budweiser, 27 x 19 . . . . . . . . . . . .4.00
2000 Budweiser, Villwock, Bernstein & Earnhardt Jr, 27 x 19 . . . . . . . . . . . . . . . . . . . . . . .4.00
1999 Busch Beer, 1998 Busch Series Winners, 16 drivers, 27 x 19 . . . . . . . . . . . . . .3.00
1991 Busch Clash, 14 drivers, 18 x 35 . . . . . . . . . . . . . . . . . . . . . . .20.00
1994 Busch Clash, 13 drivers, Daytona in background, 22 x 34 . . . . . . . . . . . . . . . .20.00

1999 Bud Shootout, 15 drivers, 27 x 19 . .4.00

1995 Busch Clash, pole winners of 1994, 18 drivers, 28 x 20 . . . . . . . . . . . . . .10.00
1995 Busch Clash, 19 drivers, Daytona in background, 22 x 34 . . . . . . . . . . . . . . . .25.00
1996 Busch Clash, pole winner's of 1995, 17 drivers, 22 x 34 . . . . . . . . . . . . . .10.00
1997 Busch Clash, pole winners of 1996, 14 drivers, 30 x 20 . . . . . . . . . . . . . . . . .5.00

1994 Busch Clash, 13 drivers, Daytona in background, 22 x 34, . . . . . . . . . . .20.00

1996 Charlotte Motor Speedway, Coca-Cola 600 at night, 20 x 16 . . . . . . . . . . . . . .2.00
1997 Charlotte Motor Speedway, Tribute to Champions, 14 x 25 . . . . . . . . . . . . . . . .10.00

1995 Busch Clash, 19 drivers, Daytona in background, 22 x 34, . . . . . . . . . . . 25.00

1996 Busch Clash, pole winners of 1995, 17 drivers, 22 x 34 . . . . . . . . . . . . . .10.00

1990 Coca-Cola 600, "You Can't Beat The Real Thing," 22 x 34 . . . . . . . . . . . . . .35.00
1994 Chevrolet, Brickyard 400, 5 drivers, 36 x 24 . . . . . . . . . . . . . . . . . . . . . .30.00
1997 Clevite, Winston Cup, Drag & Indy cars & drivers, 21 x 28 . . . . . . . . . . . . . .20.00
1998 Coca-Cola Racing Family, 8 drivers, 16 x 20 . . . . . . . . . . . . . . . . . . . . . .5.00
1999 Coca-Cola Wall of Speed at Ocean Center, Daytona, 22 x 14 . . . . . . . . . . . . .5.00
1999 Coca-Cola Racing Family, 11 drivers, 18 x 24 . . . . . . . . . . . . . . . . . . . . .5.00
2000 Coca-Cola Racing Family, 10 drivers, 24 x 36 . . . . . . . . . . . . . . . . . . . . .4.00
1991 Darlington, State Newspaper, Southern 500 Winners, 13 x 18 . . . . . . . . . . . . . .5.00
1992 Daytona RaceFest, 21 drivers, 22 x 28 . . . . . . . . . . . . . . . . . . . .10.00

1994 Chevrolet, Brickyard 400, 5 drivers, 36 x 24 . . . . . . . . . . . . . . . . . . . . .30.00
1993 Daytona Motorsports Expo, 22 old time drivers, 33 x 22 . . . . . . . . . . . . . . .10.00
1998 Daytona News Journal, 50th Anniversary logo, 12" x 18" . . . . . . . . . . . . . . . . .5.00
1998 Daytona News Journal, Night Moves, July 2, 11 x 17 . . . . . . . . . . . . . . . . . . .3.00
1995 Dixie Sports, 1995 WC schedule with 4 drivers, 23 x 17 . . . . . . . . . . . . . . . .5.00
1997 Exide Batteries, 20 drivers, 36 x 24 . . . . . . . . . . . . . . . . . . . . .7.00
2000 Florida Today, 7 drivers with cars & 1 truck, 21 x 13 . . . . . . . . . . . . . . . . . . . .2.00
1992 Ford, Manufacturers Champion, 15 drivers, 36 x 24 . . . . . . . . . . . . . . . . . . .20.00
1993 Ford, Thunderbird, 20 drivers & their cars, 24 x 36 . . . . . . . . . . . . . . . . . . . .10.00
1993 Ford, "Racing Into The Future," 24 x 36 . . . . . . . . . . . . . . . . . . . . . . .10.00
1995 Ford, 21 drivers & their Winston cup cars, 22 x 36 . . . . . . . . . . . . . . . . . . . .10.00
1997 Ford, 23 drivers & their Winston cup cars, 36 x 24 . . . . . . . . . . . . . . . . . . . .7.00
1997 Ford, 14 drivers & their NASCAR trucks, 36 x 24 . . . . . . . . . . . . . . . . . . . .7.00

1998 Coca-Cola Racing Family, 8 drivers, 16 x 20 . . 5.00

1995 Ford, 23 drivers & their Winston Cup Cars, 22 x 36 . . . . . . . . . . . . . . . . . . . . . . .10.00

1990 Gatorade, 1989 Circle Of Champions, 23 x 18 . . . . . . . . . . . . . . . . . . . . . . .25.00

1993 Gatorade, 1992 Circle Of Champions, 36 x 23 . . . . . . . . . . . . . . . . . . . . . . .20.00

1994 Gatorade, 1993 Circle Of Champions, 24 x 16 . . . . . . . . . . . . . . . . . . . . . . .20.00

1995 Gatorade, action art & 1995 WC schedule, 24 x 16 . . . . . . . . . . . . . . .2.00

1997 Gateway, Gateway 300 Inaugural Year, 28 x 22 . . . . . . . . . . . . . . . . . . . . . . .10.00

1999 Gateway, Carquest 250, #3 & #17 Busch Series cars, 26 x 17 . . . . . . . . . . . . .8.00

1977 GoodYear ad, Foyt, Gant, Allison & Yarborough, 18 x 23 . . . . . . . . . . . . . . .100.00

1993 GoodYear, Wallace, Foyt, Mansell, Gurney & Glidden, 28 x 22 . . . . . . . . . . . . . . .40.00

1999 GoodYear, "Wherever Thunder Rolls," 46 drivers, 11 x 38 . . . . . . . . . . . . . . .5.00

2000 GoodYear, Class of 2000, 47 drivers, 11 x 34 . . . . . . . . . . . . . . . . . . . . . . .4.00

1993 Goody's Powders, race card offer ad, 23 x 18 . . . . . . . . . . . . . . . . . . . . . . .15.00

1990 IROC, IROC Breakthrough Dodge Daytona, 31 x 18 . . . . . . . . . . . . . . . . . . . . . . .3.00

1992 IROC, Dodge IROC cars, 34 x 22 . . . .3.00

1993 IROC, Wallace, Earnhardt & Rudd, with IROC cars, 36 x 23 . . . . . . . . . . . . . .25.00

185

1977 GoodYear ad, Foyt, Gant, Allison & Yarborough, 18 x 23 . . . . . . . .100.00

1995 IROC, Dodge IROC cars, 16 x 32 . . . .3.00

1999 IROC, Pontiac IROC car, 12 drivers, 22 x 34 . . . . . . . . . . . . . . . . . . . . . . . .5.00

1992 "The Front Row Gang," Bill Elliott & Sterling Marlin, 16 x 24 . . . . . . . . . . . . . . . . .6.00

2000 Lowe's Motor Speedway, CarQuest 300, 29 x 23 . . . . . . . . . . . . . . . . . . . . . .4.00

1994 McCord Gaskets, #11, #75, #21, #31 & assorted racers, 20 x 28 . . . . . . . . . .8.00

1999 Memphis Motorsports, #3 & #16 trucks, 23 x 17 . . . . . . . . . . . . . . . . . . . . . . .2.00

1999 Memphis Motorsports, #3 & #17 Busch Series, 23 x 17 . . . . . . . . . . . . . . . . . .3.00

1996 Miller Genuine Draft, "Awesome Threesome," 30 x 20 . . . . . . . . . . . . . . . . .5.00

1996 Moog, 30 Years, 30 Champions, One Ball Joint, 24 x 16 . . . . . . . . . . . . . . . . . . .6.00

1997 Moog, 31 Years, 31 Champions, One Ball Joint, 24 x 16 . . . . . . . . . . . . . . . . . . .2.00

1998 Moog, 32 Years, 32 Champions, One Ball Joint, 24 x 18 . . . . . . . . . . . . . . . . . . .2.00

1999 Moog, 33 Years, 33 Champions, One Ball Joint, 24 x 16 . . . . . . . . . . . . . . . . . . .2.00

1998 Nashville, Tailgate '98, #16 & #86 trucks, 23 x 18 . . . . . . . . . . . . . . . . . . . . . . .4.00

1979 Native Tan, "Great Moments In Racing," 24 x 35 . . . . . . . . . . . . . . . . . . . .100.00

1994 North Carolina, The Motorsports Capital of the World, 20 x 25 . . . . . . . . . . . . . . .7.00

1998 Pennzoil, Team Pennzoil 13 drivers, 11 x 35 .5.00

2000 GoodYear, Class of 2000, 47 drivers, 11 x 34 . . . .4.00

1999 IROC, Pontiac IROC car, 12 drivers, 22 x 34 . . . . . 5.00

1988 Pontiac, #27, #43, #50, #62, #75 & #89 cars, 24 x 18 . . . . . . . . . . . . . . . .15.00

1994 Pontiac, #22, #30, #40, #42 & #43 cars, Sam Bass art, 28 x 21 . . . . . . .3.00

1997 The Post-Crescent, Legends of WIR, 15 drivers, 14 x 22 . . . . . . . . . . . . . . . .15.00

1997 Quaker State, Labonte, Hendrick, Gordon, & Schrader, 23 x 30 . . . . . . . . . . . .20.00

1997 Star, Telegram, Texas 500, Wanted, three horsemen, 23 x 18 . . . . . . . . . . . . . .10.00

1986 Stewart-Warner, B. Elliott, J. Rutherford & D. Garlits, 28 x 22 . . . . . . . . . . . . . .30.00

1995 Stock Car Racing, Atlanta Speedway, 1st lap action shot, 21 x 16 . . . . . . . . . . . . . .2.00

1996 Sunoco, National Missing Children's Day, 17 x 23 . . . . . . . . . . . . . . . . . . . . . . .3.00

1997 Quaker State, Labonte, Hendrick, Gordon & Schrader, 23 x 30 . . .20.00

1997 Star-Telegram, Texas 500, Wanted, three horsemen, 23 x 18 . . . . . . . . . . . . .10.00

1986 Stewart-Warner, B. Elliott, J. Rutherford & D. Garlits, 28 x 22 . . . . . . . . . . . . .30.00

1994 Team Manheim, Robert Pressley & Harry Gant, 22 x 28 . . . . . . . . . . . . . . .10.00
1993 Team Valvoline, Mark Martin, Joe Amato & Al Unser Jr., 22 x 18 . . . . . . . . . . . .5.00
1998 UAW, GM, #3, #5, #24, #43 & #44 cars, Sam Bass, 25 x 24 . . . . . . . . . . . . . .5.00
1999 UAW, GM, #3,#24 & #44 cars, Sam Bass art, 21 x 22 . . . . . . . . . . . . . . . . .4.00

1990 Unocal, "We Fuel The Winners," #27, #3 & #6 Cars, 35 x 23 . . . . . . . . . . .5.00
2000 Virginia Lottery, Virginia drivers, 9 drivers, 28 x 20 . . . . . . . . . . . . . . . . . .5.00
1986 The Winston, 10 drivers, Atlanta, 24 x 30 . . . . . . . . . . . . . . . . . . .200.00
1987 The Winston, 20 drivers, 24 x 30 . .50.00
1988 The Winston, 20 drivers . . . . . . . .75.00
1989 The Winston, 20 drivers . . . . . . .65.00
1990 The Winston, 20 drivers . . . . . . . .50.00
1991 The Winston, 20 drivers . . . . . . . .50.00
1992 The Winston, 20 drivers, "The Winston At Night," 23 x 39 . . . . . . . . . . . . . .50.00
1993 The Winston, 20 drivers, 26 x 28 . .35.00
1996 Winston Cup Wives, 2nd Annual Cruise, 12 drivers, 16 x 20 . . . . . . . . . . . . . .10.00
1994 Winston Select, 20 drivers, 37 x 24 . . . . . . . . . . . . . . . . . . . . .35.00

1995 Winston Select, 21 drivers, 20 cars, 23 x 23 . . . . . . . . . . . . . . . . . . . . .20.00
1996 Winston Select, The Waltrips plus 19 other drivers, 39 x 24 . . . . . . . . . . . . . . .20.00
1997 Winston Select, 20 drivers, 16 x 72 . . . . . . . . . . . . . . . . . . . . .20.00
1998 Winston Select, 20 drivers, 12 x 39 . . . . . . . . . . . . . . . . . . . . .15.00
1999 Winston Thunder Theater, 15 x 23 . . . . . . . . . . . . . . . . . . .5.00
1993 WTQR, Charlotte at Night, 10 x 17 . .2.00

### INDIVIDUAL

Glenn Allen, 1997 Luxair, with #99 Busch Series car, 18 x 24 . . . . . . . . . . . . . . . . . .7.00

Loy Allen, 1995 NC Highway Patrol, "Click It Or Ticket," 27 x 19 . . . . . . . . . . . . . . .5.00
Bobby Allison, 1994 Pit Stop, Pit Stop Thirst Refresher ad, 24 x 18 . . . . . . . . . . .20.00

Bobby Allison, 1984 Quaker State, headshot art, 18 x 12 . . . . . . . . . . . . . . . . . . .25.00
Bobby Allison & Hut Stricklin, 1992 Raybestos, #12 WC car, 18 x 24 . . . . . . . . . . . . .5.00
Davey Allison, 1988 IROC XII, Chevrolet, IROC schedule, 26 x 36 . . . . . . . . . . . . . . .5.00

Davey Allison, 1994 IROC, introducing Dodge, 16 x 40 . . . . . . . . . . . . . . . . . . . . .25.00
Buddy Baker, 1985 Gunk, with #88 Liquid Wrench Car, 16 x 20 . . . . . . . . . . . . . . . .25.00
Johnny Benson, 1996 Homestead, 2nd annual Jiffy Lube Miami 300, 36 x 24 . . . . . .10.00
Brett Bodine, 1995 Team Lowe's, Lowe's Building Supply, 22 x 28 . . . . . . . . . . . . . . .3.00
Todd Bodine, 1995 Adidas, with #75 Winston Cup car, 25 x 16 . . . . . . . . . . . . . . . .5.00
Neil Bonnett, 1987 Team Valvoline, #75 car, 22 x 17 . . . . . . . . . . . . . . . . . . . . .20.00
Chuck Bown, 1993 Nescafe/Nestea, with #63 Busch Series car, 16 x 20 . . . . . . . . .5.00
Jeff Burton, 1994 Raybestos, #8 WC, pit stop 18 x 24 . . . . . . . . . . . . . . . . . . . .10.00
Jeff Burton, 2000 SKF/CR, 2000 schedule, 24x18 . . . . . . . . . . . . . . . . . . . . . . .2.00
Rick Carelli, 1993 Chesrown, 1993 Winston West Champion, 18 x 24 . . . . . . . . . . .7.00
T. J. Clark, 1996 TJ Clark Racing, with #23 SuperTruck, 16 x 23 . . . . . . . . . . . . .5.00
Ricky Craven, 1998 Budweiser, #50 Budweiser car, 27 x 19 . . . . . . . . . . . . . . . . . .2.00
Wally Dallenbach Jr., 1992 Keystone Beer, #16 car on track, 15 x 22 . . . . . . . . . . . .3.00
Wally Dallenbach Jr., 1992 Keystone Beer, #16 car with 5 girls, 20 x 15 . . . . . . . . . .3.00
Bobby Dotter, 1995 Hyde Tools, NC Air National Guard, 26 x 38 . . . . . . . . . . . . . .10.00
Dale Earnhardt, 1991 Sam Bass, 5-Time Champion, 24 x 20 . . . . . . . . . . . . . . . .25.00
Dale Earnhardt, 1999 Bud, "Countdown to E Day," Sam Bass art, 24 x 18 . . . . . . . .20.00
Dale Earnhardt, 1995 Busch Beer, "True Champion" at Brickyard, 26 x 16 . . . . . . . . . . . . . . . . . .25.00
Dale Earnhardt, 1999 Busch Beer, in hunting gear, 27 x 19 . . . . . . . . . . . . . . . . .35.00
Dale Earnhardt, 2000 Busch Beer, "Legends of the Track," 27 x 19 . . . . . . . . . . . . .25.00

Davey Allison, 1989 Havoline, side view of #28 car, 15 x 39 . . .20.00

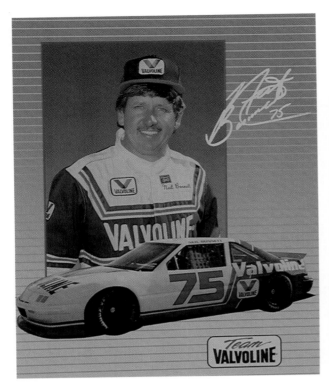

Neil Bonnett, 1987 Team Valvoline, #75 car, 22 x 17 . . . . . . . . . . . . . . . . . . . . . . .20.00

Dale Earnhardt, 1986 Cannon Libraries, "READ," 25 x 19 . . . . . . . . . . . . . . . . . . . . .300.00

Dale Earnhardt, 1998 Daytona News Journal, Daytona 500 Win, 23 x 15 . . . . . . . .20.00
Dale Earnhardt, 2000 Florida Today, 13 x 11 . . . . . . . . . . . . . . . . . . . . . .10.00

Crew Chief Kirk Shelmerdine and the GM Goodwrench team: World record holders and winners of four consecutive Unocal 76 Pit Crew Championships.

**General Motors Parts**

Dale Earnhardt, 1989 GM Parts, Flying Aces, #3 car, 34 x 24 . . . . . . . . . . . . . . . . . .85.00
Dale Earnhardt, 1997 Good Year, "What It Takes To Win," 20 x 24 . . . . . . . . . . . . . .25.00
Dale Earnhardt, 1999 GM Goodwrench, Dale & Dale Jr., 16 x 20, 15,000 . . . . . . . . .40.00
Dale Earnhardt, 1994 Goodwrench Racing, Six-Time Champion, 21 x 28 . . . . . . . . .30.00
Dale Earnhardt, 1991 Heinz, 1989, 90 Winner Southern 500, 24 x 16 . . . . . . . . . .35.00
Dale Earnhardt, 1992 High Point Police, 24 x 18 . . . . . . . . . . . . . . . . . . . . . .100.00
Dale Earnhardt, 1995 Monte Carlo, "An American Racer Reborn," 17 x 22 . . . . . . . . . .20.00
Dale Earnhardt, 1986 Unocal, '86 Pit Crew Champ, #3 Wrangler, 22 x 28 . . . . . .75.00
Dale Earnhardt, 1991 Unocal, "King of the Hill," 36 x 24 . . . . . . . . . . . . . . . . .100.00
Dale Earnhardt, 1992 Unocal, "Still King of the Hill," 36 x 24 . . . . . . . . . . . . . . . . .50.00

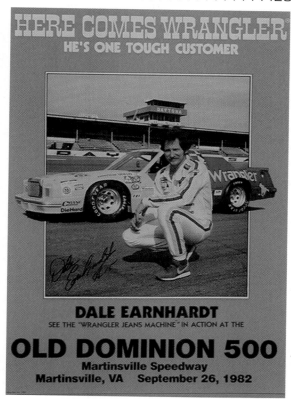

Dale Earnhardt, 1994 Unocal, Earn It,
28 x 22 . . . . . . . . . . . . . . . . . . . .50.00
Dale Earnhardt, 1994 Unocal, #3 WC car,
36 x 26 . . . . . . . . . . . . . . . . . . . .25.00

Dale Earnhardt, 1991 Heinz, 1989 – 90 Winner
Southern 500, 24 x 16 . . . . . . . . . .35.00

Dale Earnhardt, 1982 Wrangler, Old Dominion
500 ad, 22 x 16 . . . . . . . . . . . . . . .75.00

Dale Earnhardt, 1992 Unocal, "Still King of the
hill," 36 x 24 . . . . . . . . . . . . . . . .50.00

Dale Earnhardt, 1994 Western Steer, 1993
Champion, 24 x 18 . . . . . . . . . . . . .35.00

Dale Earnhardt, 1993 White/GMC, #3 WC car & transporter, 36 x 24 . . . . . . . . . . . . .30.00
Dale Earnhardt, 1996 David Peeler, American Stars Olympic, 32 x 24 . . . . . . . . . .25.00

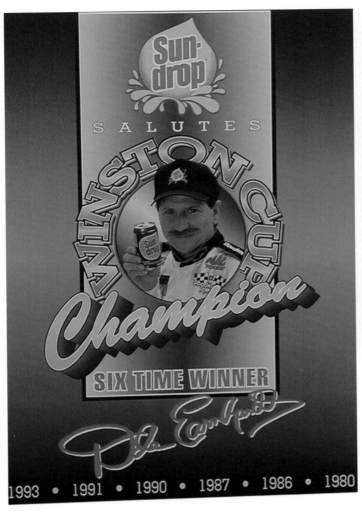

Dale Earnhardt, 1993 Sun Drop, Salutes Six-Time Champion, 28 x 18 . . . . . . . . . . .80.00
Dale Earnhardt, Jr., 1999 Budweiser, leaning on side of car, 19 x 27 . . . . . . . . . . . . .7.00
Dale Earnhardt, Jr., 1999 Budweiser, leaning on back of car, 27' x 19 . . . . . . . . . . . .7.00
Dale Earnhardt, Jr., 2000 Budweiser, "Born To Run," 19 x 27 . . . . . . . . . . . . . .4.00
Dale Earnhardt, Jr., 2000 Budweiser, Inaugural Season, 27 x 19 . . . . . . . . . . . . . .5.00
Bill Elliott, 1992 Budweiser, with #11 car & 4 girls, 20 x 28 . . . . . . . . . . . . . .7.00
Bill Elliott, 1993 Budweiser, with Junior Johnson, car & 2 girls, 20 x 28 . . . . . . . . . . .7.00
Bill Elliott, 1992 Budweiser, #11 car & 1992 schedule, 16 x 24 . . . . . . . . . . . . .5.00
Bill Elliott, 1989 Coors, 1988 Champion, 20 x 16 . . . . . . . . . . . . . . . . .15.00

Dale Earnhardt, Jr., 1999 Budweiser, leaning on back of car, 27 x 19 . . . . . . . . . . . . .7.00

Bill Elliott, 1990 Coors, display for legends poster, 31 x 22 . . . . . . . . . . . . . . . . .20.00
Bill Elliott, 1991 Fitzpatrick, art contest winner, 22 x 28 . . . . . . . . . . . . . . . . .10.00
Bill Elliott, 1996 Reese's, with assortment of #94 WC car shots, 16 x 24 . . . . . . . . . . .4.00
Tim Fedewa, 1997 Kleenex, with #33 Busch series car, 16 x 20 . . . . . . . . . . . . .4.00
Tim Fedewa, 1998 Kleenex, with #33 Busch series car, 16 x 20 . . . . . . . . . . . . .4.00
A.J. Foyt, 1992 Ray Ward, collage of A.J. Foyt stuff, 26 x 25 . . . . . . . . . . . . .20.00
Harry Gant, 1993 Farewell Tour, 25 x 20, 1 of 5000 . . . . . . . . . . . . . . . . . .5.00
Jeff Gordon, 1995 Brickyard 400, Signature Series, 21 x 17 . . . . . . . . . . . . .15.00
Jeff Gordon, 1995 Carolina Chevy Dealers, 36 x 24 . . . . . . . . . . . . . . . . . .25.00
Jeff Gordon, 1998 Darlington, The State Newspaper, 14 x 11 . . . . . . . . . . . . . . . .6.00
Jeff Gordon, 1992 Dupont, Winston Cup Debut, 18 x 23 . . . . . . . . . . . . . . . . .75.00
Jeff Gordon, 1998 Edy's Ice Cream, 24 x 18 . .7.00
Jeff Gordon, 2000 Florida Today, 13 x 11 . . .2.00
Jeff Gordon, 1994 FMC, #24 Dupont car, 24 x 30 . . . . . . . . . . . . . . . . .15.00

Dale Earnhardt, Jr., 2000 Budweiser, Inaugural
Season, 27 x 19 . . . . . . . . . . . . . . . . .5.00

Jeff Gordon, 2000 Food Lion Speed Street,
28 x 18 . . . . . . . . . . . . . . . . . . . . . . .5.00

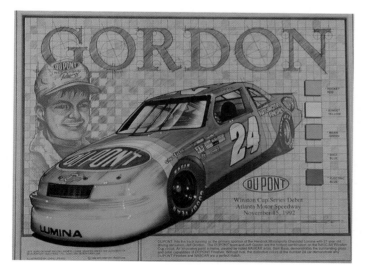

Jeff Gordon, 1992 Dupont, Winston Cup Debut,
18 x 23 . . . . . . . . . . . . . . . . . . . . . .75.00

Jeff Gordon, 1995 Carolina Chevy Dealers,
36 x 24 . . . . . . . . . . . . . . . . . . . . . .25.00

Jeff Gordon, 1999 Pepsi, Jeff Gordon & Ray
Evernham, 38 x 25 . . . . . . . . . . . . . .4.00
Robby Gordon, 1997 Coors Lite, Daytona Bike
Week, 24 x 18 . . . . . . . . . . . . . . . . .3.00
David Green, 1995 Busch Beer, girl with #95 Car,
28 x 20 . . . . . . . . . . . . . . . . . . . . . .3.00
David Green, 1997 Caterpiller, with #96 Cater-
piller car, 13 x 19 . . . . . . . . . . . . . .3.00
David Green, 1999 Kodiak, #41 car & David
green posed, 24 x 18 . . . . . . . . . . . .2.00
Jeff green, 1999 Kleenex, with #32 Busch Series
car, 36 x 24 . . . . . . . . . . . . . . . . . .4.00
Allan Grice, 1990 Thunder Dome, Debut Winner,
25 x 17 . . . . . . . . . . . . . . . . . . . . .10.00
Bobby Hamilton, 1999 Kodak, 22 x 38 . . . .2.00
Andy Hillenburg, 1994 Budget Gourmet, with #42
BGN car, 25 x 18 . . . . . . . . . . . . . .3.00
Bobby Hillin, 1993 Heilig-Meyers, Bobby Hillin &
Junie Donlavey, 22 x 28 . . . . . . . . . .10.00
Ernie Irvan, 1993 Kodak, 14 x 15 . . . . . .5.00

Allan Grice, 1990 Thunder Dome, Debut Winner, 25 x 17 . . . . . . . . . . . . . . . . . . . . . . .10.00

Ernie Irvan, 1997 Krispy Kreme, 11 x 17 . . .4.00
Kenny Irwin, 2000 BellSouth Mobility, Kenny Irwin with car, 17 x 11 . . . . . . . . . . . . . . . . . . .3.00

Dale Jarrett, 1999 Fleetwood, 36 x 24 . . . .3.00
Dale Jarrett, 2000 Florida Today, 13 x 11 . . . . . . . . . . . . . . . . . . . . . .2.00
Dale Jarrett & Dale Earnhardt, 1993 Wix Filters, Daytona 500 Finish, 12 x 40 . . . . . . .10.00
Dale Jarrett, 1995 photo file, Havoline, 35 x 23 . . . . . . . . . . . . . . . . . . . . . .7.00
Dale Jarrett, 1998 Quality Care, with action shot of #88 car, 24 x 36 . . . . . . . . . . . . . .5.00
Matt Kenseth, with Andy Hillenburg, 1999 Luxair, 24 x 17 . . . . . . . . . . . . . . . .4.00
Matt Kenseth & Jason Schuler, 2000 Visine, 27 x 18 . . . . . . . . . . . . . . . . . . . . . .3.00
Alan Kulwicki, 1993 Charlotte Motor Speedway, 18 x 26, 10,000 . . . . . . . . . . . . . .10.00
Alan Kulwicki, 1993 Hooter's, "Forever Champi- ons," 28 x 22 . . . . . . . . . . . . . . . . . .25.00
Alan Kulwicki, 1993 Toro Wheel Horse, In Memoriam, 18 x 24 . . . . . . . . . . . . .20.00
Bobby Labonte, 2000 Florida Today, 13 x 11 . . . . . . . . . . . . . . . . . . . . . .2.00
Bobby Labonte, 1993 Maxwell House, store aisle hanging ad, 21 x 31 . . . . . . . . . . . .80.00
Bobby Labonte, 1992 Sunoco, All Stars, #44 & assorted racers, 22 x 17 . . . . . . . . .4.00
Terry Labonte, 1998 Darlington, The State News- paper, 14 x 11 . . . . . . . . . . . . . . . . .3.00
Tracy Leslie, 1993 Michigan Speedway, Detroit Gasket 200, #72 Busch, 34 x 24 . . . . .7.00
Dave Marcis, 1996 Prodigy, #71 car, 31 x 24 . . . . . . . . . . . . . . . . . . . . . .3.00
Sterling Marlin, 1998 Coors Lite, Welcome Race Fans Daytona, 24 x 18 . . . . . . . . . . .2.00
Sterling Marlin, 1998 Coors Lite, "Flag One Down," 19 x 27 . . . . . . . . . . . . . . . . .2.00

Alan Kulwicki, 1993 Toro Wheel Horse, In Memoriam, 18 x 24 . . . . .20.00

Sterling Marlin, 2000 Coors Lite, WC schedule, #40 car on can, 28 x 22 . . . . . . . . . .2.00
Sterling Marlin, 1994 Kodak, transporter & equipment, 14 x 37 . . . . . . . . . . . . . .4.00
Sterling Marlin, 1995 Kodak Gold, Perfectly Focused, 20 x 38 . . . . . . . . . . . . . .3.00

Mark Martin, 1994 York Barbell, with #6 car, 27 x 36 . . . . . . . . . . . . . . . . . . . . . .20.00

Sterling Marlin, 1991 Maxwell House, with Junior Johnson, 26 x 20 . . . . . . . . . . . . . .10.00
Mark Martin, 2000 Florida Today, #60 Busch Series, 13 x 11 . . . . . . . . . . . . . .2.00
Mark Martin, 1999 Good Year, Mark Martin & Dennis Ritchie, 28 x 22 . . . . . . . . . . .3.00
Mark Martin, 1999 Valvoline, A Decade Of Speed, 1 car, 19 x 26 . . . . . . . . . . . . .3.00
Mark Martin, 1999 Valvoline, A Decade Of Speed, 3 cars, 19 x 26 . . . . . . . . . . . . .3.00
Mark Martin, 2000 Valvoline, 19 x 26 . . . .3.00
Mark Martin, 1994 York Barbell, with #6 car, 27 x 36 . . . . . . . . . . . . . . . . . . . .20.00
Rick Mast, 1997 Remington, #75 car in bullet shape, 10 x 28 . . . . . . . . . . . . . .2.00
Jeremy Mayfield, 1997 K-Mart, Go Straight To The Winner's Circle, 33 x 24 . . . . . . .2.00
Mike McLaughlin, 1994 Hyde Tools, NC Air National Guard, 26 x 38 . . . . . . . . . .10.00

Jimmy Means, 1991 Alka-Seltzer, Thunder & Thrills, car #52, 18 x 22 . . . . . . . . . . .3.00
Michigan Speedway, 1970 Motor State 500, 36x24 . . . . . . . . . . . . . . . . . . . . .100.00
Miss Mopar, 1991 Mopar, 23 x 39 . . . . . .4.00
Miss Mopar, 1992 Mopar, 36 x 27 . . . . . .4.00
Miss Mopar, 1993 Mopar, 22 x 17 . . . . . .4.00
Rob Moroso, 1990 Busch Beer, 1989 BGN Champion, 20 x 28 . . . . . . . . . . . . . .10.00
Ted Musgrave, 1998 Polaris, with #75 car & ATV on trailer, 11 x 16 . . . . . . . . . . . . . .5.00
None, 1994 Brickyard 400, Signature Series, 21 x 17 . . . . . . . . . . . . . . . . . . . .15.00
None, 1997 Budweiser, #25 car, 28 x 20 . .2.00
None, 1998 Budweiser, "Take the Lead," 27 x 19 . . . . . . . . . . . . . . . . . . . . . . .2.00
None, 1998 Budweiser, Bud car with girl taking off uniform, 28 x 20 . . . . . . . . . . . . .4.00
None, 2000 Exxon Superflo, #63 Busch Grand National Car, 20 x 30 . . . . . . . . . . . . .2.00
None, 1990 Days Of Thunder, movie poster, art, 32 x 21 . . . . . . . . . . . . . . . . . . . .20.00
None, 1997 WTQR, The Future is Now, Texas & California Tracks, 26 x 17 . . . . . . . . . .2.00
Steve Park, 1999 Homestead Pennzoil 400, Inaugural Race, 24 x 18 . . . . . . . . . . . . . .5.00
Steve Park, 1998 Pennzoil, Rookie of Year Canidate, 16 x 21 . . . . . . . . . . . . . . . .2.00
Kyle Petty, 1997 Rick Locklair, "Leading the Way," 16 x 12 . . . . . . . . . . . . . . . . . .5.00
Kyle Petty, 1991 Mello-Yello, Drink Price Ad, 28 x 18 . . . . . . . . . . . . . . . . . . . . . .5.00
Kyle Petty, 1998 Kyle Petty Charity Ride Across America, 28 x 20 . . . . . . . . . . . . . .3.00
Kyle Petty, 1999 Kyle Petty Charity Ride Across America, 28 x 20 . . . . . . . . . . . . . .3.00

Lee Petty, 1995 Living Legends, #42 car beach
racing, 17 x 11 . . . . . . . . . . . . . . . .8.00
Richard Petty, 1989 American Motors, "Has A
Checkered Past," 32 x 21 . . . . . . . .30.00
Richard Petty, 1992 Atlanta Journal, "Long Live
The King," 17 x 11 . . . . . . . . . . . .10.00
Richard Petty, 1992 Champion, Sam Bass art,
19 x 12 . . . . . . . . . . . . . . . . . .10.00
Richard Petty, 1991 Goody's, with #43, J.Dilling-
ham, 24 x 18 . . . . . . . . . . . . . . .35.00
Richard Petty, 1997 Homestead, Florida Dodge
Dealers 400, 36 x 24 . . . . . . . . . .10.00

Richard Petty, 1983 Hot Rod Magazine, "The
Racer's Edge," 17 x 24 . . . . . . . . .100.00
Richard Petty, 1992 L Tech, with Tech Welding &
Cutting Systems, 30 x 19 . . . . . . . .10.00

Richard Petty, 1987 Oakwood Homes 500, Charlotte, 24 x 19 . . . . . . . . . . . . . . .150.00

Richard Petty, 1987 Oakwood Homes 500, Char-
lotte, calendar, 24 x 18 . . . . . . . . . .40.00
Richard Petty, 1992 Pepsi, Pepsi Bottle Price ad,
22 x 12 . . . . . . . . . . . . . . . . . .10.00
Richard Petty, 1992 Fan Appreciation Tour, Geor-
gia Dome, 24 x 18 . . . . . . . . . . . .7.00
Richard Petty, 1993 "King Of The Rock," Food
Lion, Pepsi, 36 x 24 . . . . . . . . . . .15.00

Richard Petty, 1993 Pontiac, "The King Will
Always Rule," 24 x 26 . . . . . . . . . .15.00
Richard Petty, 1985 STP, 7 Time Champion, 21 x
28 . . . . . . . . . . . . . . . . . . . .100.00
Richard Petty, 1988 STP, #43 car at wind tunnel,
WC schedule, 18 x 24 . . . . . . . . . .50.00

Richard Petty, 1994 Thomasville Police, R.
Petty/D.A.R.E., 18 x 24 . . . . . . . . .20.00
Shawna Robinson, 1993 Polaroid, with #35
Busch Series car, 24 x 18 . . . . . . . .10.00
Ricky Rudd, 1987 Robert B. Neiman, Motorcraft
500, #15 WC car, 18 x 24 . . . . . . . .25.00
Ricky Rudd, 1992 Tide, 1992 schedule, art work
of #5 Tide car, 24 x 18 . . . . . . . . . .5.00

Ricky Rudd, 1993 Tide, Ricky Rudd with #5 car & Tide racing boat, 21 x 29 . . . . . . . . . .5.00
Ricky Rudd, 1995 Tide, Ricky Rudd with #10 car, 19 x 28 . . . . . . . . . . . . . . . . . .4.00
Ricky Rudd, 1996 Tide, Ricky Rudd with #10 car, 19 x 27 . . . . . . . . . . . . . . . . . .2.00
Ricky Rudd & Darrell Waltrip, 1997 Tide, 10th Anniv. of Tide Racing, 19 x 27 . . . . . . .2.00
Ricky Rudd, 1998 Tide, Ricky Rudd with #10 car, art work, 19 x 27 . . . . . . . . . . . . . .2.00
Ricky Rudd, 1999 Tide, Ricky Rudd with #10 car, 19 x 27 . . . . . . . . . . . . . . . . . .2.00
Joe Ruttman, 1999 Dana, #18 Craftsman Truck, 24 x 33 . . . . . . . . . . . . . . . . . .2.00
Felix Sabates, 1999 Coors Lite, with #40 car, 19 x 27 . . . . . . . . . . . . . . . . . .2.00
Elton Sawyer, 1998 Barbasol, with #38 BGN car, 20 x 30 . . . . . . . . . . . . . . . . . .7.00
Ken Schrader, 1994 Budweiser, #25 car pit stop, 20 x 28 . . . . . . . . . . . . . . . . . .3.00
Ken Schrader, 1995 Budweiser, #25 car, 20 x 28 . . . . . . . . . . . . . . . . . .3.00
Ken Schrader, 1992 Kodiak, #25 car pit stop, 24 x 16 . . . . . . . . . . . . . . . . . .5.00
Ken Schrader, 2000 M&M's, in car action, 34 x 22 . . . . . . . . . . . . . . . . . .2.00
Ken Schrader, 1995 Pedigree, Ken Schrader with dog, 18 x 24 . . . . . . . . . . . . . . . .4.00
Ken Schrader, 1994 photo file, Kodiak, 23 x 35 . . . . . . . . . . . . . . . . . .5.00
Ken Schrader & Steve Kinser, 1995 Tulsa Speedway, in midgets, 17 x 21 . . . . . . . . . .4.00
Tony Stewart, 2000 Florida Today, 13 x 11 . .2.00

Linda Vaughn, 1994 Hurst, 24 x 18 . . . . .4.00
Linda Vaughn, 1999 Prolong, with hot rod Lincoln, 18 x 24 . . . . . . . . . . . . . .5.00
Linda Vaughn, 1996 Hurst, 24 x 18 . . . . .2.00
Rusty Wallace, 2000 Florida Today, 13 x 11 . . . . . . . . . . . . . . . . . .2.00
Rusty Wallace, 1997 Mead, 14 x 17 . . . . .5.00
Rusty Wallace, 1996 Miller Genuine Draft, #2 Thunderbird, 30 x 20 . . . . . . . . . . .3.00

Rusty Wallace, 1996 Miller Genuine Draft, Over The Wall Gang, 20 x 30 . . . . . . . . . . .5.00
Rusty Wallace, 1997 Miller Genuine Draft, #2 Thunderbird, 30 x 20 . . . . . . . . . . . .3.00
Rusty Wallace, 1996 Miller Lite, #2 car, 30 x 20 . . . . . . . . . . . . . . . . . .2.00
Rusty Wallace, 1997 Miller Lite, "Flying Colors," 18 x 33 . . . . . . . . . . . . . . . . . .3.00
Rusty Wallace, 1997 Miller Lite, "Wanted," Inaugural Texas 500, 26 x 19 . . . . . . . . .10.00

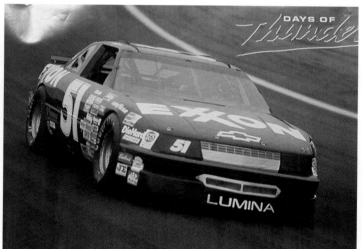

Cole Trickle, 1990 Days Of Thunder, movie poster, #51 Exxon car, 32 x 21 . . . . . . . . . .20.00
Unocal, 1990 1st Induction Ceremony, International Hall of Fame, 25 x 19 . . . . . . . . .10.00
Unocal Racestoppers, 1992 Unocal, with Camaro Z 28, 18 x 30 . . . . . . . . . . . . . . . .5.00
Linda Vaughn, 1990 Hurst, 24 x 18 . . . . .10.00

Rusty Wallace, 1997 Miller Lite, "Carolina's Most Wanted," 23 x 18 . . . . . . . . . . . . .10.00

Rusty Wallace, 1998 Miller, 25th Anniversary of Miller Racing, 30 x 20 . . . . . . . . . . .5.00

Rusty Wallace, 1998 Miller Lite, with girls, Speedweeks, 18 x 24 . . . . . . . . . . . . .5.00

Rusty Wallace, 1998 Miller Lite, with girls, Smooth Ride Clean Finish, 20 x 30 . . . .3.00

Rusty Wallace, 1998 Miller Lite, with girls, July 4th, 18 x 24 . . . . . . . . . . . . . . . .3.00

Rusty Wallace, 1998 Miller Lite, WC schedule & #2 car, 30 x 20 . . . . . . . . . . . . .2.00

Rusty Wallace, 1998 Miller Lite, "Adventures of Rusty," car in space, 30 x 20 . . . . . . .2.00

Rusty Wallace, 1998 Miller Lite, Rusty's Angels, #2 car in space, 30 x 20 . . . . . . . . . .3.00

Rusty Wallace, 1999 Miller Lite, car with two girls on Daytona Beach, 18 x 24 . . . . . . . .4.00

Rusty Wallace, 1999 Miller Lite, Rusty in bank, 30 x 20 . . . . . . . . . . . . . . . . . . .2.00

Rusty Wallace, 1999 Miller Lite, We Race For Beer, 20 x 30 . . . . . . . . . . . . . . . .3.00

Rusty Wallace, 2000 Miller Lite, with #21 Crawfish Crider, 18 x 24 . . . . . . . . . . . . .3.00

Rusty Wallace, 2000 Miller Lite, July 2000, 18 x 24 . . . . . . . . . . . . . . . . . . . . .3.00

Rusty Wallace, 1995 Keith Porter, with MGD #2 car, 28 x 22 . . . . . . . . . . . . . . .15.00

Rusty Wallace, 1995 Keith Porter, MGD #2, driver & artist, 28 x 22 . . . . . . . . . . . .20.00

Darrell Waltrip, 1981 Mountain Dew, pit stop, 22 x 17 . . . . . . . . . . . . . . . . . . . .35.00

Michael Waltrip, 1995 Homestead, Inaugural Jiffy Lube Miami 300, 24 x 24 . . . . . . . .20.00

Michael Waltrip, 1996 Winston Select, Michael plus Wood brothers, 26 x 20 . . . . . . . .5.00

Smokey Yunick, 1999 Prolong, with 1964 Indy Capsule Car, 24 x 36 . . . . . . . . . . . .3.00

Smokey Yunick, 1998 Prolong, with black & gold #13 car, 24 x 36 . . . . .5.00

# PROGRAMS

Souvenir programs have been a part of NASCAR racing from day one. Hence, programs were probably stock car racing's first collectible. Programs from Daytona's beach races are the clearly the most sought after. Traditionally, publications from inaugural events also earn high appraisals. So do programs from races that marked events — like Dale Earnhardt's first Winston Cup start, for instance.

Condition is extremely important when determining values for programs. Collectors should also be aware that race tracks have re-printed quite a few significant programs over the years.

Atlanta, fall race, 1992, Richard Petty's last race
& Jeff Gordon's first WC race . . . . . . .45.00

Atlanta, fall race, 1960 . . . . . . . . . . .110.00
Atlanta, fall race, 1961 . . . . . . . . . . . .85.00
Atlanta, fall race, 1962 . . . . . . . . . . . .65.00
Atlanta, fall race, 1963 . . . . . . . . . . . .60.00
Atlanta, fall race, 1964 . . . . . . . . . . . .50.00
Atlanta, fall race, 1965 . . . . . . . . . . . .45.00
Atlanta, fall race, 1966 . . . . . . . . . . . .45.00
Atlanta, fall race, 1967 . . . . . . . . . . . .40.00
Atlanta, fall race, 1968 . . . . . . . . . . . .40.00
Atlanta, fall race, 1969 . . . . . . . . . . . .35.00
Atlanta, fall race, 1970 . . . . . . . . . . . .30.00
Atlanta, fall race, 1971 . . . . . . . . . . . .30.00
Atlanta, fall race, 1972 . . . . . . . . . . . .30.00
Atlanta, fall race, 1973 . . . . . . . . . . . .25.00
Atlanta, fall race, 1974 . . . . . . . . . . . .25.00
Atlanta, fall race, 1975 . . . . . . . . . . . .25.00
Atlanta, fall race, 1976 . . . . . . . . . . . .20.00
Atlanta, fall race, 1977 . . . . . . . . . . . .20.00
Atlanta, fall race, 1978 . . . . . . . . . . . .20.00
Atlanta, fall race, 1979 . . . . . . . . . . . .20.00
Atlanta, fall race, 1980 . . . . . . . . . . . .15.00
Atlanta, fall race, 1981 . . . . . . . . . . . .15.00
Atlanta, fall race, 1982 . . . . . . . . . . . .15.00
Atlanta, fall race, 1983 . . . . . . . . . . . .15.00
Atlanta, fall race, 1984 . . . . . . . . . . . .15.00
Atlanta, fall race, 1985 . . . . . . . . . . . .15.00
Atlanta, fall race, 1986 . . . . . . . . . . . .15.00
Atlanta, fall race, 1987 . . . . . . . . . . . .15.00
Atlanta, fall race, 1988 . . . . . . . . . . . .15.00
Atlanta, fall race, 1989 . . . . . . . . . . . .15.00
Atlanta, fall race, 1990 . . . . . . . . . . . .15.00
Atlanta, fall race, 1991 . . . . . . . . . . . .15.00
Atlanta, fall race, 1992, Richard Petty's last race
& Jeff Gordon's first WC race . . . . . . .45.00
Atlanta, fall race, 1993 . . . . . . . . . . . .15.00
Atlanta, fall race, 1994 . . . . . . . . . . . .15.00
Atlanta, fall race, 1995 . . . . . . . . . . . .15.00
Atlanta, fall race, 1996 . . . . . . . . . . . .15.00

Atlanta, fall race, 1997 . . . . . . . . . . . .15.00
Atlanta, fall race, 1998 . . . . . . . . . . . .15.00
Atlanta, fall race, 1999 . . . . . . . . . . . .15.00
Atlanta, spring race, 1960 . . . . . . . . . .85.00
Atlanta, spring race, 1961 . . . . . . . . . .65.00
Atlanta, spring race, 1962 . . . . . . . . . .50.00
Atlanta, spring race, 1963 . . . . . . . . . .45.00
Atlanta, spring race, 1964 . . . . . . . . . .45.00
Atlanta, spring race, 1965 . . . . . . . . . .45.00
Atlanta, spring race, 1966 . . . . . . . . . .40.00
Atlanta, spring race, 1967 . . . . . . . . . .30.00
Atlanta, spring race, 1968 . . . . . . . . . .25.00
Atlanta, spring race, 1969 . . . . . . . . . .25.00
Atlanta, spring race, 1970 . . . . . . . . . .25.00
Atlanta, spring race, 1971 . . . . . . . . . .25.00
Atlanta, spring race, 1972 . . . . . . . . . .20.00
Atlanta, spring race, 1973 . . . . . . . . . .20.00
Atlanta, spring race, 1974 . . . . . . . . . .20.00
Atlanta, spring race, 1975 . . . . . . . . . .20.00
Atlanta, spring race, 1976 . . . . . . . . . .20.00
Atlanta, spring race, 1977 . . . . . . . . . .20.00
Atlanta, spring race, 1978 . . . . . . . . . .20.00
Atlanta, spring race, 1979 . . . . . . . . . .20.00
Atlanta, spring race, 1980 . . . . . . . . . .15.00
Atlanta, spring race, 1981 . . . . . . . . . .15.00
Atlanta, spring race, 1982 . . . . . . . . . .15.00
Atlanta, spring race, 1983 . . . . . . . . . .15.00
Atlanta, spring race, 1984 . . . . . . . . . .15.00

| | | |
|---|---|---|
| Atlanta, spring race, 1985 | . . . . . . . . . | .15.00 |
| Atlanta, spring race, 1986 | . . . . . . . . . | .15.00 |
| Atlanta, spring race, 1987 | . . . . . . . . . | .15.00 |
| Atlanta, spring race, 1988 | . . . . . . . . . | .15.00 |
| Atlanta, spring race, 1989 | . . . . . . . . . | .15.00 |
| Atlanta, spring race, 1990 | . . . . . . . . . | .15.00 |

| | | |
|---|---|---|
| Atlanta, spring race, 1991 | . . . . . . . . . | .15.00 |
| Atlanta, spring race, 1992 | . . . . . . . . . | .15.00 |
| Atlanta, spring race, 1993 | . . . . . . . . . | .15.00 |
| Atlanta, spring race, 1994 | . . . . . . . . . | .15.00 |
| Atlanta, spring race, 1995 | . . . . . . . . . | .15.00 |
| Atlanta, spring race, 1996 | . . . . . . . . . | .15.00 |
| Atlanta, spring race, 1997 | . . . . . . . . . | .15.00 |
| Atlanta, spring race, 1998 | . . . . . . . . . | .15.00 |
| Atlanta, spring race, 1999 | . . . . . . . . . | .15.00 |
| Atlanta, spring race, 2000 | . . . . . . . . . | .15.00 |
| Atlanta, spring race, 2001 | . . . . . . . | .45.00 |
| Charlotte 600, spring race, 1960 | . . . . | .300.00 |
| Charlotte 600, spring race, 1961 | . . . . | .140.00 |
| Charlotte 600, spring race, 1962 | . . . . | .100.00 |
| Charlotte 600, spring race, 1963 | . . . . . | .85.00 |
| Charlotte 600, spring race, 1964 | . . . . . | .80.00 |
| Charlotte 600, spring race, 1965 | . . . . . | .65.00 |
| Charlotte 600, spring race, 1966 | . . . . . | .60.00 |
| Charlotte 600, spring race, 1967 | . . . . . | .55.00 |
| Charlotte 600, spring race, 1968 | . . . . . | .60.00 |
| Charlotte 600, spring race, 1969 | . . . . . | .50.00 |
| Charlotte 600, spring race, 1970 | . . . . . | .40.00 |
| Charlotte 600, spring race, 1971 | . . . . . | .35.00 |
| Charlotte 600, spring race, 1972 | . . . . . | .35.00 |

| | | |
|---|---|---|
| Charlotte 600, spring race, 1973 | . . . . . | .35.00 |
| Charlotte 600, spring race, 1974 | . . . . . | .35.00 |

| | | |
|---|---|---|
| Charlotte 600, spring race, 1975 Dale Earnhardt's first Winston Cup race | . . . . . | 120.00 |
| Charlotte 600, spring race, 1976 | . . . . . | .30.00 |
| Charlotte 600, spring race, 1977 | . . . . . | .30.00 |
| Charlotte 600, spring race, 1978 | . . . . . | .30.00 |
| Charlotte 600, spring race, 1979 | . . . . . | .30.00 |
| Charlotte 600, spring race, 1980 | . . . . . | .25.00 |
| Charlotte 600, spring race, 1981 | . . . . . | .25.00 |
| Charlotte 600, spring race, 1982 | . . . . . | .20.00 |
| Charlotte 600, spring race, 1983 | . . . . . | .20.00 |
| Charlotte 600, spring race, 1984 | . . . . . | .20.00 |
| Charlotte 600, spring race, 1985 | . . . . . | .20.00 |
| Charlotte 600, spring race, 1986 | . . . . . | .20.00 |
| Charlotte 600, spring race, 1987 | . . . . . | .20.00 |
| Charlotte 600, spring race, 1988 | . . . . . | .20.00 |
| Charlotte 600, spring race, 1989 | . . . . . | .20.00 |
| Charlotte 600, spring race, 1990 | . . . . . | .15.00 |
| Charlotte 600, spring race, 1991 | . . . . . | .15.00 |
| Charlotte 600, spring race, 1992 | . . . . . | .15.00 |
| Charlotte 600, spring race, 1993 | . . . . . | .15.00 |
| Charlotte 600, spring race, 1994 | . . . . . | .15.00 |
| Charlotte 600, spring race, 1995 | . . . . . | .15.00 |
| Charlotte 600, spring race, 1996 | . . . . . | .15.00 |
| Charlotte 600, spring race, 1997 | . . . . . | .15.00 |
| Charlotte 600, spring race, 1998 | . . . . . | .15.00 |
| Charlotte 600, spring race, 1999 Dale Earnhardt Jr. first Winston Cup race | . . . . . . . . | .30.00 |
| Charlotte 600, spring race, 2000 | . . . . . | .15.00 |

Charlotte 500, fall race, 1960 . . . . . . . .125.00
Charlotte 500, fall race, 1961 . . . . . . . .85.00
Charlotte 500, fall race, 1962 . . . . . . . .70.00
Charlotte 500, fall race, 1963 . . . . . . . .70.00
Charlotte 500, fall race, 1964 . . . . . . . .50.00
Charlotte 500, fall race, 1965 . . . . . . . .45.00
Charlotte 500, fall race, 1966 . . . . . . . .45.00
Charlotte 500, fall race, 1967 . . . . . . . .35.00
Charlotte 500, fall race, 1968 . . . . . . . .45.00
Charlotte 500, fall race, 1969 . . . . . . . .30.00
Charlotte 500, fall race, 1970 . . . . . . . .30.00
Charlotte 500, fall race, 1971 . . . . . . . .25.00
Charlotte 500, fall race, 1972 . . . . . . . .25.00
Charlotte 500, fall race, 1973 . . . . . . . .25.00
Charlotte 500, fall race, 1974 . . . . . . . .25.00
Charlotte 500, fall race, 1975 . . . . . . . .25.00
Charlotte 500, fall race, 1976 . . . . . . . .20.00
Charlotte 500, fall race, 1977 . . . . . . . .20.00
Charlotte 500, fall race, 1978 . . . . . . . .20.00
Charlotte 500, fall race, 1979 . . . . . . . .20.00
Charlotte 500, fall race, 1980 . . . . . . . .20.00
Charlotte 500, fall race, 1981 . . . . . . . .20.00
Charlotte 500, fall race, 1982 . . . . . . . .15.00
Charlotte 500, fall race, 1983 . . . . . . . .15.00
Charlotte 500, fall race, 1984 . . . . . . . .15.00
Charlotte 500, fall race, 1985 . . . . . . . .15.00
Charlotte 500, fall race, 1986 . . . . . . . .15.00
Charlotte 500, fall race, 1987 . . . . . . . .15.00
Charlotte 500, fall race, 1988 . . . . . . . .15.00

Charlotte 500, fall race, 1990 . . . . . . . .15.00
Charlotte 500, fall race, 1991 . . . . . . . .15.00
Charlotte 500, fall race, 1992 . . . . . . . .15.00
Charlotte 500, fall race, 1993 . . . . . . . .15.00
Charlotte 500, fall race, 1994 . . . . . . . .15.00
Charlotte 500, fall race, 1995 . . . . . . . .15.00
Charlotte 500, fall race, 1996 . . . . . . . .15.00
Charlotte 500, fall race, 1997 . . . . . . . .15.00
Charlotte 500, fall race, 1998 . . . . . . . .15.00
Charlotte 500, fall race, 1999 . . . . . . . .15.00
Darlington Southern 500, 1950 . . . . . . .500.00
Darlington Southern 500, 1951 . . . . . . .250.00
Darlington Southern 500, 1952 . . . . . . .260.00
Darlington Southern 500, 1953 . . . . . . .220.00
Darlington Southern 500, 1954 . . . . . . .175.00
Darlington Southern 500, 1955 . . . . . . .175.00
Darlington Southern 500, 1956 . . . . . . .200.00

Darlington Southern 500, 1957 . . . . . . .110.00
Darlington Southern 500, 1958 . . . . . . .100.00
Darlington Southern 500, 1959 . . . . . . .100.00
Darlington Southern 500, 1960 . . . . . . .75.00
Darlington Southern 500, 1961 . . . . . . .65.00
Darlington Southern 500, 1962 . . . . . . .60.00
Darlington Southern 500, 1963 . . . . . . .50.00
Darlington Southern 500, 1964 . . . . . . .45.00
Darlington Southern 500, 1965 . . . . . . .35.00
Darlington Southern 500, 1966 . . . . . . .35.00
Darlington Southern 500, 1967 . . . . . . .35.00
Darlington Southern 500, 1968 . . . . . . .30.00
Darlington Southern 500, 1969 . . . . . . .25.00

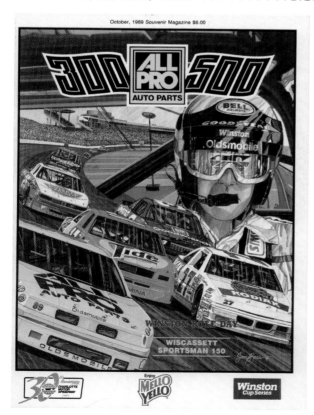

Charlotte 500, fall race, 1989 . . . . . . . .15.00

Darlington Southern 500, 1970 . . . . . . .25.00
Darlington Southern 500, 1971 . . . . . . .25.00
Darlington Southern 500, 1972 . . . . . . .25.00
Darlington Southern 500, 1973 . . . . . . .25.00
Darlington Southern 500, 1974 . . . . . . .25.00
Darlington Southern 500, 1975 . . . . . . .20.00
Darlington Southern 500, 1976 . . . . . . .20.00
Darlington Southern 500, 1977 . . . . . . .20.00
Darlington Southern 500, 1978 . . . . . . .20.00
Darlington Southern 500, 1979 . . . . . . .20.00

Darlington Southern 500, 1980 . . . . . . .20.00
Darlington Southern 500, 1981 . . . . . . .15.00
Darlington Southern 500, 1982 . . . . . . .15.00
Darlington Southern 500, 1983 . . . . . . .15.00
Darlington Southern 500, 1984 . . . . . . .15.00
Darlington Southern 500, 1985 Bill Elliott's Million
   Dollar Win . . . . . . . . . . . . . . . . . . .30.00
Darlington Southern 500, 1986 . . . . . . .15.00
Darlington Southern 500, 1987 . . . . . . .15.00
Darlington Southern 500, 1988 . . . . . . .15.00
Darlington Southern 500, 1989 . . . . . . .15.00
Darlington Southern 500, 1990 . . . . . . .15.00
Darlington Southern 500, 1991 . . . . . . .15.00
Darlington Southern 500, 1992 . . . . . . .15.00
Darlington Southern 500, 1993 . . . . . . .15.00
Darlington Southern 500, 1994 . . . . . . .15.00
Darlington Southern 500, 1995 . . . . . . .15.00
Darlington Southern 500, 1996 . . . . . . .15.00
Darlington Southern 500, 1997 . . . . . . .15.00
Darlington Southern 500, 1998 . . . . . . .15.00
Darlington Southern 500, 1999 . . . . . . .15.00

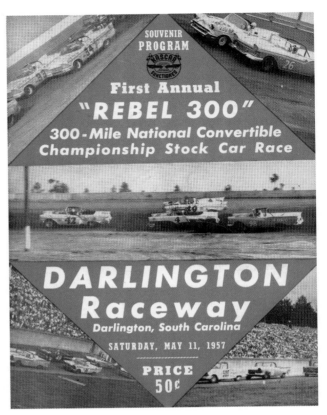

Darlington, spring race, 1957 . . . . . . . .300.00
Darlington, spring race, 1958 . . . . . . . .150.00
Darlington, spring race, 1959 . . . . . . . .100.00
Darlington, spring race, 1960 . . . . . . . .80.00
Darlington, spring race, 1961 . . . . . . . .70.00
Darlington, spring race, 1962 . . . . . . . .75.00
Darlington, spring race, 1963 . . . . . . . .45.00
Darlington, spring race, 1964 . . . . . . . .35.00
Darlington, spring race, 1965 . . . . . . . .35.00
Darlington, spring race, 1966 . . . . . . . .40.00
Darlington, spring race, 1967 . . . . . . . .40.00
Darlington, spring race, 1968 . . . . . . . .40.00
Darlington, spring race, 1969 . . . . . . . .35.00
Darlington, spring race, 1970 . . . . . . . .30.00
Darlington, spring race, 1971 . . . . . . . .20.00
Darlington, spring race, 1972 . . . . . . . .20.00
Darlington, spring race, 1973 . . . . . . . .20.00
Darlington, spring race, 1974 . . . . . . . .15.00
Darlington, spring race, 1975 . . . . . . . .15.00
Darlington, spring race, 1976 . . . . . . . .15.00
Darlington, spring race, 1977 . . . . . . . .15.00
Darlington, spring race, 1978 . . . . . . . .15.00
Darlington, spring race, 1979 . . . . . . . .15.00
Darlington, spring race, 1980 . . . . . . . .15.00
Darlington, spring race, 1981 . . . . . . . .15.00
Darlington, spring race, 1982 . . . . . . . .15.00
Darlington, spring race, 1983 . . . . . . . .15.00
Darlington, spring race, 1984 . . . . . . . .15.00
Darlington, spring race, 1985 . . . . . . . .15.00
Darlington, spring race, 1986 . . . . . . . .15.00

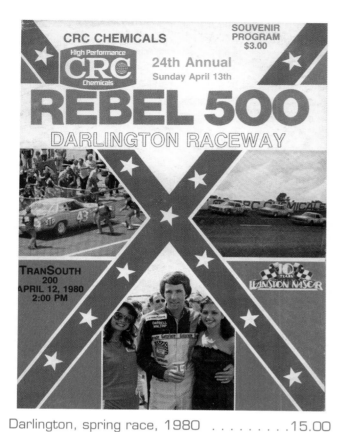

Darlington, spring race, 1980 . . . . . . . .15.00

Darlington, spring race, 1987 . . . . . . . .15.00
Darlington, spring race, 1988 . . . . . . . .15.00
Darlington, spring race, 1989 . . . . . . . .15.00
Darlington, spring race, 1990 . . . . . . . .15.00
Darlington, spring race, 1991 . . . . . . . .15.00
Darlington, spring race, 1992 . . . . . . . .15.00
Darlington, spring race, 1993 . . . . . . . .15.00
Darlington, spring race, 1994 . . . . . . . .15.00
Darlington, spring race, 1995 . . . . . . . .15.00
Darlington, spring race, 1996 . . . . . . . .15.00
Darlington, spring race, 1997 . . . . . . . .15.00
Darlington, spring race, 1998 . . . . . . . .15.00
Darlington, spring race, 1999 . . . . . . . .15.00
Darlington, spring race, 2000 . . . . . . . .15.00
Daytona Beach Course, 1948 first NASCAR
　　race . . . . . . . . . . . . . . . . . . . .1500.00
Daytona Beach Course, 1949 first . . . . .525.00
Daytona Beach Course, 1949 second . . .575.00
Daytona Beach Course, 1950 . . . . . . . .425.00
Daytona Beach Course, 1951 . . . . . . . .400.00
Daytona Beach Course, 1952 . . . . . . . .350.00
Daytona Beach Course, 1953 . . . . . . . .325.00
Daytona Beach Course, 1954 . . . . . . . .250.00
Daytona Beach Course, 1955 . . . . . . . .200.00
Daytona Beach Course, 1956 . . . . . . . .200.00
Daytona Beach Course, 1957 . . . . . . . .200.00
Daytona Beach Course, 1958 . . . . . . . .200.00
Daytona 500, 1959 . . . . . . . . . . . . . .600.00
Daytona 500, 1960 . . . . . . . . . . . . . .250.00

Daytona 500, 1961 . . . . . . . . . . . . . .150.00
Daytona 500, 1962 . . . . . . . . . . . . . .150.00
Daytona 500, 1963 . . . . . . . . . . . . . .150.00
Daytona 500, 1964 . . . . . . . . . . . . . .170.00
Daytona 500, 1965 . . . . . . . . . . . . . .100.00
Daytona 500, 1966 . . . . . . . . . . . . . . .85.00
Daytona 500, 1967 . . . . . . . . . . . . . . .75.00
Daytona 500, 1968 . . . . . . . . . . . . . . .75.00
Daytona 500, 1969 . . . . . . . . . . . . . . .55.00
Daytona 500, 1970 . . . . . . . . . . . . . . .50.00
Daytona 500, 1971 . . . . . . . . . . . . . . .60.00
Daytona 500, 1972 . . . . . . . . . . . . . . .55.00
Daytona 500, 1973 . . . . . . . . . . . . . . .50.00
Daytona 500, 1974 . . . . . . . . . . . . . . .50.00
Daytona 500, 1975 . . . . . . . . . . . . . . .45.00
Daytona 500, 1976 . . . . . . . . . . . . . . .45.00
Daytona 500, 1977 . . . . . . . . . . . . . . .45.00
Daytona 500, 1978 . . . . . . . . . . . . . . .45.00
Daytona 500, 1979 . . . . . . . . . . . . . . .45.00
Daytona 500, 1980 . . . . . . . . . . . . . . .25.00
Daytona 500, 1981 . . . . . . . . . . . . . . .25.00
Daytona 500, 1982 . . . . . . . . . . . . . . .25.00
Daytona 500, 1983 . . . . . . . . . . . . . . .25.00
Daytona 500, 1984 . . . . . . . . . . . . . . .25.00
Daytona 500, 1985 . . . . . . . . . . . . . . .25.00
Daytona 500, 1986 . . . . . . . . . . . . . . .25.00
Daytona 500, 1987 . . . . . . . . . . . . . . .25.00
Daytona 500, 1988 . . . . . . . . . . . . . . .25.00
Daytona 500, 1989 . . . . . . . . . . . . . . .25.00
Daytona 500, 1990 . . . . . . . . . . . . . . .25.00

Daytona 500, 1991 . . . . . . . . . . . . . . .55.00

| | |
|---|---|
| Daytona 500, 1992 | .20.00 |
| Daytona 500, 1993 | .20.00 |
| Daytona 500, 1994 | .20.00 |
| Daytona 500, 1995 | .20.00 |
| Daytona 500, 1996 | .20.00 |
| Daytona 500, 1997 | .20.00 |

Daytona 500, 1998 50th Anniversary, Dale
  Earnhardt win . . . . . . . . . . . . . . . . .70.00
Daytona 500, 1998 hardback edition . . .100.00
Daytona 500, 1999 Tony Stewart's first Winston
  Cup race . . . . . . . . . . . . . . . . . . . . .30.00
Daytona 500, 2000 . . . . . . . . . . . . . . .20.00
Daytona 500, 2001, Dale Earnhardt's last
  race . . . . . . . . . . . . . . . . . . . . . . .80.00
Daytona 400, July race, 1959 . . . . . . .200.00
Daytona 400, July race, 1960 . . . . . . .145.00
Daytona 400, July race, 1961 . . . . . . .125.00
Daytona 400, July race, 1962 . . . . . . .85.00
Daytona 400, July race, 1963 . . . . . . .80.00
Daytona 400, July race, 1964 . . . . . . .65.00
Daytona 400, July race, 1965 . . . . . . .50.00
Daytona 400, July race, 1966 . . . . . . .40.00
Daytona 400, July race, 1967 . . . . . . .40.00
Daytona 400, July race, 1968 . . . . . . .35.00
Daytona 400, July race, 1969 . . . . . . .35.00
Daytona 400, July race, 1970 . . . . . . .30.00
Daytona 400, July race, 1971 . . . . . . .30.00
Daytona 400, July race, 1972 . . . . . . .30.00
Daytona 400, July race, 1973 . . . . . . .30.00
Daytona 400, July race, 1974 . . . . . . .30.00
Daytona 400, July race, 1975 . . . . . . .30.00

Daytona 400, July race, 1976 . . . . . . .25.00
Daytona 400, July race, 1977 . . . . . . .25.00
Daytona 400, July race, 1978 . . . . . . .25.00
Daytona 400, July race, 1979 . . . . . . .25.00
Daytona 400, July race, 1980 . . . . . . .20.00
Daytona 400, July race, 1981 . . . . . . .20.00
Daytona 400, July race, 1982 . . . . . . .20.00
Daytona 400, July race, 1983 . . . . . . .20.00
Daytona 400, July race, 1984 . . . . . . .35.00
Daytona 400, July race, 1985 . . . . . . .20.00
Daytona 400, July race, 1986 . . . . . . .20.00
Daytona 400, July race, 1987 . . . . . . .20.00
Daytona 400, July race, 1988 . . . . . . .20.00
Daytona 400, July race, 1989 . . . . . . .20.00
Daytona 400, July race, 1990 . . . . . . .20.00
Daytona 400, July race, 1991 . . . . . . .25.00
Daytona 400, July race, 1992 . . . . . . .15.00
Daytona 400, July race, 1993 . . . . . . .15.00
Daytona 400, July race, 1994 . . . . . . .15.00
Daytona 400, July race, 1995 . . . . . . .15.00
Daytona 400, July race, 1996 . . . . . . .15.00
Daytona 400, July race, 1997 . . . . . . .15.00
Daytona 400, July race, 1998 . . . . . . .30.00
Daytona 400, July race, 1999 . . . . . . .15.00
Daytona 400, July race, 2000 . . . . . . .15.00

Indianapolis, Brickyard 400, 1994 . . . . . .40.00
Indianapolis, Brickyard 400, 1995 . . . . .30.00
Indianapolis, Brickyard 400, 1996 . . . . .30.00
Indianapolis, Brickyard 400, 1997 . . . . .30.00
Indianapolis, Brickyard 400, 1998 . . . . .25.00
Indianapolis, Brickyard 400, 1999 . . . . .25.00

Indianapolis, Brickyard 400, 2000 . . . . . .20.00
Japan, November 1996 . . . . . . . . . . . .60.00
Japan, November 1997 . . . . . . . . . . . .50.00

Japan, November 1998 . . . . . . . . . . .45.00
Riverside 500, 1963 . . . . . . . . . . .125.00
Riverside 500, 1964 . . . . . . . . . . .100.00
Riverside 500, 1965 . . . . . . . . . . . .65.00
Riverside 500, 1966 . . . . . . . . . . . .55.00
Riverside 500, 1967 . . . . . . . . . . . .55.00
Riverside 500, 1968 . . . . . . . . . . . .50.00
Riverside 500, 1969 . . . . . . . . . . . .45.00
Riverside 500, 1970 . . . . . . . . . . . .45.00
Riverside 500, 1971 . . . . . . . . . . . .40.00
Riverside 500, 1972 . . . . . . . . . . . .35.00
Riverside 500, 1973 . . . . . . . . . . . .35.00
Riverside 500, 1974 . . . . . . . . . . . .35.00
Riverside 500, 1975 . . . . . . . . . . . .35.00
Riverside 500, 1976 . . . . . . . . . . . .25.00
Riverside 500, 1977 . . . . . . . . . . . .25.00
Riverside 500, 1978 . . . . . . . . . . . .20.00
Riverside 500, 1979 . . . . . . . . . . . .20.00
Riverside 500, 1980 . . . . . . . . . . . .15.00
Riverside 500, 1981 . . . . . . . . . . . .15.00
Riverside 500, 1982 . . . . . . . . . . . .15.00
Riverside 500, 1983 . . . . . . . . . . . .15.00
Riverside 500, 1984 . . . . . . . . . . . .15.00
Riverside 500, 1985 . . . . . . . . . . . .15.00
Riverside 500, 1986 . . . . . . . . . . . .15.00
Riverside 500, 1987 . . . . . . . . . . . .15.00

Riverside 500, 1988, closed track down . .20.00
Rockingham, spring race, 1966 . . . . . . .95.00
Rockingham, spring race, 1967 . . . . . . .75.00
Rockingham, spring race, 1968 . . . . . . .50.00
Rockingham, spring race, 1969 . . . . . . .40.00
Rockingham, spring race, 1970 . . . . . . .40.00
Rockingham, spring race, 1971 . . . . . . .35.00
Rockingham, spring race, 1972 . . . . . . .35.00
Rockingham, spring race, 1973 . . . . . . .25.00
Rockingham, spring race, 1974 . . . . . . .25.00
Rockingham, spring race, 1975 Ricky Rudd's first
    Winston Cup race . . . . . . . . . . . . . .30.00
Rockingham, spring race, 1976 Elliott's first Winston Cup race . . . . . . . . . . . . . . . . .30.00
Rockingham, spring race, 1977 . . . . . . .20.00
Rockingham, spring race, 1978 . . . . . . .20.00
Rockingham, spring race, 1979 . . . . . . .20.00
Rockingham, spring race, 1980 . . . . . . .15.00
Rockingham, spring race, 1981 . . . . . . .15.00
Rockingham, spring race, 1982 . . . . . . .15.00
Rockingham, spring race, 1983 . . . . . . .15.00
Rockingham, spring race, 1984 . . . . . . .15.00
Rockingham, spring race, 1985 . . . . . . .15.00

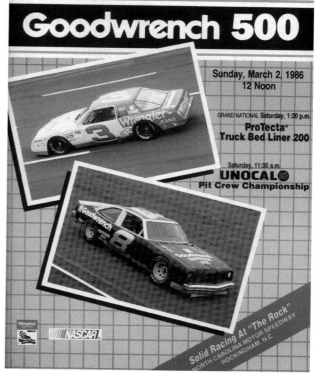

Rockingham, spring race, 1986 . . . . . . .15.00
Rockingham, spring race, 1987 . . . . . . .15.00
Rockingham, spring race, 1988 . . . . . . .15.00
Rockingham, spring race, 1989 . . . . . . .15.00
Rockingham, spring race, 1990 . . . . . . .15.00
Rockingham, spring race, 1991 . . . . . . .15.00
Rockingham, spring race, 1992 . . . . . . .15.00
Rockingham, spring race, 1993 . . . . . . .15.00

Rockingham, spring race, 1994 . . . . . . . .15.00
Rockingham, spring race, 1995 . . . . . . . .15.00
Rockingham, spring race, 1996 . . . . . . . .15.00
Rockingham, spring race, 1997 . . . . . . . .15.00
Rockingham, spring race, 1998 . . . . . . . .15.00
Rockingham, spring race, 1999 . . . . . . . .15.00
Rockingham, fall race, 1965 . . . . . . . . .120.00
Rockingham, fall race, 1966 Ned Jarrett's last
   race . . . . . . . . . . . . . . . . . . . . . .85.00
Rockingham, fall race, 1967 . . . . . . . . .65.00
Rockingham, fall race, 1968 . . . . . . . . .50.00
Rockingham, fall race, 1969 . . . . . . . . .45.00
Rockingham, fall race, 1970 . . . . . . . . .40.00
Rockingham, fall race, 1971 . . . . . . . . .35.00
Rockingham, fall race, 1972 . . . . . . . . .35.00
Rockingham, fall race, 1973 . . . . . . . . .25.00
Rockingham, fall race, 1974 . . . . . . . . .25.00
Rockingham, fall race, 1975 . . . . . . . . .25.00
Rockingham, fall race, 1976 . . . . . . . . .25.00
Rockingham, fall race, 1977 . . . . . . . . .20.00
Rockingham, fall race, 1978 . . . . . . . . .20.00
Rockingham, fall race, 1979 . . . . . . . . .20.00
Rockingham, fall race, 1980 . . . . . . . . .15.00
Rockingham, fall race, 1981 . . . . . . . . .15.00
Rockingham, fall race, 1982 . . . . . . . . .15.00
Rockingham, fall race, 1983 . . . . . . . . .15.00
Rockingham, fall race, 1984 . . . . . . . . .15.00
Rockingham, fall race, 1985 . . . . . . . . .15.00
Rockingham, fall race, 1986 . . . . . . . . .15.00
Rockingham, fall race, 1987 . . . . . . . . .15.00
Rockingham, fall race, 1988 . . . . . . . . .15.00
Rockingham, fall race, 1989 . . . . . . . . .15.00
Rockingham, fall race, 1990 . . . . . . . . .15.00
Rockingham, fall race, 1991 . . . . . . . . .15.00
Rockingham, fall race, 1992 . . . . . . . . .15.00
Rockingham, fall race, 1993 . . . . . . . . .15.00
Rockingham, fall race, 1994 . . . . . . . . .20.00
Rockingham, fall race, 1995 . . . . . . . . .15.00
Rockingham, fall race, 1996 . . . . . . . . .15.00
Rockingham, fall race, 1997 . . . . . . . . .15.00
Rockingham, fall race, 1998 . . . . . . . . .15.00
Rockingham, fall race, 1999 . . . . . . . . .15.00
Talladega, spring race, 1969 . . . . . . . .200.00
Talladega, spring race, 1970 . . . . . . . .120.00
Talladega, spring race, 1971 . . . . . . . . .60.00
Talladega, spring race, 1972 . . . . . . . . .40.00
Talladega, spring race, 1973 . . . . . . . . .40.00
Talladega, spring race, 1974 . . . . . . . . .30.00
Talladega, spring race, 1975 . . . . . . . . .30.00
Talladega, spring race, 1976 . . . . . . . . .25.00
Talladega, spring race, 1977 . . . . . . . . .25.00
Talladega, spring race, 1978 . . . . . . . . .20.00
Talladega, spring race, 1979 . . . . . . . . .20.00
Talladega, spring race, 1980 . . . . . . . . .15.00
Talladega, spring race, 1981 . . . . . . . . .15.00
Talladega, spring race, 1982 . . . . . . . . .15.00
Talladega, spring race, 1983 . . . . . . . . .15.00

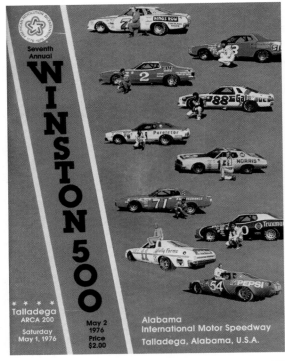

Talladega, spring race, 1976 . . . . . . . . . .25.00

Talladega, spring race, 1984 . . . . . . . . . .15.00
Talladega, spring race, 1985 . . . . . . . . . .15.00
Talladega, spring race, 1986 . . . . . . . . . .15.00
Talladega, spring race, 1987 . . . . . . . . . .15.00
Talladega, spring race, 1988 . . . . . . . . . .15.00
Talladega, spring race, 1989 . . . . . . . . . .15.00
Talladega, spring race, 1990 . . . . . . . . . .15.00

Talladega, spring race, 1991 . . . . . . . . . .15.00
Talladega, spring race, 1992 . . . . . . . . . .15.00
Talladega, spring race, 1993 . . . . . . . . . .15.00

Talladega, spring race, 1994 . . . . . . . . . .15.00
Talladega, spring race, 1995 . . . . . . . . . .15.00
Talladega, spring race, 1996 . . . . . . . . . .15.00
Talladega, spring race, 1997 . . . . . . . . . .15.00
Talladega, spring race, 1998 . . . . . . . . . .15.00
Talladega, spring race, 1999 . . . . . . . . . .15.00

# SHEET METAL

## WINSTON CUP HOOD

1 Steve Park, Pennzoil . . . . . . . . . . . .1200.00
2 Rusty Wallace, Miller Lite . . . . . . . .1800.00
4 Bobby Hamilton, Kodak . . . . . . . . . . .750.00
5 Terry Labonte, Kellogg's . . . . . . . . .1400.00
6 Mark Martin, Valvoline . . . . . . . . . .1400.00
7 Michael Waltrip, Phillips . . . . . . . . .700.00
7 Alan Kulwicki, Hooters . . . . . . . . . .4000.00
9 Jerry Nadeau, Cartoon Network . . . .1000.00
10 Ricky Rudd, Tide . . . . . . . . . . . . . .900.00
11 Brett Bodine, Paychex . . . . . . . . . . .500.00
12 Jeremy Mayfield, Mobil 1 . . . . . . . . .850.00
16 Kevin LePage, Primestar & TV Guide .600.00
18 Bobby Labonte, Interstate . . . . . . .1000.00
20 Tony Stewart, Home Depot . . . . . .2700.00
21 Elliott Sadler, Citgo . . . . . . . . . . . .700.00
22 Ward Burton, Caterpillar . . . . . . . . .900.00
22 Ward Burton, MBNA . . . . . . . . . . . .800.00
23 Jimmy Spencer, Winston . . . . . . . . .900.00
24 Jeff Gordon, Dupont . . . . . . . . . . .3500.00
25 Wally Dallenbach, Budweiser . . . . .1000.00
26 Johnny Benson, Cheerios . . . . . . . .700.00
29 Cartoon Network . . . . . . . . . . . . .1000.00
30 Derrike Cope, Bryan Foods . . . . . . .550.00
31 Mike Skinner, Lowe's . . . . . . . . . . .800.00
33 Ken Schrader, Skoal . . . . . . . . . . . .900.00
36 Ernie Irvan, M&M's . . . . . . . . . . .1500.00
40 Sterling Marlin, Coors Light . . . . . . .900.00
41 Steve Grissom, Kodiak . . . . . . . . . .500.00
42 Joe Nemechek, BellSouth . . . . . . . .550.00
43 John Andretti, STP . . . . . . . . . . . .1250.00
44 Kyle Petty, Hot Wheels . . . . . . . . .1500.00
45 Rich Bickle, Lucky Dog 10-10-345 . . .750.00
50 Budweiser, Louie the Lizard, 1998 . . . . . . . . . . . . . . . . . . . .1600.00
55 Kenny Wallace, Square D . . . . . . . . .500.00
66 Darrell Waltrip, K-Mart . . . . . . . . . .750.00
75 Rick Mast, Remington . . . . . . . . . . .500.00
77 Robert Pressley, Jasper . . . . . . . . . .500.00
88 Dale Jarrett, Quality Care . . . . . . .1500.00
94 Bill Elliott, McDonald's . . . . . . . . .1200.00
97 Chad Little, John Deere . . . . . . . . .1500.00
99 Jeff Burton, Exide . . . . . . . . . . . .1000.00

## BUSCH GRAND NATIONAL HOOD

1 Jeff Gordon, Baby Ruth . . . . . . . . . .2500.00
1 Jeff Gordon, Carolina Ford . . . . . . . .3000.00
3 Dale Earnhardt, Jr, AC Delco . . . . . .2700.00
3 Steve Park, AC Delco . . . . . . . . . . .1500.00
27 Casey Atwood, Castrol . . . . . . . . . .1200.00
44 Tony Stewart, Shell . . . . . . . . . . . .1800.00
60 Mark Martin, Winn-Dixie . . . . . . . . .1000.00

## WINSTON CUP NOSE OR REAR BUMPER

1 Steve Park, Pennzoil . . . . . . . . . . . .350.00
2 Rusty Wallace, Miller Lite . . . . . . . . .400.00
4 Bobby Hamilton, Kodak . . . . . . . . . .150.00
5 Terry Labonte, Kellogg's . . . . . . . . .350.00
6 Mark Martin, Valvoline . . . . . . . . . . .400.00
6 Mark Martin, Folgers . . . . . . . . . . . .450.00
7 Michael Waltrip, Phillips . . . . . . . . . .200.00
9 Jerry Nadeau, Cartoon Network . . . . .250.00
10 Ricky Rudd, Tide . . . . . . . . . . . . . .300.00
11 Brett Bodine, Paychex . . . . . . . . . . .150.00
12 Jeremy Mayfield, Mobil 1 . . . . . . . . .300.00
16 Kevin LePage, Primestar & TV Guide .200.00
18 Bobby Labonte, Interstate . . . . . . . .350.00
20 Tony Stewart, Home Depot . . . . . . .800.00
21 Elliott Sadler, Citgo . . . . . . . . . . . .200.00
22 Ward Burton, Caterpillar . . . . . . . . .300.00
23 Jimmy Spencer, Winston . . . . . . . . .350.00
24 Jeff Gordon, Dupont . . . . . . . . . . . .900.00
26 Johnny Benson, Cheerios . . . . . . . .200.00
30 Derrike Cope, Bryan Foods . . . . . . .300.00
31 Mike Skinner, Lowe's . . . . . . . . . . .250.00
33 Ken Schrader, Skoal . . . . . . . . . . . .450.00
36 Ernie Irvan, M&M's . . . . . . . . . . . .500.00
40 Sterling Marlin, Coors Light . . . . . . .300.00
41 Steve Grissom, Kodiak . . . . . . . . . .200.00
42 Joe Nemechek, BellSouth . . . . . . . .250.00
43 John Andretti, STP . . . . . . . . . . . . .350.00
44 Kyle Petty, Hot Wheels . . . . . . . . . .450.00
45 Rich Bickle, Lucky Dog 10-10-345 . . .200.00
55 Kenny Wallace, Square D . . . . . . . .200.00
66 Darrell Waltrip, K-Mart . . . . . . . . . .250.00
77 Robert Pressley, Jasper . . . . . . . . . .200.00
88 Dale Jarrett, Quality Care . . . . . . . .400.00
94 Bill Elliott, McDonald's . . . . . . . . . .400.00
97 Chad Little, John Deere . . . . . . . . . .300.00
99 Jeff Burton, Exide . . . . . . . . . . . . .350.00

## BUSCH GRAND NATIONAL NOSE OR REAR BUMPER

1 Jeff Gordon, Baby Ruth . . . . . . . . . .400.00
1 Jeff Gordon, Carolina Ford . . . . . . . .400.00
3 Dale Earnhardt, Jr, AC Delco . . . . . . .500.00
3 Steve Park, AC Delco . . . . . . . . . . . .400.00

27 Casey Atwood, Castrol . . . . . . . . . .250.00
44 Tony Stewart, Shell . . . . . . . . . . . .450.00
60 Mark Martin, Winn-Dixie . . . . . . . . .250.00

## SOFT DRINK BOTTLES

Commemorative soft drink bottles make up one of racing's most popular and most interesting collectible categories. The first NASCAR-themed soft drink bottle appeared a dozen years ago when Bill Elliott's brother Dan convinced the local Coca-Cola bottler to produce a bottle celebrating Bill's 1988 NASCAR Winston Cup championship.

Just a few years later, Pepsi released a series of bottles recognizing milestones in the career of Richard Petty. Pepsi has also produced a couple of bottles featuring three-time NASCAR champion Jeff Gordon.

The most coveted series of drink bottles was produced by Sun Drop — a regional brand distributed throughout the southeast. Released in 1992, the six-bottle ensemble chronicles the accomplishments of the legendary Dale Earnhardt.

Coca-Cola has produced the greatest number of NASCAR-themed bottles saluting both races and drivers who are part of the Coca-Cola Racing Family. An extremely limited edition bottle produced exclusively for Coca-Cola employees in honor of the Inaugural Brickyard 400 at Indianapolis ranks as the most popular general production piece.

In addition, Sunbelt Marketing has produced an assortment of limited production gold and crystal Coke bottles.

As one might expect, emptying a collectible soda pop bottle drastically reduces its appraised value — in most cases by 70 – 90%.

### COCA-COLA

Bill Elliott, 1988 Winston Cup Champion . .27.00
Bill Elliott, 8 oz. size, 1998 . . . . . . . . .2.00
Bobby Labonte, 8 oz. size, 1998 . . . . . . .2.00
Coca-Cola 300, Inaugural, April 5, 1997,
    Texas . . . . . . . . . . . . . . . . . . . . . . . . .6.00
Coca-Cola Racing Famliy, 8 oz.
    1999 . . . . . . . . . . . . . . . . . . . . . . . . .2.00
Coca-Cola 300, Texas . . . . . . . . . . . . . .4.00
Cracker Barrel 500, March 14,1999, Atlanta .2.00
Dale Earnhardt, 8 oz. size, 1998 . . . . . . 10.00
Dale Earnhardt, Dale Earnhardt, Jr., 8 oz.
    1999 . . . . . . . . . . . . . . . . . . . . . . . . 15.00
Dale Jarrett, 8 oz. size,1998 . . . . . . . . . .2.00
Dover Downs, 30th Anniversary . . . . . . . .6.00
Homestead Motorsports Complex, Nov. 5,
    1995 . . . . . . . . . . . . . . . . . . . . . . . . .6.00

Bill Elliott, 1988 Winston Cup Champion . .27.00

Inaugural Brickyard 400, employee edition .75.00
Jeff Gordon, Time To Refuel . . . . . . . . . . . .6.00
Jeff Gordon, 1995 Winston Cup Champion .5.00
Jeff Burton, 8 oz. size, 1998 . . . . . . . . . .3.00
Kentucky Motor Speedway, June 2000 . . . .4.00
Kyle Petty, 8 oz. size, 1998 . . . . . . . . . . .2.00
NAPA 500, 1998 . . . . . . . . . . . . . . . . . .3.00
New Hampshire Speedway, 1993 Inaugural WC
    300 . . . . . . . . . . . . . . . . . . . . . . . . . .8.00
"Official Soft Drink of NASCAR," 8 oz. size,
    1998 . . . . . . . . . . . . . . . . . . . . . . . . .4.00
Ricky Rudd, 8 oz. size, 1998 . . . . . . . . . .2.00
Todd Bodine, 8 oz. size, 1998 . . . . . . . . .8.00
1 Steve Park, 8 oz., 1999 . . . . . . . . . . . .3.00
3 Dale Earnhardt, 8 oz., 1999 . . . . . . . .10.00
3 Dale Earnhardt Jr, 8 oz., 1999 . . . . . . .5.00
10 Ricky Rudd, 8 oz., 1999 . . . . . . . . . . .2.00
10 Ricky Rudd, mini bottle, from McDonald's .5.00
12 Jeremy Mayfield, 8 oz., 1999 . . . . . . .2.00
18 Bobby Labonte, 8 oz., 1999 . . . . . . . .2.00
18 Bobby Labonte, mini bottle, from
    McDonald's . . . . . . . . . . . . . . . . . . . .5.00
20 Tony Stewart, 8 oz., 1999 . . . . . . . . . .5.00
28 Kenny Irwin, 8 oz., 1999 . . . . . . . . . .2.00
28 Kenny Irwin, mini bottle, from McDonald's .5.00
44 Kyle Petty, 8 oz., 1999 . . . . . . . . . . . .2.00
44 Kyle Petty, mini bottle, from McDonald's .5.00
50th Anniversary of NASCAR, 8 oz., 1998 .40.00

88 Dale Jarrett, 8 oz., 1999 . . . . . . . . . .2.00
88 Dale Jarrett, Mini bottle, from
    McDonald's . . . . . . . . . . . . . . . . . .5.00
94 Bill Elliott, 8 oz., 1999 . . . . . . . . . .2.00
94 Bill Elliott, mini bottle, from McDonald's .5.00
99 Jeff Burton, 8 oz., 1999 . . . . . . . . . .3.00
2000 NASCAR Racing Family . . . . . . . . . .3.00

### COCA-COLA CRYSTAL BOTTLE

Coca-Cola 600, 100 . . . . . . . . . . . . . .150.00
Coca-Cola 300, Texas, 300 . . . . . . . . .125.00

50th Anniversary NASCAR, 5,000 . . . . . .75.00
3 Dale Earnhardt, Goodwrench Plus,
    1,999 . . . . . . . . . . . . . . . . . . . . . .140.00
20 Tony Stewart, Home Depot, 1,999 . . .125.00
94 Bill Elliott, McDonald's, 1,999 . . . . . .115.00

### COCA-COLA GOLD BOTTLE

1 Dale Earnhardt, Jr., Coca-Cola, Japan,
    10,000 . . . . . . . . . . . . . . . . . . . . . .30.00
3 Dale Earnhardt, Coca-Cola, Japan,
    10,000 . . . . . . . . . . . . . . . . . . . . . .60.00
3 Dale Earnhardt, 1999, 10,000 . . . . . .60.00
18 Bobby Labonte, 1999, 10,000 . . . . . .25.00
20 Tony Stewart, 1999, 10,000 . . . . . . .30.00
88 Dale Jarrett, 1999, 10,000 . . . . . . . .25.00
99 Jeff Burton, 1999, 10,000 . . . . . . . .25.00
1996 Brickyard 400, 2,500 . . . . . . . . . .45.00
1997 Coca-Cola 300, 1,997 . . . . . . . . .40.00
1997 Coca-Cola 600, 600 . . . . . . . . . .60.00
1997 Interstate Batteries 500, 1,997 . . .40.00
Charlotte Motor Speedway . . . . . . . . . . .25.00
NASCAR 50th Anniversary, 10,000 . . . . .25.00

1 Dale Earnhardt, Jr., Coca-Cola, Japan,
    10,000 . . . . . . . . . . . . . . . . . . . . . .30.00

1997 Coca-Cola 600, 600 . . . . . . . . . .60.00

## DR. PEPPER

1998 Dr. Pepper Racing, Inaugural Season  .5.00

## MOUNTAIN DEW

1992 Mountain Dew Southern 500  . . . . .10.00
Dew Crew, 4 drivers, 12 oz. 1999 . . . . . . .3.00

## PEPSI

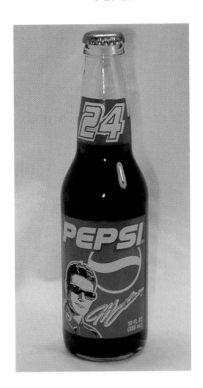

Jeff Gordon, BGN car, 12 oz., 1999 . . . . . .4.00
Richard Petty, 33 Years of Stock Car Racing,
    1992 . . . . . . . . . . . . . . . . . . . . . . .2.00
Richard Petty, 7-Time Winston Cup Champion
    1992 . . . . . . . . . . . . . . . . . . . . . . .2.00
Richard Petty, First Winston Cup Race, 1992 .2.00
Richard Petty, First Winston Cup Victory,
    1992 . . . . . . . . . . . . . . . . . . . . . . .2.00
Richard Petty, Most Career Victories, 200,
    1992 . . . . . . . . . . . . . . . . . . . . . . .2.00
Richard Petty, Most Wins in Single Season, 27,
    1992 . . . . . . . . . . . . . . . . . . . . . . .2.00
Richard Petty, Most Poles in a Career, 127,
    1992 . . . . . . . . . . . . . . . . . . . . . . .2.00
Richard Petty, Most Popular Driver, 9 Times,
    1992 . . . . . . . . . . . . . . . . . . . . . . .2.00
Richard Petty, Most Consecutive Wins, 10,
    1992 . . . . . . . . . . . . . . . . . . . . . . .2.00
Richard Petty, Pepsi 400, July 4, 1984, 200th
    Win, 1992 . . . . . . . . . . . . . . . . . .2.00
Richard Petty, 1,000 NASCAR Start,
    1992 . . . . . . . . . . . . . . . . . . . . . . .2.00
Richard Petty, Fan Appreciation Tour,
    1992 . . . . . . . . . . . . . . . . . . . . . . .3.00
Jeff Gordon, bust shot, 12 oz., 1999 . . . . .5.00

## SUNDROP

Dale Earnhardt, 6 bottle set . . . . . . . . . .135.00
Dale Earnhardt, Series #1, 1979 Rookie of
    Year . . . . . . . . . . . . . . . . . . . . . . .30.00

Dale Earnhardt, 6 bottle set.....................................135.00

Dale Earnhardt, Series #2, 1980 Winston Cup
Champion . . . . . . . . . . . . . . . . . . . .25.00
Dale Earnhardt, Series #3, 1986 Winston Cup
Champion . . . . . . . . . . . . . . . . . . . .25.00
Dale Earnhardt, Series #4, 1987 Winston Cup
Champion . . . . . . . . . . . . . . . . . . . .25.00
Dale Earnhardt, Series #5, 1990 Winston Cup
Champion . . . . . . . . . . . . . . . . . . . .25.00
Dale Earnhardt, Series #6, 1991 Winston Cup
Champion . . . . . . . . . . . . . . . . . . . .25.00

## STATUES

Only a few dozen NASCAR driver statues have been produced, but those have been created by some of the most respected folks in the business, names like Salvino, Tom Clark, Ralph Williams, Arnold, and Sports Impressions.

Living legend Richard Petty has proven to be the favorite subject. Salvino alone has produced seven different Petty statues. While some individual pieces appraise for more, the Sports Impression series of autographed statues rates the most consistent appraisals across the board. The six-driver line-up is limited to a scant 975 pieces featuring NASCAR most gifted racers.

**ARNOLD**

Richard Petty, STP, holding helmet, 1974 .390.00

**TOM CLARK**

Davey Allison . . . . . . . . . . . . . . . . . .100.00
Bill Elliott, Budweiser . . . . . . . . . . . . . .125.00

Bobby Hamilton, Country Time . . . . . . . . .99.00
Jeff Gordon, Dupont . . . . . . . . . . . . . .125.00
Harry Gant, Skoal . . . . . . . . . . . . . . .99.00

### HAMILTON SALVINO

A.J. Foyt, Copenhagen, autographed,
   1,500 . . . . . . . . . . . . . . . . . . . .190.00

Richard Petty, STP, 200 Wins, white & blue uniform, 1,500 . . . . . . . . . . . . . . . .250.00

Richard Petty, STP, 200 Wins, red & blue uniform,
   300 . . . . . . . . . . . . . . . . . . . . . .400.00

Richard Petty, STP, Farewell Tour, 2,500 .260.00
Richard Petty, STP, Farewell Tour, 6," 2,500 .78.00
Richard Petty, STP, 8" cold-cast pewter,
   2,500 . . . . . . . . . . . . . . . . . . . . .95.00
Richard Petty, STP, 6" cold-cast pewter,
   5,000 . . . . . . . . . . . . . . . . . . . . .40.00
Richard Petty, STP, cold-cast pewter plaque,
   5,000 . . . . . . . . . . . . . . . . . . . . .25.00

Darrell Waltrip, Western Auto, autographed,
   1,500 . . . . . . . . . . . . . . . . . . . .200.00

### SPORTS IMPRESSIONS

Jeff Gordon, autographed, 975 . . . . . . .180.00

Dale Jarrett, autographed, 975 . . . . . . .155.00
Kyle Petty, autographed, 975 . . . . . . . .150.00

Rusty Wallace, autographed, 975 . . . . . .160.00
Darrell Waltrip, autographed, 975 . . . . .150.00
Bill Elliott, autographed, 975 . . . . . . . .155.00

### RALPH WILLIAMS

Harry Gant, Skoal Bandit . . . . . . . . . . . .45.00
Ernie Irvan, Kodak . . . . . . . . . . . . . . . . .60.00
Flossie Johnson, 1,000 . . . . . . . . . . . . .30.00
Junior Johnson, Maxwell House . . . . . . .35.00
Junior Johnson, Maxwell House, with white
   jacket . . . . . . . . . . . . . . . . . . . . . . .50.00
Terry Labonte . . . . . . . . . . . . . . . . . . . . .65.00
Kyle Petty, Mello Yello . . . . . . . . . . . . . .35.00

Maurice Petty, standing beside engine, 3,000 . .75.00

## STEINS

The beer stein is a prime example of a mainstream collectible that has found a niche in the NASCAR arena. The three top brands of NASCAR steins are Anheuser-Busch, Dramtree-CUI, and Hunter. Franklin Mint entered the market just last year with its first offering.

Hunter is best known for its ongoing line of NASCAR champion steins. The popular collection includes an annual stein for each year's champion, going all the way back to 1949.

Arguably the most collectible of all racing steins are those produced by Anheuser-Busch. That's because Anheuser-Busch's Budweiser brand is one of the most collected licensed properties in the world — much like Coca-Cola, Harley-Davidson, or Disney. Anheuser-Busch steins feature drivers of Budweiser-sponsored race cars, or commemorate races like the Daytona 500, Brickyard 400, or the Busch Clash/Budweiser Shootout.

## ANHEUSER-BUSCH

### 1990 DAYTON

Kenny Bernstein, #CS406, 2000, Ceramarte,
   20,000 . . . . . . . . . . . . . . . . . . . . . .55.00
Brickyard 400, #N4842, 1994, USA,
   7,500 . . . . . . . . . . . . . . . . . . . . . . .85.00
Brickyard 400, #N5359, 1995, USA,
   3,500 . . . . . . . . . . . . . . . . . . . . . . .45.00
Brickyard 400, #N5359, 1995, Gerz, 1,500 .65.00
Brickyard 400, #N/A, 1996, USA . . . . . .30.00

Bud Shootout, 1998, USA, 650 . . . . . . .200.00

Bud Shootout, 1999, USA . . . . . . . . . .250.00

Busch Clash, 1996, USA, 500 . . . . . . .350.00
Busch Clash, 1997, USA, 500 . . . . . . .250.00

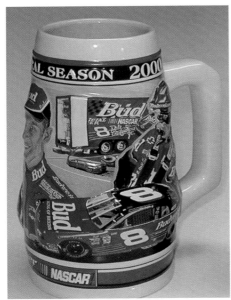

Bill Elliott, #CS196, 1993, Gerz, 25,000 .105.00

NASCAR 50th Anniversary, #CS360, 1998,
    Ceramarte, 25,000 . . . . . . . . . . . .125.00
NASCAR 50th Anniversary, #CS371, 1998, Cera-
    marte . . . . . . . . . . . . . . . . . . . .30.00
Ken Schrader, #N5054, 1995, Gerz, 4,400 .35.00
Ken Schrader, #N5510, 1995, Gerz . . . . .30.00
Speed Weeks, Gerz, 4,005 . . . . . . . . . .35.00

## DRAMTREE-CUI, INC.

Dale Earnhardt, 1994 Champion, 1995,
    Hoffbrau . . . . . . . . . . . . . . . . . . .35.00
Dale Earnhardt, #43DE98, 1998, white
    ceramic . . . . . . . . . . . . . . . . . . . .30.00
Dale Earnhardt, #43EARN, 1996, white
    ceramic . . . . . . . . . . . . . . . . . . . .25.00
Dale Earnhardt, #8298DE, 1998, lidded,
    1,998 . . . . . . . . . . . . . . . . . . . . .70.00
Dale Earnhardt, #DE593, 1996, lidded,
    numbered . . . . . . . . . . . . . . . . . .70.00
Dale Earnhardt, #DESIG1, 1997, Hoffbrau,
    10,000 . . . . . . . . . . . . . . . . . . . .35.00
Dale Earnhardt, #DESIG2, 1998, Hoffbrau .35.00
Dale Earnhardt, #EARNHF, 1996, Hoffbrau 35.00
Dale Earnhardt, Texas, 1997, Hoffbrau . . .40.00
Dale Jarrett, #102DJ, 1997,Hoffbrau . . .25.00
Jeff Gordon, 1995 Winston Cup, 1995 & 1996
    lidded, numbered . . . . . . . . . . . . . .60.00
Jeff Gordon, #1995 WCCR, 1995 & 1996
    Hoffbrau . . . . . . . . . . . . . . . . . . .25.00

Dale Earnhardt, Jr., #CS428, 2000,
    Ceramarte . . . . . . . . . . . . . . . . . . .45.00
Dale Earnhardt, Jr., #CS450, 2000, Cermarte
    lidded, 25,000 . . . . . . . . . . . . . . . .80.00
Bill Elliott, #N3553, 1992, USA . . . . . . .30.00
Bill Elliott, #CS194, 1993, Ceramarte . . . .30.00
Bill Elliott, #CS196, 1993, Gerz, 25,000 .105.00
Bill Elliott, #CS196SE, 1993, autographed, Gerz,
    1,500 . . . . . . . . . . . . . . . . . . . .240.00

Dale Earnhardt, #DE593, 1996, lidded numbered . . . . . . . . . . . . . . . . . . .70.00

Jeff Gordon, #8298JG, 1998, lidded, 1,998 . . . . . . . . . . . . . . . . . . . . . . .59.00
Jeff Gordon, #82JG98, 1998, white ceramic . . . . . . . . . . . . . . . . . . . . .18.00
Jeff Gordon, #97WCC43, 1997, white ceramic . . . . . . . . . . . . . . . . . . . . .20.00
Jeff Gordon, #97WCCB82, 1997, lidded, 1,997 . . . . . . . . . . . . . . . . . . . . . . .30.00
Jeff Gordon, #97WCCR, 1997, Hoffbrau ..25.00
Jeff Gordon, #JGSIG1, 1997, Hoffbrau, 10,000 . . . . . . . . . . . . . . . . . . . . . .30.00
Jeff Gordon, #JGSIG, 1998, Hoffbrau . . . .25.00
Jeff Gordon, Jurassic Park, 1997, white ceramic, 12,500 . . . . . . . . . . . . . . . . . . . . . .25.00
Jeff Gordon, Texas, 1997, Hoffbrau . . . . .30.00
Jeff Gordon, #WCCJG, 1995 & 1996, white ceramic . . . . . . . . . . . . . . . . . . . . . .15.00
Terry Labonte, #102TL, 1997, Hoffbrau ..25.00
Terry Labonte, Texas, 1997, Hoffbrau . . . .25.00
Mark Martin, #102MM, 1997, Hoffbrau ..25.00
NASCAR 50th Anniversary, 1998, Hoffbrau .30.00
NASCAR 50th Anniversary, #43NAS50 W, 1998 ceramic . . . . . . . . . . . . . . . . . . . . . .20.00
Kyle Petty, #43KP, 1995, white ceramic ..15.00
Kyle Petty, #KYLEHF1, 1995, Hoffbrau . . .20.00
Richard Petty, #59RICH, 1995, lidded . . . .50.00
Richard Petty, #PETTYHF1, 1995, Hoffbrau .20.00
Rusty Wallace, 1994, Hoffbrau . . . . . . .22.00
Rusty Wallace, #43RW98 W, 1998, ceramic . . . . . . . . . . . . . . . . . . . . . .18.00

Rusty Wallace, #43RW, 1995, white ceramic . . . . . . . . . . . . . . . . . . . .15.00

Rusty Wallace, #8298RW, 1998, lidded, 1,998 . . . . . . . . . . . . . . . . . . . . . .59.00
Rusty Wallace, #RUSTYHF1, 1995, Hoffbrau .20.00
Rusty Wallace, #RWFORD59, 1995, lidded, numbered . . . . . . . . . . . . . . . . . . . . .55.00
Rusty Wallace, #RWSIG2, 1997, Hoffbrau, 6,000 . . . . . . . . . . . . . . . . . . . . . .25.00
Rusty Wallace, Texas, 1997, Hoffbrau . . . .25.00
Winston Cup, #43JWIN W, 1995, ceramic .15.00

### FRANKLIN MINT

Dale Earnhardt, Goodwrench, lidded, 1st .200.00
Dale Earnhardt, Goodwrench, lidded, 2nd .200.00

Dale Earnhardt, Bass Pro Shops, lidded, 2nd . . . . . . . . . . . . . . . . . . . . . .200.00

### HUNTER

1949 –1999 Champions, different stein for each year, white ceramic . . . . . . . . . . . . .20.00

Davey Allison, Memorial, 1993, white ceramic . . . . . . . . . . . . . . . . . . . .25.00

John Andretti, K-Mart, 1996, white ceramic .15.00

Brickyard 400, 1997, white ceramic . . . . .15.00

Bristol, 1996, white ceramic . . . . . . . . . .15.00

Charlotte Motor Speedway, 1998, white ceramic . . . . . . . . . . . . . . . . . . . .18.00

Richard Childress Racing, 1996, black ceramic . . . . . . . . . . . . . . . . . . . .25.00

Daytona USA, 1995, white ceramic . . . . .15.00

Daytona USA, 38th Annual, 1995, white ceramic . . . . . . . . . . . . . . . . . . . .15.00

Dale Earnhardt, 1980 Champion, white ceramic . . . . . . . . . . . . . . . . . . . .45.00

Dale Earnhardt, 1986 Champion, white ceramic . . . . . . . . . . . . . . . . . . . .45.00

Dale Earnhardt, 1987 Champion, white ceramic . . . . . . . . . . . . . . . . . . . .45.00

Dale Earnhardt, 1990 Champion, white ceramic . . . . . . . . . . . . . . . . . . . .35.00

Dale Earnhardt, 1991 Champion, white ceramic . . . . . . . . . . . . . . . . . . . .35.00

Dale Earnhardt, 1993 Champion, white ceramic . . . . . . . . . . . . . . . . . . . .35.00

Dale Earnhardt, 1994 Champion, white ceramic . . . . . . . . . . . . . . . . . . . .35.00

Dale Earnhardt, 1998 black ceramic, pewter logo . . . . . . . . . . . . . . . . . . . .30.00

Dale Earnhardt, #3, 1996 black ceramic . .30.00

Dale Earnhardt, Brickyard, 1995 white ceramic . . . . . . . . . . . . . . . . . . . .30.00

Dale Earnhardt, Brickyard 400, 1997, white ceramic . . . . . . . . . . . . . . . . . . . .30.00

Dale Earnhardt & Richard Petty, 7&7, 1995, white ceramic . . . . . . . . . . . . . . . . .30.00

Bill Elliott, 1996, black ceramic . . . . . . . .18.00

Bill Elliott, Budweiser, 1993, white ceramic .18.00

Bill Elliott, Fan Club, 1995, white ceramic . .25.00

Bill Elliott, Gotham City, 1995, white ceramic . . . . . . . . . . . . . . . . . . . .15.00

Bill Elliott, McDonald's, 1995, white ceramic .15.00

Ford Manufacturer Championship, 1993, white ceramic . . . . . . . . . . . . . . . . . . . .25.00

Harry Gant, Skoal, 1993, white ceramic . .18.00

Jeff Gordon, 1997, white ceramic . . . . .18.00

Jeff Gordon, Brickyard 400, 1997, white ceramic . . . . . . . . . . . . . . . . . . . .20.00

Ernie Irvan, #28, 1996, white ceramic . . .18.00

Dale Jarrett, 1997, white ceramic . . . . . .18.00

Dale Jarrett, Brickyard 400, 1997, white ceramic . . . . . . . . . . . . . . . . . . . .20.00

Bobby Labonte, 1998, white ceramic, pewter logo . . . . . . . . . . . . . . . . . . . .18.00

Terry Labonte, 1998, white ceramic, pewter logo . . . . . . . . . . . . . . . . . . . .18.00

Sterling Marlin, Back to Back, 1995, white ceramic . . . . . . . . . . . . . . . . . . . .12.00

Mark Martin, #6, 1996, black ceramic . . .18.00

Mark Martin, 1998, white ceramic, pewter logo . . . . . . . . . . . . . . . . . . . .18.00

Rick Mast, Skoal, 1995, white ceramic . . .10.00

NASCAR 50th Anniversary, 1998, white ceramic . . . . . . . . . . . . . . . . . . . .19.00

Kyle Petty, 1997, white ceramic . . . . . . . .18.00

Kyle Petty, Coors Light, 1995, white ceramic . . . . . . . . . . . . . . . . . . . .10.00

Ricky Rudd, Brickyard 400, 1997, white ceramic . . . . . . . . . . . . . . . . . . . .20.00

Mike Skinner, Truck Champ, 1996, black ceramic . . . . . . . . . . . . . . . . . . . .15.00

Rusty Wallace, #2, 1996, black ceramic . .18.00

Rusty Wallace, 1998, white ceramic, pewter logo . . . . . . . . . . . . . . . . . . . .18.00

## TICKETS

In October of 1992, Lowe's Motor Speedway issued a specially designed ticket to commemorate Richard Petty's last season as a driver in NASCAR's Winston Cup Series. The concept was an instant hit with race fans. Consequently, the Concord, North Carolina, race track has offered a unique commemorative ticket for every event since.

In 1994, Atlanta Motor Speedway adopted the

practice, followed a year later by Darlington Raceway. Other tracks offering collectible tickets include Bristol Motor Speedway, Daytona International Speedway, Talladega Superspeedway, and North Carolina Speedway.

None of the tickets released so far carry any extraordinary appraisal, but they are still a favorite for race fans seeking to preserve a piece of history.

### ATLANTA MOTOR SPEEDWAY COMMEMORATIVE

1994 Rusty Wallace & Dale Earnhardt, March race . . . . . . . . . . . . . . . . . . . . . .25.00
1994 Bill Elliott, November race . . . . . . .15.00
1995 Dale Earnhardt & Richard Petty, March race . . . . . . . . . . . . . . . . . . . . . .50.00
1995 "Generations of Greatness," November race . . . . . . . . . . . . . . . . . . . . . . .20.00

1996 Jeff Gordon, March race . . . . . . .20.00
1996 Dale Earnhardt, November race . . . .40.00
1997 Bobby & Terry Labonte, March race .15.00
1997 Hendrick's Team cars, November race . . . . . . . . . . . . . . . . . . . . . . .20.00

### BRISTOL SPEEDWAY COMMEMORATIVE

1997 Darrell Waltrip, August race . . . . . .20.00
1998 Jeff Gordon, August race . . . . . . .20.00
1999 Dale Earnhardt Sr. & Earnhardt Jr., April race . . . . . . . . . . . . . . . . . . . . . . .50.00

### CHARLOTTE-LOWES SPEEDWAY COMMEMORATIVE

1992 Richard Petty, October race . . . . . .30.00
1993 The Allison Family, May race . . . . . .30.00
1993 Alan Kulwicki, October race . . . . . .30.00
1994 May Winston Select race . . . . . . .25.00

1993 The Allison Family, May race . . . . . .30.00

1994 Dale Earnhardt, May race . . . . . . . .40.00
1994 Jeff Gordon, October race . . . . . . . .25.00
1995 Dale Earnhardt & Richard Petty, May race . . . . . . . . . . . . . . . . . . . . . . .60.00
1995 Rusty Wallace, October race . . . . . .20.00
1996 Bobby Labonte, May race . . . . . . . .20.00
1996 Jeff Gordon, Dale Earnhardt & Alan Kulwicki, October race . . . . . . . . . .30.00
1997 Darrell Waltrip, May race . . . . . . . .20.00
1997 11 Drivers, "Tribute to WC Champions" October race . . . . . . . . . . . . . . . . .20.00
1998 NASCAR 50th Anniversary, May race . . . . . . . . . . . . . . . . . . . . . . .20.00
1998 Richard Petty & A.J. Foyt, July Indy race . . . . . . . . . . . . . . . . . . . . . . .15.00
1998 The Earnhardt's, Ralph, Dale, & Dale, Jr. October race . . . . . . . . . . . . . . . . .50.00

2000 10 drivers, "Men of the Millennia," May race . . . . . . . . . . . . . . . . . . . . . . .20.00
2000 The Petty's, Richard, Lee, Kyle & Adam, October race . . . . . . . . . . . . . . . . .20.00

### DARLINGTON SPEEDWAY COMMEMORATIVE

1995, David Pearson, March race . . . . . .20.00

1995 Cale Yarborough, September race . .15.00
1996 Dale Earnhardt, March race . . . . .40.00
1996 Richard Petty, August race . . . . . .15.00
1997 Darrell Waltrip, March race . . . . . .15.00
1997 Terry Labonte, August race . . . . . .15.00
1998 Fireball Roberts, March race . . . . . .15.00
1998 8 Drivers, Southern 500 Champions,
    September race . . . . . . . . . . . . . .15.00
1999 Benny Parsons, March race . . . . . .15.00
2000 Dale Earnhardt & David Pearson,
    September race . . . . . . . . . . . . . .30.00

### DAYTONA SPEEDWAY COMMENORATIVE

1998 Jeff Gordon, July race . . . . . . . . .15.00

### ROCKINGHAM SPEEDWAY COMMENORATIVE

1997 Richard Petty, February race . . . . . .15.00

1997 Dale Earnhardt & Richard Childress,
    October race . . . . . . . . . . . . . . . .40.00

### TALLADEGA SPEEDWAY COMMENORATIVE

1998 Bill Elliott, October race . . . . . . . . .20.00

## UNIFORMS

Nobody personifies the term "dressed for success" like the drivers and crewmen who compete on the NASCAR circuit. Both driver and crew uniforms are popular collectibles.

Most better-financed teams actually have three distinct sets of crew uniforms. One outfit — a very basic ensemble — is worn at the race shop. It usually displays the crewman's name, team specific graphics, and in some cases logos of major sponsors.

A second uniform is worn by at-the-track personnel for practice, qualifying, and events leading up to the race itself. Known in collector's jargon as a "Saturday shirt," this uniform is a watered-down version of the race day uniform. It usually features sponsor colors and logos of primary and major associate sponsors. The race day uniform is obviously the most elaborate — adorned with a full complement of sponsor logos and custom embroidery work.

Many collectors consider event-used driver uniforms to be the the Holy Grail of racing collectibles — and the price tags show it. Very few firesuits are valued at under $1000. Indeed, uniforms from the three or four most popular sellers easily command over $5,000 – 12,000 each.

## PIT CREW

### WINSTON CUP RACE DAY

1 Steve Park, Pennzoil . . . . . . . . . . . . .350.00
2 Rusty Wallace, Miller Lite . . . . . . . . . .400.00
5 Terry Labonte, Kellogg's . . . . . . . . . .450.00
6 Mark Martin, Valvoline . . . . . . . . . . .350.00
6 Mark Martin, Folgers . . . . . . . . . . . .450.00
7 Michael Waltrip, Phillips . . . . . . . . . .200.00
7 Alan Kulwicki, Hooters . . . . . . . . . . .650.00
7 Geoff Bodine, QVC . . . . . . . . . . . . .200.00
7 Kyle Petty, 7-Eleven . . . . . . . . . . . .250.00
9 Jerry Nadeau, Cartoon Network . . . . .400.00
9 Bill Elliott, Coors . . . . . . . . . . . . . .350.00
10 Ricky Rudd, Tide . . . . . . . . . . . . . .400.00
11 Brett Bodine, Paychex . . . . . . . . . . .200.00
11 Bill Elliott, Budweiser . . . . . . . . . . .250.00
12 Jeremy Mayfield, Mobil 1 . . . . . . . . .300.00
12 Bobby Allison, Miller . . . . . . . . . . . .300.00
16 Kevin LePage, Primestar, TV Guide . .250.00
17 Darrell Waltrip, Western Auto . . . . .275.00
17 Darrell Waltrip, Tide . . . . . . . . . . .250.00

18 Bobby Labonte, Interstate . . . . . . . .350.00

20 Tony Stewart, Home Depot, 1999 . . .750.00
21 Elliott Sadler, Citgo . . . . . . . . . . .200.00
22 Ward Burton, Caterpillar . . . . . . . .350.00
22 Bobby Allison, Miller . . . . . . . . .250.00
23 Jimmy Spencer, Winston . . . . . . . .500.00

24 Jeff Gordon, Dupont, 1998 . . . . . .1050.00
24 Jeff Gordon, Dupont, 1999 . . . . . . .950.00
25 Wally Dallenbach, Budweiser . . . . . .250.00
25 Ken Schrader, Budweiser . . . . . . . .275.00
25 Tim Richmond, Folgers . . . . . . . . .600.00

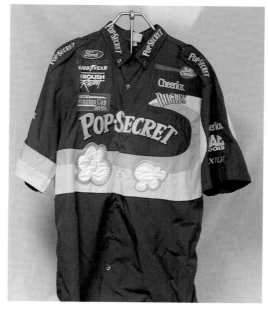

26 Johnny Benson, Pop Secret . . . . . . .250.00
28 Ernie Irvan, Texaco . . . . . . . . . . .300.00
28 Davey Allison, Texaco, black & white .500.00
28 Davey Allison, Texaco, black & orange 550.00
30 Derrike Cope, Bryan Foods . . . . . . .250.00
31 Mike Skinner, Lowe's . . . . . . . . . .300.00
33 Ken Schrader, Skoal . . . . . . . . . .400.00
33 Harry Gant, Skoal . . . . . . . . . . .375.00

26 Johnny Benson, Cheerios . . . . . . . .250.00

36 Ernie Irvan, M&M's . . . . . . . . . . .550.00
40 Sterling Marlin, Coors Light . . . . . .350.00
41 Steve Grissom, Kodiak . . . . . . . . .250.00
42 Joe Nemechek, BellSouth . . . . . . . .300.00
42 Kyle Petty, Mello Yello . . . . . . . .300.00
42 Kyle Petty, Coors Light . . . . . . . .275.00

43 Richard Petty, STP, 1960 – 1969 . . .300.00
43 Richard Petty, STP, 1970 – 1979 . . .300.00
43 Richard Petty, STP, 1980 – 1991 . . .350.00
43 Richard Petty, STP, 1992, Final Year .450.00
43 John Andretti, STP . . . . . . . . . . . .350.00
44 Kyle Petty, Hot Wheels . . . . . . . . .400.00
45 Rich Bickle, Lucky Dog 10-10-345 . .275.00
55 Kenny Wallace, Square D . . . . . . . .250.00
66 Darrell Waltrip, K-Mart . . . . . . . . .350.00
75 Rick Mast, Remington, . . . . . . . . .250.00
88 Dale Jarrett, Quality Care . . . . . . .350.00
94 Bill Elliott, McDonald's . . . . . . . . . .400.00

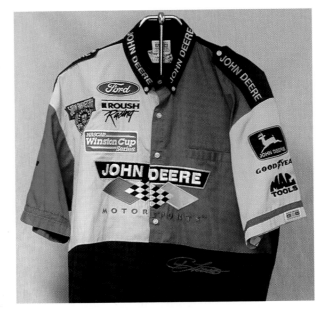

97 Chad Little, John Deere . . . . . . . . . .400.00

99 Jeff Burton, Exide . . . . . . . . . . . . . .350.00

## BUSCH GRAND NATIONAL

1 Jeff Gordon, Baby Ruth . . . . . . . . . .800.00
1 Jeff Gordon, Carolina Ford . . . . . . . .800.00
3 Dale Earnhardt, Jr., AC Delco . . . . . .650.00
3 Steve Park, AC Delco . . . . . . . . . . .500.00

44 Tony Stewart, Shell . . . . . . . . . . . .450.00
45 Adam Petty, Spree . . . . . . . . . . . . .650.00
60 Mark Martin, Winn-Dixie . . . . . . . . .350.00

# DRIVER

## WINSTON CUP

1 Steve Park, Pennzoil . . . . . . . . . . . .1700.00
1 Dale Earnhardt, Jr, Coca-Cola, Japan
    race . . . . . . . . . . . . . . . . . . . .10,000.00
2 Rusty Wallace, Miller Lite . . . . . . . .3500.00
4 Bobby Hamilton, Kodak . . . . . . . . . .1400.00
5 Terry Labonte, Kellogg's . . . . . . . . .2500.00
6 Mark Martin, Valvoline . . . . . . . . . .2700.00
6 Mark Martin, Strohs Light . . . . . . . .1800.00
6 Mark Martin, Folgers . . . . . . . . . . .4000.00
7 Michael Waltrip, Phillips . . . . . . . . .1400.00
7 Alan Kulwicki, Hooters . . . . . . . . . .6000.00
7 Geoff Bodine, QVC . . . . . . . . . . . . .800.00
7 Kyle Petty, 7-Eleven . . . . . . . . . . .1400.00
9 Jerry Nadeau, Cartoon Network . . . .1750.00
9 Bill Elliott, Coors . . . . . . . . . . . . . .2000.00
10 Ricky Rudd, Tide . . . . . . . . . . . . .1800.00
11 Brett Bodine, Paychex . . . . . . . . . .750.00
11 Bill Elliott, Budweiser . . . . . . . . . .1600.00
12 Jeremy Mayfield, Mobil 1 . . . . . . .1800.00
16 Kevin Lepage, Primestar, TV Guide . . .800.00
17 Darrell Waltrip, Western Auto . . . . .1400.00

2 Rusty Wallace, Miller Lite . . . . . . . . .3500.00

6 Mark Martin, Folgers . . . . . . . . . . .4000.00

17 Darrell Waltrip, Tide . . . . . . . . . . .1500.00
18 Bobby Labonte, Interstate . . . . . . . .1900.00
20 Tony Stewart, Home Depot . . . . . . .4500.00
21 Elliott Sadler, Citgo . . . . . . . . . . .1000.00

21 Kyle Petty, Citgo . . . . . . . . . . . . . .2500.00
22 Ward Burton, Caterpillar . . . . . . . . .1200.00
22 Ward Burton, MBNA . . . . . . . . . . .750.00
22 Bobby Allison, Miller . . . . . . . . . . .1500.00
23 Jimmy Spencer, Winston . . . . . . . .1500.00
23 Jimmy Spencer, Smokin' Joes . . . . .2700.00
24 Jeff Gordon, Dupont, 1993, Rookie .12,000.00
24 Jeff Gordon, Dupont, 1998 . . . . .10,000.00
24 Jeff Gordon, Dupont, 1999 . . . . .10,000.00
25 Wally Dallenbach, Budweiser . . . . . .1000.00
25 Ken Schrader, Kodiak . . . . . . . . . .1500.00
25 Tim Richmond, Folgers . . . . . . . . . .2600.00
26 Johnny Benson, Cheerios . . . . . . . .900.00
27 Rusty Wallace, Kodiak . . . . . . . . . .1400.00
28 Ernie Irvan, Texaco . . . . . . . . . . . .1400.00
28 Davey Allison, Texaco, black & white .4500.00
28 Davey Allison, Texaco, black & orange .5000.00
30 Derrike Cope, Bryan Foods . . . . . . .850.00
31 Mike Skinner, Lowe's . . . . . . . . . . .1000.00
33 Ken Schrader, Skoal . . . . . . . . . . . .1400.00

33 Harry Gant, Skoal . . . . . . . . . . . .1400.00
36 Ernie Irvan, M&M's . . . . . . . . . .2800.00

40 Sterling Marlin, Coors Light . . . . . . .1000.00
41 Steve Grissom, Kodiak . . . . . . . . .750.00
42 Joe Nemechek, BellSouth . . . . . . . .800.00
42 Kyle Petty, Mello Yello . . . . . . . . . .1500.00
42 Kyle Petty, Coors Light . . . . . . . . . .1200.00
43 Richard Petty, STP, 1960 – 1969 . .2000.00
43 Richard Petty, STP, 1970 – 1979 . .1800.00
43 Richard Petty, STP, 1980 – 1991 . .2000.00
43 Richard Petty, STP, 1992, final year .3000.00
43 John Andretti, STP . . . . . . . . . . . . .1800.00
43 Rick Wilson, STP . . . . . . . . . . . . .1500.00
44 Kyle Petty, Hot Wheels . . . . . . . . .2600.00
45 Rich Bickle, Lucky Dog 10-10-345 . . .900.00
55 Kenny Wallace, Square D . . . . . . . .1000.00
60 Geoff Bodine, Power Team . . . . . . .800.00
66 Darrell Waltrip, K-Mart . . . . . . . . .1500.00

55 Kenny Wallace, Square D . . . . . . . .1000.00

75 Rick Mast, Remington . . . . . . . . . .900.00
77 Robert Pressley, Jasper . . . . . . . . . .750.00
88 Dale Jarrett, Quality Care . . . . . . . .2800.00
94 Bill Elliott, McDonald's . . . . . . . . .2500.00
97 Chad Little, John Deere . . . . . . . .1800.00
99 Jeff Burton, Exide . . . . . . . . . . . .1600.00

## BUSCH GRAND NATIONAL
### DRIVER

1 Jeff Gordon, Baby Ruth . . . . . . . . . .7500.00
1 Jeff Gordon, Carolina Ford . . . . . . .7500.00

3 Dale Earnhardt, Jr, AC Delco, 1998 . .5500.00
3 Dale Earnhardt, Jr, AC Delco, 1999 . .5500.00
3 Steve Park, AC Delco, 1997 . . . . . . .1700.00
44 Tony Stewart, Shell, 1998 . . . . . . .3000.00
60 Mark Martin, Winn-Dixie . . . . . . . .1800.00

3 Dale Earnhardt, Jr, AC Delco, 1998 . .5500.00

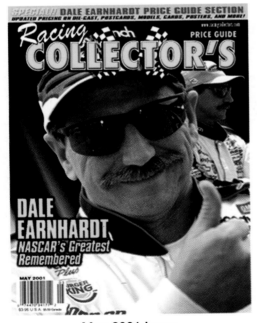